CANADIAN COURTS

Law, Politics, and Process

LORI HAUSEGGER

MATTHEW HENNIGAR

TROY RIDDELL

OXFORD
UNIVERSITY PRESS

OXFORD
UNIVERSITY PRESS

70 Wynford Drive, Don Mills, Ontario M3C 1J9
www.oupcanada.com

Oxford University Press is a department of the University of Oxford.
It furthers the University's objective of excellence in research, scholarship,
and education by publishing worldwide in

Oxford   New York

Auckland   Cape Town   Dar es Salaam   Hong Kong   Karachi   Kuala Lumpur   Madrid
Melbourne   Mexico City   Nairobi   New Delhi   Shanghai   Taipei   Toronto

With offices in

Argentina   Austria   Brazil   Chile   Czech Republic   France   Greece
Guatemala   Hungary   Italy   Japan   Poland   Portugal   Singapore
South Korea   Switzerland   Thailand   Turkey   Ukraine   Vietnam

Oxford is a trade mark of Oxford University Press
in the UK and in certain other countries

Published in Canada
by Oxford University Press

Copyright © Oxford University Press Canada 2009

Library and Archives Canada Cataloguing in Publication

Hausegger, Lori, 1970-
Canadian courts : law, politics, and process / Lori Hausegger, Matthew Hennigar, Troy Riddell.

Includes index.
ISBN 987-0-19-542373-0

1. Courts—Canada. 2. Judicial process—Canada. 3. Law—Political
aspects—Canada. I. Hennigar, Matthew A. (Matthew Aaron), 1971-
II. Riddell, Troy Q. (Troy Quinn), 1969- III. Title.

KE8200.H39 2008   347.71'01   C2008-905044-4
KF8700 ZA2 H39 2008

1 2 3 4 – 12 11 10 09

This book is printed on permanent (acid-free) paper ♾.

Printed in Canada

Contents

Preface

The genesis of this book has its roots in informal conversations between the three authors (all former graduate school colleagues) over a number of years about our desire for a book that we could use in our political science courses—a book that would take a comprehensive look at the Canadian judiciary. In contrast to the United States, there are almost no texts in Canada that examine carefully the institutions and actors in the judicial process and analyze the role of law and courts from a political perspective. Of those that do, most focus narrowly on specific courts (usually the Supreme Court of Canada) or on the interpretation and application of the Charter of Rights and Freedoms. Although, like many in our field, we embraced Peter Russell's seminal *The Judiciary in Canada: The Third Branch of Government* (1987) for its ground-breaking and comprehensive treatment of the courts as political (rather than purely legal) institutions, that book has become outdated in light of structural reforms to the judicial system. The nature of litigation has also evolved with society and, in particular (and as Russell had predicted), with the adoption of the Charter. Subsequent important contributions to the study of law, politics, and the judicial process in Canada (McCormick 1994; Morton 2002; Greene 2006) are also becoming dated or are not as wide-ranging as the book we envisaged.

Our goal with this book was thus to provide a comprehensive and authoritative overview of the contemporary Canadian judicial process and its relationship to law and politics. More specifically, our principal aims are to foster an understanding of the actors and institutions in Canada's judicial process; to demonstrate that the judicial process is a crucial part of Canada's governing process; to reveal the relationship between law, politics, and the judicial process; and to help readers, particularly students, engage in the theories, concepts, and debates that surround the judicial process and its relationship to law and politics. Our intended audience is primarily other academics and mid-level undergraduate and graduate students in the social sciences; although the book will appeal most obviously to political scientists, it is also suitable for those in socio-legal and criminal justice studies programs. It is also intended to be accessible to practitioners and educated general readers with an interest in law, courts, and politics. When possible, we have incorporated information from government reports and court records, interviews with important players in the process, secondary research by other academics, and some original research by the authors. Where relevant, reference is made to practice and research from other countries to help enhance the reader's understanding of law, politics, and the judicial process in Canada.

The book is divided into three parts. The first part introduces the foundational concepts of 'law' and 'politics' and the basic logic, structure, and processes of courts. The organization of the current judicial system in Canada and its historical development are detailed in this section, as are alternative dispute resolution (ADR) mechanisms. We consider this last topic an important and novel feature of this book, because most texts on the judicial system neglect these increasingly prevalent quasi-judicial institutions, which function both with the traditional judiciary and as an alternative to it. The second part of the book examines the most important actors in the judicial system, namely, the judges themselves—how they make their decisions, how they are chosen, and how their ability to function as impartial 'third parties' is protected while keeping judges accountable to the society and law they serve—and two important categories of litigants, interest groups and governments. The third and final part focuses on the role of the judicial process within the broader policy process in two key contexts—criminal law and civil (or 'private') disputes. This part closes by exploring the influence of courts on public policy, particularly in light of the Constitution. Throughout, 'real-world' examples or case studies are used to highlight the main concepts and issues of each chapter.

Although this book offers the most comprehensive discussion of the Canadian judicial system and its actors to date, we should acknowledge that because of the limitations of space, time, and our own expertise, some issues do not receive as full coverage as perhaps they deserve. Among these are the issues of court administration and trial delay, which, although referred to in several chapters, do not receive their own chapter. Although the Canadian literature in this field is underdeveloped compared to that in the United States, excellent work has been done by scholars such as Carl Baar, and we have endeavoured to incorporate it where applicable. Another area we do not cover in great detail is administrative law disputes (although, again, examples are discussed throughout), mostly because the book is concerned more with the judiciary's structures, processes, and role in the governing process than with various substantive areas of law. Furthermore, teachers and readers who desire more coverage of administrative law (or other areas of law) can choose from a number of other books dedicated to their topic of interest. Finally, we do not devote a chapter or specific section to the relationship between the media and the court, though we do discuss briefly the implications of the relationship—along with public opinion about the courts—in the context of judicial decision making, policy-making, and accountability. Unfortunately, although recent work by Sauvageau et al. (2006) examines media coverage of the Supreme Court of Canada, there is still relatively little analysis in Canada of this important relationship to draw upon.

This was a major learning experience for us, and we hope that readers will come away with increased knowledge of and a greater appreciation for the relationship between law, politics, and the judicial process.

Acknowledgements

We would like to thank several people for their contributions to this project. Most notably, our students at several universities (including Boise State, Brock, Calgary, Guelph, Louisiana State, McGill, and Ohio State) who have provided enormous inspiration and countless thoughtful comments over the years that we have been teaching courses about the Canadian judicial system. We are indebted to their influence on our ideas about the relationship between law, politics, and courts, and for helping us to identify issues of particular interest to those on the other side of the lectern. We also owe a debt of gratitude to our own advisers, whose expertise has informed our view of the courts that shapes the pages of this book. Thanks as well are due to Yaroslav Diduch at Brock University, from whom we received valuable research assistance on the number of judges and court organization. We are also very grateful to our interview subjects and contact personnel in a number of government departments, courts, and law schools for sharing their time and knowledge with us. Finally, thanks to our anonymous reviewers and the staff at Oxford University Press, in particular our copy editor Freya Godard, who worked quickly and carefully to save us from our mistakes, and our editor Jennifer Charlton, who guided us through our first book publication project with great patience and good cheer.

—◆—

For Craig, Connor, Samantha, and my parents.

—L.H.

For Kathleen and my parents.

—M.H.

For Carolyn, my parents, and my brother.

—T.R.

PART I

Introduction to Canada's Courts

Chapter 1

An Introduction to Politics, Law, and the Judicial Process

Within a few hours of his birth on 30 May 1996, Jonathon Drummond developed a severe infection. An X-ray taken by puzzled medical staff showed that the young boy had a small metal object lodged in his brain, and further investigation revealed a small injury to the boy's scalp. After initially claiming that she did not know how her son had been injured, the boy's mother, Brenda Drummond, revealed that on 28 May she had inserted a pellet gun into her vagina and fired it. The doctors removed the pellet surgically, and Jonathon's life was saved; Brenda Drummond, however, was charged with attempted murder.

An initial psychiatric report concluded that Mrs Drummond, who appeared to be a good mother with no history of criminal activity, was very depressed and inattentive to the functioning of her body to the extent that she was unaware that she was even pregnant.[1] Before the trial began, however, her defence lawyer, Lawrence Greenspon, tried to convince the trial judge that Mrs Drummond should not be tried because there was no law against what she had done. S. 223(1) of the *Criminal Code* of Canada states: 'A child becomes a human being within the meaning of this Act when it has completely proceeded, in a living state, from the body of its mother. . . .' According to s. 223(2) of the *Criminal Code*, however, a person is guilty of homicide if a child dies after birth from injuries inflicted by that person before birth. Mr Greenspon pointed out that Jonathon had no legal status when he was inside the womb, according to s. 233(1), and that since he had not died from his injuries, s. 223(2) did not apply.[2] Mr Greenspon cited legal precedents in support of his argument. In the 1980s, two British Columbia midwives were charged with criminal negligence causing the death of a child after the baby they were delivering died in the birth canal. The Supreme Court of Canada ruled that the midwives could not be convicted because the child was not born alive and therefore was not a human being for the purposes of the *Criminal Code*.

The Crown prosecutors in the *Drummond* case argued that a literal reading of the law made no sense. A Manitoba man had been convicted of manslaughter after a child died twenty minutes after being born because the man had stabbed the child's mother in the abdomen before the birth. Should Brenda Drummond be treated differently simply because her child did not die from his injuries? The Crown lawyers urged the trial judge, Judge Hansen, to interpret the *Criminal Code* in a manner that, they argued, would correct this anomaly in the law and provide for greater fairness.

Judge Hansen decided ultimately not to alter the law as it was written by Parliament. In her decision she stated: '[N]o matter how desirable it may be, I cannot construe s. 223 in a manner that removes the words at the end of s. 223(2): '[A]s a result of which the child *dies* after becoming a human being' (emphasis added). Justice Hansen stressed that although some people would see Brenda Drummond's act as immoral, the court was required to deal with the law and not morality. According to Judge Hansen, it should be up to Parliament to change law and policy. The defence motion to dismiss the charges was granted.[3]

Not surprisingly, the decision attracted attention and commentary with some groups supporting and other groups denouncing the decision.[4] Still others argued that the decision was legally correct but called on Parliament to change the law to prevent further injustice.[5] The *Drummond* case raises the question of 'what is and what should be the role of courts in the governing process'? Do courts adjudicate disputes by interpreting and applying the law, or do they alter public policy if the rules lead to unjust results? Should courts change the rules to reach a desirable policy outcome? What role do governments, practitioners, organized interests, and the general public want them to play—how much do these views depend on the outcome of a particular case? These questions have become particularly contested since the adoption of the Charter of Rights and Freedoms in 1982. The debate about the role of the courts in the governing process under the Charter was illustrated dramatically in June of 2005, when the Supreme Court of Canada in its *Chaouilli* decision was split on the question of whether a government policy that limited access to private health care was unconstitutional because it violated the right to 'life, liberty and security of the person' found in s. 7 of the Charter.[6] The case attracted a huge amount of political and media attention as political, legal, and medical experts speculated on whether the decision would lead to the end of Canada's public health-care system in its current form. In doing so, the case highlighted the intersection of politics, law, and the judicial process.

The next section of this chapter discusses the concepts of 'politics', 'law', and 'judicial process', which are central to our discussion of courts in Canada, before explaining the potential links between them. This explanation considers the various theoretical perspectives that attempt to explain the interaction of law, politics, and judicial process. The final section of the chapter presents a brief overview of the book.

Politics

It has been said that politics is about 'who gets what, when, and how'.[7] In other words, politics is about making decisions that distribute resources, such as how much money should go to education, health care, national defence, local police forces, the environment, and so on. It is also about creating rules, which often have associated economic, social, environmental, and moral consequences: for example, whether physician-assisted suicide should be allowed or not, whether companies have to undergo an environmental assessment before starting an energy project, whether airlines in Canada can be owned by foreign companies, whether refugee claimants should be allowed a hearing if their claim is rejected, or whether abortion is legal and under what circumstances. Politics is also concerned with how authoritative decisions are made. Should there be an elected Senate that is involved in decision making? Should Aboriginal Canadians be self-governing? Should courts have the authority to strike down laws? Explicitly or implicitly, decisions and the decision-making process are value-laden—they involve making choices, which often entail difficult trade-offs, about the value and meaning of human life, the environment, the economy, individual choice, the place of communities, and the role of various groups in society. It is not surprising that another well-known definition of politics states that politics is about the 'authoritative allocation of values' (Easton 1971).

The study of politics, therefore, focuses on two interrelated subjects: the processes surrounding the making of decisions and the outcomes of the decision-making process. In studying the process of decision making, a crucial question is, Who has the legitimate authority to make decisions for the community? In a representative democracy, the theory is that citizens vote for representatives who then make political decisions on their behalf. While this sounds simple enough, thinking about legitimacy and other process issues becomes much more complicated upon closer examination. How are the wishes of individuals and communities aggregated and articulated—what roles do political parties, interest groups, the media, and electoral rules play in reflecting and shaping input into the process? Would it make the political system more or less legitimate to take active measures to promote the input of minority groups, for example by funding them to take their issues before the courts or even including guaranteed representation in government? How should such institutions as the executive, legislative, and judicial branches, be designed to facilitate decision making but also to maintain mechanisms of accountability and to prevent the abuse of power? How should decision making authority be allocated between the local, regional, and national levels in states, such as Canada, that contain regionally distinct social and economic arrangements? In many democracies, including Canada, constitutional rights place constraints on decision makers. Who should have the authority to determine the application and scope of those constitutional rights?

The study of politics also entails an examination of the outcomes of decisions. Is political power distributed in such a way that certain groups or interests tend consistently to be the 'winners' of political decisions? Various theories in political science attempt to explain and perhaps even predict political outcomes, and theories are often related to views about the political process. Some theories propose that outcomes reflect the interests of the social elite who are said to dominate the political process, while other theories argue that political outcomes reflect open competition among groups and political parties. Yet others suggest that institutions and state actors (political, bureaucratic, and judicial leaders) are the key to understanding political outcomes.

A less abstract way of viewing decisions made in the political arena is to study public policy from an applied perspective. Public policy is defined as 'a course of action or inaction chosen by public authorities to address a given problem or interrelated set of problems' (Pal 2006, 2). The range of public policy varies enormously. Policies can involve anything from the banning by cities of smoking in restaurants to provincial education policy to federal defence policy to issues such as environmental and criminal justice policies that involve several levels of government. A conscious decision to do nothing about a particular problem can also be considered a public policy.

It deserves noting that formulating, implementing, and evaluating policies involve political choices. Decisions about what problems to tackle and how to try to solve them involve questions such as 'who gets what when and how' or the 'authoritative allocation of values' described above. Take, for example, the debate over how best to reduce the harm of illicit drug use. Critics of a prohibitionist approach argue that too much money is spent on policing and prisons and that outlawing drugs creates a black market that contributes to gang violence. They argue that responsible drug use should be an individual's choice and that more money should be directed towards health, prevention, and treatment centres. Defenders of a prohibitionist approach argue that legalizing or decriminalizing drugs could signal that drug use is acceptable, or even encouraged, and would lead to increases in drug abuse, which would result in significant social and economic costs. They call for more funding for the police and prosecutors to combat drug use and for stronger drug laws.

Law

There are various philosophical perspectives on the nature of law. Classical 'natural law' theorists held that for a law to be valid it had to be morally permissible—St Augustine argued that an 'unjust law is no law at all'—and that moral duties can be discovered in the natural order (as perhaps fixed by God) through reason (Murphy and Coleman 1990, 11–19). Owing to various potential difficulties with the natural law approach, particularly in finding agreement on what might be 'moral', legal 'positivists' argued for distinguishing analytically between 'what the law *is*' and 'what the law *ought* to be'. Although positivists like H.L.A. Hart (1961) recognized that normative considerations could not be totally divorced from the study of law, he argued that law 'as is' should be viewed as a set of rules that are created by a sovereign through a recognized set of procedures (secondary rules) (Hall 2001, 272; Murphy and Coleman 1990, 19–33). A positivist view of law has four characteristics. First, law is a *body of rules* as distinct from customs or conventions. Second, these rules are *enacted and applied by public officials*. Law, therefore, is the domain of government actors. Private groups and institutions such as the family, churches, businesses, social groups, professional organizations, and sports organizations often have sets of rules, but these rules are not considered to be 'law' and cannot be enforced as such unless the government sanctions them as law. Third, rules must be enacted *in a legitimate manner*. Legal rules developed according to specified procedures by government actors can be distinguished from rules or orders developed by terrorists, criminal gangs, or other groups not recognized as having the authority to make rules for a political community. Fourth, law is *backed by the force of the state*. Although many people feel an obligation to obey the law out of a sense of duty, laws ultimately can be backed with the threat of penalties (fines, imprisonment, a requirement to pay monetary damages and so on) (Neubauer 1997, 23–4; Vago and Nelson 2004, 7–8).

Contemporary natural law theorists, such as Lon Fuller (1969), argue that a legal system with those characteristics would also have to abide by certain procedures of justice or fairness in order to be considered legitimate. For example, the law should not be applied retroactively, the law should be reasonably precise, and like cases should be treated alike by courts. If we add this view to the positivist model, we get something called the 'rule of law'. A country that is governed by the 'rule of law' is one in which the law is a body of rules enacted and applied by public officials in a legitimate manner and backed by the force of the state; every person, no matter what his or her political, social, or economic status, is considered to be equal before the law; government officials must act according to the law; the law must be made publicly accessible before its enforcement and cannot be enforced retroactively; and the law must be applied by fair and impartial judges. The importance of the rule of law was illustrated in the famous *Roncarelli v. Duplessis* (1959) case. In 1946, Maurice Duplessis, the Premier and Attorney General of Quebec, ordered the Quebec Liquor Commission to revoke Frank Roncarelli's liquor licence for his restaurant. Mr Duplessis was angry that Mr Roncarelli, who was a Jehovah's Witness, had helped hundreds of his co-religionists to be released on bail for charges that stemmed from the ongoing dispute between the Jehovah's Witnesses and the Quebec government (and the Catholic Church). Mr Roncarelli's restaurant went bankrupt, and he had to sell his home. He then sued Mr Duplessis for damages, arguing that the Premier had overstepped his authority. The case eventually made its way to the Supreme Court of Canada, which ruled in favour of Roncarelli, finding that there was no legitimate reason for the revocation of Roncarelli's liquor licence (that is, he had not violated any of the conditions set by law for holding a liquor licence). The Court noted that there would always be some discretion associated with the administration of government, but that public officials, including the Premier, could not act with untrammelled discretion, because this could lead to abuse of power and destroy the rule of law.[8]

Although the positivist view of law has gained ascendancy, some modern legal theorists argue that even a version of the 'rule of law' that incorporates procedural justice is incomplete. The neo-classical natural law school, for instance, argues that laws should be evaluated as to whether they advance human good and prosperity— notions that are eternal but that are identified by practical reason (Hall 2001, 270). Members of this school accept that laws passed by a sovereign create legal obligations to follow them, but they suggest that to the extent that a law fails to advance the common good (as defined by practical reason), citizens or subjects of the law are not fully obliged to follow the law (see Himma 2002).[9] Natural law theory may best explain why former Nazi officials were found guilty for their actions during the Second World War at the Nuremberg trials even though they argued that they had been following orders and the law that they were charged with violating—the London Charter of 1945—was not in existence when they committed their actions (Finnis 2007).[10]

A somewhat different but naturalist-oriented perspective that also critiques legal positivism comes from Ronald Dworkin. Dworkin argues that when making decisions judges are obliged to do so according to rights based on principles, which in turn can be found in legal traditions, and on 'moral principles that underlie the community's institutions' (see Murphy 1990, 39–51 for a discussion of Dworkin's natural law tendencies). As an example, Dworkin (1978) points to the decision by the Court of Appeals of New York in *Riggs v. Palmer* (1889), which declared that an heir who murdered his grandfather would not be entitled to his inheritance even though the statutes (laws legitimately passed by the New York government) concerning wills had clearly been satisfied. Dworkin notes approvingly that the court had based its decision on the general principles, found in legal precedents, that a person should not profit or benefit from fraud or from his or her own crime; this decision would not be contemplated under a positivist view that laws are simply rules passed by the sovereign.[11]

As explained near the end of the chapter, though, analyses of the law grounded more in socio-legal studies and the social sciences than philosophy argue that the law has more to do with socio-economic power and the discretion of judges than is acknowledged by legal positivists or natural law theorists.

Categories of Law

From a practical rather than philosophical point of view, law can be divided into international law and domestic law and then further divided into public and private law.

International and Domestic Law

International law consists of rules that govern relationships and disputes between states or between people, businesses, and organizations in more than one state.

These rules may come from accepted customs and norms of international behaviour. They may also come from agreements entered into by two or more states, such as the North American Free Trade Agreement (NAFTA), the United Nations Convention on the Rights of the Child (1989), or the United Nations Convention for the Suppression for the Financing of Terrorism (1999). Finally, these rules can come from decisions made by international organizations, such as the World Trade Organization (WTO). Compared to domestic law—rules that are made by individual sovereign states for a given territory—international law can at times be somewhat difficult to deduce and enforce. International law is said to include norms or customary practices of states, but it is not always clear what those norms or customs are and states may disagree over their precise content and meaning.[12] And whereas individual sovereign states have a 'monopoly on the legitimate use of violence within a given territory' (Weber 1965) and can use this power to enforce domestic laws, there is no equivalent world power to induce or force a country to abide by international law. In these ways, international 'law' does not conform completely to the definition of 'law' (at least from the positivist viewpoint described above as a set of rules passed and enforced by a sovereign).

Nevertheless, the distinction and differences between international law and domestic law are shrinking in an era of globalization. International conventions and trade agreements are covering more and more areas of social, economic, and political activity. Though enforcement mechanisms are still relatively recent and underdeveloped, new international organizations like the International Criminal Court are being created, and some international organizations, such as the WTO, are developing more robust enforcement mechanisms. The European Union (EU) is an example of a transnational organization that has a strong set of institutional arrangements, such that many EU laws are binding on member states and are enforced by EU-level institutions.

Moreover, in countries like Canada, domestic law-making and interpretation by the courts are influenced to some degree by international law. For example, passage of Canada's anti-terrorism legislation was justified partly on the ground that it helped implement UN conventions against terrorism that Canada had signed. As well, the Supreme Court has looked to international law in making its decisions. For example, in a 2007 Charter of Rights and Freedoms decision supporting the collective bargaining rights of unions, the Court stated that the Charter 'should be presumed to provide at least as great a level of protection as is found in the international human rights documents that Canada has ratified' (*Health Services and Support—Facilities Subsector Bargaining Assn.*, 2007 at para. 70).[13]

The growth of international travel, trade, and communications is also requiring countries to consider such questions as which countries' laws apply to complex commercial transactions involving various countries, and to what extent a domestic law can apply to citizens abroad. For example, can the Canadian government pass and enforce a law banning its citizens from participating in sex with minors outside of Canada?

A related question involves the degree to which one country's domestic laws can be applied to citizens or organizations of other countries. The US Helms-Burton (1996) law, for example, which contains punishments for even non-US companies that are engaged in certain trade practices with Cuba, has been much criticized by Canada, the European Union, and Mexico as a violation of international law. A Canadian company, Research In Motion (RIM), maker of the popular BlackBerry device, tried to defend a patent-infringement lawsuit by arguing that American patent law should not apply because parts of the alleged infringement occurred on its relay and routing system, which is based in Canada. However, both the US federal district and appeals courts have rejected this argument (Avery 2005).

Private versus Public Law

Both international and domestic (national) law can be subdivided into 'private law' (sometimes referred to as 'civil law')—rules that govern relationships and disputes between individuals, groups, and corporate entities—and 'public law'—rules that govern relationships and disputes involving the state.[14] The main types of public law are constitutional law, criminal law, administrative law, and tax law. The main types of private law are torts ('responsabilité civile'), contract law, family law, and property law. These categories of law are summarized in Table 1.1.

Table 1.1   Public and Private Law

Public Law		Private Law	
Constitutional Law	Rules that define the type of government system (such as presidential or parliamentary) and the functioning of government. Constitutions also govern the relationship between citizens or groups and the state, including rights and freedoms. Finally, in federal systems, constitutions define the division of powers and jurisdiction between the national and regional governments.	Torts 'responsabilité civile'	Rules that govern under what circumstances a wrong committed against the person, property, or reputation of another, either intentionally or unintentionally, can result in the injured party obtaining a remedy from the party at fault. These rules also specify what kinds of remedies are available.
Criminal Law	Rules that define what is criminal, what the penalties are for violations of the criminal law, and what the procedures are for investigating crime and conducting a trial.	Contract Law	Rules that define what is a legitimate and binding agreement between two or more parties and how such agreements can be enforced.

Continued

Table 1.1   Public and Private Law (*Continued*)

Public Law		Private Law	
Administrative Law	Provides legal standards to govern the actions of governmental officials and remedies to those affected by the failure of government officials to follow legal standards.	Family Law	Rules that govern marriage and divorce, and the rights and obligations within a domestic relationship. the rights and obligations upon the dissolution of a relationship.
Tax Law	A specialized subset of administrative law with rules governing the collection of revenue by the state from individuals and businesses.	Property Law	Rules that are concerned with rights and obligations attached to ownership and possession of real and personal property.

In both private and public law, certain rules are concerned more with substance (for example, what is a crime or what is a valid contract), whereas other rules are concerned more with procedure (such as how a case is initiated, what kind of evidence can be produced, and so on).

Where those various kinds of rules come from and how they are applied depends on the system of law that a particular jurisdiction uses.

Systems of Law

The different legal systems in the world are characterized by differences in legal cultures and traditions, in the sources of legal rules, and in the reasoning used to adjudicate disputes based on the rules (see Glenn 2007). The two dominant systems of law in the world today are common law and civil law.[15] The common law system is used in Great Britain and many of Britain's former colonies, such as Canada, the United States, Australia, and India. The civil law system is dominant in most of Europe, Central and South America, in many parts of Asia and Africa, and even in some areas of the common law world (such as Quebec, Louisiana, and Scotland). Religious systems of law, which are somewhat less prevalent, exist in the Middle East and to some degree in south Asia, though elements can be found in other areas of the world, including Canada. In the past, the socialist legal system would have been included, but since the collapse of the Soviet Union in the early 1990s, socialist legal systems can be found in only a very few places, such as Cuba and Vietnam. Countries in the former Soviet bloc have adopted the civil law system and are in the midst of trying to establish systems of governance based on the rule of law. Table 1.2 summarizes the main differences in the major systems of law.

A brief discussion of these systems, including a historical overview and some examples of the legal systems at work, will help to make the similarities and differences between these systems more apparent.

Table 1.2   Systems of Law

	Source of Law	Legal Reasoning
Common Law Systems	Judicial decisions (judge-made law called common law), legislation, written constitutions (in some countries)	Finding legal principles from previous examples— 'does the present case resemble the previous case(s) "sufficiently" in the "relevant" aspects?' (using precedent)
Civil Law Systems	Written codes; legislation; written constitutions (in some countries)	Deductively applying principles in code to the dispute before the court
Religious Law Systems	Rules created by religious authorities with guidance from divine texts	Varies

Civil Law System

The origins of the modern civil law system can be traced back to the Corpus Juris Civilis of the Roman Emperor Justinian in the sixth century. Justinian's project collected existing and former laws of the Roman Empire along with the commentaries of legal scholars, thus creating a comprehensive code of laws that removed contradictions in the law to produce a more ordered legal system. During the Renaissance in Italy, Justinian's Code was used as a foundation upon which to build a system of law based on principles that foreshadowed the age of the Enlightenment. The idea of having legal rules set out in a rational and comprehensive code (or set of codes) that could be applied with the help of legal commentaries from experts began to spread from Italy to other countries. In 1804 in France, Napoleon introduced a comprehensive civil code containing 2,281 articles that governed private relationships and disputes involving such matters as family law, delict (torts), contracts, and property. Other codes covering civil procedure, commercial law, criminal law, and criminal law procedure soon followed. The five major codes remain the main basis of French law today. The Napoleonic Code served as a model for the drafting of the Civil Code of Lower Canada (now Quebec) in 1866, though some of the content was changed to reflect the more conservative values of Lower Canada at the time (Tetley 2000, 695–6).[16] In 1955, the Government of Quebec began to modernize the Civil Code in a comprehensive fashion. After much study and consultation and the inclusion of incremental changes that were made along the way, a thoroughly revised Civil Code was adopted in 1992 and came into force in 1994.[17]

Since the civil law system is built on the premise that codes contain a concise, but comprehensive, expression of rules governing relationships and disputes, judges in civil law systems are expected to resolve disputes by applying the legal principles in the codes to the facts of the case before them (using deductive reasoning). Dissenting opinions (where a judge disagrees with the decisions of his or her colleagues) or concurring opinions (where a judge agrees on the results reached by his or her colleagues but for different reasons) are not usually found in judicial decisions in civil law systems. Generally, in civil law judgments, references are made to legal commentaries and treatises about the codes, but not to how the code was applied in past judicial decisions.

In common law systems, however, dissenting and concurring opinions are allowed in judgments involving more than one judge and frequent references are made to past legal decisions, called precedents. The reliance on past cases in common law systems can be explained by the fact that, unlike the civil law system, the common law system is built upon a system of inductive reasoning (reasoning from example) where the legal principles developed in past cases are applied or modified as necessary to the facts of the case before the court. This reliance on precedent stems from the origins of the common law system.

Common Law System

The origins of the common law system can be traced back to twelfth-century England. At that time the courts of Henry II, administered by judges who travelled the country in regular circuits, began to base their decisions on the common customs of the entire realm rather than the parochial traditions of a particular shire or village that the courts of the nobles used for making decisions. Henry II's judicial and legal reforms bolstered the power and influence of the king's courts. By the fourteenth century it was established that judges of the king's courts would look to the legal principles from previous cases (precedents) to the case before them. The laws of England, therefore, were not contained in any one document but could be found mostly in the decisions of judges of the Crown—these rulings comprised the 'common law' (Abraham 1993, 7–12).[18]

Judicial decisions began to circumscribe the kinds of claims—defined in a series of 'writs' (such as writs of trespass)—that the courts would hear under the common law.[19] Because of the increasing complexity of the common law system, due particularly to the highly technical writ system under which a claim had to be fitted into one of the specific writs to gain access to the royal courts, more people began to approach the King's Chancellor to settle disputes.[20] At first, the Chancellor and his assistants would dispense justice without resorting to past decisions or technical procedures; eventually, though, the Chancery courts started following precedent and created a system called 'equity'. In doing so, they developed different ways of starting a court claim, as well as some novel remedies for claimants, such as the injunction, which is an order compelling or prohibiting an activity (for example, prohibiting trespassing on someone's property) (Yates, Yates, and Bain 2000, 8–10).

Friction developed between the common law courts and the Chancery courts over which rules would prevail if they conflicted. Similar questions were raised as to what would happen if legislation passed by Parliament conflicted with common law. After the Glorious Revolution of 1688–9, which established the principle of parliamentary supremacy, it became clear that laws passed by Parliament would trump common law made by judges if there was a conflict between the two

(Yates, Yates, and Bain 2000, 35). In time, Parliament passed legislation that made judges more independent of the executive (that is, the Crown) (*Act of Settlement, 1701*) and that combined common law courts and equity courts, the latter being given primacy in cases of conflict (*Judicature Acts* of 1873 and 1875).[21]

The growth of the British Empire spread the common law system of law to places like Canada, the United States, Australia, India, Malaysia, and South Africa. These countries developed a system of law that contained both legal rules in statutes passed by legislative bodies and legal rules developed by judges (common law). Some of these countries, such as Canada, the United States, and India, also added written constitutions to their legal systems.

Common Law Compared with Civil Law

Over time, there has been some convergence between the common law and civil law systems. In common law countries, much legislation has been passed that supplants common law made by judges; for example, Canada has legislation called the *Criminal Code* that was passed by the federal Parliament and that contains substantive and procedural criminal laws. Meanwhile, judges in civil law systems are looking, either formally or informally, to past judicial decisions as guides for their judgments in order to provide consistency in the application of the codes, which are written in relatively general terms.[22]

Nevertheless, important differences remain between the two systems. Most legislation passed in common law countries does not often resemble the concise and comparatively abstract codes of civil law systems. Furthermore, legislation created in common law countries is often influenced by common law decisions by judges, as executive and legislative bodies decide which common law rules to 'codify' in legislation and which common law rules need to be altered by legislation. Although judges in civil law systems are increasingly looking to past decisions for guidance as to how to interpret codes, in the common law systems, precedents and reasoning from example still play a more fundamental and important role since judges use precedents to interpret legislation (as illustrated in the *Drummond* case) and to create rules in areas where legislation does not apply.[23] Finally, as will be briefly noted in subsequent chapters, the two systems differ in the selection and training of judges and in both private (civil) and criminal law procedure.

Religious Legal Systems

Religious legal systems differ from the common law and civil law systems in that an important source of law for a country or region is a set of rules developed by religious authorities.[24] Nearly a thousand years ago, religious legal systems were important in the governance of large parts of the world. The Catholic Church during the Middle Ages was a powerful legal and political institution in Europe. Canon law—rules developed by Church leaders that were codified over time—and enforced by ecclesiastical (church) courts applied to many different relationships and disputes beyond strictly religious or church matters. Ecclesiastical courts made decisions involving such matters as heresy, witchcraft, marriage, adultery and other sexual sins, libel, and weights and measures, though jurisdiction was often shared with non–religious courts in issues not directly related to the Church or for individuals who were not part of the clergy.[25] Box 1.1 illustrates that the ecclesiastical courts also dealt with 'pesky' matters.

Box 1.1   Ecclesiastical Intervention

'Where infestations of pests became an epidemic, Mother Church sometimes invoked divine intervention to deal with the problem. Some examples from the late medieval period include: in 1479 Cockchafers indicted before the ecclesiastical court at Lausanne and condemned to banishment; in 1485 High Vicar of Valence commanded caterpillars to appear before him, gave them a defence counsel and finally condemned them to leave the area; in 1488 High Vicar of Autun commanded the weevils in neighbouring parishes to stop their attacks on crops and grain and excommunicated them.

Stupid medievals eh? It's more accurate to say that they were trying to find a way of curing something that they could observe without understanding why it was actually happening. Many pests go through a boom-bust cycle, the population increasing in size during one year and being markedly less the next year as their food runs out or the number of predators catches up. Once a plague of pests had reached bad enough proportions to warrant ecclesiastical attention, the epidemic was already on the wane. The intervention of the priests, and hence God too, seemed to have paid off . . .'

(Source: http://www.florilegium.org/files/ANIMALS/Pest-Control-art.html).

Islamic law (Sharia law)—legal doctrine created by religious legal scholars who tried to understand the divine law articulated in the Koran and the teachings of the Prophet Mohammed—was the basis of all laws in areas ruled by the Arabic and later Ottoman Empires (Badr 1977–8; Vogel 2003).[26]

For a variety of reasons, including the Protestant Reformation and the rise of representative government, the power of the ecclesiastical courts waned in Europe though canon law left an imprint on the development of civil law. The prevalence of Islamic law declined as European countries expanded their colonies and imported their laws, which were based predominantly on the civil law system. The spread of the civil law system was often aided by local rulers who used the civil codes to reduce the influence of rivals, including Islamic legal scholars. Islamic law did remain, however, for issues of family law and inheritance in many countries (Vogel 2003, 365).

Throughout the world there are continual debates about how much freedom individuals and groups should have to practise their religion; how closely laws should reflect the moral principles of religious faiths; and how much, if at all, governments should be allowed to support religious groups or causes. In India, for example, the constitution declares the country to be secular, but differences in personal laws, such as those pertaining to marriage and divorce, between religious groups, such as Hindus, Muslims, and Christians, have generated legal and political controversy. Chapter 3 explores briefly the debate over whether the government of Ontario should allow Muslims in Ontario to decide family-law disputes through alternative dispute resolution based on Sharia law. Nevertheless, in countries with a Judeo-Christian, Hindu, or Confucian tradition, no serious thought is given to basing a system of law and government on religious authority.[27]

The situation is somewhat more complicated in the Muslim world, where there is considerable discussion about the role of Islamic law in the system of governance. Some argue that it should be the basis of all political, social, and economic life. In Iran, for example, the Islamic revolution of 1979 ushered in a constitution that declared Iran to be an Islamic republic and provided for a system of government that gave significant power to Muslim clerics and lawyers, especially those who sit on the Council of Guardians and review laws to ensure their conformity with Islamic principles. Even in Iran, though, the role and application of Sharia law is contested, particularly as it concerns the place of women in politics and society (Halper 2005).[28] Other countries struggling with the role of Islamic law in government include Turkey, Egypt, and Iraq. An amendment to Egypt's constitution in 1980, for instance, made Sharia law the principle source of law, but the system remains largely secular and based on the civil law system. Family law, however, is based on Sharia law for the Muslim majority; family law for the Christian and Jewish minorities is based on their religions.

Egypt, therefore, could be said to have a mixed legal system, a not uncommon situation. As noted above, some countries allow religious law to govern family relationships. Other jurisdictions, including Scotland, South Africa, Louisiana, and Quebec, have mixtures of civil and common law systems.

The Canadian Legal System

In Quebec, private law that does not involve matters of federal jurisdiction as defined in the Constitution (such as the definition of marriage, copyright, and interest on money) is governed by the civil law system. Rules are set out in the Quebec Civil Code, and judges make decisions by applying the Code with less reliance on past cases than one would find in common law systems (though the use of precedent even in purely civil law cases appears to be increasing in Quebec).[29] In 2001 and 2004, Parliament passed laws—*Federal Law Harmonization Act No. 1 and No. 2*—that were designed to ensure that laws passed by Parliament involving private law reflected the wording and concepts of the Quebec Civil Code as well as those of the common law used in the other provinces and territories (Raaflaub 2004). Public law in Quebec (whether federal or provincial) is based primarily on the common law system. Elsewhere in Canada, the common law system is used for both private and public law.

So, if a person (Smith) in Alberta hit his neighbour (Jones) over the head with a bat during an argument, Jones could be charged under the *Criminal Code* of Canada, which is a federal law (because the Constitution of Canada gives the federal government power over criminal law). If the case came to trial, the judge would base his or her decision on the *facts* of the case and the *law*. The case would involve the common law legal system because it is public law. The judge would find the legal rules of assault in the *Criminal Code* and in precedents about assault (such as how past judges interpreted the *Criminal Code* or how long a sentence other judges gave for an assault conviction). In this example, Jones could also sue Smith for the assault under tort law. In Alberta, the case would also use the common law system. The judge would determine whether the facts of the case were analogous to those found in common law precedents (though provinces also have legislation that shapes private law); if they were, the judge would invoke the legal principles in the precedents to determine an outcome.

If, however, the same case between neighbours were heard in Quebec, the civil law system would be used—the judge would apply the law as stated in the Quebec Civil Code (perhaps with some references to how the Code has been applied in similar cases) to the facts of the case to determine an outcome.

Box 1.2 provides an example of Canada's system of laws at work using legal rules surrounding privacy as a case study.

Box 1.2   Rules about Privacy

While Canadians enjoy enhanced safety, convenience, and entertainment from modern technology such as cell phones, digital cameras, web cams, and computers, these technologies can also threaten their privacy. Electronic devices allow businesses and governments to collect and store large amounts of data on individuals in Canada. Individuals and organizations can purchase technology that allows them to take photographs or make audio or video recordings of others without their consent. The rules that have been created to protect privacy can highlight the different kinds of legal systems and categories of law in Canada. They also reveal that the creation of legal rules is an ongoing enterprise.

A number of laws in Canada designed to protect privacy fall under the category of 'public law'; therefore, the common law system applies in such situations. For example, in July 2005 the federal government amended the *Criminal Code* by adding 'voyeurism' as a criminal offence: s.162(1)(c) makes it an offence to observe 'surreptitiously' or make a visual recording of a person 'in circumstances that give rise to a reasonable expectation of privacy' if that is done 'for a sexual purpose'. The *Criminal Code* also makes it an offence to eavesdrop electronically on others without their consent. This means that the rules that judges use in every province, including Quebec, to decide cases in which people have been charged with voyeurism or electronic eavesdropping will be found in legislation (i.e., the *Criminal Code*) and in precedents that have interpreted and applied the legislation to real-life situations.

Is there any way for individuals to prevent others from spying on them or using their images in ways not covered by the *Criminal Code*? Or, even if there are rules in the *Criminal Code*, can individuals obtain compensation from other individuals, groups or businesses that violate their privacy? These questions involve private law, rather than public law. Under the Canadian Constitution, these issues tend to fall more under provincial jurisdiction. Quebec has addressed this issue by including the protection of privacy in its human rights law and by stating in article 3 of the Civil Code of Quebec that individuals have the 'right to the respect' of their 'name, reputation and pri-vacy'. Therefore, in Quebec a person can obtain redress against others for invasion of privacy and judges will base their decisions on the principles codified in the Civil Code (and in other laws such as Quebec's human rights law). A Quebec school teacher, for example, was able to recover damages from a newspaper that printed a story revealing he was suffering from AIDS (Craig 1997, 332).

The situation in the common law provinces remains somewhat in flux. Courts outside of Quebec have come to different conclusions about whether a privacy tort exists in common law. Common law courts in Canada, unlike courts in the United Kingdom and Australia, have not rejected outright the notion that a common law tort of invasion of privacy exists. The Alberta Court of Appeal, though, in its *Motherwell* (1976) decision was willing to recognize protection of privacy only as it related to other torts, such as the tort of nuisance, which protects property interests. The plaintiff in the case had been subjected to harassing phone calls, and the court argued that this diminished the use of her telephone system. As Craig (1997) points out, this ruling limits the application of privacy guarantees and does not recognize personal autonomy and dignity as important principles. Other judges have gone further. In January 2006, for example, Judge Stinson, an Ontario trial court judge, argued:

With advancements in technology, personal data of an individual can now be collected, accessed (properly and improperly), and disseminated more easily than ever before. There is a resulting increased concern in our society about the risk of unauthorized access to an individual's personal information. The traditional torts such as nuisance, trespass, and harassment may not provide adequate protection against infringement of an individual's privacy interests. Protection of those privacy interests by providing a common law remedy for their violation would be consistent with Charter values and an 'incremental revision' and logical extension of the existing jurisprudence . . . [T]he time has come to recognize invasion of privacy as a tort in its own right. (Quoted in Cameron 2006, 1).

In a different case, Judge Stinson rejected an argument by McDonald's Restaurants that a case against it alleging that it had breached a person's privacy for conducting a credit check on an employee without his consent should be dismissed because a tort of privacy does not exist in the common law (*Somwar v. McDonald's* 2006). However, since Judge Stinson is a trial court judge and the case was settled before a full hearing could be held, it does not establish a strong precedent (Cameron 2006).

Some common law provinces—British Columbia, Saskatchewan, Manitoba, and New Brunswick—have passed legislation, that is, statutes, that provide for statutory privacy torts. S. 1 of the British Columbia *Privacy Act*, for example, states: 'It is a tort, actionable without proof of damage, for a person, willfully and without a claim of right, to violate the privacy of another.' The Act states generally that the 'nature and degree of privacy to which a person is entitled in a situation or in relation to a matter is that which is reasonable in the circumstances, giving due regard to the lawful interests of others' (s. 1(1)). Specific examples of violations of privacy given in the Act include eavesdropping and surveillance (s. 1(4)). The Act also stipulates that an act or conduct is not a violation of privacy under certain circumstances, such as if consent was given or if a matter was published in the 'public interest' (see ss. 2(2) and 3). A woman in British Columbia used the *Privacy Act* to initiate an action against the BC government's insurance agency. The agency had hired private investigators to determine whether she was pretending to be injured in order to collect insurance. The woman alleges that the video surveillance conducted by private investigators is a violation of the tort of privacy established in the *Privacy Act*, and she is seeking damages.

Judicial Process

Societies, both ancient and modern, have tended to rely on a third party to resolve disputes between two other parties; adjudication by courts, however, is only one possible type of 'triadic' system (Shapiro 1981, chap. 1). We can distinguish these different types of triads across a spectrum, according to the amount of coercive power the third party possesses. At one end of the spectrum is the go-between, who shuttles proposals back and forth between the parties. Next is the mediator, who actively assists both parties in fashioning a mutually agreeable solution to their dispute. Farther along the spectrum is the arbitrator, who can impose a solution on the parties (which can be 'binding' or 'non-binding' depending on the type of arbitration). In the case of an arbitrator, both parties have usually consented in some fashion to such arbitration even if indirectly (for example, because they signed a contract that called for arbitration in the event of a labour dispute). Finally, at the end of the spectrum are the courts, where a judge imposes a binding decision upon the parties and often one of the parties is not before a judge voluntarily. Not only does coercion become greater along the spectrum, but the parties have less choice of who the third party will be and what rules the triad will use to resolve the dispute (Shapiro 1981). In modern courts, the parties have very little say as to who will judge their case and what law the judges will use to adjudicate the dispute. Therefore, a common understanding of courts is that they adjudicate disputes by applying laws to the facts surrounding the dispute to determine an outcome.

This relatively straightforward description of courts and judicial process, however, is complicated by various factors. (These factors are explored more fully in Chapter 3.) First, in the 'real world', alternative dispute resolution processes, particularly mediation, are becoming more common in Canadian courts. Among other things, the greater use of 'pre-trial' conferences in both civil and criminal cases is hastening this trend.

The second complicating factor involves the courts and fact-finding. It is often difficult for a judge to determine the truth of what happened between two disputing parties (these are sometimes referred to as 'historical' facts—who did what to whom and when).[30] As explained in somewhat more detail in Chapters 3, 9, and 10, a host of procedural rules about evidence have been created in private (civil) law and criminal law; these rules try to balance a variety of sometimes competing values. Just one example of where reasonable people disagree over how best to get the 'truth' and how best to balance various values and goals is the controversy over whether children testifying about alleged abuse should be able to do so behind a screen.

Another issue bound up with the courts and fact-finding is the reality that decisions made by courts involving a dispute between two parties could have wider implications for politics, society, and the economy. How much should or can judges know about these wider implications? In the *Chaoulli* (2005) case—the case regarding private health care mentioned in the introduction to this chapter—

the courts were presented with studies about the impact of various forms of health care on the efficiency, effectiveness, and equality of medical treatment. Can judges understand the methodology and conclusions of these social science studies that are traditionally used by government policy-makers? Can the adversarial process be relied upon to present and test social fact evidence?

The third difficulty with viewing courts as bodies that resolve disputes by applying the law to facts is that, as discussed more fully in Chapters 3 and 4, judicial decisions frequently involve to some extent the development of rules rather than simply the application of rules. For example, when rollerblading became popular in the 1990s, some rollerbladers were charged with breaking provincial traffic laws. When the tickets were challenged in court, the judges had to determine whether rollerblades fell under the definition of a 'vehicle' in the traffic law, in which case their users would be subject to traffic rules just like car drivers and bicyclists (Vittala 1994).[31] Judges in appellate courts are even more likely than trial court judges to be required to develop the law, because appeal-court judges are often hearing cases that have been appealed because there is a lack of clarity in the rules. Nevertheless, all judges normally have a choice as to how far to go in making rules when deciding a case. In the example outlined at the beginning of this chapter, for example, Judge Hansen was invited to alter slightly the rules in the *Criminal Code* as they applied to injuries sustained in the womb, but she argued that it was up to Parliament to decide if the rules should be changed.

The degree to which judges make law and the degree to which it is desirable for them to do so become even more significant when it is a question of constitutional law. In areas of the law other than constitutional law, like criminal law or tort law, Parliament and the legislatures are able to pass new laws to override judicial decisions they do not agree with. Constitutional law, however, is the supreme law and cannot be easily changed. And judges have the authority to strike down ordinary laws, if they believe that these laws contradict the rules set out in the Constitution, such as in the Charter of Rights and Freedoms (this is part of the power of judicial review).

Different judges have different opinions as to where the right point is on the continuum between being restraint in making rules (adjudicatory philosophy) and willingness to shape the law (policy-making philosophy). For example, in the Supreme Court's 1988 *Morgentaler* decision, Justice Wilson alone argued that the Charter of Rights should be read expansively to include the right to have an abortion. However, the two dissenting judges argued that the Charter should not be read expansively to include rights giving women access to abortion and suggested instead that the framers of the constitution deliberately refrained from including pro-choice or pro-life clauses in the Charter so that abortion policy would be determined by Parliament.

Whether a judge adopts an adjudicatory or a policy-making approach clearly has important political implications. Advocates of the policy-making approach argue that it allows judges to keep the law 'in tune with the times' and to arrive at decisions that are 'just' in the circumstances. They argue that the courts, unlike political bodies such as Parliament, are not influenced by money or votes and are therefore legitimate and important venues for making policy-related decisions. Conversely, supporters of the adjudicatory approach argue that it is undemocratic for unelected judges to be making policy decisions; and that if democratic institutions such as Parliament or the legislatures are flawed, they should be reformed rather than circumvented. They argue also that the adjudicatory approach promotes consistency, stability, and predictability in the law.

The fourth difficulty with saying that judges adjudicate disputes by applying the law to a set of facts is that social science research reveals that judicial decisions are influenced to some degree by non-legal factors. These factors can include a judge's ideology, religious background, or gender (Tate and Sittiwong 1989; Ostberg, Wetstein, and Ducat 2002; Segal and Spaeth 2002); public opinion (Mishler and Sheehan 1993; Stimson, MacKuen, and Erikson 1995); the socio-political context, including the stance of the government on an issue (Epstein and Walker 2004, 41–3); or strategic bargaining among judges on appellate courts (Epstein and Knight 1998) (see Chapter 4 for a discussion of the influence of each of these factors). For example, some observers have suggested that the willingness of judges to expand access to abortion in the *Morgentaler* (1988) case given above was due to their personal characteristics and ideologies. Notably, Justice Wilson was the only woman on the Court and the only judge to endorse the idea that the Charter gives women the right to an abortion (Morton 1992, 236–46).

The degree to which non-legal factors influence decision making has consequences for the intersection of law, politics, and judicial process. The process of selecting judges to the US Supreme Court, for example, is heavily politicized because each side wants to appoint a judge who shares its ideology—the premise being that ideology matters when Supreme Court judges decide a case. Some argue that contests over the ideology and characteristics of Canadian Supreme Court judges have already begun and will accelerate.

The fifth and final difficulty with the traditional notion that judges adjudicate disputes by applying the law to a set of facts involves the related questions of what constitutes a 'legal dispute' and how easy it is to gain access to the courts for the adjudication of disputes. Courts themselves have created a number of rules concerning what is a 'legal dispute'. These rules will be discussed at greater length in Chapter 3, but together they stipulate that access to a court depends on being a party to a sufficiently developed and 'live' dispute that involves 'legal' and not 'political' questions. Depending on how strictly these rules are applied, the barriers to getting into court are higher or lower. Lower barriers make it easier for individuals, groups, or businesses to challenge laws in court, thereby making the courts potentially more important and relevant in the political and policy processes. Chapter 3 discusses how these rules, although they are applied somewhat inconsistently, have generally been relaxed over the last few decades. In fact, one judge of the Canadian Supreme Court warned that the courts could turn into 'political battlegrounds' for competing interests after his colleagues granted access to a man who wanted to challenge Canada's abortion laws (from the pro-life perspective) even though he had no clear legal connection with the abortion law; that is, he was not a doctor who was charged under the law, nor was he the husband or father of a woman who wanted an abortion.

Subsequent chapters also consider other issues surrounding access to the courts. These include the rules for how interested third parties can participate in a court case, the ability of governments to ask the courts questions about the law without being involved in an actual legal dispute, and how legal cases are funded.

Theoretical Understandings

The preceding sections of this chapter discussed politics, law, and judicial process independently, though potential links between them were highlighted. This section of the chapter explores some theories and frameworks that attempt to explain and perhaps even predict the relationship between politics, law, and judicial process. These general theories will help inform the more specific discussions about the interaction between law, judicial process, and politics in subsequent chapters. The approaches discussed here are legal realism, critical legal studies, feminism, and new institutionalism.

Legal realists—as their name implies—tend to reject the philosophical orientations of natural law and legal positivism as 'unrealistic' views of law. Realists argue that the law and its impact are are shaped by the political, social, economic, and technological context (Devlin 1994, 606–7). From this perspective, because the theory of natural law is too abstract and legal positivism simply focuses on what the law 'is', both approaches tend to isolate law and courts from their political, social, and economic context. Likewise, the legal realist movement questioned the positivist assumption that legal decisions were determined largely by the systematic application of rules. As the American jurist Oliver Wendell Holmes maintained, 'the life of the law has not been logic, but experience.' The realists argued that decisions made by judges were influenced by the individual attitudes of judges and other external forces, such as the political circumstances surrounding the facts of a dispute (Devlin 1994, 607).

The critical legal studies (CLS) approach shares some assumptions with the realists, particularly concerning the influence of political and socio-economic factors on the law and the idea that law is contingent. However, CLS scholars emphasize that the law tends to constitute and legitimate the interests of those who are already powerful—politically, economically, and socially.[32] According to CLS scholars, laws tend to protect property and individual rights, thereby undermining social democracy. Some CLS scholars also point out that many judges and lawyers tend to be drawn from privileged socio-economic backgrounds, and those who are not are often socialized during their legal training to think like members of a privileged group (Mandel 1994). CLS scholars acknowledge that groups can use the law (such as human-rights law) and courts to pursue social change, but they are rather pessimistic about their chances of success.

A number of feminist legal scholars share the basic assumptions of CLS scholars, but they apply those particular insights to the relationship between gender, politics, and law. As Brettel-Dawson (2002, 58) puts it:

> Law reproduces underlying contradictions/complexities in the (social) situation of women (and men) as mediated by the intersectionality of gender, class, race/ethnicity, sexual orientation and (dis) ability. . . . The use of law and legal forums, to the extent that they are premised upon the very structures being challenged, can, in fact, further entrench oppression. Instead, refocusing on integrated political, economic and social action, of which legal engagement is but one part has been urged.

Feminists argue that the law and courts have traditionally been biased toward men and have reinforced traditional gender roles and sexual inequality, but not all legal feminist scholars or activists focus on gender differences and postmodern conceptions of discourse and power relations as Brettel-Dawson and others do. More liberal legal feminists argue that the law and legal system should treat men and women the same and they work to change discriminatory laws (Audain 1992, 1024–7). They hope that as more women become lawyers and judges, the process will continue to evolve towards this kind of equality. Chapter 7 discusses the legal strategies of Canadian women's groups, including one that supports more socially conservative policies and argues that radical feminists have unduly influenced the law and legal system.

Finally, the new institutionalist (NI) approach to law and courts, which has some elements that can be found in the legal realist or CLS schools, investigates the ways in which courts are political institutions and how they are connected to the larger political governing system. The NI approach makes a number of assumptions:

1. Laws to some degree are the product of political and socio-economic forces, but laws are also constitutive in the sense that they can privilege certain groups or ideas above others, can influence the strategies of actors in the political and socio-economic systems, and can also shape the attitudes and goals of actors in the political process.[33] Canadian constitutional scholars, for example, have pointed out that the introduction of the Charter of Rights into Canada's legal system not only gave groups another strategic option by which to try to shape government policy, but also transformed Canada's political culture and political

discourse with greater emphasis on rights for individuals and groups in society (Cairns 1992, Russell 2004b).

2. A second assumption is that judicial decision making is influenced by the formal and informal rules of courts and the relationship of the courts with other levels of government. Like the realists, NI scholars agree that the attitudes and preferences of individual judges can influence their decisions, but NI scholars argue that decisions are also shaped by a number of institutional features of courts. These include how much discretion the law provides in various cases, whether a court is at the top or bottom of the judicial hierarchy, the power of the Chief Justice of appellate courts to assign responsibility for writing judicial opinions (and the voting rules for appellate-court decision making), and the methods by which judges are selected and held accountable. (For example, if judges are elected or face confirmation elections as they do in some American states this may affect their decisions.)

3. Another basic assumption of the NI approach is that the courts have an important role in the governing process (Kritzer 2003a); however, the nature of that role depends on various factors. One of the precursors of the NI approach was Robert Dahl's argument that because American courts were linked to other branches of government, especially through the government's power to appoint judges, the courts tended to reaffirm the policies created by the dominant political coalition and this was an important political role played by the courts. Although there is some validity to that argument, the NI approach considers it to be overly simplistic and incomplete (McCann 1999, 69). NI scholars point out that judicial decision making is complex and that courts have acted independently in political conflicts when governments cannot act or refuse to. Moreover, courts can help set the political agenda, provide (or restrict) strategic options and resources in a dispute, shape discourse and goals, and prompt counter-mobilization to a decision (or series of decisions) (McCann 1999).

The potential for courts to influence politics and policy is dependent upon various institutional factors (both formal and informal). Various institutional rules created by either the government or the courts about access to court, evidence, how much discretion courts have to hear a case, whether interest groups receive government funding to challenge laws, or how creative judges should be in applying the law can increase or decrease the potential for courts to be policy-makers. Whether courts have the power of judicial review, particularly the ability to compare government laws and actions against constitutions, is another important factor in the policy-making potential of courts. How the court system is structured, particularly how much influence national courts have over the development of sub-national (provincial) laws (or how much influence provincial and state courts have over national laws) also has political implications. Furthermore, since courts do not have power over 'the purse or the sword' (in Alexander Hamilton's famous phrase from the American *Federalist Papers*), NI scholars note that the 'real world' effects of judicial decisions will be dependent upon various interrelated factors such as public opinion, the reaction of government organizations to a decision (including whether resources are provided to implement a decision), the reactions of the litigants to a decision, the reaction of the media to a decision, and the use that interest groups make of a judicial decision (Rosenberg 1991; Riddell 2004).

How would each of these theories explain the relationship between law, judicial process, and politics exhibited in the *Drummond* case (discussed at the beginning of the chapter) about the baby that was born with a pellet in his brain? A legal realist would go beyond the legal-positivist perspective (Judge Hansen simply applied the law 'as is') to consider whether Judge Hansen's decision was influenced by her personal attitudes about fetal rights and reproductive rights, attitudes that to some degree may have been shaped by her gender—she may not have wanted to make a legal decision that could have led to restrictions on reproductive rights. Critical legal studies scholars and critical feminist scholars might argue that although the decision not to change the law is positive in the sense that it could not be used in the future to restrict reproductive rights, such court cases divert attention from fundamental factors that affect women's equality, such as gendered labour markets, a lack of affordable day care, and inadequate social programs. New institutionalist theorists, like the legal realists, would consider whether Judge Hansen's personal views affected her decision. However, NI theorists would also suggest that perhaps her decision rested in part on a genuine conviction that a judge should not be making law and that maybe this view was shaped by institutional structures—the fact that she is a trial court judge at the bottom of the judicial hierarchy. An NI theorist, particularly from outside of Canada, would find it interesting that a judge appointed by the province of Ontario was able to interpret and apply a federal law (the *Criminal Code*). Finally, NI scholars would also note the difficulty of predicting how the decision would affect policy surrounding criminal law and reproductive rights. Much would depend on such interrelated factors as media reporting of the decision, lobbying by interest groups after the decision, and the decisions by various government officials as to whether the law should be changed or not.

Conclusion

The premise of this book is that law and judicial process are indeed political. Although the book does not endorse one particular theory about the political nature of law and judicial process, it does focus on legal rules, judicial structure and process (the organization of the Canadian courts, rules for selecting judges, rules of accountability, and the civil and criminal law processes), and the behaviour of actors in the system (judges, lawyers, interest groups, and government officials) and it sees them (rules, structures, processes and behaviours) as interrelated. Thus, there is an underlying new-institutionalist strain running throughout the text. This theoretical orientation is particularly evident in the next chapter, which provides an overview of the structure of the Canadian judiciary and discusses how the structure has shaped and been shaped by legal and political forces.

Chapter 2

The Structure of Canadian Courts

On 24 August 1993, in the coastal waters north of Nova Scotia, two men landed 463 pounds of eels, which they sold for $787.10. They were promptly arrested for violating several federal fisheries regulations, including fishing without a licence, fishing with a prohibited net, fishing eels out of season, and selling eels without a licence. At trial before a judge of the Nova Scotia Provincial Court, the men conceded all of these facts. However, the two—both Mi'kmaq Indians—argued that they were exempt from the Canadian government's regulations, citing a clause in the Treaties of Peace and Friendship between the Mi'kmaq and the British Crown, signed between 1760 and 1761, which bound the Mi'kmaq not to 'traffick, barter or Exchange any Commodities in any manner but with such persons or the managers of such Truck-houses as shall be appointed or Established by His Majesty's Governor at Lunenbourg or Elsewhere in Nova Scotia or Accadia.' They contended that this phrase entitled the Mi'kmaq of Nova Scotia to fish and trade eels, an activity their people had engaged in since their initial contact with Europeans. One of the men, Donald John Marshall, Jr, was already well-known in Canadian legal circles for his wrongful murder conviction in 1971 and subsequent acquittal twelve years later, which had led to a Royal Commission that found widespread racism in the Nova Scotia justice system. The case regarding eel fishing came to bear his name, and ultimately it reached the highest court in Canada.

The only issue at Marshall's trial was whether he actually possessed a treaty right to catch and sell fish. The treaties of 1760–1 were not worded generously and were in fact designed to prevent the Mi'kmaq from trading with anyone other than the British—namely, the French, with whom the Mi'kmaq had been allied continuously during the frequent struggles between the two European powers to control North America. The Treaties of Peace and Friendship, which had been signed shortly after the British conquest of Quebec, were as the Canadian government's expert witness testified, intended to consolidate the peace and reduce Mi'kmaq dependence on Britain by ensuring that the native inhabitants could sustain themselves economically. Viewed from the perspective of the 1990s, however, there was an obvious legal problem: the Treaties limited Mi'kmaq trade to exchanges with 'Truckhouses' (a barter-based trading post), but truckhouses disappeared from Nova Scotia shortly after the treaties were signed. A replacement system of government-licensed traders had also disappeared by 1780. This fact led the trial judge to conclude that, although Marshall and his fellow Mi'kmaq had a right to take fish to the truckhouse to trade, that right had effectively expired along with the truckhouses and subsequent special arrangements. Moreover, the trial judge ruled that the Mi'kmaq did not have a treaty right to fish or to hunt, because the 1760–1 treaties did not specify any rights to obtain the *means* to trade. Without a treaty exemption from the various fisheries regulations, Marshall was convicted on all counts. Notably, however, the judge granted a sentence of 'absolute discharge'—not only would Marshall serve no jail time or pay any fine, but the conviction would not appear on his record.

Yet the case did not end there. Marshall's primary concern was the court's interpretation of the treaties, and he appealed the ruling to the Nova Scotia Court of Appeal—the highest court in the province—where it was reviewed by three judges. He did not fare any better than at trial. In fact, the appellate judges not only upheld his conviction, but denied that the 1760–1 treaties granted any rights *whatsoever*. The Court of Appeal concluded unanimously that, rather than granting rights, the trade clause was a limit imposed upon the Mi'kmaq to help keep the peace with the British. Echoing his earlier determination when struggling against the Canadian justice system, Marshall persisted and appealed to the Supreme Court of Canada, the highest court in the land.

Like most appellants, Marshall needed 'leave to appeal', that is, the Supreme Court's permission to bring his case, which it granted. The Court has increasingly chosen to focus on constitutional law cases over the past thirty years, and since the adoption of the 1982 Constitution, this includes treaties with Canada's First Nations. The only issue at this stage was whether the lower-court judges had interpreted the treaties correctly. By a vote of 5–2[1] the Court found that they had committed 'errors of law' by ignoring other historical sources—including other treaties and the Mi'kmaq's own oral history—and it overturned the decisions of the lower courts (*Marshall v. The Queen* 1999a). The Court acquitted Marshall and also found an aboriginal treaty right to obtain a moderate livelihood through hunting, fishing, and trading the products of those traditional activities.

Marshall v. The Queen had an unusual and striking epilogue: shortly after the Supreme Court's decision, Mi'kmaq began fishing without licences or regard for conservation regulations in the lucrative lobster trade, not only in Nova Scotia but in neighbouring provinces as well. Non-native fishermen reacted violently to this threat to their livelihood, destroying the cars and boats of Mi'kmaq fishermen, who were equally determined to continue fishing. While rejecting the request of a coalition of non-native fishermen, who wanted Marshall's acquittal suspended until the government could establish fisheries regulations for the Mi'kmaq, the Supreme Court issued an extremely rare clarification of its earlier ruling (*Marshall v. The Queen* 1999b). The Court unanimously denied that its first *Marshall* ruling 'had established a treaty right "to gather" anything and everything physically capable of being gathered'. Although Donald Marshall's acquittal would remain, unregulated fishing (not to mention hunting, logging, and mining) by natives would not.

The saga of Donald Marshall, Jr's case illustrates several fundamental features of Canada's judicial system:

1. *Federal but unified court system.* By *federal*, we mean that the judicial system reflects the official division of governmental authority in Canada between two levels, the provinces and the national (or 'federal') government. Each province in Canada (as well as the Yukon, Northwest, and Nunavut Territories) has its own system of courts, and as we will see shortly, there is also a system of federal courts, including the Supreme Court of Canada. By *unified*, we mean that there are features of Canada's judicial system which operate so as to break down the strict divisions of federalism. Two features are particularly important in this respect. First, provincial courts can rule on federal laws, as seen in *Marshall* when the Nova Scotia courts enforced the Canadian government's fisheries regulations (and, of course, provincial courts can also rule on provincial laws). Second, the Supreme Court of Canada has unlimited jurisdiction over both provincial and federal law; for example, even a fairly routine case about a speeding ticket can end up before Canada's highest court (see Box 2.3). This is unlike the United States Supreme Court, which, as a federal court, can rule on a state law only when it raises an issue under the United States Constitution. We will examine some additional unifying features of the Canadian judicial system later in this chapter.

2. *Hierarchies of courts.* Canada's courts are arranged in a system of increasing authority, such that a court higher up the ladder has the power to review the ruling of a lower court, and lower courts are bound by the decisions of the higher courts. Trial courts, where virtually all cases begin, occupy the lowest level of the hierarchy, and there are multiple levels of courts of appeal, also called 'appellate courts'; the number of levels depends on the legal issue. Cases therefore proceed on a predetermined path through the levels of the judicial system. In Marshall's case, his trial took place in the Nova Scotia Provincial Court, with subsequent appeals to the Nova Scotia Court of Appeal and the Supreme Court of Canada. However, most cases that begin in a province's court system end in it without reaching Canada's highest court. In fact, although more than 10,000 cases are appealed every year (Greene et al. 1998, 44), this represents only a small fraction of the number of potential appeals.

3. *Different courts perform primarily different but overlapping functions.* Recall from Chapter 1 our distinction between disputes of *fact* and disputes of *law*. The first requires courts to engage in fact-finding: What happened? Did the accused commit the crime he is charged with? Disputes of law,

however, require judges to engage in legal interpretation, that is, clarifying (or sometimes defining) the 'rules of the game' for law enforcement officials, other judges, and the public. Fact-finding is the primary responsibility of trial courts—it is typical, for example, for the appeal court simply to accept the trial court's factual findings.[2] Nevertheless, legal interpretation is the main role of appeal courts, in two senses. First, as we saw in *Marshall*, appeal courts are expected to correct 'errors of law' committed by lower-court judges. Second, even if the lower-court judge has not technically made an 'error', appellate judges may re-interpret the law on the basis of new information or changes in society or because they disagree philosophically with the lower court. However, Canadian trial courts are also empowered to interpret the law. We saw this in *Marshall*, where the trial judge tried to determine what the 1760–1 treaties meant in the context of the contemporary eel fishery. Indeed, *Marshall* was unusual in that the accused conceded the facts of the case at trial and rested his defence entirely on an interpretation of treaty law. This illustrates that the functions of trial and appeal courts can overlap, although appeal courts have the final say.

4. *Multiple legal systems and bodies of law.* A natural consequence of federalism is that each provincial and national unit of government creates its own body of law. We also make a distinction between *statutes* and *regulations*. Statutes are laws passed by the legislative branch, such as Parliament or a provincial legislature. Regulations are rules created by the executive branch, such as government departments or agencies (Fisheries and Oceans, for example), which are designed to clarify and implement statutes. In addition, Canada has a body of constitutional law, which establishes the basic features of our legal and political systems, including the federal division of powers itself, the rights of citizens and other residents of Canada, and since 1982, the unique rights of First Nations. A case can involve more than one of these bodies of law at the same time. *Marshall*, for example, concerned fisheries regulations passed by the federal government as well as constitutional law in the form of native treaties. Unlike *Marshall*, a case may also simultaneously involve both federal and provincial laws. For example, people caught driving while intoxicated are routinely charged under both the federal *Criminal Code* and the province's traffic regulations (in Ontario, the *Highway Traffic Act*).

5. *High degree of judicial discretion in system.* The Canadian legal system is designed to give judges control over a great number of issues that come before them. This feature of the system will be a recurring theme of this text, but we can already observe from the most recent journey by Donald Marshall, Jr through the judicial system that judges have flexibility regard-

ing legal interpretation, sentencing, granting leave to appeal, and even determining how many judges on a court of appeal will hear a case.

Overall, to paraphrase Russell (1987, 333), we can think of the Canadian judicial system as a pyramid-shaped filter, with the Supreme Court at the tip: many cases pass through the wide layer of trial courts, but access and capacity narrow sharply as one moves further, through the appellate courts, so that the system receives progressively fewer cases.

With these basic principles of the Canadian judicial system in mind, we next take a closer look at the different trial and appeal courts that make up the system.

The Canadian Judicial System—Provincial, Federal, and Integrated Courts

Figure 2.1 provides a general overview of the structure of the Canadian judicial system, which is composed of three general categories of courts, known by the sections of the 1867 Constitution that authorized their creation: the 'purely provincial' section 92 courts; the 'purely federal' section 101 courts, and the section 96 'provincial' courts, which are actually the shared responsibility of the provincial and federal governments. Section 92 courts are 'purely provincial' in the sense that they are created, organized, administered, appointed, and paid by their provincial government; each province has its own set of s. 92 courts. The federal government performs all of these functions for the s. 101 courts. The s. 96 courts, however, represent a type of unified, or integrated, judicial federalism that is unique among the federations of the world. As with the s. 92 courts, each province has its own set of s. 96 courts, which it administers and may reorganize. However, the judges of these courts are appointed and paid by the federal government (we examine the appointment systems of each type of court in greater detail in Chapter 5). For a brief period after Confederation in 1867, s. 96 courts were the *only* significant category of courts in the country, but this quickly changed with the creation and growth of both the 'purely' provincial and the 'purely' federal courts. The following sections detail the historical background and current jurisdiction, structure, and size of all three categories of courts. The workloads of the various courts are also discussed.

Box 2.1   The Constitutional Foundations of the Canadian Judiciary: Sections 92.14, 96, and 101

The following sections of the *Constitution Act, 1867* (formerly the *British North America Act, 1867*) established the basic contours of the Canadian court system:

s. 92.   In each Province the Legislature may exclusively make Laws in relation to Matters coming within the Classes of Subject next hereinafter enumerated; that is to say,—

...14.   The Administration of Justice in the Province, including the Constitution, Maintenance, and Organization of Provincial Courts, both of Civil and of Criminal Jurisdiction, and including Procedure in Civil Matters in those Courts.

s. 96.   The Governor General shall appoint the Judges of the Superior, District, and County Courts in each Province, except those of the Courts of Probate in Nova Scotia and New Brunswick.

s. 101. The Parliament of Canada may, notwithstanding anything in this Act, from Time to Time provide for the Constitution, Maintenance, and Organization of a General Court of Appeal for Canada, and for the Establishment of any additional Courts for the better Administration of the Laws of Canada.

Figure 2.1   The Structure of the Canadian Court System

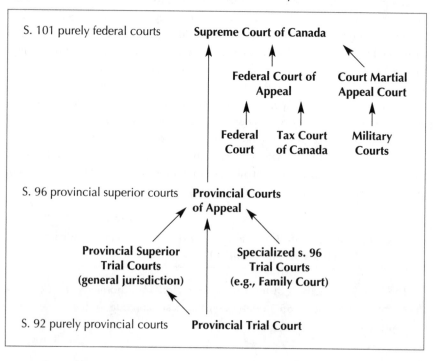

Before beginning to review the various courts, however, it is important to discuss briefly the meaning and relevance of the term 'jurisdiction' since it is central to understanding the structure of Canada's courts. 'Jurisdiction' here refers to the responsibilities of the court, or what matters it is authorized to hear. We will examine three dimensions of jurisdiction: territorial, hierarchical, and subject matter. *Territorial jurisdiction* refers to the geographic area over which the court has authority. When we say that s. 92 courts are 'provincial' courts, it is primarily because they may only hear cases arising within their own province. *Hierarchical jurisdiction* refers to the court's rank in the judicial system, that is, whether it is a trial or appeal court (or both). A trial court has 'original jurisdiction', which, as noted above, means that it is the first court to hear the case, whereas courts with 'appellate jurisdiction' may review the rulings of lower courts (the specific standards of review used by appeal courts are elaborated in Chapter 4). Of our three categories of courts, s. 92 courts are unique in having *only* original jurisdiction—there are no s. 92 appeal courts. Finally, *subject-matter jurisdiction* is the set of legal issues heard in that court, for example, criminal law, civil law, administrative law, family law, and so forth. Within subject-matter jurisdiction, we can make a distinction between whether a court has 'exclusive' jurisdiction over an issue or 'concurrent' (shared) jurisdiction with another court.

This chapter will demonstrate that since the early days of Confederation there have been questions, struggles, and negotiations over jurisdiction (particularly surrounding the jurisdiction of the s. 96 courts compared to the s. 92 courts or the s. 101 federal courts). Why are there disputes over jurisdiction—a seemingly arcane matter of legal process? Sometimes litigants challenge the jurisdictional authority of a court as a legal tactic to win their cases (at least temporarily). More important, for the purposes of this text, disputes and negotiations over court jurisdiction between the federal and provincial governments are driven in no small measure by political considerations. Recall from Chapter 1 that politics, among other things, is concerned with the process of decision making and influence over decision making. Since courts are important decision makers within a system of governance, it is not surprising that governments may try to maximize the influence of the courts that they administer and to which they appoint judges (and judges tend to favour expansions of their court's influence as well.) For example, as noted in the opening chapter, in the twelfth century, Henry II used his system of 'King's courts' to undermine the power and authority of the nobles and their courts. That said, governments will sometimes accept a reduction in the jurisdiction of their courts for certain purposes, such as cost savings (judges do not come cheap, after all) or recognizing the need for more efficient and effective justice given constitutional constraints. Whether it is expanding or contracting, the jurisdiction of courts is intimately connected to larger political issues.

Finally, it must be stressed that although disputes over court jurisdiction are usually between the federal and provincial governments, they are frequently played out within the judicial system itself, particularly in the highest courts of appeal. As will be demonstrated repeatedly throughout this chapter, the institutional structure and processes of the Canadian judiciary have been shaped significantly by decisions of the Supreme Court of Canada (and, before 1949, the Judicial Committee of the Privy Council in Britain) in the course of resolving jurisdictional disputes—a process which has necessarily entailed interpreting the Constitution and the various statutes governing the courts.

The Section 92 Provincial Trial Courts

Trial courts are the front line of a judicial system in that they handle the most cases. They are the first court (as distinct from an *administrative tribunal*,[3] discussed in Chapter 3) to hear a case, and so are also known as 'courts of first instance' or 'courts of original jurisdiction'. As Figure 2.1 shows, there are s. 92, s. 96, and s. 101 trial courts (in contrast, there are no s. 92 appeal courts). Within these categories, Canadian trial courts usually include a mixture of specific-jurisdiction courts—that is, those created to deal with only a given area of law, such as family law—and general-jurisdiction courts. We shall look at each category in turn.

Historical Background

Soon after Confederation, provincial and municipal governments began creating local courts for minor civil and criminal cases. These were initially known as 'magistrates' courts' or 'police courts' (the latter because they were often located in the same building as the police department). Later, in the first half of the twentieth century, magistrates were also empowered to hear cases involving child protection, deserted wives, and spousal abuse, which became the body of family law. Early criminal and family courts were often staffed by 'lay-benchers', that is, people without legal training and who were not judges. An exception was in Quebec, where, in addition to lay magistrates' courts, there was a Court of Sessions of the Peace staffed by judges with legal qualifications and tenure, to hear criminal cases. In English Canada, as late as 1968 an Ontario Royal Commission chaired by Chief Justice James McRuer found that patronage appointments (for example, the appointment of former politicians) to the magistracy were the norm for governments of all political parties. This, in turn, raised concerns about the quality of justice being rendered by magistrates, concerns that were compounded by the magistrates' close connections to the police, inadequate facilities, and lack of institutional independence. Partly in response to McRuer's findings, magistrates' courts were 'judicialized' in Ontario and later in all provinces (except Alberta) between the 1960s and early 1980s, with the requirement that provincial court judges have legal training and experience.[4] (This had already occurred in 1962 for Quebec's Magistrates' Court.) Although this has improved the technical skill on the provincial benches, the degree to which patronage still plays a major role in appointment to these courts is an open question.

The constitutionality of these provincially-appointed courts was challenged early and often after their creation, usually by litigants who had lost their case in such a court, but also by the federal government. The grounds for these challenges were that the only explicit mention of the power to appoint judges in the 1867 Constitution appears in section 96, which assigned this power to the *federal* government (see Box 2.1). The provinces' position, however, was based on s. 92(14), which, while not mentioning appointment, grants provincial governments wide authority over the creation and administration of provincial courts. The dispute over the validity of provincially appointed courts was ended in 1892 by the ruling of the Judicial Committee of the Privy Council (JCPC)[5] in the *Maritime Bank Case*. The case was not specifically about judicial appointment but rather about the general nature of Canadian federalism. The JCPC enforced what it argued was the essence of a federal system of government: the equal constitutional status of the national and regional governments, or 'dual sovereignty'. It followed that if the federal government had the power to appoint judges to courts it created (under s. 101), then the provincial governments must have the same power for their courts.[6] However, the JCPC's ruling did not end litigation over the *jurisdiction* of provincially appointed courts, which continues to this day.

Jurisdiction

S. 92 courts have extensive and diverse subject-matter jurisdiction, which they have accumulated slowly but continuously since Confederation. Although the specific details vary from province to province, the legal issues heard in these courts today usually fall into the following five categories:

Provincial Offences

In every province, the s. 92 court has original exclusive jurisdiction over all provincial and municipal offences. Examples include traffic infractions (driving without a licence, speeding, and so on), littering, underage drinking, and literally thousands of other 'summary' offences (less serious offences, similar to misdemeanours in the US).

Federal Offences

As Box 2.2 shows, federal offences may be found not only in the *Criminal Code*, but also in many other statutes and regulations. The *Marshall* case provides three non-Code examples: fishing without a licence, fishing out of season, and fishing with an illegal net. Every province's s. 92 court has original exclusive jurisdiction over all summary offences created by Parliament. Parliament (but not the provinces) can also create 'indictable', or more serious offences that carry heavier punishment.

Jurisdiction over indictable offences is more complicated. There are three categories of indictable offences, and legislation determines where each is heard. The least serious (illegal betting for example) are assigned exclusively to s. 92 courts, whereas the most serious (murder, treason, sedition, war crimes, and 'alarming the monarch') must be heard in a s. 96 trial court, usually before a judge and jury.[7] For all other indictable offences, the accused can choose between trial before a s. 92 court judge alone, a s. 96 court judge alone, or a judge and jury in a s. 96 court (there are no jury trials in s. 92 courts). Even for cases tried in a s. 96 court, the case may begin with a 'preliminary inquiry' to determine if there is enough evidence against the accused to proceed with a trial; these inquiries are usually heard before a s. 92 court judge or justice of the peace (see below).

To complicate matters further, there are a large number of 'hybrid' or dual-procedure offences, such as theft under $5,000, where the Crown (prosecution) decides whether to charge the accused with a summary or indictable offence. Summary, indictable, and hybrid offences are discussed more fully in Chapter 9.

In all, s. 92 courts hear the overwhelming majority—over 95 per cent—of trials involving federal offences. It must be stressed that this trend has been actively driven by the *federal* government, which for several decades has willingly shifted judicial jurisdiction over federal offences to the s. 92 courts. As this suggests, the federal government overcame its initial opposition to these courts and has in fact been the actor most responsible for their growth. The reasons for this, and other factors behind the growth of s. 92 courts, are discussed below.

Box 2.2   What's an 'Offence'?

In Canada, 'offence' is the technical term for a law or regulation that, if broken, is punishable by fine or imprisonment. Although people often associate offences with 'crimes', in Canada crimes are only those offences contained in the federal *Criminal Code*. Provincial governments can also create offences, for example, speeding while driving, and the federal government can create non-*Criminal Code* offences, such as fishing without a licence (*Fisheries Act*) or drug possession (*Controlled Drugs and Substances Act*). A useful way to think of it is this: all crimes are offences, but not all offences are crimes.

Young Offenders

Under Canada's *Youth Criminal Justice Act* (YCJA), which replaced the *Young Offenders Act*, persons aged 12 to 17 who are charged with committing a crime are usually treated differently than adults. This reflects the view that young people, by virtue of their relative immaturity and level of development, require greater procedural protections during trials. By the same token, the sentencing of people aged 12 to 17 is usually aimed less at punishment than at rehabilitation and reintegration into society. The YCJA designates 'youth justice courts' to apply these special rules; all provinces have classified their s. 92 trial courts as such courts, and some have even created special courts to deal with young people exclusively.

Family Law

Most s. 92 trial courts have been given jurisdiction over a range of legal issues related to families, which may include marriage, adoption, child custody (in cases of neglect, endangerment, abuse, or separation of the parents), and child support payments ('maintenance'). Notably, however, proceedings related to divorce may be heard only in s. 96 courts. This exception is discussed further in the section below on s. 96 courts.

Civil Law

Except in Manitoba, Nova Scotia, Ontario, and Prince Edward Island, s. 92 courts have been empowered to hear civil cases involving relatively small monetary claims, ranging from less than $5,000 (in Newfoundland and Labrador and Saskatchewan) to less than $25,000 (in Alberta). In addition to small claims, the Civil Division of Quebec's s. 92 court also has jurisdiction over more formal cases in which the amount in dispute is up to $70,000, except cases for spousal support and those cases against the federal government (which are reserved for the s. 96 and s. 101 courts respectively).

Structure

The subject-matter jurisdiction of s. 92 courts is a striking example of integrated judicial federalism in Canada. As we saw, the federal government can assign *federal* offences, most notably under the *Criminal Code*, to *provincial* s. 92 courts. In fact, the only area of criminal law that has been kept from these courts is jury trials, and even they often begin in s. 92 courts with the preliminary inquiry (see Chapter 9). On the other hand, the provinces determine how their courts will deal with these issues, organizationally speaking—for example, in specialized divisions or general courts.

Twenty-five years ago, the most notable structural feature of s. 92 courts was their tremendous size, for there were far more judges in this than any other category after a sustained period of jurisdictional expansion, particularly in criminal law. According to Russell (2007b), in 1982 there were 1,013 s. 92 judges in Canada, compared to only 657 s. 96 trial *and* appellate judges. The expansion of s. 92 courts had been caused by several factors in the preceding decades, including, as noted above, the federal government's eagerness to transfer jurisdiction over federal offences to these provincially appointed courts. The federal government's behaviour in this respect seems illogical, since vigorous competition between the federal and provincial levels of government for jurisdiction is perhaps the defining feature of Canada's constitutional history. The rapid growth of s. 92 courts may itself provide a clue, however, for unlike s. 96 court judges, s. 92 judges are not paid by the federal government. This fiscal reality certainly explains the more recent trend, discussed below, of the provinces 'downloading' routine administrative matters to lower-paid justices of the peace and part-time judges. The expansion of s. 92 courts also reflected larger political trends, especially the phenomenon of 'province building': that is, the growth of provincial welfare states and bureaucracies after the Second World War, in large part as a result of the growth of regionalism and Quebec nationalism. Provincial governments were wary of having their new laws and programs enforced (and possibly undermined) by federally appointed s. 96 judges. As well, judicial appointment provided an enticing opportunity for political patronage.

As Table 2.1 illustrates, the numerical imbalance between the s. 92 and s. 96 courts has shrunk, defying earlier expectations that the growth of s. 92 courts would continue to outpace that of the other courts, especially the s. 96 courts.[8] In fact, there are now *fewer* s. 92 court judges, especially in Ontario and Quebec, than there were in the 1980s, whereas the s. 96 courts have grown (see Table 2.1). The full reasons for this development are not yet clear, but Peter Russell (2007b) identifies at least one part of the explanation: massive off-loading of what were s. 92 court responsibilities (for example, search and arrest warrant applications) to justices of the peace (JPs) in criminal law and prothonotaries in civil law. In Ontario at the end of 2006, for example, there were 309 full-time and 19 part-time JPs, outnumbering the 289 full-time and 37 part-time s. 92 judges. Another factor, given the s. 92 courts' wide criminal law jurisdiction, may be the steady decline in crime rates over the past three decades. It is less clear why there has been a resurgence of s. 96 judges, since it cannot be explained by crime rates (especially since those judges' criminal law caseload has been shrinking (Webster and Doob 2003)). Some possibilities, however, could be an increase in private litigation, family law, or judicial review of provincial tribunals, since, as we shall see below, s. 96 courts have jurisdiction over these issues.

The provinces also vary in the degree to which they have specialized s. 92 courts. Perhaps not surprisingly given its small number of judges, Prince Edward Island has the least specialization. Its three judges each hear all matters within the jurisdiction of the PEI Provincial Court (notably, this includes only criminal and provincial offences by adults and youths), and they sit in only four locations. At the other end of the spectrum, the Alberta Provincial Court contains five specialized divisions: Civil Court (civil claims under $25,000); Criminal Court (bail hearings, preliminary inquiries, trials and sentencing of all summary and most indictable offences); Family Court (spousal and child support, child custody and access, and child welfare and protection); Traffic Court; and Youth Court (cases under the YCJA). The Court of Québec has a similar level of specialization, with Civil, Criminal and Penal, and Youth (child protection and YCJA cases) Divisions, as well as a unit called Tribunal des professions, which can review the decisions of professional conduct committees, such as those for doctors and lawyers.[9] In addi-

Table 2.1   Number of Full-Time Canadian Judges, 2006

Section 101 Courts		Province	Court of Appeal	Section 96 Lower Courts	Section 92 Courts
Supreme Court of Canada	9	Alberta	15	75	114
Federal Court of Appeal	11	BC	15	102	135
Federal Court	33	Manitoba	7	33	40
Tax Court of Canada	21	New Brunswick	7	21	26
(The Court Martial Appeal Court draws its judges from other s. 101 courts)		Newf. & Lab.	6	20	23
		Nova Scotia	8	33	34
		Ontario	24	289	283
		PEI	3	5	3
		Quebec	20	144	270
		Saskatchewan	9	32	46
		Nunavut	—[a]	3	—[d]
		N.W.T.	—[b]	3	3
		Yukon	—[c]	2	3
Total Number of Judges	**74**		**114**	**762**	**980**

Notes:
1. Figures are based on statutory guidelines where possible, and otherwise most recent information from the court.
2. Figures do not include supernumerary judges.

[a] The Nunavut Court of Appeal is composed of justices from the Courts of Appeal of Alberta and Saskatchewan and the judges and ex officio judges of the s. 96 lower courts of the Northwest Territories, Yukon, and Nunavut.
[b] The NWT Court of Appeal, like the Nunavut Court of Appeal, is composed of justices from the Courts of Appeal of Alberta and Saskatchewan and the judges and ex officio judges of the s. 96 lower courts of the Northwest Territories, Yukon, and Nunavut.
[c] The Yukon Court of Appeal is made up of justices of the British Columbia Court of Appeal and justices from the s. 96 lower courts of Yukon Territory and Northwest Territories.
[d] The Nunavut Court of Justice is Canada's first unified, single-tier court.

tion, a municipality in Quebec can choose, either individually or in collaboration with other municipalities, to establish Municipal Courts for cases involving local by-laws, taxes, and less serious provincial and federal offences, such as shoplifting and contraventions of traffic rules. All provinces mix permanent court locations with travelling (or 'circuit') courts, with judges travelling periodically to the latter to administer justice for small communities in more remote areas.[10]

A final issue regarding the structure of s. 92 courts worth elaborating is the existence of *justices of the peace*, as noted above. Historically, even before

Confederation, JPs were members of the local elite who performed many of the same functions as magistrates. Today, JPs hear a surprisingly large number of matters, particularly under the *Criminal Code*, which assigns them the same jurisdiction as provincial court judges. Their precise role differs from province to province, but in Ontario, for example, a part-time 'non-presiding' justice of the peace issues search warrants, presides over bail hearings, and issues subpoenas, while full-time 'presiding' justices of the peace, in addition to these duties, hear cases involving provincial offences. Despite these judicial functions, JPs do not usually require a background in law (practising lawyers are actually precluded from becoming JPs in some provinces[11] to counter-balance the influence of the legal profession), although they receive special training and usually work with legally trained clerks. Writing in 1987, Peter Russell predicted that the 'judicialization of magistracy' might actually increase the use of lay JPs, because they offered a cheaper and more flexible solution than appointing tenured, full-time judges to deal with the heavy workload of administering criminal justice. Although exact figures are not available nationally, it is certainly the case that JPs vastly outnumber s. 92 court judges in some provinces, as indicated for Ontario above. The situation is even more extreme in Saskatchewan, where in 2006 there were 175 JPs, many working in remote communities, compared to only 46 provincial court judges. The same features that make JPs administratively and economically attractive to government, however, prompt concerns about their independence. Beginning in the late 1990s, some provinces introduced reforms to address both issues, including independent councils of judges and laypersons to make recommendations to the government regarding JP appointments, salaries, and alleged misconduct; these reforms mirror measures taken since 1997 to enhance judicial independence (see Chapter 6). In 2005, the Supreme Court's ruling in *Bodner v. Alberta* (2005) confirmed that JPs must enjoy the same independence as judges, even though it ultimately allowed the Alberta government to reject a salary recommendation by that province's JP compensation commission.

Workload

Unfortunately for students of Canada's provincial courts (both s. 92 and s. 96), public reporting on the workload of these courts is poor or relatively inaccessible (especially to non-residents). Only British Columbia, Manitoba, New Brunswick, Newfoundland, and Ontario publish data on-line, and of these only Ontario provides the more useful information about number of cases actually heard, decisions issued, and size of backlog. (British Columbia, New Brunswick, and Newfoundland and Labrador report only cases 'received' or 'filed', and Manitoba only hourly courtroom use statistics.) The remaining provinces issue no information of any kind, and inquiries to their courts and governments proved unsuccessful.

The Canadian Legal Information Institute (CanLII) maintains an excellent website (www.canlii.org), which contains the published decisions of most courts in Canada, going back several years. However, most decisions by trial courts—and recall, all s. 92 courts are trial courts—are not published. Given the social and political importance of administering justice—not to mention the public expense of the judicial system—this lack of transparency is troubling. While it is true that the number of cases in these courts is very large and potentially difficult to track, the fact that two of the largest provinces are able to do so suggests it is possible. Indeed, it is hard to imagine that such statistics are not kept, since they are necessary for assessing the performance and resource needs of the judicial system. This suggests that the problem is rather one of public access.

A full accounting of these courts' workload is therefore impossible, but the data from British Columbia, New Brunswick, and Ontario provide some useful insights that are likely representative of the other provinces. The first is the sheer number of s. 92 trials compared to those in s. 96 courts: in Ontario in 2004/5, for example, judges in the Ontario Court of Justice heard over 4.7 *million* 'events',[12] compared to only 284,667 in Ontario's (s. 96) Superior Court of Justice (Ministry of the Attorney General 2006, App. B). This discrepancy is astonishing in light of the fact, reported in Table 2.1, that there are actually *fewer* s. 92 judges than s. 96 judges in Ontario. In British Columbia, 3.5 times as many cases are filed in the s. 92 court as in the s. 96 trial court, yet the former has only a third more judges. This would seem to imply that the types of cases handled in s. 92 courts are less complicated and therefore take less time to resolve.

The second insight provided by the data for these provinces is the predominance of 'criminal' cases (those involving either federal or provincial offences) on the s. 92 court docket—over 99 per cent in Ontario, where most civil, family, and small-claims cases are heard in the Superior Court of Justice. The s. 92 docket is slightly more balanced in New Brunswick and considerably more so in British Columbia, where criminal cases filed constituted roughly 93.5 per cent and 68 per cent of the respective totals in 2004/5; of these, a significant proportion (roughly 37 per cent in British Columbia) are traffic offences. The big difference in British Columbia is that 22 per cent of the cases filed were related to family law or small claims, a percentage that is probably more representative of most provinces.[13] The large proportion of criminal (and small-claims) cases in the s. 92 workload also helps explain those courts' disproportionately higher output given their number of judges, since criminal matters are usually less complicated than the civil (and often family) litigation and criminal jury trials that predominate in the s. 96 courts. Before we move on to the next category of courts, it must be stressed that when we speak of administering criminal justice in later chapters, we are referring almost entirely to s. 92 courts—not only are they the workhorses of the criminal justice system, but 99 per cent of criminal cases which begin in these courts also end there.

The Section 96 'Provincial' Courts

Historical Background

The distinguishing feature of s. 96 courts, among Canadian courts as well as the judicial systems of other federations, is their blend of provincial administration and federal appointment. As appointment has the most direct influence on the ideological (or more problematically, partisan) orientation of the judiciary, this arrangement reflected the dominant view among the Fathers of Confederation, most notably Sir John A. Macdonald, that Canada should be a quasi-federation dominated by the national government. As Peter Russell (1987) observes, Macdonald wanted the federal–provincial relationship to mirror that between the Imperial government in London and her colonies. In this sense, s. 96 is consistent with other centralizing provisions of the 1867 Constitution, such as federal disallowance, reservation, and the 'Peace, Order, and Good Government' (POGG) clause.[14] Like those provisions, s. 96 has been eroded since 1867 as Canada has been transformed from Macdonald's vision into a more classical federation, with greater equality between the national and regional governments.

The 'Superior, District, and County Courts in each Province' identified in s. 96 of the *Constitution Act, 1867* (formerly the *British North America Act*) were the new country's primary courts. It is therefore striking how little s. 96 actually says about the composition of these courts. Ss. 97–100 establish the foundations of judicial independence for these courts: tenure of office (s. 99, but only for 'Superior' courts); 'fixed' salaries (s. 100); and the requirement that these judges be members of their respective provincial bar (that is, that they have legal training). Otherwise, the 1867 Constitution is silent about the actual functions and organization of these courts. However, as Russell (1987, 47) observes, 'the Canadian Constitution did not purport to be a comprehensive plan for a new and ideal system of government', unlike its US counterpart. This is because Canada's founders were content to adopt the main features of the British state—responsible parliamentary government, the British monarch as the head of state, and the English court system (including the JCPC as the highest court of appeal)—while trying to blend them with the federal division of power and the specific legal and cultural needs of French Quebec. Indeed, the courts listed in s. 96 already existed (sometimes by other names) at the time of Confederation and, particularly the superior courts, had been functioning as colonial courts for many years. S. 129 of the 1867 Constitution makes this judicial continuity explicit, with its provision that '. . . all Courts of Civil and Criminal Jurisdiction, . . . and all Officers, Judicial, Administrative, and Ministerial, existing therein at the Union, shall continue in Ontario, Quebec, Nova Scotia, and New Brunswick respectively, as if the Union had not been made.'

The 'Superior' courts were already British North America's oldest judicial institutions in 1867, existing in every province and largely mirroring the structure of their English counterparts. They were assigned to deal with the most serious issues in criminal and civil law. This helps explain why s. 99 of the *Constitution Act, 1867* provided them with greater independence than any other court, guaranteeing only their judges security of tenure. Superior courts have also long possessed appellate jurisdiction, for panels of trial judges could review rulings of a fellow superior court trial judge, or of an 'inferior' county or district court judge (see below). In 1874, Ontario was the first to create an appeal court staffed with its own judges, and all provinces have since followed suit.

In contrast, the 'inferior' s. 96 county and district courts handled less serious criminal and civil trials, in more remote areas. Except in Upper Canada/Ontario, they were also less extensively developed than superior courts, and they did not exist at all in Quebec. In Quebec, the functions of county and district courts were performed by the provincially appointed Court of Sessions of the Peace and magistrates' courts, which later became the Court of Québec. As the other provinces witnessed the massive shift of less serious criminal cases into s. 92 courts, they all began folding their county and district courts and judges into the superior courts, beginning with British Columbia in 1969. There was also support for this merger movement from county and district court judges themselves, because the functions of these and the superior courts had become somewhat blurred. County and district courts no longer exist in any province today, Nova Scotia being the last to merge its s. 96 courts in 1992.

Jurisdiction

Recall our three dimensions of jurisdiction introduced above, *territorial, hierarchical,* and *subject matter.* As provincial courts, s. 96 courts have territorial jurisdiction only within their province, although some provinces have developed procedures for superior courts to hear cases arising outside that province to prevent duplication or if the case otherwise could not be heard. S. 96 courts have thicker hierarchical jurisdiction than s. 92 courts, for this category contains both trial and appeal courts. In some cases, the same court has both original and appellate jurisdiction, depending on the issue. For example, the Ontario Superior Court of Justice has trial jurisdiction over the most serious criminal cases, but it hears appeals from the s. 92 trial court in cases involving less serious offences; a similar structure exists in all provinces (see Box 2.3). On the other hand, the Courts of Appeal have original jurisdiction over 'references' by their respective provincial governments, which occur when the cabinet asks the Court for an 'advisory opinion' (technically non-binding, but usually respected as a formal ruling) on the legality of proposed or existing legislation. The subject matter jurisdiction of s. 96 courts is constitutionally unlimited, reflecting the fact that they were intended to be the primary type of court. In other words, s. 96 courts can hear virtually any legal issue, criminal or civil, public or private, federal or provincial.

Box 2.3   'Speeding' through the Canadian Judicial System

On 11 July 1991, while driving in New Brunswick, Réjean Richard was stopped and given a ticket for speeding. He failed to pay the fine or appear in the New Brunswick Provincial Court at the time stated on the ticket and was convicted without a trial, as required by s. 16 of New Brunswick's *Provincial Offences Procedure Act.* (As in other provinces, speeding is a provincial traffic offence and is prosecuted in a s. 92 provincial trial court.)

Richard appealed his conviction to the (s. 96) New Brunswick Court of Queen's Bench (CQB) on the grounds that his conviction without trial violated s. 11(d) of the Canadian Charter of Rights and Freedoms, which guarantees any person charged with an offence the 'right to be presumed innocent until proven guilty according to law in a fair and public hearing by an independent and impartial tribunal' (notably, and confusingly, the meaning of 'tribunal' here is the more general traditional one, which includes 'courts', and not the specialized one cited earlier.) The CQB agreed, but found that s. 16 was a 'reasonable limit' on Richard's rights, given the importance of 'establishing a more expeditious and efficient and less costly scheme for minor provincial offences'.

Richard then appealed to the (s. 96) New Brunswick Court of Appeal (NBCA), which reversed the Court of Queen's Bench by a vote of 2–1. The majority of the NBCA concluded that the violation of Richard's rights could not be justified, since s. 16 violates the independence of the judiciary by requiring judges to convict people who fail to appear for their trial date or pay their fine.

The government of New Brunswick appealed this decision to the Supreme Court of Canada, which unanimously reversed the NBCA and threw out Richard's Charter-based challenge to s. 16. Stressing that this was a regulatory offence without the possibility of imprisonment, the Supreme Court ruled that under New Brunswick's ticketing system, Richard was fully aware of the consequences of failing to pay or appear in court, and therefore he had waived his right to a trial when he failed to appear. Moreover, the law allows convictions to be set aside if the person applies to the court within forty-five days of the conviction and can satisfy a judge that their failure to appear was not their fault. (See *R. v. Richard* 1996.)

All that for a speeding ticket!

This is an accurate description of the subject matter dealt with by the highest s. 96 appeal courts in each province, but there is a large gap between the unfettered constitutional jurisdiction of s. 96 *trial* courts and what they actually hear. We have already seen one major example—the s. 92 courts' near-monopoly over trials involving offences. It is not that s. 96 *could* not hear these cases, but that the provincial and federal governments have chosen to assign them to 'purely provincial' courts instead. This and other jurisdictional transfers have not been without controversy, often leading to litigation (ironically, sometimes in the very courts whose jurisdiction is at stake). We will examine three areas that have been particularly contentious: the creation and review of administrative tribunals, criminal trials, and family law.

Creation and Review of Administrative Tribunals

Aside from the criminal cases shifted to s. 92 courts, the greatest threat to s. 96 jurisdiction has been the creation of many provincial and federal administrative tribunals to settle legal disputes that used to be heard in the superior courts. Perhaps because federal tribunals and s. 96 courts are appointed by the same authority and because s. 101 empowers the 'Establishment of any additional Courts for the better Administration of the Laws of Canada', litigation has typically focused on the creation of provincially appointed tribunals. In a 1938 case on the matter, the JCPC tried to sharply restrict further erosion of s. 96 court jurisdiction, in effect 'freezing' it at its 1867 levels (*Toronto v. York* 1938). The JCPC's rationale was that, unlike provincially appointed judges at that time, s. 96 judges were protected by 'the three principal pillars in the temple of justice, and they are not to be undermined': appointment by the Governor General (in reality, the federal cabinet or Prime Minister), tenure, and 'fixed' salaries.

This restrictive approach was significantly liberalized over several cases in the following decades.[15] The changes were synthesized in the Supreme Court's 1981 ruling in the *Residential Tenancies Act Reference*, which produced a three-part test for determining when superior court jurisdiction could be removed to a provincially appointed court or tribunal. This test, with minor subsequent revisions, is as follows:

(1) *Historical Inquiry*: Was the subject matter assigned to the tribunal one that was decided exclusively by a superior, district, or county court at Confederation?[16]

This is roughly the same standard as that proposed by the JCPC in 1938, although there is judicial flexibility at this stage since 'subject matter' is usually a matter of interpretation.[17] However, even if a tribunal fails at this stage, there are two more chances for it to survive constitutional review:

(2) *Judicial Function Test*: Is the tribunal's assigned task 'judicial', which is defined as the adjudication of a dispute through the application of a recognized body of rules in a fair and impartial manner? If so, the task cannot be transferred to a tribunal.

A body designed to settle disputes between landlords and residential tenants by applying an existing statute is a good example of a 'judicial'-type tribunal that would fail this part of the test.[18] That said, there are many examples of tribunals that would pass. Take, for one, the Canadian Radio-television and Telecommunications Commission (CRTC), a federal administrative tribunal charged with regulating Canada's airwaves and telecommunications network and promoting Canadian culture. To begin with, the CRTC is responsible for *creating* many of the regulations and standards that it then enforces through its power to grant (and deny) broadcast licences and to issue fines. Therefore, it cannot be said to resolve disputes through the impartial application of a recognized body of rules. Furthermore, in its role as a promoter of Canadian culture, it cannot be said to be 'impartial' when granting licences; it is, by definition, biased toward broadcasters that promote Canadian content, and against those that do not. For these reasons, the CRTC would be considered an 'administrative' (and, in part, 'legislative') rather than a 'judicial' tribunal.

Failing the above tests, however, a 'judicial' tribunal could still pass constitutional muster if it prevailed at the third stage of the test.

(3) *Institutional Setting Test*: Is the tribunal a crucial part of a wider regulatory system, so long as the 'sole and central function' of the tribunal is not adjudicating disputes? If so, a jurisdictional transfer is allowed.

A positive example was the Ontario Municipal Board in the late 1970s. Although the Board had been given the authority to resolve certain disputes over assets between amalgamating municipalities, this adjudicatory role was, according to the Supreme Court, merely one part of 'the overall picture of the general restructuring of the municipalities in which the Municipal Board is given an important part to play' (*The Corporation of the City of Mississauga v. The Regional Municipality of Peel et al.* 1979).

As the reader may have already guessed, this three-part test is actually a fairly easy hurdle to clear. Only the most overt incursions into s. 96 court jurisdiction would fail by this measure, and thus, there have been few constitutional impediments to the growth of administrative tribunals. Possibly in response, the Supreme Court raised the hurdle in 1995 by adding an additional step to the *Residential Tenancies Act Reference* test. In *MacMillan Bloedel v. Simpson* (1995), a slim majority of the justices ruled that the superior courts' 'core jurisdiction' could not be transferred away without a formal constitutional amendment. Unfortunately, they provided very little guidance about what 'core jurisdiction' means, beyond the vaguely worded phrase 'those powers which are essential to the administration of justice and the maintenance of the rule of law [without which] s. 96 of the Constitution Act could not be said either to ensure uniformity in the judicial system throughout the country or to protect the independence of the judiciary.' As Peter Hogg (2003) has argued, this shift creates a great deal of uncertainty about the constitutionality of existing tribunals.

Another restriction the Supreme Court has imposed concerns judicial review of (that is, appeals to a court from) tribunal decisions. Some provinces, most notably Quebec, have attempted to prevent such appeals to s. 96 courts, but have been blocked by the Supreme Court from doing so completely (A.G. Quebec v. Farrah 1978; Crevier v. A.G. Quebec 1981). As it currently stands, superior courts cannot be prevented by the provincial legislatures from reviewing provincial tribunal decisions to determine whether they are within that tribunal's assigned jurisdiction, or whether the tribunal's powers violate the Constitution (most notably, the federal-provincial division of powers). Parliament is less constrained in this regard—the only judicial review of federal tribunals it cannot remove is that done on constitutional grounds (A.G. Canada v. Canard 1976; CLRB v. Paul L'Anglais 1983).

Criminal Trials

A second contentious area for s. 96 jurisdiction revolves around criminal trials. Given the extremely high percentage of criminal trials ('criminal' here referring to all federal and provincial offences) heard in s. 92 courts, one might ask why a complete transfer has not occurred. There was in fact an initiative by the provinces in the early 1980s to create a s. 92 unified criminal trial court. This move was linked to provincial dissatisfaction at the time with the federal government's unfettered power to appoint s. 96 court judges, a power that it exercised with no provincial input (as we shall see in Chapter 5, this was changed in the late 1980s). It also reflected the combative relationship between Prime Minister Trudeau and the provincial premiers during this extended period of constitutional negotiations that culminated in the 1982 Constitution, including the Charter of Rights and Freedoms. Shortly thereafter, the provinces proposed major jurisdictional transfers from the s. 96 courts at a constitutional conference in 1983, but the negotiations focused on aboriginal rights and the judicial reform proposals were never discussed (Russell 1984a, 248).

The issue came to a head in the 1983 reference case McEvoy (1983), in which the Supreme Court considered the constitutionality of a hypothetical scenario where the federal Parliament and the New Brunswick Legislature agreed to shift all trials of indictable offences to s. 92 courts. The Court surprised many observers by ruling that 'Parliament can no more give away federal constitutional powers than a province can usurp them', even if only to create concurrent jurisdiction. The decision turned on the Court's finding that s. 96 courts cannot be stripped of their 'core or inherent' jurisdiction and 'essential character' as those existed at

Confederation. These standards parallel the 'historical inquiry' in the *Residential Tenancies Act Reference* test; the second and third parts of that test could not save a s. 92 'unified' criminal court, however, as it would clearly be a 'judicial' body whose only function was to adjudicate (criminal) disputes.

The finding in *McEvoy* is problematic, in light of how much of the s. 96 courts' 1867 jurisdiction had *already* been transferred away to purely provincial courts. The Supreme Court recognized this tension but drew a distinction between 'one or a few transfers of criminal law power' (which was understating the matter considerably) and 'a complete obliteration of Superior Court criminal law jurisdiction', which would have the effect of transforming the 'inferior' s. 92 court into a superior court in criminal cases. The *McEvoy* ruling was buttressed by the Court's subsequent decision in *MacMillan Bloedel* (see above), where the Supreme Court explicitly indicated for the first time that they would use the *Residential Tenancies Act Reference* test, along with the 'core jurisdiction' standard, for deciding jurisdictional transfers to 'inferior' courts as well as administrative tribunals. A bigger problem remains, however, in that *McEvoy* and subsequent Supreme Court rulings failed to define precisely the 'inherent jurisdiction' or 'essential character' of the superior courts.

As it currently stands, while the s. 96 superior courts have unlimited criminal law jurisdiction under the Constitution, Parliament and the provinces have assigned jurisdiction over many offences exclusively to the s. 92 trial courts and have created a system where either the Crown (the prosecution) or the accused can 'elect', or choose, their venue for most other offences. Sections 469 and 473 of the *Criminal Code* list only a handful of serious offences that must be tried in the s. 96 courts; those offences include murder, various forms of treason, intimidating government officials, and piracy, all of which must be tried with a jury unless both the Crown and accused choose otherwise. Section 553 further provides that s. 96 courts must hear any case where the accused elects for trial by judge and jury. The exception is in Nunavut, which has the only unified s. 96 trial court in Canada (the Nunavut Court of Justice).[19] While there are therefore no jury trials in s. 92 courts, this prohibition has not been explicitly challenged on constitutional grounds in the Supreme Court of Canada, and constitutional scholar Patrick Healy (2003) argues compellingly that nothing in *McEvoy* or subsequent cases precludes jury trials from being heard in s. 92 courts.[20]

Although several scholars have recently advocated consolidating criminal trials in the provincial s. 92 courts,[21] most provinces do not appear to have much interest in this option. In 1990, the provincial Attorneys General unanimously proposed assigning all criminal trials to the superior, federally appointed courts. As Baar (1996, 293) observes, 'this proposal was supported by the Canadian Association of Provincial Court Judges, whose membership—provincially appointed judges—[stood] to gain more prestige and higher salaries from the change', since most of them would have been assigned to the s. 96 courts as part of the process. Although the provinces altered their court unification strategy partly in light of *McEvoy*, ballooning judicial salaries were at least as influential, if not more so. The economic situation for the provinces in the early 1990s was fairly bleak as Canada experienced a major economic recession, and the federal government made deep cuts in its transfer payments to the provinces. The federal government, not surprisingly, was not interested in taking on the cost of funding about 1,000 new judges, and it rejected the proposal. Baar (1996, 294) observes that the failure of the s. 96 unification efforts led directly to the decision by most provinces to cut their number of s. 92 judges and download routine criminal work to lower-paid justices of the peace.

Notably, the federal government's decision in 1990 was supported by the superior court judges themselves, 'who feared they would be inundated by high volumes of routine criminal work' (Baar 1996, 294). Similarly, in 2000 the Ontario Superior Court of Justice issued a scathing report rejecting the suggestion by the then Ontario Attorney General James Flaherty that unification would improve the efficiency of the criminal justice system. These events illustrate that the politics surrounding judicial administration are not simply federal–provincial struggles, but include the judges themselves as represented through their various professional associations. The federal government appeared to recognize this in the mid-1990s, when it rejected the New Brunswick government's proposal to create a s. 96 unified criminal trial with the surprising explanation that it would not amend the federal *Judges Act* without the support of both the superior court and provincial bar (Baar 1998, 117).

Family Law

The third area of s. 96 jurisdictional contention is family law. As noted above, s. 92 courts in many provinces have significant jurisdiction over family law, including adoption, child custody, and support payments, but some matters related to divorce must be heard in a s. 96 court. The result is that families undergoing divorces may find themselves bounced back and forth among a confusing, time-consuming, and (given lawyers' and court fees) expensive array of s. 92 and s. 96 courts. Why is this the case?

To begin with, Canadian family law is a bewildering hodgepodge of federal and provincial laws. Under the *Constitutional Act, 1867*, Parliament has jurisdiction over 'marriage and divorce' (s. 91(26)). Parliament accordingly makes rules for child support, custody, alimony, and so forth when associated with divorce, but provincial legislatures make the rules if these things are associated with separations short of or outside of divorce (the latter arises with 'common-law' relationships). By virtue of provincial authority over 'the solemnization of marriage in the province' (s. 92(12)) and 'property and civil rights in the province' (s. 92(13)), the province can make laws regarding adoption, the division of matrimonial assets, the civil obligations of husbands and wives, and the guardianship and protection of children (Russell 1987, 226). To further complicate matters, the federal criminal law power (s. 91(27)) covers certain family disputes (domestic assault, for example) and offences committed by youths.

How, then, does all of this affect the family law jurisdiction of courts? The provincial and federal governments can assign adjudicative jurisdiction over their laws, with the caveat that they cannot remove such jurisdiction from a s. 96 court if doing so runs afoul of the rules laid down in the *Residential Tenancies Act Reference*, *McEvoy*, and *MacMillan Bloedel*. The real complication is that the Supreme Court allowed *some* aspects of family law to be moved to s. 92 courts—most notably, adoption and maintenance for children and deserted wives (*Reference re Adoption Act and Other Acts* 1938), and guardianship, child custody, and access to children (*Reference re B.C. Family Relations Act* 1982)—on the grounds that these issues were either 'novel' or, before 1867, were heard by provincially appointed JPs or magistrates. Although there has not been any litigation specifically about the jurisdiction to hear divorce cases, it is widely accepted that this is within the 'core jurisdiction' of s. 96 courts and cannot be transferred. Thus, closely related issues involving a family—such as divorce, allegations of abuse, child support, and custody—might result in more than one court case proceeding simultaneously before different judges, creating inefficiencies and frustration for family members and the legal officials involved.

Prompted by the problems created by a fragmented system of family courts, a movement began in the 1960s to create a 'unified' family court (UFC), with the provinces urging that such bodies be provincially appointed s. 92 courts. The federal government was not receptive to this argument, and at the time, neither were leading members of the legal profession, who held the 'purely' provincial courts in lower esteem than the superior courts (Russell 1987, 226). An innovative attempt by British Columbia to blend s. 96 and s. 92 courts into a single provincial family court was frustrated by the Supreme Court's decision in the *Reference re B.C. Family Relations Act* (1982), which restricted the authority of the provincially appointed judges (specifically, they could not make orders regarding the occupying or entering of the family home in divorce cases). This ruling, with the others cited earlier, made it clear that the creation of a provincially appointed unified family court would require an amendment to s. 96 of the Constitution. However, a UFC at the *s. 96 level* would not, because there are no constitutional limits on the jurisdiction that can be exercised by a superior court. Many provinces have developed such courts on a limited scale, usually in their largest urban centres; at present, only New Brunswick and Prince Edward Island have province-wide UFCs (and in Prince Edward Island they are simply incorporated into the regular s. 96 trial courts rather than as a separate division), although Ontario is committed to expanding its current network of UFCs to the entire province.

To summarize, s. 96 trial courts usually possess the following exclusive jurisdictions: civil cases involving large sums of money, where they are the main courts (except in certain cases involving the claims against the Government of Canada, discussed in the section below on s. 101 courts); the most serious criminal trials, usually involving a jury (murder cases being the most common); review of provincial administrative tribunals (except in Quebec); cases related to divorce, and all family law in selected UFCs; and appeals from s. 92 provincial courts regarding summary offences, civil cases, and family law.

Structure

We can distinguish at least two structural dimensions of provincial superior courts. The first is the hierarchical or vertical structure, that is, how many levels of trial and appeal courts make up the s. 96 courts within the province. The various provincial superior courts are quite similar in this respect, in that every province except Ontario has a single appeal court (the highest court within the province) and, below it, a layer of superior trial courts (which, confusingly, also often serve as courts of appeal for the s. 92 courts, as noted above). As detailed in Box 2.3 and Figure 2.2, New Brunswick's system provides an example: the Court of Queen's Bench is the superior 'trial' court, and the Court of Appeal is what its name implies. Ontario is unique for retaining an additional intermediate-level s. 96 appeal court, called the Divisional Court, which hears appeals from the lower s. 96 Superior Court of Justice in civil cases when less than $50,000 (raised from $25,000 in 2006) is at stake. In most provinces, there used to be more than one level of s. 96 trial courts in the form of the district and county courts, but this ended when these courts were merged with the superior courts.

The second dimension is the lateral or horizontal structure, which may include issue-specialized courts at each level, and the geographical centralization or decentralization of the court. The courts of appeal are the simplest in both regards, since (with the exception of Ontario's Divisional Court) there is only a single court in

Figure 2.2   Chart of Section 96 Courts in New Brunswick

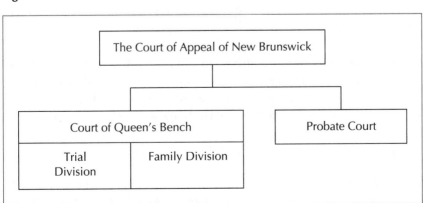

each province and territory dedicated to hearing appeals, and it usually sits in the provincial capital, although some divide their time between major centres.[22] Judges in these courts usually sit in panels of three or, less frequently, five to review decisions by lower courts.[23]

Things are more varied at the trial level. In terms of issue specialization, some provinces, including Alberta, British Columbia, Quebec, Prince Edward Island, and all three territories have only a single superior trial court, which hears all matters falling within its subject matter jurisdiction. In Manitoba, the Court of Queen's Bench is a single court but has a family division with its own judges and a general division for all matters not relating to family law; in Winnipeg, the family division is effectively a unified family court. In Saskatchewan and Newfoundland and Labrador, there is a single general-jurisdiction s. 96 trial court but with separate UFCs in certain urban centres. In the remaining provinces, there are multiple specialized courts although with overlapping judicial membership. Ontario and Nova Scotia have specialized s. 96 small claims courts (nominally, at least[24]) for cases involving less than $10,000 and $15,000 respectively, and Nova Scotia and New Brunswick have probate courts to deal with wills and to supervise the administration and distribution of estates. New Brunswick has the country's only province-wide UFC system, although Ontario is committed to such a system and currently has UFCs in 17 centres; Nova Scotia's UFCs are limited to the Halifax region and Cape Breton. Even in New Brunswick, Nova Scotia, and Ontario, however, the bulk of s. 96 court trials *not* dealing with family law, including both criminal and civil cases, are heard in a court of general jurisdiction (see Table 2.2).

With respect to the degree of geographic centralization, all provinces' s. 96 trial courts are fairly decentralized. Judges, who are usually assigned to a particular region of the province, preside over a 'circuit' of courts in smaller communities within that region, travelling throughout the year. Prince Edward Island, which is the exception to this model, has three permanent superior trial courts. In most other provinces, the largest urban centres constitute their own region or district, and their judges would therefore travel less. Saskatchewan is somewhat different in this regard, for even the 'resident' judges assigned to urban courts work the circuit to help clear backlogs. Notably, decentralization among superior courts (except in Quebec) has increased quite dramatically since the mid-1980s, when they were concentrated in the major cities. The shift can be attributed to the 'merger movement' mentioned earlier, when the district and county courts were converted wholesale into superior courts. As Quebec never had district and county courts, its superior court system has always been highly decentralized.

Workload

As with the s. 92 courts, there is little published data on the workload of the s. 96 courts, with the exception of those in British Columbia, New Brunswick, and

Table 2.2   Names of Section 96 Trial Courts

Province or Territory	General Jurisdiction Trial Court	Unified Family Court?
Alberta	Court of Queen's Bench	No
British Columbia	Supreme Court	No
Manitoba	Court of Queen's Bench (General Division)	Winnipeg (and Family Div. outside capital resemble UFCs)
New Brunswick	Court of Queen's Bench (Trial Division)	Province-wide: Court of Queen's Bench (Family Division)
Newfoundland & Labrador	Supreme Court	St John's
Nova Scotia	Supreme Court	Halifax and Cape Breton
Ontario	Superior Court of Justice	17 locations
Prince Edward Island	Supreme Court (Trial Division)	Effectively, in Supreme Court (Trial Div.)
Quebec	Superior Court	No[a]
Saskatchewan	Court of Queen's Bench	Regina, Saskatoon, Prince Albert[b]
NWT	Supreme Court	No
Nunavut	Nunavut Court of Justice	No
Yukon	Supreme Court	No

[a] However, Quebec excludes only child protection and adoption from the Superior Court. These matters are heard in the Quebec Court, Youth Division.
[b] Outside these cities, the Court of Queen's Bench hears all family law matters except child protection.

Ontario. These provinces reveal some consistent patterns for the s. 96 trial courts. First, criminal law makes up a very small fraction of the s. 96 trial court workload, confirming the dominance of the s. 92 courts in this field. In Ontario, the Superior Court of Justice (SCJ) heard just under 285,000 'events' (see above) in 2004/5, and only 6.7 per cent (19,027) of these were in criminal law. New Brunswick reported an almost identical proportion (6.8 per cent of 11,023 cases filed) in 2004/5, while in British Columbia only 3 per cent of new trials in 2005 concerned criminal law. Since, as pointed out above, jury trials must be held in s. 96 courts, the evidence reveals that the continuing presence of s. 96 courts in the criminal-law field relies heavily on such trials, as they make up just over half of all criminal trials in the Ontario SCJ (*Report of the Ontario Superior Court of Justice*, in Russell 2007b). The judges of the Ontario SCJ stressed in a 2000 report that they remain an important part of the criminal justice system—especially since they hear jury trials for the most serious crimes, and appeals from the s. 92 courts—but there is no denying that a relatively small share of criminal cases is heard in these courts. Moreover, this proportion is shrinking rapidly, at least in Ontario. As Webster and Doob (2003) observe, the SCJ's criminal caseload fell 26 per cent from 1998 to 2000/1, while the s. 92 caseload fell only 3 per cent. From 2000 to 2005, the number of criminal cases heard in the Superior Court remained almost unchanged (19,000 a year), despite large increases in Ontario's population. In part, this can be explained by a troubling situation concerning the Superior Court of Justice (SCJ), which was flagged recently by its Chief Justice (Smith 2007): the number of judges in this court has remained static at 289 during a period when Ontario's population has grown by over five million. This also helps explain why the SCJ's criminal case backlog has grown by 22 per cent in five years. In short, the court is under-staffed.

With the relatively small criminal caseload, it is no surprise that s. 96 trial courts are preoccupied with civil and family law. These make up 60 per cent and 34 per cent respectively of the events heard in the Ontario SCJ, and a third of the civil proceedings are in the small claims court. Unlike criminal law, some of these areas have seen large increases in the number of cases over the past five years in Ontario: 40 per cent in small claims, and 14 per cent for family law (Ministry of the Attorney General 2006). The exception is larger civil suits, where the number of new proceedings has remained stable for five years, perhaps reflecting a shift to

Figure 2.3   Selected S. 96 Trial Court Workloads

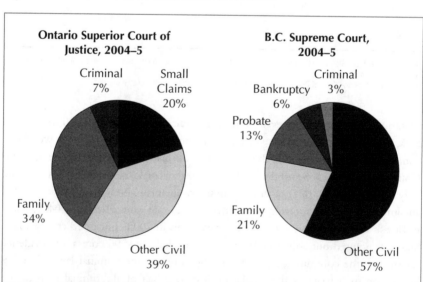

Source: Based on figures from Ministry of the Attorney General (2006) and Supreme Court of British Columbia (2006). Percentages are of 'events heard' in Ontario and new filings in British Columbia.

small claims court or alternative dispute resolution. Despite this, the number of civil law events heard annually has actually dropped by 8 per cent in five years, providing further evidence that the SCJ is understaffed (Ministry of the Attorney General 2006, B7, note 3). In British Columbia, where small claims are heard in a s. 92 court, the workload distribution is a bit different than in Ontario, but the dominance of civil matters is clear: 56 per cent of the cases are civil suits, 21 per centfamily, 13.5 per cent probate (estates and wills), and 6.5 per cent bankruptcy (see Figure 2.3). Although civil and family law cases are increasingly the focus of s. 96 courts at the expense of criminal law, we should be careful not to overstate this trend, in light of the number of courtroom hours dedicated to each in Ontario. In 2004/5, civil cases occupied 62,643 courtroom hours, family law 49,008 hours, and small claims 30,336 hours; criminal cases, at only 7 per cent of the docket, nevertheless took up 49,706 hours, or more than family law. This measure is imprecise because it does not include the many hours of judicial work in chambers (as opposed to open court), but it does suggest that the actual workload of the s. 96 courts may be more balanced than the number of 'events' or cases suggests.

The most notable feature of the workload of the s. 96 appeal courts is how small it is, compared to the massive number of potential appeals from the lower s. 96 and

Table 2.3   Number of Appeals Filed in S. 96 Courts of Appeal, 1995–7

Province	Civil Appeals		Criminal Appeals	
	1995	1997	1995	1997
BC	1,284	1,122	590	580
Alberta	669	613	759	580
Saskatchewan	314	269	269	279
Manitoba	289	215	184	204
Ontario	1,321	1,229	1,543	1,225
Quebec	2,556	n.a.	667	n.a.
New Brunswick	210	n.a.	119	n.a.
Nova Scotia	163	203	132	92
NF & Lab.	n.a.	122	n.a.	81
PEI	33	31	n.a.	20
Totals	**6,839**	**3,804**	**4,263**	**3,061**

Source: Adapted from Greene et al. (1998).

s. 92 courts. Table 2.3 provides an overview of the appeals filed in the highest s. 96 courts of appeal in each province roughly a decade ago; unfortunately, comprehensive data are not available after this point. More recent information from the Ontario Court of Appeal reveals that in 2004/5 that court decided 1,765 cases (with a roughly even split between criminal and civil matters), while the lower courts of Ontario together received roughly half a million new cases (Ministry of the Attorney General 2006). This demonstrates how rare appeals really are. As McCormick (1994) notes, our legal system assumes that one receives a fair and just verdict from the trial judge, and as Greene et al. (1998) observe, the financial cost of appealing (especially since legal aid is often unavailable) and the prospect of losing prevent many potential appeals.[25] Furthermore, almost all court of appeal decisions are final, that is, are not appealed in turn to the Supreme Court of Canada—in Ontario, the figure is 98 per cent. This fact has a very practical significance, given the workload figures cited above: most civil law cases are heard in provincial courts and even if appealed are ultimately resolved in the provincial Court of Appeal. The result has been the 'checkerboard' or decentralized development of civil law across the provinces, in spite of the 'unified' Canadian court system. This has also occurred to some degree in criminal law, but since the *Criminal Code* is a federal statute, Parliament, the federal Attorney General, and the Supreme Court have all endeavoured to eliminate provincial disparities in the criminal process. (As we will see in Chapters 8 and 9, however, there are major limitations to such efforts, because law enforcement and prosecution usually fall to provincial police and Crown attorneys, and trials and sentencing to s. 92 provincial court judges.)

The Section 101 Federal Courts

Historical Background

Unlike s. 96, s. 101 does not establish or recognize existing courts but rather empowers the federal government to create two distinct kinds of courts: a 'general court of appeal for Canada' and 'any additional courts for the better administration of the laws of Canada.' Parliament created both in 1875 with, respectively, the Supreme Court of Canada and the Exchequer Court of Canada. Many Canadians are surprised to learn that the Supreme Court was not created until eight years after Confederation, and then by a simple statute (in contrast, the Supreme Court of the United States was established and its powers clearly defined by the US Constitution). In Canada, however, there was no pressing need for such a court, because there was already a 'general court of appeal' that sat at the top of the judicial hierarchy: the Judicial Committee of the Privy Council (JCPC), in London. Since the JCPC was Canada's highest court of appeal from 1867 to 1949, during this 'long adolescence' (Russell 1987, 335) the Supreme Court of Canada was supreme in name only. Moreover, before 1875, any legal question could be addressed by a province's s. 96 Court of Appeal. Even after 1875, it was possible to bypass the Supreme Court and appeal directly from a s. 96 Court of Appeal to the JCPC in what was known as a *per saltum* appeal. In part, this reflected provincial suspicion of the new court, which was seen by some as an attempt by the federal government to create a court that would be favourable to central authority. Jennifer Smith's research reveals that some proponents of the Supreme Court openly admitted that they had political motives for the creation of the Court. They hoped that the Supreme Court would become 'a substitute for the failing remedy of disallowance' since the latter—which gives the federal government the remarkable authority to 'veto' provincial laws—was politically risky to use because it was often unpopular and provoked provincial resistance (Smith 1983). This factor, along with the federal government's ability to 'refer' legal questions directly to the Court (see below) and an early pattern of patronage-based appointments of low-calibre judges to the Supreme Court, help explain why the Court was widely viewed as a second-rate institution until the mid-twentieth century. Since becoming Canada's highest court and expanding from seven to nine judges in 1949, however, the Supreme Court has shed this image and become a highly respected judicial institution. In the chapters that follow, we will return to the Supreme Court to examine its roles and internal processes in greater detail.

The Exchequer Court of 1875 had very limited jurisdiction: cases against the federal government involving revenue it collected. This was gradually expanded to include virtually all civil cases against the federal government, all federal tax cases, citizenship and immigration matters, and admiralty law. The Exchequer Court was replaced and greatly expanded in 1971 with the creation of the Federal Court of Canada (FCC), which included a trial and appeal division; these were formally divided into the Federal Court of Appeal and the trial-level Federal Court in 2003. A major responsibility of the new FCC was judicial oversight of the growing body of federal administrative tribunals, which paralleled the growth of similar institutions in the provinces. The growth of both was driven by the massive expansion of welfare state programs and state regulation of the economy in general, beginning in earnest during the 1960s. This trend has also led to the creation of other s. 101 courts, whose structure and jurisdiction are detailed below.

Jurisdiction

Unlike the provincial courts, the s. 101 courts have unlimited *territorial* jurisdiction, reflecting the fact that these are national courts. With respect to *hierarchical* jurisdiction, the s. 101 courts include courts of both original (that is, trial) and appellate jurisdiction. Unlike the lower s. 96 courts, the purely federal courts are, with a few exceptions, *either* trial or appeal courts. One notable exception is that the Supreme Court of Canada has original jurisdiction over references by the federal government, as exemplified by the recent reference on same-sex marriage.

Another important exception is that the Federal Court of Appeal has original jurisdiction to review the actions and authority of a large number of federal tribunals listed in s. 28 of the *Federal Courts Act*. On *subject matter*, the Supreme Court has unlimited jurisdiction, which distinguishes it from high courts in most federations, which are often restricted to hearing cases related only to national laws (in the United States) or regional laws (in Switzerland), though most have jurisdiction over constitutional law, which may involve either. As well, the Supreme Court's jurisdiction over both constitutional and non-constitutional cases, while consistent with other common law high courts in, for example, the United States, Australia, and Israel, is quite different from most civil law countries, which usually have a specific 'constitutional court' to resolve matters related to constitutional interpretation.[26] With the exception of the Supreme Court, however, the distinguishing feature of the s. 101 courts is their narrow authority, which has been the result of often surprising decisions by the Supreme Court.

As Peter Hogg explains, the wording of the phrase 'for the better administration of the laws of Canada' in s. 101 itself imposes some limits on the federal courts (other than the Supreme Court; see Hogg, 2003, section 7.2(b)). First, it means that these courts have only the jurisdiction explicitly given to them by Parliament, unlike the s. 96 courts, which have virtually unlimited jurisdiction by default, and even the s. 92 courts, which possess inherent jurisdiction over matters handled by provincially appointed courts and magistrates before Confederation. Second, these courts can be given jurisdiction only over matters arising under 'the laws of Canada', a simple phrase that has spawned a considerable amount of litigation. An early argument by the federal government that it meant *all* laws in Canada, regardless of which level of government had passed them, was rejected by the Supreme Court. Today, it is well established that it can, at most, refer to *existing* (and not 'potential') federal legislation and regulations. In several cases at the end of the 1970s (in particular *Quebec North Shore Paper Co. v. Canadian Pacific* 1977, *McNamara Construction v. The Queen* 1977, and *R. v. Thomas Fuller Construction* 1980), the Supreme Court also rejected the argument that the federal courts could preside over cases where the federal government had constitutional jurisdiction over the legal issue but no actual legislation, even when the statute creating the federal courts granted them general authority over such issues. For example, in *McNamara*, the federal government attempted to sue a company it had hired to build a penitentiary for breach of contract. Penitentiaries are a federal responsibility under the *Constitution Act 1867*, but because the case turned on common law rather than a federal statute, the Supreme Court denied the s. 101 court jurisdiction over the case.[27]

These rulings have had the result of severely constraining the subject matter jurisdiction of the federal courts and fragmenting civil law cases. The *McNamara* ruling removed the federal government's ability to initiate a civil suit in the s. 101 courts unless Parliament has enacted a law allowing it to do so in that specific matter; a general grant of authority in the legislation that establishes the federal courts was deemed insufficient by the Supreme Court. However, the federal Crown can *be* sued in the s. 101 courts, a jurisdiction they have shared with the s. 96 courts since Parliament amended the law in 1992. (Before 1992, this was exclusively the jurisdiction of the s. 101 courts, so the Supreme Court is not solely responsible for narrowing the jurisdiction of the federal courts.) What this means is that if someone sues the federal Crown in a s. 101 court, the government can almost never counter-sue or sue a third party involved in the dispute—as is frequently done in civil cases—in the same court. Similarly, and unlike their American counterparts, Canadian federal trial courts have been denied 'ancillary' and 'pendent' jurisdiction, which, as Peter Russell (1987, 69) puts it, 'make it possible for courts exercising a constitutionally limited federal jurisdiction to deal with issues of state [provincial] law if these are closely associated with the main action concerning federal law.' In other words, these doctrines allow courts to hear legal issues they normally could not if they arise from a common set of facts (for example, the building of a federal penitentiary), in order to consolidate all the diverse but related claims in a civil law matter. As a result, a single situation can give rise to multiple cases spread across different courts, not unlike the fragmentation described above in the field of family law.

An obvious question is *why* the Supreme Court has adopted such a rigidly restrictive attitude toward the federal courts, particularly since it has produced so much wasteful and confusing fragmentation of civil cases. Leading court observers, such as Hogg and Russell, are quite critical of the Supreme Court's approach to this issue, and attribute it to the Court's desire to protect the jurisdiction of the s. 96 superior courts and limit the emergence of a 'dual' system. As we saw with family law, the Supreme Court's approach means that any consolidation of civil cases involving both provincial and federal law must take place in the s. 96 superior courts. Thus, some (again, including Hogg and Russell) advocate eliminating the federal courts altogether in order to streamline the civil justice system, particularly since the federal government appoints the judges of both the s. 96 and s. 101 courts. There is merit to this argument, but it overlooks at least one advantage of having a system of national courts for adjudicating national laws: cross-regional consistency. A decision by a s. 101 court applies equally anywhere in Canada, regardless of where the case originated. In contrast, a decision by a provincial court, *even if it involves federal law*, applies only in that province. This can produce a checkerboard effect of inconsistent interpretation and application of national laws, as it has already done with criminal law and, because of the s. 96 courts' concurrent jurisdiction, federal civil law.

Thus far, we have not addressed a question often asked about s. 101 courts: what about criminal law? After all, since criminal law is a federal responsibility under the Constitution and the *Criminal Code* is a federal law, it would seem to fall within the scope of the 'laws of Canada'. Section 4 of the *Federal Courts Act* does, in fact, designate the Federal Court 'as a superior court of record having civil and criminal jurisdiction', and the federal courts have some criminal jurisdiction, most notably over the recently added anti-terrorism provisions. The explanation therefore seems to be more a matter of choice by Parliament than a constitutional barrier, and this choice is certainly consistent with the federal government's willingness to shift these cases to the provincially appointed s. 92 courts. However, given the political stakes that the federal government has in the anti-terrorism laws, it will be interesting to see if the new political context since September 11 produces some shift of authority towards the Federal Court.

The preceding discussion has focused on what the s. 101 courts below the Supreme Court do *not* hear, but what *do* they have jurisdiction over? As noted, they have concurrent jurisdiction with the s. 96 courts in civil suits against the federal Crown. However, they have exclusive jurisdiction for judicial review of a wide range of federal administrative tribunals, commissions, and agencies, such as the Immigration and Refugee Board, Employment Insurance umpires, the National Parole Board, and the Canada Revenue Agency. The s. 101 courts also hear interprovincial and federal–provincial disputes and many cases arising from federal legislation, including cases pertaining to taxation, immigration and citizenship, labour relations, intellectual property, admiralty law, parole and penitentiaries, national defence, and telecommunications, to name just a few. That said, recall that Parliament has opted to have many federal laws and regulations enforced through the provincial courts, as we saw in the *Marshall* case at the outset of this chapter. The result is that the lion's share of cases in s. 101 courts are brought by individuals or companies that are challenging the legality (often the constitutionality) of a federal law or administrative tribunal, or a decision of a specific tribunal.

Structure

As mentioned above, there are both s. 101 trial and appeal courts. The Supreme Court of Canada is, of course, the most well-known appeal court in the country, but below it, there are the Federal Court of Appeal (FCA), which hears appeals from the trial-level Federal Court (FC) and the Tax Court of Canada (TCC); and the Court Martial Appeal Court of Canada, which hears appeals from courts martial. As the court names suggest, there is some issue specialization at both the trial and appeal level. The Tax Court was established in 1983 to hear cases pursuant to (not surprisingly) federal taxes, and since 1991 it has had exclusive jurisdiction in this regard.[28] The TCC's original exclusive jurisdiction has been expanded since its creation to include cases arising from aspects of Employment Insurance, the Canada Pension Plan, veterans' affairs, Old Age Security, and cultural property. Courts martial, which are disciplinary bodies for military personnel, are essentially criminal law courts. There are four types of courts martial within the Canadian Forces: the General Court Martial (GCM), the Disciplinary Court Martial (DCM), the Standing Court Martial (SCM), and the Special General Court Martial (SGCM). Their jurisdictions largely overlap in that they try individuals for 'service offences', which are offences under the *National Defence Act*, the *Criminal Code,* or any other Act of Parliament committed by a person while subject to the military Code of Service Discipline. The Special General Court Martial is exceptional in that it can try only civilians (for example, non-military personnel in war zones where regular courts are not available), and it issues punishments of fines and imprisonment, whereas the most severe punishment issued by the DCM and SCM is 'dismissal with disgrace'. The courts martial also differ in their membership—the GCM and DCM use a mix of military judges and officers, the SCM a single military judge in a less formal and expedited hearing, and the SGCM a single military judge but in a formal hearing. At the appellate level, the CMAC, created in 1959 to help 'civilianize' military courts, hears appeals only from these courts martial; since 1991 it also has the power to review the severity of sentences and to substitute new sentences. Notably, this 'civilianizing' extends to the CMAC's membership, which is drawn from the civilian judges of other s. 101 courts. The Federal Court and Federal Court of Appeal, which have more general-issue jurisdiction, hear federal law cases that have not been explicitly assigned to the other s. 101 courts. Until 2003, these last two courts were technically two divisions (trial and appeal) of the Federal Court of Canada, and judicial membership did overlap, especially early in the Federal Court's history (see Bushnell 1997). Although the 2003 change formally divided the personnel of the two courts, it was otherwise an administrative reform with little jurisdictional impact.

Geographically, the federal courts are headquartered in Ottawa, but with the exception of the Supreme Court of Canada, they are actually fairly decentralized to enhance their accessibility. All lower s. 101 courts (even the FCA and CMAC) are circuit courts that hear cases in several locations across the country throughout the year. In addition to its sixteen local offices, the FCA has also adopted a network of tele-conference and video conference facilities in Canada's ten largest cities to reduce the need for travel by litigants and judges.

A final note on structure concerns the number of judges who preside over each case. Like their provincial counterparts, the FCA and CMAC usually hear appeals in panels of three judges, and five in extraordinary cases, whereas trial court cases (except some courts martial) have a single judge. As discussed in more detail in Chapter 4, the Supreme Court has only nine members but has historically heard a large share of its docket with smaller panels of five or seven justices, full-court hearings being reserved for its most important cases. The quorum of justices for a case is only five, but four is permitted with the permission of the parties to the case.[29] In more recent years, Chief Justices have increased the number of cases heard by a full court, but panels of seven are still used frequently. The rationale for regularly assigning fewer than nine justices is ostensibly to alleviate the heavy workload of the individual justices so that the Court may hear more cases (and is sometimes done because of illness or judicial vacancies caused by retirements. Given the finality and importance of the Supreme Court's rulings and the fact that closely divided decisions are not unusual, the use of incomplete panels troubles many Court observers. Moreover, the workload rationale for incomplete panels is not particularly compelling in light of evidence from the US Supreme Court (although, to be fair, the Canadian justices seem to write more opinions per case—that is, concurring and dissenting—than their American counterparts). All nine justices of the US Supreme Court must preside over every case and participate in every petition for *certiorari* (request to appeal to the Court), which today number over 8,000 per year. The Canadian Supreme Court, with the same amount of help from law clerks, hears only about 600 leave-to-appeal requests per year (see below), and these are dealt with in panels of only three justices (see Flemming 2004). Yet, the US Court renders roughly the same number of judgments each year as its Canadian counterpart. The Supreme Court has been endeavouring in recent years to hear more cases as a full court, particularly in contentious or high-profile matters, although frequent departures of justices have made this difficult.

Workload

In stark contrast to the other categories of courts, the federal courts regularly publish detailed workload reports (four times a year for the Federal Court) on the Internet. Given their relatively narrow jurisdiction, it should come as no surprise that the s. 101 courts collectively have the lightest workload of the three categories of courts. Russell (1987, 317) reports that the average number of cases initiated per year in the Federal Court (trial division) between 1971 and 1985 was only 2,957. As we can see in Figure 2.4, that number had almost quadrupled to over 11,522 by 2003–6, with almost another 5,000 initiated in the Tax Court of Canada. The Federal Court's docket includes cases involving aboriginal treaties, admiralty law, intellectual property, patented medicines, civil suits against the federal Crown, and review of federal tribunal decisions (most notably, regarding immigration and Employment Insurance). The FC's workload, however, consists primarily of immigration-related cases, which are the only category of its docket that has increased significantly since the mid-1990s. Immigration cases make up between 75 per cent and 80 per cent of all proceedings begun in the FC, and 50 per cent to 60 per cent of its annual backlog ('Pending' in Figure 2.4). Judicial review of decisions by visa officers alone jumped so much—from 149 in 1995 to 890 in 2000—that in 2002 Parliament made such review by leave of the court instead of automatic upon the claimant's request.[30] Notably, this and other changes to the immigration and refugee process contributed to a 27 per cent drop in new cases in the Federal Court from 2002 to 2006, allowing the court to cut its backlog in immigration cases by over 40 per cent (4,380 to 2,491). This progress notwithstanding, the lower s. 101 courts continue to struggle with heavy backlogs (see Figure 2.4). In all three courts with available data, the annual backlog is close to the number of new proceedings,

Figure 2.4   Average Annual Workload of S.101 Courts, 2003–6

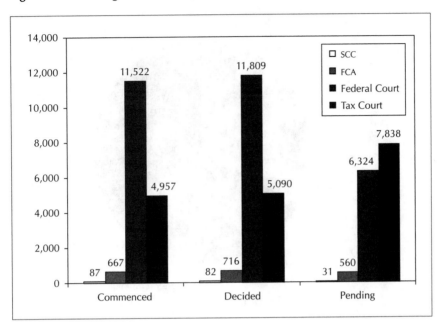

Source: Calculated from data in Court Administration Service (2006) and Supreme Court of Canada (2006).

and it is actually significantly larger in the TCC. As well, the TCC backlog is even larger than the number of cases resolved annually, suggesting that that court does not have the institutional resources it requires.

Unlike the lower s. 101 courts, which have fairly limited docket control (although the FCA has more than the trial divisions), since 1974 the Supreme Court of Canada has enjoyed almost complete control over which cases it will hear. In that year, Parliament amended the *Supreme Court Act* to eliminate the right of appeal to the Supreme Court in civil law cases involving claims over $10,000. Instead, those seeking access to the Supreme Court must apply for 'leave' to appeal from the Court's Justices. Although accused persons and the Crown still have a limited right to appeal in serious criminal matters (see Chapter 9), 80 per cent to 90 per cent of the Supreme Court's docket is now determined by the Court itself (Supreme Court of Canada 2006, 4). On the basis of the 'elastically worded and vaguely defined' (Flemming and Krutz 2002b, 233) guidelines in s. 40(1) of the *Supreme Court Act*, the case must raise an issue of 'public importance' (see the discussion in Chapter 4).

Docket control has clearly permitted the Court to shift its focus to public law matters, such as criminal law, administrative law, and constitutional law (see Figure 2.5). For example, in 2005, despite the fact that applications for leave to appeal in private law were three times the number in public law, over 60 per cent of the cases heard by the Supreme Court concerned public law (Supreme Court of Canada 2006, 6). Notably, 70 per cent of these, or 42 per cent of the total docket, were

Figure 2.5   **Supreme Court of Canada, Appeals Heard by Issue Area, 2005**

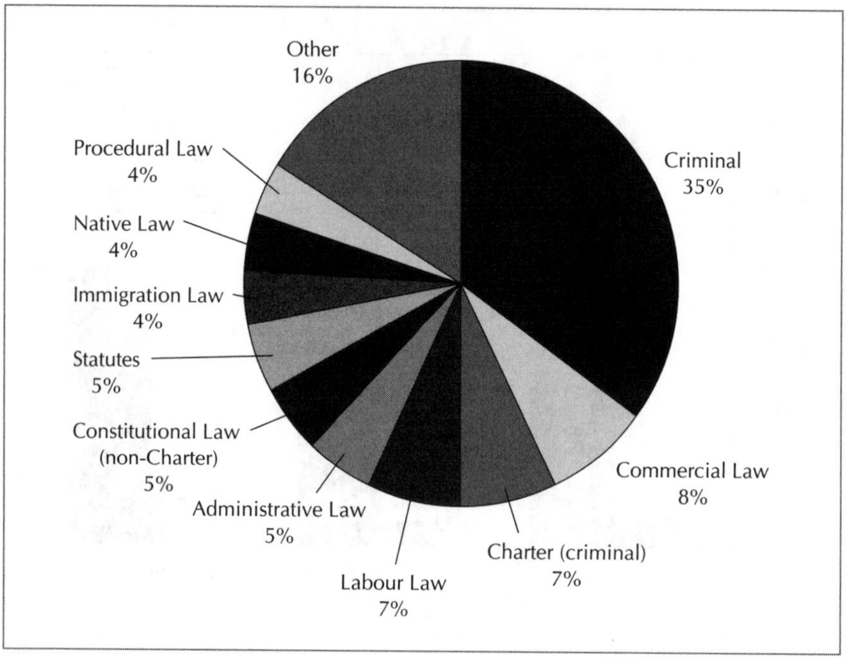

Other
16%

Procedural Law
4%

Native Law
4%

Immigration Law
4%

Statutes
5%

Constitutional Law
(non-Charter)
5%

Administrative Law
5%

Labour Law
7%

Charter (criminal)
7%

Commercial Law
8%

Criminal
35%

Source: Adapted from Supreme Court of Canada (2006).

criminal matters. While cases involving the Charter of Rights and Freedoms continue to occupy a significant portion of the Supreme Court docket—roughly 15 per cent—this is down from 25 per cent to 30 per cent a decade ago.[31]

Another major development in the Supreme Court's workload has been its declining output over several years. In 1990 the Court issued 144 decisions, which dropped to about 100 a year in the mid-1990s and hit a new annual low in 2006 with only 59. The explanation for this trend has not been determined, but there are several possibilities, including the increasing complexity of cases; high turnover for several years among the Court's justices, including the departure of two of the most frequent decision writers, Justices Iacobucci and L'Heureux-Dubé; efforts to craft more consensual decisions, which take longer; and greater deference to lower-court rulings (Makin 2006b, A4). In the US, where their Supreme Court has exhibited a similar trend, commentators suggest that the aging justices prefer a lighter workload and are spending more of their time travelling to academic and non-bench professional events. Another possibility is the steep drop in appeals 'as of right' from fifty-seven in 1995 to the low teens in the early 2000s, despite the fact that leave-to-appeal applications have consistently numbered between 550 and 650 since 1995 (Supreme Court of Canada 2006, 4). Since appeals as of right are usually disposed of in a paragraph with a single opinion for the Court, the number of significant cases being ruled on may not actually be dropping much. As Makin notes, however, the number of pages written annually by the Court in its published judgments has fallen by over 1,000 in the past decade, a trend which cannot be attributed solely to the falling number of appeals by right.

From a Unified to Dual Court System?

At several points in this chapter, we have made reference to the 'unified' nature of Canada's judicial system, at least as laid out in s. 96 of the 1867 Constitution, and the subsequent development of 'purely' provincial and federal courts. So where do we stand today? How far has Canada moved toward the 'dual' court system of (largely) separate national and regional courts seen in the United States? To answer this question, it is important to be accurate about just how unified the Canadian system really was in 1867. Although there were no 'purely' federal courts, we saw that there were already provincially appointed local magistrates and justices of the peace in most provinces, or they were created almost immediately after Confederation. Peter Russell correctly observes that the s. 92 provincial courts do not threaten the unified system to the extent that they enforce federal laws such as the *Criminal Code*. Indeed, having provincially appointed judges apply federal laws is even *more* 'unified' in terms of federalism than having these cases heard by the federally appointed judges of the s. 96 courts. The same cannot be said, however, when provincially appointed judges adjudicate cases arising from provincial offences, family law, and civil law. The Supreme Court of Canada seems to have recognized this, as indicated by its refusal to allow the consolidation of family law in s. 92 courts. The emergence of s. 96 united family courts in some provinces is, in fact, a move toward a more unified court system in general. As Healy (2003) argues, a consistent approach by the Supreme Court to the matter of unification would see it allow all federal indictable offences to be heard in s. 92 courts, especially since s. 92 courts now hear criminal trials as complex as those heard in s. 96 courts (Webster and Doob 2003). Unification of the criminal trial courts has not occurred, however, nor does there seem to be any interest within the federal government for such a reform, especially since some contend that it would require a constitutional amendment to s. 96.

In any case, the effect of s. 92 courts on unification seems to be mixed, and we do not have separate 'purely' provincial court systems for provincial law. It should be noted that some provinces—especially Alberta, British Columbia, and Quebec—are closer to such a system than other provinces. Even in these provinces, though, the effect is limited to the trial courts since appeals from the s. 92 courts are heard by s. 96 courts. In other words, the appellate courts in Canada continue to exercise a strong unifying influence on the judicial system. The provincial courts of appeal have wide jurisdiction over disputes arising from both provincial and federal law. The Supreme Court of Canada, which has broader jurisdiction than its American counterpart, is the ultimate symbol of a unified system, although this image is somewhat undermined by the fact that it hears a very small number of cases and is entirely a creature of Parliament, in contrast to the s. 96 Courts of Appeal. Greater provincial involvement in Supreme Court appointments, as proposed in the failed Meech Lake Accord (1987–90) and Charlottetown Accord (1992), would counteract the latter of these shortcomings, although it could generate other criticisms, which are discussed in Chapter 5.

What about the lower s. 101 courts? Russell and Hogg both contend that these pose the greatest threat to the unified system, first, because s. 96 courts used to review federal administrative bodies, and second, because there is no provincial influence at any point as cases pass from federal trial to appeal courts, while the reverse is not true for the provincial courts. It is likely for these reasons that the Supreme Court has been so hostile to the lower s. 101 courts, and why it has precipitated the fragmentation of civil cases involving the federal government, which encourages litigants to consolidate cases in the s. 96 courts. As late as 1987, however, Russell (1987, 53) could only call the Federal Court of Canada 'the thin edge of the wedge', and it does not appear to have thickened much since. Though there are certainly more cases in the Federal Court now than in 1987, they remain a small percentage of the total number of cases in the judicial system. It should be noted that the Canadian system *is* 'federal' or dualistic in the sense of how cases move up the judicial hierarchy, in that the provincial and federal systems are like parallel train tracks (albeit leading to the same 'station', the Supreme Court): once a case begins in a provincial trial court (either s. 92 or s. 96), it must be appealed to that province's (s. 96) appeal court(s) and federal trial rulings must proceed to the Federal Court of Appeal. In short, one cannot 'switch tracks' halfway through the journey.

Conclusion

Even to those familiar with Canada's legal system, the structure of the judiciary is complex and frequently confusing. Part of the problem is the misleading labels: 'Supreme' and 'Superior' courts in some provinces are actually lower- or intermediate-level trial courts (see Table 2.2). 'Federal' laws and regulations are frequently enforced by 'provincial' courts, and some 'provincial' courts are actually appointed by the federal government in Ottawa. Furthermore, responsibilities and authority within the Canadian judicial system often overlap, and the courts in which a case is ultimately heard involves a considerable amount of choice by the parties to a case and, at the higher levels of the judicial hierarchy, the judges themselves. We hope that this chapter has helped dispel some of this confusion while illustrating that court workloads and structural features are inherently tied up in the larger political context. With this foundation, we can proceed with our examination of the actors and internal processes of these courts.

Chapter 3

Judicial Process and Alternative Dispute Resolution

A couple in Alberta was planning a divorce after a five-year separation and had some divergence of opinion about child custody and visitation. Twin sisters in Manitoba disagreed with the decision by the Manitoba High School Athletics Association to prevent them from playing on the boy's hockey team. Marcel was charged with drug possession in Vancouver and therefore was in conflict with the state. A lesbian woman who had broken up with her partner sued the government of Ontario because its *Family Law Act* created legal obligations for support payments when opposite-sex couples broke up but not same-sex couples. Doctors in Newfoundland went on strike for higher salaries from the government.[1]

What do all these seemingly different disputes have in common? All of them featured dispute-resolution processes by third parties that differed slightly or significantly from the traditional adjudicative model of courts. In the adjudicative model, a neutral and passive judge, who is not chosen by the parties, makes a binding decision by applying established legal principles to a set of facts that are presented by opposing parties in conformity with strict and formal procedural rules. Trials shown on television—real or fictional—are often representative of the adjudicative model. In the example of the divorce, however, the couple did not go to court. They used a variation of mediation called 'collaborative law', which differs from adjudication in a court in all important respects: the couple chose their third-party mediators; the process was informal; the agreement they reached was based on their expressed desires and interests, not the law; and the agreement was not forced upon them. The doctors in Newfoundland and the government resolved their dispute through arbitration, which sits somewhere between adjudication by a court and mediation. The doctors and government together chose an arbitrator to hear their submissions, the process for presenting arguments and evidence was semi-formal, the decision was based largely on the principles of labour law, and the decision was binding on the parties. The twin sisters who wanted to play hockey made a human rights complaint before an administrative tribunal, the Manitoba Human Rights Commission. They made their presentations, as did the athletics association, in a somewhat formal process, and the Commission ruled in the girls' favour on the basis of Manitoba's human rights legislation.

In these first three examples, the dispute-resolution processes were outside of the judicial process. The last two examples show ways in which the judicial process itself is changing. Marcel appeared before a specialized drug court in Vancouver, where the judge, instead of being a neutral and passive referee as in an adjudicative-style court, actively collaborated with the defence lawyer, the Crown attorney, and representatives of social agencies to formulate a treatment plan for Marcel. The court monitored Marcel's progress. After he had successfully completed the program, the judge and other members of the court team applauded his efforts (literally) and he was free to go.[2] This is an example of the 'problem-solving' model of court. The example of the lesbian couple in Ontario illustrates the 'policy-making' model of court. The couple had settled their financial dispute before the case reached Canada's Supreme Court, but rather than declare the case to be moot, the Court used it as an opportunity to modify existing legal principles. The Court, on the basis of an expansive interpretation of the Charter of Rights, ordered the government of Ontario to change its law so that same-sex couples would not be treated differently from opposite-sex couples.

This chapter compares the objectives and procedures of three models of court—policy-making, problem-solving, and adjudicative—as part of an analysis of four key components of the judicial process: (1) access to court, (2) the role of the judge and number of parties, (3) fact-finding, and (4) mode of reasoning. After highlighting how the policy-making and problem-solving models are challenging the adjudicative model of courts, the chapter next demonstrates how the adjudicative model is also being challenged outside of the judicial process by alternative dispute resolution (ADR) mechanisms, such as mediation and arbitration, and adjudication by administrative tribunals.

Throughout the chapter we note particular impetuses for the rise of challenges to the adjudicative model from within and outside the judicial process. The chapter also pays attention to the political implications of these trends. Are certain political, legal, or social actors or interests privileged over others by changes in the judicial process or the use of alternative dispute resolution systems as opposed to courts? What kinds of values are promoted in each type of dispute-resolution process? The chapter concludes with some possible theoretical explanations for the rise of other dispute-resolution processes that challenge the adjudicative model.

Judicial Process

At any moment in Canada or any other country, individuals, families, groups, businesses, and government agencies have untold numbers of grievances with one another. However, only a tiny fraction of these disputes ever reach a court or are even discussed with a lawyer. There are a whole host of reasons why a dispute may not escalate into a legal one—socially constructed norms may militate against taking a dispute farther, some individuals or organizations may just decide to put up with their grievances, and others may not have the financial means to engage in a legal fight (see McCormick 1994, 40–3). Even for those with the willingness and financial capacity to initiate litigation, there are still procedural and substantive limits to the kinds of disputes that the courts will hear. Chapter 1, for example, noted that in a number of provinces there is no clear legal basis for a lawsuit based on a claim that another individual, such as a neighbour using a digital camera, had breached one's 'privacy'. The discussion on 'access to courts' below highlights various procedural and substantive limits to getting into court, particularly to challenge the validity of government law and policy.

Access to court is one of the four aspects of judicial process that are crucial to understanding the role of courts in the larger system of governance. The others are how many parties are involved and what the role of the judge is; what kinds of facts are collected and how are they collected; and what mode of reasoning judges use to arrive at a conclusion. Each of these dimensions of the judicial process is discussed in somewhat greater detail below. As part of those discussions, this section of the chapter traces how the traditional 'adjudicative' model of courts is being challenged by the 'policy-making' and 'problem-solving' models of courts.

In the adjudicative model, each of the four key aspects of the judicial process is predicated on the normative assumption that the proper and legitimate role of courts is to resolve disputes and not to solve underlying problems or to make policy. First, judges adjudicate 'concrete legal disputes'. In other words, they do not adjudicate disputes that are hypothetical, no longer exist, or involve a disagreement that is not legal in nature. Access to courts, especially to challenge government policy, is difficult. Second, the legal dispute involves two parties and, in the common law system, the judge acts as a passive 'referee' who makes decisions on the basis of submissions from the parties in an adversarial process. Third, the facts presented by each party must follow established legal procedures and involve 'who did what to whom' (adjudicative facts). Finally, the judge arrives at a conclusion by applying established legal principles to the facts of the case. This does not mean that judges never play some role in defining the legal principles—rules may need to be clarified or adjusted incrementally—but it does mean that judges are quite limited in the degree to which they create rules, even in appellate courts.

Conversely, the 'policy-making' model assumes that it is proper and desirable for courts to be involved in the articulation of public values through policy development. Thus, policy-making courts operate less like adjudicators and more like legislatures or executive bodies. It relatively easy to obtain access to the court to challenge government policy, third-party interest groups are allowed to make presentations to the court, social-science data are used in decision making, and judges try to balance various social interests in their decisions.

A more recent model of courts is the 'problem-solving' model. This model sees value in the courts' trying to address the underlying problems or issues that give rise to legal disputes. The problem-solving court makes use of ADR techniques, such as mediation, before the trial, and trials themselves are presided over by judges who are actively involved in the collection of evidence and in trying to fashion a solution to problems in their decision making. The models are summarized in Table 3.1.

Table 3.1 Models of Judicial Process in the Common Law System

	Adjudicative	Policy-making	Problem-solving
Access to courts	Strict rules of standing, mootness, ripeness, and political questions that make access difficult	Liberalized rules of standing, mootness, ripeness, and political questions that make access easier	—
Number of parties and role of the judge	Bi-polar (two parties to the dispute)	Multi-polar (third parties allowed and even encouraged)	'Team'-based approach
	Formal procedural rules	—	Less formal rules, especially in pre-trial ADR processes
	Passive judge	—	Judge more actively involved in promoting pre-trial settlements. More active at trial.
Fact-finding	Adjudicative facts	Social facts	More contextual knowledge of the litigants
	Parties present facts, strict rules of judicial notice	Parties (and interveners) present facts, but rules of judicial notice relaxed	Judge more active in fact-finding
Mode of Reasoning	Applying well-established legal principles	Creating rules to balance interests and achieve 'justice'	Focusing on solving problems of the litigant and building relationships
	Incremental law-making	Relatively greater law-making	
	Deference to legislatures	Less deference to legislatures	

Of course, the real world of judicial process does not tidily reflect these different models—different courts and judges exhibit different tendencies, and even one case may have elements from more than one model. However, the models are useful in that they help us to detect trends in judicial process, sharpen our ability to understand the potential benefits and drawbacks of each of the models, and aid us in understanding the tensions and difficulties that can arise as changes are introduced, sometimes haphazardly, to the traditional adjudicative processes to accomplish goals that the adjudicative process was not designed to accomplish.

Access to Court: Standing, Mootness, Ripeness, and Political Questions

The adjudicative model of courts would suggest that courts should confine themselves to deciding live, concrete legal disputes, because that model views the function of courts as adjudicating legal disputes between two parties who have a direct interest in the outcome. Conversely, the policy-making model of courts features more relaxed versions of these requirements (discussed below) because that model proposes that the courts have a legitimate and important role in shaping and disseminating public values. As long as an important issue with differences of opinion on each side is well-argued in court, technical requirements about there being a live, concrete legal dispute become less important in the policy-making model (Sossin 1999, 3).

The requirement that one must be party to a legal dispute in order to have a case heard in court is called *standing*. In the context of public law and the ability to challenge the constitutional validity of a law, the test was quite restrictive until it was liberalized in the 1970s and early 1980s. In *Smith v. Ontario Attorney General* (1924), the Supreme Court argued that a person could ask a court to declare a law of general applicability invalid only if the law 'exceptionally prejudiced' the plaintiff and directly affected the personal, property, or pecuniary interests of the plaintiff. This restrictive test was changed by three Supreme Court decisions—*Thorson* (1975), *McNeil* (1976), and *Borowski* (1981)—that culminated in a much more relaxed rule of standing.

Joe Borowski was a man who wanted to challenge the federal government's abortion law from the 'pro-life' perspective. Even though he was not directly affected by the law (for example, he was not a doctor or a woman wanting an abortion) or even indirectly affected (for example, he did not have a wife or a child wanting an abortion against his wishes), he was allowed to challenge the law. In its *Borowski* (1981) decision, the Court said that standing should be granted if a person is affected directly by a law or has a 'genuine interest as a citizen in the validity of the legislation and that there is no other reasonable and effective manner in which the issue may be brought before the Court.' The majority argued that there was no other reasonable way that Borowski's perspective would get into court (for example, if a doctor was charged under the abortion law for performing abortions illegally, the doctor would not argue for a more restrictive abortion law). Chief Justice Laskin (along with Justice Lamer) dissented and argued that the decision would allow the judicial arena to become a political battleground over the issue.[3]

A little more than a decade after the *Borowski* (1981) decision, the Supreme Court stated that allowing public-interest standing by individuals and interest groups was even more important after the Charter of Rights and Freedoms was added to the constitution in 1982; otherwise, 'Charter rights might be unenforced and Charter freedoms shackled' (*Canadian Council of Churches* 1992). The Supreme Court also said, however, that 'blanket approval' should not be given to requests for standing. The decision to grant standing should be guided by the role of the courts in the system of government, the desirability of having both sides of the issue presented by those most directly affected by the law, and the resources needed to hear and decide cases. In this particular case, standing was denied to the Canadian Council of Churches to challenge rules that made it harder for individuals to get refugee status, because the Court believed that such a claim could and would be brought by individuals who were actually denied refugee status. While this ruling denied standing to a group, it generally reaffirmed the principle of standing created in *Borowski* (1981) and stated that the discretion to grant standing should be used in a 'generous and liberal manner'. Compared to the original rule of standing, such an approach makes it easier for individuals and groups to use the courts to challenge laws, and this, in turn, increases the potential for courts to become more involved in shaping public policy. In the *Chaoulli* (2005) case, for instance, although Dr Chaoulli was not 'exceptionally prejudiced' by Quebec's laws against private medical services, the Supreme Court stated that he had public-interest standing, on the basis of the *Borowski* precedent, to challenge rules against private health care.[4]

The Supreme Court also has affirmed that courts have the discretion to make decisions in *moot* cases where the dispute is no longer 'live'. Ironically, the case again involved Joe Borowski. He had challenged Canada's abortion law (unsuccessfully) in a Saskatchewan trial court and the Saskatchewan Court of Appeal after being granted standing by the Supreme Court in 1981. Yet, by the time his case got back to the Supreme Court level, the Court had already struck down Canada's abortion law in its 1988 *Morgentaler* decision, thereby rendering the case moot. Borowski, however, wanted the Supreme Court to hear his case because he had wanted to attack the law from the pro-life side and hoped for a favourable ruling on the rights of the fetus or unborn child.

Ultimately, the Supreme Court declined to accept Borowski's case. In announcing that decision, however, the Supreme Court maintained that courts could hear moot cases, and it created a three-part guideline (similar to the one for standing) to help judges determine whether moot cases should be heard and decided. First, judges should consider whether an adversarial situation would exist if a court were to hear a moot case—would both sides of the issue be effectively represented? Second, judges need to determine whether the issues raised by the case are important enough to warrant the use of scarce judicial resource to hear and decide a moot case. If the underlying issue is one that will likely reappear before the courts, then that favours hearing and deciding the issue, especially if the issue tends to evade appellate review. (For example, cases involving legal issues surrounding striking workers often become technically moot before reaching the upper echelons of the judiciary because the labour dispute is often over by the time the case moves up the appellate ladder). Deciding these kinds of cases can save the courts' time (by reducing the chances that the same issue will continue to be litigated) and clarify disagreements about the law that otherwise may not be resolved. Third, judges are encouraged to think about the courts' 'proper law-making function' and to be sensitive to the judiciary's role as the 'adjudicative branch in our political framework'. When the Supreme Court applied these guidelines to Borowski's case specifically, it ruled that it should not make a decision in the absence of new abortion legislation that would likely be passed by Parliament and subsequently challenged in the courts.

The specific result in *Borowski* (1989) represented more the 'adjudication of disputes' approach to mootness, but a review of the case law in Canada found decisions not to hear moot cases 'surprisingly rare' (Sossin 1999, 103). An example of a decision to hear a moot case comes from the *M. v. H* (1999) decision referred to at the beginning of this chapter. The case of *M. v. H.* began when a lesbian couple ended their relationship and M. discovered that she could not apply for spousal support payments from her former partner because Ontario's *Family Law Act* applied only to opposite sex-couples. Shortly before the Supreme Court was going to hear the case about whether the Ontario law violated equality rights in the Charter of Rights, M. and H. reached a financial settlement to their dispute, thereby rendering the case moot since a live legal dispute no longer existed. The Supreme Court decided to hear the case anyway, and it ruled that Ontario's law did violate the Charter of Rights. This not only led governments across the country to alter their social policies but also created an important legal and political resource for proponents of same-sex marriage. Although courts in Canada have been inconsistent in applying the Borowski guidelines (Sossin 1999, 130), the fact that they have discretion to decide moot cases and do so frequently suggests movement toward the policy-making approach.

Whereas mootness is concerned with whether a live legal dispute still exists, the doctrine of *ripeness* is concerned with whether a dispute has had enough time to develop a sufficient legal and factual foundation (or if that is even possible). In the early 1960s, for example, the Supreme Court argued that a member of the Jehovah's Witnesses, Laurier Saumur, could not challenge a Quebec law that threatened religious freedoms because he had not yet been charged under the law. In other words, Saumur's case was not sufficiently ripe. (In turn, this also meant that he did not have standing because he was not party to a legal dispute). In the Charter era, courts have at times declined to hear public law cases because they were premature or have ruled against claimants because the factual allegations were overly speculative. In *Operation Dismantle* (1985), for example, the Supreme Court dismissed a claim that the Canadian government's decision to allow the United States to test cruise missiles in Canada violated the Charter's rights to life and security of the person by increasing the chances of nuclear war, because it was not possible to determine whether the Canadian government's decision would or would not increase the chances of nuclear war. In other instances, however, the Court has been amenable to deciding cases that were somewhat speculative or hypothetical. For instance, in *Smith* (1987) the Court struck down the mandatory seven-year minimum sentence in the *Narcotic Control Act* for importing drugs on the basis of a hypothetical scenario in which someone received a seven-year prison term for importing a 'joint of grass'.[5] The Supreme Court also has been willing to be somewhat more lenient about ripeness in 'reference' cases—cases in which the federal government has asked it for an advisory opinion. The Court, for example, decided to give its opinion about whether Quebec could secede unilaterally from Canada even though the reference case was based only on the possibility that Quebec might try do so (*Quebec Secession Reference* 1998). Overall, Sossin describes the Supreme Court's ripeness jurisprudence as a 'quilt of piecemeal and partial rules', and he urges the Court to think carefully about the concept because it goes to fundamental questions about the role of the judiciary in the process of governing (1999, 99).

Another doctrine that raises questions about the role of the judiciary in the governing process is the *political questions* doctrine. In thinking about its relationship to the executive and legislative branches of government, the US Supreme Court developed the 'political questions doctrine', which stipulated that if an issue was the clear responsibility of another branch of government or if an issue lacked 'judicially discoverable and manageable standards for resolving it', then it was a non-justiciable political issue (see *Vieth v. Jubelirer* 2004). The US Supreme Court has used the political questions doctrine to decline to make decisions involving such issues as the impeachment process used by the Senate and various foreign affairs and military decisions. However, the doctrine has been diluted over time, for the Court has heard cases about how electoral districts are drawn (*Baker v. Carr* 1962) and who should win the presidency in a contested election (*Bush v. Gore* 2000).

There is a strain of Canadian jurisprudence that stipulates that 'purely political' matters or matters that do not raise a 'sufficient legal component' should not be heard (Sossin 1999, 171). However, the Canadian Supreme Court has rejected the direct applicability of the American 'political questions doctrine' in Canada on various occasions, such as when it said in *Operation Dismantle* (1985) that foreign-policy decisions are not automatically immune from judicial scrutiny under the Charter of Rights.[6] The Supreme Court's willingness to hear certain cases, particularly ones involving the existence and enforcement of constitutional conventions, has drawn criticism from commentators who argue that these are political issues that do not lend themselves to principled, legal resolution (Mandel 1994; Russell 1983).

The Supreme Court's rejection of a strict political questions doctrine is consistent with lower barriers to standing, readiness to hear moot cases, and flexibility in hearing premature or speculative cases. Notwithstanding inconsistencies in applying each of the doctrines of standing, mootness, ripeness, and political questions, the Canadian judiciary has moved closer to the policy-making model by making it generally easier for individuals and organizations to challenge laws and government policy than under the adjudicative model. This does not mean, of course, that every challenge will succeed just because a court decides to hear it. The group Operation Dismantle found this out when it lost its bid to stop cruise missile testing in Canada. However, as discussed in Chapter 11, rights claimants win a fair amount of the time (approximately a third of the time at the Supreme Court level) and even a loss in court can raise the profile of an issue and re-frame the policy discourse.

Role of the Judge and Number of Parties

One of the most prominent victories in a rights-based case in the last several years came in the *Chaoulli* decision, in which the Supreme Court struck down Quebec's limits on access to private health care.[7] The *Chaoulli* case featured a number of third-party interveners that appeared before the Supreme Court to make arguments. Interveners in the case included various provincial governments, Senators, medical associations, private health clinics, and anti-poverty groups. It is not surprising that governments and interest groups were concerned about the case, for it had important policy implications. The increased willingness of Canadian courts to allow intervener groups, particularly in Charter of Rights cases, signals a shift towards the policy-making model of courts. Because the policy-making model views the balancing of competing interests and the articulation of policy values as legitimate functions of courts, it is helpful to have a number of parties express their viewpoints in court. By way of contrast, the adjudicative model of courts views the existence of more than two parties in a case as antithetical to the role of the courts to adjudicate disputes between two parties whose legal rights and obligations are directly at stake. (See Chapters 4, 7, 8, and 11 for more information about interveners.)

The remainder of this discussion focuses more on the role of the judge in the process. It tracks the movement in the Canadian judiciary towards a 'problem-solving' model of courts. Judges described in this model participate actively in the process as managers; resolve disputes by ADR processes before trial (or send litigants to court-affiliated ADR sessions); and are more actively involved in the trial than in the adjudicative model, especially in specialized courts created to deal with specific issues, such as drug addiction.

The emphasis increasingly placed on 'case management' by judges, facilitated primarily by pre-trial conferences (or pre-hearing conferences at the appeal level), opens the door for a move away from the adjudicative model. Whether these conferences are mandatory or simply available at the request of one of the parties or the judge varies somewhat from jurisdiction to jurisdiction and by area of law (civil, family, small claims, criminal, and so on), but they are becoming more common in the judicial process. The British Columbia Court of Appeal, for example, allows a judge to convene a pre-hearing conference in criminal law cases to simplify issues on appeal and to address any matter that might expedite the appeal. In family law cases in superior trial courts in Alberta, pre-trial conferences are mandatory and have two components: case management and settlement (Alberta Court of Queen's Bench 2006).

In this last example, judges in the Alberta superior trial courts hearing family law cases are clearly instructed to 'encourage and promote settlement of the matters in issue' in the settlement component of the pre-trial conference. This is not a typical function of a judge in the adjudicative model. The degree to which judges behave more as facilitators to expedite the process (by clarifying issues, setting timetables, and making sure procedures have been followed) or behave more proactively to help achieve a settlement depends somewhat on how the pre-trial conference rules are written. The style and the philosophy of individual judges and the local legal culture are also important determinants of whether pre-trial conferences are relatively procedural, directed more at evaluating the legal claims of each side, or used to actively encourage a settlement through various dispute-resolution mechanisms (Macfarlane 2008).[8]

While individual judges and courts vary, the trend in civil (non-criminal) cases is toward more active judicial participation in dispute resolution. In a number of cases, such as the Judicial Dispute Resolution program (JDR) started by Alberta judges (Agrios 2004), judges have taken the initiative to introduce pre-trial dispute-resolution processes even in the absence of specific court rules. Some provincial appellate courts are also conducting pre-hearing mediation sessions if both parties so request (Greene et al. 1998, 69–70). In other instances, the rules of the court place judges more clearly in the role of resolving a dispute. In Manitoba, for example, the parties may jointly request judicially assisted dispute resolution for certain civil law disputes in the superior court. This assistance may come in various forms, such as mini-trials or an early evaluation of the claims; generally, the judge is allowed to explore creative solutions to the dispute with both parties (Aikins Report 2002). In the Federal Court of Canada, a judge may order the parties to engage in a dispute-resolution conference overseen by a case-management judge who will undertake mediation, early neutral evaluation of the merits of each side's case, or a mini-trial.[9]

In contrast to civil litigation, judges in criminal law cases have generally been discouraged from actively resolving disputes before trial. As explained further in Chapter 9, though, there is some uncertainty as to how far judges should go in facilitating resolution and plea discussions between the Crown and the accused in criminal cases during pre-trial conferences. In the US, some jurisdictions are experimenting with having judges take a more direct role in negotiations between the prosecution and the accused before trial (Gottsfield and Michkowski 2007).

Although the degree of direct involvement by judges in resolving disputes differs between civil and criminal cases, both criminal and civil processes are making increased use of alternative dispute resolution or therapeutic processes that are associated with the courts but not conducted by judges. The use of diversion programs in criminal law is referred to at various points below as well as in Chapter 9. In civil litigation, many jurisdictions encourage or even require mediation before trial. These mediation programs are often referred to as 'court-annexed' or 'court-affiliated' programs because the people who participate in them have already started the process of resolving their disputes through the courts, but non-judges conduct the mediation while the legal case is on hold within the judicial process. Saskatchewan and Ontario, for example, both have mandatory mediation for non-family civil cases that are initiated in their superior trial courts.[10] Other jurisdictions, such as British Columbia, make mediation a requirement in non-family disputes in superior trial court upon the request of one of the parties. In Nova Scotia and Quebec, judges may order the parties to undertake mediation in family law cases before a trial in superior trial court. Governments have created bureaucratic support systems to help individuals obtain and pay for mediation services when they are required to do so by the judicial process.

The trend towards the greater use of case management or settlement conferences and court-affiliated ADR techniques before trial (or the appeal hearing) in Canada and elsewhere can in part be explained by concerns over delays in the court system and the harmful effects of those delays, including increased costs and stress (CBA 1996; Mack 2003, 15–17; Moldaver 2006). In addition to greater efficiency, it is argued that the use of ADR techniques in the judicial process can lead to an enhanced quality of justice by being responsive to the needs and interests of the litigants rather than focusing on the procedural requirements of the adversarial judicial process (CBA 1996; Mack 2003, 15-17).

Determining whether these goals are being achieved or not is complicated by a whole host of difficulties, so it is not surprising that different research studies have come to different conclusions (Mack 2003).[11] Evaluations of mandatory, court-annexed mediation in Saskatchewan and Ontario, though, have been generally positive (Macfarlane 2003; Hann and Baar 2001). Hann and Baar (2001), for example, claim that mandatory mediation in Ontario has resulted in reduced times to dispose of cases and decreased costs to litigants.[12] In Saskatchewan, clients of mandatory mediation consistently mentioned the benefit of being able to hear and be heard by the other side in an informal setting (Macfarlane 2003, 14–15).

However, not all clients were satisfied with the process. One client (the plaintiff in an abuse case) said that 'she hated going through the process of telling her story again, and that the anticipation of having to meet with her alleged abuser face-to-face produced enormous anxiety for her' (Macfarlane 2003, 19). This anecdote raises larger questions about the introduction of ADR processes in the judicial process, including whether people should be forced to participate in ADR proceedings. More generally, critics of the trend towards introducing ADR into the judicial process argue that such processes could lead to the 'privatization' of justice, which could have a disproportionate impact on individuals from disadvantaged groups who would be forced to accept dispute-resolution processes that did not allow them to press their legal rights fully (Farrow 2006). This could result in 'second-class' justice. A related concern is that by encouraging pre-trial settlements, the judicial branch abrogates its function of explicating the law and enforcing procedural protections and legal rights in a public and transparent dispute-resolving forum. In turn, this can undermine the rule of law and accountability (Farrow 2006). More specific concerns are raised about aspects of the judicial process. Can judges maintain their independence and impartiality when acting more as managers and mediators than as adjudicators of disputes? Will individuals in civil litigation or criminal cases feel pressured to accept the recommendations of a judge in a pre-trial forum even if it goes against their expectations of justice? Will appellate courts be able to supervise the work of trial courts effectively if dispute resolution increasingly takes place without a trial decision that can be appealed? Do judges have adequate training to undertake new roles (Landerkin and Pirie 2003, 281–96)?

A number of responses have been offered to such critiques. It has been pointed out that very few cases get to trial under the traditional adjudicatory system anyway and that trials do not guarantee that justice will be achieved. Furthermore, proponents remind us that a trial is still an option after court-affiliated ADR. They also argue that ADR processes can help the disadvantaged (and even those in the middle class) by offering simpler and less costly dispute-resolution alternatives—an especially useful development for the increasing number of Canadians not able to afford a lawyer (BC Justice Review Task Force 2005; BC Justice Review Task Force 2006). According to Landerkin and Pirie (2003), the flaws in the traditional process—cost, complexity, and an emphasis on adversarial confrontation that can undermine relationships—leave room for alternative measures that still fit within the ambit of the judicial function and complement the adjudicatory function of courts. A number of suggestions have been made to mitigate the potential drawbacks of ADR processes within the judicial process; those include more training for both judges and lawyers in ADR techniques; careful thinking about what kinds of ADR techniques are best suited to being part of the judicial process; continued adherence to judicial ethics of fairness and impartiality; incorporating transparency and accountability into the processes as appropriate; and sustaining the adjudicatory aspect of courts (Landerkin and Pirie 2003; Farrow 2006; Agrios 2004; Mack 2003).[13]

The increased emphasis on trying to settle or solve disputes, often by addressing underlying issues or problems, is not confined to pre-trial processes but is becoming more prevalent during the trial stage as well. The most prominent manifestation of the trend towards a 'problem-solving' or 'therapeutic' approach to justice in the courtroom is the rise of 'specialized' courts. Canada, following the lead of the US, has established a number of different specialized courts to process cases involving drugs, mental health, domestic violence, and aboriginal offenders (Bakht 2005).

Although the actual functioning of specialized courts can vary considerably, they tend to be characterized by (1) attention to seeking 'tangible outcomes for victims, for offenders and for society', along with active judicial monitoring to try to ensure that those goals are met; (2) collaboration of the courts with criminal justice agencies, government service providers, and community organizations to help achieve goals set for individuals and the community by providing integrated planning and implementation of programs; and (3) non-traditional roles being played in the courtroom by lawyers and judges (some of whom have been given special training in the area or are assigned for long enough stretches of time to provide continuity to the system) (Berman and Feinblatt 2001, 121–2; Eaton and Kaufman 2005). The Mental Health Court of New Brunswick, for example, has a 'team' whose members have mostly participated in the court since its inception in 2000, and who work on each file. The team includes the judge, crown prosecutor, duty counsel, psychiatrist, mental health officials, probation officer, and community caregivers. Those eligible to be in mental health court (individuals who are criminally responsible and fit to stand trial but who have committed an offence linked to mental illness or intellectual disability) must take responsibility for their offence and then enter a specifically designed program to address their needs. The court monitors their progress carefully. Upon successful completion of the program, the charges are dismissed or a non-custodial sentence is given (Walker 2006).

As with the study of ADR before trial, assessing the effectiveness of problem-solving courts is not easy, but early studies (mostly from the US, but some in Canada) have generally shown positive results in keeping individuals in treatment, reducing recidivism, and assisting victims and communities (Berman and Feinblatt 2001, 132–3; Walker 2006; United States Government Accountability Office 2005). Nevertheless, criticisms have been levelled against problem-solving courts. Some argue that such courts are too lenient towards defendants, while others argue that such courts are overly paternalistic and deprive defendants (often from a lower socio-economic background) of due process protections, which can lead to coerced admissions of guilt. A related concern is that problem-solving courts force lawyers on each side into roles that may conflict with their professional duties and also with the duties of a judge to act as an impartial and neutral adjudicator. Judges may also lack the proper training and personalities for this different role. And, finally, there are concerns about the erosion of judicial independence or the usurpation of policy-making power by judges if they act as part of a team and help organize and broker community meetings to address problems (Berman and Feinblatt 2001, 134–5; Eaton and Kaufman 2005; Bakht 2005, 252–3).

Despite these reservations, the trend towards such courts is accelerating. In the summer of 2005, for example, the federal Department of Justice announced millions of dollars in funding to expand drug treatment courts in Canada beyond Toronto and Vancouver (Canada, Dept. of Justice 2005). Family courts also continue to become more and more problem-solving in orientation. Pre-trial mediation is becoming more commonplace, and the trial process itself more informal. Recently, for instance, a judge did not allow a lawyer to represent his client in family court because the lawyer had a reputation for being difficult and making the process highly adversarial (Doolittle 2007). Decisions in family court, as noted above, are often based less on technical legal requirements and more on the welfare of the litigants and the best interests of the child. Governments have made efforts to integrate social-service organizations with these courts, often making them available in the same building. A report by the British Columbia Justice Review Task Force released in 2005 called for further problem-solving reforms. The report recommended even greater integration between (unified) family courts and social-service organizations, improved and simplified information dissemination on family law, mandatory consensual dispute resolution session(s) before the parties entered the judicial process, and mandatory pre-trial case management and settlement hearings before trial. For those small number of cases for which a trial is appropriate (because of an intractable problem that requires legal rights to be enforced, or a need to clarify the law), the trial would be held before a judge with specialized training who would be more actively involved in the trial and conduct a more informal trial than in the traditional process (BC Justice Review Task Force 2005).[14]

A number of judges and commentators are now arguing that problem-solving approaches can and should be used in regular courtrooms through such means as the use of clear and plain language and active listening by judges[15]; showing empathy and treating people with respect and dignity; setting goals and monitoring progress; co-ordination with service organizations; more use of restorative justice principles in the criminal context; and a more team-based, non-adversarial approach in the courtroom (Farole et al. 2005; Thompson 2005). Even appellate courts could engage in therapeutic jurisprudence by writing opinions in a way that treats each party's viewpoint with respect (Bahkt 2005, 251).

The spread of such principles in regular courtrooms might be inhibited, though, by institutional and resource constraints; an unwillingness of some judges to adopt 'therapeutic' values, especially in regard to punishment; and a concern that too much of a problem-solving, team-based approach might undermine their role as impartial adjudicators of disputes. Proponents agree that this latter objection is one that needs to be addressed carefully, but they suggest that a balance can be achieved by encouraging lawyers to be team players without sacrificing their clients' interests while judges remain committed to hearing both sides and not imposing their will on the proceedings (National Judicial Institute 2005, 26).

What about those litigants that are not represented by a lawyer? The increasing numbers of individuals who are not represented by counsel pose a challenge for judges (McLachlin 2007). How can judges help such litigants without sacrificing their impartiality? Rollie Thompson (2005), a law professor at Dalhousie law school, argues that there are certain things judges can do for unrepresented litigants that would be relatively uncontroversial, such as providing legal information and innocuous pieces of legal advice and making procedural rulings that help to get at the substantive issues. Beyond that he acknowledges that proposals become contentious. Thompson himself favours more systematic changes to regular court processes that would involve judges more actively in the process—such reforms would follow the trends in pre-trial case management and settlement conferences and problem-solving orientations in courts. Particularly owing to the complexity of rules of evidence, Thompson also argues that in some circumstances judges should adopt a more 'inquisitorial' approach, in which they would examine witnesses, prove documents, call experts, and suggest possible arguments.

The judge's function in the evidence-gathering process, the kinds of evidence that are allowed into court, and the rules of evidence have important value and policy implications for the judicial process and the role of courts in the governing process. The next section briefly explores these issues.

Fact-Finding

Suggestions that judges become more involved in the collection and examination of evidence might strike some readers as odd, especially those used to watching US or Canadian courtroom dramas (real or fictional) where a passive judge (or judge and jury) renders a decision by applying the law to what he or she believes happened on the basis of the presentation and examination of evidence by two parties in an adversarial process. However, historical and comparative perspectives would suggest that it is reasonable and may even be desirable for fact-finders to play a more active role in trial or pre-trial processes. Judges and juries in the first few centuries of the common law system were central in generating and evaluating evidence (the jury, for example, was originally a group of locals who could be relied upon to remember what happened between the two parties in dispute), but owing to various historical circumstances and developments the system evolved so that the parties in the case became solely responsible for the collection and examination of evidence (Langbein 2003). In the civil law system judges have always had an integral role in gathering and testing evidence, including participating in criminal investigations, facilitating the exchange of documents in civil litigation (which often leads to a decision without any sort of courtroom trial), and asking questions of witnesses during 'trials' that are not like the adversarial trials in the modern common law system.[16]

Fact-finding differs between the two systems at the appellate level as well. In civil law systems, intermediate appeal courts will undertake a *de novo* review of the case—these courts will re-examine both the law and the facts from the lower court and may even collect new evidence and hear new testimony—whereas the general principle in common law countries is for all appeal courts to focus on the trial judge's application of the law and not on factual determinations (Apple and Deyling 1995, 29).[17] Of course, in the real world of Canadian courts there are exceptions and nuances to this general principle. For one thing, the line between 'law' and 'fact' is often blurry. Many legal concepts, such as the 'reasonable person' in tort law or 'self-defence' in criminal law, require a consideration of the factual context when they are applied. Also, trial judges have complained that appellate courts have retried the facts of the cases even though appeal judges usually have only the written transcript of the trial (Greene et al. 1998, 191).[18] It has been suggested that experiments with audio and video transcripts of trials may lead to more frequent fact determinations by appellate courts since it would reduce the relative disadvantage that appellate judges have in trying to determine the credibility of witnesses (Greene et al. 1998, 192). Indeed, the US Supreme Court recently used videotape from a police cruiser in a high-speed pursuit to render a decision and even posted the video on its website (*Scott v. Harris* 2007).[19] Recent Canadian Supreme Court judgments, however, have rebuked appeal courts for interfering with trial findings about what happened between parties in legal dispute (*Housen v. Nikolaisen* 2002; *H.L. v. Canada* 2005). Critics of these decisions argue that too much appellate deference to trial court fact-finding could result in injustice or suppression of the truth. Supporters counter that trial judges are in the best position to separate fact from fiction and that appellate deference to their fact-finding conclusions (as is the general tradition in the common law system) brings efficiency and finality to the process. In doing so, it reduces the incentive for wealthy litigants to 'roll the dice' and appeal any adverse trial court decision (Makin 2005).

There is considerable debate about whether the modern common law system or the civil law system is better at fact-finding, especially in getting at the 'truth' of what happened between disputing parties. Does the common law approach, emphasizing the presentation and cross-examination of evidence at an adversarial trial before a passive judge, supported by rules of evidence like the hearsay rule (a rule that generally precludes the introduction of third-party statements because they cannot be cross-examined for reliability) and the 'judicial notice' rule (stipulating that judges can take into consideration only facts not presented at trial that are not subject to dispute)—offer the best chance of revealing the truth? Or does the civil law system, with fewer and less restrictive rules of evidence, more influence of judges in gathering and collating evidence, less emphasis on adversarial trials, and more scope for appeal court fact-finding offer the best hope of finding out what happened between the parties?

Aside from being difficult to resolve,[20] the debate about truth seeking overlooks two important features of fact-finding in the judicial process. First, fact-finding is ancillary to one of the central functions of courts, which is to resolve or bring finality to disputes. Resolving disputes on the basis of the certainty of what happened is desirable, but this is not the primary objective, especially considering that it is often very difficult to know with absolute certainty what happened between parties in a dispute (Summers 1999; Damaska 1986, 122–3). Modern societies, whether they use common law or civil law systems of law, have moved away from procedures that try to invite divine guidance as to what absolutely happened (such as trial by ordeal) to processes that accept decisions based on what 'probably' happened (Shapiro 1981, 46–8). Furthermore, these fact-finding processes cannot allow every detail that may have had an impact on the dispute to enter into the process, or the judicial system would be completely overwhelmed (McCormick 1994, 45-6).

Second, as the need for some efficiency in the process suggests, the search for 'truth' is only one value or objective of the rules created to govern the collection and examination of evidence. Such rules are often political in the sense that value choices are associated with the balancing of various priorities. The political battles waged in Canada over evidence and sexual assault trials in the last couple of decades—under what circumstances, if any, should the defence be allowed to bring up a woman's sexual history or access third-party medical and psychological records—contained arguments about what rules would best help find the 'truth' about what happened, but they also featured arguments about due process rights, women's equality, and expectations of privacy (Hiebert 2002, Chap. 5). While the value-laden nature of evidentiary rules is particularly striking in criminal law (also see Chapter 9), evidentiary rules and values are also intertwined in various kinds of civil litigation, such as constitutional and family law. For example, former Canadian Supreme Court justice L'Heureux-Dubé remarked that in 'family law it must be recognized that fact-finding is an essentially value laden concept' (1994, 564–5).

After making that observation, L'Heureux-Dubé argued that judges in family law cases should take greater notice of social realities in order to counter what she characterized as the male-based rules of family law that disadvantaged women and children. This could be done by expanding the concept of 'judicial notice' to allow judges more latitude to consider social factors that were not presented by the parties to a case (L'Heureux-Dubé 1994, 575). According to L'Heureux-Dubé, this would allow judges to focus on justice more broadly than is allowed by the process-oriented adversarial model and its emphasis on adjudicative facts—who did what to whom when and with what motive and intent.

L'Heureux-Dubé's comments illustrate more generally the proposition that if we value problem solving or the shaping of rules (policy-making) by courts beyond their traditional function of adjudication of disputes, then fact-finding will change in two ways: (1) judges are likely to become more active in the fact-finding process than in the adjudicative model, and (2) social (or legislative) facts—concerned with social contexts and the causes and effects of public policies—will supplement or even supersede the adjudicative facts in decisions. Over the last few decades, Canadian courts have responded to critiques about the overly legalistic tendencies of the adjudicatory model. They have adopted more active judicial involvement in fact-finding—whether through greater use of judicial notice or of judges in specialized courts who communicate directly with the accused—and more use of social facts in various legal contexts. In criminal law, for example, judges have considered the social conditions of aboriginals in Canada when sentencing aboriginal offenders. In family law, judicial notice has been taken of literature on access and child development, and expert opinion on various family-related issues is frequently allowed (Thompson 2003).

The use of social facts is particularly prominent in Charter cases. The text of the Charter itself implicitly calls for social-fact evidence, such as the right to 'equal benefit of the law' in s. 15 or the right to official minority-language programs and schools 'where numbers warrant' in s. 23. The Supreme Court's interpretation of the Charter, backed by groups hoping to use the Charter to pursue policy change, has further encouraged the use of social facts. In particular, the use of social facts is required by the Court's interpretation of the s. 1 'reasonable limits' clause to make the government demonstrate that it has a 'pressing and substantial' objective and 'proportional' means to achieve that objective for legislation that has been found to violate rights (Morton 2002, 367–8). More generally, the Supreme Court signalled early in its Charter decisions that the often criticized legalistic approach to the 1960 Bill of Rights should not be followed and instead judges should take a 'contextual' and 'purposive' approach in Charter decisions. Thus, the Supreme Court encouraged the presentation and use of social facts in Charter cases (see *MacKay v. Manitoba* 1989). Not surprisingly, Charter cases have featured a wide variety of social-fact evidence, such as the possible effects of pornography on violence against women; the number of francophone children in Edmonton; and the social, medical, and economic implications of private health-care delivery, to name but a few.

Social facts enter the judicial process by three primary methods: judicial notice, expert witnesses, and factums. Generally, appellate courts will give less deference to trial findings about social facts than adjudicative facts, and sometimes appellate courts, especially the Supreme Court, will collect additional social facts not presented at trial through one of the three methods (Jamal 2005). A brief overview of each of these methods reveals that there are pitfalls to their use and that the courts are struggling to create rules and procedures that allow for social facts to facilitate policy-making and problem-solving while trying to preserve the basic tenets and benefits of the adjudicatory approach.[21]

After some contradictory decisions about judicial notice by the Supreme Court, a trend is developing for judicial notice of social facts, such as those contained in government reports, to be generally subject to somewhat less stringent admissibility requirements than adjudicative facts; however, judicial notice still should not be used when the social facts are controversial or dispositive (Jamal 2005, 7–9). For example, the Ontario Court of Appeal stated that a trial judge should not have based his decision that a company did not give sufficient notice to a clerical employee that her employment was being terminated on research found by the trial judge suggesting that lower-level workers would have a harder time in finding new employment than more skilled, managerial workers (Thomson 2003).[22] Nevertheless, the rules surrounding the judicial notice of social facts are still far from clear and remain controversial (Jamal 2005).[23] There are concerns that judicial notice can be a conduit by which biases, whether personal or systemic, can enter into decision making (McCormick 1994, 47; Williams 1996, 4).

Because this evidence is not subject to cross-examination, the use of judicial notice can also harm the procedural rights of the litigants in the dispute and allow untested (or contradictory) evidentiary assumptions to guide decision making.[24] The dissenters in the *Trochym* (2007) case accused their Supreme Court colleagues of taking judicial notice that hypnosis-induced evidence is unreliable (on the basis of US court decisions) without any expert evidence being introduced on the topic at trial or even on appeal.

Expert witnesses retained by one or both sides of a dispute are commonly used to present scientific and social-scientific data at the trial level, and their testimony constitutes an exception to the hearsay rule. The use of such experts poses challenges as well, however. Experts often disagree with one another, judges may find it difficult to ensure that experts do not offer opinions that stray beyond the facts and reasonable inferences, and judges may not be well-equipped to understand or evaluate all of an expert's testimony (McLachlin 2007). In recognizing some of these difficulties, the Supreme Court in the 1990s began cautioning judges to be mindful of the relevance, reliability, and necessity of the expert opinion and the qualifications of the experts, but the effect on lower-court use of expert testimony appears uneven (Thompson 2003, 14–18).

Another way of introducing social-fact evidence into a case is through the submission of factums (sometimes called 'Brandeis briefs,' after the US lawyer who pioneered the practice) that contain social-fact data compiled by the litigants or interveners, though this practice is more common at the appellate level than at the trial level (Williams 1996). This technique of introducing social facts suffers from some of the same problems as judicial notice and expert witnesses: the information may be biased, the information may not reflect the interests of other groups that will be impacted by a court's decision, judges may not have the training and expertise to assess the data adequately, and the studies are not subject to examination through the adversarial process. Furthermore, the rules for the admission and use of Brandeis briefs are not clear (Williams 1996, 9–10).

Former Supreme Court justice Bertha Wilson hoped that the increased use of third-party interveners would mitigate some of the limitations on social fact-finding by courts by presenting social-fact evidence from various viewpoints. However, getting social facts into court is still no guarantee that they will be properly understood (Morton 2002, 368). That was illustrated dramatically by the aftermath of the Supreme Court's *Askov* decision (see Box 3.1).

Box 3.1   *R. v. Askov*

In November 1983 Elijah Askov and his co-accused threatened an individual with guns and knives in an effort to retain control over the supply of exotic dancers to the Toronto region. After being arrested and charged with extortion and weapons offences, Askov and the others chose to have a trial before a judge and jury in a s. 96 district trial court. Following a preliminary inquiry in Brampton Provincial Court that was completed in September 1984, the accused were told that the earliest trial date available at the District Court would be October 1985. When that date arrived, their place on the list had not been reached so the date of the trial was moved to September 1986. At the beginning of the trial, the accused argued successfully that their right to trial within a reasonable time guaranteed in s. 11(b) of the Charter of Rights had been violated by the twenty-three-month delay in getting to trial after the preliminary inquiry.

As the case worked its way up the judicial hierarchy, Askov's lawyer discovered that political scientist Carl Baar was just completing research on trial times in Canada. Baar's research showed that the Brampton court was the slowest of the eight districts that he had studied for the year 1987 (five from Ontario, two from British Columbia, and one from New Brunswick). Since the research showed that Askov's case took longer than 90 per cent of other cases in the already very slow Brampton district, Askov's lawyer asked Baar to summarize his research findings in an affidavit. The findings in the affidavit were accepted by the Crown, and Askov's lawyer incorporated them into his presentation to the Supreme Court in March 1990.

When the Supreme Court released its decision in *Askov* in October of 1990, it ruled that the rights of the accused to trial within a reasonable time under s. 11(b) of the Charter had been violated by excessive delay caused by a lack of institutional resources. In rendering its decision, the Supreme Court also suggested a guideline of six to eight months as the 'outside limit of what is reasonable' for normal criminal cases.

The decision turned out to be a public policy disaster. As a direct result of *Askov*, over 40,000 criminal cases, largely from Ontario, were dismissed. The media and the public were outraged. How did this happen? The Court misused and misunderstood social-fact evidence. In a rather extreme example of judicial notice, Justice Cory, after oral argument and without the knowledge of the parties to the case, phoned a friend in Montreal to obtain some information about court times in that city. He then doubled the time it took an average case to get to trial in Montreal to create the six-to-eight-week guideline. In an appendix to his affidavit, though, Baar had stated that Quebec data would not be comparable because of differences in the way that Quebec processed criminal cases compared to other provinces. Furthermore, the

Court seemed not to understand the implications of its decisions in light of Baar's data. Justice Cory said that Toronto courts were already operating acceptably, though Baar's data showed that over 25 per cent of Toronto's cases were over the six-to-eight-month guideline. The policy ramifications of the decision were exacerbated when Ontario judges and Crown lawyers read the decision as applying to provincial courts as well as s. 96 courts.

How could this debacle have been avoided? The Court could have used the adjudicative facts of the case—the accused were arrested for extortion and weapons charges, and it took twenty-three months to get to trial after the pre-liminary inquiry—to create a precedent that could have been supplemented by future decisions. This would have been an adjudicative approach that built the rules incrementally on the basis of adjudicative facts in successive cases. Alternatively, if the Court wanted to create guidelines to reduce uncer-tainty in future cases using a policy-making approach, it could have sched-uled the case for re-argument and asked the parties and interveners to concentrate on the issue of guidelines. This would have allowed social facts about trial-time trends to be introduced, challenged, and clarified in a more systematic way.

(Adapted from Baar 2002). Used with permission of the University of Calgary Press.

Modes of Reasoning

The Supreme Court used (or misused) social facts in the *Askov* decision to create a general policy about how long it should take for a case to get to trial. The decision tried to weigh the need for the criminal justice system to process cases against the right of individuals to a trial within a reasonable time. The decision illustrates two important and related features of a policy-making model of decision making: first, there is a focus on the creation of rules to govern future behaviour (with the help of social facts), with less attention paid to the immediate dispute between two par-ties (and the adjudicative facts surrounding the dispute); and second, there is an attempt to balance competing interests when creating the policy (again, with the aid of social facts). Notice that this mode of reasoning resembles that of legislative and executive actors in the political system. Legislators, cabinet ministers, and bureaucrats try to create rules that govern future behaviour and balance the inter-ests of different parties. When making policy about university tuition fees, for example, governments design rules that try to balance various values and interests (particularly equality of access to education for students versus the need for revenue to provide for quality education), using predictions informed by social facts about how different increases in fees may influence student enrolment and university revenues. How governments determine and justify their policy goals (the balancing of interests) and the means to achieve them (in this example, say a cap of 5 per cent increases in fees per year) can include various considerations, including ideology, public opinion, and expert opinion. As Paul Weiler notes, government actors 'do not feel institutionally committed to the creation of new legal rules only if they can be justified by a reasoned opinion relating the development of accepted doctrinal premises' (1968, 438).

The creation of new legal rules by *judges*, however, is legitimate, according to the adjudicative model, only if it is done incrementally and is based on accepted legal principles in an attempt to resolve a dispute between two parties (on the basis of the adjudicative facts of what happened). Notice that the adjudicative model accepts that judges do shape the law. This model views this as necessary and desirable because rules cannot be written with enough specificity to govern all disputes that may arise in a society—a difficulty that is compounded by the need to adapt rules in light of socio-economic and technological changes. Again, though, rule development by judges must only be incremental and based on existing legal principles. More fundamental policy choices should be made by the legislative and executive branches of government.

Of course, sometimes there will be disagreement about what constitutes an acceptable level of rule development within an adjudicative framework. For example, in a tort case that began when a motor vehicle hit some cows on a road in rural Ontario, Paul Weiler (2002) thought that it was within the boundaries of an adjudicative approach for the Supreme Court to override an ancient British precedent, which stated that a farmer's livestock had a right to be on the road, and replace that rule with the general rule of torts that blame should be apportioned according to fault (roughly fifty-fifty in this case). Weiler argued that the issue was a narrow one: there was no requirement for complex social facts, and the Supreme Court based its decision on well-established general principles of tort, as opposed to creating something like a 'no fault' scheme of liability, which would be a more radical, complex, and value-laden rule change. Some judges who heard the case, though, including all three Ontario Court of Appeal judges and a dissenter on the Supreme Court, argued that while the law may be outdated and lead to unjust results, it was up to elected legislators and not judges to change those rules.

In the policy-making model, courts are less concerned with showing deference to the legislative branch because judges are considered to have a legitimate and important role to play in the development of policy (hence the comfort with lower barriers of access to court, interveners, and social facts) with less emphasis on existing legal principles than under the adjudication-of-disputes model. Many commentators and judges argue that the introduction of the Charter of Rights in 1982 moved the courts somewhat towards the policy-making model by requiring judges to evaluate the constitutionality of laws and government actions against vaguely worded rights guarantees in the Charter. However, as discussed in Chapter 11, there are serious disagreements about how judges should interpret the Charter and about how deferential or not they should be to government policy. In other words, the Charter may have shifted the baseline somewhat towards giving judges a greater role in shaping policy, but judges still have a large degree of choice as to how active they want to be in creating policy under the Charter.

Compared to the policy-making and adjudicative models, the 'problem-solving' model does not have as well-defined a mode of reasoning. The role of law and the judges' relationship to it is different and more variable in the problem-solving approach because of its focus on managing or addressing the underlying issues in a dispute. When an attempt is made to resolve a dispute before trial, the law is a more or less an important backdrop, depending on which ADR process is used. In mediation, for example, more emphasis is placed on the needs and interests of the parties than on the law, whereas mini-trials often work best when the applicable legal rules are quite clear and the parties, understanding those legal conditions, are willing to work for a solution (Yates, Yates, and Bain 2000, 133–6). When disputes enter the actual courtroom in the problem-solving model, the applicable legal principles themselves emphasize a therapeutic approach and leave room for judges to fashion a solution tailored to the problem. In family law, for instance, a key legal concept in guiding judicial decision making is the 'best interests of the child'. In criminal law, judges, particularly in specialized courts, take advantage of the discretion in sentencing rules to prescribe solutions, such as an aboriginal healing circle or treatment for drug addiction.

Clearly, the dominance of the adjudicative model of judicial process is under pressure from the policy-making and problem-solving models. There are ongoing debates about the desirability and possibility of modifying the values and associated processes of the adjudicative model or replacing them with those of the other two models. The adjudicative model is also facing pressure from three dispute-resolution methods outside of the judicial process: mediation, arbitration, and administrative dispute resolution.

Alternative Dispute Resolution (ADR) Systems

Alternative dispute resolution (ADR) processes are considered alternatives to the traditional adjudicative model of judicial process. There are various types of ADR processes that involve third parties. The two most prominent forms are mediation and arbitration, but there are various hybrids and variations of those two methods, including mini-trials, early neutral evaluation, med-arb (or arb-med), and collaborative law (Menkel-Meadow 2005, 101; Perrin 2002; Vago and Nelson 2004, 220–1). ADR techniques like mediation have ancient roots in various societies around the world, including those of the aboriginal peoples in North America

(Landerkin and Pirie 2003, 252-3). The modern use of ADR in Canada is relatively recent, however. Some ADR processes were in use by the 1970s and 1980s—the ADR Institute of Canada grew out of an organization started in the mid-1970s—but ADR did not become more popular and mainstream in Canada until the 1990s (see Farrow 2005).

Of the various ADR processes that involve third-party resolution of a dispute, mediation differs the most from traditional court adjudication. In mediation, the parties choose the mediator; the process is relatively informal; mediators actively offer possible solutions to problems in light of a variety of factors, including the needs and interests of the parties to the dispute; and finally, a mediator cannot impose a decision on the parties—a resolution is reached only if the parties consent to an agreement after discussions facilitated by the mediator. Arbitration rests somewhere between mediation and court adjudication, though it is somewhat closer to the latter. The formality of the arbitration process varies but tends to be more akin to the formal process of a trial where the arbitrator listens relatively passively to the submission of the parties. The decision making in arbitration is based more on legal rights and responsibilities than on a mediated process. The arbitrator, as in the adjudicative model of courts, imposes a decision on the parties except when the parties have agreed to make the arbitration non-binding. Unlike the adjudicative model of courts, however, arbitration offers the parties the power to choose who the third-party decision-maker will be (Cooley 1986).

Individuals or organizations in a dispute enter into ADR primarily in one of three ways: they agree to do so, a contract stipulates that ADR must be used as a first resort to resolve problems, or legislation or court rules force disputants who have entered the judicial process into court-affiliated or judicially-run ADR (or require it upon the request of the judge or one of the parties). When arbitration is undertaken outside of court, laws such as the *Alberta Arbitration Act* or the federal *Commercial Arbitration Act* provide rules for the conduct of arbitration and set out conditions about the possibility of appealing an arbiter's decision to a court. No laws govern the conduct of mediation. Organizations like the ADR Institute of Canada, though, have produced guidelines for mediation and have designations that recognize training and experience of ADR practitioners.

ADR processes are used for a wide variety of disputes involving both private and public law. Proponents claim that ADR is more efficient and economical than litigation, gives more control over the process to the parties in the dispute, and allows for greater privacy. Advocates also maintain that ADR practices, particularly those closer to the mediation end of the spectrum, are very helpful in situations where dialogue and a holistic, forward-looking approach to issues, rather than the formal adversarial process of litigation, would be more likely to find elements of agreement and disagreement, allow for the expression of feelings, and open the possibilities for both mutual understanding and self-understanding. This could in turn promote more long-lasting resolutions to disputes than the adjudicative model. Family law, because it often involves disputants who will likely have an ongoing relationship, has become an especially fertile ground for mediation. Mediation and related processes have been successful in helping divorcing or separating couples to focus on important issues and reach agreements that they can live with and that are best for their children with fewer costs and less resentment compared to adversarial litigation (Yates, Yates, and Bain 2000, 133–4; Perrin 2002). Mediation is used in various other situations, however. A Crown lawyer in Saskatchewan, for example, diverted a mischief case involving a youth to mediation 'because it would allow the victims to confront the youth and show him how frightened they were' and 'it may do the youth some good' (Moyer and Basic 2004, 32). Arbitration has long been a popular method of resolving labour disputes and is a prominent method of resolving commercial and consumer disputes, both domestically and internationally. Like mediation, though, arbitration is used in various legal situations. For instance, it has been used to deal with compensation for industrial pollution (Yate, Yates, and Bain 2000, 137). The controversy over the application of Sharia law in Ontario involved arbitration and family law (see Box 3.2).

Box 3.2   The Use of Religious Tribunals for Family Law in Ontario

In 2004, the Islamic Institute of Civil Justice (IICJ) proposed the establishment in Ontario of arbitration panels based on Sharia law for personal and family law. Although Syed Mumtaz Ali, the president of the IICJ, maintained that the laws of Ontario and Canada would bind the proposed 'Sharia court', he also said that individuals within the Muslim community who wanted to be considered 'good Muslims' would have to resolve their disputes in such a court. This announcement generated considerable media attention and controversy. The government of Ontario responded by establishing a review of its *Arbitration Act* as it pertained to family and personal law by former Attorney General Marion Boyd. Boyd, who heard from various groups, submitted her report in December 2004 (Ontario, Ministry of the Attorney General 2004). The report noted that family law arbitration was already being conducted by Jewish tribunals and even in some Muslim settings in Ontario under existing arbitration laws.[25] Boyd acknowledged that understandable concerns about the application of Sharia law in family matters had been created by some comments by Muslim leaders that justified the unequal treatment of women and some practices under Muslim family law that provided less support for women and children than under Ontario law, such as the requirement that a divorced man support his divorced wife only for three menstrual cycles or until the birth of a child already conceived. However, she had also heard from some Muslim women who argued that it was not Sharia law that was at fault for the unequal treatment of women and children but cultural practices and traditions that were being challenged by women within Islam.

The heart of the issue, according to Boyd, was about allowing minority cultural groups and individuals within that group to practise their religious beliefs in accordance with multiculturalism, while maintaining protection of individual rights and the equality of women and children under Canadian and Ontario law. Boyd aimed to balance these tensions by recommending that religious family law arbitration continue to be allowed but that the legal safeguards surrounding the process be bolstered. Among other things, she recommended that the Ontario *Family Law Act* be revised to allow an arbitration decision to be set aside by a court if it was unconscionable, if the best interests of the child were not respected, or if an individual was not aware of the nature and consequences of the agreement. She also called for more regulations to be placed on the arbitration process and for greater public education about arbitration. The report aimed to give Muslims and other religious groups the choice to use an ADR process that reflected their religious principles, even if others might not agree with the outcomes of the arbitration, while trying to ensure that the choice was informed and protected by legal safeguards.

Reaction to the report was volatile. Supporters and opponents of the plan clashed in the media and even during demonstrations over the next several months. The legal counsel for the Canadian Council of Muslim Women argued that the report was naïve. She claimed that Muslim women would be pressured into using arbitration for family law and this would result in unequal treatment for women. There were complaints from some Muslim organizations that family law arbitration would privatize and ghettoize dispute resolution to the detriment of already disadvantaged people, especially new refugees. Others within and outside the Muslim community argued that it was wrong to have various legal regimes based on particular ethnic or religious principles. Finally, some argued that allowing the application of Sharia law in family law would provide a foothold for radical Islamists to promote Islamic law and identity.

Others defended the plan. A *Globe and Mail* editorial suggested that the report struck a proper balance between allowing for the religious practices and the protection of rights. The editorial further opined that it would be wrong to prevent a group of people from using an alternative form of dispute resolution that is often faster, cheaper, and less irritating than going to court.

Iman Mubin Shaik, who had already been conducting family mediation and arbitration at the Majid El-Noor Arbitration Centre, maintained that his Islamic beliefs did not go 'hand in hand with the oppression of women.' At a rally, Wahida Valiante said that if Jews and Christians could arbitrate family matters, then Muslims should have that right as well.[26] For her part, Marion Boyd responded to critics by arguing that her plan would help ensure that arbitrations were not driven underground and that there were legal protections in place. She emphasized that Muslims would have a choice whether to use the arbitration panels or not. Boyd also warned that if arbitration was not allowed for Muslim family and personal law, the rights of other religious groups to arbitration would likely be denied as well.

Indeed, shortly after a demonstration that drew 300 protestors to the Ontario legislature as part of a global series of protests against Sharia law, Ontario Premier Dalton McGuinty announced in September 2005 that there would be no arbitrations based on Sharia law and no religious arbitration in general in Ontario. Various religious groups vowed to fight the ban on religious arbitration in the courts.

Sources: CBC 2004; CTV 2005; Freeze and Howlett 2005; *Globe and Mail* 2004; Mallan 2004; Ontario, Ministry of the Attorney General 2004; Wente 2004.

Some of the arguments made by opponents of Sharia-based arbitration in Ontario reflect the broader concerns expressed by those who are critical or at least skeptical about ADR. There are worries that ADR privatizes dispute resolution, thereby reducing public accountability and impeding the development and articulation of legal norms by the courts (Fiss 1984). A related objection is that dispute resolution out of the public eye can lead to pressures to settle when one party has more power than the other and the weaker party has less reliance on legal rights, compared to dispute resolution in an adjudicative court (which would feature a neutral judge applying strict legal rules). This is a significant reason why some feminist commentators are wary of mediation in family law (Goundry, Peters, and Currie 1998). Advocates for battered women in particular have been very vocal about the dangers of mediation; although some progress is being made in making mediators understand the inherent power imbalance in abusive relationships, there are fears that the often subtle methods of control in such relationships will not be recognized by mediators (Goundry, Peters, and Currie 1998, 45–6). More generally, there are worries that ADR can result in 'second-class' justice for disadvantaged groups in society. And there are more immediate questions about whether ADR is as efficient and economical as proponents claim.

Despite these objections and some concern by supporters that the increased interest in ADR by the legal profession will result in increased legalism and costs (Vago and Nelson 2004, 218), the popularity of ADR continues to grow and is increasingly supported by government policy. For example, the *Canada Divorce Act* now requires that lawyers talk about mediation with their clients, the recent *Youth Criminal Justice Act* promotes the use of diversion programs, the new *Ontario Residential Tenancies Act* gives power to the Landlord and Tenant Board to mediate disputes, and the *Canada Labour Code* continues to endorse arbitration as the primary method of resolving disputes between labour and management in federally regulated industries. As discussed above, rules of judicial process are being changed to mandate or encourage court-affiliated or judicial ADR. Governments have created offices that facilitate ADR within and outside the judicial process through such means as providing information about ADR and maintaining lists of ADR practitioners. Examples of such offices are British Columbia's Dispute Resolution Office and the Dispute Resolutions Services (DRS) office in the federal Department of Justice. Restorative justice initiatives in the criminal justice context, such as Nova Scotia's Restorative Justice program, are also indicative of the trend towards ADR processes. Ontario's decision to remove the possibility of arbitrating family law issues through religious tribunals, prompted by a rather unusual political firestorm, was an exception to this trend.

Dispute Resolution in Administrative Tribunals

Dispute resolution by administrative tribunals is another prominent method of resolving disputes outside of the courtroom in Canada and other modern societies. Adjudication by administrative agencies, boards, commissions, and tribunals (all of which we shall call simply 'tribunals') became more prevalent as government became more and more involved in regulating social and economic activity, especially after the Second World War. Governments believed that granting adjudicative functions (with relaxed procedural requirements and without the need to adhere formally to precedent) to arm's-length tribunals would allow for judgments that were made efficiently, were informed by expertise in specialized social, environmental, or economic fields, and were consistent with other administrative and policy decisions that the tribunal might render.

Whereas adjudication has been called the 'defining function' of administrative tribunals (Barker 2006, 110), the term adjudication in administrative tribunals is used to describe a wide range of decisions. Adjudication is being used when the Canadian Radio and Telecommunications Commission decides to grant a television licence from amongst various proposals supported by various companies and groups, the Canadian Transportation Agency decides whether an airline can make passengers with a large girth pay for two seats, the Alberta Energy Resources Conservation Board decides whether or not a pipeline can be built in the face of opposition from landowners concerned with the environmental impact, the Quebec Labour Relations Board decides whether a union should be certified at a Wal-Mart over the objections of the company, the Canadian Immigration and Refugee Board decides whether a refugee claimant should be allowed to stay in the country or not, or the Newfoundland and Labrador Human Rights Commission decides whether an organization has discriminated in its employment practices.

The Supreme Court has ruled that administrative tribunals have to follow the principle of 'fairness' when making decisions, but that the requirements of fairness depend on the circumstances. Costs, the complexity and importance of the issue, efficiency, the nature of the statutory scheme that created the tribunal, the rights and interests of the parties, and the public interest in a just administrative system must all be balanced against one another. The more that an administrative decision is quasi-judicial in nature—when the rights of individuals are directly affected and legal standards, rather than administrative or policy considerations, are the predominant basis of the decision—the greater are the procedural requirements (Bryant and Sossin 2002, 168–74; Gall 2004, 543–4). In its *Singh* (1985) decision, for example, the Supreme Court said that an initial determination of a person's refugee status without a hearing and partly on the basis of administrative and policy considerations (such as concern for efficiency in the process and the government's relationships with other countries) and information about international events may be appropriate; however, if a person was being denied refugee status, there had to be an oral hearing that had stricter procedural rules and at which the claimant could contest the case against him or her more on legal grounds.

The normative requirements of adjudication may justify, in the administrative context, more procedural guarantees, more emphasis on legal standards instead of policy considerations, and unbiased decision makers who are not beholden to government (Russell 1987, 17–18). Concern has been expressed, though, that too many procedural requirements are being placed on administrative tribunals by courts and government officials, and that these requirements can increase costs, time, and complexity; lead to more adversarial proceedings often attended by legal counsel for each side; and detract from the flexibility needed by tribunals to balance their adjudicative, regulatory, policy-making, and administrative duties (Mullan 2005; Jacobs 2003). Indeed, the *Singh* decision was widely criticized for increasing costs and backlogs in the refugee-determination process (Knopff and Morton 1992; Simpson 2004). David Mullan (2005) speculates that these procedural requirements result from the increased use (both officially and unofficially) of ADR processes by many tribunals. Though Mullan is troubled with turning tribunals into courts, he is also concerned that over-reliance on ADR by administrative tribunals could lead to a dearth of guidance in written decisions and the possibility that parties with greater economic or social power could unfairly determine the outcomes of cases behind closed doors.[27] He therefore calls for more middle-ground approaches.

For a decision rendered by an administrative tribunal (as opposed to the dispute being settled through ADR), the possibility that the decision can be appealed to a court depends on what the 'enabling statute' that created the tribunal says about the conditions, if any, under which a decision can be appealed. A different kind of judicial supervision of administrative tribunals is available through judicial review. Whereas an appeal allows a court to assess the merits of the tribunal's decision,[28] judicial review allows the courts to review only 'how the decision was reached, and by whom' (Bryant and Sossin 2002, 160–1, 188). Whether an administrative tribunal acted outside of its authority granted by its enabling statute, whether a tribunal failed to follow the requirements of fairness, or whether tribunal members abused their discretion are common bases for judicial review (Gall 2004, 545–55). The power of judicial review derives from a superior court's inherent jurisdiction over executive action, though legislation sometimes defines the process for asking for judicial review (Bryant and Sossin 2002, 188).

Governments have tried to limit or preclude the judicial oversight of various administrative tribunals by denying or limiting appeals from an administrative tribunal and by using 'privative' clauses to reduce or eliminate judicial review of administrative decisions. A privative clause is a clause inserted into a tribunal's enabling statute that attempts to nullify or limit the jurisdiction of a superior court to perform judicial review on the tribunal's decisions. For example, the *Canada Labour Code*, which legally creates the Canada Industrial Relations Board, specifies that 'every order or decision of the Board is final and shall not be questioned or reviewed in any court, except in accordance with the *Federal Courts Act* on the grounds referred to in paragraph 18.1(4)(*a*), (*b*) or (*e*) of that Act.' At times courts have resented privative clauses and have read them narrowly, often prompting governments to strengthen the language of the clause (Gall 2004, 559). At other times, though, the courts have been somewhat more deferential. Although courts have not accepted that their power of judicial review can be denied completely, they have at times expressed the need for deference to administrative tribunal decisions when a privative clause is present in the enabling statute (Bryant and Sossin 2002, 159–60).

Conflict over judicial oversight of administrative tribunals has been particularly present in the area of labour relations. In Ontario, for example, a select committee on labour relations with a majority of Conservative Party members recommended in 1958 that changes be made to the *Labour Relations Act* to allow appeals from the Ontario Labour Relations Board to the courts. The recommendation was supported by various business groups (Smith 2006, 25). Labour groups, however, were opposed because labour had representation on the Board and they believed that the courts were dominated by judges who favoured business interests. Indeed, Ontario courts had tended to resist encroachment on the scope of their decision-making power when requested to do so by business interests. Over time, though, the courts became more deferential to the decisions of the Ontario Labour Relations Board.

Conclusions

The struggles involving privative clauses, like the controversy over arbitration by religious tribunals, or debates about policy-making or problem-solving by judges, remind us that dispute resolution has political dimensions. Since legal decisions reflect different value choices, it matters who the decision makers are, what the objectives of dispute resolution are, and what the processes are for making decisions. It is clear that the objectives of the traditional adjudicative model of courts—to bring finality to a dispute through the application of established legal principles to the adjudicative facts of the dispute—and the processes of the traditional adjudicative model—an adversarial process steeped in procedural rules culminating in a trial before a passive judge—are being challenged from within and outside of the judicial process. Outside the judicial process, ADR and administrative tribunals purport to offer more efficient and less complex processes that offer the possibility for more holistic and diverse decisions facilitated by non-judges (in the case of certain ADR processes) or decisions by tribunals that reflect expertise in a certain area of policy and administration (in the case of administrative tribunals). Within the judicial process, the problem-solving model of court seeks to address underlying problems of individuals, family, and community by using less formal processes where judges with specialized knowledge and training act as part of a team. At the very least, the problem-solving model advocates that there be ADR processes within the judicial process to increase the chances of an efficient and possibly more meaningful settlement. The policy-making model views the role of courts as contributing to the development of fair rules that balance different interests by lowering barriers of access to court and incorporating social facts into the decision making. In addition to reviewing the potential benefits of challengers to the adjudicative model, this chapter also noted criticisms of these challengers, including the possibility of unintended economic, social, or political consequences. The aftermath of the *Askov* decision was described as an example of a specific unintended consequence brought about by a policy-making approach.

What remains to be addressed are potential explanations for the turbulence surrounding dispute resolution by third parties in Canada. In his well-known study of the Canadian judiciary, Peter Russell argued that the 'environment' surrounding Canada's judicial system, consisting of social and economic development, dominant currents of political philosophy and ideology, and legal culture, both supported the powers and functions of the judicial branch and created pressures for change in the judicial system (1987, Chap. 2). Russell noted that the rise of a professional judicial branch independent of government to adjudicate disputes was associated with economic and social modernity, which eroded more informal social methods of dealing with disputes (such as customs or family). This required specialized expertise for dealing with a wide range of socio-economic conflict and was based on the liberal principle of protecting all individuals against government power. A strong and independent legal profession and the prestige of being a judge supported the judicial system. Although these environmental factors have remained somewhat constant and therefore continue to support the adjudicative model of court, there have been changes in the environment, sometimes contradictory, which can help begin to explain recent trends in third-party dispute resolution in Canada.

Compared to when Russell wrote roughly two decades ago, Canada now operates in a more globalized world, which is even more demographically diverse and which is more highly educated. These developments could help explain the speed at which the ADR movement spread from the United States to Canada and other countries and the increased use of ADR in multinational business and trade disputes (Bradbeer and Shackleton 2005). It could also help explain the desire of individuals to have more control over how they resolve their disputes and the aspirations of minority groups to use their own tribunals to settle conflict. The dominant political philosophy to which Russell referred has since been attacked from opposite directions. Conservative-minded thinkers argued for a contraction of the state. Philosophically, conservatives encouraged people to reduce their reliance on the state to solve problems (which would support ADR as a private dispute-settling approach) and critiqued policy-making courts for conducting 'social engineering'. Practically, the rise of the conservative movement precipitated government spending cuts, thereby reducing legal aid budgets. In turn, this drove people to look for more economical forms of dispute resolution like ADR and led to calls for judges to be more active in levelling the playing field for litigants not represented by lawyers (Thompson 2005). From the other side, the liberal paradigm was challenged by a 'post-liberal' philosophy that demanded that the state use its power to do more, not less, especially to help the disadvantaged. Adherents of this philosophy tend to distrust majoritarian institutions like legislatures and therefore advocate that courts play a greater role in solving societal problems and shaping social policy, especially through the Charter of Rights (Bateman 2002). Many law professors supported an expanded policy-making role for the court. However, Canadian legal culture was more apprehensive about ADR dispute resolution. This has changed, though, as evidenced by the number of law schools now offering programs in ADR (Farrow 2005). As noted above, for better or worse, the increasing role of lawyers in ADR and administrative tribunals may make them function more like adjudicative courts.

Environmental factors help to shape expectations about the role and value of various dispute resolution mechanisms. More proximate signals about what is expected of courts and other dispute-resolution processes come from the discourse and actions of actors in the political system. This chapter has shown that governments have responded to complaints about the costly, slow, and overly legalistic nature of adjudication culminating in a trial by increasing, to varying degrees, their support for ADR within and outside the judicial process (including in administrative tribunal processes) and their support for problem-solving courts. As discussed further in Chapters 8 and 11, governments have shown some comfort with more of a policy-making role for courts by entrenching the Charter of Rights in the constitution and opportunistically using the courts for political advantage. However, elected politicians have on numerous occasions also expressed unhappiness with courts for usurping their law-making role. Public opinion, interest groups, and the media also influence the extent to which the policy-making model is considered to be legitimate or desirable.

Finally, environmental forces and other actors in the system of governance shape the attitudes and actions of judges, but judges also independently shape dispute-resolution processes. This chapter pointed out, for example, how judges sometimes initiated the introduction of ADR mechanisms into the judicial process. Some judges are also at the forefront of championing problem-solving or policy-making approaches for the courts. These initiatives likely reflect some combination of an altruistic desire to provide better 'justice' and an attempt to strengthen judicial power (or at least an attempt to retain the relevance of courts in the face of a changing society and critiques of the adjudicative model).

Given that the environment of the courts has experienced rapid change over the last few decades, that the courts have received mixed signals about their dispute-resolving role from members of the political system, and that judges often disagree at least somewhat about the nature of the judicial role, it is not surprising that the institutional norms and rules of judicial process—covering access to court, role of the judge and number of parties, fact-finding and mode of reasoning—are being contested. In turn, the institutional connections between the judicial branch and the broader system of governance, involving rules about judicial appointments, independence, and accountability, which were predicated on courts as adjudicators of disputes, are also coming into question. These and other aspects of judicial process are explored in subsequent chapters.

PART II

Actors in the Process

Chapter 4

Judicial Decision Making

In 1989, Jean Tremblay applied for an injunction from a Quebec Superior Court to prevent his former girlfriend, Chantal Daigle, from obtaining an abortion. As the father, Tremblay was deemed to have the proper 'interest' to apply for the injunction. His injunction was granted after a judge interpreted the term 'human being' in the Quebec Charter of Human Rights and Freedoms as applying to the fetus—thus granting it the right to life. The injunction was appealed, and less than three weeks later, the Quebec Court of Appeal upheld the lower court's decision. Thirteen days later, the Supreme Court of Canada interrupted its summer vacation to hear arguments in the case—making *Tremblay v. Daigle* the speediest case in Canadian history (Morton 1992).

Chantal Daigle was twenty-two weeks pregnant when her case was heard by the Supreme Court. She was not the perfect test case for supporters of abortion rights. She had deliberately tried to get pregnant while with Tremblay and had sought an abortion only after they broke up (Morton 1992). However, she did make allegations of abuse by Tremblay.[1] Daigle was supported by intervener briefs from the Women's Legal Education and Action Fund (LEAF), the Canadian Abortion Rights Action League (CARAL), and the Canadian Civil Liberties Association (CCLA), while Tremblay's position was supported by Campaign Life, REAL Women, and Physicians for Life. Midway through the first day of oral arguments, it was announced that Daigle had defied the injunction and obtained her abortion in the United States. This effectively made the case moot and the case could have ended there. The Supreme Court, however, decided to continue hearing the case; it announced its decision at the end of oral arguments—another unusual event for such a high-profile case.

The Court's decision struck down the injunction against Daigle, and three months later, the Court added its reasoning to this outcome in a unanimous 'judgment of the Court'. According to the Court, nothing in Quebec legislation supported Tremblay's claim that his interest in the fetus gave him 'the right to veto a woman's decisions in respect of the foetus she is carrying' (*Tremblay v. Daigle* 1989). The Court went on to rule that a fetus was not a 'human being' and, therefore, did not have the right to life under the Quebec Charter of Human Rights and Freedoms. The Court stated that nothing in the Charter or Civil Code 'display[ed] any clear intention on the part of its framers to consider the status of a foetus' (*Tremblay v. Daigle* 1989, 555) and it seemed unlikely that if they had intended this, they would have left it to chance.

Why did the Supreme Court continue to hear this case once it became moot even though it had refused to decide another case in the abortion area (*Borowski v. Canada (Attorney General)* 1989) on this basis? What influenced the justices' decision? Were the legal arguments particularly compelling? Did the interveners before the Court have an influence? Did the justices merely decide according to their own policy preferences?

The Court's opinion makes reference to legal factors such as the framers' intent when drafting the legislation. But do the opinion's justifications for the decision tell the whole story? According to Sharpe and Roach, Chief Justice Dickson was furious upon learning that Daigle had obtained an abortion in defiance of the injunction and was inclined to end the case right then. Beverley McLachlin, however, apparently changed the Chief Justice's mind, and perhaps others on the Court, when she suggested that 'the Court put themselves in Daigle's shoes' (2003, 393). McLachlin pointed out that Daigle's pregnancy was already well advanced, making her 'a desperate young woman' determined not to bear the child of the man who had beaten her. Added to that, there was no way to know how long the Court would take to make its decision. Thus 'could she really be blamed for going to the United States to have her abortion?' (Sharpe and Roach 2003, 393). These behind the scenes events, and the implication that Justice McLachlin changed minds with her arguments, suggest that more than legal factors may be at work in judicial decisions. Justices, and their arguments, may influence the vote of their colleagues. McLachlin suggests that gender may also play a role: 'that you need a different variety of perspectives on the Court . . . maybe you need to look at it . . . in this case [from] a woman's point of view. Not that a man couldn't have seen it that way—ultimately they did, but it wasn't the way it immediately hit them' (as quoted in Sharpe and Roach 2003, 394).

Was *Tremblay v. Daigle* unique? Or do factors other than legal considerations regularly influence judicial decisions? This chapter will concentrate on judicial decision making and, in particular, the influences on judges' decisions. After a brief consideration of the differences between trial and appellate courts, the first part of the chapter discusses the process of accepting and deciding cases at the appellate courts. The remaining parts of the chapter focus on the factors that may determine the path judges take in their decisions. Traditional approaches to decision making emphasize the importance of legal factors. However, more recent scholarship has suggested that other factors may play a prominent role, including the judges' own policy preferences, their personal attributes, and the external environment (for example, the likely response of the media, public opinion, and political institutions). We will consider several influences in turn and the evidence that has been put forward to support them. Although we will make reference to trial courts where appropriate,[2] the focus of this chapter will be primarily on appellate courts, particularly the Supreme Court. More information is available on appellate courts since these courts regularly publish written opinions that help explain their decisions, and scholars have spent more time attempting to identify the influences on them.

Distinguishing Trial and Appeal Court Decisions

Although a lot of a trial judge's job involves activity outside the courtroom—for example, helping to negotiate settlements in civil cases—their decision making, wherever it occurs, is concentrated primarily on resolving disputes (see Chapters 9 and 10 for a more detailed discussion of trial courts in criminal and civil cases). McCormick identifies three important steps in a trial judge's decision making: identifying the relevant facts in the case, identifying the relevant law, and combining the facts and the law to produce the right result (1994, 44). For trial courts, the emphasis is on the first step, determining the facts of the case, which judges do by listening to the testimony of the parties and witnesses in the case. Trial judges use the information given to them to make the best decision they can, although this information is often incomplete or even inaccurate (Baum 2008a, 176). Witnesses may not exist, may fail to show up to court, or may have inaccurate recollections. Where differing accounts exist, choosing the proper interpretation of the facts may also be difficult. The adversarial nature of the common law system ensures that lawyers have an incentive to 'obscure the facts, rather than illuminate them' if it helps build a stronger case (Baum 2008a, 177). The difficulty judges have in determining the relevant facts means that mistakes are common: in fact one judge and legal scholar suggests that 'facts are guesses' (Jerome Frank as quoted in Baum 2008a, 177).[3]

Appeal courts are responsible for reviewing lower-court decisions. They read briefs and listen to oral arguments by the lawyers in the case rather than listening to witnesses. Therefore, the emphasis at the appellate level is generally on applying the law to the facts already determined at trial. On questions of law, appellate judges review *de novo*[4]—'as if it were new'—and do not need to defer to the trial judge in the case (Solum 2003). However, on findings of fact, appellate judges are supposed to defer to the trial judge unless those findings are 'clearly erroneous'. Since trial judges are the ones actually hearing the testimony of the parties and witnesses, their decisions on such matters as the credibility of witnesses and the proper weight to give conflicting pieces of evidence are accepted. Appellate judges are also supposed to abide by discretionary decisions of trial judges unless there was an 'abuse of discretion' (Solum 2003). Thus, decisions by trial judges on issues such as discovery, or the admission of evidence, are more difficult to challenge on appeal. Of course, distinctions between law, facts, and discretion are not always clear, and clever lawyers may frame questions to invoke the law and make deference to the trial judge less likely.

The trial judge's emphasis on the facts is the main distinction between this level of judge and that of the appellate courts. Justices Iacobucci and Bastarache sum up this distinction in their opinion in *Housen v. Nikolaisen* (2002): 'While the primary role of trial courts is to resolve individual disputes based on the facts before them and settled law, the primary role of appellate courts is to delineate and refine legal rules and ensure their universal application' (as quoted in MacIvor 2006, 100). Whereas trial judges are responsible for applying settled law, appellate judges are there primarily to correct errors in law and to clarify the law (though sometimes trial judges complain that an appellate court has retried the facts of their case when rendering a decision). They generally face more complex legal questions (Tarr 2006). This is particularly true of the Supreme Court of Canada. The lower level courts of appeal (such as the Alberta Court of Appeal or the Federal Court of Appeal) are the first level of appeal for most cases, and so these courts spend much of their time on the necessary correction of errors (for example, problems with a trial judge's instruction to a jury). Indeed, by one judge's account, at least 80 per cent of a provincial appellate judge's time is spent on the correction of errors (Greene et al. 1998, 106). High-level courts of appeal, such the Canadian Supreme Court, by contrast, direct their attention more to clarifying the law and developing it (Baum 2008a).

Appellate decision making also differs from decision making at the trial level, in the number of participants. Since cases before appellate courts are heard by panels of at least three judges, decisions require consultation—and outcomes are determined—by a group. This stands in stark contrast to trial judges, who have sole influence over how things are handled and decided in their courtroom. Yet appellate judges are often described as being more isolated than trial court judges. This refers generally to the number of case participants the judge sees from day to day. In the course of their work, trial judges are in contact with the parties in the case, witnesses, opposing counsel, and—occasionally—jury members. Particularly in criminal cases, where the same prosecutors and defence lawyers are frequently before the court, trial judges may develop a 'working group' of sorts. The judge and lawyers may 'socialize' during their workday, aiding in the smooth processing of the large number of cases they see (Tarr 2006). Appellate judges, by contrast, are in contact mostly with written briefs and court records, and they spend most of their time researching and writing their opinions in their own chambers, enjoying only limited contact with others (primarily their own law clerks). Since their focus is generally on the law, rather than the facts of the case, 'life on the court of appeal is a highly cerebral one. One addresses issues and arguments without being subject to many of the human pressures and the unpredictables with which a trial judge must cope' (Dickson 2000, 380).

Deciding to Take a Case: The Appellate Court's First Decision

As a general rule, the higher the level of appeal court, the more discretion judges have in deciding which cases they want to hear. In many countries around the world, including Canada and the United States, 'it is considered a matter of fundamental fairness . . . that the party who loses at trial . . . is entitled to an appeal'

(Greene et al. 1998, 43). As a result, the provincial appeals courts and the appeal division of the Federal Court hear cases primarily 'as of right' rather than 'by leave' (Greene et al. 1998, 43). Appeals 'as of right' are cases that courts must hear; appeals 'by leave' are cases that require the court's approval to be heard.

In 1974, Parliament gave the Supreme Court much more control over its docket by amending the *Supreme Court Act* to eliminate most 'appeals as of right' (these changes took effect in 1975). Appeals as of right are still allowed in a few circumstances in criminal cases, such as when a lower appeals court overturns an acquittal,[5] but the Court now exercises discretionary jurisdiction over the majority of its cases.[6] Table 4.1 illustrates the decreasing number of cases heard 'as of right' over the past decade. Indeed, in 2007, these cases made up only 18.9 per cent of the Court's docket. [The fact that most Supreme Court cases today are accepted 'by leave' rather than 'as of right' sets it apart from the lower appellate courts.]

Table 4.1   Supreme Court of Canada Caseload by Year

	Applications for Leave Granted[a] (%)	Cases Heard as of Right (%)	Judgments Allowing Appeal	Unanimous Judgments (%)
1996	12.1	41.5	45.2	78.2
1997	11.2	35.6	49.5	70.1
1998	12.3	28.3	51.1	76.1
1999	13.4	25.3	50.7	72.6
2000	13.2	17.9	45.8	72.2
2001	12.0	17.7	30.8	82.4
2002	10.9	22.2	53.4	69.3
2003	12.5	19.5	43.2	76.5
2004	15.1	15.7	55.8	73.1
2005	11.7	14.0	52.8	73.0
2006	11.9	16.3	62.0	79.7
2007	11.9[b]	18.9	51.7	62.1

[a] These percentages may be slightly high because the numbers do not include applications for leave that were quashed, adjourned, discontinued, or remanded to a lower court.
[b] The 2007 percentage does not include 83 cases that were still pending at the end of 2007.

Source: Supreme Court of Canada 2008a.

So how does the Supreme Court set its agenda and decide which cases to hear? The next section outlines the process used by the Court for granting review, and considers the factors that may influence the decision to accept a case.

Supreme Court 'by Leave'

Each year the Canadian Supreme Court receives hundreds of applications for leave to appeal. In the past decade, the number of applications has generally been between 500 and 600, with a high of 642 applications in the year 2000, and a low of 506 applications in 2006 (www.scc-csc.gc.ca). As Table 4.1 demonstrates, however, the Court grants very few of these applications. The highest proportion of applications for leave granted in a year since 1996 has been 15 per cent, and in most years it has been closer to 12 per cent. While low, this is actually a much better success rate than that found in the US Supreme Court. That Court receives a much greater number of appeals (over 7,000 a year since the late 1990s) but accepts a much lower percentage of them (fewer than 1 per cent in recent years) (Baum 2007). Thus, while the Canadian Supreme Court has fewer applications for leave to consider, it places a higher proportion of these applications on its docket, 'which means that their agenda is much more accessible to litigants than that of the US Supreme Court' (Flemming 2004, 12).

The Canadian Supreme Court's leave-to-appeal process has been studied extensively by Roy Flemming (2004). Flemming has detailed the necessary steps in the process, beginning with the first step: the decision to appeal.[7] Once that decision is made, an application for leave to appeal must be filed with the process clerk of the Court's Registrar's Office. If the application meets the strict formatting and presentation rules, it is forwarded on to the Law Branch of the office. The lawyers in this branch review the application and prepare a summary of its contents, generally including the history of the case, the facts, and legal issues (Flemming 2004, 14–15). They also make a recommendation as to whether the application should be granted or denied. Thus, there is a permanent specialized unit within the Supreme Court responsible for the preliminary screening of appeals. This unit performs a function roughly equivalent to that done by law clerks at the United States Supreme Court.[8] The use of staff lawyers in Canada not only frees the law clerks for other business, but also ensures that more experience is brought to the summaries and recommendations.[9]

In the next step of the process, the summary and recommendation for an appeal application are forwarded to a panel of three justices. The Chief Justice of the Court assigns the nine justices to panels of three at the start of the Court's fall term and reshuffles them each year (or more frequently as required by illness and retirements) (Flemming 2000, 50). The decision as to which three justices should sit on a panel has not been widely studied, but at least in one instance, it is not completely random: one panel of three is usually made up of at least two justices from Quebec (Flemming 2004, 73). When the summaries and recommendations of the staff lawyers are forwarded to the panels of justices, applications for leave coming out of Quebec are usually given to the panel made up of the Quebec justices. This panel's composition and application assignment is understandable given Quebec's different civil law tradition, but it does ensure there is very little anglophone participation in the Quebec appeals (Flemming 2004). Other applications for leave are distributed amongst the panels with an effort to equalize the workload. However, an application dealing with a specialized issue may be assigned to a panel with a justice whose expertise is in that area (Flemming 2004).

Since the 1980s, oral arguments have been a rare event in the leave-to-appeal process, and the three justices on the panel do not usually meet to discuss the applications for appeal they are assigned (Flemming 2004). Instead decisions are reached through memorandum, with two votes needed for an appeal to be granted. Decisions at the leave-to-appeal stage tend to be unanimous. Indeed, in his study of over 1,200 applications for leave, Flemming found only thirty with a dissenting justice (2004, 15).[10] Justices can use the conference (a meeting of all nine justices) to try to change the panel's decision on an application; however, the panels do appear to have the final say on whether an application is granted or denied leave (this discussion relies on Flemming 2004 and Bastarache 2007).

The use of panels of justices to decide applications for leave to appeal sets the Canadian Supreme Court apart from its US counterpart, where all nine justices hear appeals and four justices must agree before leave can be granted. The result in Canada is a more decentralized process, where the potential exists for the appeal decision to depend on which panel hears the application.[11] This potential is furthered by the widespread discretion justices have as to which applications to accept. As shown in Box 4.1, the *Supreme Court Act* provides only limited guidance on what cases the Supreme Court will accept on appeal.

Box 4.1   Applications for Leave to Appeal to the Supreme Court

An appeal lies to the Supreme Court from any final or other judgment of the Federal Court of Appeal or of the highest court of final resort in a province . . . where, with respect to the particular case sought to be appealed, the Supreme Court is of the opinion that any question involved therein is, by reason of its public importance or the importance of any issue of law or any issue of mixed law and fact involved in that question, one that ought to be decided by the Supreme Court or is, for any other reason, of such a nature or significance as to warrant decision by it, and leave to appeal from that judgment is accordingly granted by the Supreme Court.

Source: *Supreme Court Act*, s. 40 (1)

The *Supreme Court Act* does suggest that the Court will accept applications for leave if they raise issues of 'public importance'; however, what causes an issue to be of 'public importance' is not defined. The late John Sopinka offered some guidance on what might qualify when he was sitting on the Supreme Court (see also Bastarache 2007). According to Sopinka, the public importance criterion is triggered by constitutional challenges, appeals raising issues on which there is conflict among the provincial courts of appeal, appeals raising a new point of law, appeals requiring interpretation of 'important' federal or provincial laws (if the law exists in more than one province), and appeals requiring the definition of aboriginal rights (Crane and Brown 2004). Sopinka also said that factors other than public importance could lead the Court to grant leave to appeal. In criminal cases, for example, the Court was likely to grant leave to cases not meeting the public importance threshold if they involved the possibility of a defendant's being unfairly convicted (Crane and Brown 2004; Flemming 2004).

Flemming tested several jurisprudential factors in his models of the appeal decision. He found that applications suggesting there was lower-court conflict on the issue (between two provincial courts of appeal) were more likely to be granted leave to appeal, as were applications where a judge on the lower-court panel had dissented from the panel's decision (2004, 68–70). Appeals linking the lower court's decision to provincial or federal government interests were also more likely to be granted leave, as were appeals asking the Supreme Court to 'revisit' its previous decisions (Flemming 2004, 70). Thus, jurisprudential factors appear to have an influence on the leave-to-appeal decision.

It appears that in Canada, in contrast to the US, jurisprudential factors play a greater role in the decision to grant an appeal than more litigant-centred factors (such as the status and resources of the parties) (Flemming 2004, 99–100; for descriptions of the influence of these and other factors in the United States, see McGuire 1993; Galanter 1974; Salokar 1992; Caldeira and Wright 1988). This finding is complicated, however, by institutional features—in particular, the Canadian Supreme Court's use of panels for the leave-to-appeal decision. In his 2004 study, Flemming examined variations in the decisions of different panels. His results show that while panels may not differ greatly in the number of applications they grant, they do differ significantly in the criteria they use to reach their decisions (Flemming 2004, 75). Different panels emphasize different rules in making their decisions.

The institutional feature of panels makes strategic manoeuvring (a justice voting on leave on the basis of the expected outcome of the case if accepted) unlikely in Canada. Since panels are often used to decide the merits of a case, it becomes extremely difficult for a justice to predict how the Court will vote if the panel grants leave to an application. Flemming suggests that strategic considerations may play a different role in Canada than in the US. Since the Chief Justice may not assign justices to panels to hear cases in which they voted to deny leave, Flemming suggests there is an incentive for a justice who does not agree with his two colleagues to vote with them anyway (2004, 87) so that he will at least have a chance to take part in the decision on the merits. And since Canadian Supreme Court justices often volunteer to write opinions (rather than having them assigned to them), this might be extensive input indeed. Thus, the practice of using panels to hear cases may contribute to the high rate of unanimous decisions at the leave-to-appeal stage.

Table 4.2 demonstrates some characteristics of the cases accepted by the Supreme Court and heard during the 2007 term (see Chapter 2 for a more detailed description of the workload of the Supreme Court, as well as that of the lower appellate and trial courts). Cases arising in British Columbia, Quebec, and Ontario dominated the Supreme Court's docket, and the single highest category of cases involved criminal law (although when all the civil issue categories are added together, they outweigh criminal issues).

Table 4.2   Supreme Court of Canada Characteristics of Cases, 2007

Origin of Case	Appeals Heard (no.)	Type of Case	Appeals Heard (%)
British Columbia	13	Criminal Law	45
Ontario	11	Torts	9
Quebec	11	Charter (Criminal)	9
Federal Court of Appeal	7	Administrative Law	4
Alberta	5	Charter (Civil)	4
Manitoba	2	Procedural Law	4
Saskatchewan	2	International Law	4
New Brunswick	1	Commercial Law	4
Nova Scotia	1	Constitutional Law	4
Newfoundland & Labrador	0	Taxation	4
Northwest Territories	0	Others	9
Nunavut	0		
Prince Edward Island	0		
Yukon	0		

Source: Supreme Court of Canada 2008a.

The Process of Hearing and Deciding Cases

Once a case is appealed (and once leave is granted by the Supreme Court), the parties must make their written submissions[12] to the court. For each case, an appeal court judge must wade through trial transcripts, factums[13] from both the appellant and respondent, and lists of authorities. As discussed in Chapter 7, the judges may also have several intervener factums to read as well. Once all the documents are filed, a date is set for oral argument. The *Supreme Court Act* dictates that the Supreme Court must sit in three sessions each year: fall (October through December), winter (late January through March), and spring (late April to the end of June). During its sessions, the Court alternates between two weeks of hearings and two weeks of writing decisions and preparing for hearings (www.scc-csc.gc.ca). The provincial courts of appeal differ widely in their schedules. British Columbia, Alberta, and Newfoundland also alternate between two weeks of hearings and two weeks of writing decisions, but Nova Scotia hears cases during five six-week terms every year (www.courts.ns.ca/dockets_on_line).

The Use of Panels

At the appeal-court level, each case is heard by more than one judge. Provincial courts of appeal typically use panels of three judges to hear and decide a case.[14] In all provinces except Prince Edward Island (which has only three judges sitting on its appeals court), the Chief Judge of the court must select which three judges will hear the case. The procedure for doing this varies to some extent from province to province, but usually, the clerk of the court creates lists of all the possible combinations of judges[15] (Greene et al. 1998, 65).

One difference between the provinces that may influence case decisions is the timing of the notification of counsel as to which judges will hear a case. In Alberta and Quebec, this notification is done ahead of time, whereas in the other provinces counsel find out the makeup of the bench only when they walk into the courtroom. This difference is significant because lawyers who know in advance which judges will be hearing their case may invent reasons to reschedule a hearing in the hopes of being assigned to a different panel (Greene et al. 1998, 66). Advance notification of the makeup of the panel may also influence the content of briefs, because lawyers will tailor their arguments to the judges sitting on the bench (Revesz 2000).

At the Supreme Court level, cases may be heard by five, seven, or nine justices. The number of justices assigned to hear a case is always odd in order to prevent the possibility of a tie vote on the outcome of the case. Very occasionally, cases have been heard by six or eight justices when a situation—such as a justice's illness—that prevents one of the panel from hearing the case has arisen late in the process. (If a tie were to result from such a situation, the lower court's decision would stand.) Although more recent Chief Justices have expressed a preference for having cases heard by the full Court of nine (Ostberg and Wetstein 2007; McCormick 2000), the most frequent size of a panel is seven.[16] As the Court's prominence and power have increased in the years since the passage of the Charter, so has the preference for larger panels. At least for cases judged to be of high public importance, there is now unease with a panel of only seven, since it is possible for four justices—a minority of the Court—to determine the outcome of a case and it is possible that the presence of the two non-participating justices would have produced a different decision. An example is the controversial *Chaoulli v. Quebec* case, which struck down Quebec's ban on private health insurance, particularly since only six of seven justices hearing the case addressed the Charter of Rights and Freedoms and those six divided 3–3 on the issue.[17]

The Chief Justice is responsible for deciding both the size of a panel and who will be on it. The decision to have a case heard by a panel of justices rather than by the Court *en banc* (that is, all nine justices) is sometimes forced on a Chief Justice by the absence of justices due to illness or other commitments. Models controlling the potential influences on the decision to sit as a panel suggest that Chief Justices are more likely to assign all nine justices to hear a case when the Charter is at issue or when an intervener is present (indicating an issue of widespread interest), and are more likely to assign only a panel of justices when the case is coming to the Court as an 'appeal as of right' (cases forced on the Court that are often disposed of in short, one-page decisions) (Hausegger 2000).

The decision as to who will sit on a panel is usually made several weeks before oral arguments are heard in a case, but it is not made public. Lawyers do not discover which justices will be hearing their arguments until the day of the hearing. If the Chief Justice wished to, he or she could exercise some influence on the outcome of the case by assigning justices strategically: assigning those that are likely to decide in a particular way while leaving others off the bench. In their study of panel-assignment decisions from 1986 to 1997, Hausegger and Haynie suggest that for cases involving salient civil rights and liberties issues, Chief Justices Dickson and Lamer were more likely to assign justices with similar policy preferences to themselves (2003, 651). Other factors found to play a role in the choice of a panel include the expertise of the justice, their home province, and their gender (Hausegger 2000). Justices with expertise in a particular issue area were more likely to sit on a panel hearing a case dealing with that issue, and justices were also more likely to sit on cases appealed from their home province (this, of course, was particularly true for the Quebec justices in cases originating in Quebec that involved civil law). Interestingly, both Chief Justice Dickson and Lamer appear to have been more likely to assign female justices to panels (Hausegger 2000). Perhaps this was an effort on their part to increase the representativeness of the panels hearing cases.[18]

Oral Arguments and Preliminary Votes

After the panels are constituted, the next step for all levels of appellate court is oral arguments. Whereas trial court judges listen both to the arguments of opposing lawyers and to the testimony of witnesses, in appellate courts only the parties' lawyers attend and make arguments (with the exception of intervener lawyers if they are given permission to briefly present their arguments to the court). Lawyers are given a specified amount of time to present their arguments. At the provincial Courts of Appeal, time limits vary by province and by type of appeal. In the Ontario Court of Appeal, for example, sentencing appeals have time limits of thirty minutes for the appellant, twenty minutes for the respondent, and ten minutes for an appellant's rebuttal. However, in appeals such as conviction appeals on indictable offences, these limits do not apply (www.ontariocourts.on.ca/coa/en). Lawyers in these appeals are asked to give the court a time estimate before a judge of the court decides the time to be allowed for each side.

Unlike judges in trial courts, appellate court judges are very active during the oral arguments, frequently interrupting and asking questions. Although Supreme Court justices often ask questions during oral argument, they have tended to be not as expansive as judges on lower courts of appeal, owing to the stricter time limits that are placed on the parties arguing the case before them (Greene et al. 1998, 118).[19] The justices' questions are intended to clarify issues from the factums and perhaps to bring attention to particular aspects of the law. Justice Bastarache points out that oral argument can be particularly important in areas of law where the justices do not have as much expertise, such as admiralty law and Internet crime. He also notes that while oral arguments may not often change the justices' minds on the outcome of a case, it can have an influence on the reasoning they use in their opinions (2007).

After oral argument, appeal court judges meet in conference to discuss the case. Since they make their decisions in groups, (unlike trial court judges, who have only themselves to satisfy) they need to find out their colleagues' positions on the cases. At the provincial appeal courts, the three judges sitting on the panel will meet quickly, vote on how the case should be decided, and determine whether judgment should be reserved (in which case a written decision will be released at a later date instead of an oral decision being announced immediately).[20]

Although at the Supreme Court, decisions are less likely to be announced immediately, it does occur, as in the *Tremblay* case described in the introduction to this chapter. However, even if the judgment is announced immediately from the bench, an opinion may follow at a later date, as it did in *Tremblay*. According to the Supreme Court's own statistics, the number of decisions delivered from the bench has decreased significantly since the mid-1990s. In recent years, roughly 20 per cent of judgments have been delivered from the bench (www.scc-csc.gc.ca).

As might be expected, many of the cases decided in this manner have come to the Court 'as of right' rather than 'by leave'.

Supreme Court justices also have a conference after hearing a case. In that conference, the justices go around the table from most junior to most senior, each describing his or her view on how the case should be disposed. The votes indicate who will make up the majority on the case, and one of that number will often volunteer to write the opinion. If someone does not volunteer then the presiding justice—the Chief Justice if he or she is on the panel hearing the case—will assign the task. In the United States, there is an extensive literature on the opinion-assignment decision by Chief Justices and the potential influences on it. Several of these studies suggest that Chief Justices are more likely to assign tasks to justices with similar ideological preferences—particularly in important cases (see for example, Maltzman, Spriggs, and Wahlbeck 2000; Davis 1990). However, Supreme Court conferences are not public, so the only information we have on them comes from the justices' own writings. Whereas in the United States, Supreme Court justices have released their papers containing detailed notes on conferences, not much is known about the votes and discussions of conferences of the Canadian Supreme Court.[21] Thus, there are no detailed statistics on the number of times an opinion is assigned by the Chief Justice (rather than being written by a volunteer) and we do not yet know whether Canadian Supreme Court Chief Justices have taken advantage of their power to influence the direction of the reasoning in a case through their opinion assignment.

Crafting Opinions in a Case

Since appellate courts are involved in collegial decision making, opinion assignment is not the final step in the process. Rather the author of the majority opinion will circulate the draft of his opinion to all the justices in an effort to get as many justices as possible to sign it. Justices may send memoranda around discussing the opinion, and majority-opinion authors may rewrite their opinions in response to those comments.[22] In the *Tremblay* case described at the beginning of the chapter, Chief Justice Dickson originally circulated a draft that argued the fetus did not have legal status under s. 7 of the Charter. However, Justice LaForest objected to the Court's discussing the issue of fetal rights under the Charter, and said that he would write separately on narrower grounds. Preferring a unanimous decision from the Court for such a controversial issue, Chief Justice Dickson rewrote his opinion leaving out any discussion of fetal rights under s. 7 (Sharpe and Roach 2003).

In each of the last ten years, the Supreme Court has rendered unanimous opinions on the disposition of the case over 70 per cent of the time (except in 2002 when it was 69 per cent). (See Table 4.1.) Though high, this number shows that there are a significant number of cases in which the majority-opinion author was unable to get everyone to sign on. If a justice does not agree with the majority on the outcome of the case, he or she will cast a vote in dissent and will likely write (or join) a dissenting opinion that outlines the problems with the majority opinion and the reasons why the dissenting position is superior.[23] These opinions will also be circulated amongst the members of the Court for them to consider signing. Dissenting opinions are rarer in the provincial courts of appeal. For example, the Ontario Court of Appeal has recently reached unanimity in 93 per cent of all sexual assault cases and 99 per cent of all narcotics cases (with an average of 95 per cent for all cases; Stribopoulos and Yahya 2007).

Former Justice Iacobucci argues that dissenting opinions are valuable because they make the majority opinion stronger: '[C]larity of thought, in short, is not improved by agreement but by disagreement' (2002, 14). Dissents are also championed for the guidance they can provide to future courts, as well as to legislatures that are intent on overturning the Court's decision. This was the case in the aftermath of *R. v. O'Connor*, a case that Parliament felt struck the wrong balance between defendants' and victims' rights by setting too low a threshold for the disclosure of a victim's medical and therapeutic records. In drafting legislation intended to correct the balance and still comply with the Charter, the government relied on Justice L'Heureux Dube's dissenting opinion in *R. v. O'Connor* (Iacobucci 2002, 14). This legislation was later upheld by the Court in *R. v. Mills*.

Of course, if there are no dissenting opinions and the Court votes unanimously on the disposition of the case, this does not imply complete agreement. Justices voting in the majority also have the option of writing a concurring opinion. Usually a concurring opinion is written by a justice who agrees with the outcome of the case but not with the reasoning used by the majority to reach that outcome.[24] The existence of these opinions is significant, because the Supreme Court's reasoning is often thought to be more important than the actual outcome of the case. The outcome directly affects the immediate parties before the Court, but the reasoning has much broader implications for future court decisions (McCormick 2004a, 103). The 'right' outcome is not nearly as valuable without the 'right' reasoning to support it. Arguing that concurring opinions are as much an example of judicial disagreement as are dissenting opinions and that they are just as important to study, McCormick quotes US Justice Antonin Scalia, who says, 'An opinion that gets the reasons wrong gets everything wrong which it is the function of an opinion to produce' (2004a, 104).

Concurring opinions are more frequent at the Supreme Court than at lower courts of appeal. In the current period under Chief Justice McLachlin, however, concurrences occur on average only about ten times a year. This is significantly lower than the rate under Chief Justice Dickson and Chief Justice Lamer (1984 to 2000), when the average was over thirty times a year (McCormick 2005b).

Outcome of the Case

Appellate courts can vote to uphold the lower court's decision (in effect dismissing the appeal) or to overturn it (allowing the appeal). The provincial courts of appeal usually dismiss more appeals than they allow. The British Columbia Court of Appeal, for example, has allowed only 37 per cent to 41 per cent of appeals over the last six years (British Columbia, Court of Appeal 2007). The Supreme Court has split relatively equally between allowing and dismissing appeals in the past decade (see Table 4.1). The number of appeals allowed has been slightly higher in recent years, but even during this period the highest proportion has been 62 per cent in 2006. The low rate of appeals allowed in most of the years (for example, 31 per cent in 2001 and 43 per cent in 2003) is interesting given the Supreme Court's discretion over its docket. One might expect the Court to accept cases because it disagreed with the outcome of the court below. Indeed, the United States Supreme Court votes to allow an appeal (reversing the lower court's decision) in over two-thirds of its cases (Baum 2007, 94).

The Determinants of Judicial Decision Making

The first part of this chapter discussed the process of decision making. The chapter now changes direction to focus on the decisions themselves and the possible influences on the judges making the decisions.[25] As mentioned earlier, most of the discussion concerns the Supreme Court level (see Chapters 9 and 10 for more in-depth analysis of trial court behaviour in the criminal and civil areas).[26] With no higher court overseeing their decisions and no chance of promotion to a higher court, Supreme Court justices face fewer restrictions when they decide cases, and different factors may play a greater role in their decisions compared to those of trial judges (and even provincial appeal-court judges). Thus, whereas the justices' legal training and experience may ensure legal factors are emphasized in their decisions, the cases heard by the Supreme Court are likely to be more complex and to have no clear solution.

Legal Factors

Judges at all levels of courts are responsible for settling questions of law. They are called on to interpret the meaning of statutes, precedents, and constitutional provisions and to apply that meaning to settle the case before them. Judges themselves often suggest that the law is the sole basis of their decisions—that they merely apply the proper interpretation of the law to the question before them. John Roberts, the Chief Justice of the United States Supreme Court, suggested just this at his confirmation hearing, when he compared judges to umpires:[27] 'Judges and justices are servants of the law, not the other way around. Judges are like umpires. Umpires don't make the rules; they apply them' (as quoted in Baum 2007, 114).

The suggestion that justices base their decisions entirely upon legal factors has been subject to criticism. The law is often ambiguous and open to different interpretations. Judges, particularly at the Supreme Court, are often faced with choices, and these choices may be influenced—consciously or unconsciously—by factors other than the law. However, if not definitive, the law is surely important to judges and their decision making, given that the parties in court cases make their arguments with reference to legal principles, and court decisions are framed in the language of the law. Justices are also part of the legal community, a community that often produces written evaluations of the justice's treatment of the law (Baum 2007).[28] But the fact that law matters might be best illustrated by the justices' own words. In some cases, the justices will say that though they are deciding the case as they 'have to', in order to honour the proper interpretation of the law, the result is unfortunate, and something that should be altered by those in a proper position to do so (usually Parliament).[29] As discussed below, the willingness of judges to follow the law, rather than to change it, may be related to how they see their role as a judge.

A variety of approaches are adopted by judges in interpreting statutes and constitutional provisions, and these approaches can give insight into the role that law plays in judicial decision making (Baum 2007). This section discusses some of these approaches.

Precedent

The Supreme Court's decisions create precedents to be followed by it and other courts. The doctrine of *stare decisis* ('let the decision stand') suggests that like cases should be decided alike. Under this doctrine, lower courts are expected to follow the rulings of higher courts, and the Supreme Court is expected to follow its own precedents when making decisions.[30] The provincial courts of appeal, however, are not bound to follow one another's opinions. Thus, in similar cases dealing with hate speech, the Alberta Court of Appeal struck down the section of the Criminal Code preventing the distribution of hate literature as an unconstitutional infringement on freedom of expression (*R. v. Keegstra*), whereas later that same year, the Ontario Court of Appeal ruled the section was constitutional (*R. v. Andrews*).[31] Decisions by provincial appellate courts on other courts at this level are considered merely 'persuasive'. Decisions by the Ontario Court of Appeal would also not be binding on the lower Alberta courts, although they might be considered 'strongly persuasive' (Gall 2004, 433–7).

Precedent generally refers to the legal reasoning necessary to decide the case: the *ratio decidendi*. Court decisions also contain discussions of law that are not the basis of the court's decisions. These statements are considered *obiter dictum*, and judges are not bound by this in future decisions.[32]

Most judges champion precedent and the doctrine of *stare decisis*. Even Chief Justice Dickson, who believed the Charter required justices to 'go beyond abstract logic and disembodied precedent' in their decision making, argued that 'change need not, and should not, take place at breakneck speed' (Sharpe and Roach 2003, 311). Dickson's comments suggest one of the values of following precedent: stability in law. There can be an advantage to making only incremental changes in the law. The consistency in result allows litigants and governments alike to predict the courts' responses as they contemplate bringing cases or writing legislation. The courts' predictability may prevent fruitless appeals and litigation (Gall 2004). Courts that are seen to follow precedent closely can also enhance perceptions of their legitimacy since they appear to apply neutral principles to their decision making and to decide cases without personal bias. Therefore, following precedent is believed to further the fairness of the law in that similar parties undertaking similar litigation are expected to be treated the same.

Supreme Court precedent is particularly important to lower courts, which are expected to follow the Court's decisions. Several Supreme Court justices interviewed by Greene et al. (1998) suggested that the influence of precedent is one of the main differences between the Supreme Court and lower appellate courts. According to these justices, there was far less pressure to follow precedent at the Supreme Court and far more pressure to 'get it right' (Greene et al. 1998, 104–5). However, since the Supreme Court decides fewer than 100 cases each year, some of the influence of precedent on lower courts may be weakened as well. Lower-court judges can feel relatively assured that their decisions will not be overturned, given the low number of cases actually accepted (and then reversed) by the Court each year. Even if lower-court decisions are reviewed, the courts have little power to ensure their precedent is followed. Thus, a provincial court of appeal may overturn a trial court judge's decision if he does not follow a precedent established previously by the higher court. But there is nothing the appeal court can do to ensure that he follows that precedent in his next case. The appeal court must wait for cases to be brought to it in order to correct their outcome, and it is powerless to punish the trial judge for ignoring its decisions. In fact, as McCormick suggests, trial judges who feel they are correct in their decisions may respond to any rebuke from the higher court with a sense of 'martyrdom' that they wear 'with pride rather than shame' (1994, 57).

Of course, following precedent is not always preferable or even possible. While there is a 'hard core' group within the Canadian judiciary who believes they 'must slavishly adhere to precedent and *stare decisis*', most justices recognize that the practice of following *stare decisis* 'when pushed to doctrinaire limits becomes utter nonsense' (Gall 2004, 456). Many argue that a single-minded pursuit of precedent would keep the courts out of step with the times and might even lead to problematic results. They suggest that precedent should be modified if it is leading to unjust results.[33]

If a justice believes that that some aspect of the case before the Court is different from that seen previously, he or she can 'distinguish' the precedent and argue that it does not apply. Justices distinguish precedent far more frequently than they overturn it. In some instances justices appear to 'distinguish' cases simply to avoid following a precedent. The legitimacy that the use of precedent is thought to convey on courts makes justices much more reluctant to overturn it than to ignore it on occasion.

Some scholars suggest that precedent is not a real factor in judicial decisions, arguing that justices merely reach the decision they want, and then use precedent to 'justify' their result. (See, for example, American champions of the 'attitudinal model' discussed in the next section, such as Segal and Spaeth 2002.) Others suggest justices cite precedent because they feel the need to appeal to others who value precedent in order to maintain the legitimacy of the court. (This is suggested by some who argue that justices undertake a strategic approach to decision making—see the discussion in Baum 2008b.) Stier and Brenner argue, however, that scholars advocating these viewpoints are suggesting an unrealistic amount of cognitive effort on the part of the justices to work on both planes—to determine their own policy preferences and then identify the relevant legal arguments to justify their decision (Stier and Brenner 2008). Instead, Stier and Brenner suggest that 'the culture of law [with its emphasis on legal reasoning and precedent] shapes the decision making of Supreme Court justices' (2008, 5).

As noted in Chapter 1, precedents play an important role in the common law system in developing judge-made law, because legal principles are developed on a case-by-case basis over time. However, with more and more legal rules being found in written constitutions and legislation in common law countries, how do judges decide how to apply these rules? Eventually, the interpretations given by appellate courts will provide guidance (and will be considered precedents), but how do judges decide initially how a constitutional or legislative provision should be interpreted and applied?

Framers' Intent

One approach that justices may adopt for interpreting the provisions that are brought before them is the inferred intent of the framers. When faced with interpreting provisions within the Constitution, justices could ask what the framers intended when writing the 'supreme law of the land'. Similarly, in statutory interpretation, justices could ask what the legislators intended in drafting legislation as they did. This factor has received a lot of attention in the United States, where it is referred to as 'original intent'. American scholars argue that the framers' and legislators' intent can be discovered by looking at records surrounding the drafting of the Constitution and at legislative history (committee reports, debate, speeches, and the like). Supporters of original intent argue it allows for the neutral interpretation of legal principles (Bork 1971). Justices determine what the framers intended by the constitutional section, or piece of legislation, and apply that intent to resolve the case in front of them without reference to their own beliefs or preferences. Original intent is also attractive to its supporters since it implies the Court is following the intent of drafters that were elected by a majority, rather than substituting the judgment of the non-elected justices (Manfredi 2001; Bork 1971). And, like the arguments surrounding precedent, original intent is thought to promote stability in law, allowing for greater predictability over time for litigants and other players in the legal system.

Opponents of original intent, however, argue that the interpretation of the Constitution should not be restricted to the time it was passed. Rather, its meaning should be kept current and in touch with today's societal values. Opponents also point to the difficulty of using the original-intent approach. To determine the framers' intent, one first has to decide who the framers were, not an easy task considering the dozens—or even hundreds—of people that may be involved in drafting a constitution, or drafting and passing legislation. And even if one is successful in deciding which participants should be at the forefront and labelled 'framers', it is still necessary to narrow down the intent of the group, which may vary by individual. A further difficulty, of course, is trying to identify intent decades, or even centuries, after the fact (Hogg 1987. Even if the information is available, the reliance placed on records may steer one astray if they reflect those writing them (for example, legislative staff), more than the framers themselves (Baum 2007). Thus opponents suggest there is room for subjective judgment in the pursuit of original intent.

Historically, the framers' intent has not been a dominant factor in Canadian constitutional jurisprudence. The Judicial Committee of the Privy Council (JCPC), which acted as Canada's final court of appeal until 1949, seemed to ignore the intent of the framers of the *British North America Act* (the *BNA Act*, which is now referred to as the *Constitution Act 1867*). Their dismissal of intent was consistent with the British courts' reluctance to consider legislative history (reports, testimony, speeches, and the like) when determining the meaning of statutes, and the *BNA Act* was, after all, a statute of British Parliament and treated as such by the JCPC (Hogg 2006b; Walton 2001). Refusing to look at evidence such as legislative debates at the time the document was written, the JCPC would have been unable to determine the framers' intent even if it had wanted to use it. The approach taken by the JCPC had profound effects on the interpretation of the document. Critics have argued that the British justices, none of whom had ever been to Canada, were 'quite ignorant of the history, geography and society' of the country, and interpreted the Constitution according to their own 'preconceived notion of what a federal system should look like, a notion that would have been contradicted by much of the legislative history' (Hogg 2006b, 75).[34]

The JCPC did speak of the division of powers laid out in sections 91 and 92 of the *BNA Act 1867*, as being 'watertight compartments'—sections whose meaning was set at the time of Confederation. However, scholars point out that the Court was not greatly concerned with what that meaning was intended to be, mentioning intent instead only 'in cases where it sought to prove what Parliament could not have intended' (Walton 2001, 318). Indeed, by 1929, the JCPC appeared to take a very broad approach to interpreting the Act—and one very much removed from original intent. In that year, the JCPC interpreted the 'Person's Case'. This case was instigated by five Alberta women who wanted the Prime Minister to appoint a woman to the Canadian Senate. The Prime Minister refused, citing s. 24 of the *BNA Act*, which required the appointment of 'qualified persons'. The Prime Minister argued that women were not persons in the legal sense of the word. When the question was brought before the Canadian Supreme Court, the Court sided with the Prime Minister, ruling that women were not persons, because they had not been considered such when the Act was drafted (MacIvor 2006). The five women appealed their case to the JCPC, which in 1929, ruled in their favour. In that decision, the JCPC suggested the proper approach to interpreting the Constitution was not 'narrow and technical,' arguing instead that 'the British North America Act planted in Canada a living tree capable of growth and expansion within its natural limits' (*Henrietta Muir Edwards v. Attorney General for Canada* 1930). Thus, the Constitution should be interpreted in 'tune with the times,' responsive to changing beliefs in society. (For a detailed discussion of the Person's Case see Sharpe and McMahon 2007.)

In the decades since its ascension to final court of appeal for Canada, the Supreme Court has essentially rejected the idea of original intent in its constitutional interpretation in favour of the 'living-tree' doctrine.[35] Thus, the justices have rejected the notion that the meaning of the Constitution is 'frozen'—set at the meaning the framers would have intended. Instead, the Court has taken a 'progressive' approach to constitutional interpretation, which involves adjusting the meaning of the documents' provisions to keep up with changes in society and its values. Whereas adherents of framers' intent argue that the original understanding should guide justices and only be changed through amendments to the document, adherents of the 'progressive' (or living tree) approach give the courts the power to adapt the meaning as needed (Hogg 2006b).

The idea of framers' intent hit a new difficulty with the passage of the Charter of Rights and Freedoms in 1982. The recent enactment meant that the framers of the Constitution were still present on the scene when the courts started making decisions in the early 1980s, and their intent might well be knowable. Right from the start, however, there were indications that the Supreme Court would not adopt an approach of 'framers' intent'. In 1984, Justice Dickson, for example, argued that while statutes are focused on the present, the Constitution was written with 'an eye to the future . . . [and] must, therefore, be capable of growth and development over time to meet new social, political and historical realities often unimagined by its framers' (*Hunter v. Southam* 1984, 155). A year later, Justice Lamer wrote a decision for the Court which rejected the notion that the Court should interpret s. 7 of the Charter narrowly (as a purely procedural guarantee), to comply with the intent of government officials writing the Charter. Lamer argued that the passage of the Charter had been a complex affair, carried out by such a wide variety of individuals and institutions that 'the comments of a few federal civil servants' could not be determinative' (Sharpe and Roach 2003, 319). Since the Charter was meant to last for generations to come, the meaning of its provisions and values should not 'become frozen in time to the moment of adoption with little or no possibility of growth, development and adjustment to changing societal needs' (*Re B.C. Motor Vehicle Act* 1985). Thus, the living tree doctrine is alive and well in the Charter era.

Justice Lamer's opinion in the reference case described above makes the Court's preference for the progressive approach clear, but also suggests there are difficulties in following the framers' intent, even for a recent enactment. This difficulty is demonstrated by the issue of sexual orientation. The Charter of Rights and Freedoms does not explicitly mention sexual orientation in s. 15, the section guaranteeing equality rights. However, in 1995, the Supreme Court added sexual orientation to the list of grounds protected against discrimination by s. 15 (*Egan v. Canada* 1995). Critics argue this decision was a direct violation of the framers' intent. They suggest that the federal government deliberately left sexual orientation out of the Charter, despite repeated requests by the gay community to include it[36] (Morton and Knopff 2000, 43). Other scholars argue that the framers intended to leave the list open-ended so that the courts could add grounds of discrimination, such as sexual orientation, over time. Kelly, for example, quotes then Justice Minister Jean Chrétien, who suggested, 'If legislatures do not act, there should be room for the courts to move in. . . . Because of the difficulty of identifying legitimate new grounds for discrimination in a rapidly evolving area of the law, I prefer to be open-ended rather than adding some new categories with the risk of excluding others' (2005, 98).

Despite their critique of the framers' intent approach, however, the Supreme Court—unlike the JCPC—has made use of legislative history in its constitutional decisions over the last few decades. When interpreting the *BNA Act 1867*, for example, the Supreme Court has consulted the confederation debates (*A. G. (Can.) v. Can. Nat. Transportation Ltd.* 1983), among other records (Hogg 2006b). Of course, the *Constitution Act 1982* has an extensive legislative history because of its recent enactment, including various drafts of the document, testimony before committees, and legislative debate, and the Supreme Court has made use of these records as it has interpreted the Constitution. For example, in *Reference re Public Service Employee Relations Act (Alta.)*, Justice McIntyre looked to evidence from the Special Joint Committee hearings on the Constitution to help determine whether the right of association in s. 2(d) of the Charter should be interpreted as a protection for the right to strike. In his concurring opinion, McIntyre argued:

> [I]t is apparent from the deliberations of the committee that the right to strike was understood to be separate and distinct from the right to bargain collectively. And, while a resolution was proposed for the inclusion

of a specific right to bargain collectively, no resolution was proposed for the inclusion of the right to strike. This affords strong support for the proposition that the inclusion of a right to strike was not intended' (*Reference re Public Service Employee Relations Act (Alta.)* 1987).[37]

However, in general, the majority of the Court has used legislative history only as 'part of the context', as a 'starting point', and does not necessarily feel 'bound by even a clear indication of what the framers intended' (Hogg 2006b, 79).

Statutory Interpretation: Legislative Intent and Textualism

In Canada, judges interpreting ambiguous statutes follow the 'cardinal principle in statutory interpretation. . . . [A] legislative provision should be construed in a way that best furthers its objects . . . a judge must ascertain the intent of the legislature in enacting the statute' (Gall 2004, 479–80). However, that opens the question of how a justice should determine the object of a statutory provision. As mentioned above, while serving as Canada's final court of appeal, the JCPC refused to look at legislative history, concentrating instead on the text of legislation. The 'textualism' approach suggests that the text of the provision is authoritative—that 'the only reliable indicator of legislative intention is the meaning of the legislative text. Therefore, to the extent this meaning is discernable, it should govern outcomes' (Sullivan 1998). When using this approach, justices may examine the 'plain meaning' of the text and interpret the words in their 'ordinary sense.' The late Chief Justice Antonio Lamer stated:

> [T]he first task of a court construing a statutory provision is to consider the meaning of its words in the context of the statute as a whole. If the meaning of the words when they are considered in this context is clear, there is no need for further interpretation. The basis for this general rule is that when such a plain meaning can be identified this meaning can ordinarily be said to reflect the legislature's intention. (*Ontario v. Canadian Pacific Ltd.* 1995)

When the meaning of the text is clear, it must be taken as the intent of the legislature without any reference to outside evidence. However, if following the plain meaning of the text produces an absurd or unjust result, the 'golden rule' allows justices to modify the meaning but only to the extent necessary to avoid the absurdity (Gall 2004, 481). If the meaning of the text is ambiguous, 'the mischief rule' allows outside material to be introduced to guide the choice of the proper meaning. This rule directs justices to look at the common law before the passage of the disputed provision, and determine what 'mischief' or defect existed that the provision was meant to remedy. They must then interpret the provision so as to best resolve the mischief and further the remedy (Gall 2004, 481).[38] In looking to external sources in the statutory area, however, Canadian courts do not make extensive use of legislative history. It is considered inappropriate to study legislative debates, speeches, or committee reports (Gall 2004)—any of the material that might be used to determine particular legislators' intent. This stands in stark contrast to the United States, where any aspect of legislative history, including Congressional committee reports and floor debates, can be used.[39]

Textualism, and the plain meaning approach in particular, have been subject to criticism. Ruth Sullivan, for example, argues that 'one of the most frustrating aspects of the plain meaning rule is trying to understand what sort of meaning interpreters have in mind when they label a meaning plain' (1998, 192). Is it literal meaning or dictionary meaning, audience-based meaning or some other form? In the 1990s, plain meaning was interpreted as literal meaning by Chief Justice Lamer, who suggested that 'the best way for the courts to complete the task of giving effect to legislative intention is usually to assume that the legislature means what it says, when this can be clearly ascertained' (*Ontario v. Canadian Pacific Ltd.*; Sullivan 1998–9, 181). For Justice LaForest plain meaning was dictionary meaning, and he referred to definitions of words within legislation he was interpreting. However, during that same period, Justice L'Heureux-Dubé conceived of plain meaning as 'audience-based meaning' and wrote, for example, about language having 'a well-defined 'plain meaning' within the business community' (*Manulife Bank of Canada v. Conlin*; Sullivan 1998–9, 195).[40]

Thus, critics point out that different types of meaning can lead to different results by justices who are all applying the 'plain meaning' approach (see the *Ontario Mushroom Co.* case described at the beginning of Chapter 11 for a good example of this as the justices attempt to interpret the words of a minimum wage law and determine its application to mushroom workers). The approach also assumes that those drafting the statute chose each word carefully—and that the words chosen have a clear meaning. Things become more difficult when words with more than one meaning are placed in a text, or when phrases with no readily apparent meaning (such as 'due process of law' in the constitutional realm) are used. Some argue that plain meaning is not as objective as its supporters suggest, but often requires interpretation and choices by the justices (Segal and Spaeth 2002).[41]

Policy Preferences

The concept that judicial decisions are based entirely on legal rules—whatever the approach—was prevalent in the early literature on the courts and is still championed by many judges themselves, who often suggest their job consists of merely 'following the law'. However, the existence of dissenting and concurring opinions suggests that there is no one 'knowable' legal rule for a case situation: different interpretations of the same set of facts, words, and precedents are possible. What, then, accounts for these different interpretations? Since the mid-twentieth century, the dominant answer in the American judicial literature has been the justice's own policy preferences (at least at the Supreme Court). Indeed, some scholars argue that the justices' policy preferences are the only explanation for their decisions and that legal factors are used merely to justify a decision they wish to take. (See, for example, the discussion of the attitudinal model in Segal and Spaeth 2002.)

Even court scholars who do not go to that extreme will usually agree that policy preferences play some role in the justices' decisions. These preferences are usually measured in terms of ideology, liberal versus conservative. Thus, a justice supporting the rights of criminal defendants would be described as voting liberally, while justices voting against rights claimants would be described as voting conservatively.[42] Those suggesting that a justice's preferences (ideology) matter often point to the consistency that exists between the positions justices take in cases and the attitudes they convey in their speeches and articles off the bench (Baum 2007). Ideology is also a good predictor of the outcome of cases. American scholars who have studied the ideology of US Supreme Court justices for decades have found that knowing the relative ideological makeup of the Court has allowed them to predict fairly accurately how the Court will rule in a case. Perhaps the best example of this is *Bush v. Gore* (2000), where the five justices who were considered conservative (Justices Scalia, Thomas, Rehnquist, Kennedy, and O'Connor) lined up against the four justices considered liberal (Justices Stevens, Ginsburg, Souter, and Breyer) in allowing the appeal by the conservative (Republican) candidate, George W. Bush.

In Canada, at least until the late 1980s, a more traditional view of the courts was prevalent, for the 'role of the judiciary [was] perceived as being essentially technical and non-political . . . there to apply the laws made by the political branches of government' (Russell 1987, 3). In the past, the ideology of Supreme Court justices has not been widely discussed, and Canadian scholars have suggested that ideological leanings have been neither obvious nor consistent—even at the Supreme Court (see for example, Morton, Russell and Riddell 1994). In addition, traditionally, ideology was not thought to play a large role in judicial appointments and was believed to be overshadowed by influences such as region and patronage. This viewpoint may be changing, however, as evidenced by the increased interest in how justices are selected in Canada (see the discussion in Chapter 5). As calls are heard for a more open process, there appears to be at least an implicit understanding that the various potential appointees will behave differently on the Court. Interest groups have now joined the process, lobbying for judges holding particular values (a commitment to equality rights, for example) to be appointed to the bench (Morton and Knopff 2000). This increased activity by interest groups indicates that they, at least, believe judicial ideology matters. Scholars have also started examining the Supreme Court in terms of the justices' policy preferences and ideology (see, for example, Ostberg and Wetstein 2007; Songer and Johnson 2002; Manfredi 2001). There is more agreement today that the policy preferences of Canadian justices may influence their decisions.

Adherents to the 'attitudinal model' suggest that 'judicial outcomes [are] the product of the ideology of individual justices [as well as] the result of attitudinal responses to specific case facts that can be triggered in different areas of law' (Ostberg and Wetstein 2007; Segal and Spaeth 2002). However, a difficulty exists with the preferences approach: how does one determine the policy preferences, or ideology, of a justice? Indeed, justices are loath to speak of themselves in ideological terms, and they often argue that ideology is irrelevant since they focus on legal factors when deciding cases. For example, Justice Binnie from the Supreme Court said, 'I don't know that I can pigeonhole myself as a conservative or liberal or activist' (*Ottawa Citizen* 1998), and former Justice LeDain suggested that 'judges don't come to each case with a predisposition or general tendency or drift' (*Ottawa Citizen* 1984).[43]

Scholars usually turn to outside measures of ideology as they build models to test its influence on judges' decisions. A recent approach, one that has been used on both sides of the border, looks to newspaper editorials at the time of a justice's appointment, and codes the language used to describe the justices to come up with an ideological score (Segal and Cover 1989; Ostberg and Wetstein 2007). However, scholars are constantly searching for a better measure of judicial preferences (see, for example, the discussion of the 'personal attribute model' below).

A further difficulty with determining the policy preferences of justices is that they may change over time, or by issue. Thus, Justice L'Heureux-Dubé can be categorized as conservative in the area of criminal law but liberal in the civil rights and liberties area (Morton, Russell, and Riddell 1994; Ostberg and Wetstein 2007). The Court's decisions themselves can also be divided on an ideological scale (Epstein and Walker 2007). Cases such as *Egan v. Canada* (1995), which challenged the denial of old age security benefits to a same-sex couple, are difficult to classify. Though the Court ruled against the rights claimant (a conservative outcome), they did recognize sexual orientation as a protected ground under the equality section (s. 15) of the Charter (a liberal outcome).

Testing Policy Preferences in Canada

Ostberg and Wetstein (2007) tested the attitudinal model on the Canadian Supreme Court for decisions made between 1984 and 2003. They constructed an ideological score for each justice on the basis of a content analysis of newspaper articles at the time of each justice's appointment to the Supreme Court.[44] Comments on the justices were placed on an ideological continuum ranging from liberal to conservative, with comments such as 'strong believer in the Charter', 'champion of the rights of the criminally accused', and 'liberal judge', placed at the far liberal end of the scale (Osberg and Wetstein 2007, 50). The authors then used their measure to try to predict liberal votes on the bench. Their results suggest that ideology played a significant role in criminal and economic cases. For example, an extremely liberal justice was 40 per cent more likely to cast a liberal vote in a right to counsel case (in favour of the criminal defendant) than an extremely conservative justice (2007, 86). However, surprisingly—given findings in the United States—judicial ideology did not play a significant role in voting on civil rights and liberties cases. Instead, measures such as the gender of the justice and the presence of government and interveners before the Court had more of an influence on the outcome of the case (133). Ostberg and Wetstein conclude that the importance of the attitudinal model in Canada 'is more complex and less pronounced than found in the United States' (2007, 216).

Ostberg and Wetstein (2007) also studied the interplay between case facts and the attitudinal model. Even the strictest adherent to the attitudinal model in the United States will acknowledge that the facts of the case matter as well. In a right-to-counsel case, for example, the fact that the police had failed to inform the defendant that he had a right to counsel will make judges of all ideological predilections more likely to rule in favour of the defendant (Ostberg and Wetstein 2007, 87). However, Ostberg and Wetstein discovered that liberal and conservative justices respond to different factual cues before the Court. They also found that conservative justices respond to fewer factual cues, a finding that led them to conclude that 'conservative justices are more prone than their liberal colleagues to base their votes on their ideological predispositions' (2007, 223).

Strategic Model of Decision Making

Although the study of judicial decisions in terms of policy preferences is a much more recent phenomenon in Canada than in the United States, most judicial scholars today, on both sides of the border, argue that a judge's policy preferences do matter. However, there is not complete agreement on how those policy preferences influence decision making. Recently, another model of decision making has gained prominence—the strategic model—which answers this question differently than the attitudinal model (see, for example, Eskridge and Frickey 1994; Epstein and Knight 1998; Maltzman, Spriggs, and Wahlbeck 2000). Like the attitudinal model, the strategic model believes justices have goals they are pursuing.[45] However, this model argues that the justices, in their pursuit of their goals, face constraints, which cause them to 'adjust their positions where doing so might advance the policies they favor' (Baum 2007, 121). Put differently, this model suggests that justices actually vote strategically. Thus, a justice may move slightly away from their preferred position in order to get other justices to sign on to their opinions. Strategic justices will write decisions that are as close to their ideal point as possible without provoking the executive and legislature to overturn the result. They may also modify their position slightly if it increases the likelihood their decision will be enforced by the government.

Scholars have not yet done extensive work on the strategic model of decision making in Canada. However, anecdotal evidence suggests that such behaviour probably exists. Remember, for example, how Chief Justice Dickson tried to get agreement on his opinion in *Tremblay v. Daigle*.

Role Orientations

Judicial decisions may also be influenced by the justices' 'role orientation'. This role orientation, which may act as a constraint on justices, is their conception of what is 'appropriate behavior' for a judge, how they believe they should act (Baum 2007, 131). There are various ways to think of role orientation—the previous chapter, for example, discussed the 'adjudicative' role and the 'policy-making' role. Judges who adopt the latter role are more comfortable with the idea of shaping law and balancing interests than judges closer to the adjudicative side of the continuum, who prefer to base their decisions on established legal principles and to shape law only incrementally as a by-product of adjudication. In the area of constitutional law, especially if constitutional rights are involved, a justice's role orientation is usually discussed in terms of activism and restraint. A justice is labelled activist if he or she believes it is proper for the Court 'to assert independent positions in deciding cases, to review the actions of the other branches vigorously, to strike down unconstitutional acts willingly, and to impose far-reaching remedies for legal wrongs whenever necessary' (Epstein and Walker 2007, 36). A justice is considered 'restraint-oriented', by contrast, if he or she prefers to defer to the legislature when interpreting the legislature's actions and would reject broad remedies, correcting only that which is absolutely necessary (Epstein and Walker 2007, 36). A justice who considers him- or herself to be more of an 'adjudicator of disputes' will tend to be more restrained in Charter of Rights cases, whereas a justice with a more policy-making orientation will tend to be more activist in Charter cases. The role-orientation approach suggests that a justice's view of the appropriateness of judicial activism may shape their decisions as illustrated in Box 4.2, which briefly outlines the Supreme Court's decision in *Chaoulli v. Quebec (Attorney General)* (2005). The justices' opinions in *Chaoulli* provide examples of both activism and restraint in the same case.

**Box 4.2   Role Orientation in Terms of Activism and Restraint:
The *Chaoulli* Example**

Chaoulli v. Quebec (Attorney General) (2005) involved a challenge to Quebec legislation banning private health insurance in the province. The challenge was brought by George Zeliotis, a 61-year-old man who had waited a year to have hip surgery, and Dr Jacques Chaoulli, a Quebec physician who had been refused a licence to operate an independent private hospital. (Chaoulli had once gone on a three-week hunger strike to protest the decision of the health board not to grant recognition to his 'home delivered' medical services: Manfredi and Maioni 2006.) The Supreme Court was asked to consider the constitutionality of the Quebec ban. One year after hearing oral arguments, the Court released its decision. The seven justices hearing the case voted four to three to strike down the ban as unconstitutional. The case provoked widespread controversy over both the ruling and its reasoning. Critics forecast the end of Canada's health-care system and spoke angrily about the Court's poor treatment of health-care research and government debates.

Three opinions were written in *Chaoulli*, each suggesting a different role orientation. The 'majority' opinion was written by Justice Deschamps, who had cast the deciding vote on the divided court. This opinion based its decision on a section of the *Quebec Charter of Human Rights and Freedoms*, arguing that long waiting times violated the rights to life and personal inviolability. Both the majority and concurring opinions interpreted rights broadly in striking down the law, but the majority opinion confined itself to the Quebec Charter, while the concurrence brought in the Canadian Charter of Rights and Freedoms. In voting to strike down the law, Justice Deschamps argued that when 'social policies infringe rights that are protected by the charters, the courts cannot shy away from considering them' (at para. 89). She went on to argue that the Court had heard ample evidence about health-care policy to inform its decision and that the government had failed to act on reforming health-care waiting times. Government 'inertia' could not be used to justify judicial deference, according to Deschamps, who also noted that courts were the 'last line of defence for citizens'.

In dissent, Justices Binnie, Lebel, and Fish argued the ban was not unconstitutional and suggested the Court should defer to the provincial legislature. These justices suggested the health-care questions at issue in the case had been a matter of extensive debate throughout Canada and that this debate was not something the justices could resolve 'as a matter of constitutional law'. No constitutional standard existed that could tell judges what was 'reasonable' access to health care. The issue was one of social policy, which was best left to the legislature to decide.

Source: *Chaoulli v. Quebec (Attorney General)* (2005); Manfredi and Maioni 2006.

Judicial activism has been highly criticized by many scholars, and it tends to be vilified in the media—the Court is seen as overstepping its bounds and usurping the elected legislature. In recent years, judicial activism has been equated with liberal justices' running amok with the Court's new-found power under the Charter. However, it should be noted that activism is a judicial philosophy, rather than a political one, and can thus be associated with either liberal or conservative justices. Indeed, in their study of judicial decisions from 1984 to 2003, Ostberg and Wetstein found that 'when it comes to some of the most high-profile legal controversies, conservative justices are just as likely as their liberal colleagues to be activists' (2007, 213). The *Chaoulli* decision provides an example of this as well, for one of the most conservative justices on the Supreme Court, Justice John Major, voted to strike down the Quebec legislation banning private health insurance programs—joining the opinion that has been characterized as activist.

Whether one is speaking in terms of adjudicative versus policy-making, or activism versus restraint, the question remains whether these different 'role orientations' actually matter. Are justices' decisions influenced by their perception of what is proper for a justice to do? The American literature is skeptical that a strong connection exists (see the discussion in Baum 2007). It is difficult, of course, to determine a separate influence for these orientations. Does a justice vote to uphold a piece of legislation because he is a restraint-oriented judge who believes the right behaviour of the court is to defer to the legislature? Or does he vote to uphold the legislation because he has conservative or liberal policy preferences and this outcome would best fulfill his goals?

Personal Attributes

According to Judge Rosalie Abella, '[e]very decisionmaker who walks into a courtroom to hear a case is armed not only with the relevant legal texts but with a set of values, experiences and assumptions that are thoroughly embedded' (as quoted in Wilson 1990, 507). The personal attribute model argues that a judge's career experience, education, partisan affiliation, social background (for example, religion), and other related factors shape a justice's attitudes, and those attitudes—the embedded factors—can influence that justice's decisions (Tate and Handberg 1991). Social scientists advocating this model 'contend that pre-court life experiences play a prominent role in shaping the personal values and policy preferences of judges, and that such biographical factors can be useful in predicting judicial decisions' (Brudney, Schiavoni, and Merritt 1999, 1682).

Tate and Sittiwong (1989) tested the personal attribute model on the Canadian Supreme Court for its non-unanimous decisions between 1949 and 1985. They discovered that for cases dealing with both economic and civil liberties issues, justices that were Catholic, were from outside Quebec, had been appointed by Liberal Prime Ministers (other than Mackenzie King), had political experience, and had extensive judicial experience voted more liberally than their judicial colleagues. Songer and Johnson (2007), testing the same factors in the more recent era, found some of these measures worked only in the time period in which they were originally tested. However, their updated model found that a broader measure of region (Quebec, Ontario, the West, and the Atlantic provinces—rather than just Quebec and non-Quebec)—and party affiliation had a significant influence on the justices' decisions, particularly in the criminal and economic areas. In criminal cases, for example, justices from Ontario and the West voted more liberally than those from the east (Songer and Johnson 2007, 927). Party and region had an interactive effect on these decisions: among justices appointed by a Progressive Conservative Prime Minister, those from Quebec were more likely to vote conservatively than those from other regions.

Gender

In the United States several studies have examined the influence of gender on voting behaviour. Though there have been some contradictory findings,[46] much of the literature suggests that female judges vote differently in certain issue areas. Songer, Davis, and Haire (1994), for example, found that female judges on the federal courts of appeal voted liberally in civil rights cases more often than their male colleagues.[47] Similarly, Davis, Haire, and Songer (1993) found that female appellate court judges voted for the rights claimant in employment discrimination cases more often than their male colleagues, but they did not find a difference between the genders in obscenity cases. The American literature has also discovered some indirect effects of gender on decision making. In particular, having female judges on the panel hearing cases at the federal appellate courts has been found to affect the voting behaviour of the male judges on the panel. Thus, male judges on panels with one or more females were more likely than judges on all-male panels to support rights claimants in employment discrimination cases (Farhang and Wawro 2004). This held true for sexual harassment and sex discrimination cases as well (Peresie 2005).[48]

In Canada, a recent study of the Ontario Court of Appeal found that differences did exist in the voting behaviour of male and female judges (Stribopoulos and Yahya 2007), although an earlier study by McCormick and Job (1993), found no such differences for the Alberta Court of Appeal. According to Stribopoulos and Yahya (2007), female judges were more likely than their male counterparts to support the complainant in sexual and domestic violence cases and more likely to support mothers in family law cases. At the Supreme Court, the first female justice to be appointed to the Court, Bertha Wilson, suggested that the values, experiences, and assumptions a justice brings to the Court may vary with gender. While she acknowledged that there are some areas of law where it is very difficult to find a 'uniquely feminine perspective'—such as contracts or laws affecting corporations—she suggested that other areas exhibit a 'distinctly male perspective' (Wilson 1990). Interestingly, when the Supreme Court struck down s. 251 of the Criminal Code, Canada's 'abortion law', Wilson stood alone in suggesting women had a constitutional right to abortion (*R. v. Morgentaler* 1988). Her male colleagues focused instead on procedural-fairness guarantees under s. 7 of the Charter (in particular, the problem of unequal access and delay). The *Tremblay* case cited at the start of this chapter also suggests gender may matter. It has been reported that Justice Beverley McLachlin's arguments to her colleagues ensured the case was decided (after Chantal Daigle's abortion was revealed), instead of being declared moot, and McLachlin has suggested it was her viewpoint as a woman that allowed her to see things differently (Sharpe and Roach 2003, 394).

A few studies have tested the influence of gender on judicial decisions at the Supreme Court level. Songer and Johnson (2007) discovered that gender did have an effect in one of the issue areas they studied: civil rights and liberties. Female justices tended to vote more liberally than their male colleagues in cases involving civil rights and liberties. However, there was not a significant difference between the votes of male and female justices in either criminal or economic cases (Songer and Johnson 2007, 928).

In their study of Supreme Court decisions, Ostberg and Wetstein (2007) also found that gender had an influence on the outcome of cases in the civil rights and liberties area. Examining cases decided by the Supreme Court from 1984 to 2003, the authors found that controlling for factors such as ideology and party background, female justices were more supportive of rights claimants in equality cases and contentious (that is, non-unanimous cases) free speech cases than their male colleagues. In fact, female justices were 27 per cent more likely to rule in favour of discrimination claims in all equality cases, and 54 per cent more likely to rule in favour in models including only non-unanimous cases (2007, 134–9).

The Courts and Inside Influences

In the appellate courts, of course, a decision is not rendered by a single judge, and thus, judges must work with their colleagues in resolving the cases before them. These colleagues may influence a judge's ultimate vote in a case, or at least persuade him to join an opinion he might not have otherwise chosen. The *Tremblay* case described at the beginning of this chapter provides a good example of the influence of colleagues. The Supreme Court might not have gone on to decide the case, after learning of Daigle's abortion, if Justice McLachlin had not asked her colleagues to put themselves in her shoes, and Chief Justice Dickson's opinion in the case might have been very different (or at least more expansive) had he not been pursuing Justice LaForest's vote.

Chief Justice Dickson's decision to alter his opinion to attract Justice LaForest's support reflects institutional rules and norms. At the Supreme Court level, majority rules. Therefore, a justice needs four other justices (if the full Court has heard the case) to sign on to his or her opinion for it to be adopted as the Court's outcome and reasoning.[49] This requirement may induce justices to tailor their decision in a way that will appeal to at least four other justices. However, in *Tremblay*, Chief Justice Dickson wanted to write more than a majority opinion: he wanted to achieve unanimity on the Court, and he modified his opinion to that end.

Unanimous decisions are believed to have more legitimacy and to carry more force than divided results. As a result, appellate court justices are thought to pursue larger winning coalitions than the simple majority needed to decide the case. This implies a need for justices to work together, to negotiate, and to make concessions.[50]

Some scholars have attempted to measure the influence of justices on their colleagues by examining the number of times a justice is cited and the number of times a justice is specifically named in subsequent Supreme Court decisions (McCormick 2000); others have looked at opinion authorship rates (Ostberg and Wetstein 2007).[51] Ostberg and Wetstein argue that the pattern of shifting leadership they found (according to justices' areas of expertise) shows that the Supreme Court 'is a collegial institution that is willing to work as a coordinated team when resolving cases, and that individual justices may be willing to sacrifice the overt expression of their own attitudes and values more readily than their U.S. counterparts, for the good of the team' (2007, 211). Thus there appears to be support for the influence of colleagues on judicial decision making at the Supreme Court of Canada.

The Courts and Outside Influences

Do groups from outside the courts influence the decisions of judges? This might be expected to be less of an influence at the Supreme Court level than at lower courts. Although lower-court judges in Canada are appointed for long terms (usually until age 70 or 75), other courts stand above them. Ambitious judges, interested in promotion, may be concerned with their portrayal in the media and the response of government officials to their opinions. They may be anxious to make a favourable impression on those reporting about, or involved in, the judicial selection process. Appointed until age 75 and with no chance of promotion to a higher court, Supreme Court justices should feel relatively secure in ignoring outside forces when making their decisions—they are difficult to remove no matter how much the public or the government dislikes their opinions. However, this section suggests that one cannot rule out the potential influence of outside forces on Supreme Court decisions. As they are 'possessed of neither the purse nor the sword', the Supreme Court may be concerned with the external environment to ensure enforcement of their decisions and to further their policy goals. Of course, justices may well value the approval of external audiences for its own sake and may be influenced in their decisions by their perception of what will win the approval of outside audiences that are important to them (Baum 2006, 163).

Public Opinion

For many court decisions, such as those dealing with patent law or trucking regulations, the public may not hold a strong opinion. Many court decisions—even Supreme Court decisions—fly under the average Canadian's radar. In these types of cases, it seems unlikely that public opinion would have any influence on judicial decision making. There is very little opinion for the Court to consider and very few consequences for not considering it. However, for more high-profile cases, like those involving the Charter, the public may have a very strong opinion, and media coverage may keep them well informed of the courts' behaviour. Does the court then consider public opinion in making its decisions—at least in controversial cases?

American scholars have studied extensively the influence of public opinion on judicial decisions. Many studies (among them, Mishler and Sheehan 1993; Stimson, MacKuen, and Erikson 1995; Flemming and Wood 1997) suggest that justices should pursue positive public opinion to their decisions because it leads 'to better implementation of [their] decisions, reduces the chances that the other branches will limit or reverse those decisions, and deters action by the legislature and executive against the Court itself' (Baum 2006, 63). Justices influenced by public opinion might avoid making controversial decisions that divide public opinion (although Canada's Supreme Court has made many of these types of decisions, for example, the *Morgentaler* abortion case and the *Chaoulli* health-care case). They may try to match the ideology of the Court's decisions to that of the general public, or they may avoid controversial decision practices—such as striking down precedents (Baum 2006, 64). There has not been a definitive answer on whether public opinion is, in fact, influencing any of this behaviour. Part of the difficulty is to determine causality: did the Court's decision mirror the public's ideology because the Court was following public opinion, or did it mirror the public's ideology because the 'same social forces' moving the ideology of the public were also moving the ideology of the court (Baum 2007, 144)?

Would the effect of public opinion on judicial decisions be more readily apparent if judges were elected? Since many state court judges in the United States face retention elections, research has been directed at this question. It appears that elections do influence judicial behaviour, but the nature and extent of that influence are dependent upon various factors, such as whether a judge has had an electoral loss before, how knowledgeable the voters are, how competitive the elections are, and how soon the next election is (Hall 1992, Huber and Gordon 2004).

Studies of public opinion and the courts in Canada have tended to focus on the public attitude towards the Supreme Court, and not its potential influence on it (Sniderman et al. 1996; Fletcher and Howe 2001). However, former Chief Justice Antonio Lamer suggested in an interview that public and media attention in controversial cases may influence decisions: 'It is in these cases I am concerned that as a result of virulent or harsh comments by the press or the public, the most popular thing to do might become the outcome' (Makin 1999).

The Media

Bridging the gap between the Court and the public is the media. The courts, and particularly the Supreme Court, have seen a significant increase in coverage by the media in the Charter era. As the Supreme Court has made more controversial decisions on subjects such as abortion, gay rights, pornography, and language rights, the media has increased its coverage and its critiques of the decisions. Although not all Supreme Court justices are favourably disposed towards the media,[52] many do realize its importance to them. It is from the media that most Canadians learn about both the Court and its decisions. Justices recognize that public attitudes towards the Court may depend, in part, on how it is portrayed in the media, and they recognize the truth behind Peter Russell's observation that 'journalists are the managers of the political life of judicial decisions' (Sauvageau, Schneiderman, and Taras 2006, 8). As the above comment by Chief Justice Lamer suggests, this fills some justices with concern, because they worry that 'inaccurate or sensationalist handling of judicial decisions by the media . . . [puts] pressure on them to make decisions that [will] result in 'good press' (Greene et al. 1998, 184).

Justices may have different incentives for cultivating the media. They may want to ensure favourable attitudes to increase the likelihood that their decisions will be enforced. However, like other citizens, the justices may also get satisfaction from being portrayed positively in the media (Baum 2007, 145). Whatever the incentive, there is evidence that the justices notice their media coverage. In the United States, Justice Clarence Thomas is said to be able to remember the 'dates of unflattering articles written about him, and the names of the reporters who wrote them . . . with near photographic memory' (cited in Baum 2007, 145).

When Brian Dickson became Canada's Chief Justice in 1984, he worked to better the relationship between the Court and the media. He established a press room, altered the procedure for releasing decisions (the Court now gives advance warning to the press and avoids releasing more than a couple of decisions at a time), and assigned the Court's executive legal officer to deal with 'media relations' (among other things, the ELO generally 'walks' the media through a decision's legal reasoning at its release) (Sharpe and Roach 2003, 293). The current Chief Justice, Beverley McLachlin, has regularly interacted with the media, and enjoys a friendlier relationship with them than many of her predecessors.

The Legal Community

Justices are more likely to care about the opinion of those who are close to them. The legal community may be of particular importance to justices because it is *their* community. Made up of lawyers, judges, and law professors, this group is not only composed of many of the people with whom the justices will regularly associate, but it is also the group that will most closely evaluate the justices' decisions. Appellate court judges frequently attend conferences and give speeches attended by members of the legal community. Visits to law schools are particularly common. These events are opportunities for discussion of legal principles that may later influence a judge's decision. Through publications in law reviews and other academic writing, the legal community may provide information to the judges and may even persuade them to an interpretation (particularly if it is the obviously dominant approach) (Baum 2007,

144). Baum (2006) suggests that law professors may be an important audience to judges who care about how they are perceived and evaluated (2006, 101).

In Canada, decisions by the provincial courts of appeal tend to be short—on average six pages—and most do not contain any reference to academic writing (Greene et al. 1998, 131–7). Although some provincial courts, such as Quebec, do use such references,[53] it is not a common practice anywhere, and there is reason to doubt this factor influences decisions to any large degree. In its early decades, the Canadian Supreme Court also did not make widespread use of academic writing; on the contrary, the citing of living scholars was particularly discouraged (Sharpe and Roach 2003, 213). The Court's opinions used very technical language and were directed more towards practising lawyers (McCormick 2000, 143). This began to change when Bora Laskin—himself a former legal scholar—became Chief Justice, and under Chief Justices Dickson and Lamer, citation of legal academics became much more the norm. Scholars studying the area have found that nearly half of all the Lamer Court's decisions contained citations of academic sources, totalling about 400 citations a year (McCormick 1998a). This openness to academic sources was accompanied by an effort on the part of the justices to make their decisions less technical and more accessible, thereby broadening the targeted audience to include academics and the 'educated public' (McCormick 2000, 143).

More recent Supreme Court justices have likely been influenced by the writing of legal academics. Chief Justice Dickson regularly read both legal periodicals and academic writing. There is evidence that when Dickson wrote decisions dealing with the equitable distribution of property in divorce, for example, he was heavily influenced by this academic writing. His working notes were peppered with sections taken from academic sources published in Canada, the United States, and England (Sharpe and Roach 2003, 184). Of course, Dickson is not alone in his attention to scholarly work. Most other recent Supreme Court justices have frequently made use of academic writing. Marc Gold has suggested that it sometimes appeared as if the Court was 'writing for the academy' (1985: 460). Whatever the motivation—the desire to achieve their policy goals or to get the law 'right', in order to earn respect amongst the legal community—justices do appear to consider academic analysis in their decisions.

Interest Groups

Chapter 7 discusses in detail the activity and influence of interest groups on court decisions. In the lower courts, interest groups participate by sponsoring a case (in effect providing a lawyer and other resources to a potential litigant, support that allows them to become a party in the case) or by intervening in the case (submitting a brief as an interested third party). At the Supreme Court, however, most groups are present as interveners. Even the Women's Legal Education and Action Fund (LEAF), which is the most frequent litigator before the Supreme Court, has only rarely sponsored a case before it. In the great majority of cases, groups participate before the Supreme Court by submitting a brief on behalf of themselves in an attempt to further their goals. But do the justices listen?

The American literature has produced mixed results. As detailed in Chapter 7, some studies have found that litigants that have an interest group on their side are more successful (Songer and Kuersten 1995; Wolpert 1991), while others have not found the same effect (Songer and Sheehan 1993; Tauber 1998). The debate over interest-group influence continues to be waged. There is some agreement, however, that interest groups are influential in setting the agenda. Particularly in the United States, 'many cases would not get into any court, much less the U.S. Supreme Court, without the help of an interest group' (Epstein and Walker 2007, 43). Furthermore, studies have found that interest-group participation at the leave-to-appeal stage increases the likelihood that the US Supreme Court will accept a case—regardless of whether the group is arguing for leave to be granted or against it (Caldeira and Wright 1988).

As mentioned earlier, this potential influence is less available to Canadian interest groups, because the Supreme Court does not allow groups to participate at the leave-to-appeal stage. Epp (1998), however, has argued that interest groups are influential in setting the agenda in Canada. He argues that the 'rights revolution' that has occurred in Canada is largely a result of interest-group mobilization, suggesting that these groups have brought cases to the courts that have shaped the state of Canadian law.

Some studies have suggested that interest groups have also influenced the Canadian justices' decisions. Manfredi (2004), for example, suggests that LEAF has made a difference through the type of evidence the group brings to Court—evidence that the Supreme Court frequently cites. Ostberg and Wetstein have found that, controlling for other factors such as judicial ideology and case characteristics, LEAF appears to have exerted some influence on Supreme Court decisions in the equality area from 1984 to 2003 (2007, 133, 136). These authors found similar results for the Canadian Labour Congress in union cases decided by the Court (2007, 169, 173). Ostberg and Wetstein suggest that interest groups may affect the importance of other influences as well. They argue that 'attitudinal responses by the justices are partially a byproduct of the types of claims advanced by some interest groups' (2007, 219–20). The Charter era has brought new areas of law before the Court, as well as increased litigation by interest groups that 'push the rights envelope' before the Court. In this scenario, Ostberg and Wetstein argue justices will be more likely to fall back on their own attitudinal predispositions when deciding cases, and they believe that the increased rights-based litigation has increased the attitudinal disagreement amongst the justices (2007, 33).

Parliament and the Executive
The government of the day may influence judicial decisions in a variety of ways. Governments are responsible for appointing judges at all levels of court—provin-

cial governments appoint s. 92 judges, and the federal government appoints s. 96 and s. 101 judges. This appointment power provides the means for governments to shape the courts' approaches and decisions over the long term. By placing judges on the federal bench with viewpoints similar to that of the government of the day (or at least to the Prime Minister and his cabinet), that government could influence policy for years to come (given the judicial retirement age of 75). As discussed in Chapter 5, governments, historically, have not taken advantage of their appointment power to select only judges with ideologies similar to their own. Even at the Supreme Court, other factors—such as region—have generally been of more importance in Canada. However, in the current era of high-profile judicial decisions, this could change—and the government's power of appointment creates the potential for significant influence.

Although judicial independence is explicitly intended to limit government influence on judicial decisions, Chapter 6 discusses another possible means by which governments might influence those decisions: through their role as 'administrators of courts' and, in particular, their control over judicial salaries and administrative support. Appellate judges interviewed by Greene et al. expressed concern about this power, and 'more than one judge reported an impression that provincial governments had cut back on administrative support services to the appellate courts because they were unhappy about the direction of appellate court decisions' (1998, 184–5). One example noted by the judges was the reduction of secretarial support. And Chapter 6 examines the sometimes contentious discussions between judges and governments about salaries. Certainly, judges have seen the connections between their decisions and the use of government power. Whether these connections are deliberate or not, the perception that they are might influence the decisions of the judges.

Government positions might also be considered by judges concerned about the enforcement of their decisions. The courts rely on the other branches of government to implement their rulings. Chapter 11 discusses the relationship between courts and legislatures, and the aftermath of decisions. It is possible that justices try to anticipate the reaction of the government to their decisions and tailor their decisions to achieve the greatest probability that it will be enforced.

Governments may also try to influence the outcome of particular cases. Although considered improper, direct attempts by members of government to influence cases pending before the courts, have occasionally been made throughout history. In 1976, for example, it was brought to the public's attention that three Liberal ministers had contacted members of the judiciary about cases before them. Marc Lalonde, principal secretary in the Prime Minister's Office, called a judge at home on a Sunday morning to discuss the trial of a number of Trinidad citizens charged with destroying a university computer. Lalonde informed the judge of a message from Canada's High Commission to Trinidad that 'expressed concern that violent riots might occur in Trinidad if a guilty verdict was rendered at that time' (Russell 1987, 79). When the judge said he was going to proceed with jury instructions the next day and would not take steps to delay the verdict, Lalonde replied that 'the situation was one of grave concern' (Russell 1987, 79). This, and other 1976 contacts between cabinet ministers and members of the judiciary resulted in Prime Minister Trudeau drafting guidelines prohibiting Cabinet ministers from contacting the judiciary. Two years later, Trudeau accepted the resignation of the Minister of Labour, John Munro, after it was discovered that Munro had contacted a judge to argue on behalf of a constituent the judge was due to sentence the next day (Russell 1987, 80).

However, this type of direct attempt to influence the judiciary is rare. Governments more commonly try to influence judicial decisions through litigation. Governments at both federal and provincial levels are in court frequently, and this frequency is thought to build up an expertise, and—at the lower court level, at least—a working-group relationship, which may increase their success rate (see the discussion in Chapter 8 of governments as litigators). The federal government, for example, has an enviable success rate before the Supreme Court (McCormick 1994), and this success rate appears to hold true at the leave-to-appeal stage as well (Flemming 2004). In Charter cases, the federal government has a high success rate in defending its legislation and actions from challenge at the Supreme Court (Kelly 2005; Hennigar 2007), and at lower courts as well (Hennigar 2007).

Conclusions

Of course, to really understand judicial decision making and the influences on it we need to ask the justices. We would want to interview all the justices sitting on a panel and probe the factors that went into their decision (Epstein and Walker 2007). One difficulty with this approach, of course, is that justices are not particularly accessible and would likely refuse a request to detail the reasons behind their decisions. However, a second difficulty is that, as social scientists, we would probably not believe what they told us anyway. Individuals may not be very self-aware or they may want to paint themselves in the most positive light. Thus, the influences they reported would have to be viewed with caution.

A traditional view of judicial decision making, which would emphasize the importance of legal factors, would suggest that justices merely interpret the law as they attempt to 'get it right'. For several decades, however, the dominant models of judicial decision making have emphasized that courts, like legislatures, are part of the political system and that justices do care about policy. Today, it is recognized that justices do not make their decisions in a vacuum, and scholars have suggested many factors that may influence judicial decisions; those include not only legal factors and policy preferences, but also other factors such as interest groups, the legal community, and the gender of the judge.

Gibson suggests that 'judges' decisions are a function of what they prefer to do, tempered by what they think they ought to do, but constrained by what they perceive is feasible to do' (1983, 9). Like many judicial scholars, Gibson's theory is premised on the idea that judges pursue policy goals. Pursuing these goals is what they 'prefer to do' (Segal and Spaeth 2002). The facts of the case, however, act as a constraint—setting the boundaries (Segal 1984). Role orientation, conceptualized in terms of activism and restraint, describes what the judge feels he or she 'ought to do'. The actions and expectations of colleagues, the rules and norms of the institution and the external environment, all put restraints on judicial decision making. They help to determine what is 'feasible to do'.

This suggests a complicated picture of decision making, one where many factors can play a role. In the courts, as in other areas of society, 'individuals make decisions, but they do so within the context of group, institutional and environmental constraints' (Gibson 1983, 32). As the Canadian courts have become more prominent players in the political system, the way in which they make decisions has attracted increased interest. However, much more work needs to be done and better measures need to be derived before we can reach a more complete understanding of the decision-making process.

Chapter 5

Judicial Selection

In Canada, judicial appointments, at both the provincial and federal levels, are executive appointments. As noted in Chapter 2, the provincial governments are responsible for staffing the 'purely provincial' s. 92 courts, whereas the federal government is responsible for staffing all federal courts and each province's s.96 superior trial and appellate courts. As courts, and particularly the Canadian Supreme Court, come to be perceived more as 'policy-makers', in addition to 'adjudicators', more and more interest (and controversy) surrounds these court appointments. Virtually every major newspaper in the country has commented on the growing political influence of Canadian judges and has criticized the secretive, in-house method of appointing them.

When the election of the new Conservative federal government in 2006 coincided with a vacancy on the Supreme Court, changes were sure to occur. The new Prime Minister, Stephen Harper, had been very vocal in his criticism of the Supreme Court's power and the selection process. So, in March 2006, we saw for the first time in Canadian history, a Supreme Court nominee required to submit to a public hearing, where he faced questions from representatives of the four political parties in the House of Commons—a televised confirmation hearing of sorts.

This change generated a widespread outcry against the move towards an American system of judicial selection. Canadians have watched the US Senate battle over nominees in recent decades, and many remember how the 1991 Clarence Thomas nomination had played out, with almost soap-opera-like drama, on their television sets.[1] Indeed, in the fall of 2005, only a few months before the Canadian hearing, the United States had filled two vacancies on its Supreme Court, and the controversy surrounding the Roberts and Alito confirmation battles (with Justice Alito confirmed by only a 58 to 42 vote) was still fresh in people's minds. Many feared the kind of overt 'politicization' of the judiciary they felt accompanied the US method of appointment. Judges (including the Chief Justice of the Canadian Supreme Court) expressed concern that good candidates would be scared away by the prospect of being exposed to this kind of political process. (For more on the controversy see the section in this chapter on Supreme Court appointments.)

However, the event itself was very tame—particularly compared to its American counterpart. In the United States, the Roberts hearings, for example, lasted for nearly a week before the Senate Judiciary Committee. On the Monday, the nominee gave an opening statement, and the Committee senators also gave opening statements of ten minutes each. On the Tuesday and Wednesday, each senator had thirty and twenty minutes respectively to question Judge Roberts. On the Thursday, other witnesses were heard (the Republicans and Democrats each invited about fifteen). Throughout the process, senators asked probing questions about hot-button issues, the Democrat minority being particularly aggressive as they tried to determine Roberts' stance on issues likely to appear before the Supreme Court.

In Canada, the politicians were much more restrained—there was one three-hour session with a well-respected moderator (Peter Hogg) who was a constitutional expert and the former dean of a law school. The moderator outlined what kinds of questions the nominee, Marshall Rothstein, could not be expected to answer. He said Rothstein could not tell them his views on controversial issues or his position on hypothetical cases or why he had decided a particular case the way he had.[2] (One could argue that that rules out almost everything of interest!) The nominee then made a twenty-minute opening statement. This was followed by questions from twelve Members of Parliament (MPs) representing each of the parties in the House of Commons. The MPs went around the table twice, before the Minister of Justice (who chaired the session) asked whether there was any need to go around the table a third time. The members agreed there was not—which in itself surely sets the Canadian experience apart from its American counterpart.

The whole hearing, including the opening and closing statements, took just over three hours. In stark contrast to the more aggressive questioning of US senators, the MPs were extremely polite and deferential to the candidate. Indeed, during the first round of questioning, a few of the opposition MPs began by apologizing to the nominee for putting him through the process at all. A few MPs did ask questions on such controversial topics as abortion, same-sex marriage, and gun control, but the Minister of Justice was quick to remind the nominee that he did not have to answer the questions, and Rothstein sidestepped each of them adroitly. In the end, it was Prime Minister Harper's choice whether Rothstein was appointed to the Supreme Court or not. The committee was invited to submit its comments to the Prime Minister about the candidate, but it had no veto power over the appointment. Thus, executive appointment continued in Canada—although much more publicly than before.

The quiet conduct of the hearing could not have been better for those advocating change in the selection process, and Marshall Rothstein was an excellent choice to produce just such a hearing. Rothstein's conservative legal philosophy made him attractive to Harper's Conservative government, but his name had actually been included on a short list of candidates by an advisory committee formed by the previous Liberal government. Thus the government's major opposition could not criticize the choice of Rothstein with any credibility. In addition, Rothstein's professional qualifications were above reproach. The Canadian bar viewed him with respect 'not only for his competence and conscientiousness but also for his civility to counsel appearing before him' (Ziegel 2006, 548).

However, it was probably Rothstein's own performance that did more to defuse concern about public hearings than anything else. Rothstein 'charmed the members of the committee and the large television audience with his informality, self-deprecating sense of humour, and willingness to explain his judicial philosophy in simple terms which were readily comprehensible even to non-lawyers' (Ziegel 2006, 549). This, and Rothstein's good-natured handling of questions on more controversial issues, meant that viewers were able to learn more about a Supreme Court nominee without any of the partisan ugliness many feared. In the end, there was a large consensus built around this very 'judge-like' 65-year-old, and he was appointed to the Supreme Court in March 2006.

Justice Rothstein's appointment to the Supreme Court brings out some of the major questions that will be considered in this chapter, including the various possible methods of judicial selection and the debate surrounding their use. Different selection systems often demonstrate different values and, in particular, different emphasis on judicial independence and judicial accountability. Whereas Chapter 6 discusses the competing values of judicial independence and accountability in depth, in this chapter we highlight their connection to different selection systems.

This chapter will also consider the question of what executive branches use as the basis of selection for judgeships. Are nominees chosen on the basis of their competence, with merit (however defined) the only consideration? Or do the politicians choosing judicial nominees let politics play a role in their decision? If politics does play a role, what form does it take? It may be that the provincial and federal executive branches pick people for judgeships on the basis of their political connections: a 'who you know' kind of selection system. Political executives may also choose people on the basis of their ideology. Thus, Prime Minister Harper may have chosen Marshall Rothstein for the Supreme Court because—knowing Rothstein's conservative legal philosophy—he felt Rothstein's values would mirror his own on issues that might come before the Court. Alternatively, Harper may have chosen Rothstein because of his previous connections to the Conservative Party as a Winnipeg lawyer (Flanagan 1985, 46). Of course, it is also possible that the only consideration in Rothstein's appointment was his standing in the legal community and the high respect he had earned as both a lawyer and a Federal Court judge. This chapter will examine these possible bases of selection as well as others, such as the newer idea of group representation—the idea that factors such as gender, ethnicity, and language may also influence judicial nominations (an idea which in itself has provoked a debate about the appropriateness of such considerations).

After a brief consideration of some different selection systems used in other countries, this chapter will detail the methods the Canadian provincial governments and the federal government have used to select judges—both historically and today. Within each major category of court (s. 92, s. 96, and Supreme Court), we consider the basis of selection used by the appointing government, as well as the makeup of the judiciary, to get a sense of what the different selection methods have produced on the bench.

Throughout the chapter, debates on changing the system of selection are highlighted, and some of the major alternatives that have been suggested—at least at the federal level—are discussed. Traditional considerations have been with the effect of systems of selection on competence and judicial independence (Baum 2008a, 93–4). Is there a particular system that produces more competent judges?[3] And which system promotes—or appears to promote—an independent judiciary capable of making impartial decisions? In Canada, judicial independence has historically been the focus of much more attention than judicial accountability. Indeed, a look at the index of several books on the courts finds entries for judicial independence but not accountability. This is especially compatible with a more traditional view of the role of justices, the idea that justices merely interpret the law without considering their own policy preferences or external influences. In this view, accountability would be a problematic notion since judges' decisions 'should be based on their reading of the law rather than the views of their constituents' (Baum 1995, 19).

However, both this traditional view, and the heavy emphasis on independence in Canada, may be changing. Champions of judicial accountability argue that Canada's current unelected and nearly untouchable judges make policy and thus should be held accountable for their decisions. There has been increasing interest in and concern about judicial selection as Canadian courts have played a much different, and more visible, role in the years since the 1982 adoption of the Charter of Rights and Freedoms. As courts—and particularly the Supreme Court—issue decisions on such controversial issues as same-sex marriage and abortion, we hear more and more accusations of judicial policy-making and more and more calls for changes in how those judges are chosen. This chapter concludes with an examination of some of these calls for change at Canada's highest court: the Supreme Court. Does the Charter era require a different method of judicial selection, and if so, which method will best choose justices who embody the qualities that Canadian want in their judiciary? These questions will again be at the forefront in the summer and early fall of 2008 as Prime Minister Harper and his government work to fill a vacancy on the Supreme Court left by the retirement of Justice Michel Bastarache in June 2008.

The Judicial Selection Process in Comparative Perspective

This section examines judicial selection from a comparative perspective. Studying other countries—particularly the United States with its array of different selection methods—can provide a quick tutorial on the alternatives available for selecting judges. It can also offer an insight into the values underlying the choice of a particular method. With judicial selection in Canada coming under more and more scrutiny in recent years, these considerations are necessary to further our understanding of both the current process and the possible reforms to the system.

Judicial appointments in Canada are executive appointments and a reflection of the country's English roots. In England, historically, the 'monarch was regarded as the fountain of justice. The courts were the King's courts and the judges were the King's judges. So it was natural that all the superior court judges should be appointed by the reigning monarch or his designate' (Ziegel 1999, 8). While continuing with executive appointment, Canada put its own stamp on its selection system with its division of the appointment power between provincial and federal executives. Provincial executives have the power to appoint all s. 92 provincial court judges,[4] while the federal government has the power to appoint judges to the federal (trial and appeal) courts, the Tax Court, and the Supreme Court. However, in a more unusual arrangement, the federal executive branch also has the power to appoint all s. 96 provincial superior court judges.

United States Federal Court Selection

The United States, the other federal system that is most familiar to Canadians and most similar to the Canadian system, follows a more obvious division of selection. The federal government appoints judges to all levels of federal court (district, circuit, and Supreme Court, as well as judges for specialized federal courts such as the Tax Court), while the state governments are responsible for selecting judges to all state-level courts. This division of responsibility has led to a wide variety of methods of judicial selection in the United States. Indeed, state governments have so much discretion in the area that it is difficult to find two states that select judges in exactly the same way. This makes the United States an excellent source for comparison, because it provides a glimpse into the workings of a wide range of alternatives, each with a different place on the scale between judicial independence and judicial accountability.

US federal court judges are selected by a process most like that of Canada, in that it involves appointment by the executive branch. It differs, however, in the constitutional requirement that presidential appointments be confirmed by the Senate. The process has three major steps: the President nominates an individual, the Senate Judiciary Committee holds hearings on the nominee and makes a recommendation, and then a vote takes place on the Senate floor, with the nominee confirmed by a simple majority vote. The actual role played by the President and the senators, however, has varied depending on the level of court. There are ninety-four lower federal courts (district courts) spread throughout the United States, with at least one in each state. The large number of judges involved in these courts and the application of each court to just a single state has led Presidents to be less personally involved in these appointments—usually assigning the task to their White House (and/or Justice Department) staff instead. (For a more detailed description of the process of judicial selection for both US federal and state courts, see Baum 2008a and Tarr 2006.)

Traditionally, lower federal court appointments have been dominated by the norm of 'senatorial courtesy'. This norm imbues the senators from the state in which the lower federal court vacancy occurs with an almost veto-like power—particularly if they are from the President's party. If such a senator objects to the President's nominee, the Senate as a whole will vote against the confirmation. With this in mind, the President's staff discusses potential nominees with the home-state senators and often takes recommendations from them—thus reversing the primary power of judicial selection and creating 'senatorial appointment with the advice and consent of the Senate' (Attorney General Robert Kennedy quoted in Tarr 2006, 73). Those championing more legislative involvement in Canadian judicial appointments probably do not have this kind of legislative control in mind.

Senators generally play a weaker role in federal circuit (appeals) court appointments. Since these courts stretch over state lines, control by any particular state's senators is lessened. Although a convention has developed of reserving certain seats for particular states (and, therefore, treating a vacancy of that seat as a vacancy for the state), the President's greater interest in these courts tends to increase the role of the executive (Baum 2008a). With the US Supreme Court taking fewer and fewer cases in recent years, the importance of the federal courts of appeal has grown. These courts now provide the final word on more cases—and, therefore, more policies—than ever. The fact that the US Supreme Court did not accept a major abortion case, for example, between 1992 and 2000, suggests the importance of decisions by appeals courts during that time. In addition, the eleven years without a Supreme Court vacancy meant that all the action in judicial selection was happening at lower courts—something that did not go unnoticed by interest groups (Epstein and Segal 2005). With Presidents now more likely to elevate judges to the Supreme Court from the lower federal courts, both interest groups and politicians can see higher stakes in circuit court appointments. Fighting the appointment of the 'wrong' circuit court judge today is much preferred to facing a more high-profile and contentious Supreme Court nomination of the same candidate in a few years time.

These factors have significantly increased the attention paid to lower-court appointments. Although few circuit court appointees are defeated by a majority vote in the Senate, there has been a growing use of other methods to prevent a confirmation. For example, in the 1990s, the Republican majority on the Senate's Judiciary Committee (the committee that first screens the nominee before sending its recommendation to the Senate floor) failed to hold hearings on a large number of President Clinton's nominees—and without a hearing, a floor vote will not be held. In the last two years of his presidency, only 47 per cent of nominees were granted a hearing by the committee (Epstein and Segal 2005, 25). When President Bush took office the Democrats did not control the Senate Judiciary Committee.

Therefore, they turned to the filibuster[5] to stall confirmation of the President's nominees. In President Bush's first term, ten lower-court nominations were blocked by this method (Epstein and Segal 2005, 25). It is this kind of inherent competition between the branches of government and the 'gamesmanship' it produces, that many fear from the prospect of legislative confirmation of judicial appointments in Canada (although the integrated nature of Canada's executive and legislative branches would probably affect this relationship in a different way).

Of course, Presidents and senators pay most attention to Supreme Court appointments. Although the actual process is the same for all federal judges, the importance of the Supreme Court means the stakes are higher with its appointments. Presidents tend to be personally involved in the appointment process and often have meetings with potential candidates before settling on their nominee (Baum 2008a). The media, the general public, and interest groups all play a more significant role in these appointments—increasing the pressure on decision makers at both the appointment and confirmation stage. (See Chapter 7 for a more in-depth discussion of interest-group activity and influence on federal court appointments.) With heightened public attention on Supreme Court vacancies, interest groups are quick to point out to Presidents and senators their constituents' opinion on the nominee and to spend much time and money trying to influence that opinion (Caldeira, Hojnacki, and Wright 2000; Caldeira and Wright 1998; Scherer 2003).

Although most Supreme Court nominations have been confirmed by the Senate, there have been some notable exceptions (Robert Bork's 1987 defeat is the most high-profile recent one). In the decades since Franklin D. Roosevelt came to office, there have been three defeats and three more candidates withdrawn from consideration (Baum 2007). There have also been, particularly recently, some very close votes (Clarence Thomas was confirmed by a vote of 52 to 48 in 1991 and Samuel Alito was confirmed by a vote of 58 to 42 in 2005). In recent decades, at least, the ideology of the nominee and its possible influence on the justice's vote while on the Court, has been the main point of contention before the Senate,[6] and nominations that will change the ideological balance of the Court have been the most controversial. When reformers argue for legislative involvement in Canadian Supreme Court appointments, it is to these more contentious appointments that their opponents refer.

The fact that American federal judges are appointed for life is often credited with making them more immune to outside pressures. The US federal selection system does appear to emphasize independence more than accountability. The confirmation process, however, might well be thought of as adding a layer of accountability missing in Canada. Though the general public is unable to punish federal judges for unpopular opinions, their representatives in the Senate do have a voice at the start about the type of decision maker chosen for the position and, at least in the case of judges being considered for elevation, may hold appointees responsible for their previous decisions while on a lower court.

United States State Court Selection Systems

The selection systems of a majority of the states put a much heavier emphasis on judicial accountability, as they involve some type of public election at some point in the process. A few states do practise executive appointment (with or without confirmation by the state senate),[7] and legislatures in two states (Virginia and South Carolina) select judges for their courts, but these methods are rare and confined primarily to the eastern seaboard.[8] Indeed, at the end of their term, as many as 87 per cent of all state judges must face some form of election in order to remain on the bench (Baum 2006, 61). Some states use 'partisan elections' where the party of the judicial candidate is printed right on the ballot. Still others use 'retention elections' as part of some form of 'merit selection'. A retention election is held after a judge has sat on a court for some period of time. In a merit selection system, a committee composed of lawyers and lay persons[9] sends a list of names (usually three to six) to the governor, who then selects one of those names to fill the vacancy on the bench. After some period of time, voters are asked whether they wish to retain the judge—no other candidates appear on the ballot.

Judicial elections are heavily favoured by the American public (Baum 1995). Students asked to debate their use produce long lists of the disadvantages of electing judges, but the majority continue to champion their use—believing the main advantage of holding judges accountable far outweighs a longer list of problems with the system. Judges do face some unique problems when running for their positions, however, including the difficulty of talking about their stance on issues of importance to the public. Judges are constrained by the need to appear neutral, in the event one of these issues later presents itself to their court in a case. As a result, judicial campaigns are often characterized by a lack of information amongst the voters (Sheldon and Lovrich 1999).

Judges also have difficulty with fundraising. The most obvious source of funds is the legal community, but there are major problems with taking money from someone who may soon appear before the court.[10] This is a particularly important issue since judicial elections have become more and more expensive over the years (for example, candidates alone spent over $13 million for four seats on the Alabama Supreme Court in 2000) (Tarr 2006). Studies have found campaign contributions may be the biggest determinant of the outcome of judicial elections (see, for example, Cheek and Champagne (2000), who studied judicial elections in Texas from 1980 to 1998 and discovered that in twenty-four of twenty-eight races, the candidate with the most money won).

Elections are the selection method closest to the accountability end of the spectrum. This heavy emphasis often raises concerns about the effect of elections on judicial impartiality. A great deal of scholarly work has been done on the influence elections may have on justices and their behaviour. Huber and Gordon (2004), for example, examined the relationship between judicial elections and judicial impartiality in sentencing behaviour at the trial court level. The authors discovered evidence that judges 'become significantly more punitive the closer they are to standing for reelection. [In fact] in Pennsylvania, for the time period and crimes, [they] analyze, [they] attribute more than two thousand years of additional incarceration to this dynamic' (Huber and Gordon 2004, 261). Hall (1992) discovered a link between elections and the voting behaviour of judges on state supreme courts. Judges facing competitive elections were more likely to vote with the majority and avoid unpopular dissents on politically sensitive issues (see also work by Hall 1995 and Langer 2002 among others). More recently Paul Brace and Brent Boyea have found that the percentage of votes for the reversal of death sentences is much higher one year before an election than it is during an election year (at least for judges who are less secure in their positions). However, the number of votes for reversal rebounds to a higher level the year after the election (2007, 194).

Of course, many judges in states with judicial elections actually come to the bench first through appointment. Most states grant their governor the power of interim appointment. This power allows governors to appoint someone in the event of a mid-term resignation. The person appointed serves until the regularly scheduled election. Indeed, in Idaho, the governor made ten consecutive interim appointments to the state's supreme court between 1968 and 1998 (www.ajs.org). Thus, in a state that elects its supreme court, an election for an open seat was not held for decades.[11] This is significant given the advantage incumbent judges tend to enjoy.[12] In many states it is relatively uncommon for a sitting judge to face competition in an election—particularly in the lower courts (Baum 2008a). These patterns suggest that elections may not be accomplishing what many hope, for if an uninformed electorate is not regularly given a choice of candidates to select from, accountability is minimal.

There is some suggestion that the love of elections and judicial accountability is a uniquely American phenomenon—a result of their history and their greater distrust of government. It should be noted, however, that a 2007 *Globe and Mail*/CTV poll found that 63 per cent of Canadian respondents were in favour of electing judges in Canada.[13] Currently, no judges in Canada are selected this way. Indeed, most Canadian jurists recoil at the idea (Makin 2007b). Many of these jurists point to concerns with impartiality—particularly given the demands for fundraising in elections. Former Ontario Chief Justice, Roy McMurtry, for example, worried that re-election pressures could influence judges' verdicts and sentences. McMurtry suggested that 'the potential for abuse is horrific . . . [reelection pressures] could really destroy the very best traditions of an independent judiciary' (Makin 2007b). It is unlikely that a change this dramatic will be made to judicial selection in Canada, since even the party most critical of judicial power has suggested that elections are not part of Canadian 'tradition' (Makin 2007b).

Many who worry about the disadvantages of electing judges but still favour some aspect of accountability champion instead the merit selection method for selecting judges. With its combination of committee nomination, gubernatorial appointment, and retention election, merit selection is often thought to provide an attractive balance between judicial accountability and judicial independence. It does not, however, remove politics from the process. Studies have found that the nominating committees (which provide the list of names to the governor for appointment) tend to be made up of politically active people, who are chosen with political considerations in mind, and who often base their own choice of nominees on those same political considerations (Reddick 2002; Maute 2007).[14] Thus, while American systems may vary along the judicial independence and judicial accountability continuum, no system is removed from politics.

The presence of politics in selection systems is not, in itself, necessarily problematic. It only becomes a problem if politics produces candidates without the skills and qualities needed to be a judge (Friedland 1995). Studies have not conclusively demonstrated which selection system produces 'better' judges[15] (probably, at least in part, because of the difficulty of defining 'better'). However, the American selection systems generally place a heavy emphasis on accountability and very little on legal competence (Baum 2008a). No specialized training is needed to be a judge, and the general public is probably not well equipped to judge legal competence when they are voting for candidates.

Other Comparisons

In many parts of Europe, by contrast, accountability is a more foreign concept and instead judicial independence and competence are given much greater weight. In France, for example, people train to be judges[16] at a specialized school (the École Nationale de la Magistrature), just as one would train to be a lawyer or a doctor (Provine and Garapon 2006). Prospective students must pass an entrance examination, and training—which includes both coursework and 'trainee' judicial positions—lasts nearly three years. Upon finishing their training, French judges usually take positions at the lowest level of court in the provinces. They gain these positions on the basis of examination scores (Provine and Garapon 2006, 183). The Conseil Supérieur de la Magistrature (CSM) governs the nomination and promotion of judges in France. CSM is made up of four lay people, six judges, and six prosecutors who sit for (four-year) non-renewable terms (Provine and Garapon 2006, 184).

Similar processes exist in Spain and Portugal, while in Germany, those who wish to become a judge must apprentice with the judiciary before being selected through a competitive examination (Volcansek 2006). In Italy, by contrast, becoming a judge is based entirely on a competitive examination, where new judges 'enter the magistrature . . . with no practical experience or training, and receive [their] entire professional socialization from within the established ranks of the judiciary' (Volcansek 2006, 163). Although the use of competitive examinations (which are graded anonymously) suggest an emphasis on competence, judicial promotion in Italy is based on seniority, not performance (Volcansek 2006). Overall, however, the European civil law systems tend to emphasize technical expertise. In some other European countries—for example, France and Germany—'higher ranking magistrates' are responsible for regularly evaluating the work of their lower judicial counterparts, and these evaluations are made available to those responsible for promotion (Guarnieri 2001, 129). It is possible in these systems that judges consider their superiors when making decisions in an effort to receive favourable performance reviews—a different kind of accountability. However, none of the systems suggests that accountability—at least, in its traditional sense—is an important consideration, and in Italy, the judges themselves have prevented efforts to reform the system (Volcansek 2006).

Most common law countries (particularly Commonwealth countries such as Britain, Australia, New Zealand, and Canada) have traditionally emphasized technical expertise less than the civil law countries and accountability less than the United States. Instead, these countries have tended to speak more about the goal of judicial independence. Judges are appointed from the ranks of lawyers (or barristers) by the country's executive and are appointed for long terms.

Methods of judicial selection have increasingly come under discussion in several of these countries, however. Britain recently made changes to their process, decreasing the role of the executive branch in favour of an independent, nongovernmental body (Maute 2007). In England, for example, a fifteen-member commission, the Judicial Appointments Commission, is responsible for recommending one name (based on merit) to the Lord Chancellor for each judicial vacancy below the new Supreme Court[17] (they are responsible for about 900 judicial positions in total (Maute 2007). This commission increases the influence of lay persons on the process, for it requires seven of the fifteen to be from outside the legal field (selected by an 'open competition' application process), and also requires a lay person to chair the commission (Maute 2007, 413–14). According to Kate Malleson (2006), the goals of the establishment of the new commission are to 'strengthen judicial independence, diversify the composition of the judiciary, maintain and enhance the quality of appointments, and raise public confidence in the system' (45–6). Thus, the focus remains judicial independence—and, increasingly, competence—rather than accountability. Has Canada followed a similar path? The next several sections examine, for each level of court in Canada, the current process of judicial selection, the changes that have occurred over the years, and the changes that have been proposed more recently.

Canadian Provincial Court (s. 92) Judges

As mentioned above, the provincial governments are responsible for appointing judges to all s. 92 provincial courts. Chapter 2 discusses the importance of these courts today and highlights the differences found in the size of courts and in the number of judges. Provincial governments appoint 48 per cent of all judges in Canada (Greene 2006, 9), and in 2006 at least four of the provinces appointed more judges to their s. 92 courts than the federal government did to all the s. 96 courts within their province (see Chapter 2).[18] Given the responsibilities of the s. 92 courts today, this suggests provinces are exercising significant power with their appointments. How have provinces exercised this power?

Selection for s. 92 courts has followed the more traditional pattern of Commonwealth countries: executive appointment. In all provinces this means, in principle, appointment by the cabinet. However, the actual process differs by province and time period. The first century of provincial appointments was best characterized as political. Patronage appears to have dominated the process, for judges reached the bench through their political connections. For example, a 1968 report in Ontario suggested that 'there have been isolated cases where one who has not been a supporter of the party in power has been selected for the office, but such cases are unusual' (*Ontario Royal Commission Inquiry into Civil Rights* 1968, 539; see also Friedland 1995, 243).

The Ontario Model

In response to this report, Ontario became the first province to change its selection process significantly. As mentioned in Chapter 2, the province first replaced its magistrate's courts with a provincial court featuring 'better facilities and higher qualifications for judges' (Greene 2006, 14). Judicial candidates now had to be experienced lawyers. The province also introduced, in 1968, an additional step in the selection process: a seven-person Judicial Council. This council was responsible for evaluating potential candidates for the bench and reporting its conclusions to the Attorney General (Friedland 1995, 243). The Attorney General would then make appointments based presumably on those evaluations. There was nothing requiring the Attorney General to appoint the candidate with the highest evaluation, but the new system was thought at least to weed out very poor candidates (Greene 2006, 14). The significance of this 1968 change is debatable since the council served essentially as a screening committee—evaluating only the names of candidates given to it by the province's Attorney General. While an independent council that evaluates candidates suggests the idea of merit, the candidates being evaluated by such a process may still be chosen entirely by patronage.

In 1988, Ontario maintained its position at the forefront of judicial-selection reform, when it established a three-year pilot project to undertake a new method of appointing provincial court judges. The Judicial Appointments Advisory Committee (JAAC) was initially chaired by Professor Peter Russell, a political scientist and leading scholar on the courts. The committee had as its mandate 'first, to develop and recommend comprehensive, sound and useful criteria for selection of appointments to the judiciary, ensuring that the best candidates are considered; and, second, to interview applicants selected by it or referred to it by the Attorney General and make recommendations' (www.ontariocourts.on.ca/judicial_appintments/where.htm). The committee issued its final report in 1992, and in 1995, the Judicial Appointments Advisory Committee was established by statute.

The Judicial Appointments Advisory Committee is made up of thirteen members, seven of whom are laypersons selected by the Attorney General.[19] The remaining six members are two provincial judges (selected by the Chief Judge of the province), a member of the Ontario Judicial Council (appointed by that Council), one lawyer appointed by the province's Law Society, one lawyer appointed by the Ontario branch of the Canadian Bar Association, and finally, one lawyer appointed by the County and District Law Presidents' Association (Devlin, MacKay, and Kim 2000, 772). The high number of lay people on the committee has been a source of concern to some who worry these members may not be capable of evaluating the professional excellence of the candidates (this view was expressed, for example, by the Ontario branch of the Canadian Bar Association: see Friedland 1995, 246). However, others argue that this may even be an advantage since an 'overemphasis on professionalism' can put too much focus on legal technique and not enough on other judicial skills that might be evaluated better by non-lawyers (Devlin, MacKay, and Kim 2000, 785).

The Judicial Appointments Advisory Committee advertises judicial vacancies widely across the legal profession and accepts the applications for the positions. Applicants must have been a member of the bar for at least ten years. They also need 'a sound knowledge of the law, an understanding of the social issues of the day and an appreciation for the cultural diversity of Ontario' (www.ontario courts.on.ca). The applications are reviewed, references and criminal records are checked, and a short list of candidates is composed. The committee then meets to select candidates from that short list to interview. After each interview, the committee votes on the candidate, and at the end of the process, it submits a ranked list of at least two names to the Attorney General (Devlin, MacKay, and Kim 2000). The Attorney General must select a judge from this list (although he is free to ask the committee to create a new list for him to choose from).

There is an extensive list of criteria used to evaluate candidates. The committee is, of course, interested in professional excellence, and it examines everything from the candidates' professional achievements and experience, to their involvement in professional activities that keep them up to date with the law. The ability both to undertake administrative tasks and to write and communicate well is also necessary (www.ontariocourts.on.ca). The committee is also interested in a candidate's community awareness, which it judges by a variety of criteria. Among other things, members attempt to determine a candidate's knowledge of and interest in social problems that lead to cases before the courts. They also examine a candidate's 'sensitivity to changes in social values relating to criminal and family matters' (www.ontariocourts.on.ca). Personal characteristics are another factor used by the committee, including criteria such as 'an ability to listen, respect for the essential dignity of all persons regardless of circumstances, moral courage and high ethics, punctuality . . . [and] an absence of pomposity and authoritarian tendencies' (www.ontariocourts.on.ca). Finally, the committee examines demographics and attempts to overcome under-representation of groups, such as women and racial minorities. The goal is to make the Ontario bench more representative of the Ontario population.

The Ontario committee is a true nominating committee, and the executive is limited to choosing an appointee from a list drawn up by this independent body. This reduces the executive's discretion and limits political influence on the process. It does not erase politics from the process, however. Since the majority of the members of the committee are lay people nominated by the Attorney General, the door is open to political considerations. In addition, the Attorney General's ability to request a new list of candidates can keep politics in play. In the late 1990s, for example, the Harris government became convinced that the committee had a bias towards more liberal candidates who were 'too soft on crime' (Morton 2006; Greene 2006). As a result, the government required the committee to submit more names to the Attorney General, so the cabinet would have more choice.

Some observers suggest politics also plays a role in the Ontario committee because of its mandate to increase diversity on the bench (Morton 2006, 71). During the committee's first six years, the percentage of women appointed to the bench increased from 3 to 22 per cent and those appointed included 'Canada's first aboriginal woman judge, Ontario's first black woman judge, and Canada's first East Asian woman judge' (Morton 2006, 70). Some critics suggest that these appointments were influenced by politics, with the demographic criteria being weighed more heavily than those based on merit.

However, even if it is impossible to remove politics entirely from the process, the current Ontario system has reduced patronage appointments significantly. It has also been successful in improving the quality of appointments to the bench and increasing the judiciary's representativeness of the Ontario population as a whole (Friedland 1995; Greene 2006).

Other Provinces

The other provinces followed Ontario's 1968 lead and reformed their judicial appointment systems to include judicial councils or committees of various forms. The provincial committees vary in the number of members (from three to thirteen), but all include a combination of judicial, legal, and lay members. The trend has been towards making these provincial committees nominating committees, and not just screening committees. Today, four provinces—British Columbia, Manitoba, Nova Scotia, and Newfoundland—have systems similar to that of

Ontario.[20] These provinces' committees recruit applicants, review and evaluate the applications, and produce (nominate) a list of potential nominees to the executive of the province (Devlin, MacKay, and Kim 2000; see also each province's website for provincial courts). Quebec also has a nominating committee. However, it differs from the other provinces in that the committee is not responsible for recruiting applicants. Instead, that duty falls to a person chosen by the province's minister of justice (Devlin, MacKay, and Kim 2000, 773).

In 1999, Alberta introduced a slightly different nominating committee system. In that province, the Judicial Council[21] accepts applications, checks references, and interviews candidates. It then ranks candidates as either approved or not approved and sends this information to the Attorney General (Devlin, MacKay, and Kim 2000, 768). When a judicial vacancy occurs, the Attorney General convenes the Provincial Court Nominating Committee. This committee has eleven members, including judicial and legal representatives and members of the public (see http://justice.gov.ab.ca/courts for details). The committee chooses individuals to interview from the Judicial Council's list of approved candidates. It then recommends three to six names to the Attorney General. The executive must appoint from amongst the recommended names, although it can request another list of candidates.

Thus, today, seven of the ten provinces have nominating committees working on judicial appointments. The other three provinces (Saskatchewan, New Brunswick, and Prince Edward Island) have committees which perform more of a screening function than a nominating one. In Saskatchewan, for example, the provincial Judicial Council provides only advisory opinions for the executive. The council accepts nominations and evaluates the applicants, but it is required to send the executive all of the names and evaluations rather than creating a short list (it, therefore, is closer to the 1968 Ontario system, with all its drawbacks).

The increased emphasis on nominating committees in the majority of provinces suggests an emphasis on the quality of judges rather than political connections. The same qualifications need to be made here, however, as those made with regard to the Ontario system described above. In addition, it should be noted that of the seven provinces using a nominating committee (including Ontario), only Manitoba requires the provincial executive to choose from the original list of candidates submitted to it by the committee, rather than allowing it to request a new list (Devlin, MacKay, and Kim 2000, 786).

Direct accountability is not the goal of any province's selection system. The general public is unable to vote for a judicial candidate and is not given the opportunity to vote against judges if they disapprove of the job they are doing on the bench. Except in exceptional circumstances (see Chapter 6), governments are also unable to hold judges accountable for their job performance (disapproval of a judge's decisions would not, ordinarily, be sufficient grounds for removal).

Makeup of the Judiciary

While accountability is not emphasized at the provincial level, there has been greater concern for diversity on the bench in recent years. In 1999, all provincial courts together, had an average of 20 per cent female judges, with a low of 12.5 per cent in Newfoundland and a high of 33 per cent in Prince Edward Island (Devlin, MacKay, and Kim 2000, 761; see also provincial court websites in each of the provinces). In Ontario, with its mandated emphasis on diversity, 23 per cent of provincial court judges were female. In British Columbia, the percentage of female judges is second only to Prince Edward Island, at 26 per cent.

Interestingly, the introduction of nominating committees in the provinces appears to have significantly increased the number of women on the bench (Matisz 2005). In Manitoba, for example, in the years immediately preceding the nominating committee, roughly 30 per cent of appointees were female. This jumped to 52 per cent in the years immediately after the installation of the nominating committee (Matisz 2005). The number of minorities appointed to the bench has also started to increase but is still very low across the country. Members of designated minority groups (based on race, culture, disability, and sexual orientation) made up roughly 27 per cent of British Columbia applicants from 2004 to 2006 (most of whom were members of visible minorities), and 18 per cent of those were approved for appointment (British Columbia Judicial Council 2004–6, 10). However, that 18 per cent translates to only four candidates.

Box 5.1 profiles the backgrounds of a few provincial court judges in British Columbia, which uses a true nominating committee, and in New Brunswick, which does not. This small sample is fairly typical, in that all of the provincial judges were appointed in the province they grew up in, and all went to law school in the province of their appointment. The judges are also fairly typical, however, in that there is no one path to the bench. Before their appointment, they practised different forms of law (although many had been prosecutors at one time in their past) and did so for varying lengths of time.

Box 5.1   Profile of Select Provincial Court Judges

HARBANS K. DHILLON, British Columbia
Born in Hong Kong
Raised in Vancouver
BA, University of British Columbia
Law degree, University of British Columbia, 1987
Private practice, 1988–99
First Indo-Canadian woman appointed to BC Provincial Court, 1999

RONALD WEBB, British Columbia
Born in Cranbrook, BC
Played semi-professional hockey, Albuquerque Chaparrals
BComm., University of Calgary
Law degree, University of Victoria, 1985
Private practice 1986–90
Prosecutor Crown Counsel Office, 1991–2004
Appointed to the BC Provincial Court, 2004

PATRICIA L. CUMMING, New Brunswick
Born in Bathurst, NB
BBA, University of New Brunswick
Law degree, University of New Brunswick, 1973
Crown Prosecutor 1973–6
Special Prosecutions Branch 1976–82
Director Policing Services, 1982–1985
Appointed to the NB Provincial Court, 1985

J.L. JACQUES DESJARDINS, New Brunswick
Born in Grand Falls, NB
BA, Collège de Bathurst
Law degree, University of New Brunswick, 1974
Private practice
Appointed to the NB Provincial Court, 1981

Federal Section 96 Court Judges

Officially, s. 96 judges (the provinces' superior court judges) are appointed by the Governor General of Canada. This, of course, actually means appointment by the federal cabinet and primarily involves the appointment of candidates recommended by the Minister of Justice.[22] The federal government's appointment power over these provincially created and administered courts was originally granted in an effort to protect the courts from 'local politics or prejudice' (Morton 2006, 57). Indeed, several of the men participating in the Confederation conferences suggested that appointments made by the federal government were likely to be of higher quality than those by the provincial governments—for the federal government was more likely to choose competent, well-known and respected men (Friedland 1995, 234). However, federal government appointments to the superior provincial courts also served the interests of some of the country's founders by further weakening the position of the provinces versus the federal government (Morton 2006). In addition, it is possible that the division was pursued by 'key players in Confederation' in order to keep the power of patronage for themselves. This may be inferred from the reception received by Sir Samuel Tilley when he suggested a selection method that would insulate judicial appointments from party politics: 'considerable reluctance . . . was exhibited by several of the legal members of the conference to forego prizes now apparently within their grasp' (Friedland 1995, 234).

Whatever the reason, the provincial governments' inability to appoint judges to their own superior courts seems somewhat incongruous with a federal system of government. Indeed, this arrangement has been subject to controversy. In 1982, for example, a new Progressive Conservative government in Saskatchewan began protesting the federal Liberal government's appointments in that province, arguing the Liberals were dumping members and supporters in Saskatchewan superior courts (Simpson 1988). In response to this alleged patronage, the Saskatchewan government began using its power of administration of the courts to decrease the number of available s. 96 judgeships. First, the provincial government reduced the number of judges on the Saskatchewan Court of Appeal from seven to five. Then it turned its attention to the lower superior court, the Court of Queen's Bench. If a judge died or retired from that court, Saskatchewan would eliminate the position, thus precluding the federal government from making an appointment. For two years the federal Liberal government and provincial Conservative government knocked heads over this issue, and the number of judges on the Court of Queen's Bench dwindled from thirty to twenty-four (Simpson 1988). The dispute only ended with the election, in 1984, of the federal Progressive Conservative party, which promised to consult Saskatchewan and the other provinces when making appointments. The Saskatchewan Progressive Conservatives then increased each s. 96 court's membership to its original levels and saw some of their own prominent supporters appointed to the newly restored vacancies (Simpson 1988).

Appointment Process Historically

The Saskatchewan controversy over s. 96 appointments brings up the question of whether federal government appointments to s. 96 courts were really 'better' than those that provincial governments could have made. Indeed, the federal government made political appointments right from the start, and its appointments were subject to criticism. In 1872, one writer said: 'The system is radically bad: for in lieu of good lawyers, worn-out politicians are placed on the bench. If a man is a political failure, presto he is made a judge.' (Friedland 1995, 235). Criticism of federal appointments continued, and in 1918 the Canadian Bar Association (CBA) recommended that changes be made to emphasize legal achievements and other qualities of merit, rather than political or financial considerations (Friedland 1995, 235). In 1930 the CBA gained a prominent ear when its president, R.B. Bennett, became Prime Minister. Bennett believed that judicial appointments should be based on merit. However, after only two years in office, he acknowledged that patronage was hard to escape, suggesting that the 'test whether a man is entitled to a seat on the Bench has seemed to be whether he has run an election and lost it' (Friedland 1995, 236).

Patronage remained a significant influence on appointments for the next several years. A study of appointments made to federal courts from 1945 to 1965 concluded that 'all but a few of the judges appointed during the period were affiliated with the party in power at the time they were appointed, and most were actively engaged in politics' (study by R.C.B. Risk, quoted in Friedland 1995, 236). However, changes began to be made to the process in 1967, when the Minister of Justice, Pierre Trudeau, asked the National Committee on the Judiciary, a committee of the CBA, to review the candidates he was considering and rate whether they were qualified for the position—thus adding a screening committee of sorts (Greene 2006, 14). The next year, in an attempt to make the process more systematic, the government created the position of special assistant to the Minister of Justice. This person was responsible for 'prescreening' candidates interested in a judgeship and collecting information on other potential candidates from a variety of sources, including members of the legal profession and provincial Attorneys General (Greene 2006; Ziegel 1999).

Though appointments were thought to have improved with these changes, patronage was not eliminated. The Minister of Justice often felt pressure from cabinet ministers to appoint particular candidates from their region (CBA 1985, 40–2). There was also no actual requirement for the Minister of Justice to consult the CBA's National Committee on the Judiciary, and there were instances in which this review process had been bypassed. In 1984, for example, the Trudeau government made six appointments to the bench right before the election, and one of these appointments was never seen by the committee. All six appointees were former Liberal politicians, and reaction was intense. The next year, a CBA study interviewed lawyers, judges, and provincial and federal officials, concluding that patronage was the main factor in appointments in the Atlantic provinces and Saskatchewan and was a significant influence in Alberta and Manitoba (CBA 1985, 37–40). Change was called for by the CBA, the Canadian Association of Law Teachers (CALT), and political scientists. Political scientist Peter Russell summed up the feelings of most reformers when he said that 'the vulnerability of the appointing process to the personalities and whims of the governing party which [the Trudeau appointments] so vividly demonstrates, is a strong part of the case for a more enduring institutional reform: that is, for the establishment of true nominating commissions' (Russell 1987, 120).

However, despite making change in judicial appointments an election issue, the new Prime Minister, Brian Mulroney, did not make changes in the process during his first term from 1984 to 1988. Indeed, a study by Peter Russell and

Jacob Ziegel found that significant patronage continued during that time. Russell and Ziegel (1991), who examined the Mulroney government's appointments (to the s. 96 and federal courts), found that 24 per cent of appointees had 'major' involvement with the appointing party. Major involvement included running for office, acting as a party official, or participating actively in election or leadership campaigns. An additional 23 per cent of appointees had 'minor' involvement with the party, such as constituency work, financial contributions, or close professional or personal ties with the party leadership (Russell and Ziegel 1991). Thus, 47 per cent of the government's appointees had some partisan political connection to the party appointing them.

It appears that before 1988 competence was not emphasized in federal judicial appointments to nearly the same degree as patronage.[23] And the degree of patronage present in these appointments has implications for the traditional Canadian goal of judicial independence. If judicial independence provides the basis for impartiality, problems can ensue in a system where judges gain their positions because of their connections with the appointing party, as well as when judges depend on the executive for promotion.

1988 Changes to the Appointment Process

In April 1988, after consultations with the legal community and other interested groups, Mulroney's Minister of Justice, Ray Hnatyshyn, announced changes to the federal government's appointment process (although it was 1989 before the changes were fully implemented). Some suggest it was the reforms undertaken at the provincial level—particularly in Ontario—that spurred Prime Minister Mulroney to order a review of the process (Greene 2006, 15). According to Hnatyshyn, the purpose of the new system was 'to enable all interested and qualified individuals to be considered for appointment, and to provide a means by which the Minister of Justice can receive broadly-based and objective advice about their qualifications for appointment' (as quoted in Millar 2000, 617).

Under the post-1988 system, s. 96 (and federal court)[24] appointments involve the Office of the Commissioner for Federal Judicial Affairs (OCFJA), as well as judicial advisory committees in each of the provinces and territories (the larger provinces, Ontario and Quebec, have more than one such committee). The Commissioner for Federal Judicial Affairs is more at arm's length from the Minister of Justice than the pre-1988 special assistant was, and this may insulate the process more from politics. The commissioner is responsible for accepting applications for court vacancies (a new addition, for applications had not been required before this time). The commissioner then verifies that the applicants meet the required qualifications to be a federal judge—including having at least ten years' experience as a lawyer—before referring the names to the judicial advisory committee in the appropriate province (Friedland 1995). Applications from s. 96 trial court judges for seats on s. 96 appellate courts (judges seeking promotion), are not evaluated by the committees. Until 1999, applications from provincial court judges for s. 96 courts were also left unrated. That year, however, a practise sprang up of providing non-binding comments on such candidates (Millar 2000).

The judicial advisory committees serve as screening committees, reviewing the personal history questionnaires of candidates sent to them by the commissioner (rather than recruiting candidates themselves) and forwarding all assessments to the Minister of Justice, rather than composing a short list of potential nominees. When the committees evaluate candidates, they focus on professional competence and merit and use a list of criteria under four main categories: professional competence and experience (for example, proficiency in the law, standards and reputation, work habits, and scholarly ability); personal characteristics (for example, ethical standards, tolerance, common sense, and tact); social awareness[25] (including sensitivity to gender and racial equality, and public and community service); and potential impediments to appointment (such as drug or alcohol dependency, financial difficulties, or sexual harassment complaints). (For a full list of the criteria, see Millar 2000, 653.)

In 1991,[26] the committees began rating candidates on a three point scale: 'unable to recommend', 'recommended', or 'highly recommended'. From this point until 2006, roughly 40 per cent of candidates were rated as 'recommended' or 'highly recommended' (Office of the Commissioner for Federal Judicial Affairs 2008; Millar 2000). This rating system has been changed again, however. In autumn 2006, Stephen Harper's Conservative government eliminated the top category of 'highly recommended'. Candidates are now judged more on a pass-fail system, 'recommended' or 'not recommended'. Once candidates receive an assessment by the committee, the list is forwarded to the Minister of Justice, who can choose appointees from the list for up to two years. Though there are no rules preventing a Minister of Justice from selecting a candidate rated as 'not recommended', every Minister of Justice has appointed candidates that have received at least a 'recommended' rating from the committee (Millar 2000, 620). The Minister can, however, ask for a reassessment of a candidate.[27]

Judicial advisory committee members are appointed for a three-year term, although they can be reappointed for an additional term. Until 2006, each committee had seven members: one nominated by the provincial branch of the CBA, one by the provincial law society, a judge nominated by the province's Chief Justice, a member nominated by the province's Attorney General, and three members, two of whom had to be lay people, appointed by the federal Department of Justice (Millar 2000). When appointing the committees, the Minister of Justice attempted 'to reflect a balance of factors appropriate to the jurisdiction, including geography, language, and multiculturalism, in addition to gender' (Millar 2000, 621). In autumn 2006, Stephen Harper's Conservative government made changes to the membership of the committees by adding an additional member appointed by the federal Minister of Justice. This member was to be someone from the police community. The Conservative government also changed the judicial member of the committee into a non-voting chair.

Assessments of the 1988 Reform and Recent Changes to the Appointment Process

Have the 1988 changes been successful in decreasing patronage and increasing the influence of merit on appointments? The system did create a more systematic screening process that allowed more provincial input. However, the changes did not go as far as the legal community had hoped and controversy still surrounds the appointment process. Perhaps the largest problem with the new system is that the committees are screening committees rather than nominating committees. The committees can only review the names submitted to them by the federal government (rather than recruit those they feel will be the best candidates), and they must submit all their assessments, instead of composing a list of the 'best' nominees to give to the Minister of Justice. Patronage has room to flourish in this system because the Minister has widespread discretion to overlook the best-qualified candidates. Indeed, according to Peter Russell, governments have frequently chosen candidates that were merely 'recommended', rather than 'highly recommended', when that has allowed them to appoint party supporters (Russell 2007a). Since being 'recommended' in this system means the candidates have merely met some very minimal requirements, this suggests the reforms have not achieved a dominant emphasis on merit.

Patronage can also be introduced into this system through the membership of the judicial advisory committees. Partisanship appears to be a factor in the federal government's choice of who sits on the committee. When the committees' membership expired in 2006, for example, about half of the people appointed to the committees by the Conservative government's Minister of Justice were Conservative partisans, including defeated Conservative candidates and Conservative political staffers (Clark 2007a). Similar ties were found between the previous members of the committees and the Liberal government that had appointed them (Clark 2007b). This practice adds to the potential for patronage since ratings may be affected by the composition of the committee.

Though a complete systematic study of the post-1988 federal government appointments does not yet exist, preliminary work does suggest that patronage has continued unabated since the 1988 changes to the process. From 1989 to 2003, 723[28] judges were appointed to the s. 96 (and federal) courts, and approximately 30 per cent were found[29] to have donated money to the party that appointed them within five years of their appointment (Riddell, Hausegger, and Hennigar 2008). Although donating to a political party is a relatively low level of political involvement, 30 per cent is considerably higher than the average of 0.65 per cent of eligible voters who donate money to a political party during some of those same years

(Riddell, Hausegger, and Hennigar 2008, 20). The importance of connections to the appointing government does not appear to depend on who is Prime Minister. Indeed, Peter Russell argues that 'in terms of patronage appointments to the judiciary, there is nothing to choose from among the Mulroney Conservative governments and the Martin and Chrétien Liberal governments. They all gave undue influence to political considerations in making judicial appointments' (Russell 2007a, A21).[30]

The latest changes made by the Harper government to the s. 96 (and federal court) appointment system are unlikely to reduce the role of patronage in appointments,[31] and they have been subject to widespread criticism from the legal community. Both Beverley McLachlin, the Chief Justice of the Supreme Court of Canada, and the Canadian Judicial Council she chairs have been vocal in their criticism of the Harper government's changes. For McLachlin and the Council, the biggest objection is to the government's failure to consult the legal community before introducing changes to the system (Makin 2006c). The Canadian Judicial Council and other individuals and groups have also criticized the specific changes themselves, such as the elimination of the 'highly recommended' category in assessments. Opponents of this change argue that it turns the judicial advisory committees' assessment into a choice between pass and fail, making it even more difficult to determine whether the government is appointing good candidates. Although governments could appoint 'recommended' over 'highly recommended' candidates in the past, the existence of that third category ensured they could be held accountable for their choice not to appoint the most qualified individuals. (Russell 2007a).

The addition of a member of the police community to the committees has also come under fire, uniting the legal community in their opposition to the plan. Prime Minister Harper has argued that he is interested in judges who are 'tough on crime'. A member of the police community would presumably have the same values and would apply that to his or her assessment of candidates. The Conservative government has also argued that the police community is such a prominent part of the legal system that it deserves a voice in the appointment of judges. However, opponents such as former Chief Justice Antonio Lamer have criticized the government's plan as being 'counter-intuitive and counter-productive' (Telus 2007). Testifying before a House of Commons committee, Lamer pointed out that the vast majority of the work of the s. 96 courts (and federal courts) involves civil cases. Thus, justices need to be experts in subjects such as torts, contracts, and taxation rather than criminal law (see also Russell 2007a).[32]

The decision of the Harper government to make the judicial member of the committee a non-voting chair has also come under criticism. According to Russell and Lamer, this effectively silences the one member who is best informed about the qualities needed in a judge (Russell 2007a). This change, and the addition of the police representative, also effectively give the federal government an extra vote on the committee. The committee now has four government appointees, who, if voting as a block, could prevent any candidate not favoured by the government from receiving a favourable rating (Makin 2006c). With a majority of voting members now appointed by the Minister of Justice, some argue that the advisory committees are no longer independent of the government (Canadian Judicial Council 2007).

Makeup of the Judiciary

The criteria used by the judicial advisory committees in s. 96 (and federal) court appointments do not include gender, race, or ethnicity. However, as mentioned above, the Minister of Justice does take multiculturalism and gender into account when appointing members to the committees themselves. That, and criteria such as 'non-mainstream legal experience', 'bilingualism', and 'sensitivity to gender and racial equality', have probably contributed to the trend of appointing greater numbers of women and minorities in the past few decades. In the early 1980s, only 3 per cent of federally appointed judges were women, by 1990 this number had increased to 10 per cent, and by 2000 this number had more than doubled again (Morton 2006, 68). By 2004, 26 per cent of judges sitting on s. 96 trial courts and 33 per cent of judges on s. 96 appeals courts were female (Baar 2006).

In their study of judicial appointments from 1984 to 1988, Russell and Ziegel found that 17.5 per cent of appointments were women—which, they suggest, reflects a conscious effort on the part of the Mulroney government to increase diversity on the bench (1991, 12). Table 5.1 illustrates that this trend continued, for the s. 96 courts, through Mulroney's subsequent term and those of the Chrétien government. The percentage of women appointed during Chrétien's second term (1997–2000), was particularly high (approximately 39 per cent to s. 96 trial courts, and 40 per cent to s. 96 appeals courts), given that, on average,

Table 5.1   Federal Judicial Appointments by Gender, 1988–2003

	S. 96 Trial Courts (%)	S. 96 Appeal Courts (%)	Supreme Court (%)
Mulroney 1988–93	M: 77.8 F: 22.2	M: 67.9 F: 32.1	M: 85.7 F: 14.3
Chrétien 1993–7	M: 64.1 F: 35.9	M: 73.3 F: 26.7	M: 0 F: 0
Chrétien 1997–2000	M: 61.1 F: 38.9	M: 60.0 F: 40.0	M: 60.0 F: 40.0
Chrétien 2000–2003	M: 67.1 F: 32.9	M: 70.0 F: 30.0	M: 50 F: 50

Source: Compiled by the authors from lists of appointments (Riddell, Hausegger, and Hennigar 2008).

women have made up only 24 per cent of applicants for federally appointed courts (Riddell, Hausegger, and Hennigar 2008, 15). These numbers suggest that a search for diversity may be a factor in appointments.

The number of visible minority judges and aboriginal judges has also increased during this period, although both groups remain very under-represented in relation to their percentage of the general population (Greene 2006).[33]

Justices sitting on s. 96 courts still tend to be a fairly elite group. In their study of judges appointed from 1984 to 1988, Russell and Ziegel found that a significant number had studied law at Dalhousie (17.4 per cent) or Osgoode Hall (12.6 per cent), two of the most prestigious law schools (1991, 17). Although these numbers have declined to some extent, these two law schools continue to be the most represented, with 9.9 per cent of appointees having attended Dalhousie and 10.4 per cent Osgoode Hall (Riddell, Hausegger, and Hennigar 2008, 17).

Supreme Court Justices

The appointment of Supreme Court justices is not addressed in the Constitution, but rather is guided by the *Supreme Court Act of 1875*. As with the federal courts and the s. 96 courts, it is by executive appointment—that is, by the Governor in Council. However, unlike the practice in those other courts, the actual choice of which candidate will sit on the Supreme Court bench is made by the Prime Minister (although he receives help with the process from his Minister of Justice). Indeed, the Prime Minister exercises great control over these appointments. According to Peter Russell, Canada is the 'only constitutional democracy in the world in which the leader of government has an unfettered discretion to decide who will sit on the country's highest court' (2004a, 17). Traditionally appointments have been made by the Prime Minister without legislative input or confirmation hearings. The Prime Minister even has the power to change the appointment process, as Prime Minister Stephen Harper did when he imposed a three-hour legislative hearing on the 2006 Supreme Court appointee—a change he made with no need for legislative approval or a constitutional amendment.

There are only a few prerequisites for becoming a Supreme Court justice. Appointees to the Supreme Court must either be a sitting s. 96 court judge or have at least ten years' 'standing at the bar' of their province (Supreme Court of Canada 2008b). The *Supreme Court Act* also dictates that three justices must come from Quebec. Quebec has a civil law tradition unfamiliar to the rest of Canada, and the requirement of the three justices is intended to facilitate judgments on appeals from that province. By convention, the three justices from Quebec have been matched by three justices from Ontario. Indeed, the Supreme Court exhibits regional representation. Of the remaining three justices, two traditionally come from the West,[34] and one from the Atlantic provinces. When a justice retires, he or she is replaced by someone from his or her region.[35]

For all but the last three Supreme Court appointments, the process has been the same. Guided by these requirements, or conventions, when a Supreme Court vacancy occurred, the Minister of Justice consulted with a variety of individuals, many from the region of the retiring justice. Among others, advice was sought from the Chief Justice of the Supreme Court, Attorneys General from the appropriate region, senior members of the law societies and bar associations of that region, and chief justices from the courts in the area (Cotler 2004). The Minister then created a list of candidates and discussed their merits with the Prime Minister. These candidates were often judges sitting on the provincial court of appeal, senior members of the province's bar, or academics (Cotler 2004). After evaluating the list, the Prime Minister chose a candidate and recommended that person to the cabinet for appointment. As discussed later in this chapter, this procedure has been altered recently. The last three appointments have included additional steps and participants in the process.

Once chosen, justices must move to the National Capital Region (if they do not already live there) or within forty kilometres of it. They sit on the Supreme Court, 'during good behavior' until the mandatory retirement age of seventy-five (unless they choose to retire earlier).[36] As detailed in Chapter 6, they can be removed only for incapacity or misconduct by the Governor General 'on address' of the Senate and House of Commons (Supreme Court of Canada 2008b).

Influences on Appointment

Aside from the experience and regional requirements, Prime Ministers generally have free rein in making their appointments. So what influences their choice of justice from the list of candidates they are given? Patronage was originally a very heavy consideration. William Lyon Mackenzie King, who was Prime Minister from 1921 to 1930 (for all but a few months in 1926) and from 1935 to 1948, is said to have based his appointments to the bench on 'no preference for judicial experience, considerable weight to service to the Liberal Party, some minimum level of ability, and influential friends' (Snell and Vaughan 1985, 154). Indeed, before 1949, the membership of the Supreme Court looked very political, for 55 per cent of the justices had been elected politicians at some point in their past (Friedland 1995, 236).[37] Pierre Trudeau (as Minister of Justice and later as Prime Minister) is often credited with removing patronage as a consideration in Supreme Court appointments (see, for example, Greene 2006; MacIvor 2006). While a candidate's viewpoints on issues such as federalism and civil rights may have influenced some of Trudeau's appointments, their connections to the party did not (at least at the Supreme Court level).

Partisan considerations have probably not been completely absent in recent decades. Patronage is thought to have played a role in at least one more recent appointment. In 1979, Prime Minister Joe Clark appointed Julien Chouinard, who had run for election as a Conservative candidate in 1968. His appointment came after Clark had first invited him to become a member of his cabinet (McCormick 2000, 85). However, since the 1960s, such appointments have been rare.[38]

Then what has replaced patronage as a consideration? According to Irwin Cotler, Minister of Justice for the Liberal government from 2003 to 2006, three main criteria are used when potential candidates are being considered: professional capacity (including proficiency in the law, superior intellectual ability, analytical and written skills, and capacity to manage stress), personal characteristics (honesty, integrity, patience, tact, and tolerance among others), and membership in an under-represented group (Cotler 2004). This suggests an emphasis on the merits of a candidate, and indeed, the credentials of the average Supreme Court justice are much different today than before the 1960s. Modern Supreme Court justices' credentials tend more to be 'appellate experience, an academic connection, and some demonstration of public service' (McCormick 2005a, 10).[39] However, the criteria also suggest a more recent consideration: diversity—often in the form of group representation.

At the Supreme Court, that diversity has been demonstrated mostly in terms of language and gender.[40] The choice of Chief Justice has traditionally alternated between the most senior French and English members of the Court.[41] And, more recently, a pattern has developed of appointing at least one francophone amongst the non-Quebec justices—on the most recent Court there were two, Michel Bastarache (who retired on 30 June 2008) and Louise Charron (McCormick 2005a, 22). The first female justice, Bertha Wilson, was appointed to the bench in 1982. She was later joined by Claire L'Heureux-Dubé in 1987 and Beverley McLachlin in 1989. In 1991, this number declined to two when Bertha Wilson retired and was not replaced with another woman, despite pressure from feminists (Morton 2006, 58). However, in 1999, the number again increased to three with the appointment of Louise Arbour to replace a retiring male justice (Peter Cory). Since that time, the retired L'Heureux-Dubé has been replaced by another female justice, Marie Deschamps and an additional woman has been put on the bench to increase the number to four. (When Louise Arbour resigned to take a position with the UN, and Frank Iacobucci retired, they were replaced by Rosalie Abella and Louise Charron.) Whether replacing a female justice with another woman has attained the status of convention, it has now been done twice. The influence of gender on Supreme Court appointments seems firmly entrenched—it is unlikely that the number of female justices will be reduced significantly in the future.

The focus on group representation in Supreme Court appointments has been the subject of criticism. As Peter McCormick notes, 'the representational factors, however defensible and well-intentioned, inevitably complicate the professionalism of a merit-based system' (2005a, 22). There are also choices that have to be made about which groups deserve attention. Recently, ethnicity and gender have been more heavily emphasized, but some critics question why these factors are more important than others such as social status. Ted Morton asks, for example, whether 'a white woman lawyer from a secular, upper-class family bring[s] more diversity to the bench than a son of recent Eastern European immigrants with strong religious beliefs' (2006, 72).

Interestingly, ideology has not, historically, played a prominent role in Supreme Court appointments, something which stands in stark contrast to the practice in the United States. Though this may be changing, Ostberg and Wetstein note that newspaper accounts of even 'recent judicial nominations in Canada spend as much time discussing a prospective appointee's regional fit on the Court, bilingual skills, gender, and legal experience as they do ideological pro-clivities of the new appointees' (2007, 35). There are, of course, exceptions to this, as illustrated by Prime Minister Trudeau's choice of Bora Laskin for Chief Justice in 1973. This choice violated the convention of appointing the most senior anglophone justice, for Laskin had been on the Court less than four years. However, the most senior anglophone justice, Ronald Martland, had written opinions that were supportive of provincial rights, as well as opinions that were unsympathetic to the Bill of the Rights (Morton 1992). Laskin, by contrast, had ideas more similar to those of Trudeau on federalism and civil rights. Trudeau did, however, appoint other justices to the bench—Jean Beetz, for example—who were strong champions of provincial rights.

As the Supreme Court's increased policy-making role becomes more apparent, ideology may play a greater role in the process. In the Charter era, the stakes are raised, and groups may become more concerned with what type of justice is hearing cases in their issue or area of interest. For example, EGALE (Equality for Gays and Lesbians Everywhere) recognized early the importance of getting the 'right' justices on the bench, and it has lobbied the government for candidates 'committed to equality issues' (Morton and Knopff 2000, 107). Faced with this pressure and in light of their own interest in getting favourable decisions from an increasingly powerful Court, governments may begin to consider ideology more heavily than in the past.

Reform of the Process

The Canadian public is not particularly well-informed about the selection of Supreme Court justices. Indeed, Fletcher and Howe (2001) found that only 13 per cent of Canadians knew who selected Supreme Court justices. However, when asked who should appoint Supreme Court justices, most respondents do not choose the current system. Most would like to see either provincial input or some form of legislative involvement (Fletcher and Howe 2001, 289).

These preferences may soon begin to be expressed more strongly as the media pay greater attention to the Supreme Court appointment process. Calls for reform have increased steadily in the years since the enactment of the Charter. As Jacob

Ziegel points out, 'it is now abundantly clear that the open-ended norms of the *Charter* require members of the Supreme Court to make critical policy decisions on questions affecting the conduct of Canada's political, economic and social affairs' (2006, 551). And with this recognition has come concern for how Court members are chosen. Critics argue that 'Canada now has an American-style Supreme Court with an unreformed British-style appointments system' (Morton 2006, 57).

Many proposed reforms for Supreme Court appointments are directed at making the process more open and accountable. In 2004, the Standing Committee on Justice heard testimony from academics, the Canadian Bar Association, and retired Supreme Court Justice L'Heureux-Dubé on the appointment process. The two main reforms recommended by the committee were the creation of a commission to recruit and evaluate candidates and legislative scrutiny of the prospective appointee before their official selection by the Prime Minister (Morton 2006). When two justices announced their retirement in June of 2004, the Martin government responded to the committee's report by adding a new step to the process. Once the Prime Minister chose the two replacements, the Minister of Justice would meet with a committee formed from the House of Commons to answer questions about the nominees, thus opening up the process to public scrutiny. However, the committee could not question the nominees directly, and it could not veto their appointment, so this was purely an informational meeting—what one journalist called, 'sending your mother to do your job interview' (as quoted in McCormick 2006, 543).

In 2005, another vacancy occurred on the Supreme Court, and the Liberal government announced another change to the process. After consulting with the usual individuals within the region with the vacancy, the Minister of Justice submitted a list of approximately eight names to an advisory committee. This committee had members from each of the parties in Parliament, as well as nominees from the provincial law societies and the provincial Attorneys General. Two 'prominent' Canadians, who were not members of the legal community, also sat on the committee (Hogg 2006a, 529). This committee was then responsible for reducing the list to three names. The committee did this, but before the Prime Minister could make his selection, an election was called and the Liberal government was defeated. The new Conservative government decided to fill the vacancy with a candidate from the short list created before the election. However, whereas the Liberal government had intended that the Minister of Justice should appear before the House of Commons Standing Committee on Justice to outline the qualifications of the appointee, the new Conservative government announced that the chosen candidate, Marshall Rothstein, would participate in a public interview process.

This interview, described at the beginning of this chapter, was the subject of controversy. The Chief Justice of the Supreme Court, Beverley McLachlin, voiced her opposition to public hearings of nominees to the Court, as did past and present presidents of the Canadian Bar Association and other prominent members of the legal community (Ziegel 2006). Most feared such hearings would 'politicize' the Court and hamper judicial independence. There was also concern that the best candidates would be deterred from pursuing the job because of the potential invasion of their privacy. However, supporters pointed out advantages to public hearings, including educating the public and promoting democracy with a more open system (Malleson 2006; Hogg 2006).

In the end, the hearings did not live up to the opponents' fears, and public hearings may now become a permanent part of the process. Marshall Rothstein himself has suggested that his appointment has meant that it will be difficult for future nominees to the Supreme Court to be appointed through a less transparent process (as quoted in Nejatian 2007). In Rothstein's eyes, however, this is not something that should be viewed with fear. He argues that the 'politicization' of the American Supreme Court appointment process is unlikely to be replicated in Canada because of the 'active dialogue between the legislature and the judiciary in Canada, the different political environment in [Canada] and the existence of the notwithstanding clause' (Nejatian 2007).

The retirement of Justice Michel Bastarache in June 2008 leaves another vacancy on the Court for the government to fill. It remains to be seen whether Stephen Harper—or some future Prime Minister—will keep the advisory committee, created by the Liberal government, to narrow the list down to three candidates. The inclusion of nominees of provincial Attorneys General and provincial law societies, on the committee, may be one solution to another demand for reform: greater provincial input on Supreme Court appointments. Provinces pushed hard for—and secured—the power to nominate Supreme Court justices in the 1987 Meech Lake Accord. However, with the failure of Meech Lake and the subsequent Charlottetown Accord, this issue has lost a lot of its momentum (Morton 2006). Although Quebec remains interested in having a more direct say in Supreme Court appointments, this is no longer a prominent issue in other provinces.

Makeup of the Judiciary

Table 5.2 briefly outlines some of the backgrounds of the current Supreme Court justices. Many of the justices on this Court look very different from those sitting on the bench during the Court's first 100 years. Most Supreme Court justices have been white men of British or French descent. The first real break in this pattern came in 1970 with the appointment of Bora Laskin—the first Jewish judge. Currently three Jewish justices sit on the Court: Morris Fish, Rosalie Abella, and Marshall Rothstein. Other breaks in the British-French pattern include the appointment of the first justice of Ukrainian background, John Sopinka, in 1988, and the first justice of Italian background, Frank Iacobucci, in 1991 (McCormick

Table 5.2   Profile of Supreme Court Justices, 2008

	Year of Birth	Year Appointed	Province Appointed From	Appointing Prime Minister	Prior Judicial Experience	Law School
C.J. Beverley McLachlin	1943	1989 2000 (CJ)	British Columbia	Mulroney Chrétien (CJ)	BC Supreme Court BC Court of Appeal	University of Alberta
Michel Bastarache[a]	1947	1997	New Brunswick	Chrétien	NB Court of Appeal	University of Ottawa
Ian Binnie	1939	1998	Ontario	Chrétien	None	Cambridge & Toronto
Louis LeBel	1939	2000	Quebec	Chrétien	Quebec Court of Appeal	Laval University
Marie Deschamps	1952	2002	Quebec	Chrétien	Quebec Superior Court & Court of Appeal	Université de Montréal
Morris Fish	1938	2003	Quebec	Chrétien	Quebec Court of Appeal	McGill University
Rosalie Abella	1946	2004	Ontario	Chrétien	Ont. Prov. Court & Court of Appeal	University of Toronto
Louise Charron	1951	2004	Ontario	Chrétien	Ont. Court of Justice & Court of Appeal	University of Ottawa
Marshall Rothstein	1940	2006	Manitoba	Harper	Federal Court (Trial & Appeal)	University of Manitoba

[a] Justice Bastarache will retire from the Supreme Court effective 30 June 2008.

Source: Supreme Court of Canada 2008b.

2005a, 22). As mentioned above, the first woman, Bertha Wilson, was appointed in 1982, and the number of women on the Court has grown steadily since. The current Court has four female justices, the highest number in its history, and four times the number sitting on the US Supreme Court.

Table 5.2 also demonstrates a strong pattern of previous judicial experience. All but one of the current justices sat on a lower court before their appointment. It is also interesting that the previous judicial experience came, almost entirely, on provincial courts of appeal, rather than the s. 101 federal courts.

Conclusions

This chapter began by outlining a variety of different methods that have been used to select judges. Each method places a slightly different emphasis on values ranging between judicial independence and judicial accountability, and each places a different weight on merit. In Canada, judicial appointments have traditionally emphasized judicial independence over accountability. No judges in Canada are elected, and even confirmation hearings of the sort used for the federal courts in the United States have, as yet, been rejected. Instead, Canadian judges are selected by executive appointment, and are thus insulated from the public whose cases they hear.

This traditional focus may be changing, however, as the courts acquire a more policy-making role in the Charter era. As courts delve more into the controversial issues of the day, more and more calls for accountability are heard. Most members of the legal community fear even parliamentary confirmation hearings—where MPs could vote for or against a candidate—let alone elections. However, surveys show that the majority of the Canadian public would like to have more say in judicial appointments. While drastic changes are unlikely to occur in the selection process of judges in Canada, it may be that compromise solutions, such as public hearings where appointees face questions from the people's representatives, are here to stay.

Recent years have also seen an increased focus on merit, rather than patronage, in Canadian judicial appointments. The provinces have perhaps gone furthest towards this goal, for many have instigated true nominating committees to recruit and recommend candidates for their s. 92 courts. Though federal government appointments are evaluated more by a screening committee, rather than a nominating committee, there has been more emphasis on professional qualifications at that level as well. Since an appointment system based on patronage calls into question the integrity and quality of the process, these changes are seen as progress. One must be careful, though, to recognize that all selection systems are political to some extent. Even in provinces with true nominating committees that heavily emphasize merit, politics can exist in the selection of members for the committee or the choice among candidates on the short list. The more recent championing of diversity also introduces politics into the system. Among other things, decisions must be made as to which characteristics to pursue. It is important to remember, however, that the presence of politics in judicial selection is not necessarily a bad thing. It only becomes problematic when politics trumps professional capability as a basis of appointment. Current Canadian selection systems have been moving away from that situation, but—at least at the federal level—more changes may need to be made if patronage is to be eliminated.

Chapter 6

Judicial Independence and Accountability

> Suffice it to say that independence of the judiciary is an essential part of
> the fabric of our free and democratic society. It is recognized and pro-
> tected by the law and the conventions of the Constitution as well as by
> statute and common law. Its essential purpose is to enable judges to ren-
> der decisions in accordance with their view of the law and the facts
> without concern for the consequences to themselves. This is necessary
> to assure the public, both in appearance and reality, that their cases will
> be decided, their laws will be interpreted, and their Constitution will be
> applied without fear or favour.[1]

A provincial government announces that judicial salaries will be reduced as part of
across-the-board cuts to the salaries of public sector workers to reduce ballooning
government deficits and debt. The government requires judges to start contributing to their own pension plans. Semi-retired judges will no longer be able to collect their full salary while only working part-time. Judges are summoned to testify
before a Royal Commission about their role in a miscarriage of justice. A judge is
reprimanded by his fellow judges for his conduct on the bench. The federal government announces it is unilaterally changing the appointment method for lower-
court judges by including the input of a representative of the policing community.
In a speech to a law school audience, a judge criticizes the reluctance of the government of the day to recognize same-sex marriage.

Do any of these situations—all of which actually occurred in Canada—violate
judicial independence?

To answer this question, we must of course first know what is meant by 'judicial independence'. What does it require, why is it important, and how do we
protect it in Canada? This chapter discusses these central questions, and the complex relationship between independence and judicial accountability: is it possible
to 'enable judges to render decisions in accordance with their view of the law and
the facts without concern for the consequences to themselves' but still ensure
meaningful answerability for their actions? And what are the implications for
independence and accountability when judges shift from their traditional 'adjudicatory' role toward policy- and law-making?

Impartiality versus Independence

As noted in Chapter 1, judicial independence is the foundational concept of adjudication or any other 'triadic' dispute-resolution mechanism. Simply put, adjudication requires that the third party who resolves the decision must be independent of the other two parties. That is, he or she must be in a position to be *impartial*, or neutral as to the outcome of the dispute. We would probably not trust a ruling in favour of party A if we knew that the judge was A's wife or best friend. Similarly, if a judge ruled in favour of a corporation in a costly civil suit, we would question the legitimacy of that ruling if we discovered that the judge owned a lot of stock in the company and stood to lose a large amount of money if the corporation lost. In *R. v. Valente* (1985), the first major case involving judicial independence brought under s. 11(d) of the Charter of Rights and Freedoms, Justice Le Dain usefully distinguished between independence and impartiality, while stressing their intimate connection:

> Although there is obviously a close relationship between independence and impartiality, they are nevertheless separate and distinct values or requirements. Impartiality refers to a state of mind or attitude of the tribunal in relation to the issues and the parties in a particular case. The word 'impartial' . . . connotes absence of bias, actual or perceived. The word 'independent' . . . reflects or embodies the traditional constitutional value of judicial independence. As such, it connotes not merely a state of mind or attitude in the actual exercise of judicial functions, but a status or relationship to others, particularly to the executive branch of government, that rests on objective conditions or guarantees. (1985, para. 15)

Impartiality, in other words, refers to a subjective frame of mind, whereas independence refers to more objective (or external) institutional relations between courts and other actors which *permit* such impartiality (or, in R. MacGregor Dawson's more colourful phrase, judges should be 'placed in a position where [they have] nothing to lose by doing what is right and little to gain by doing what is wrong' (1954, 486)).

Though it is important for judges to approach cases as impartially as possible, it is equally important that they *appear* to do so. As the old saying goes, 'justice must not only be done; it must also be seen to be done.'[2] Justice Le Dain, who addressed this point in *Valente* (1985, para. 12–13), established the standard that to be valid, an apprehension of bias must be 'reasonable', that is, that a reasonable person, fully informed of the issues and viewing the situation realistically and practically, would conclude that the judge could not make an independent and impartial adjudication. It is debatable whether this standard actually clarifies the matter for a layperson, but it is other judges (on appeal or in a disciplinary hearing), not laypersons, who ultimately decide if there is a 'reasonable apprehension of bias'. In other words, the 'reasonable person' referred to by Justice Le Dain is inevitably a judge, and judges are assumed to be reasonable people (although judges nevertheless disagree with one another about what is 'reasonable').[3]

The primary concern today is judicial independence *from government*, although impartiality still requires judges not to have extensive connections to private parties appearing before them. Governments pass the laws enforced by courts, appoint and (in extraordinary circumstances) remove judges, authorize funding for court infrastructure and legal aid, and appear in court more than any other class of litigant. And because courts are an organ of the state, judicial salaries are paid by the government from public revenues. All of this means that there is an uncomfortable potential for courts to appear institutionally too close—and possibly vulnerable—to government. This becomes particularly problematic in light of the modern function of courts, which includes enforcing limits on the government (another crucial part of the rule of law). The most familiar of these limits are the constitutional rights contained in the 1982 Charter of Rights and Freedoms (which, for example, forbid unreasonable discrimination or censorship by the state) and the federal division of powers, but there are many others, including aboriginal rights, statutory human rights codes, and especially in the criminal law, common law protections developed by the courts. Although 'checks and balances' is an American term, Canadians have largely adopted the idea that courts should act as a 'check' on the elected government and that this function requires a certain amount of institutional separation between the two—what we call judicial independence.

Before we detail some of the institutional requirements of judicial independence, it is important to recognize that, as Russell (2001, 6–8) notes, political scientists refer to two concepts of judicial independence. The first, which is a *relational* concept, refers to the formal institutional protections for judges, both individually and collectively, from interference by other individuals and institutions in the political system. The second is a *behavioural* concept; that is, it refers to actual judicial behaviour and whether it clearly displays autonomous decision making. The two concepts are obviously related, as it is widely believed that institutional protections foster autonomous behaviour while a lack of institutional independence will deter it.[4] However, we know from international examples that the relationship is not that simple or automatic. Some courts that have strong institutional protections, such as Japan's, nevertheless exhibit little autonomy from the ruling government (O'Brien and Ohkoski 2001; Ramseyer and Rasmusen 2003); others—ironically including England, the 'original' example of judicial independence—have formidable judges with relatively weak institutional protections. The fact of the matter is that we have an incomplete understanding of how institutional independence actually affects judicial behaviour, and how much of the former is necessary to ensure that judges will uphold the rule of law by resolving disputes fairly and by enforcing limits on government. This point is revisited near the end of the chapter. For now, let us turn to the main features of institutional independence and how they are secured in Canada.

What Does Judicial Independence Require?

It is important to begin by recognizing that there is no single definition of 'judicial independence' that is universally agreed upon by either judges or academics, and thus, no universally accepted set of comprehensive criteria (Russell 2001, 1). There are, however, some features which are commonly accepted, and which roughly parallel those identified by the Supreme Court of Canada in *Valente*. These are job security (or 'tenure'), financial security, and some measure of administrative control by the judges themselves over the workings of the court, although the precise nature of this last aspect of independence is more contested than the other two. It is also well established that judicial independence has both an individual and collective dimension; that is, it must protect not only individual judges, but also the judiciary as a whole. It is axiomatic that job security is essential if judges are to be impartial—and *seen* to be impartial—in their rulings, particularly in cases involving other branches of the state. The judge who fears removal simply for deciding against the government of the day has much to lose personally, and a reasonable person would rightly question the fairness of rulings that favoured the government. As this example implies, job security does not mean that judges must be permitted to serve indefinitely (or until death), just that they should be insulated against removal at the whim of the government. Accordingly, pre-set age or term limits do not violate judicial independence, but *renewable* term limits which are at the discretion of the government—as is common in continental European high courts—arguably do. As Friedland writes, 'the ability of the government to extend a term is not significantly different from the ability of the government to curtail a term. Both put pressure on the judge to favour the government' (1995, 41). As well, job security does not mean that judges cannot ever be removed from office, but the process must make removal extremely difficult and require reasons—supported by evidence—that are as severe as misconduct (including unethical behaviour), incapacity, or gross incompetence.

Similarly, it is common sense that judicial independence would be threatened if the salaries of judges were vulnerable to cuts by the government for any reason of its choosing. Independence in a democratic state is also commonly held to require that judicial salaries be set by the government (which is responsible for public spending), but for the entire group of judges rather than for individual judges (McCormick 1994, 841). The salary issue nicely exemplifies the distinction between the individual and collective dimensions of independence. If a single judge's salary were to be cut because the government was unhappy with that judge's rulings, this would clearly violate judicial independence. But it is equally problematic if *all* judges' salaries were cut simultaneously and by the same amount if it was intended to punish the courts for, say, repeatedly constraining the government in cases involving human rights or for issuing sentences in criminal trials that the government felt were too lenient. As these examples suggest, however, the rationale for the government's actions is important, because reasonable people may well find across-the-board salary cuts (or freezes) justifiable and non-threatening to judges in certain circumstances. This issue is explored in greater detail later in the chapter.

As a separate branch of the state, there is a strong argument for what Justice Le Dain characterized in *Valente* as 'the institutional independence of the tribunal [court] with respect to matters of administration bearing directly on the exercise of its judicial function' (para. 47). While noting the lack of consensus among existing studies on the matter, he concluded that 'judicial control . . . over assignment of judges, sittings of the court and court lists—as well as the related matters of allocation of court rooms and direction of the administrative staff engaged in carrying out these functions—has generally been considered the essential or minimum requirement for institutional or 'collective' independence' (para. 49). Some, such as Deschênes (1981) and former Chief Justices Bora Laskin and Brian Dickson (cited in *Valente*, para. 50), argue for an even more expansive definition of *administrative autonomy*, including preparing the court's budget and allocating related expenditures, and the recruitment, classification, promotion, remuneration, and supervision of support staff. When it ruled in the 1985 *Valente* case, the Supreme Court (like the Canadian Judicial Council (see below under 'Removal of Federally Appointed Judges'), which had commissioned Deschênes's report) did not agree that such additional powers were essential to judicial independence, but such issues are likely to resurface (McCormick 2004b). Indeed, in its 2006 report *Alternative Models of Court Administration*, the Canadian Judicial Council (CJC)—an organization representing federally appointed judges—called for replacing the 'executive model' currently in place with greater judicial autonomy over court budgets and administration, while acknowledging that such autonomy raises concerns over budgetary accountability (see the discussion near the end of this chapter regarding judicial accountability). It is also worth noting that, ironically, administrative or collective independence carries a potential threat to the independence of individual judges. Of particular concern is the influence of Chief Justices, which may create situations where an individual judge fears negative repercussions for defying his or her immediate superior (a concern that has been mitigated in recent years on some courts by having Chief Justices serve for limited, fixed, and non-renewal terms and allowing judges of the court to participate in the selection of their Chief). There is also some concern that the growing trend toward judicial peer review on issues of salaries and discipline, which is discussed below, poses a threat to individual independence.

McCormick (2004b) identifies three additional components of judicial independence as it developed in the Anglo-American tradition to which Canada belongs. First, judges are not answerable to the bureaucracy for judicial matters; that is, the sole justification for judicial rulings appears in their oral or written decisions. Second, as originally noted by Shapiro (1981), judges are drawn from or part of an 'aggressively independent legal profession'. Lawyers in Canada are a largely self-regulated profession, with tight controls over who is permitted to join and remain members of the bar, and s. 97 and s. 98 of the *Constitution Act, 1867* (see Box 6.1 below) and similar provisions in various statutes require judges to be members. Third, judges traditionally adhered to 'formalistic' decision making that maximized deference to Parliament, even allowing for the high degree of judicial creativity inherent in the common law (McCormick 2004b, 842). This meant that judges applied statutes without significantly modifying them, and any disputes about what the law meant were resolved by reference to the actual text. Thus, 'the judicial role was internally and voluntarily constrained', which limited the adverse consequences for the government of judicial independence (McCormick 2004b, 842).

Judicial Independence in Canada

The main provisions guaranteeing judicial independence in Canada are contained in constitutional law (both from 1867 and 1982), statute law, and common law (judicial decisions), the last of which includes a recent controversial ruling by the Supreme Court of Canada (*Remuneration Reference* 1997) recognizing an 'unwritten constitutional principle of judicial independence' rooted in our British origins. Judicial independence was 'invented' in England in 1701 with the *Act of Settlement* (McCormick 2004b, 839)—at least for a very few judges[5]—and it provided that judicial appointments were valid *quamdiu se bene gesserint* (Latin for 'during good behaviour') and that judges who misbehaved could be removed only by both Houses of Parliament. Upon Confederation in 1867, Canada explicitly reproduced the main provisions of British judicial independence in sections 97 to 100 of the *B.N.A. Act* (later the *Constitution Act, 1867*). Notably, the provision guaranteeing tenure (s. 99) applies only to the 'superior' courts, which, as we saw in Chapter 2, were originally just the s. 96 higher trial and appeal courts in each province that were appointed by the federal government. This of course excluded the (now defunct) s. 96 county and district courts, as well as the provincially appointed s. 92 courts.

Box 6.1   Protections for Judicial Independence in Canada

Constitutional Law

Act of Settlement, 1701 (England)—judges' commissions are valid *quamdiu se bene gesserint* (during good behaviour), and if they do not behave themselves they can be removed only by both Houses of Parliament.

Constitution Act, 1867

97.   Until the Laws relative to Property and Civil Rights in Ontario, Nova Scotia, and New Brunswick, and the Procedure of the Courts in those Provinces, are made uniform, the Judges of the Courts of those Provinces appointed by the Governor General shall be selected from the respective Bars of those Provinces.

98.   The Judges of the Courts of Quebec shall be selected from the Bar of that Province.

99.   (1) Subject to subsection two of this section, the Judges of the Superior Courts shall hold office during good behaviour, but shall be removable by the Governor General on Address of the Senate and House of Commons.

(2) A Judge of a Superior Court, whether appointed before or after the coming into force of this section, shall cease to hold office upon attaining the age of seventy-five years, or upon the coming into force of this section if at that time he has already attained that age.

100.   The Salaries, Allowances, and Pensions of the Judges of the Superior, District, and County Courts (except the Courts of Probate in Nova Scotia and New Brunswick), and of the Admiralty Courts in Cases where the Judges thereof are for the Time being paid by Salary, shall be fixed and provided by the Parliament of Canada.

Charter of Rights and Freedoms, 1982

11.   Any person charged with an offence has the right

d)   to be presumed innocent until proven guilty according to law in a fair and public hearing by an independent and impartial tribunal [*applies only in criminal trials*]

Federal Statutes

Canadian Bill of Rights, R.S.C. 1960, c. 44, C-12.3

2.   . . . no law of Canada shall be construed or applied so as to

f)   deprive a person charged with a criminal offence of the right to be presumed innocent until proved guilty according to law in a fair and public hearing by an independent and impartial tribunal, or of the right to reasonable bail without just cause

Judges Act, R.S.C. 1985, c. J-1 [now protects salaries as well]
Federal Courts Act, R.S., 1985, c. F-7
Supreme Court Act, R.S., 1985, c. S-26

Provincial Statutes and Regulations (may be several in each province)
Ex: *Courts of Justice Act*, R.S.O. 1990, c. C.43 (Ontario)
Alberta Provincial Judges Compensation Commission Regulation, Alta. Reg. 111/2006

Common Law Doctrines
The Rule of Law—the government must act through recognized legal channels (Parliament) and not arbitrarily, and is bound by its own laws, as enforced by an independent judiciary.

'Unwritten constitutional principle' implied in preamble to 1867 Constitution (*Remuneration Reference*)

Other case law (see Box 6.2)

Whether the federally appointed s. 101 courts, including the Supreme Court of Canada, are protected by ss. 99 and 100 remains a matter of some debate. Lederman (1956) states emphatically that they are, since they are clearly designated as 'superior courts' in the statutes that authorize their creation (the *Federal Courts Act* and *Supreme Court Act*).[6] The courts have been almost silent on this issue, but in one trial-level case (*Addy v. Canada* 1985), the Federal Court of Canada ruled that s. 99 applied to federal as well as provincial superior courts. In any case, the independence of the s. 101 courts is explicitly guaranteed by federal statutes—the *Federal Courts Act* and *Supreme Court Act*—which contain provisions mirroring ss. 97 to 100.

As noted, however, it is unequivocal that the 1867 protections do not apply to the s. 92 courts. This became highly problematic as they acquired almost exclusive jurisdiction over criminal trials (where the state, or 'Crown', is a party to the case), and a significant family law caseload. A Royal Commission report by Ontario's Chief Justice James McRuer in 1968 blasted that province's lack of formal protections for provincially appointed judges (and justices of the peace and administrative tribunals), after finding widespread patronage appointments, judicial under-education, and salary tampering by government officials (Ontario 1968). McRuer's report led to sweeping statutory reforms of Ontario's judicial system, which were emulated in the other provinces (Greene 2006, 81-2). The constitutional shortcomings of the independence of s. 92 courts, at least in criminal law, were corrected in 1982 by the adoption of s. 11(d) of the Charter of Rights and Freedoms, which guarantees those charged with an offence a trial by an 'independent and impartial tribunal [court]'. S. 92 courts that hear civil law, however, remained constitutionally unprotected, but in many provinces, the same s. 92 court hears both criminal and civil cases. Notably, s. 11(d) echoes a similar guarantee in the statutory *Canadian Bill of Rights, 1960* (s. 2(f)), but the leading compendium of Canadian constitutional law (Hogg 2003) lists no cases in which the independence of a s. 92 court was challenged under this provision.[7] Most of the case law on judicial (as distinct from administrative tribunal) independence since 1982 has concerned the s. 92 courts and the practical implications of s. 11(d).

Box 6.2   Leading Canadian Cases on Judicial Independence

Landreville v. Canada, [1977] 1 F.C. 419—Federal Court (Trial Division) decision rejecting Justice Landreville's argument that s. 99 was violated when the government appointed an inquiry before a Joint Address of Parliament; the ruling was not appealed.

R. v. Valente, [1985] 2 S.C.R. 673—Whether s. 92 court judges in Ontario are 'independent and impartial tribunals' under s. 11(d) of the Charter (see discussion above).

Beauregard v. Canada, [1986] 2 S.C.R. 56—Supreme Court ruling that the federal government did not violate s. 100 by requiring judges to contribute to their own pension plans.

Mackeigan v. Hickman, [1989] 2 S.C.R. 796—Judges cannot be compelled by Royal Commissions to testify about their past decisions.

R. v. Lippé, [1991] 2 S.C.R. 114—It does not undermine judicial impartiality or its appearance if part-time municipal court judges in Quebec maintain a private legal practice.

R. v. Généreux, [1992] 1 S.C.R. 259—The ad hoc nature of General Courts Martial does not satisfy the conditions of judicial independence laid down in *Valente*.

Gratton v. Canadian Judicial Council, [1994] 2 F.C. 769 (Federal Court, Trial Division)—Permanent incapacity due to infirmity or sickness prevents a judge from holding office 'during good behaviour' and is therefore legitimate grounds for removal; the decision affirmed Parliament's authority to delegate investigation of complaints to the Canadian Judicial Council.

Ruffo v. Conseil de la magistrature, [1995] 4 S.C.R. 267—The chief judge's authority to file a complaint with a judicial council against a judge of his own court does not violate the principles of judicial impartiality and independence guaranteed by s. 7 of the Charter.

Remuneration Reference, [1997] 3 S.C.R. 3—Judicial independence is an 'unwritten constitutional principle', and changes to judicial salaries must be approved by an independent judicial compensation commission and, if they are not, must be reasonably justified to a court of law.

Canada (Minister of Citizenship and Immigration) v. Tobiass, [1997] 3 S.C.R. 391—Meetings between a government official and a chief justice regarding delays in judicial proceedings interfere with judicial independence.

Re Therrien, [2001] 2 S.C.R. 3—Following the *Valente* ruling on s. 11(d) of Charter, Quebec did not require a legislative vote to remove a provincial court judge. Judge Therrien argued that the 'unwritten constitutional principle' of judicial independence required a legislative vote, and s. 11(d) must conform if the unwritten principle provided broader protection. The Supreme Court disagreed, also establishing that the standard contained in s. 11(d) should be used for both civil and criminal cases in inferior courts.

Ocean Port Hotel v. British Columbia (General Manager, Liquor Control and Licensing Branch), [2001] 2 S.C.R. 781—The legislative branch determines an administrative tribunal's degree of independence, and when the intention of legislature is unequivocal, courts must not import common law doctrines of judicial independence.

Moreau-Bérubé v. New Brunswick (Judicial Council), [2002] 1 S.C.R. 249—Independent disciplinary commissions may recommend stiffer discipline than that of the initial inquiry panel, in this case, removal rather than reprimand.

Mackin v. New Brunswick, [2002] 1 S.C.R. 405—Abolition of supernumerary (semi-retired) status for provincial court judges and requiring current supernumerary judges to adopt full-time workload or retire does not violate 'unwritten principle' of judicial independence.

Ell v. Alberta, [2003] 1 S.C.R. 857—Removing current justices of the peace who do not meet newly enacted job qualifications does not violate their independence, because the new criteria were rationally designed by an independent Judicial Council to enhance public confidence in the justice system.

Provincial Court Judges' Assn. of New Brunswick v. New Brunswick (Minister of Justice); Ontario Judges' Assn. v. Ontario (Management Board); Bodner v. Alberta; Conférence des juges du Québec v. Quebec (Attorney

General); Minc v. Quebec (Attorney General), [2005] 2 S.C.R. 286— Governmental rejections of judicial compensation commission recommendations accepted when supported by 'reasons that are complete and that deal with the commission's recommendations in a meaningful way'. Also, justices of the peace warrant the same constitutional protections regarding financial security as judges.

Canada (Attorney General) v. Cosgrove, [2007] FCA 103 (F.C.A.)—Provincial Attorneys General cannot bypass the CJC's usual screening procedure for complaints and order a full inquiry into a judge's conduct.

Tenure

Job security is implicated in a variety of issues, including mandatory retirement and removal for incapacity, incompetence, and misconduct. As noted earlier, a mandatory retirement age that applies to all judges of the same court equally does not, in itself, threaten independence since it cannot be construed by any reasonable person as a 'threat' or attempt to influence a judge's decisions. S. 96 judges were appointed for life under s. 99 until 1960, when the Constitution was amended to require retirement at age 75. In Ontario, Nova Scotia, and British Columbia, the federal *Judges Act* permits s. 96 lower-court judges to retire at age 70, but 75 is still the maximum age. Judges of the Supreme Court of Canada and the lower federal s. 101 courts must also retire at age 75, but the age of mandatory retirement is usually lower in the s. 92 provincial courts. In Alberta and Ontario, for example, it is set at 70 and 65 respectively, but it is possible for judges to apply to continue until age 75 with either a part- or full-time workload, often at their full pre-retirement salary. Such 'supernumerary' judges provide an important source of experience, and they help to alleviate personnel shortages without creating long-term financial commitments for governments. In most courts, however, this continuation is subject to annual reappointment, usually by the Chief Justice of that court. From the perspective of judicial independence, though this practice is preferable to leaving reappointment to the Attorney General, it does raise the spectre, discussed above, of intra-judicial violations associated with collective independence.

A more overt threat to independence is the ability to remove a judge from office. As noted earlier, the very first form of independence established in England in 1701 entailed protecting judges from arbitrary removal. Until the 1970s, however, provincially and federally appointed 'inferior court' judges in Canada could in practice be removed simply by order of the provincial Attorney General (Greene 2006, 100); the practice was only declared unconstitutional in the 1985

Valente decision. Though judges were not frequently removed, 'certainly more than a handful were' according to Greene (2006, 100). Superior court judges, as noted above, were guaranteed tenure by s. 99 of the 1867 *Constitution Act*.

The requirement of 'bad behaviour' on the part of the superior court judge before removal by a joint address of Parliament introduces a large measure of uncertainty, however. What exactly constitutes 'bad behaviour', which is not defined in the Constitution? Presumably this cannot be defined by the government of the day since this would provide little independence for judges facing a government with a partisan majority in both Houses (although one cannot assume the appointed Senate would follow the House of Commons). The implication is that 'bad behaviour' is best determined (either alone or in collaboration with Parliament) by some party independent of the executive branch. The Supreme Court of Canada came to the same conclusion in *Valente*: 'the essentials of security of tenure for purposes of s. 11(d) of the Charter [are] that the judge be removable only for cause, and that cause be subject to *independent review and determination* by a process at which the judge affected is afforded a full opportunity to be heard' (para. 31, emphasis added). As Canada's parliamentary system subordinates the legislative branch to the cabinet executive, this leaves only one obvious option to conduct an 'independent review': the judiciary itself.

In what will become a recurring theme in this chapter, judicial peer review has emerged as one of the major trends in the last four decades of judicial politics. The first 'judicial council' in Canada was established in Ontario in 1968, the federal Canadian Judicial Council shortly afterwards in 1971, and councils were created in all of the provinces except Prince Edward Island by the mid-1980s.[8] Composed of senior judges[9] from the respective federally or provincially appointed courts (and in some cases, also lawyers and laypersons), judicial councils perform a wide range of tasks associated with judicial administration; they emerged from a desire to introduce a buffer between individual judges and the government. They are responsible for conducting judicial education, nominating candidates for appointment, identifying problems with court administration and recommending improvements, and, since 1997, making salary recommendations (see the next section). One of their primary tasks, however, is to handle complaints against judges—including allegations of unethical behaviour, incompetence, and incapacity due to permanent disability—and to make recommendations to Parliament or the provincial government regarding removal or other disciplinary measures permitted by law.

McCormick writes, 'The very best way to approach the problem of judicial discipline is to appoint judges who do not need to be disciplined. . . . The best disciplinary mechanism is a ruthless and rigorous appointment process; everything else is backstop' (1998b, 113). While he makes a good point, human fallibility makes it inevitable that a system for investigating complaints and recommending disciplinary action will be necessary. Judicial peer review offers an appealing option, partly because it lessens the threat to judicial independence from the other branches, but also because it leaves the assessment of judicial conduct to those most familiar with the requirements of the job. This is not to say that discipline by judicial councils is unproblematic. Judges may be reluctant to discipline each other, which helps explain the practice of appointing both judges and non-judges to a judicial council—a practice followed only partially in Canada, but found in all European civil law countries, whose councils mostly predate Canada's (Guarnieri and Pederzoli 2002, 165). Judicial peer review also creates the potential for another instance of 'collective' independence violating the independence of an individual judge. This is particularly the case when the Chief Justice of a court files a complaint with a judicial council against one of his or her own colleagues, seeking his or her removal. That occurred in *Ruffo* (1995, discussed below) and *Gratton* (1994). In *Gratton*, the Chief Justice of the Ontario Court of Justice (a s. 96 court, later renamed the Superior Court of Justice) sought to remove Justice Fernand Gratton because the latter had been unable to perform his duties for over eighteen months due to various medical problems, including a severe and debilitating stroke. When the CJC began an inquiry, Justice Gratton challenged this on the grounds that Parliament could not 'delegate' its authority to remove judges under s. 99 and that infirmity was not a valid ground for removal since it did not violate 'good behaviour'. As noted in Box 6.2, the Federal Court trial judge ruled against Gratton on both issues, and Gratton resigned shortly thereafter, ending the CJC's inquiry. In this case, the Chief Justice's actions were proper, and since Gratton was not actually hearing cases, owing to his infirmity, his independence and impartiality on the bench were not really threatened. Notably, in a report for the CJC a decade later, Friedland (1995, 262) recommended treating judicial incapacity due to illness or infirmity differently from misconduct, in part because disability or illness may be temporary, while removal through impeachment is effectively permanent. Instead, he preferred that such cases be treated as they are in the rest of society, through long-term disability status and appointment of a replacement while leaving the determination of incapacity in the hands of fellow judges (as is the practice in the US federal courts). Today, though the CJC can still recommend removal on grounds of incapacity, the government can grant a leave of absence with full pay for as long it (but not the judge or her peers) deems appropriate (*Judges Act*, s. 66(2)). However, since Gratton, this has not occurred for any federally appointed judge.

Of greater concern than incapacity is judicial misconduct, which also arises more often, though it is still quite rare. The types of misconduct that have received the most media attention include apparent bias (for example, sexist or racist comments during the trial,[10] or taking a political stand off the bench), inappropriate conduct (especially towards court staff[11]), and conflicts of interest.[12] However, more common complaints include judicial treatment of litigants, delays in rendering decisions, and criticizing other judges or higher-court judgments. Removal of a judge for misconduct is extremely rare in Canada. The following sections consider, in turn, removal for federally appointed judges, removal of provincially appointed judges, and two disciplinary issues that have emerged in the past three decades—judicial codes of conduct and discipline short of removal.

Removal of Federally Appointed Judges

Among federal appointments, no judge has ever been removed for misconduct, but it has almost happened on two occasions. The first instance, and the closest we have come to removal, involved Judge Leo Landreville in Ontario in the 1960s. After his appointment to the bench, allegations arose that Landreville had received 'kickbacks' when he was the mayor of Sudbury from a natural gas distributor for whom Landreville's city council approved a franchise. Charges were laid against him but were dismissed by a judge at the preliminary hearing (see Chapter 9); however, rumours and allegations of wrong-doing persisted, particularly in the legal community. At the urging of the Law Society of Upper Canada, which advocated Landreville's removal, the federal Minister of Justice appointed a Royal Commission—consisting of a single justice of the Supreme Court of Canada, Ivan Rand—to examine the matter and make a recommendation regarding impeachment. Rand concluded that Landreville 'has proven himself unfit for the proper exercise of his judicial functions' (in Friedland 1995, 85), and a special joint committee of the House of Commons and Senate met nineteen times, interviewing Landreville extensively in eleven meetings. It too recommended impeachment, and the then Minister of Justice, Pierre Trudeau, tabled a resolution for removal in June 1967. Still protesting his innocence, Landreville resigned at this point, thus ending the impeachment proceedings, although he successfully challenged, through the courts, Rand's conduct—which was often unprofessional (Russell 1987, 180)—and jurisdiction during the inquiry. The authority of Parliament to conduct such an inquiry, however, was upheld (*Landreville v. The Queen (No. 2)*, 1977). Political dissatisfaction with how the matter was handled led to the creation in 1971 of the CJC, which has statutorily defined jurisdiction and uses panels of more than one judge to investigate complaints.

The CJC's first full inquiry was held in 1981, when it investigated a complaint (by another judge) about criticism voiced during a convocation address by BC Supreme Court judge Thomas Berger of the Trudeau government's proposed constitutional amendment package for not recognizing aboriginal treaty rights. (The subsequent amendment in 1982 did enshrine those rights, in s. 35.) The CJC found that Berger's comments were 'indiscreet' but did not warrant removal (he resigned anyway) and that judges should avoid criticizing politicians from off the bench. But it rejected the position of its own committee of inquiry that in the future removal should be required in similar circumstances. Though Russell (1987, 87) agrees that Berger displayed poor judgment, he observes that subjecting him to an unprecedented level of investigation 'in circumstances when it may appear that such a procedure was adopted under pressure from the prime minister, also showed questionable political judgement' and may have itself violated

Berger's independence. The issue of judicial off-bench commentary is discussed later in this chapter in the section headed 'Is Judicial Independence a "Two-Way Street"?' The only time the CJC has recommended that Parliament remove a judge was in the case of Justice Jean Bienvenue of the Superior Court of Quebec, who made sexist and anti-Semitic comments while presiding over a case, and who afterwards demonstrated 'an aggravating lack of sensitivity to the communities and individuals offended by his remarks or conduct' (Canadian Judicial Council 1997, 70). Before Parliament could vote on whether to impeach him, Bienvenue retired in 1996 with his pension intact.

This is not to say that there have not been additional cases of misconduct by federally appointed judges. In 1999, Justice Robert Flahiff of the Superior Court of Quebec resigned after his conviction for laundering money ($1.6 million) from narcotics trafficking, thereby ending the CJC's inquiry. In 2002, Justice Bernard Flynn, also of the Quebec Superior Court, was investigated by the CJC for comments he made to the media regarding a property transaction that involved his wife and a municipal government.[13] While the inquiry found Flynn's statements 'inappropriate and unacceptable' because they violated 'his duty to act in a reserved manner', it did not recommend his removal from the bench.

The Bienvenue and Flahiff incidents highlight the problem that federally appointed judges can retire or resign (with pension intact as in Bienvenue's case) before the inquiry and removal processes have run their course. It would be preferable for the CJC to be able to hear such matters to their conclusion, in part to establish standards of conduct for others and to enhance the transparency of, and public confidence in, the complaints process.

Most recently, in 2004 the Attorney General of Ontario ordered the CJC to conduct an inquiry into Justice Paul Cosgrove of the Ontario Superior Court for his bizarre conduct in a murder case. Cosgrove demonstrated apparent bias in favour of the accused and stayed the case in 1999 on the grounds that the Crown, police, immigration officials, and even forensic scientists had committed over 150 Charter violations during a complex conspiracy against the accused (*R. v. Elliot* 1999). The Ontario Court of Appeal overturned the ruling in *Elliot*, but Cosgrove challenged in the Federal Courts the provincial Attorney General's power to order the CJC to initiate a full inquiry of a s. 96 court judge.[14] The FCA confirmed what the CJC had decided for itself in a previous inquiry (involving Justice Boilard—see below), that the commission can summarily dismiss a provincial Attorney General's complaint 'if it is obviously unmeritorious or does not disclose judicial conduct warranting removal from office' (*Cosgrove v. Canadian Judicial Council* 2007).[15] This change also echoes Friedland's recommendation to the CJC (1995, 265), including retaining the *federal* Minister of Justice's power to demand a full inquiry by the CJC, since Ottawa is formally responsible for appointing and disciplining s. 96 and s. 101 court judges. In November 2007, the Supreme Court of Canada refused Cosgrove's application for leave to appeal the FCA's ruling, and the CJC resumed its inquiry.

Despite the fact that relatively few full inquiries have been conducted by the CJC since 1971, complaints against federally appointed judges are not uncommon; however their number is tiny in comparison to the tens of thousands of decisions made by these judges each year. Since 1996, there have been between roughly 150 and 200 complaints filed per year, usually by litigants (half of all complaints arise from family law proceedings (CJC 2002, 15)) but also by fellow judges, Attorneys General, and occasionally politicians. The vast majority of complaints are dismissed early in the screening process for being completely baseless or for pertaining to matters that are properly appealed to a higher court rather than a judicial council (usually these are allegations of judicial error). In addition to the cases cited above, there have been some instances of judges resigning or retiring while the CJC was deliberating on whether to conduct a full inquiry, but on the whole, the complaints statistics suggest that Canada's superior court judges have conducted themselves in a highly professional manner. As further evidence of this, the number of complaints has remained fairly stable over the past decade, even though 'increasing numbers of self-represented litigants have appeared before judges, individuals have become more conscious of their rights generally, and the opportunity to register complaints with the Council has become better known' (CJC 2002, 14).

A final point worth noting about the federal impeachment process is that it requires a final stage never reached in our history: the Governor General must *accept* the joint address of Parliament requesting removal. Though he or she presumably would, this separate step does add a check against egregious abuses of parliamentary power. A Governor General who invoked this check would almost certainly spark a constitutional crisis, however, and further litigation on the matter would be virtually certain.

Removal of Provincially Appointed Judges

Alberta Premier Ralph Klein caused a considerable stir in 1994 when he commented on a popular call-in radio program that 'whoever appoints should be able to un-appoint. . . . It seems to me if we have the power to hire, then we ought to have the power to fire' (in Renke 1998, 121).[16] While Klein did not act on these sentiments, provincially appointed judges have been removed more often than their federally appointed counterparts, particularly before the adoption of the Charter of Rights and Freedoms and the *Valente* decision. Even today, removal procedures are easier than those laid out in s. 99 for federally appointed judges. According to *Valente*, although the removal procedure requires an independent assessment of the impugned judge's conduct, in which the judge is permitted to present his or her perspective, a legislative vote is not necessary to protect judicial independence. In fact, only in Ontario does the legislature have to approve the judicial council's recommendation to remove a judge. Elsewhere, either final authority over removal rests with the provincial Attorney General and cabinet, or, as in Manitoba and British Columbia, the judicial council's recommendation is *binding* on the government (so that a judge is prevented from resigning before the government can act). Since *Valente*, removals of provincially appointed judges have occurred, but they are rare. Some notable examples in recent years include the following cases:

- Jocelyne Moreau-Bérubé was removed in New Brunswick in 2002 for characterizing the majority of Acadians in her area as 'drunks', 'crooked', and 'dishonest'.
- Richard Therrien was removed in Quebec that same year for failing to disclose during his application for judicial appointment that he had been arrested in 1970 for illegally assisting the FLQ terrorists who had just murdered Pierre Laporte (although he had been pardoned and his conviction 'vacated' in 1987).
- In 2005 the Quebec Court of Appeal, echoing a recommendation from Quebec's judicial council (Conseil de la magistrature), urged the government to remove controversial family court judge Andrée Ruffo for her latest breach of judicial ethics in a long career of such violations and disregard for the law.[17] She resigned in 2006 after the Supreme Court of Canada refused to hear her appeal and before the government could remove her.

Like federally appointed Justice Bienvenue, some provincial court judges simply resign before they can be removed. Two examples of this occurred in 2004, the first when Ontario judge Kerry Evans resigned before a full inquiry of the judicial council could be held but after a preliminary investigation heard testimony from several female members of the courthouse staff that Evans had sexually harassed them. In British Columbia, Judge David Ramsay resigned shortly before pleading guilty to multiple counts of sexual assault and having sex with a minor, for which he received a seven-year sentence.

Judicial Codes of Conduct

The removal of Judge Ruffo illustrates an important development with respect to judicial discipline and accountability: the emergence of judicial *codes of conduct* or *codes of ethics*. In Ruffo's case, the ultimate justification given for her removal was her repeated violations of Quebec's Code of Ethics, which was adopted in 1981, following British Columbia's 1976 'Code of Judicial Ethics'. Quebec's code, for example, sets out the following ten rules:[18]

1. The judge should render justice within the framework of the law.
2. The judge should perform the duties of his office with integrity, dignity and honour.
3. The judge has a duty to foster his professional competence.

4. The judge should avoid any conflict of interest and refrain from placing himself in a position where he cannot faithfully carry out his functions.
5. The judge should be, and be seen to be, impartial and objective.
6. The judge should perform the duties of his office diligently and devote himself entirely to the exercise of his judicial functions.
7. The judge should refrain from any activity which is not compatible with his judicial office.
8. In public, the judge should act in a reserved, serene and courteous manner.
9. The judge should submit to the administrative directives of his chief judge, within the performance of his duties.
10. The judge should uphold the integrity and defend the independence of the judiciary, in the best interest of justice and society.

British Columbia's code is very similar, but in addition it emphasizes the need for judicial punctuality when attending hearings and rendering decisions.

Although such codes are viewed by some judges as encroachments on their independence, they establish a written standard by which to assess allegations of judicial misconduct, and thus they bolster judicial accountability. Moreover, the process by which Quebec's code was developed showed considerable sensitivity to the desire to protect judicial independence—it was a shared endeavour of all three branches of state, with the legislature establishing the broad rationale for the code, the judiciary drafting the precise details and overseeing its enforcement through the Conseil de la magistrature, and the executive retaining the power of final approval of the code but without the power to amend it. Nonetheless, most provinces and the federal government have not adopted enforceable judicial codes of ethics, although the CJC (1998) and the Ontario Judicial Council (1996) have published 'guidelines' for their judges.

Discipline Short of Removal

Before her removal, Judge Ruffo had been 'censured' by Quebec's judicial council on several occasions—in effect, reprimanded and instructed not to do it again. This raises another emerging issue in judicial discipline: discipline short of removal. In the absence of a duly authorized and enforceable code of conduct, such practices raise jurisdictional concerns at the federal level since neither Parliament nor the CJC has any clear disciplinary authority beyond removal under s. 99 of the *Constitution Act, 1867*. Nonetheless, the CJC has adopted the practice of criticizing judicial conduct even when that conduct does not, in the council's view, warrant removal. In at least one case, this informal practice had disastrous consequences. The incident involved Quebec Superior Court Justice Jean-Guy Boilard, while he was three months into hearing the very high-profile *Beauchamp* case in 2002—the first prosecution of the Hells Angels under Ottawa's anti-organized crime legislation, for which an entirely new, more secure courthouse had been built. One of the defence lawyers filed a complaint that Boilard had demonstrated bias against his client (in another, unrelated case), and though the CJC found Boilard's conduct was not serious enough to warrant removal from office, the council expressed via an official letter to the judge concern about his conduct. Unfortunately, this was publicized in the media before the judge had read the Council's letter, and Boilard recused himself from the *Beauchamp* case on the grounds that he had lost the 'moral authority' to preside over the court. A new multi-million dollar trial was subsequently ordered, with a considerable waste of time and money. In an ironic epilogue, the Attorney General of Quebec was so infuriated at this turn of events that he ordered the CJC to investigate Boilard for misconduct, but the Council found the judge's recusal was ethically acceptable.

At the provincial level, many jurisdictions have explicitly empowered their judicial councils with a wide range of disciplinary tools short of recommending removal. Ontario's judicial council, for example, can 'warn', 'reprimand', suspend with or without pay (though only for thirty days for the latter, and with benefits), order the judge to apologize to the complainant, or require the judge to receive education or treatment (*Courts of Justice Act*, s. 51.6(11)). Similar provisions exist in most provinces. Notably, in his report to the CJC in the mid-1990s, Martin Friedland (1995, 139–40) argued that the federal CJC should not follow the provincial example and that a written 'expression of disapproval', publicized in the most serious cases, is sufficient sanction if removal is not warranted.

Financial Security

Like job security, financial security for judges is intended to insulate them from threats to one of their most fundamental needs, the ability to earn a living, but also from pressure based on financial incentives. This means that judicial salaries are not subject to arbitrary reduction by the government and also that incentives or rewards cannot be given by the government to only some judges. Furthermore, salaries must be high enough to at least limit judicial susceptibility to bribery by private parties (although this can never be completely eliminated). All of this is similarly true for judicial pensions upon retirement. As Friedland (1995, 263) notes, it is important that judges not be 'not unduly concerned about their financial security and can thus act completely independently, according to their consciences and not their future prospects'.

At the federal level, there have been two major issues that arose regarding financial security. The first was related to s. 100's phrase that judicial salaries 'shall be fixed', with the result that they literally did not move—even to account for inflation, which effectively eroded their value. As Russell (1987, 150–1) notes, there were usually large stretches of time—as much as twenty-six years (1920–46)—between increases by Parliament, even during periods of very high

inflation, as in the 1970s. This problem was corrected in 1981 with an amendment to the *Judges Act* (s. 25(2)) which established automatic annual increases tied
to the industrial 'aggregate' (a composite price index), with a guaranteed annual
raise of 7 per cent. That same year Parliament established the Triennial
Commission, which met every three years to make non-binding salary recommendations to the Minister of Justice for federally appointed judges. This system,
which was considered unsatisfactory by the judges (Friedland 1995, 56–7), has
been replaced by a judicial salary commission as required by the Supreme Court
of Canada in the *Remuneration Reference* (see below).

The second major issue concerned the pensions of federally appointed judges,
the premiums of which were initially paid entirely by the government (that is to
say, taxpayers). This changed in 1975, when Parliament voted that judges should
contribute 6 per cent of their salary toward their own pensions. This was challenged by Quebec Superior Court Justice Marc Beauregard on the grounds that it
violated s. 100, which states that the 'Salaries, Allowances and Pensions' of s. 96
court judges 'shall . . . be provided by the Parliament of Canada.' He argued that
this meant by Parliament *exclusively*, which was the practice from 1867 until 1975.
His case eventually reached the Supreme Court of Canada (*Beauregard v. Canada*
1986), which rejected his argument by citing the 'living tree doctrine' that 'the
Canadian Constitution is not locked forever in a 119-year old casket' (*Beauregard*,
para. 46). Moreover, the Court concluded that s. 100 requires Parliament only to
provide *a* pension but not necessarily *all* of that pension, and that it is widely
accepted in our society that workers should contribute something toward their
own retirement income (*Beauregard*, para. 49).

In the provinces, legislative measures taken after the McRuer Report
improved the financial security of s. 92 court judges but not to the level enjoyed
by their s. 96 and s. 101 counterparts. This fact became evident in the 1990s,
when a number of provincial governments—in particular Alberta, Manitoba, and
Prince Edward Island—reduced all of their judges' salaries, without prior consultation, as part of widespread salary rollbacks of all publicly paid employees.[19] Soon
afterwards, several accused in criminal trials being heard in s. 92 courts challenged
the constitutionality of their proceedings, alleging that because of the salary reduc-
tions, the court was not an 'independent and impartial tribunal' under s. 11(d) of
the Charter. About the same time, the Association of Provincial Court Judges in
Manitoba launched a constitutional challenge, also under s. 11(d), against the
salary cuts, and in Prince Edward Island the government referred the issue to that
province's Appeal Division of the Supreme Court. All of these cases eventually
reached the Supreme Court of Canada, which heard them together in what
became known as the *Remuneration Reference* (1997).

The Supreme Court's ruling in 1997 accepted that judicial salaries could be
reduced if it were done across the board so that individual judges were not targeted, but it surprised even veteran court watchers when it declared that any

changes to judicial salaries (either up or down) must be reviewed by a 'judicial compensation commission' (JCC) 'interposed between the judiciary and the other branches of government' that is 'independent, effective, and objective.' While leaving the precise composition of JCCs (albeit within these criteria) to the executive and legislative branches, the Court ordered that all governments must establish such institutions to prevent the appearance of salary 'negotiation' between judges and governments, and that the existing cuts were unconstitutional because they had not been reviewed by such a body. Finally, JCC recommendations are not binding upon government, but any rejection must be for clearly articulated 'reasonable' grounds, where the courts would ultimately determine what is 'reasonable.'

This was a top-down 'revolution' in the Court's approach to judicial independence (McCormick 2004b), but only one justice (La Forest) dissented. The judicial creation of a constitutionally required institutional reform was itself controversial, but it was rendered even more so by the shaky legal arguments employed by Chief Justice Lamer and endorsed by the majority. Although the cases were based on challenges under s. 11(d) of the Charter—which applies only to criminal matters—the Court's ruling found a broader 'constitutional principle of judicial independence' in the rather unlikely location of the preamble to the *Constitution Act, 1867*. This preamble reads that Canada has a 'Constitution similar in Principle to that of the United Kingdom', and Lamer contended that therefore Britain's long tradition of judicial independence should be shared by all Canadian courts, not just the s. 96 courts recognized in our original Constitution. There are several flaws in this argument, which we will only briefly summarize here. To begin with, preambles are by definition not enforceable rights, let alone a proper legal foundation for mandating wholesale institutional reform. Moreover, Lamer's reasoning resurrects an old legal argument in Canada known the 'implied bill of rights theory' (that is, that rights enjoyed in Britain are implicitly shared by Canadians by virtue of the preamble), which a majority of the Supreme Court had repeatedly rejected since the 1930s. Second, the strong form of judicial independence in Britain applies only to the superior courts (upon which our 'superior' s. 96 and 101 courts were modelled), and not the inferior courts, which are analogous to our s. 92 courts. And, in any case, Britain has never adopted JCCs, so they cannot possibly be part of our constitutional tradition.

As Greene (2006, 91) argues, 'for the judiciary to state that JCCs are required by the Constitution not only underlines the potential scope of judicial discretion but also illustrates its potential for abuse.' Part of the Supreme Court's abuse of its discretion in this case was its decision to apply its entirely new constitutional interpretation retroactively by declaring unconstitutional the salary freezes which had not been vetted by a JCC. Retroactive application of the law violates a central tenet of the rule of law— ironically in this case, since the Court majority argued that a key rationale for judicial independence is the protection of the rule of law (*Remuneration Reference*, para. 10).

Notwithstanding all of this, Greene (2006) suggests that JCCs are 'without a doubt, a good idea', and governments at both the provincial and federal levels quickly moved to establish JCCs and salary review procedures. For example, Parliament passed s. 26(1) of the federal *Judges Act* in 1998, creating the Judicial Compensation and Benefits Commission, which meets every four years to assess judicial salaries. Its three members—one nominated by the judiciary, another by the Minister of Justice, and a third by the other two members—serve fixed terms of four years (but, like federally appointed judges, 'on good behaviour'). The fear that requiring governments that reject a JCC's recommendation to defend their actions to a court 'makes the judges the final arbiters of their own remuneration' (Greene 2006, 91) has been only partially realized. After Ontario's JCC recommended a 55 per cent salary raise (from $110,000 to $170,000) for its s. 92 judges in order to bring them closer to s. 96 court judges, the Ontario government tried to limit the raise to 2 per cent but was overruled in court (Greene 2006, 92; *Ontario Conference of Judges v. Ontario (Chair of Management Board)* 2004). In contrast, in 2005 the Supreme Court of Canada accepted the rationales presented by the governments of Manitoba and Alberta—including that s. 92 court judges perform simpler functions than s. 96 court judges and therefore do not deserve the same pay—for their refusal to implement the steep salary increases recommended by their JCCs (*Provincial Court Judges' Assn. of New Brunswick v. New Brunswick (Minister of Justice); Bodner v. Alberta*, 2005). The Court established the fairly relaxed standard that a government's 'reasons [for not following a JCC recommendation] that are complete and that deal with the commission's recommendations in a meaningful way will meet the standard of rationality' so long as those reasons 'rely upon a reasonable factual foundation' (para. 25).

Though the creation of constitutionally required JCCs was a striking example of judicial activism, which essentially removed legislative control over salaries, it did put an end to concerns that 'inferior' court judges lacked financial security. Though cuts to judicial salaries are not theoretically inconceivable, it would take a truly dire emergency for the government to rationalize such cuts, and let us recall, the recession of the early 1990s was insufficient. Thus, McCormick (2004b, 851) concludes, the salary issue is 'definitively settled.'

Administrative Autonomy

It cannot be said, however, that a myriad of issues related to judicial administration have been settled; those include the role of the Chief Justice, case management, court budgets, courthouse facilities, and human-resource matters pertaining to court support staff. Neither the 1867 Constitution nor the 1982 amendments clearly address the day-to-day administration of the courts. Under s. 92(14) of the *Constitution Act, 1867*, provinces have jurisdiction over the 'Administration of Justice in the Province, including the Constitution, Maintenance, and

Organization of Provincial Courts, both of Civil and of Criminal Jurisdiction,' but it is not clear that this wording implies absolute administrative authority, especially since case assignment to judges, case scheduling, and supervision of court support staff have traditionally been the responsibility of the court itself. Moreover, s. 92(14) applies only to the ss. 92 and 96 'provincial' courts, and not the federal s. 101 courts. In part because of this ambiguity—and also, perhaps more important, the growing assertiveness of the judges themselves—the extent of judicial control over court administration has already begun to emerge as the next big issue in judicial independence (McCormick 2004b; CJC 2006a, Greene 2006).

The key concern is that there is, as Friedland (1995, 175) puts it, 'an 'inherent conflict' when the courts are run by the department that is the chief litigator before the courts' and that court staff experience 'conflicting loyalties' when directed by both the provincial Attorney General's office (for s. 92 and 96 courts, and the Minister of Justice for the federal courts) and the judiciary. In *Valente*, the Supreme Court suggested that the minimum requirements for the 'collective' or institutional independence of the judiciary were judicial control over assignment of judges to cases, sittings of the court, court lists (scheduling of case hearings, which may include docket control for higher appeal courts), allocation of court rooms, and direction of administrative staff engaged in carrying out these functions. The Court also recognized that there 'must necessarily be reasonable management constraints' on judicial self-administration since courts are an expensive publicly funded institution, and a fundamental principle in our system of government—arguably undermined by the *Remuneration Reference* decision—is that elected, accountable governments are responsible for the public purse. Moreover, courts are just one component of the larger system of justice, along with, in the criminal law, police, prosecutors, legal aid, and corrections and, in both criminal and civil law, other dispute-resolution mechanisms (Friedland 1995, 219).

The *Valente* decision regarding administrative independence was, however, at odds with the views of some senior judges (including the then Chief Justice, Brian Dickson) and with the way in which the Supreme Court itself is administered, as well as with subsequent recommendations by the 1987 Zuber Report on judicial administration in Ontario (Ontario 1987) and Friedland's 1995 report for the CJC. The key points of disagreement were the level of judicial control over the preparation of court budgets and distribution of allocated resources, and over human-resources matters such as the hiring and supervision of court support staff. Dickson, perhaps reflecting his own management experience in the military during the Second World War and in private business (Sharpe and Roach 2003), called for full control by chief judges over these matters in a speech to the Canadian Bar Association the same year *Valente* was decided. (Curiously, though, Dickson agreed with Le Dain's more limited view in *Valente*) (Friedland 1995, 179). Rather than empower chief judges to this degree, the Zuber Report called for the creation of a provincial and several regional 'courts management committees' staffed by a

mixture of judges, government representatives, lawyers, and laypersons with control over preparing budgets and human resources. In a similar recommendation
that he made to the CJC, Friedland (1995) argued not only that the huge resources
involved—up to half a *billion* dollars, 4,000 employees and 200 offices in Ontario in
1995 alone—make complete judicial self-administration inappropriate (181), but
also that administrative decisions should be decentralized to 'those who have to live
with them' as much as possible (219). Budget estimates, in particular, should be
prepared initially by the judiciary before going to the Minister of Justice or
Attorney General, Treasury Board, and legislature, although he suggests chief
judges should do this in collaboration with other judges on their court rather than
in isolation (1995, 218–20).

As it currently stands, the Supreme Court of Canada is the most independently
administered court in the country, for since 1977 it has been a separate government
agency with a full-time, tenured registrar trained in administration who assists the
Chief Justice. Since the late 1980s, the Court's budget has been established by the
Court in conjunction with the Treasury Board, the Minister of Justice acting primarily in a politically supportive role (Friedland 1995, 179–80). The lower federal
(s. 101) courts were not granted the same level of independence, though in 1978
they were somewhat insulated from the federal Minister of Justice by the creation
of the Commissioner of Federal Judicial Affairs (CFJA). This is an agency that is at
arm's length from the Minister and is mandated to promote judicial independence
and better administration. This does not protect s. 96 court judges from interference by provincial governments, however, such as when the Quebec government
tried to fire half of the superior court judges' secretaries and most of their ushers,
with no prior consultation, as part of across-the-board cuts to all departments
(Greene 2006, 85).[20] Friedland's proposal to the CJC would have required any such
change to be approved by a judicial management commission staffed to a significant degree by judges themselves, but to date, the federal government has not
adopted his recommended institutional reforms. In 2006, the CJC reiterated its call
for greater collective independence but recognized the need for public accountability over budgeting; it advocated 'limited autonomy for the judiciary within an
overall budget for court administration set by the appropriate legislative authority,'
featuring assignment of professional court administrators to chief justices and an
independent commission 'for the prevention and resolution of disputes related to
the overall size of the budget allocated to the judiciary' (CJC 2006a, 3).

In the provinces, no court has extensive administrative autonomy, although
chief judges (for example, in Ontario) have acquired some direct responsibility for
drafting parts of the court budget and for greater 'human resources functions for
court support staff' (Greene 2006, 85). Since 1993, the chief judge of the (s. 92)
Ontario Court of Justice has had an executive co-ordinator (reporting to the
chief), who helps 'to liaise with senior court services personnel regarding administrative issues' (Greene 2006, 85). Though Ontario did create the committees

recommended by the Zuber Report, it accorded them only advisory, rather than managing, authority. A dispute in 2002 between the provincial chief judge of British Columbia and the government over the latter's unilateral decision to close several courthouses resulted in a negotiated settlement by which the judiciary would be consulted before any future changes to the budget or courthouse administration (McCormick 2004b, 851). This is a far cry, however, from ceding decision making authority over resource management to the judges. McCormick (2004b, 851) reports a similar event in Alberta in 2001, when the Calgary court-house of the Court of Appeal was closed for several months because of health concerns, with the result that the court was unable to function and the provincial government was threatened with legal action. As he notes, ultimately 'neither episode was decided through litigation, but either could have been' (2004b, 851). These are but snapshots of the provincial scene, but there are no comprehensive studies which assess the level of collective independence among the provincial courts. Notably, however, at its annual meeting in August 2007 the Canadian Bar Association passed a resolution calling on provincial and territorial governments to transfer control over court administration to judges.

Other Issues Related to Independence

Judicial independence is, arguably, threatened by several additional issues that do not fit comfortably into the previous three categories. Some (but by no means all) of these, which are addressed briefly below, are a mix of *direct* and *indirect* threats to judicial independence. A direct threat exists when the government tries directly to influence the decision making of sitting judges, *and* can back up its efforts with some form of sanction or punishment. Threats to a judge's continued employ-ment or pay are classic direct threats. Indirect threats, on the other hand, lack any immediate effect—rather, they usually operate to erode judicial legitimacy in such a way as to make direct threats more feasible. The first several of the issues below, for example, represent direct threats to a judge's ability to make decisions impar-tially, whereas the judicial appointment system and public criticism of judges are at worst indirect threats when judges enjoy tenure, financial security, and some measure of administrative autonomy. Others, such as the reference procedure, present both direct and indirect threats to judicial independence.

Judicial Exposure to Civil or Criminal Proceedings
Severe pressure could be brought to bear on individual judges if they were subject to civil suits or criminal prosecution for decisions they made in the course of legit-imately performing their duties. One can imagine civil claims for 'pain and suffer-ing' because of trial delays or adverse child custody decisions, or charges of 'false imprisonment' if judges refused bail for someone ultimately acquitted (Friedland 1995, 37). For this reason, judges in the English tradition have enjoyed immunity

from such proceedings since 1607, and it is now a well-established principle in common law (Friedland 1995, 33). This immunity does not extend, quite rightly, to actions unrelated to their judicial function or to criminal misconduct in office such as accepting bribes.

Politicians Contacting Judges about Cases

The fundamental principle of judicial independence is that judges should be free from interference by state officials when rendering their decisions. It follows logically that members of Parliament and especially cabinet ministers and staff of the Prime Minister's Office should not contact judges directly regarding cases over which they are presiding. Nonetheless, three of Pierre Trudeau's cabinet ministers (including future Prime Minister Jean Chrétien) did so, ultimately prompting him to announce in 1976 a prohibition on such contact on penalty of removal from cabinet (none of the three ministers was removed, however).[21] Prime Minister Jean Chrétien reiterated these guidelines in 1994 while extending them to contact with administrative tribunals (Friedland 1995, 29). Similar prohibitions were introduced in Ontario by Premier William Davis in 1978, and reinforced by Premier Bob Rae in 1990. The prohibition on contacting judges was tested—and upheld—at the federal level when John Munro and Jean Charest resigned their cabinet posts in the Mulroney government after telephoning judges about cases concerning their constituents.

Judicial Education

Unlike some civil law countries, such as France, Canada does not offer training for prospective judges. Rather, people train to be *lawyers*, and only become judges by somehow—through their meritorious reputation or political connections or both—coming to the attention of nominating committees or appointing officials in the political executive (see Chapter 5). Therefore newly appointed judges require some education to be able to perform their duties properly and to avoid misconduct which might result in discipline. Similarly, it is likely that judges require supplemental training in law over the course of their career to keep pace with substantive developments in their fields or as they move into new positions, including judgeships in appellate courts or chief justiceships. Whereas technical training is uncontroversial among judges—so long as it is *directed and conducted* by judges (Friedland 1995, 167)—the same is not true for 'social-context education', which is concerned with sexism, racism, and other forms of discrimination. Some judges, including the Alberta Provincial Judges' Association in 1991, have complained publicly that such education violates judicial independence when it is taught with a 'unilateral' or one-sided view, or by civil society actors who also appear as litigants before the court (Morton and Knopff 2000, 127). These complaints appear to focus on the inclusion of feminist legal academics who are also members of LEAF (the Women's Legal Education and Action Fund)—an interest group that advocates substantive sexual equality (see Chapter 7)—in seminars on 'gender sensitivity' and equality rights offered by the National Judicial Institute (NJI) and the Western Judicial Education Centre (WJEC). The NJI, which was established in 1988 and is funded by both the federal and provincial governments, offers a wide range of judicial education programs for all judges in Canada. The WJEC has provided training for western provincial court judges since 1984. LEAF's access to judges, according to their critics, 'represents a resource that is denied to all other social interests' (Morton and Knopff 2000, 127). Partly because of such complaints, the CJC and Canadian Bar Association have resisted making social-context education mandatory, while nevertheless emphasizing that it is crucial for judges to remain aware of changes in law and society. Notwithstanding the concerns of some critics, the rate of participation in judicial-education programs is very high, roughly 80 per cent according to the most recent available data (in Morton and Knopff 2000, 125). While it is fairly obvious that judicial independence requires that judicial education not rest with the executive or legislative branches, misgivings have emerged in the United States over 'all-expenses-paid' seminars offered by members of the private sector who present only 'a particular point of view', usually a conservative or pro-business one (Dowling 2008; MacLean 2006). To date, there is little evidence that this is considered a problem, or even an issue, in Canada.

Structural Threats

Structural threats to judicial independence refer to 'the power of governmental bodies outside the judiciary to create and modify judicial institutions' (Russell 2001, 13). Some of these, such as the rules governing judicial discipline and removal, we have already discussed; judicial appointment systems are discussed below. Others, however, include reorganizing, modifying, or abolishing categories of courts or altering the composition of the court. According to conventional wisdom, the classic example of this last one occurred in 1937, when President Franklin Delano Roosevelt threatened to 'pack' the US Supreme Court by adding six new seats and appointing people more sympathetic to his Depression-fighting economic reforms. This was clearly designed to pressure the court to stop striking down parts of the President's New Deal on constitutional grounds, and it appeared successful—the court's jurisprudential shift became known as the 'switch in time that saved nine'. More recent research by Cushman (1998) suggests that the conventional view is mistaken, for the 'switch' was actually evident in the justices' conferences well before Roosevelt's plan was announced, and the plan had so little political support that it could not have had an influence on the justices. Other governments, however—particularly in Latin America (for example, Peru and Argentina in the 1990s)—have successfully 'packed' their courts in the style threatened by F.D.R.

Many countries, including Canada, have stringent constitutional amending formulas that are intended to prevent or at least hinder structural threats of this type. Our 1982 Constitution makes such tampering with the Supreme Court of Canada extremely difficult by requiring the consent of both Houses of Parliament and all provincial legislatures to alter that Court's composition (s. 41(d)); any other structural change to the Supreme Court requires the consent of Parliament and two-thirds of the provincial legislatures that represent at least 50 per cent of the total population. (This said, the method of appointing Supreme Court justices, which is a very important institutional dimension of the Court, can and has been changed by the federal government without recourse to the amending formula—see Chapter 5). The existence of an amending formula, on the other hand, permits determined elected governments that have wide public support to reform the Supreme Court, and this is as it should be in a democracy. The lower courts, however, have no constitutional protection against most structural reforms, because provincial governments have wide authority under s. 92(14) of the *Constitution Act, 1867* to reorganize the s. 92 and s. 96 courts, and the federal government may do the same with the lower s. 101 courts. As noted in Chapter 2, provincial governments have eliminated the s. 96 county and district courts (though the judges were reassigned and promoted to superior court judges) and have created a number of specialized courts, including family courts, municipal courts, small claims courts, and so forth. This is not to suggest that these reforms undermined judicial independence, but they do point to the vulnerability of the system to structural reforms by the other branches of government.

Reference Cases

Writing two decades ago, Peter Russell (1987, 91–2) questioned the legitimacy of the political executive's power to 'refer' questions to the court (the Supreme Court federally; for provinces, their top appeal court) 'on any matter whatsoever' since it blurs the separation of powers between the judicial and executive branches. Implicit in his allusion to the separation of powers was that references may violate judicial independence by forcing them to hear cases at the executive's request. Barry Strayer (1988, 140) is more explicit that courts 'do not perform strictly judicial functions' when deciding reference cases, but he also comes to the conclusion that 'it is equally apparent that there is no constitutional bar to their making decisions not arising out of litigation.'

Many of the most important constitutional cases in our history have been reference cases, but the reason why helps illustrate the problem: references tend to be launched on politically controversial issues (French-language rights in Manitoba in 1985; the patriation of the Constitution in 1981; Quebec secession in 1998; same-sex marriage in 2003; and so on), where the courts are effectively being dragged into a debate in the hope that they will legitimize the side that initiated the reference. However, in the process of ruling, the court inevitably creates discontented political actors, particularly since the judges are often asked to make a decision with few or no facts (Strayer 1988), which may threaten the court's long-term legitimacy. The courts, it should be noted, bear part of the responsibility for this concern because they have welcomed the opportunity to participate in major policy and constitutional debates—a trend broken only recently when the Supreme Court refused to answer whether the Charter's equality rights require the recognition of same-sex marriages (*Reference re Same-Sex Marriage* 2004).

The argument that references violate judicial independence was rejected unanimously by the Judicial Committee of the Privy Council (JCPC) early in the last century (*A.G. Ontario v. A.G. Canada* 1912), but that decision turned on the JCPC's assertion that rulings in references are only non-binding 'advisory opinions', which the court itself may ignore in subsequent 'real' litigation. The fact that references have always been cited by the courts and recognized by governments just like any 'real' case suggests that the JCPC's logic may no longer hold. In 1998, however, the Supreme Court of Canada affirmed the JCPC's decision, at least with respect to federally initiated references, when deciding to rule on the *Reference re Quebec Secession* (Hogg 2003, 206). Whether this affirmation will survive the expanding definition of judicial independence remains to be seen, but it is unlikely that reference cases will be considered problematic in that regard in the near future, particularly now that the Court has made it clear that it will decline to answer questions when it so chooses.

Judicial Appointments

How judicial independence might be threatened by the judicial appointment system is not self-evident, and as McCormick (2004b, 852) writes, it is 'perhaps reaching a bit' to link them. Nonetheless, some have done so, and as detailed below, the Chief Justice of the Supreme Court of Canada has recently hinted in the media that she may as well. The traditional view is that so long as a judge has security of tenure and the other fundamental guarantees of independence once on the bench, then it does not matter how he or she was appointed. Moreover, at least for candidates vying for their first judgeship, they are not judges yet, so how can their judicial independence be violated by the appointment process? Friedland (1995) offers a contrary view that emphasizes the *indirect* connections between appointment and independence. First, appointing lower-quality judges makes it more likely that they will require disciplinary action later for unethical behaviour or incompetence. Second, and associated with this, lower-quality judges or overt patronage appointments undermine public confidence in the courts 'and create a climate for interference with the necessary independence of the judiciary' (Friedland 1995, 233). The central importance of public support for the judicial independence is revisited in the conclusion to this chapter.

Chapter 5 explained that judicial appointments in Canada are at the discretion of the political executive, with only minor constraints exercised by judicial nomination committees (for example, in the case of Ontario's s. 92 courts), or, to a lesser extent, judicial screening committees (in the case of s. 96 and lower s. 101 courts). When Stephen Harper's Conservative government announced in the fall of 2006 that it was reforming, without prior consultation with the judges, the Judicial

Advisory Committees (JACs) that it uses to screen candidates for appointment to the s. 96 and lower s. 101 courts, criticism from the Canadian Judicial Council—chaired by Chief Justice Beverley McLachlin of the Supreme Court of Canada—came swiftly (CJC 2006b). She expressed concern that Harper's plan, which added a representative of the police force appointed by the federal government and reduced the committee rankings to just 'recommend' or not (eliminating the 'highly recommend' category), will compromise the independence of the advisory committees (CJC 2006b). Leading judicial scholar Peter Russell and the Criminal Lawyers Association also criticized the reforms, the latter contending that '[this] is a transparent attempt to broaden [the Minister's] discretion and reduce the power of the committees. . . . Inevitably, you get more patronage and less qualified appointments' (in Makin 2006c, A1). Three months later, the CJC issued a press release which explicitly linked a merit-based appointment system to 'public confidence in the independence and impartiality of Canada's judges' (CJC 2007).

The important question, of course, is whether the courts might decide at some point in the future that judges appointed under the new system—or under some other system that only minimally limits executive discretion over appointment—do not meet the standards of an 'independent and impartial tribunal' under s. 11(d) of the Charter, or the 'unwritten constitutional principle of judicial independence'. Concerning the federal government, this argument would run up against the hard reality of s. 96, which gives the executive the authority to appoint judges, with no mention of JACs. It would be an odd argument to say that the Constitution prevents governments from designing JACs to their liking, when it is clearly constitutionally permissible for the government to abolish JACs altogether. However, the Court was not constrained by the clear constitutional text of s. 100 regarding judicial salaries in the *Remuneration Reference* (it is never truly constrained in constitutional cases, frankly), so it is conceivable that the 'unwritten principles of the Constitution' might again be invoked to create a required institution. Although this would be a striking assertion of judicial power, and a judicially designed appointment system would raise serious doubts about its democratic legitimacy, wholesale restructuring of the appointment system by the executive may indeed pose a structural threat to the courts' independence. This threat could operate either indirectly or directly. Indirectly, a structural change that undermined the quality of the judges appointed could erode the court's legitimacy, as suggested above. Structural changes to the appointment system could cross over into a direct threat in a couple of ways, most obviously if the proposed change, such as retention elections or renewable terms of appointment, would violate security of tenure or financial security. Alternatively, even if sitting judges were protected, a government might try to pressure judges to alter their rulings by threatening a change to the appointment system which it knows the judiciary opposes. For example, a government that was upset at what it considered light criminal sentences might propose that judges be chosen through popular elections (though once elected, they would have tenure), if it knew the public wanted 'tougher' sentences. Judges could of course exercise their independence and refuse to change their approach to sentencing, but the government's reforms could alter the complexion of the court considerably (especially appeal courts, where judges sit in panels). Note, however, that the threat in this example is the government's *proposed change* to the appointment system. It must be emphasized that an *existing* judicial appointment system which protects tenure and financial security does not directly threaten judicial independence in its proper institutional sense.

Judicial Promotions

Most appeal court judges are drawn from the lower trial and appeal courts,[22] and chief judges are routinely elevated from the 'regular' judiciary. As repeatedly recognized in the academic literature (see, for example, Russell 1987, 135–41; the McRuer Report; and Friedland 1995), promotions raise the same concerns for independence as appointment, plus another, more serious one: that 'ambitious judges might worry that a particular decision or a string of decisions could affect their prospects' (McCormick 2004b, 852; see also Friedland 1995, 255). Russell suggested this risk was 'rather far-fetched' when writing in 1987, but he acknowledged that '[s]till, . . . the risk is there' and might increase as Charter cases raise the stakes of judicial review for governments (137). Moreover, since elevations by the federal government of existing judges do not pass through the JAC screening process, a check against lower-quality appointments is removed. The important administrative role of chief judges and the increasingly complex and politicized issues reaching appeal courts suggest that this issue may acquire greater importance to the judicial establishment.

Criticism by Other Judges

The main concern about internal criticism is when it is backed by the spectre of disciplinary proceedings, as when a chief judge—who can launch such proceedings and often participates in them—criticizes a member of his or her own court. Judge Ruffo made this very argument during one of her earlier disciplinary hearings, and although the Supreme Court of Canada ultimately backed the Chief Judge, Justice Sopinka in dissent found a troubling appearance of bias (*Ruffo v. Conseil de la magistrature* 1995). Another incident occurred in Newfoundland in 2002, when the province's Chief Justice, former Liberal Premier Clyde Wells, wrote to the *Globe and Mail* to 'clarify' a ruling by three of his Court of Appeal subordinates in which they criticized the Supreme Court's interpretation of the Charter's 'reasonable limits' provision for allowing too much judicial discretion. Wells argued that because two of the justices concurred with the third (Justice Marshall) without providing reasons, Marshall's criticism of the Supreme Court was his alone. Though this is debatable, it is well established in our legal tradition that a judge's reasons must be entirely contained in his or her ruling from the bench; comments off the bench are not part of the official record and carry no legal weight or precedential value. A 'clarification' by a judge not even presiding over the case was 'unprecedented' (Greene 2006, 99), notwithstanding the fact that Wells had framed his input as 'correcting an error in the media' in his capacity as Chief Justice. John Crosbie, a lawyer and former Minister of Justice in the Mulroney government—and old political adversary of Wells since their disagreement over the Meech Lake Accord—made this point in his complaint as a private citizen against Wells to the CJC, which hastily dismissed it.

Public Criticism of Judges

Until fairly recently, there was a strong tradition in the Anglo-American legal system that politicians should not publicly 'scandalize'—that is, criticize—judges for their rulings, and this was backed up (at least in theory, if not much in practice) by the threat of being charged with 'contempt of court' by the judge—the only offence still defined exclusively by the courts rather than Parliament (Friedland 1995, 30–2). For example, the 'Judges Affair' of 1976 (see note 21), was sparked, in part, when Justice Kenneth MacKay cited Minster of Corporate and Consumer Affairs André Ouellet for contempt of court after Ouellet publicly called MacKay's ruling 'a complete disgrace'. This tradition has faded, probably for a number of reasons: the growth of a 'rights culture' that values free expression; the movement of courts into previously 'political' areas of social policy, particularly under the Charter of Rights and Freedoms, where social commentary on rulings is to be expected; the rise of a neo-conservative (and often populist) ideology and its expression in political parties at the provincial and federal level; and the 'decline of deference' (Nevitte 1996) within society toward all traditional institutions of authority. To be sure, public support for courts has usually remained higher than for the elected branches, but there has been a crescendo of criticism of judges by elected governments and the media (Hughes 2001). Patricia Hughes (2001) contends that such criticism may eventually cross the line into a violation of judicial independence, because it either intends to erode or has the effect of seriously eroding the legitimacy of the courts. In particular, she expresses concern about commentary that questions the very legitimacy of judicial decision making: 'Seen . . . as a comprehensive challenge to the judiciary, a certain type of public commentary is meant to influence legislatures and fuel demands for more control over judges. In short, it has the potential to lead us back to the more traditional threats to judicial independence emanating from the executive and legislature' (Hughes 2001, 202). In this sense, the connection between public criticism and judicial independence parallels the indirect, long-term relationship between judicial appointment and independence. She does not clearly indicate the point at which legitimate criticism becomes excessively corrosive, but she recognizes that the bar should be set high since public criticism of any state institution is not only protected by the right to free expression but is also crucial to democracy.

Is Judicial Independence a 'Two-Way Street'?

Just as politicians were traditionally expected to refrain from criticizing judges for their rulings, judges were expected to reciprocate by discussing political matters only when they became legal ones, and then only insofar as it was necessary to resolve the dispute (McCormick 1998b). To do otherwise would expose judges to allegations of bias should a related issue come before the court, potentially undermining the court's legitimacy as a whole. This principle was affirmed by the CJC in the 1981 Berger Affair, discussed above. The CJC reiterated the standard of judicial 'self-restraint' in its report criticizing Justice Flynn's comments to the media about a property deal between his wife and a municipal government, but again it declined to recommend Flynn's removal or any other discipline. Moreover, in several previous complaints against members of the Supreme Court of Canada for their off-the-bench political commentary, the CJC did not even criticize the justices. REAL Women—an anti-feminist conservative women's group—launched a complaint about Justice Bertha Wilson in 1990 for her speech at Osgoode Hall Law School endorsing feminist principles, and another against Justice Beverley McLachlin in 1991 for her criticism in a speech to the Elizabeth Fry Society of male bias in the criminal law (Greene 2006, 97; Sopinka 1996, 167–8). In 2000, the CJC rejected a complaint by well-known conservative academic and court critic Ted Morton (now a Progressive Conservative MLA and cabinet minister in Alberta) regarding Justice L'Heureux-Dubé's support for 'gay rights and homosexual marriage' in a series of public speeches, in which she also criticized existing government policy on these matters (Morton 2002, 206–9). Thus, the CJC appears unwilling to enforce the standards of judicial impartiality laid down during the Berger Affair; indeed, it is unlikely that Berger would even be investigated today (McCormick 1998b, 111).[23] Instead, the CJC has adopted the attitude of the former Supreme Court justice John Sopinka, who criticized the Berger rule as unrealistic in the Charter era: 'No longer can we expect the public to respect decisions from a process that is shrouded in mystery and made by people who have withdrawn from society' (1996, 169). That said, even Sopinka recognized that judges should avoid off-bench participation in 'controversial current political issues' (1996, 171), and it is fair to say that L'Heureux-Dubé's speeches on the equality rights of same-sex couples fell into this category.

There is now before the CJC a case that may clarify the council's position on the limits of free speech in political affairs for judges as public citizens. In May 2008 a full inquiry of the CJC recommended the removal of Justice Ted Matlow of the Ontario Divisional Court because of his heavy involvement in a community group opposed to the City of Toronto's urban development plans in his neighbourhood. Among other things, the inquiry criticized Matlow for identifying himself as a judge—including using the title 'Justice Matlow' and Ontario Court of Justice stationery—in his contact with media and politicians on behalf of the group. More basically, however, the inquiry concluded that 'by organizing and leading community opposition to . . . a controversial municipal government decision, Justice Matlow has placed himself in a position incompatible with the due execution of the office of judge' (CJC 2008, 63). At the time of writing, Justice Matlow has requested judicial review of the inquiry committee's report on several grounds, including that it violates his freedom of expression under the Charter.

Although the inquiry revealed some questionable conduct by Matlow, it should be noted that the original complaint carried more than a whiff of political interference with the judiciary. A City of Toronto official launched the complaint with the CJC after Matlow had refused to recuse himself from a 2005 case involving the city government. The official had requested the recusal on the grounds of Matlow's involvement in his community group, which was 'wholly unrelated' to the case in which the judge was asked to recuse himself (Schmitz 2007). However, the city did not demand Matlow's recusal until *after* he had ruled against it in the unrelated case. Adding to the sense that the city targeted Justice Matlow is the fact that his two co-panelists on the case agreed with his judgement and that during his dispute with the city Matlow had ruled in its favour in four out of five cases (Schmitz 2007). This complaint thus raises a larger institutional issue for the judiciary, as noted in Matlow's submission to the CJC: 'If a judge's ruling with respect to recusal are [*sic*] allowed to become the subject of investigations into judicial ethics and the basis for discipline or removal from office, this will encourage litigation tactics of intimidation, which will undermine the security and independence of the judiciary and encourage judgeshopping' (in Tyler 2007c, B1).

Independence and Accountability

Independence is crucial to the effectiveness and legitimacy of the judiciary, but there is simultaneously a strong desire for judges to be 'accountable' for their actions. This presents a paradox: there is a 'natural tension' between accountability and independence since 'accountability could have an inhibiting effect on proper judicial action' (Friedland 1995, 264). How then might we achieve some measure of judicial accountability? A good place to start is by considering what we mean by 'accountability': to whom, and for what purpose? Burbank's (2007) definition, in Box 6.3, provides a number of options.

Box 6.3   Are Judges 'Accountable', and to Whom?

[J]ust as independence must be conceived in relation to other actors (independence from whom or what?), so must accountability (accountability to whom or what?). As a result, judicial accountability should run to the public, including litigants whose disputes courts resolve, and who therefore have a legitimate interest in court proceedings that are open to the public and in judicial decisions that are accessible. Judicial accountability should also run to the people's representatives, who appropriate the funds for the judiciary and whose laws the courts interpret and apply, and who therefore have a legitimate interest in ensuring that the judiciary has been responsible in spending the allotted funds and that, as interpreted and applied by the courts, public laws are functioning as intended. Finally, judicial accountability should run to courts and the judiciary as an institution, both because individual judicial independence exists primarily for the benefit of institutional independence and because appropriate intra-branch accountability is essential if potentially inappropriate interbranch accountability is to be avoided.

Stephen Burbank (2007, 913), 'Judicial Independence, Judicial Accountability and Interbranch Relations'

We can derive from these what we term a 'weak' and a 'strong' form of accountability. The weak form is that judges must render their decisions, and provide justifications for those decisions, publicly; they are also expected to ground their rulings in established precedent and law and to justify it when they do not. The Supreme Court's unanimous decision in *Sheppard* (2002) made such justification a requirement, on the grounds that judges are accountable to the broader society. (The Court has also, however, imposed limits on the degree to which judges can be made to justify publicly their rulings *off* the bench: in *Mackeigan v. Hickman* (1989), the justices ruled that judicial independence prevented Royal Commissions—in that case, regarding the wrongful conviction of Donald Marshall, Jr—from compelling judges to testify about their past decisions.) This also implies that the rule of law factors into judicial accountability since we should not accept as legitimate judicial decisions that are unconstrained by law (Burbank and Friedman 2002, 12). The strong form of accountability entails more direct answerability to the public, other judges, or the non-judicial branches of government, such as through elections, disciplinary peer review mechanisms, the appeal process, confirmation votes,[24] legislative overrides of judicial rulings, structural reforms to the judiciary, evaluations of judges, or impeachment of individual judges. The distinction between weak and strong accountability is related to (but does not perfectly overlap) another conceptual distinction, between *professional* accountability and *democratic* accountability. This concerns *to whom* judges are accountable: their peers and the legal community, or the wider public and their elected representatives? A recent poll by the *Globe and Mail* found surprisingly that two-thirds of respondents were in favour of judges being elected, with roughly a quarter being 'strongly' so (Makin 2007b). Notwithstanding the widespread use of judicial elections in the United States, it is difficult to reconcile the practice with judicial impartiality and independence, at least in the context of an adjudicative model of courts. As discussed in the last chapter, evidence from the United States that the prospect of an election alters judicial behaviour tends to support this view. Moreover, a judge elected by electoral majorities is in an apparent conflict of interest when called upon in a case to uphold the rights of an unpopular minority.

With respect to accountability for misconduct, the disciplinary procedures described earlier in this chapter strive to balance accountability with independence, and professional with democratic accountability through the use of peer review. However, these have arguably been of low visibility and limited effectiveness because only full inquiries are made public and 95 per cent of complaints against judges are disposed of before reaching this stage (Friedland 1995, 135). Tied to this is the risk that the existing system is too 'cozy' since judges are often reluctant to discipline their colleagues or do more than issue a criticism. As Greene (2006, 99) observes, the CJC's perfunctory handling of Crosbie's and Morton's complaints against its own members 'raises the suspicion that the council was circling the wagons' and applying a different standard than in the full inquiries ordered into Berger, Flynn, and Matlow (none of whom were CJC members).

The trend toward greater judicial administrative autonomy raises a different form of accountability: responsibility to elected officials and the taxpayers for the court's budget and allocation of resources. This form of accountability is not related to the conduct of individual judges on the bench but rather to decisions made by the judicial administrative elite on behalf of the entire court. This parallels the concept of bureaucratic accountability, but the direct supervision and disciplinary actions possible within the public service would be absent in the judicial context, precisely because of concerns about judicial independence (Greene 1995). Notably, the federal courts in the US have enjoyed almost complete administrative autonomy for several decades—including drafting and allocating their court budgets—but, as Greene (1995, 362) observes, such control 'has been purchased at the price of having to account for the budget', and judges 'must lobby, like other government services, for a fair share of the federal budget.' Concern among both judges and governments about how to achieve meaningful budgetary accountability while avoiding US-style judicial lobbying is the major reason why, to date, judges (other than on the Supreme Court) do not have—and are not seeking full administrative autonomy (CJC 2006a). Instead, judges have promoted 'half-way' measures where overall court budgets would be determined through commissions staffed by representatives of the judges and the government, but specific expenditures from that budget would be allocated by the judiciary; disputes over the budget would be heard by special panels to avoid the appearance of 'negotiation'. Such proposals echo the approach taken with judicial salaries after the *Remuneration Reference*, although it should be noted that disputes over judicial salaries remain, and as noted earlier, that ruling has been criticized for usurping Parliament's authority over the public purse.

Summing up, although judicial independence can co-exist with professional accountability—albeit with some risk of internal threats to individual judges—it is extremely difficult, in light of the factors discussed throughout this chapter, to reconcile it with meaningful democratic accountability.

Judicial Impartiality Revisited: Independence in an Era of Judicial Policy-Making

Before concluding, it is worth considering the implications for judicial independence when judges are no longer deciding only traditional disputes as 'neutral umpires' who apply the law to a set of historical facts that occurred between two parties (the adjudicative model), but are also hearing cases that entail significant policy-making, social facts, and third-party interveners (the policy-making model: see Chapter 3). To phrase it differently, and recalling McCormick's (2004b) point above, what are the consequences when judges abandon traditional formalistic decision making where law-making is only incremental ('filling in the blanks') and instead embrace the creation of rules and articulation of public values as an important part of the judicial function? It is clear that this opens the door to judicial attitudes, biases, and ideology, as is well documented by legal realist scholars. An example is provided by Justice L'Heureux-Dubé's comments that prompted Professor Morton's complaint to the CJC: regardless of whether one agrees with her position on same-sex relations, it is indisputable that she did not approach cases on this issue free of preconceived attitudes. Judicial policy-making further implies that the judge considers the long-range policy and social implications of his or her ruling as much as or more so than the facts, laws, and immediate parties before him or her. In neither sense is the judge still 'impartial' in the traditional sense. The accumulation of these types of cases inevitably exposes courts to the perception that they are 'politicized'.

What is more, Shapiro (1981, 34) contends that 'lawmaking and judicial independence are fundamentally incompatible,' since governmental elites will not indefinitely tolerate the exercise of political power 'by an isolated judicial corps free of political restraints'. This, and the erosion of traditional impartiality, tend to lead governments and the public to demand greater democratic accountability of the courts or to try to curtail judicial authority. Such calls for accountability are threats to the judicial independence that was developed for courts as adjudicators of disputes, but they are natural responses when courts make authoritative value (that is, political) decisions as policy-makers (Weiler 1968, 439–43). For example, our notions of independence and accountability would likely be different when judges strike down limits on private health care, as the Supreme Court did in a case brought by Dr Chaoulli (which featured relaxed rules of standing, social facts, interveners, and policy-making), than they would if Dr Chaoulli's case had involved a medical malpractice lawsuit or a regulatory body trying to revoke his medical licence. (The latter case would probably feature a concrete legal dispute, historical facts, two parties, and the application of established law.)

Though this seems a disconcerting thought, it is perhaps useful to recall the views of the framers of the 1789 Constitution of the United States, as articulated in *The Federalist Papers* (1787–8). While they did recognize that the 'separation of powers' was necessary to prevent the concentration of too much power in any single institution, they also realized that 'checks and balances' are not possible when this separation is absolute. In other words, *some* overlapping of function and authority between the executive, legislative, and judicial branches is necessary to enable one branch to limit another (*Federalist Papers*, No. 48). Thus, while we must certainly be wary of attempts by the other branches to put undue pressure on the judiciary, we should not expect—nor desire—judicial independence to isolate the courts from the broader political environment completely. And the more the judiciary's role overlaps that of the legislature and executive, the more we can expect conflict between those branches of government.

Conclusions

It is important to remember the broader political and social context in which judicial independence exists. Judicial independence is important because of society's need for legitimate, accessible dispute resolution, although the growing popularity of alternative dispute resolution suggests that societal demands are not being met by the traditional adjudicatory 'triadic' model. The major disputes about judicial independence in the last three decades have been driven by two highly political factors: first, resource scarcity and the fiscal priorities of elected governments and the electorate itself, in which the justice system is a low priority for spending compared to health care and education; and second, the increased assertiveness of the judiciary itself, through its development of the case law and advocacy via judicial councils and chief judges. Even as judicial independence has been fortified and expanded, however, traditional judicial functions have been hived off by governments (often with the courts' blessing) to institutions—justices of the peace and administrative tribunals—that do not necessarily enjoy comparable levels of protection (Greene 2006, 93). This fact was underlined by the Supreme Court's ruling in *Ocean Port Hotel v. British Columbia* (2001), which refused to extend automatically the features of judicial independence to tribunals, leaving the latter's institutional protection up to the legislature. (But it must be stressed that the Court left the door open to extending judicial independence-level protections to tribunals in the future, and it did so with respect to financial security in *Bodner* (2005).[25]) Finally, it cannot be overemphasized that judicial independence relies ultimately not on constitutional provisions or judicial assertiveness, but on broader societal support and political respect for these measures (Geyh 2002). A judiciary which enjoys little popular legitimacy is much more easily pressured or overtly interfered with by governments (as in many Latin American regimes) since the political cost to such governments is relatively low. There is also a growing body of international scholarship which suggests that judicial independence may rely on a competitive party system. This 'insurance theory' holds that political parties that become the government are more likely to respect judicial independence if they expect to lose power in the future because the courts represent a means to influence public policy which does not depend on electoral success (Finkel 2008; Ginsburg 2003; Ramseyer and Rasmusen 2003; Sieder, Schjolden, and Angell 2005). In other words, foresighted governments will not undermine judicial authority because they expect to exploit it for their own purposes later. Canadian citizens would do well to remember their important role in protecting judicial independence.

Chapter 7

Interest Group Litigants

In 1983, 18-year-old Nigel Gayme was arrested for sexually assaulting a 15-year-old girl in the basement of his school. At his preliminary inquiry, Gayme suggested a defence of consent and honest but mistaken belief in consent. The accused sought to cross-examine the complainant about her prior sexual conduct. Gayme argued that the complainant had frequently come to his school to participate in sexual acts with students and had freely given out sexual favours. However, two sections of the *Criminal Code*, s. 276 and s. 277, limited the admissibility of evidence about a complainant's past sexual conduct. Gayme's lawyer asked the provincial court judge to declare ss. 276 and 277 unconstitutional and allow the cross-examination to proceed. The judge refused the defence's motion (arguing he lacked jurisdiction to make such a declaration), and Gayme was committed for trial.

In 1984, Steven Seaboyer was arrested and charged with sexually assaulting a woman he had been drinking with at a Toronto bar. At the preliminary inquiry for his case, Seaboyer sought to cross-examine the complainant about her previous sexual conduct. Seaboyer and his lawyer argued that the complainant's bruises and other aspects of her physical condition could have been caused by 'other acts of sexual intercourse' (*R. v. Seaboyer* 1991). However, Seaboyer came up against those same two sections of the *Criminal Code*, s. 276 and 277, which limited the use of evidence of a complainant's past sexual conduct. Accordingly, the judge at the inquiry refused to allow the cross-examination and Seaboyer was committed for trial.

Seaboyer and Gayme next turned to the Supreme Court of Ontario to request that their committal for trial be quashed. The judge granted the requests on the grounds that ss. 276 and 277 of the *Criminal Code* did violate the fair-trial guarantees of the Charter of Rights and Freedoms. The Attorney General of Ontario appealed this decision to the Ontario Court of Appeal, which unanimously reversed the lower-court decision in 1987. Seaboyer and Gayme then appealed to the Supreme Court of Canada, and the cases—bundled together because of their similar issues—were heard in 1991.

Arguing before the Supreme Court of Canada were the lawyers for the parties of the case—the two appellants, Seaboyer and Gayme, and the respondent, the Attorney General of Ontario. However, like many other Supreme Court cases since the late 1980s, the parties were not alone. Also submitting briefs[1] to the Court were lawyers for the Attorneys General of Canada, Quebec, and Saskatchewan, as well as lawyers for the two most frequent interest-group participants before the Court: the Canadian Civil Liberties Association (CCLA) and the

Women's Legal Education and Action Fund (LEAF).[2] Did the three governments and two public-interest groups participate because they felt strongly about Seaboyer and Gayme's guilt or innocence on the sexual assault charges? On the contrary, the briefs they submitted to the Court suggest that they had little interest in Seaboyer and Gayme as individuals. Rather these participants were deeply concerned about the Court's decision regarding s. 276 and s. 277 of the Criminal Code—Canada's 'rape-shield' provisions. The groups participated in the case in an effort to influence the Court's decision in an area of interest to them.

Subsections 276 and 277 were designed to prevent the cross-examination or the introduction of evidence of a complainant's sexual history during a sexual-assault trial. Specifically, s. 276 placed restrictions on the use of evidence of a complainant's previous sexual activity and s. 277 prevented a complainant's sexual reputation from being used to challenge her credibility. The provisions had been introduced in response to modern-day criticisms of the assumptions behind the traditional common law approach that allowed the admission of such evidence: the belief that a woman who had engaged in sexual activity in the past was more likely to consent to sexual activity and was less likely to speak the truth under oath (*Seaboyer and the Queen* 1987).

Seaboyer and Gayme, supported by the brief of the CCLA for s. 276[3], argued that the provisions were unconstitutional violations of the Charter's protection of fundamental justice and the right to a fair trial as guaranteed in ss. 7 and 11(d) of the Charter.[4] Why would a public-interest group like the CCLA participate in a case in support of two men accused of sexual assault? The CCLA sees itself as a 'watchdog' guarding against threats to fundamental freedoms, and the group has drawn considerable attention to the rights of the criminally accused. In this case the CCLA argued that s. 276 'arbitrarily and unconditionally excludes evidence which might be relevant to the issue of the guilt or innocence of the accused' (CCLA 1991, 7).

LEAF, by contrast, is an interest group more narrowly focused on the rights of women, and *R. v. Seaboyer* touched on one of LEAF's major concerns: violence against women. As with all of their cases, the group felt the need to participate in order to support the interests of women—something it believes it is in a better position to do than government participants. In *Seaboyer*, LEAF intervened to argue that the rape-shield provisions were necessary to prevent the introduction of evidence that was irrelevant as well as prejudicial to the victim. Their brief suggested that the introduction of such evidence made the complainant rather than the accused appear to be on trial and led to embarrassment that would discourage the reporting of sexual assaults. The group also suggested that 'empirical evidence supports the conclusion that the admission of sexual history in sexual assault trials independently reduces the possibility of conviction and lowers sentences' (LEAF 1991, 11). LEAF and the government participants took the position that a woman's past engagement in sexual activity does not mean she has consented to the activity under investigation.

The Supreme Court thus faced a difficult question that pitted the rights of the accused against the protection of the complainant in one of the most charged areas of criminal law, sexual assault. What did they decide? All four governments and a public-interest group had lined up on one side against the two criminal defendants and another public-interest group. Studies have demonstrated the high rate of success of governments before the Supreme Court (see, for example, McCormick 1993; Haynie et al. 2001);[5] so one might expect their interests to be on the winning side here as well. However, while the Supreme Court did rule that s. 277 did not infringe the Charter (holding there was no connection between a complainant's reputation and her credibility as a witness), it struck down s. 276 as an unconstitutional infringement on the Charter. The Court argued that in excluding evidence of sexual activity s. 276 had gone too far by preventing the use of evidence that might be 'essential to the presentation of legitimate defences. . . . In exchange for the elimination of the possibility that the judge and jury might draw illegitimate inferences from the evidence, it exacts as a price the real risk that an innocent person may be convicted' (*R. v. Seaboyer* 1991). In the majority's view it was not the evidence that was the problem but rather the misuse of that evidence. Thus s. 276 had excluded evidence that was necessary to a fair trial as guaranteed under ss. 7 and 11(d) of the Charter.

Was *R. v. Seaboyer* unusual for having interest-group participants before the Supreme Court? Since the passage of the Charter in 1982, interest groups have increasingly turned to litigation to pursue their interests. Although LEAF and the CCLA are the two most frequent group participants before the Court, groups of all types and sizes have appeared. Interest-group participation has not been limited to conservative or liberal groups, small or large groups or groups interested in a particular kind of issue. Both corporations and unions litigate, as do environmental groups, civil liberties groups, and social conservatives. Box 7.1 presents a brief description of a sample of organized interests that have participated in trials before the Canadian courts.

Box 7.1   A Sample of Organized Interests That Have Appeared before the Courts

---

Women's Legal and Action Fund (LEAF)[6]—Formed in 1985 after the passage of the Charter specifically to protect and further women's equality rights, LEAF litigates in the areas of equality and discrimination, family law, sexual assault, and abortion.

Canadian Civil Liberties Association (CCLA)—Formed in 1964 to protect fundamental freedoms, the CCLA litigates in a wide range of issue areas, including the rights of criminal defendants, minority rights, and freedom of expression.

Equality for Gays and Lesbians Everywhere (EGALE)[7]—Formed in 1986 to pursue equality rights for lesbians and gays, EGALE has been involved in nearly all of the major sexual orientation cases before the courts.

REAL Women—Founded in 1983, REAL is a socially conservative group with an emphasis on the family. The group has participated in court primarily in cases involving abortion and fetal rights and the rights of same-sex couples (they oppose LEAF in these cases).

Evangelical Fellowship of Canada—Formed in 1964, this group is a national association of evangelical Christians. It has appeared in court cases involving religious freedom, genetic and reproductive technology, family law, and the rights of abortion protesters.

Congress of Aboriginal Peoples—Founded in 1971 as the Native Council of Canada, CAP represents the interests of Metis and non-status Indians. It has participated in court cases involving a variety of Aboriginal issues.

Canadian Bankers Association—Established in 1891, the CBA is the representative body for banks doing business in Canada. The group has been involved in cases dealing with such issues as interest rates, contracts, income tax, banking operations, and the power of banks.

Canadian Labour Congress (CLC)—Founded in 1956, the CLC is a national organization of labour unions; the majority of Canadian unions are affiliated with it. The CLC has undertaken litigation in such areas as labour law, collective agreements, freedom of association, and freedom of expression.

Canadian Medical Association (CMA)—Formed in 1867, the CMA is the national organization of physicians and medical students. The group participates in court cases dealing with health-care issues.

Canadian Cancer Society—Formed in 1938, the Cancer Society is dedicated to fighting the disease and improving the quality of life of the victims of cancer. The group's most high-profile litigation involves the tobacco industry. For example, it has participated in cases dealing with the retail display and commercial advertising of tobacco products.

In *R. v. Seaboyer* both LEAF and the CCLA had participated before a lower court (the Ontario Court of Appeal). It should be noted, however, that most of our information on interest-group participation comes from their appearances before the Supreme Court. Indeed, interest-group participation before lower courts is still much less common in Canada—making *Seaboyer* more of the exception than the rule.

This chapter explores what we know of interest-group participation before the Canadian courts, with frequent comparisons to the United States, where interest-group litigation has been used and studied more extensively. The chapter begins by asking *why* groups would turn to the courts and then examines the various methods they have used in their efforts to influence judges. These methods include both indirect strategies for influencing the courts—such as writing articles for law reviews—and the more common direct strategies: sponsorship of cases and intervention in cases. The bulk of the chapter concerns interest groups as interveners before the Canadian Supreme Court. We focus on this form of participation and on this Court, because up to this point, Canadian interest groups have undertaken intervention more than any other form of litigation, and their intervention has been concentrated more in the Supreme Court of Canada. The chapter concludes with an examination of the success and influence of groups before the courts. There has been widespread criticism of this use of the courts by interest groups in Canada (see for example Brodie 2002 and Morton and Knopff 2000). Have groups achieved what they hoped to before the courts, or has their effect been exaggerated?

Why Groups Turn to the Courts

Why would interest groups undertake costly and time-consuming litigation?[8] Since all interest groups seek to achieve the collective goals of their group, the most straightforward answer is that the 'primary purpose of litigation is to seek a policy change or to stop a change from taking place' (Berry 1989, 155). But why turn to the courts instead of the executive or legislature? The choice of litigation suggests that the courts are considered to be policy-making bodies. Indeed, as we have emphasized throughout this book, the courts are political institutions that are frequently asked to decide on matters of such national concern as private health care, abortion, same-sex marriage, and the treaty rights of aboriginals. This has been particularly true for the Canadian Supreme Court since the adoption of the Charter of Rights and Freedoms. As Roy Flemming reflects in his study of the Supreme Court's case selection, 'which cases are heard mould the development of the law, but equally important, . . . the choice of cases and the Court's emphasis on particular areas of the law can lead to major public policy changes' (Flemming 2004, 2). American interest groups recognized the power of the courts and began litigating extensively decades earlier, and Canadian groups have been quick to recognize the increased power of the courts in the Charter era and have increased their rate of litigation in response. But even if we acknowledge the policy-making potential of the courts, why would groups choose this avenue over the more direct (and less-time consuming) access they can have to legislators?

Early on, the American literature suggested a 'political disadvantage theory' for interest-group litigation (see, in particular, Cortner 1968). According to this theory, interest groups litigate because they are unable to penetrate other branches of government. Thus groups look to litigation when 'all else fails' and they are unable to achieve their policy objectives through the more traditional routes such as the legislature (Epstein 1985).

The political disadvantage theory gained a wide following during the civil-rights era and beyond because it did appear to explain much of the early American interest-group litigation. The National Association for the Advancement of Colored People (NAACP) was often the model for this theory. Determined to end segregation and achieve equality for African Americans in the United States, this group was unable to achieve significant gains through the state legislatures or even Congress. Faced with unreceptive audiences in the traditional forums of policy making, the NAACP formed a Legal Defense Fund, the NAACP LDF, to pursue its interests through the courts. Kent Roach believes that a similar situation may have driven Canadian interest groups to the courts at various times. He argues that before the 1980s 'linguistic, religious and racial minorities, women and First Nations all made selective use of litigation . . . when they were faced with prejudice and exclusion in the legislative process' (Roach 1993, 165).

For several years, the political disadvantage theory was the dominant theory in the literature. However, scholars began increasingly to question the accuracy of this theory. In more recent years some authors have suggested it is only a partial explanation and applies only to the experience of groups such as the NAACP LDF,[9] and to the era in which it was litigating (Olson 1990). In 1985, Kim Lane Scheppele and Jack Walker, Jr attempted to test the political disadvantage theory by using their survey of 892 American interest groups. The authors examined whether groups that were considered political 'outsiders' used the courts more than political 'insiders'. They concluded that although they could not declare the political disadvantage theory wrong, 'it captures only a fraction of the interest group litigation activity' (Scheppele and Walker 1991, 182). Instead, they found that the groups in their survey that were 'most likely to use the courts [were] the wealthy and established groups that seek court favor for conservative purposes' (Scheppele and Walker 1991, 182). These were groups the authors considered political 'insiders' because of their success in using the legislative branch to achieve their goals. Lee Epstein also found that the political disadvantage theory provided a poor description of the litigation motivation of conservative groups using the courts in the 1980s (Epstein 1985).

In Canada, after the passage of the Charter of Rights and Freedoms in 1982, many groups that had traditionally been considered politically disadvantaged did turn to the courts in the hopes of achieving gains they had not won through the legislature. Several authors have written about the Charter era as one where disadvantaged groups have another point of access from which to pursue their goals (Sigurdson 1993; Hein 2000). However, groups that are more often considered politically advantaged (for example, business interests) also litigate frequently (Hein 2000), and there has been increasing notice of the need for resources in order to litigate (Roach 1993). Thus, in Canada many commentators have also suggested that the political disadvantage theory does not provide a completely accurate description of interest-group litigation. (See, for example, Brodie 2002, which provides a lengthy argument against the political disadvantage theory.)

Why else then do groups litigate? Several different answers have been suggested, each likely describing some group's experience. Groups that have traditionally been considered advantaged may litigate in response to successful litigation by those they consider opponents of their causes (Epstein and Kobylka 1992). Particularly if litigation brings constitutional wins for opponent groups, advantaged groups may find their legislative gains erased. Some suggest this helps explain the increase in litigation in the United States by corporations, trade associations, and other like groups in the 1970s (Epstein and Kobylka 1992). Litigating interest groups may even be created by other groups to pursue litigation in response to success by litigating interest groups whose views are contrary to the original groups' interests. In the United States, for example, Pat Robertson's Christian Coalition formed the American Center for Law and Justice to counteract the activities of the American Civil Liberties Union (ACLU) before the courts, and the Pacific Legal Foundation was formed in response to the litigation of liberal environmental organizations (Baum 2001; Lowery and Brasher 2004). Similarly, a substantial pro-life counter-movement was promoted in the courts as well as in the state and national legislatures in the aftermath of *Roe v. Wade*.

Groups that have been able to achieve some gains in the legislature may also litigate in order to protect those gains, since court victories are not as likely as legislation to change with the next election (Scheppele and Walker 1991). In fact, the lengthy terms served by judges and their attention to precedent suggest that most court decisions will have a long-lasting impact on a policy issue. Groups may want to participate in cases in the issue areas of interest to them to influence the direction of those long-lasting decisions. The groups may also be drawn into litigation to defend previous wins—either in the legislature or the courts—or to protect a policy that is favourable to their cause and that is being challenged. LEAF, for example, was drawn into the *Conway v. Canada* case (also known as *Weatherall v. Canada* 1993) when a male inmate challenged the constitutionality of a policy allowing female guards in male prisons but not male guards in female prisons. LEAF participated to protect the employment opportunities of the female guards (given that the number of male prisoners is several times that of female prisoners) while arguing that allowing male guards in female prisons would 'exacerbate social disadvantage' (LEAF 1993, 10) since women are more threatened by the power imbalance and fear of sexual violence. Thus, the group went to court to protect a policy that favoured its interests.[10]

Whether they litigate primarily for offensive or defensive reasons, the underlying motivation of an interest group's decision to litigate is the belief that the court is considering an issue important to its members. It may be that they participate primarily to receive publicity for their group and its position on the issue or to demonstrate to their members their activity in the area (Epstein and Rowland 1991). However, for most groups, influencing policy that is important to their members is probably at the forefront of their goals. Lee Epstein argues that groups go to court 'because they view the courts as just another political battlefield, which they must enter to fight for their goals' (Epstein 1985, 148).

Indirect Strategies for Influencing the Courts

Interest groups' efforts to 'fight for their goals' and influence policy take a different form before the courts than before legislatures. Direct lobbying of individual judges is not possible because personal contact between judges and the participants in the cases before them is highly improper. This means that the more common lobbying routes of persuading decision makers through close and regular contact and by 'wining and dining', granting favours, and making campaign contributions are impossible in Canada's courts (although campaign contributions to judges are possible in the United States since several states have elected courts). Interest groups are instead confined primarily to submitting legal briefs to the courts and making oral arguments before them.

However, there are a few indirect strategies that interest groups can use. The Canadian women's interest group, LEAF, was formed in response to a study commissioned by the Canadian Advisory Council on the Status of Women. This study, *Women and Legal Action: Precedents, Resources and Strategies for the Future*, recommended the formation of a legal action fund to litigate systematically on behalf of equality, but it also argued the group should make efforts to inform the media and 'educate' lawyers and the judiciary (Atcheson, Eberts and Symes 1984, 171). This suggests one form of indirect strategy for an interest group: attempting to influence judges by shaping their perspective on the law. One way interest groups do this is by writing articles for law reviews in which they evaluate the work of the courts and present arguments for the 'correct' legal interpretation for their issue areas. Judges are part of the legal community, and law reviews—particularly their evaluations of judicial decisions—are thought to be noticed by the judges[11] (Baum 2006, 100). There is also evidence that judges use law reviews 'to provide themselves with the legal reasoning to move in a new direction and to bolster their position on a case' (Schlozman and Tierney 1986, 363). This may have been particularly attractive to Canadian judges facing cases under the new Charter of Rights and Freedoms in the 1980s. Greene et al. (1998, 150) note a dramatic increase in Supreme Court citations to academic articles and legal periodicals between the late 1960s and the 1990s. The leaders of the Supreme Court in the early Charter years may have been predisposed to view legal articles favourably. Bora Laskin, who was Chief Justice in the early years of the Charter (until 1984), had been a law professor before becoming a judge, and this type of legal background became increasingly common during and after his tenure.[12] Of course, even justices who were not previously law professors may have viewed legal articles favourably in those early Charter years. For example, Brian Dickson, Chief Justice from 1984 to 1990, 'admired legal academics and was always interested in any assistance that their writings could provide' (Sharpe and Roach 2003, 203).

'Law review lobbying', where legal experts affiliated with (or sympathetic to) particular groups publish articles in law reviews arguing in favour of particular legal interpretations, has been practised by groups in the United States for decades (Schlozman and Tierney 1986, 363). As suggested above, interest groups use this strategy to build credibility and support for their positions. One American group that has been credited with using law reviews successfully to help achieve its goals is the NAACP. Beginning primarily in the 1940s, that group made an effort to get large numbers of favourable law-review articles published in the time leading up to its litigation in an area. The group hoped that judges would see an increase in support for its position and be persuaded to change existing unfavourable precedents (O'Connor 1980; Vose 1972). The Women's Rights Project (WRP) has also made extensive use of legal writing to advance its positions on legal issues. When the future US Supreme Court Justice Ruth Bader Ginsburg was a co-director of the WRP she frequently wrote legal articles about sex discrimination, in addition to making presentations to law students, professors, and lawyers (Cowan 1976). Again the hope was to influence the viewpoint of judges who would later hear these kinds of cases in their courts.

In Canada, LEAF in particular has attempted to 'influence the influencers' through legal writing, including law reviews, other articles, and books. The importance of this strategy to this group was emphasized from the start (Razack 1991), and its annual reports outline the legal writing undertaken by its members that year. The amount of material published by women associated with LEAF is extensive and covers a wide range of issues with an emphasis on equality. Their efforts have not gone unnoticed. In the *Seaboyer* case discussed above, the dissent cites the work of a legal academic (Elizabeth Sheehy) who has consulted for LEAF on cases, and through the years, the Supreme Court has in its majority opinions cited other academics associated with LEAF (for example, Shelagh Day, Gwen Brodsky, and Marilou McPhedran). LEAF is not alone in its use of this strategy, however, for law professors and lawyers affiliated with various other interest groups appear to have recognized the potential for legal writing in furthering their views (see for example, work by Alan Borovoy of the Canadian Civil Liberties Association).

Interest groups may also try to influence judges by participating in judicial education seminars (see Chapter 6). In Canada, an independent and non-profit organization, the National Judicial Institute (NJI) was formed in 1988 to provide judicial education. The NJI offers courses in the craft of judging, education in substantive law, and social-context education. Particularly in the social-context area, the NJI consults with legal academics who teach and do research in the area of interest (for example gender) and with groups that are part of the relevant community (Swinton 1996). Several people have both participated in interest groups and served as speakers at the National Judicial Institute.[13] This suggests another avenue by which interest groups can present their perspective to judges.

In the United States, interest groups have also devoted significant attention to an additional indirect strategy for influencing the federal courts. Particularly at the Supreme Court, groups have become increasingly active in the judicial selection process. Federal judges in the United States are nominated by the President and confirmed by the Senate. Although the emphasis tends to be on the confirmation stage, groups that are important to the President are thought to be active in the first step of the process, lobbying the executive for the 'correct' selection. Some argue that socially conservative groups were particularly active in the Supreme Court nominations of 2005 and 2006 (Baum 2007, 31). For the position of Chief Justice, the groups started early criticizing one potential candidate, Attorney General Alberto Gonzales, for his moderate views. In the end, President Bush nominated John Roberts—a candidate the administration had worked hard to sell to conservative groups over the previous year (Baum 2007; Kirkpatrick 2005).

Interest-group involvement at the confirmation stage has increased significantly since the 1960s with many groups dedicating significant time and money to influencing the ultimate vote on a candidate. Groups lobby senators by giving them information about the preferences of their constituency or the possible policy consequences of having the nominee on the bench. They run advertisements for or against the nominee and organize grassroots campaigns that send out special mailings and leaflets and organizing letters (Caldeira, Hojnacki, and Wright 2000). Several groups also testify at the confirmation hearings held by the Senate Judiciary Committee. Interest-group activity can make a significant difference in the outcome of a nominee (Caldeira and Wright 1998). For example, group activity is thought to have helped prevent the confirmation of Robert Bork in 1987 and to have mobilized significant opposition to Clarence Thomas and Samuel Alito (48 out of 100 Senators voted against Thomas and 42 against Alito) (Baum 2007).

In Canada, interest groups have not participated in the judicial selection process in the same way. The process itself is significantly different, and there have not been the access points to encourage groups to build the necessary resources for such a campaign. However, with changes to the selection process expected in the future (including perhaps a more American-style confirmation process—see Chapter 5), this may become another avenue that Canadian groups follow in order to influence the courts. F.L. Morton and Rainer Knopff (2000) suggest that some groups may already be doing this. Morton and Knopff point to a memo written by EGALE to its supporters in 1997 listing potential candidates[14] for a Supreme Court vacancy and asking supporters for any information they had about them. The memo emphasized how 'vitally important' it was for GLB (gay-lesbian-bisexual) communities 'that LaForest be replaced by someone more committed to equality issues' (Morton and Knopff 2000, 107). This implies, at least, that EGALE intended to attempt to influence the selection process—efforts that will no doubt increase with future vacancies.

Direct Strategies for Influencing the Courts— Sponsorship of Cases

Of course, the most common way that interest groups try to influence the courts is through litigation in actual cases. Litigation by interest groups differs from that by individuals in that groups are rarely the parties in a case. The ability to bring a case before the courts is governed by the rules of standing, which although liberalized by the Canadian Supreme Court in recent decades, still present significant hurdles to group activity. As noted in Chapter 3, the current rules were established in three cases (*Thorson, McNeil,* and *Borowski*) in the late 1970s and early 1980s. These rules enable a public-interest group to bring a case if three criteria are met: a serious issue is at stake, the group attempting to bring the case has a genuine interest in the issue and, finally, there is no other 'reasonable and effective' method for bringing the issue before the courts. In 1981, the liberalized rules allowed Joseph Borowski (who was neither a doctor nor a pregnant woman) to proceed with his challenge to Canada's abortion law as a violation of the 'right to life' (since it allowed some abortions to proceed). However, the Court still prefers parties that are more directly affected by an issue, and interest groups have had some difficulty meeting the third requirement, that is, that there be no other reasonable and effective method of bringing the issue before the courts (see for example *Canadian Council of Churches v. Canada* 1992 and *R. v. Morgentaler*).[15]

Therefore, instead of acting as a party in a case, groups generally pursue litigation by either sponsoring cases or intervening in existing cases. An interest group sponsors a case by providing the financial backing and legal representation for a party bringing a case; a group intervenes when it obtains the court's permission to submit a brief in a case where it is not a direct party, and thereby presents the group's arguments on the legal issues before the court.

The Canadian women's group LEAF, one of the most frequent interest-group litigators before the courts, was created to pursue litigation through case sponsorship. The group wanted to 'assist women with important test cases and to ensure that equality rights litigation is undertaken in a planned, responsible and expert manner' (Fudge 1987, 487). Case sponsorship allows groups more control over the arguments presented to the court and, ideally, over the order in which issues are brought before the court—ensuring that the court sees only the issues it is ready to decide in a favourable way. The American NAACP LDF has been the model for many groups in its pursuit of sponsorship. Particularly in its education litigation, this group chose cases carefully to allow for a step-by-step dismantling of the 'separate but equal' doctrine. Cases with desirable characteristics were chosen in order to build up favourable precedents and force the US Supreme Court to confront the group's ultimate goal—the overruling of the separate-but-equal precedent and the end of segregation. Inspired by the success of the NAACP LDF, American women's groups tried to emulate the group's strategy. LEAF, arriving on the scene much later than the American groups, deliberately patterned its strategy after that of the NAACP LDF and what was probably the most successful American women's group of the time, the Women's Rights Project (Atcheson, Eberts and Symes 1984).

Although the advantages of sponsorship have made it a preferred litigation strategy for many groups, few groups actually undertake it, and women's groups in both the United States and Canada have had difficulty doing so. Sponsorship is a long-term strategy, and the planning and litigation required by this strategy requires extensive resources and time. The successful campaign launched by the NAACP LDF, as described above, took fifteen years and over $500,000 before the group achieved its ultimate goal in 1954 with *Brown v. Board of Education* (Lowery and Brasher 2004, 237; Schlozman and Tierney 1986). In addition, since the goal of sponsorship is usually to build a favourable precedent in an issue area, the success of this strategy is affected by the ability of the group to control the litigation field. The NAACP LDF was able to bring before the courts favourable-fact cases that gradually chipped away at the separate-but-equal doctrine. With offices in many of the places that had a high African-American population, the group was able to hear of potential lawsuits, offer its assistance, and control the timing of cases. Individual African Americans in the early period were also less likely to have the financial means to bring cases on their own. This meant that, although the process was impossible to fully control, the NAACP LDF had a relatively high success rate in controlling which cases went before the courts in its issue areas of interest (Wasby 1988).

Other groups, however, have not enjoyed that same success. These groups often find themselves surprised by cases brought by litigants in their issue area, cases that either have less than favourable facts—making a favourable court decision less sure—or have been brought too early, before the courts are ready to take a step in that direction. For example, women's groups interested in liberalizing a country's abortion law would probably prefer the party in the case they sponsor to be pregnant as a result of rape or incest, rather than to be surprised by a case brought by a pregnant woman who is litigating because she does not want to have another child for economic reasons.[16]

The difficulty of having other litigants in the field and the extraordinary resources needed to sponsor cases has meant that this strategy has not been extensively used by Canadian interest groups. EGALE, for example, found it very difficult to control the litigation area in its pursuit of equality rights for gays and lesbians. EGALE was often surprised by cases brought by individual litigants (see the discussion in Miriam Smith 2005, 340). And the National Citizens Coalition discovered how costly sponsorship could be in the 1991 case, *Lavigne v. Ontario Public Service Employees Union,* when it sponsored Lavigne's challenge to mandatory union dues (Lavigne disapproved of how some of the union dues were used). Sponsoring Lavigne, the NCC not only lost the case, but was also required to pay the costs of the union it had challenged, and—more unusually—the costs of unions acting as interveners in the case (for example, the Canadian Labour Congress). Even LEAF, which was formed with sponsorship as a litigation objective, recognized very early the difficulties of litigation and the need to be open to alternatives (Eberts 1986; Atcheson, Eberts, and Symes 1984). Indeed, though the group has sponsored cases in the lower courts,[17] it has sponsored only one (*Schachter v. Canada* 1992) of the forty cases it has participated in before the Supreme Court of Canada.

Direct Strategies for Influencing the Courts— Intervention in Cases

Most interest groups that litigate before the courts do so as interveners—a less costly alternative to sponsoring a case.[18] As mentioned above, intervention requires an interest group to obtain the court's permission to submit a brief in an existing case. Thus, this form of interest-group litigation requires less direct involvement by the groups but still allows groups to alert the justices to particular legal interpretations in their issues of interest. Although interveners have long been recognized in Canada[19]—they are even mentioned in the Supreme Court's 1878 rules—interest groups made only infrequent use of intervention in the years before the Charter (Brodie 2002). Though this is no longer the case (the history and frequency of interventions are discussed below), the practice is still much more recent here than in the United States. Much of what we know about such interest-group activity comes from studies of American groups. *Amicus curiae* is the term used in the United States for interested third parties that intervene in a case. Literally meaning 'friend of the court' amicus curiae were originally intended to aid judges with their decisions. Today amici in the US tend to be friends of one of the parties. The vast majority of amici write briefs that state their support for either the appellant or respondent right on the front page of the brief.

In Canada, interveners are also more likely to support a party than to be neutral. Some Canadian judges have expressed concern about this position taking by interveners in the briefs they submit to the court. For example, former Supreme Court Justice John Major publicly lamented the tendency of interveners to support one party or the other. Major argued that interveners should take a more 'objective approach'. He suggested that 'those interventions that . . . align their argument to support one party or the other with respect to the specific outcome of the appeal are, on this basis, of no value. . . . The anticipation of the Court is that the intervener remains neutral in the result, but introduces points different from the parties and helpful to the Court' (as quoted in Crane and Brown 2004, 276).

History of Interveners before the Courts

As mentioned above, third-party intervention has been common in the United States. Indeed today well over 90 per cent of cases before the American Supreme Court have amicus curiae participation (Epstein et al. 2006). Other countries' courts have been slower to allow these interventions. Most Commonwealth countries have 'a relatively undeveloped system of public interest intervention' (Clark 2005, 72). In Britain it is only in the past six or seven years that third-party interventions have become common (Arshi and O'Cinneide 2004, 69–70). In New Zealand this form of participation is just beginning (Clark 2005, 74) and in Australia the policies regarding third-party intervention are still more restrictive (Clark 2005, 74, 83).

The rules of intervention in Canada were left nearly unchanged in the 100 years following their first enactment in 1878 (Rule 60 of the *Supreme Court Rules*) (Welch 1985). According to those original rules, interested parties could intervene by leave of the Court or a judge 'upon such terms and conditions and with such rights and privileges as the Court or Judge may determine' (Welch 1985, 215). However, it was primarily governments that were granted the right to intervene before the courts under Rule 60; interest groups were confined to participation in an occasional reference case (Welch 1985). In the 1970s the Supreme Court attracted attention when it allowed interest groups to intervene in two non-reference cases: one dealing with the right to equality, *Attorney General of Canada v. Lavell* (1974), and a second involving the abortion issue, *Morgentaler v. the Queen* (1976). This increased openness to interest-group interveners, which continued into the early 1980s, was primarily due to the attitudes and influence of Chief Justice Bora Laskin.

In 1983, the Supreme Court changed its rules of intervention. The new Rule 32 gave governments the 'right to intervene' in cases where a constitutional question had been stated. Governments merely had to file a notice stating their intention to participate in such a case. The new Rule 18 also gave an automatic right to intervene to any group that had participated as an intervener before a lower court (see Welch 1985 for a detailed description of these rule changes). However, these rules were short-lived, and by December 1983, the Court had rescinded the automatic right to intervene for interest groups participating at lower courts and suggested that group participation in 'purely criminal appeals' would not be allowed (Welch 1985, 219). Thus despite the promise of the rule changes in 1983, and the passage of the Charter, interest-group access to the Canadian Supreme Court actually became more restricted in the early to mid-1980s.[20]

In 1984, Supreme Court Justice Bertha Wilson argued for allowing more interventions before the Supreme Court. She argued that this would 'assist in legitimizing the Court's new role through a more open and accessible court process, and it would go part way to solving the counter-majoritarian problem which some see as inherent in judicial power' (Sharpe and Roach 2003, 385). However, Wilson's colleagues on the bench were less favourable to the idea. Some were concerned about the Court's new role under the Charter and felt participation by interest groups and other non-parties would distract the Court from following legal principles when deciding cases (Sharpe and Roach 2003, 384). Others were concerned about the time such interventions cost the Court and the complexity they added to the case. In 1985, Justice William Estey argued that 'this Court no longer has the time to fritter away sitting and listening to repetition, irrelevancies, axe-grinding, cause advancement, and all the rest of the output of the typical intervenant' (Sharpe and Roach 2003, 385).

After the gains they had made in the 1970s, interest groups were dismayed with the more restricted access they again faced in the early 1980s. In response, they launched a campaign to lobby the Court to allow more interventions. For example, Alan Borovoy of the CCLA submitted a brief to the Court asking it to rethink its decision to prevent his group from intervening in an early Charter case. Borovoy argued that 'the entire community will be increasingly affected . . . by decisions of the Court [and thus] larger sections of the community should be able to participate in the process which produces those decisions. [He suggested] a more inclusive process was required to ensure public respect for both the Charter and the Court' (Sharpe and Roach 2003, 386). Articles also appeared in law reviews and other academic outlets criticizing the Court's closed-door approach to interveners (see for example Welch 1985 and Bryden 1987).

After a *Globe and Mail* article reported the criticism of the Court's approach to non-government intervention, Chief Justice Brian Dickson scheduled the issue for discussion at the Court's next conference (Sharpe and Roach 2003, 388). Presumably as a result of this discussion, the justices asked the Supreme Court's Liaison Committee to the Canadian Bar Association to study the issue and make recommendations. The committee received submissions from various interest groups, including the CCLA and LEAF, which argued for a more open-door policy to interest-group interveners (Brodie 2002). These groups were disappointed with the committee's recommendation, which would have required interest groups to demonstrate that the parties in the case would not adequately represent a group's interests and legal arguments. However, the new rule on intervention adopted by the Court in 1987 was more permissive, allowing interest-group intervention as long as groups could demonstrate their 'submissions would be useful to the Court and different from those of the other parties' (Sharpe and Roach 2003, 389). This new rule also reaffirmed the right of Attorneys General to intervene in constitutional cases. After 1987, interest groups were granted permission to intervene at a much higher rate—several groups, such as the CCLA and LEAF, achieved routine acceptance by the Court.

In a 1999 case, *Lovelace v. Ontario*, the Supreme Court appeared to qualify slightly its acceptance of interveners. In that case the Court denied intervener status to several groups and denied others the right to make oral arguments before the Court. This case created a two-step process that was codified into law in 2002. Interest groups must first obtain the Court's permission to intervene in a case. The Court later decides whether oral arguments will be allowed and, if so, how long they may be (Crane and Brown 2004, 274–5).

These modest rule changes may reflect further changes in judicial attitudes. In interviews with Canadian judges, Greene et al. discovered that for Quebec Court of Appeal judges at least, opinion was divided about the appropriateness of 'the use of the courts by social and public-interest groups to achieve social change' (1998, 97). Judges who expressed support for such activity by groups argued that judges could keep it in check by denying standing to groups without real interest in a case. Judges who were less in favour of such activity tended to distinguish between public and private law cases. These judges saw fewer problems with allowing such intervention in public law cases (involving governments) than they did in private law cases.[21] Since private law cases involve parties that are individuals or corporations, these judges expressed reservations about allowing groups to participate since such participation could increase the length of the trial and thus the costs (Greene et al. 1998, 97).

The Supreme Court justices interviewed by Greene et al. were asked to rate the appropriateness of the use of the court by social and public-interest groups. On a scale of 1 to 5 (with 5 being 'extremely appropriate'), the responding justices gave an average response of 3.5 (Greene et al. 1998, 127). In the interviews, a few of the justices suggested that these groups could be helpful for the information they provide the court and another justice thought the participation was appropriate since the court was 'part of the democratic process' (Greene et al. 1998, 127).

In a 2000 interview with the *National Post*, Chief Justice Beverley McLachlin stated that 'many times the cases that come before us ask us to make rulings that affect not only the parties but a wide range of other people. So it's only just and fair that we allow those other people to present their viewpoints' (Chwialkowska 2000). However, in that same interview with the *National Post*, Justice Bastarache took a less favourable position toward group intervention. He suggested that the information provided by interveners may not be as necessary today as it may have been when the Charter was enacted in 1982. Indeed, Bastarache argued that 'there is some reason for us to reconsider our general policy on interveners simply because of the fact that we have lived with the Charter for 18 years and we have a lot of experience in interpreting the Charter' (Chwialkowska 2000). Justice Major, who appeared to agree with Bastarache in the interview, suggested that 'what has probably been a mistake is that we've opened the door probably too widely to interveners' (Chwialkowska 2000).

Debate on Intervener Participation

These differing judicial attitudes towards interveners are mirrored in the academic literature. There is a debate as to whether the participation of interest-group litigants is problematic for democratic governance. Morton and Knopff, two leading critics of interest-group litigation before the courts, argue that Canadian courts have been 'pushed' by a 'Court Party' towards a rights revolution (2000, 24). This 'Court Party' is a political minority made up of networks of individuals and groups (of which the CCLA and LEAF are two prominent members) that want to 'constitutionalize policy preferences that could not easily be achieved through the legislative process' (Morton and Knopff 2000, 25). Work by Morton and Knopff and Ian Brodie among others argues that the Supreme Court in the Charter era has used interest groups for cover when pursuing judicial activism—to portray itself 'as the defender of disadvantaged groups . . . [a move] that insulates the Court from criticisms of its activism . . . [since] criticizing the courts would be criticizing the disadvantaged' (Brodie 2002, xvii). Through this the Court has used judicial review to extend the power of the state and promote social reform. Critics of interest-group litigation argue that the groups litigating most often in Canada are anything but disadvantaged. [22] These groups have circumvented the legislature to achieve tremendous policy gains and in doing so have helped courts elevate themselves far above their traditional role in a liberal democracy.

Supporters of interest-group litigation counter that litigation by groups such as aboriginal peoples, civil libertarians, LEAF, and EGALE—what Gregory Hein (2000) calls 'judicial democrats'—can actually enhance democracy. Judicial democrats believe that litigation and court action are necessary to ensure the protection of minorities—particularly unpopular minorities—from action by unrepresentative legislatures whose majorities are 'more apparent than real' (given plurality elections) and that have a history of not being equally accessible to everyone (Hein 2000, 20). Indeed, these groups suggest that 'litigation has the potential to make our public institutions more accessible, transparent and responsive, if courts hear from a diverse range of interests, guard fundamental social values and protect disadvantaged minorities' (Hein 2000, 19).

Intervener Participation before the Supreme Court in the Charter Era

Since most research on the practice of intervention in Canada has been directed at the Supreme Court, less is known about such activity in the lower courts. But what we do know points to less interest-group activity in the lower courts, particularly at the trial level. Although groups like the CCLA and LEAF have been interveners before lower courts, as a rule, interest groups pay more attention to appellate courts, especially the Supreme Court, because it sits at the top of the judicial hierarchy. Our discussion of interveners has also concentrated on their participation at the 'merits stage' of a case (once the Court has agreed to hear a case) rather than at the earlier leave-to-appeal stage (where a party asks the Court to hear a case on appeal). Though it is theoretically possible for a group to be granted the right to intervene at the application-for-leave stage, this is a very rare occurrence. Supreme Court justices have discouraged this type of participation, and group involvement has come almost exclusively after this stage (Flemming 2004; Crane and Brown 2004).

Table 7.1 presents the percentage of cases actually accepted by the Supreme Court that had intervener participation in the year preceding and the ten years following the Supreme Court's changes to the rules on intervention. One can see that in the early years of the Charter, cases with government interveners were far more common than those with non-government interveners. However, as time went on, the percentage of cases with non-government interveners increased steadily, and for some parts of the 1990s these participants were present in a higher percentage of cases than governments. While this ten-year snapshot is meant to demonstrate the patterns of intervention after the rule changes, the actual number

Table 7.1   Percentage of Supreme Court Cases with Interveners by Type, 1986–97

	Non-Government (%)	Provincial Governments (%)	Federal Government (%)
1986	5.4	13.5	12.2
1987	2.2	17.6	11.0
1988	6.8	17.5	16.5
1989	8.7	20.5	12.6
1990	8.4	32.1	23.7
1991	16.0	17.0	11.0
1992	19.6	15.7	15.7
1993	13.0	16.0	11.5
1994	17.0	10.4	10.4
1995	18.4	18.4	11.7
1996	17.4	15.7	9.1
1997	17.3	7.1	5.4

Note:
All cases are included with the exception of reference cases, motions, and rehearings.

of interventions by non-government interveners has increased in the years since 1997. For example, of the fifty-nine cases decided in 2006, over 40 per cent had non-government interveners (government interveners remained relatively constant with percentages in the mid-teens).[23]

Table 7.2 examines the rate of participation of non-government interveners in more detail. This table illustrates the increase in the number of briefs submitted by non-government interveners in the ten years after the 1987 rule change. It also presents the total number of non-government interveners participating in cases each year. This latter number suggests that most briefs were signed by more than one intervener. The numbers have remained relatively consistent in the years since 1997. In the cases decided in 2006, for example, sixty-five non-government intervener briefs were filed and eighty-eight interveners appeared before the Court. These numbers are comparable to the higher numbers seen in 1996 and 1997.

Table 7.2   Non-government Intervener Participation in Cases before the Supreme Court, 1986–97

	# of Cases with Non-govt. Interveners	# of Briefs with Non-govt. Interveners	Total # of Non-govt. Interveners
1986	4	8	10
1987	2	2	2
1988	7	9	19
1989	11	26	29
1990	11	34	55
1991	16	28	37
1992	20	38	66
1993	17	44	60
1994	18	32	50
1995	19	43	69
1996	21	65	95
1997	17	49	84

Notes:

1. All cases decided each year are included, with the exception of reference cases, motions, and rehearings.
2. The government label is used only for interveners represented by a provincial or federal Attorney General or the corresponding justice department. Thus, some entities, such as Canada Post, that operate—and litigate—more at arm's length from the government may be included in the non-government numbers.

The vast majority of these non-government interveners are individuals or corporations. However, these participants usually appear before the Court only once; they do not undertake systematic litigation. Public-interest groups, by contrast, participate in many cases as they try to advance their interests. The non-government intervener with the highest rate of intervention from 1986 to 1997 was LEAF, followed by the CCLA. Other interest groups that participated relatively frequently in these years included such wide-ranging organizations as the Coalition of Provincial Organizations of the Handicapped, REAL Women, the Fisheries Council of British Columbia, the Canadian Jewish Congress, the League for Human Rights of B'Nai Brith, and Alliance Quebec.

Of course litigation in any form is expensive. Though intervention is a less costly alternative to sponsoring a case, it still requires a substantial amount of money. In his study of the 'rights revolution' in countries such as the United States, Britain, India, and Canada, Charles Epp points out that rights advocacy groups in Canada have benefited from government funding (1998). Through avenues such as the Court Challenges Program, groups like LEAF have received financial support for their litigation. Box 7.2 outlines the time line of the Court Challenges Program—a program that has been the focus of controversy for its funding of interest groups.

Box 7.2   The Court Challenges Program

1978—Court Challenges Program established by Prime Minister Trudeau to provide funding to those wanting to challenge Quebec language legislation in court.

1985—Prime Minister Brian Mulroney extends the mission of the program to include funding of litigation challenging federal legislation on the basis of equal rights.

1992—The program falls victim to budget cuts by the Mulroney Conservative government.

1994—The Liberal government re-establishes the Court Challenges Program as a 'national non-profit organization . . . set up . . . to provide financial assistance for important court cases that advance language and equality rights guaranteed under Canada's Constitution' (www.ccppcj.ca).

Funding is provided for case development and for case funding. To qualify for funding, a case must test equality rights under the Charter and must 'improve the way the law works for people who have suffered discrimination' (www.ccppcj.ca).

1994–2006—The Court Challenges Program comes under increasing criticism primarily from social conservatives who argue the program has been 'captured' by rights advocacy groups. Conservative groups such as REAL Women point out the difference in funding levels between themselves and groups like LEAF.

2006—The new Conservative government cancels the Court Challenges Program.

As noted in Box 7.2, the Court Challenges Program was set up by the federal government to fund groups challenging legislation (either on the basis of language or equality rights). Official-language minority groups and public-interest groups such as LEAF benefited tremendously from the program and lobbied hard for its continued survival. Some argue the program was captured by these groups, noting that—at least in its post-1994 form—its board of directors included some language-rights activists and some equality–rights activists (Morton and Knopff 2000; Brodie 2002). Indeed Ian Brodie argues that the program became more autonomous from government over the years and was instead controlled by its beneficiaries (2002, 116). Brodie and other critics have suggested that the funding decisions of the Court Challenges Program have tended to favour rights claimant groups over conservative groups, noting cases where LEAF was funded but REAL Women (LEAF's conservative counterpart) was not. Using arguments similar to those used to question the participation of interest groups before the courts, these critics question the propriety of government funding for groups that are challenging government legislation—particularly when that support does not extend to all groups. The Court Challenges Program was cancelled by Stephen Harper's Conservative government in 2006. Interestingly, Ian Brodie had left academia and was serving as Harper's Chief of Staff when the program was cancelled.

Success and Influence of Interest Groups at Court

As we have pointed out, the direct strategy of intervention has been the most common route by which interest groups pursue their interests in court. Two questions remain: have groups been successful in achieving their goals before the courts, and is any success they have enjoyed a result of their influencing the justices and their decision making? These questions are probably more complicated than they appear. First, one must ask what constitutes a group's success? Some groups may litigate in order to achieve publicity for their issue area of interest or to satisfy their members that they are active in that issue area. However, researchers usually focus on a more common definition of litigation success: winning a case.

Of course, what constitutes winning a case is also a matter of debate. In the 1988 *R. v. Morgentaler* case, the Supreme Court struck down Canada's abortion law. The outcome of this decision was considered a victory for pro-choice groups. However, the case doctrine left less room for celebration by these groups. Four of the five justices making up the majority in the case struck down the law on procedural grounds, and at least two of these justices explicitly suggested a remedied law would pass constitutional scrutiny. Only one justice, Justice Bertha Wilson, argued that women have the right to an abortion. Thus a win on outcome was not equalled by a clear win on reasoning, with the result that future decisions in the area were more uncertain; the 'right' outcome does not ensure the 'right' result in the future if the 'right' reasoning is not there to support it.

Most studies of interest-group litigation focus on case outcome in their analysis. However, studies that distinguish between outcome and doctrine often discover a different level of success for each. For example, a study of LEAF's success before the Supreme Court discovered that the group was more successful in achieving favourable case outcomes than it was in achieving favourable case doctrine (Hausegger 1999). The case presented at the beginning of this chapter is an example. In *R. v. Seaboyer*, the Supreme Court dismissed the appeal of the men accused of sexual assault—a win for LEAF in terms of case outcome. However, in their decision, the Court struck down s. 276 of the Criminal Code (one of Canada's rape shield laws) as a violation of the Charter. This reasoning was directly contrary to LEAF's interests. Nevertheless, LEAF has been quite successful in terms of doctrine—enjoying a 78 per cent success rate in cases it participated in during the 1980s and 1990s (Hausegger 1999; see Manfredi 2004 for similar findings).

Morton and Allen (2001) argue that even when LEAF and other feminist organizations have lost before the Supreme Court, most of those losses have not resulted in an unfavourable policy change. These authors argue that feminist groups have been successful in instigating changes by governments towards the groups' favoured policy. For example, after their 'loss' on doctrine in *R. v. Seaboyer*, LEAF turned to Parliament for a remedy. The group was able to have some input in a new sexual-assault law—a law that so pleased women's groups that feminists suggested *Seaboyer* may have been a 'blessing in disguise' (Morton and Allen 2001). Miriam Smith makes a similar observation in her study of lesbian and gay rights in Canada. She suggests that some litigation losses might actually help groups by raising awareness of an issue and mobilizing the community to pursue political action (1999, 46–55).

Though LEAF has been the focus of several studies, it may not be the most representative group in terms of success. Scholars have long noted the influence of different resources on the success of parties before the courts, and studies have shown that repeated appearances before a court allow parties to build up experience, creating 'repeat players' that are advantaged in their litigation (Galanter 1974). As the most frequent interest-group litigator before the Supreme Court, LEAF should enjoy more success than some of its counterparts. Individuals and groups that appear before the Court only once are unlikely to have the expertise or relationship with the Court that benefit repeat players. However, even LEAF probably does not enjoy as much success as the ultimate repeat players before the courts: governments. As noted in the next chapter, several studies have found the American federal government to be particularly advantaged before the courts (see for example, Songer, Sheehan and Haire 1999; Salokar 1992), and the Canadian governments also appear to enjoy high levels of success (McCormick 1993; Haynie et al. 2001). In a study of cases heard by the Canadian Supreme Court from 1949 to 1992, Peter McCormick discovered that the Crown[24] was the most successful litigant, followed by the federal government, big business, and provincial governments (1993, 532). As LEAF has usually intervened on the side of government parties (Manfredi 2004), the group may also be benefiting from the repeat-player status of the governments.

Influence

As the last statement suggests, success does not equal influence, and 'being on the winning side may have more to do with the type of litigants amici [interveners] choose to support than any effect of amicus [intervener] participation' (Songer and Kuersten 1995, 36). How might interest groups achieve influence over the justices' decisions? The groups are thought to gain influence by providing information to the justices. This information may be data and arguments unique to the groups' briefs that enable the courts to decide cases involving new issues such as those involving the Charter in the 1980s. Jerry DeMarco (2005), for example, partly substantiates his arguments that interveners have played a 'substantial role' in shaping environment-law decisions before the Canadian Supreme Court by pointing to the fact that the Court has referred to authorities that were cited only in intervener factums. Box 7.3 describes one of the most prominent examples of this type of influence which occurred in a US case, *Mapp v. Ohio*.

Box 7.3   *Mapp v. Ohio* (1961)

In 1957, Ohio police officers attempted to enter Dollree Mapp's home to search for a fugitive accused of bombing the house of Don King (who later became a high-profile boxing promoter). Mapp refused them entry, and the police left, only to return three hours later with more officers. When Mapp did not answer the door, the officers opened it 'forcibly'. When Mapp demanded to see the search warrant, the police waved a piece of paper at her. A scuffle then broke out between Mapp and the police, Mapp grabbing the paper and shoving it down her blouse and the police retrieving it and restraining her. At the same time Mapp's lawyer arrived at the house but was refused entry by the police. The police proceeded to conduct a thorough search, which included looking in dresser drawers and photo albums. In the process the police discovered obscene material the possession of which was illegal under Ohio law. At trial, the search warrant was not produced, and the trial court stated there was 'considerable doubt as to whether there ever was any warrant for the search of [the] defendant's home'. Nevertheless, Mapp was convicted of possession of obscene material.

Mapp then appealed her conviction to the Supreme Court. In their briefs to the court, both Mapp's lawyer and the lawyer for Ohio based their arguments on the First Amendment and the possession of obscene material in one's home. By contrast, a brief submitted by an amicus curiae, the American Civil Liberties Union, argued that Mapp's conviction should be overturned on the basis of the Fourth Amendment which protects against unreasonable search and seizure. The ACLU argued that since the evidence had been obtained illegally, it should have been excluded from the trial. In *Mapp v. Ohio* (1961), the Supreme Court picked up the arguments of the ACLU and reversed Mapp's conviction on the basis of the Fourth Amendment. The justices applied the exclusionary rule for illegally obtained evidence to the states for the first time.

Sources: *Mapp v. Ohio* (1961); Epstein and Walker (2007).

Interest groups may also act as 'signals' to the courts by letting them know that important issues are before them—issues of interest to a broader community. They can indicate to the justices 'the array of social forces at play in the litigation' (Caldeira and Wright 1988, 1111). They also provide information about public opinion—or at least their own constituency's opinion—on an issue area before the court. These signals may influence the justices' approach to the case. It is also thought that groups may exert some influence over the justices because of their ability to turn to the legislature for a remedy of a court's decision. Since justices are thought to prefer their decisions be left standing, this implicit threat may cause the justices to listen more closely to a group's arguments.

Are interest groups actually influential? Charles Epp (1998) has argued that through their litigation, organized interest groups have contributed to a 'rights revolution' in several countries, including Canada. According to Epp, the combination of organized interest groups that bring cases to courts and supportive judges has ensured the far-reaching influence of the Charter of Rights and Freedoms in the policy arena. Without the mobilizing by such groups, the Charter might have been merely a series of 'empty promises'.

However, at the individual-case level, much of the American literature has cast doubt on the influence of interest groups, focusing instead on the importance of the justices' own policy preferences when they decide cases. The few studies that have tried to test interest-group influence directly have produced mixed results. Songer and Sheehan (1993), for example, examined amici participation before the US Supreme Court, and found that litigants who were supported by amicus briefs were no more successful than those that were not. However, Songer and Kuersten (1995) found that litigants were more successful when supported by amici at state supreme courts. Robin Wolpert (1991), who examined gender discrimination cases, found that, controlling for other possible influences, the number of amicus curiae briefs supporting a particular litigant increased the probability of the court's deciding in favour of that litigant. By contrast, Steven Tauber (1998) found that the NAACP LDF did not exert influence in the capital punishment cases in which it participated.

The influence of groups before the Canadian Supreme Court has not received much systematic testing. Manfredi argues that the most frequent interest-group litigator, LEAF, has 'made a difference through the type of evidence it brought to the Court's attention', noting that from 1988 to 2000 'the Court made 108 references to extralegal material cited in LEAF factums' (2004, 150, 153). One quantitative study of LEAF discovered that, controlling for other possible influences—such as judicial preferences and the facts of the case—LEAF did influence the outcome of cases. LEAF's presence made an outcome favourable to the group's interests more likely. However, that same study discovered that LEAF's presence did not make favourable doctrine in the court's ruling more likely (Hausegger 1999). Since interest groups are probably more interested in their long term impact on an issue area, this finding suggests groups may have less influence on courts than their detractors have feared.

Whether groups do manage to influence Canadian courts is still a matter of debate and in need of more systematic study. However, some Supreme Court justices have given reasons to doubt the impact of interest-group participation. As detailed earlier, Justice Bastarache, at least, has suggested that the information provided by the groups is less useful today than it was when the Charter was first enacted—when the justices had had less experience dealing with the issues raised by the document.

Conclusions

This chapter began with *R. v. Seaboyer,* the case of two men charged with sexual assault. By the time the case reached the appellate-court level, Seaboyer and

Gayme were no longer alone before the court. Instead, governments and interest groups had joined them, each making arguments about the 'proper' disposition of the case. Why might interest groups participate in a criminal case, taking sides for and against the accused? This book suggests that courts, and particularly the Supreme Court, are political institutions that make policies with far-reaching implications. Interest groups turn to litigation to achieve their policy goals. Thus LEAF joined *R. v. Seaboyer* in an effort to support legislation that protected victims in sexual assault cases—something they believed to be vital in their campaign to end violence towards women—and the CCLA joined to further its fight for fundamental freedoms and the rights of the criminally accused.

As we pointed out, LEAF and the CCLA are not alone in their litigation—a great variety of interest groups use the courts. In *Seaboyer*, both LEAF and the CCLA adopted a direct strategy for achieving their goals: they intervened in the case. The difficulties of sponsoring a case and the almost Herculean task of controlling the litigation field mean that groups are pushed into intervention more often—forced to jump into a case already underway rather than undertake a carefully planned campaign. It is in this role as intervener that interest groups are probably most objectionable to their critics. Some scholars argue that there is a litigating 'Court Party', which is pushing the Court towards judicial activism. They worry that groups are not only increasing the time and costs involved in court cases but are also making an 'end run' around the elected legislature in the pursuit of their goals. Supporters of interest-group litigation, by contrast, suggest that group participation, even as interveners, can be advantageous to democracy. They argue that this litigation makes political institutions more accessible and ensures the protection of minorities.

Each of these views rests, to some extent, on the assumption that interest groups achieve their goals before the courts. However, as *R. v. Seaboyer* illustrates, we must be careful when measuring the success of a group. Achieving the right outcome in a case is not enough to further a group's goals—the right doctrine needs to accompany it. In addition, a careful determination of success does not end the larger debate of whether interest-group litigation is actually effective, that is, whether group participation influences the justices' decisions. The high rate of group participation before the courts suggests that groups believe they do have influence. However, this belief has not been settled definitively in the literature. In addition, *R. v. Seaboyer* suggests the need to consider the fate of a group's policy goals more broadly since groups may fail before the court and yet still achieve long-term success by exerting influence on the legislature. Thus interest-group litigation is an area in need of further study—not only to provide answers about the success and influence of interest groups, but also, perhaps more important, to facilitate a more informed debate about whether interest-group litigation itself damages or enhances democracy.

Chapter 8

Governments in Court[1]

In 2001, eight gay and lesbian couples applied to the British Columbia Director of Vital Statistics for marriage licences but were denied on the grounds that the statutory and common-law definitions of 'marriage' included only opposite-sex couples. Accompanied by the advocacy group EGALE Canada (see Chapter 7), the couples sued the governments of British Columbia—which, like all the provinces, issues marriage licences—and of Canada—which has jurisdiction over the definition of marriage—on the grounds that the laws violated their equality rights under the Charter of Rights and Freedoms. Both governments maintained that the definition of marriage was constitutional. After the claimants lost at trial, they appealed successfully to the British Columbia Court of Appeal in the spring of 2003 (*EGALE Canada v. Canada* 2003). A similar ruling was made in Ontario shortly afterwards (*Halpern v. Canada* 2003).

The federal government led by Prime Minister Jean Chrétien now had to make a decision: should it accept the losses in court, and thus have to immediately recognize same-sex marriages (but only in those courts' provinces), or appeal to the Supreme Court of Canada, where it would most likely lose again given that Court's recent record of supporting equality rights for sexual orientation (and risk setting a national precedent)? The federal government chose a third option: it drafted a bill that would recognize same-sex marriages but protect the religious freedom of churches to refuse to perform them, and before allowing Parliament to debate the bill, referred it to the Supreme Court to assess its constitutionality under the Charter and the federal division of powers.[2] The Court's opinion, released in December 2004, was that the bill would be constitutional, but it refused to answer the key question of whether the government *must* recognize same-sex marriage, on the grounds that it was unnecessary to answer since the government had already said it planned to do so (*Reference re Same-Sex Marriage* 2004). Paul Martin's Liberal minority government tabled the bill in Parliament, where it was narrowly passed in June 2005 and received Royal Assent a month later. Same-sex marriages were now legally recognized in Canadian law.

The saga of same-sex marriage hints at the complexities governments face as litigants in the courts. The cases illustrate two ways Canadian governments can appear in court—by being sued, and through the reference procedure—and some of the important strategic decisions they must make in the course of litigation. For example, should they concede the claims of plaintiffs, appeal losses to higher courts, or use the reference procedure to receive the court's advice quickly on legal questions? This chapter examines the role of the government as a litigant, that is, as a party before the courts. After discussing the various ways in which governments can become litigants, the chapter describes the government's lawyer: the Attorney General (AG). The chapter then focuses on the decisions a governmental has to make about litigation, such as whether to prosecute, initiate a reference, intervene, appeal, or concede, and whether AGs should be 'independent' of the government's leadership when handling litigation. We then examine the success rate of governments in court, which is very high. The concluding section examines the implications of these strategies for the relationship between courts and governments, and for the way we view the impact of courts on public policy and democracy itself.

Governments as Litigants: Why Do Governments Appear in Court?

Governments are the most frequently appearing class of litigants, ahead of businesses, unions, professional associations, and public-interest advocacy groups like EGALE or LEAF. There are five ways in which the government can appear in court, four of them as a 'direct party' to the case, and the fifth as a 'third-party' intervener. These are as follows:

Prosecution of Offences

The most common reason governments appear in court is to prosecute offences and enforce municipal by-laws. In Chapter 1, where we explored the different types of legal disputes, 'criminal' disputes—or more accurately, enforcement of offences—were distinguished by the fact that the case involves the accused individual and the *state*; the state represents the victim of the offence and the broader society's interest in punishing and deterring similar behaviour that undermines public peace and safety. In criminal law, the prosecuting state is usually called the 'Crown' or 'Crown Attorney', reflecting the fact that Canada's head of state is the Queen (or King).[3] As noted in Chapter 2, both the provincial and federal governments can create offences, although only the latter can create the more serious indictable offences.

A unique feature of Canadian law is that the prosecution of *criminal* offences—which, recall, are created by the federal Parliament—are usually enforced by provincial governments. This is because s. 92(14) of the 1867 Constitution gives the provinces jurisdiction over the administration of justice, as does the *Criminal Code*. This division of responsibility reflects Canada's federal nature and creates an interesting dynamic: criminal offences are created at the national level but enforced 'locally', thus allowing national standards to be influenced by the values of the smaller community in which the crime took place. Thus it is unlikely that, for example, the crime of distributing pornography is enforced to the same degree in Montreal as it is in small-town Saskatchewan. A more concrete example arose when the federal government created its gun registry, which was deeply unpopular in rural areas, where guns and hunting are common. The several provincial governments that opposed the registry, such as Alberta, Newfoundland, and Ontario, stated that they would not prosecute anyone who committed the offence of refusing to register their guns (Lindgren and Naumetz 2003, A1). This 'federalism' dynamic in criminal law has only been reinforced by the trend toward making the provincially appointed s. 92 courts primarily responsible for trials of criminal (and many other federal) offences.

Although the federal government can choose to prosecute some crimes if the province refuses—as Ottawa threatened to do with the gun registry[4]— some offences, most notably narcotics, income tax fraud, illegal fishing, and since 2001, terrorism, are usually enforced by the federal government. Another exception is that the federal government retained the power to prosecute criminal offences in territories that are administered federally, that is, the Northwest Territories, Nunavut and the Yukon, and on Indian reserves.[5] Federal authority to prosecute offences is asserted in s. 2 of the *Criminal Code*,[6] which provoked disputes between the federal and provincial governments, climaxing in a series of cases in the late 1970s and early 1980s.[7] The crux of the provinces' argument was that many federal non-Code offences—most notably, narcotics offences—were criminal law in 'pith and substance', regardless of their exclusion from the Code, and their prosecution was therefore within provincial jurisdiction over 'the administration of justice' in section 92(14). The Supreme Court of Canada resolved this dispute in favour of the federal government in three key cases, *R. v. Hauser* (1979), *A.G. (Canada) v. Canadian National Transportation, Ltd.* (1983), and *R. v. Wetmore* (1983). In *Hauser*, the first to be decided, the majority of the Court agreed with the provinces that criminal prosecutions are properly conducted by provinces, but it also found that Ottawa can prosecute offences arising under any federal jurisdiction *other than* the criminal law, such as fisheries (s. 91(12)), trade and commerce (s. 91(2)), and the 'residual power' in the s. 91 'POGG' (Peace, Order and Good Government) clause (which included the regulation and prohibition of narcotics).[8] Whereas *Hauser* appeared to work around the province's jurisdiction in s. 92(14) by preserving provincial prosecution of 'criminal' matters, the *C.N. Transportation* and *Wetmore* decisions only four years later rejected this restrictive approach. In a striking rejection of long-standing practice, the Court stated that s. 92(14) does not give provinces a monopoly over criminal prosecution, observing that this had simply been an arrangement authorized by the statutory *Criminal Code* rather than the Constitution; if the federal government wanted to change this arrangement, it could do so by simply amending the *Criminal Code* or any other quasi-criminal legislation to give itself the power to prosecute. As pointed out in notes 6 and 8,

Ottawa has done so with a number of offences, including terrorism, war crimes, crimes against humanity, membership in a gang, firearms offences, and a wide range of offences committed against international diplomats and their property. Even with these, however, provincial governments may still choose to prosecute, so the jurisdiction is effectively shared.

All of this said, the lion's share of offences are currently prosecuted by provincial governments, the major exception being drug-related offences.

Defendant in Civil Suits

It is fairly common for individuals and groups in society to sue governments for damages or unfair treatment just as they might sue another person or institution. As the state has grown, through expanded social programs, business regulation, and taxation systems, the potential for conflict between the state and society has also increased. Some examples should be familiar: Natives have been engaged in protracted suits against the federal government for abuse they sustained in the old residential schools. This system took aboriginal children from their families and communities in order to 'westernize' and Christianize them, forcibly erasing their own languages, cultures, and religious beliefs. Refugees and immigrants who are refused entry to Canada commonly challenge the decisions of government officials in court on the grounds that proper procedures were not followed or important factors in their cases were overlooked. Similarly, people who are denied government benefits (such as Employment Insurance or social assistance) or licences (whether for marriages or to run a television station) often challenge the decision in court, as we saw with same-sex marriage. Although most Charter cases (over 70 per cent) arise when someone claims his or her rights in the course of being prosecuted for a crime (for example, 'free expression' (s. 2(b)) as a defence for possessing child pornography, or protection against 'unreasonable search and seizure' (s. 8) to contest a successful drug raid), many Charter cases begin as civil suits against the government, where someone claims a government decision or law has violated his or her rights. Besides same-sex marriage, we have witnessed this with Quebec's ban on private health insurance (*Chaoulli* 2005), the denial of government-paid parental leave to biological fathers (*Schachter* 1992), and the use of 'security certificates' to indeterminately detain immigrants suspected of terrorism (*Charkaoui* 2007), amongst many other issues.

Plaintiff in Civil Suits

Just as the government can be sued, it can sue others like any other plaintiff. This occurs fairly rarely, and usually in one of two situations. The first is when the government sues a business, usually in a dispute related to some service the business was contracted to provide. In Chapter 2 we cited the example of *McNamara*

Construction v. The Queen (1977), where the federal government attempted to sue a company it had hired to build a penitentiary for breach of contract. The second situation is when one government sues another. This is very rare, because inter-governmental disputes in court are more commonly handled through the refer-ence procedure (see next section). An example of a 'regular' civil suit between governments occurred when the Peel Regional Municipality sued the federal and provincial governments for the cost of housing juvenile delinquents in group homes as part of a young offenders' program which those governments had forced the municipality to implement; Peel sued for compensation after the Supreme Court of Canada ruled that it was illegal to offload these costs onto municipalities (*Peel v. Canada and Ontario* 1992). Another example, this one involving the Constitution, arose in 1994 when British Columbia unsuccessfully sued the Government of Canada over the latter's decision to end passenger rail service on Vancouver Island, on the grounds that this service was guaranteed in the articles of British Columbia's entry into Confederation in 1871 (*British Columbia (A.G.) v. Canada (A.G.)* 1994).[9]

Recent developments in British Columbia point to a third scenario, where the government pursues civil litigation explicitly to influence public policy. In 2005, the Supreme Court of Canada upheld British Columbia's 1998 legislation (the *Tobacco Damages and Health Care Costs Recovery Act*), which allows the government to sue tobacco companies for financial damages in order to compensate the province for smoking-related health-care costs (*British Columbia v. Imperial Tobacco Canada Ltd.* 2005). The law permits not only retroactive damages, but also litiga-tion to recover the costs of future illnesses linked to 'tobacco-related wrongs'.

Reference Cases

Reference cases have been alluded to several times in this book already, but to recap, they occur when the federal government asks the Supreme Court of Canada—or a province asks its highest court of appeal—for an 'advisory opinion' on any 'question of law or fact'. As Russell (1987, 91) observes, the reference pro-cedure thus gives the executive branch of government 'privileged access' to those courts. It is important to note that the reference power is not found in the Constitution but is something governments have given themselves through regu-lar legislation and is therefore vulnerable to a court ruling that it violates judicial independence under the Charter or the Constitution's 'unwritten principles' (see Chapter 6). The first power to refer appeared in the 1875 statute creating the Supreme Court of Canada (currently s. 53 of the *Supreme Court Act*), and was first enacted in the provinces soon after by Manitoba, Nova Scotia, and Ontario in 1890 (Strayer 1988, 315–16).

A noteworthy feature of these provisions is that they are clearly designed to encourage the courts to resolve jurisdictional disputes between the various units of

Canada's federal system of government (Smith 1983; Strayer 1988, 314–15), for s. 53 explicitly allows the federal government to refer questions about *provincial* legislation or jurisdiction.[10] Provinces can reciprocate under their reference legislation;[11] for example, Ontario's Lieutenant Governor in Council may refer 'any question' to the Ontario Court of Appeal (*Courts of Justice Act*, s. 8(1)). As well, the *Supreme Court Act* (s. 53(5)) gives provinces the right to appear in any federally initiated reference case involving provincial legislation, and provincial reference legislation grants the reciprocal right to the federal government. Provincial references may be appealed to the Supreme Court of Canada, but there is not a 'right' to have the appeal heard; rather, they are handled like any other application for leave to appeal to that court, although there are no examples of such applications being denied.[12]

Although no one has conducted a comprehensive study of federal or provincial reference cases, about 170 references appear to have been either initiated or appealed to the Supreme Court of Canada (or, before 1949, the JCPC) since 1875, and Strayer (1988) reports that references represented over a third of constitutional law cases during the century after Confederation, but they declined to only 15 per cent between 1967 and 1986. Nonetheless, references are heavily over-represented in the most high-profile and contentious constitutional law cases in Canada's history. Besides same-sex marriage, the Supreme Court of Canada has heard references on such heated issues as the introduction of the GST (1992), the patriation of the Constitution (1981), the abolition of appeals to the JCPC (1940), whether Quebec can secede unilaterally (1998), whether Manitoba's entire body of statutes must be bilingual (1985), whether Ottawa can impose wage and price controls to fight inflation (1976), whether women are 'persons' under the Constitution (1928), and even whether references themselves violate judicial independence (1912; see Chapter 6). As discussed later in this chapter under 'Government Litigation Strategies', there are good political reasons why governments have shifted such issues to the courts.

Third-party Intervention

The previous chapter explained that interest groups have often opted to 'intervene' in court cases, a procedure that requires them to obtain the court's permission to present a legal argument (in writing, orally, or both) in a case where they are not a direct party. What makes intervention attractive to interest groups applies equally to governments: it is a cost-effective way to lobby the courts (usually the highest appellate courts) to adopt a particular legal interpretation. Specifically in the case of governments, intervention allows them to have input where the court is ruling on a policy very similar to the government's own, or on a legal provision—such as a Charter right—that may affect a number of its own laws. The federal and provincial governments together were actually the most frequent category of interveners until fairly recently (see Chapter 7, Table 7.1), although the federal government is the most frequent intervener in almost any year, followed closely by the AG Ontario (Brodie 2002, 38). There is a good reason for Ottawa's frequent appearances, which is related to the federal division of power over the administration of criminal justice noted earlier: whereas provinces prosecute the offences, the federal government is responsible for criminal law, including the creation of offences and defences, and for establishing the criminal process (rules regarding police procedure, evidence, appeals, sentencing, and so forth). The federal government therefore has a deeply vested interest in how the courts enforce and interpret these provisions. Particularly since the adoption of a wide range of 'due-process rights' (right to counsel, right against unreasonable search and seizure, and so on) with the 1982 Charter, the federal government has frequently been in a position to make arguments before the courts about potential changes to criminal law. To do so in the vast majority of cases where the prosecution is conducted by the province, the federal government must intervene.

Notably, however, it does not have a *right* to intervene unless the case involves a question of constitutional law. In non-constitutional cases, governments must obtain the permission or 'leave' of the court in which they wish to intervene. The guidelines that courts use when deciding whether to allow an intervener are laid out in the statutes establishing each court or their associated regulations. Since these guidelines are worded very loosely, the decision whether to admit an intervener is entirely up to the court. As a consequence, the courts have not always adhered closely to their own requirement that interveners bring distinct or novel perspectives. The Supreme Court ostensibly tightened up its criteria for government interveners in *R. v. Osolin* (1993), at least in criminal cases, by turning down Ontario's application to intervene in a case prosecuted by British Columbia on the grounds that Ontario would not add anything that would not be raised by the prosecution. This appeared to set the bar fairly high for future provincial applicants to demonstrate their 'distinct' contribution. In the same case, the Court noted that the federal government brings a 'national perspective', which prosecuting provinces cannot, giving Ottawa an advantage in its applications to intervene.

The numbers do not suggest, however, that *Osolin* had much effect. According to a senior federal government lawyer, the federal government intervenes very rarely in lower-court criminal cases that do not involve the Constitution,[13] and even at the Supreme Court, it intervened in only about forty-eight non-constitutional criminal cases from 1982 to 2008; indeed, it intervened in only sixty-three non-constitutional cases total in that period.[14] By comparison, Ontario, the largest province, intervened in non-constitutional cases forty-four times. More interesting, and contrary to the signal sent in *Osolin*, Ontario intervened in non-constitutional criminal cases fairly frequently, about two-thirds as often as Ottawa (thirty-three times).[15] Unfortunately, little is known about interventions by other provinces at the Supreme Court, and virtually nothing about interventions below the Supreme Court by any provincial government, even in constitutional law.

Governments *do* have a right to intervene in constitutional law cases at several points in the judicial hierarchy, but this right is a statutory or regulatory one, and not in the Constitution.[16] With a few exceptions (Ho 1994; Hennigar 1996; Morton, Hennigar and Ho 1996; Clarke 2006), virtually nothing has been written about governmental intervention strategies and arguments in constitutional cases, and what there is deals exclusively with cases in the Supreme Court of Canada.

Who Is the Government's Lawyer?

At both the provincial and federal level in Canada, each government is almost always represented in court by an Attorney General. Federally, according to s. 5(d) of the *Department of Justice Act*, the Attorney General of Canada 'shall have the regulation and conduct of all litigation for or against the Crown or any department, in respect of any subject within the authority or jurisdiction of Canada.' Identical language is found in s. 5(h) of Ontario's *Ministry of the Attorney General Act*, and similar provisions exist in all provinces. The Glassco Commission on Government Organization in the early 1960s found a significant gap, however, between statute and reality at the federal level. Various departments and agencies of the federal government had gradually set up their own legal services, such that by the early 1960s, 'it was estimated that more than 85 per cent of the government's lawyers . . . did not come under the responsibility of the Department of Justice' (Brunet 2000, 67). The Glassco Commission's report in 1963 recommended the integration of all federal government legal services under the direction of the Justice Department; that was begun with the 1966 *Government Organization Act*. By 1970, after extensive negotiations between Justice and other departments and agencies and the transfer of nearly 200 federal government lawyers to the Justice Department, 'the revamped Department more closely reflected the organization mandated by the *Department of Justice Act*' (Brunet 2000, 67). Today, with few exceptions,[17] the AG Canada exercises the monopoly over litigation authorized by s. 5(d).

As Hennigar (2002) details, however, AGs do not usually conduct their government's litigation themselves; this task falls primarily to lawyers under the supervision of the AG, who are either permanent members of the public service or 'agents' contracted from private practice. In some cases, the government hires a well-known lawyer or legal scholar to handle its case, as it did with Peter Hogg for the *Same-Sex Marriage Reference*. In the case of the AG Canada, the number of permanent staff litigators is staggeringly large: over 2,500, of whom roughly half are located in Ottawa and the other half in seventeen regional offices across the country (Canada, Department of Justice 2006), where the lion's share of day-to-day litigation is handled.[18] This explains the description of the AG as 'Canada's largest law firm' (Rosenberg 2003). Although comparable data are not available for the provinces, the fact that they are primarily responsible for enforcing the *Criminal Code* suggests that these offices are also very large. In Ontario for example, 900 Crown attorneys prosecute some 500,000 charges each year (Ontario, Ministry of the Attorney General 2006c).

A noteworthy feature of government litigation is which counsel represents the government before the Supreme Court. In the United States, the national government has a specialized elite corps of lawyers, the Office of the Solicitor General, who take over the handling of Supreme Court appeals from the Department of Justice lawyers who appear in the lower courts (see for example Salokar 1992, Zorn 2002, Pacelle 2003). There is no analogous body at the federal level in Canada. In Charter cases from 1982 to 2000, the original counsel from the lower-court case were replaced less than 25 per cent of the time (Hennigar 2002, 96). In recent years, however, the AG Canada has adopted a policy of having Supreme Court appeals handled by one of a dozen or so senior litigators drawn from the regional offices or the national headquarters in Ottawa, although original counsel often remain on the case to gain experience before that court. Little is known about the structure of AG offices in the provinces, but the same counsel often appear before the Supreme Court. This is particularly true of the smaller provinces, most likely because of a mixture of area specialization and the limited number of government counsel.

Attorneys General in Canada are somewhat unusual compared to government lawyers in other Anglo-American democracies, in that the AG is simultaneously a sitting member of the cabinet with wide-ranging policy responsibilities, including the criminal law and maintaining the justice system (at the federal level, this latter position is formally known as the 'Minister of Justice', but the Minister and the Attorney General are the same person[19]). Thus, AGs are appointed to their posts by their Prime Minister or provincial Premier, like any other cabinet minister. What is even more unusual, however, is that AGs are also elected members of Parliament (or the provincial legislature). In fact, some Prime Ministers and Premiers have simultaneously been the AG; among them were Sir John A. Macdonald immediately after Confederation (when the AG was considered a part-time position) and the autocratic Premier of Quebec, Maurice Duplessis (who used that position to persecute Jehovah's Witnesses: see *Roncarelli v. Duplessis* 1959[20]). The broad range of issues currently administered by AGs makes it very impractical for any First Minister today to hold both portfolios concurrently. Indeed, in light of the AG's duty to serve as the government's senior legal adviser and representative, it would likely be seen as a rather alarming concentration of power.

Concern about the Attorney General's political role (see, for example Law Reform Commission of Canada 1990; Edwards 1995) led some provinces— British Columbia, Nova Scotia, and Quebec—and recently the federal government to create the position of Director of Public Prosecutions (DPP) to handle the prosecution of offences at arm's-length from the AG/Minister of Justice. This is consistent with the practice in England, Wales, Northern Ireland, the Republic of Ireland, Australia, and South Africa. In all cases, the DPP reports to the Attorney General, who is publicly responsible for its activities (for example, in Question

Period in the House). Nova Scotia was the first province, in 1990, to create a statutorily independent DPP, following a recommendation of the Royal Commission investigating the wrongful conviction of Donald Marshall that found extensive politicization and systemic racism in that province's justice system. How much independence will be enjoyed by the new federal DPP remains to be seen since the AG may take over conduct of a case (or an intervention) from the DPP (*Director of Public Prosecutions Act*, ss. 13–15); in a review of Nova Scotia's DPP in 1998, similar provisions in the province's *Public Prosecutions Act* raised concerns about the DPP's independence (Nova Scotia, Department of Justice 1998). The issue of an Attorney General's independence when conducting litigation or prosecutions is discussed further below.

Government Litigation Strategies

This chapter opened by noting that governments can appear in court for a number of reasons, including prosecutions, civil litigation, references, and interventions. But *why* do they engage in these activities, and why do they appeal in some cases and not others? With specific reference to constitutional cases, why does the government sometimes concede that its own laws are unconstitutional? The following section considers the state of the literature on these questions, with an emphasis on the complex relationship between courts and governments in litigation and how it blurs the lines of accountability for policy changes stemming from court rulings.

Why Prosecute?

At first glance, the answer to this question seems obvious: governments prosecute offences when people or organizations break the law. This is not always the case in practice, however, for Crowns may decline to prosecute even though the police have made an arrest. This is usually because the Crown feels it does not have enough evidence to prove guilt beyond a reasonable doubt. MacNair (2002, 257) cites the well-established principle that 'the prosecutor's duty is not to seek a conviction, but to see that justice is done': 'As representatives of the Crown, they are expected to be advocates on behalf of the state and obtain convictions of the accused who are guilty; they must also ensure that innocent persons are not convicted' (258).[21]

The Crown might also decline to prosecute because it does not believe that the law can or should be enforced. For example, after juries in Montreal repeatedly acquitted Henry Morgentaler of violating the *Criminal Code*'s ban on abortions performed outside hospitals and without hospital approval,[22] the Crown announced it would no longer attempt to prosecute him. Another more recent example concerns the Mormon splinter community in Bountiful, British Columbia, which practices polygamy in violation of s. 293 of the *Criminal Code*. The AG of British Columbia has refrained from prosecuting community members for years on the grounds that its own lawyers believe the law may violate the Charter's freedom of religion. (In August 2007, British Columbia's Special Prosecutor, appointed to investigate Bountiful, recommended the use of the reference procedure to ascertain the constitutionality of the law.)

The Crown is also guided by its belief in what the 'public interest requires' although this should not be influenced by considerations of partisan advantage for the Crown's government. An example of prosecuting in the public interest would be when the Crown tries someone with whom many sympathize in order deter others from similar actions. This was arguably the case with the Crown's decision to prosecute Robert Latimer for second-degree murder (rather than the lesser charge of manslaughter) for the 'mercy-killing' of his severely disabled and chronically pain-inflicted daughter Tracy. As prosecutor Randy Kirkham stated at Latimer's first trial in 1994, condoning such an act would be tantamount to declaring 'open season on the disabled'.[23]

This principle of prosecutorial independence was given its classic exposition by British parliamentarian Lord Shawcross in 1951, and has been adopted by Canadian Crowns (in Scott 1989, 120):

> The true doctrine is that it is the duty of the Attorney General, in deciding whether or not to authorize the prosecution, to acquaint himself with all the relevant facts, including, for instance, the effect which the prosecution, successful or unsuccessful as the case may be, would have upon public morale and order, and with any other consideration affecting public policy. . . . The responsibility for the eventual decision rests with the Attorney General, and he is not to be put . . . under pressure by his colleagues in the matter.

The main reason for such independence (or 'discretion') is, of course, to prevent miscarriages of justice which may result from politically motivated prosecutions or poor police work. Examples of the former are prosecutions against critics of the government and high-profile cases where there is political pressure to 'convict someone, anyone' because of public demand (such as when there is a serial killer, rapist, or child murderer on the loose). Although Crowns and the police both represent the state and wider public in the administration of criminal justice, it is important to recognize that they serve quite different functions. One of the Crown's functions is to serve as a check on weak evidence or improper investigations by the police by refusing to prosecute such cases. This 'weeding out' also serves the interests of the court system by preventing further backlogs and delays. Finally, prosecutorial discretion allows for flexibility when dealing with accused individuals where prosecution to the fullest extent of the law would not serve the 'broader public interest' and might ruin the individual's life—for example, with first-time offenders, or when there are significant extenuating circumstances.

In 2002 the Supreme Court strongly endorsed prosecutorial discretion in the handling of cases but allowed professional lawyers' associations (in that case, the Law Society of Alberta) to discipline prosecutors (who by law must belong to such associations) for flagrant ethical violations, such as failing to disclose evidence as required by law (*Krieger v. Law Society of Alberta* 2002). This reflected a small expansion of prosecutorial *accountability*, which traditionally flowed to the AG to whom Crowns report and to the courts, which could check Crown bias or abuses of authority through the power of judicial review, although judicial oversight has been exercised rarely, even since the adoption of the Charter's legal rights (Roach 2000).[24] Crowns in Canada are also potentially accountable through civil litigation because, since the Supreme Court's decision in *Nelles* (1989), they can be sued for malicious prosecution. That case ended the absolute immunity of Crowns and AGs outside Quebec from civil liability for prosecutorial decisions. (Suits in Quebec have been allowed since 1986.) This check has not, however, proved particularly effective to date, in part because there are 'considerable hurdles to such actions' (Stuart 1995, 341): only persons who have been convicted (rather than just prosecuted unsuccessfully) can sue; such cases are expensive for individuals; and, as Justice Lamer himself noted in *Nelles*, it is inherently difficult to *prove* malicious prosecution.[25] The situation today is thus not much different from that in the mid-1990s, when Stuart observed that 'there is little effective legal, political, or administrative accountability for prosecutors' (1995, 353).

It should be noted that, beginning in the 1990s, AGs at both the federal and provincial level have attempted to check abuses of Crown discretion—and so enhance prosecutorial accountability—by giving their Crowns guidelines for prosecutorial decisions, such as the *Federal Prosecution Service Deskbook* (Canada, Federal Prosecution Service 2005) and Ontario's *Crown Policy Manual* (Ontario, Attorney General 2006). These documents lay out the general principles above but also enumerate a variety of factors that pertain to the public interest (see for example Box 8.1) and provide guidelines for specific offences. The *Crown Policy Manual*, for example, encourages vigorous prosecution of spousal abuse (in contrast to the practice in Canada for many years, when it was treated as a 'private' matter) and warns Crowns against 'long-entrenched myths and stereotypes' (for example, that 'no really means yes') when dealing with cases of sexual assault.

Box 8.1   Deciding to Prosecute

The Public Interest Criteria

Where the alleged offence is not so serious as plainly to require criminal proceedings, Crown counsel should always consider whether the public interest requires a prosecution. Public interest factors which may arise on the facts of a particular case include:

a)   the seriousness or triviality of the alleged offence;
b)   significant mitigating or aggravating circumstances;
c)   the age, intelligence, physical or mental health or infirmity of the accused;
d)   the accused's background;
e)   the degree of staleness of the alleged offence;
f)   the accused's alleged degree of responsibility for the offence;
g)   the prosecution's likely effect on public order and morale or on public confidence in the administration of justice;
h)   whether prosecuting would be perceived as counter-productive, for example, by bringing the administration of justice into disrepute;
i)   the availability and appropriateness of alternatives to prosecution;
j)   the prevalence of the alleged offence in the community and the need for general and specific deterrence;
k)   whether the consequences of a prosecution or conviction would be disproportionately harsh or oppressive;
l)   whether the alleged offence is of considerable public concern;
m) the entitlement of any person or body to criminal compensation, reparation or forfeiture if prosecution occurs;
n)   the attitude of the victim of the alleged offence to a prosecution;
o)   the likely length and expense of a trial, and the resources available to conduct the proceedings;
p)   whether the accused agrees to co-operate in the investigation or prosecution of others, or the extent to which the accused has already done so;
q)   the likely sentence in the event of a conviction; and
r)   whether prosecuting would require or cause the disclosure of information that would be injurious to international relations, national defence, national security or that should not be disclosed in the public interest.

The application of and weight to be given to these and other relevant factors will depend on the circumstances of each case.

The proper decision in many cases will be to proceed with a prosecution if there is sufficient evidence available to justify a prosecution. Mitigating factors present in a particular case can then be taken into account by the court in the event of a conviction.

Source: *Federal Prosecution Service Deskbook* (Canada, Federal Prosecution Service 2005, Part V, Chap. 15). Reproduced with the permission of the Minister of Public Works and Government Services Canada, 2008.

Such guidelines do not remove prosecutorial discretion, however, and where there is discretion there is also room for personal bias. It is well-known, for example, that Crowns were historically reluctant to prosecute domestic abuse against women (especially sexual abuse by husbands against their wives), and it was for this reason that Crown guidelines encouraging vigorous prosecution in such cases were adopted. Some have also complained that Crowns are more likely to prosecute—and to seek harsher punishments for—members of some societal groups more than others. This has been alleged with respect to aboriginals and black males in particular, and it is true that those groups are over-represented as defendants and prisoners in the criminal justice system. Whether this is due to prosecutorial (and/or police or judicial) bias, however, or because individuals from those social groups might be statistically more involved in criminal activity—or a combination of both—is notoriously difficult to determine empirically (Free 2002).[26] More to the point, there have been few rigorous studies of this contentious issue in Canada. Whereas the report of the Commission on Systemic Racism in the Ontario Criminal Justice System found that Crown lawyers, judges, and defence counsel did not believe Crown discretion resulted in systemic racism (Ontario, Commission 1995, 191), the Royal Commission into the wrongful conviction of Donald Marshall (see Chapter 2) concluded that 'the fact that Marshall was a Native was a factor' in why 'the criminal justice system failed [him] at virtually every turn' (Nova Scotia, Royal Commission 1989, 15). Though we do not intend to impugn the integrity of individual Crown attorneys with the suggestion, the existing and conflicting evidence suggests that greater and more sophisticated study of this issue is needed.

Why Launch a Civil Suit?

As explained earlier, there are three reasons a government may pursue civil litigation: to resolve a contractual dispute with a private business; to resolve a jurisdictional dispute with another government, usually regarding the federal division of powers; and to influence public policy, as with British Columbia's litigation against tobacco companies. Such litigation has not, however, been the subject of sustained academic study.

Why Use the Reference Procedure?

As noted earlier, references have a long history in Canada, and they have been politically motivated from the outset. As Jennifer Smith (1983) points out, when the federal government created the Supreme Court in 1875, it also created the reference procedure, and the hope of people like Sir John A. Macdonald was that the procedure could be used to 'police' the federal division of powers more efficiently—in short, to stop incursions by the provincial governments into federal jurisdiction. However, the provinces soon gave themselves the reference power as well, and ever since, the two levels of government have used references on highly politically charged issues, including matters unrelated to the federal division of powers.

Strayer (1988, 318–33) provides the best summary of the advantages of the reference procedure, any of which could prompt a government to launch a reference. In keeping with their originally intended function, references provide a 'flexible means for each level of Government to challenge the constitutional authority of the other level of Government', a procedure which, at least for the federal government, has replaced the now-defunct constitutional powers of disallowance and reservation (322).[27] This option is particularly attractive when one level is politically weak and cannot obtain what it wants through regular negotiation or constitutional amendment (Riddell and Morton 2004). This has occurred on several occasions, such as when Alberta objected to Trudeau's attempt to tax natural gas exports under the National Energy Plan (*Reference re Proposed Federal Tax on Exported Natural Gas* 1982; see Riddell and Morton 2004), and when several provinces opposed Trudeau's plan to amend the Constitution unilaterally in 1980 (*Patriation Reference* 1981). The reference procedure can also be used by one province against another, as evidenced by one of the most creative reference cases on record. In the so-called *Chicken and Egg Reference* (*Attorney General of Manitoba v. Manitoba Egg and Poultry Association et al.* 1971), Manitoba—a major egg exporter—attacked Quebec's egg marketing scheme that protected Quebec egg producers by restricting imports from other provinces. Whereas other provinces retaliated by restricting chicken imports from Quebec (a major chicken supplier), Manitoba took a more innovative approach: it adopted, at least on paper, a (completely unnecessary) egg marketing scheme identical to Quebec's and referred it to its own Court of Appeal in the hopes that it would be ruled an unconstitutional infringement of interprovincial trade (only the federal government can regulate interprovincial trade). Manitoba got the 'loss' it wanted and appealed it to the Supreme Court, which also found the scheme—and by extension, Quebec's—unconstitutional. The *Chicken and Egg Reference* suggests another advantage of the reference procedure—it allows governments a measure of control over the factual basis on which the case is decided. As noted in Chapter 7, one of the chief hurdles for interest groups trying to conduct strategic litigation is to find and manage 'test cases' that provide the factual context best-suited to the desired legal outcome. The reference procedure allows governments to overcome this difficulty by giving them the power to frame the issues sent to the court as they wish.

Strayer cites several other advantages of references, including that it allows a government to bring before the courts an issue that might not arise through regular litigation, either because of the expense to individual litigants or because the issue is regarded as 'non-justiciable'. The *Patriation Reference* mentioned above is a good example of the latter, because the provinces asked the court whether there was a 'constitutional convention' or tradition—by definition, not a law—requiring provincial consent to any constitutional amendment that affected their jurisdiction. The main additional advantage he notes, however, is *speed*, for it quickly gives governments the benefit of a legal opinion that might take several years to acquire through regular litigation. This is especially valuable if there are conflicting decisions in the lower courts; or if the government in question wishes to set up a complex, large-scale program, as witnessed in the *Anti-Inflation Reference* (1976) regarding federal wage and price controls; or to clarify which order of government has regulatory authority over a pressing issue (such as natural resources, as in *Reference re Proposed Federal Tax on Exported Natural Gas* 1982 and *Reference re Newfoundland Continental Shelf* 1984). In British Columbia's potential reference regarding polygamy, we can see an additional dynamic related to federalism when a province seeks clarification of a federal law that the province has the responsibility to enforce but cannot amend.

References also offer governments some political advantages not mentioned by Strayer, all of which are exemplified (if not fully realized) by the same-sex marriage reference. The first of these is 'agenda management', or the need to deal with a political issue. Although references are often lauded for their speed compared to regular litigation, they can also be used to delay government action on a potentially explosive issue, much like a Royal Commission. When the federal government amended the terms of its reference on same-sex marriage six months after the initial reference (see note 2), it was in part to postpone the expected date of the Supreme Court's decision so that it would not fall in the middle of an election campaign (a tactic that proved unsuccessful, as it turned out) (Huscroft 2004, 258).

The second political advantage of reference cases is position legitimization. As mentioned in Chapter 6, because courts enjoy greater public support than elected governments, politicians seek the court's approval of their preferred policies or legal position to enhance their perceived legitimacy and to weaken political opposition. Although this happens with any court victory, some references seem designed primarily to elicit this support in a timely fashion. This was certainly Ottawa's goal when initiating the *Reference re Quebec Secession* (1998) on whether Quebec could unilaterally separate on the basis of a referendum question designed solely by the government of Quebec. The Supreme Court's decision endorsed Ottawa's position that the federal government would not be bound to recognize any future vote in favour of separation if the referendum question were not sufficiently clear, and that Ottawa should have a say in the wording of future questions. These principles were later enshrined in the federal government's *Clarity Act*. The first version of the same-sex marriage reference questions is another example. If all the federal government wanted was to obtain the Supreme Court's position on the issue, it could have simply appealed the *Halpern* or *EGALE* cases. Instead, it drafted a bill legalizing same-sex marriage and asked the Court what was essentially a rigged question: would *recognizing* same-sex marriage violate equality rights? The short answer is that it would not, and the government knew this—the question was designed to elicit a specific response from the judges: 'same-sex marriage is consistent with the Constitution.' It should be noted that the government's critics, both within the opposition parties and its own caucus, saw through this tactic, and the government was pressured to ask the more pertinent question of whether the *traditional* definition of marriage was unconstitutional.

The third additional advantage of references, closely tied to the second, is 'buck-passing' or transferring political responsibility. By eliciting a judicial ruling, a reference case can create a situation where the government can claim that it 'has' to pursue a course of action which it already prefers ('the court made me do it'), but which is politically divisive or unpopular. Turning again to the same-sex marriage issue, Ottawa could have simply passed legislation recognizing such couples; its use of the reference procedure was clearly intended to give it political cover. Once again, however, its attempts were frustrated when the Supreme Court declined to say whether the Charter *requires* the recognition of same-sex marriage.

This points to a problem for governments with the reference procedure: the court may not co-operate, either by ruling against them, or by refusing to answer the question. s. 53(4) of the *Supreme Court Act* states unequivocally that the Court must answer any question put to it, yet the justices have carved out exceptions where the questions are overly abstract or 'would throw the law into confusion' by contradicting the (legally binding) rulings of lower courts (*Reference re Same-Sex Marriage* 2004). This latter exception would appear to defeat one of the purported benefits of references, that they quickly resolve contradictions in the lower courts, and might indicate the Court's growing resentment of being thrown such politically hot potatoes. As well, as noted in Chapter 6, references on politically contentious issues may ultimately undermine their value by hurting the Court's legitimacy. This risk is exacerbated by the highly abstract (or hypothetical) nature of most references, which occur in the absence of disputes involving facts or real people. Strayer (1988, 334) makes this point: 'Where there are few, if any, genuinely legal criteria to which courts can resort for a rationale for their decision, they may be perceived as making a political judgment which may impair their long-term credibility.'[28]

Why Intervene?

The government's motivation to intervene in a case as a third party was touched upon earlier. Like interest groups, governments intervene in an attempt to influence judicial decision making, in particular how the judges interpret the law. It is not known for sure why governments choose to intervene when they do, but their own guidelines on the matter probably provide a good idea. To begin with, governments do not intervene routinely, and their lawyers must obtain approval to do so from fairly high up the bureaucratic hierarchy (the Assistant Deputy Attorney General of Canada and the National Litigation Committee in Ottawa). According to the *Federal Prosecution Service Deskbook* (Canada, Federal Prosecution

Service 2005) and the *Civil Litigation Deskbook* (Canada, Department of Justice 2003, A-2.6),[29] 'There is no single principle which guides decisions in this area,' and different factors will weigh more heavily depending on the circumstances. The federal government is more likely to favour intervention if the issue has been raised in an appeal court, especially to the Supreme Court, and if the constitutional validity of federal legislation has been challenged (this is most likely to occur in criminal matters, where the provincial Crown is prosecuting the case). If the case involves a constitutional challenge in a court below the Supreme Court, the government is less likely to intervene, but it may if:

- the legislation is part of an important policy initiative (such as the GST or firearms registry);
- no direct party to the litigation (usually the provincial Crown) intends to defend the legislation adequately; or
- the federal government has evidence that makes it more able to defend the law than another litigant.

Federal and provincial statutes require that AGs must be informed of constitutional challenges to their legislation, in recognition of the fact that they may wish to intervene in such cases. Ottawa has also flagged as worthy of intervention cases involving aboriginal rights, language rights, provincial laws that are similar to federal laws, 'legal issues of broad importance' to federal interests, and exceptionally important social issues (abortion is cited as an example).

Intervention can also be used in a more strategic sense that is related to intergovernmental relations, because it is a way for one order of government to try to influence the laws of the other. The leading example is the federal government's recurring interventions over the past three decades to support language-rights claims against provincial governments (for example *Société des Acadiens v. Association of Parents* 1986, *Mahe v. Alberta* 1990, *Doucet-Boudeau v. Nova Scotia* 2003, and *Solski v. Quebec* 2005), which began as part of Prime Minister Pierre Trudeau's efforts to promote official bilingualism across Canada, often in the face of provincial resistance, especially in Quebec. This strategy is particularly evident with respect to minority-language education for anglophones in Quebec and francophones outside Quebec (*Mahe, Doucet-Boudreau, Solski*), because such programs are crucial to maintaining one's mother tongue but education is entirely within the constitutional jurisdiction of the provinces. To overcome this difficulty, Trudeau funded the creation of official language (that is, French and English) minority groups (OLMGs), created the Court Challenges Program in 1978 to fund OLMG litigation against provinces, and intervened in such litigation to support the claimants. The capstone to this strategy was the inclusion in the Charter (s. 23), at Trudeau's insistence, of minority-language education rights, which are exempt from the s. 33 'notwithstanding' clause and which provide a strong foundation for

OLMG litigation (see Riddell 2004). Provinces may also intervene strategically in cases involving another province to encourage a judicial ruling that will legitimize their own policy initiatives. Manfredi (1994) gives the example of interventions by Ontario and New Brunswick in support of an Alberta francophone OLMG in *Mahe*, at a time when their own pro-bilingualism policies were meeting with stiff political opposition. A Supreme Court ruling endorsing minority-language education 'could be mobilized by both provinces to dilute this opposition by allowing them to argue that their new policies were required by their constitutional obligations' (Manfredi 1994, 111).

Why Appeal?

To understand why the government might appeal in any given case, one needs to ask what the government's goals are when appealing—what does it seek to achieve? Most fundamentally, we can assume that—like any appellant—the government seeks to minimize or reverse the loss it suffered in the lower courts. All losses in litigation entail some cost to the losing party, and when governments lose in court, their costs can be sorted into two categories: financial and policy costs. Like private litigants, governments may have financial expenses if found liable in civil suits, as well as the expense of preparing and presenting the case. In addition, however, the state may bear fiscal costs associated with a policy change, for example, being ordered by a court decision to provide minority-language education. Policy costs include the loss of a particular statute to judicial invalidation or significant reinterpretation, as was the case with the abortion law in *Morgentaler*. A related policy cost is the opportunity cost (in time, personnel, and political capital) of attempting to draft replacement legislation, as the Mulroney government learned in its two unsuccessful attempts to pass a new abortion law.

There has been little rigorous examination of governmental decisions to appeal, even in the US (but see Salokar 1992; Waltenburg and Swinford 1999a, 1999b; Zorn 2002; Pacelle 2003), but recent work (Hennigar 2007) sheds some light on appeals by the federal government to the Supreme Court of Canada in Charter cases. The evidence from Canada and the US is that governments appeal—as with intervening—only selectively and on the basis of a variety of factors. In the Canadian case, the federal government seeks to appeal in only about 30 per cent of the cases where it could.[30] Its decisions to appeal are the product of calculated decisions based on costs, case importance (or 'salience'), the prospect of winning on appeal, and, in certain circumstances, the chance that the Supreme Court will grant leave to appeal ('reviewability'). Specifically, an appeal is much more likely if there was dissent among the judges of the lower appeal court; if the lower court crafted a novel interpretation of the Constitution that limits the government's power (but only, curiously, if there were interveners present in the case); and if the court 'rewrote' ('judicially amended') the government's law being challenged.[31] Appeals in civil cases are more common than in criminal cases, not surprisingly since the former tend to involve greater financial and policy costs. What is equally interesting is what does *not* influence the decision to appeal: the ideology of the Supreme Court, which party is in power, or if the lower court simply strikes down ('nullifies' or 'invalidates') a law and leaves it to Parliament to fix. This surprising finding about nullification shows that the simple fact of judicial activism is less important to government decision makers than the form this activism takes, for the government challenges only the greatest incursions on its policy authority. The evidence permits the conclusion that the AG Canada actively defends the authority of the government and, correspondingly, challenges attempts by the lower appellate courts to expand judicial power, *regardless* of the party in power. As well, government decision makers appear to actively consider strategic factors, such as minimizing or avoiding losses on appeal.

As the evidence from Canada and the US confirms, governments do not, as a general rule, waste resources or risk their credibility with the Supreme Court by litigating 'lost causes'. Winning is also important for jurisprudential reasons, namely, that losing before the country's highest court of appeal may establish an unfavourable legal rule with the widest possible application or, as Waltenburg and Swinford (1999a, 254) find, governments 'will not put good precedent at risk.' The risks of appealing are even greater for the Canadian federal government, in that its losses are limited when they occur in provincial courts of appeal, whereas a loss before the Supreme Court has consequences for the application of federal law at the national level. This is because rulings by provincial courts of appeal apply only in the jurisdiction of that court (for example, Ontario for the Ontario Court of Appeal), but the Supreme Court's decisions apply in all jurisdictions. In view of this risk, governments have an extra incentive to avoid losing in the Supreme Court.

All of these findings more or less confirm the AG Canada's own views on appealing. Departmental documents and interviews with government lawyers (see Hennigar 2002; 2007) suggest that they do not appeal routinely and that there is a thorough, centralized approval process for appeals to the Supreme Court. In particularly high-profile cases, such as that on same-sex marriage, the decision to appeal may even be debated at the highest levels of the political executive, by the cabinet and the Prime Minister, and could include calculations about the impact of the issue in an anticipated election (MacCharles 2004, H1, H4; Hennigar 2008). Moreover, department officials are cognizant of the Court's limited capacity to hear appeals and their office's institutional credibility with the Court's justices. Consequently, departmental guidelines (Canada, Federal Prosecution Service 2005) recommend seeking an appeal only when the 'public interest' requires it, as when:

- the issue raised by the case is of widespread importance, or its impact is not confined largely to the immediate case;
- the lower courts differed in interpreting the issue raised;

- the decision could impair the enforcement or administration of a significant government policy initiative if left unchallenged;
- the resources required to prepare and present the appeal do not significantly outweigh the value of pursuing the case further; and
- there are public expressions of concern about the lower-court ruling (but only where the arguments for and against appealing are evenly matched).

As with many other areas of government litigation in Canada, more research is needed to gain a fuller understanding of the decision to appeal.

Before proceeding, it is important to recognize the broader political significance of the government's appeal decisions, in particular how the government's selectivity has important implications for judicial agenda setting. A large body of recent work on judicial activism through the 'rights revolution', led by Charles Epp's (1998) comparative analysis and by Morton and Knopff (2000) in Canada, emphasizes the courts' passive nature, or the fact that judges require other actors to bring cases for adjudication. Scholars identify the crucial role of interest groups in this regard. Epp (1998, 3), for example, concludes that Canada's 'rights revolution' is explained primarily by a 'support structure for legal mobilization, consisting of rights-advocacy organizations', or what Morton and Knopff term the 'Court Party' (see also Smith 1999; Brodie 2001; Hein 2001). This conclusion ignores the fact that *governments* are by far the most frequent appellant in rights litigation. By definition, most Charter-rights claims are directed at government institutions, officials, or legislation, and, as 'the ultimate repeat player', the national government has a vested interest in broad, long-term jurisprudential development that provides an incentive to bring cases to the highest court in the land. Thus, the rise of the judiciary in Canada has, ironically, been made possible to a large extent by the very institution that stands to lose authority because of judicial activism. On the other hand, a decision by the government *not* to appeal losses in rights litigation means that important constitutional questions are kept from being heard in the highest court in the land, or at least delayed. A notable example is whether the Charter's equality rights provisions protected sexual orientation, and accordingly whether statutory human rights codes must as well. The federal government did not appeal from its loss on this issue in the Ontario Court of Appeal in 1992 (*Haig v. Canada*), and the Supreme Court of Canada was not able to address this question fully for another six years (in *Vriend v. Alberta* 1998).

Why Concede?

Any time a government is sued, it must decide whether it is willing to defend itself or whether it will concede. In typical civil litigation (see Chapter 10), conceding usually means settling out of court or seeking a resolution through alternative dispute resolution. Both strategies were employed in recent years by the federal government in response to claims by Aboriginals about abuse (both physical and cultural) resulting from state-ordered or -sanctioned residential schooling. That set of cases, though exceptional for their number and the amount of financial damages claimed—the May 2006 settlement will cost over $2 *billion*, in addition to the over $250 million already paid through litigation and ADR—point to several factors the government (like any litigant) would consider: financial costs, time, personnel required, and the consequences in terms of public relations of appearing to 'fight'.

Litigation under the Charter of Rights raises a special issue for the government with respect to concession, however, and it is the scenario that has received the most scholarly attention (Edwards 1987; Scott 1989; Huscroft 1996; Jai 1998; McAllister 2002; Roach 2000, 2006): should the government concede in court that its own legislation is unconstitutional? Most of the treatment of this issue arises in the debate over whether the AG should be able to make such concessions 'independently' over the objections of his or her own cabinet and/or Parliament. That debate is surveyed in the next section. For now, let us consider the various options government lawyers have when presented with a Charter-based challenge to a statute, as outlined by Huscroft (1996). The first is a 'full Charter defence', which sees the government arguing that the law does not violate the claimant's rights, and, should the court disagree, that the law is a 'reasonable limit' under section 1 of the Charter. (Section 1 permits the government to limit the Charter's rights so long as the limits are 'reasonable', explicit in the statute, and 'demonstrably justified.'[32]) Governments usually offer a full defence.

A second option is to give a 'limited Charter defence', which could mean either conceding the rights violation but not s. 1 or to contest the rights violation but offer no s. 1 defence. In the *Sauvé* (2002) case, the federal government conceded that the law—which denied the vote to prisoners sentenced to at least two years—violated the Charter's s. 3 right to vote, but offered a vigorous s. 1 defence based on political philosophy (social-contract theory), the importance of citizenship and voting, and the fact that the prohibition ended when the prisoner was released. An example of a case where no s. 1 defence was offered is *Chaoulli*, mentioned already several times in this volume, which concerned whether Quebec's ban on private health insurance violates the Charter's s. 7 right to 'life, liberty, and security of the person'. As co-defendant with Quebec, the federal government in *Chaoulli* denied that the ban violated s. 7 but did not address s. 1, possibly because the AG Quebec offered a full Charter defence of its law. Whereas some violations, if found, would be difficult to justify as 'reasonable', as a general rule failing to argue s. 1 is a questionable tactic because it gives the court no choice but to find the law unconstitutional if it does find a Charter violation—which occurs much more often than a finding of unreasonableness (Hiebert 1996; Kelly 2005).

The third option is a 'full concession', which entails conceding both that the law violates a Charter right and that it is unreasonable. A government might choose this strategy if the law was passed a long time ago (especially before the adoption of the Charter), or if it was passed by a previous government of a different party. An example of full concession is *Schachter v. Canada*, where the federal government accepted that its law denying parental-leave benefits to new biological (but not adoptive) fathers unjustifiably violated the Charter's equality rights. Indeed, the only reason the government even appealed the case was to challenge (successfully) the lower court's remedy of 'reading in' natural fathers; though Ottawa had already extended such benefits to all parents, it had cut the amount significantly to maintain the overall cost of the program. While this example suggests the government's full concession was motivated by the fact that it had a replacement program in place, it remains unclear why the government opts for a particular one of these three strategies at a given time.

Should the Attorney General Be 'Independent'?

It was explained earlier that the principle of prosecutorial independence is well-established in our legal tradition to prevent politically motivated prosecutions and miscarriages of justice. Our focus here, however, is on civil litigation, particularly when it involves constitutional challenges to government policies. Writing in 1987, John Edwards, the foremost scholar of Attorneys General in Canada, concluded that '[t]here appears to be considerable confusion as to whose interpretation of the law, whose assessment of the policy implications of the legal conflict should prevail' when 'a conflict of opinion arises by virtue of the Attorney General's assessment of the legal and policy issues' (51). Two decades later, this confusion persists. Edwards's widely cited argument was that the AG has a special duty to 'protect the Constitution' and to represent the 'public interest', even if this requires that he or she advance a legal position in court at odds with the wishes of the government.

His concern is understandable. Liberal democratic regimes contain an inherent tension between the government's partisan incentive to appease the voting majority (or at least a plurality, given our electoral system) and the responsibility to respect the rights and freedoms of individuals and minorities. This tension is particularly acute when the minority is an unpopular one. Edwards went so far as to advocate the creation of a separate, independent litigation office which would represent the government in all criminal and civil proceedings and whose head would report to the AG but sit outside cabinet, like the Office of the Solicitor General of the United States.[33] Edwards's position that the AG should refuse to defend laws which he or she believes are unconstitutional has been echoed by former Ontario Attorney General Ian Scott (1989) and, more recently, by Department of Justice Canada senior counsel Debra McAllister (2002), Ontario Deputy Attorney General Mark Freiman (2002), and law professor Kent Roach (2000, 2006). In the most recent contribution to this debate, however, Roach (2006) contends that AGs should concede that legislation is unconstitutional only after all attempts to resolve potential violations through other legislative means (including invoking the s. 33 'notwithstanding' clause) have been exhausted.

Edwards's position has not gone unchallenged, however. Huscroft (1996) argues that the AG should be independent from the political executive but only to the extent necessary for the AG to adhere to the will of the *legislature*. As a member of Parliament, a government minister, and the chief Law Officer of the Crown, the AG has a duty to represent the legislature, a duty that requires him or her to defend the impugned legislation and to prosecute existing laws. Huscroft criticizes Scott's argument for its 'presumption that the public interest lies only in vindicating the *Charter* rights of individuals' and for 'overlook[ing] the constitutional interest inherent in defence of the legislative process', in particular 'the effect of denying the legislative branch a voice in the judicial process' (1996, 154–5). Put simply, legislatures should repeal or amend 'obviously unconstitutional' laws, not leave it to the AG to orchestrate their judicial nullification. Huscroft is especially concerned about AGs' conceding that legislation is unconstitutional when the legislature has clearly rejected the government's attempt to amend the challenged legislation or where the law was adopted through a free vote; concessions by AGs in such circumstances, in Huscroft's opinion, undermine respect for the legislature.[34] Whether one agrees with Huscroft that the AG should serve the legislature rather than the executive (or herself) depends on what policy tools one believes the political executive can use legitimately. Elections clearly empower governments to pursue their policy goals, but can governments use only parliamentary mechanisms or litigation as well? The authors of this volume do not seek to answer this question, only to raise it.

Another criticism of Edwards's argument is that the AG's conception of the 'public interest' may be excessively legalistic. Julie Jai, herself a government lawyer, observes (1998, 18) that litigation decisions made within the AG's office usually ignore non-legal factors such as policy design, political consequences, and financial costs. Given that litigation positions—and court rulings—in Charter cases can have all of these non-legal implications, Jai concludes that questions such as whether a government action is a 'reasonable limit' on Charter rights is 'an issue involving as much policy as law, and might be most appropriately decided by Cabinet' (18).

More fundamentally, one could challenge the authority of the AG to independently ascertain and represent the public interest at all. In a society as complex and pluralistic as Canada, 'the very notion of a single public interest . . . is hotly contested' (Roach 2000, 26-7). On the one hand, the pluralistic public interest can be represented *by* the public in litigation, through the participation of citizens and interest groups. After all, why does the public interest need to be guarded by a state official—a full, partisan member of the political executive, no less—if the 'public' can appear in court to speak for itself? Over the past thirty years, the public have been encouraged in a variety of ways to do so, including by the relaxation of traditional standing rules by the Supreme Court of Canada, government funding of interest-group litigation, and the opening of the courts to third-party interveners. Take, for example, the same-sex marriage cases: in *Halpern* alone, seven same-sex couples challenged the legal status quo with the support of three interest groups (EGALE Canada, the Metropolitan Community Church of Toronto, and the Canadian Coalition of Liberal Rabbis for Same-Sex Marriage), and the Canadian Human Rights Commission. This is not to deny the importance of courts' hearing a variety of viewpoints, but there are other measures the courts can employ to this effect that do not require the AG to oppose his or her own government.

On the other hand, the AG's responsibility to serve the public interest is not unique among government officials. Carney (1997, 6) correctly observes that AGs 'are not *the* guardians of the public interest. That responsibility is shared by all who are vested, directly or indirectly, with the sovereign power of the people: parliament, the executive and the judiciary.' If the AG cannot legitimately claim a monopoly on representing the public interest, then his or her monopoly over the conduct of government litigation presents a problem when it is used to concede a law's unconstitutionality, over the objections of cabinet, on the basis of the public interest. As the government's sole legal representative before the court, the AG's assessment of the public interest is the only one presented to the court on behalf of the government, even if it is not the only assessment *within* the government. In a recent speech, Andrew Petter (2007b), the former Attorney General of British Columbia, criticized the influence government lawyers have on their lay colleagues in cabinet. He stressed that non-lawyers are risk-averse and are deferential to lawyers with respect to litigation, admitting that he had used this fact to his advantage when advancing his own policy preferences. Thus, the AG's office has a strong capacity, not only to shape the legal position taken in court on behalf of other departments, but also to secure changes to proposed legislation in the name of preventing litigation (see also Kelly 2005 on the latter scenario).

Despite its numerous advocates within the legal academic community, concrete examples of AGs' exercising independence in litigation are rare. One that we know of involved Ian Scott when he was AG of Ontario, when he conceded in the *Blainey* (1985) case, against the wishes of his government, that rules barring girls from playing in boys' hockey leagues and from challenging this under the Ontario Human Rights Code violated the Charter's equality rights (see Scott 1989, 124–5). Ironically, the Ontario High Court of Justice rejected Scott's concession and upheld the ban, although it was overturned by the Court of Appeal.[35] Although AGs Canada have conceded Charter violations in several cases, there is no evidence that they did so over the objections of their Prime Minister or the cabinet.

Governments in Court: A 'Success' Story

In large measure because of the prosecution of offences, governments appear in court more often than any other litigant. Governments are also, however, the most successful class of litigants. This section provides evidence to this effect and explores possible explanations for the government's high success rate in court, including the idea that experience as a litigant breeds success.

There are no comprehensive statistics on the success rate of litigants for every level of court in Canada in all types of cases, and the most thorough figures in existence are somewhat out of date (McCormick 1994). Nonetheless, the available data indicate that governments in Canada are extremely successful in court. McCormick's (1994) study of the provincial courts of appeals from 1920 to 1990 and of the Supreme Court of Canada from 1949 to 1992 examined the success rate of different categories of litigants in all types of cases.[36] His two main conclusions were that governments are more successful than other categories of litigants—including big business, unions, other businesses, individuals, and other interest groups—but that the *type* of government or governmental role matters. Specifically, the government was most successful in appeals from the prosecution of offences (as 'Crown'), winning roughly two-thirds of the time. In non-criminal cases, the federal government was noticeably more successful than the provinces (as a group—individual provincial figures were not given), and that municipal governments were the least successful. Indeed, provincial and municipal governments were slightly less successful than big businesses. Nonetheless, these governments still win over half the time.

McCormick also calculated a more nuanced measure of success developed by Wheeler et al. (1987) called 'net advantage', which refers to the phenomena that 'appeal courts tend to affirm rather than to reverse the lower court' and that governments appeal much less often than they are appealed against (McCormick 1994, 159). Net advantage is calculated by subtracting a litigant's *loss* rate when respondent from that litigant's *success* rate when appellant. McCormick discovered that the Crown was the most successful litigant (with a net advantage of 26.9 per cent), followed by the federal government (20.4 per cent), big business (15.0 per cent), and provincial governments (3.7 per cent) (1993, 532).

Not surprisingly given the high profile of Charter of Rights cases, especially in the Supreme Court of Canada, there is more information on success rates in those cases, although it is still woefully incomplete. In the Supreme Court, governments (taken together) have been successful at defending their laws and the actions of their officials, especially the police, against roughly two-thirds of Charter-based challenges since 1982, and they have become more successful over the last decade (Kelly 2005). The reason for the upward trend (or downward, for rights claimants) is most likely that laws drafted before the Charter, and therefore most likely to violate rights, have already been struck down, or repealed by governments, and government officials have become used to working with the Charter. Chapter 11 examines in greater detail how the threat of Charter litigation has influenced government policy-making. When it comes to defending statutes (as opposed to the conduct of government officials), the federal government is slightly more successful (65 per cent) than the provinces (60 per cent) (Kelly 2005, 148). Information on Charter cases in the lower courts is rare, but the evidence suggests governments are even more able to defend their statutes there (Kelly 2005; Hennigar 2007). The federal government, in particular, posted a remarkable 73.2 per cent Charter-case success rate (+46.5 per cent net advantage) in the provincial courts of appeal and the Federal Court of Appeal between 1982 and 2000 (Hennigar 2007). Ottawa was only slightly less successful in Charter cases involving civil litigation (168 wins of 237 cases, or 70.9 per cent) than criminal prosecutions (268 wins of 356 cases, or 75.3 per cent), with respective net advantages of 44.3 and 47.8. In the Charter cases before the Supreme Court of Canada between 1986 and 1997, the federal government enjoyed a net advantage of +38 per cent, while the provinces enjoyed a lower net advantage of 31 per cent (Hausegger 2002). Unfortunately, we have no figures for Canada's trial-level courts.

The federal success rates are comparable to that of the US national government, which has a net advantage of 45.1 per cent in the US courts of appeal (Songer and Sheehan 1992) and 35.9 per cent in the US Supreme Court (Sheehan, Mishler, and Songer 1992). On the other hand, Canadian provinces as a group are less successful than American state governments as a group, which have net advantages of 30 per cent in the courts of appeal (Songer and Sheehan 1992), 11.2 per cent in the US Supreme Court (Sheehan, Mishler, and Songer 1992), and 11.8 per cent (with large city governments) in the state supreme courts (Wheeler et al. 1987; see also Farole 1999).[37] It must be noted that there is much, much more academic study of government litigation in the US than in Canada (or really anywhere else in the world). Governments in Canada are generally more successful than those in other countries, apart from the US, although governments are usually the most privileged litigants in their own countries. This was confirmed by Haynie et al. (2001), who undertook a similar study to McCormick's in Canada, Australia, Great Britain, India, the Philippines, South Africa, and Tanzania (see also Kritzer (2003b) for a review of the existing comparative literature). The exception to this pattern is Australia, whose national, state, and local governments are all remarkably unsuc-cessful in that country's High Court. Though they all win about half of their appeals, they frequently lose when they are the respondent, resulting in a low net advantage for the national government (11.8 per cent) and *negative* scores for the states (−2.5 per cent), municipalities (−16.5 per cent), and governments as the Crown in criminal matters (−2.0 per cent) (Smyth 2000).

Another form of litigant success is getting leave to appeal to the highest courts, and here again governments fare better than other litigants (Flemming and Krutz 2002a; Flemming 2004). Who is able to secure leave to appeal has broader impor-tance for the legal system beyond simply the chance to win a particular case. Because appeal courts routinely shape the law through interpretation (and increas-ingly, make policy), those parties that get their cases heard 'will have a hand in directing the path of the law' (Flemming and Krutz 2002a, 811). Parties that are disproportionately successful in securing leave to appeal, such as governments, therefore possess more power and influence over agenda setting than others. It is important to note, however, that 'setting the agenda' is quite distinct from winning the case once the court hears it. The Supreme Court of Canada, for instance, reverses lower appeal-court rulings only about half the time, and the US Supreme Court reverses about two-thirds of its decisions (Flemming 2004, 53; Supreme Court of Canada 2008a, 8). In other words, securing leave to appeal to the Supreme Court means that one is as likely to lose one's case as win, statistically speaking, although governments are still more successful in this regard than others.

Still another measure of success is how the government fares when intervening as a third party in support of another litigant. In the simplest terms, is a party more likely to win when it has the support of a government? As Table 8.1 shows for Charter cases in the Supreme Court between 1986 and 1997, the answer is clearly yes, regardless of whether the party is the appellant or the respondent. A more nuanced analysis reveals the interesting result, however, that the federal government influences the outcome of Charter cases only when it intervenes to *oppose* the rights claimant. That is, the Court is less likely to find in favour of the rights claimant when the federal government opposes the claim. In contrast, provincial government interveners have influence when either opposing or supporting the claimant.[38]

Besides case disposition and leave to appeal, there are other, more substantive ways of measuring litigant success, such as the creation of favourable or unfavourable legal interpretations as precedents (Morton and Allen 2001). Legal interpretation is especially prevalent in appeal courts and is closely tied to law-making. Moreover, it is possible to win a dispute for the wrong legal reasons, or conversely to lose on disposition but obtain a favourable interpretation. For example, in *Egan v. Canada* (1995), a same-sex couple was unsuccessful in its claim for a spousal pension under Old Age Security, but it secured the important ruling from the Supreme Court of Canada that sexual orientation was protected under the Charter's section 15 equality rights.[39] Manfredi (1997) terms the phenomenon of judges interpreting the Constitution 'micro-constitutional politics', and likens it to amending the Constitution without going through the formal amending formula.[40] Most studies of the success of litigants regarding legal interpretation focus on interest groups (Riddell and Morton 1998; Manfredi 1994; Hausegger 2000; Morton and Allen 2001; Manfredi 2004; Riddell 2004), but Hennigar's (1996) analysis of the federal government's first decade of Charter cases is an exception. That study found that Ottawa was far more successful on case disposition (74 per cent) than at persuading the Supreme Court of Canada to

Table 8.1 Government Success as Third Party Before the Supreme Court, Charter Cases Heard 1986–97

Intervening Government	Success Rate When Supporting Appellant (%)	Success Rate When Supporting Respondent (%)
Federal	75	83
Provincial, as a whole	80	82

adopt the government's interpretations of the Charter (49 per cent). The gap was widest when the federal government intervened in criminal law cases, where the side it supported won on case disposition three-quarters of the time yet only one-quarter of its legal interpretations were adopted by the Court. This points to the need for further, more nuanced study of government success rates in court, and in particular of whether 'success' translates into 'influence' over legal interpretation by the courts (see Chapter 7 for a discussion of this distinction).

Why are governments so successful in court, at least on case disposition? Several explanations have been offered (mostly generated in the US), but the dominant one is 'party capability theory' (Galanter 1974). According to party capability theory, the judicial system favours 'repeat players' (RPs) or well-resourced 'haves' who litigate frequently. RPs develop expertise, long-term legal strategies, and institutional credibility with judges and court staff, and they have 'economies of scale', which translate into low start-up costs for any individual case (as they already have lawyers on staff), and access to legal specialists (Kritzer and Silbey 2003, 4–5). Repeat players can be businesses or organizations (for example, an interest group like LEAF), but the ultimate repeat player is a large government. At the other end of the spectrum are 'one-shot' (OS) litigants—usually individuals, small businesses, or interest groups—that appear in court only rarely. One of Galanter's key findings is that when RPs meet OS litigants in court, RPs tend to win. This is the scenario most individuals face when they sue, or are prosecuted by, the government. The party capability theory has been tested and confirmed in Canada's highest appeal courts (McCormick 1993), as well as in England (Atkins 1991), Israel (Dotan 1999), and several other countries (Haynie et al. 2001), but it has a mixed record in the US, where Sheehan, Mishler, and Songer (1992) did not confirm it, in contrast to Wheeler et al. (1987), Songer and Sheehan (1992), and Farole (1999), and it was not confirmed in Australia (Smyth 2000).[41]

Party capability theory is not without its challengers, or at least refiners. McGuire (1995; 1998) argues that the key factor determining litigant success in the US is the experience of one's counsel. Though governments tend to have more experienced counsel than other litigants, he finds that any government 'advantage' evaporates if the either side's counsel has an equal or greater amount of experience. In other words, government success rates are inflated by the large number of RP-OS cases. This is not the case in Canada. Although a recent test (Szmer, Johnson, and Sarver 2007) of McGuire's 'lawyer capability' theory in the Canadian context confirmed that lawyers' experience influences outcomes in the Supreme Court of Canada, governments are *still* disproportionately successful after taking this factor into account. Other explanations in the literature include the previous success (rather than just 'experience') of the lawyer (Haynie and Sill 2007), the ideology of the courts (Sheehan, Mishler, and Songer 1992), and the fact that most judges have conservative backgrounds that favour business, the political establishment, and the social status quo (Wheeler et al. 1987; Mandel 1994).

Kritzer (2003b), who offers the most developed challenge to McGuire and the party capability theory, however, points to several factors that favour governments. Governments make the rules by which litigation is conducted, including laws regulating the liability of government officials and the creation of tribunals that filter cases out of the regular court system. He also points to the government's selectivity about which cases it appeals (see also Zorn 2002), although this would not explain why the Government of Canada is as successful as a respondent as when it appeals (Hennigar 2002). Finally, Kritzer stresses that courts are part of the broader state, and there is a 'norm of deference' to other state agencies, in no small measure because judges rely on these other government actors to enforce their rulings (see Rosenberg 1991 for more on this relationship).

Regardless of the ultimate explanation, the high success rate of governments in court has important political ramifications. At the very least, it is a dash of cold water on those who think of the courts as a welcoming forum for citizens wishing to challenge their governments. Though some challengers do prevail, the statistical reality is that the deck is heavily stacked against those individuals, even in cases involving constitutional rights. This also implies that the prospect of fundamentally reforming public policy or the government itself through litigation must be viewed with some skepticism. Galanter's (1974) seminal article on repeat players was subtitled 'speculations on the limits of social change' for good reason.

Conclusions

As the 'ultimate repeat player' litigant, governments exercise a significant influence on the flow of cases and issues to the court system, and their success as litigants has important consequences for the prospect of policy and social change via the courts. That said, it is also important to recognize that there is a complex political relationship between governments and courts and that sometimes 'losing is winning' from the government's perspective. There are at least five situations in which the government might prefer to 'lose' in court (or at least not mind losing):

1. The government wants to change a law or policy but wants to avoid political responsibility—in short, it wants the court to do it. This might be because the issue in question is so polarizing for the public that any action the government takes will provoke considerable opposition, as with abortion. US scholar Mark Graber (1993) calls this scenario the 'nonmajoritarian difficulty'. Or, it might be an issue that would expose the government to damaging questions by opposition parties if dealt with in Parliament. Or it would save time and 'political capital', since changing a policy through the courts means that it might not be necessary to do so through Parliament. This is especially useful if the policy in question was adopted by a previous government of a different party.

2. Government leadership or some part thereof wants to silence dissent or criticisms within cabinet, caucus, or society. A good example is the same-sex marriage case, as noted earlier.

3. The government wants to mobilize its supporters. There is ample evidence that interest groups litigate in the face of almost certain failure to highlight their grievances and to foster a sense of political-group identity (Smith 1999). Similarly, governments may reap political gains with clientele or partisan supporters by appearing to 'go down fighting'. For example, the Parti Québécois appealed the invalidation of part of its mandatory French education regime ('Bill 101'; *Attorney General of Quebec v. Association of Quebec Protestant School Boards* 1984),[42] even though there was virtually no chance the federally-appointed Supreme Court would reverse a nullification under the new Charter's language rights (which had been drafted specifically to *counter* Bill 101).

4. The government wants to challenge the legitimacy of the judiciary or the larger political system. This was a secondary objective of the Parti Québécois when it pursued the 'lost cause' of Bill 101 in the Supreme Court. The court's decision allowed the separatist PQ to argue that the Québécois goal of preserving the French language and culture could not be realized within the legal and political framework of Canada and that the Supreme Court—which is entirely appointed by the federal government—could not be trusted. (This would also help the government of Quebec argue later that provinces should have more influence over Supreme Court appointments.)

5. Finally, in some lower-court cases, the government may not have preferred to lose, but having done so it decides to 'cut its losses' and not appeal. This can prevent or delay the issue from reaching a higher court (such as the Supreme Court), whose decisions get more media coverage and have wider application.

Refusing to appeal is just one of the tactics discussed in this chapter that the government has at its disposal to shift the issue—and, hopefully, responsibility—to the judiciary. It can also concede to challenges against its laws or actions or use the reference procedure, but all of these strategies raise serious questions about who is *really* responsible if the court rules against the government. This should be borne in mind when one is evaluating the effect of the court on policy-making and on debates about 'judicial activism' and the 'dialogue' between governments and courts; those issues are explored in Chapter 11.

PART III

Courts at Work

Chapter 9

Criminal Justice: Policy and Process

On 15 June 1983, Dr Henry Morgentaler opened a private abortion clinic in downtown Toronto contrary to s. 251 of the Criminal Code of Canada, which stipulated that abortions could be performed only in a hospital and if approved by a Therapeutic Abortion Committee (consisting of at least three doctors) to save the 'life or health' of the mother. Doctors faced a possible maximum life sentence if they were convicted of breaking the law. This law had been upheld during Morgentaler's first trip to the Canadian Supreme Court in 1975. The Court had ruled that the law was within the federal government's constitutional jurisdiction over criminal law and that the 1960 Bill of Rights, an ordinary piece of federal human rights legislation, did not give courts the authority to strike down such a law (*Morgentaler* 1975).

The police raided Morgentaler's new clinic on 5 July 1983. That morning two undercover officers posing as a distraught couple wanting an abortion finished paying their consulting fee to the clinic when police cruisers suddenly blocked either end of the street. A dozen police officers and detectives rushed into the clinic to make arrests and gather evidence. Media coverage of the establishment of the clinic, the police raid, and subsequent pro-choice and pro-life rallies was extensive. Pro-choice activists argued that the abortion law violated women's rights and that clinics like Morgentaler's should be legal, while pro-life activists argued that the law should be enforced and even made more restrictive to protect the rights of the fetus or unborn child (Morton 1992, 160–70).

Before entering a plea in November 1983,[1] Morgentaler's lawyer, Morris Manning, made a pre-trial motion before a superior trial court judge to have the abortion law declared unconstitutional. One of the arguments was based on the principle of federalism. Manning argued that s. 251 of the *Criminal Code* was *ultra vires* (beyond the power) of Parliament because it dealt with health, which was a provincial matter, rather than criminal law, which was federal jurisdiction under the *Constitution Act, 1867*. The other primary constitutional arguments were based on the Charter of Rights. The most important of these was that s. 251 of the *Criminal Code* violated the right to 'life, liberty and security' contained in s. 7 of the Charter by denying women the right of privacy to make a choice about terminating a pregnancy. Manning used over a dozen expert witnesses (including obstetricians and family planning counsellors) and reports about abortion policy to try to convince Justice Parker that s. 251 of the *Criminal Code* regulated a medical practice that was now very safe and created limited and unequal access to abortion services in Canada, thereby depriving women of access to health services and the right to choose to end their pregnancy. The Crown argued that these social facts were irrelevant because the Charter did not contain a right to an abortion and Canadian judges should not use the Charter to actively shape policy.

This trial within a trial took approximately five months, and it took another three months for Justice Parker to release his nearly sixty-page decision. Justice Parker upheld the law. He argued that it was within Parliament's criminal law jurisdiction to create a law that declared interference with the ordinary course of conception and birth to be 'socially undesirable' and subject to punishment, even if abortion had become medically safer in the time since the Supreme Court upheld the abortion law as valid criminal law in the mid-1970s. He then argued that the law did not violate s. 7 of the Charter. According to Justice Parker, the law did not violate the 'principles of fundamental justice' (as required by s. 7) because historically in Canada there had always been laws against abortion, from common law rules to the 1892 *Criminal Code* to the 1969 *Criminal Code* amendments (*R. v. Morgentaler* 1984).

Morgentaler's actual trial in superior court started in October 1984. After a week of jury selection, the opening remarks were made by the Crown prosecutor and by Morgentaler's defence lawyer. Manning told the jury that he would be using the common law 'defence of necessity'—Morgentaler's violation of the law would be justified as necessary because the law created delays and unequal access for women requiring abortions. To that end, Dr Morgentaler testified that a number of wives and mistresses of politicians had come to him for abortions, thus suggesting that politicians were hypocritical and knew that the law was inadequate. Once all the witnesses had been examined and cross-examined over a two-week period, it was time for the closing statements. The Crown prosecutor asked the jury to be neutral on the abortion issue and to focus only on applying the law. To acquit Morgentaler, he warned, would invite 'anarchy' and undermine democracy. By contrast, Manning told the jury that Morgentaler had broken the law to prevent greater harm to women and doctors and that the jury had a right not to apply the law—the 'right and just verdict' would be an acquittal. After a weekend break, Justice Parker gave his instructions to the jury. He told them that the 'defence of necessity' was narrower than Manning had portrayed and that no direct evidence had been presented at trial of any woman's having been denied an abortion in Ontario. Justice Parker also condemned Manning's suggestion that the jurors could ignore the law. Nevertheless, after two days of deliberations the jury returned a verdict of 'not guilty' (Morton 1992, Chap. 16).

Pro-life supporters urged the Attorney General of Ontario, Roy McMurtry, to appeal the acquittal, while pro-choice supporters asked him not to appeal. After a month, McMurtry attempted to placate both sides: he would appeal the acquittal but would not seek an injunction to prevent Morgentaler from reopening the clinic and no new charges would be filed if the clinic was reopened. Manning then announced that he would cross-appeal the trial judge's ruling that the law did not violate the constitution. The appeal hearing before a five-judge panel of the Ontario Court of Appeal began late in April 1985 and concluded on May 7. During Manning's presentation, the justices had sounded skeptical and peppered him with questions. Not surprisingly, when the court released its decision on 1 October 1985, it was a total defeat for Morgentaler. The court said that the law was within Parliament's criminal law jurisdiction and that it did not violate the Charter. It argued that 'the policy and wisdom of legislation should remain first and foremost a matter for Parliament and the Legislatures.' As for the defence against the charges, the court said that the defence of necessity was not legally available to Morgentaler because there was no 'emergency situation' that forced him to violate the law (like needing to break the speed limit to transport a seriously injured person to hospital). They also strongly chastised Manning for telling the jury that they could ignore the law (*Morgentaler* 1985).

The Supreme Court of Canada granted Morgentaler leave to appeal the Ontario Court of Appeal's decision. The hearing was held in October 1986, and it took the seven-judge panel over a year to release its decision in this controversial case. In January 1988, by a vote of 5–2, the Supreme Court struck down the abortion law as violating the Charter of Rights (*Morgentaler* 1988). One judge, Justice Bertha Wilson, argued that the 'liberty' provision in s. 7 of the Charter gave a woman the right to choose to terminate a pregnancy, at least within the first trimester. The other judges in the majority did not agree that there was a right to abortion, but they did find that the system of Therapeutic Abortion Committees (TACs) for regulating abortions placed physical and psychological stress on women seeking abortions (in no small part because there was unequal access to the committees across the country). Therefore their rights to 'security of the person' in s. 7 of the Charter were limited in a way that did not correspond to the 'principles of fundamental justice.'[2] Justices McIntyre and LaForest dissented from the conclusions reached by their colleagues. They would have upheld the law because the Charter did not speak to the abortion controversy (*Morgentaler*, 1988).

Since the majority held the law to be invalid, Morgentaler no longer had to worry about criminal prosecution for performing abortions in his clinics. In 1989 the Mulroney government proposed a new law that would have made abortion an indictable offence under the *Criminal Code* punishable by up to two years in prison unless a 'medical practioner' had approved the abortion for the sake of the 'life or health' of the woman (with health defined as physical or psychological). However, in the wake of strong criticism by pro-life and pro-choice groups, the bill was defeated by an unprecedented tie vote in the Senate (Morton 1992, 290–3).

The Morgentaler saga illustrates many important features of criminal law. It reveals that defining what is criminal can be politically contentious and that under the Charter courts are able to play an important role in shaping the content of criminal law. Morgentaler's arrest, trial, and subsequent appeals also provide a window into how the criminal justice process works after one is suspected of violating a criminal law. However, Morgentaler's case is not very representative of the criminal law process generally. Most criminal charges never result in a trial because the charges are stayed or withdrawn by the Crown or the accused pleads guilty. The small proportion of cases that do go to trial (there are still many) are usually for 'routine' offences such as petty theft or impaired driving and rarely involve juries. Overall the justice system resembles a factory with overburdened defence counsel, Crown lawyers, justices of the peace, judges, and court staff trying to prepare for various hearings and trials while also undertaking less formal discussions in the back halls of the courtroom (Makin 2003; Cole 2008).

This chapter examines the functions and influences of courts in five key stages of criminal law: (1) defining the scope and substance of criminal law; (2) shaping and monitoring investigatory procedures; (3) developing and implementing pre-trial processes; (4) conducting criminal trials and appeals; and (5) undertaking post-trial processes, particularly sentencing. Some comparisons are made with criminal law processes in other countries to put Canada's criminal law system into context. The chapter concludes with an examination of some theoretical models for explaining criminal justice policy and process with a particular focus on courts.

Scope and Substance of Criminal Law

Historically, judges played a significant role in the development of the criminal law in England. By the thirteenth century, a body of (judge-made) common law had developed that contained three kinds of offences: treason, felonies (such as murder, rape, mayhem and theft including arceny, burglary, and robbery), and misdemeanours (such as attempted suicide).[3] Over time, the British Parliament passed statutes that added to or modified criminal offences or their associated punishments. The large number of often very specific statutes (by 1826 there were over twenty acts that dealt with willful damage or theft of trees, the penalties for which ranged from a twenty-pound fine to death), and common law precedents made the criminal law tangled and confusing (Brown 1989, 12). Attempts to codify Britain's criminal law into a systematic statute were defeated, owing in large part to opposition against changing or undermining the common law.

Canada, however, used one of the proposed drafts developed in Britain as the basis for its comprehensive 1892 *Criminal Code*.[4] Nevertheless, some common law crimes were still recognized and occasionally prosecuted in Canada until the amendments to the *Criminal Code* in the early 1950s abolished common law offences (at the time, some of the remaining common law offences, such as public mischief, were incorporated into the Code) (Mewett 1988, 156–7). Although judges in Canada cannot create new crimes through judge-made law, they still exert an important influence in shaping the criminal law in four main ways: (1) by determining whether Parliament has acted outside the scope of its criminal law power when passing a law or whether a provincial legislature has encroached on the federal power over criminal law when passing a law; (2) by deciding whether a criminal law violates the Charter of Rights; (3) by interpreting and applying the *Criminal Code* and other federal statutes, such as the *Controlled Drugs and Substances Act* and the *Youth Criminal Justice Act*, that contain criminal laws; and (4) developing common law defences. We will examine the first three roles here and provide some examples of common law defences later in the 'trial' part of the chapter.

Federalism

Since the 'criminal law plays an important role in society in stating fundamental values', the framers of the Canadian Constitution expressed a desire in pre-Confederation conferences to give the power over criminal law to the federal government rather than to the provinces. In their estimation, this would help Canada avoid the mistake the Americans made in giving too much authority to the states, including the power over criminal law, which contributed to the American Civil War (Friedland 1984, 48). Although this proposal was relatively uncontroversial and was adopted in the *Constitution Act, 1867*, the parameters of the criminal law power soon generated political and legal tension between the federal government and the provinces. When such clashes arise, the courts are often asked to rule on the jurisdictional question (and they are also asked to rule in cases brought by individuals or businesses that seek to avoid regulation by having legislation declared unconstitutional on federalism grounds). In doing so, the courts must try to delineate the boundaries of the federal criminal law in the regulation of political, social, and economic activity and the boundaries of provincial power over such matters as 'property and civil rights' and 'matters of a merely local or private nature'. (Provinces also have the authority to enforce valid provincial laws through fines, imprisonment, or other penalties.)

The Judicial Committee of the Privy Council (JCPC), the British tribunal that was Canada's highest court of appeal before 1949, struggled somewhat to define the essence of 'criminal law'. In one of its later decisions involving federal prohibitions on the sale, manufacturing, and importing of margarine, the JCPC narrowed the criminal law to include only laws serving such ends as 'public peace, order, security, health and morality' (Hogg 2003: 461–4).[5]

More recently, the Supreme Court has expanded somewhat the scope of the federal criminal law power (Baier 2006, 140–2; also see Chapter 2). A majority of the Court said that a federal ban on tobacco advertising fell under the criminal-law power because it served indirectly to protect the public from a harmful product (even if the product itself remained legal) (*RJR-MacDonald* 1995). Soon after, in a challenge to the *Canadian Environmental Protection Act* brought by Hydro-Quebec (after it was charged for dumping PCBs into a river), the Court ruled that environmental protection was a valid objective of criminal law (*Hydro-Quebec*

1997). The Court then upheld the federal gun-control legislation as a valid exercise of criminal law power in its *Reference Re Firearms* (2000) decision, because the purpose of the law involved public safety and it contained prohibitions backed by penalties. In *Malmo–Levine* (2003), the Court upheld the prohibitions on the possession and distribution of marijuana in the federal *Controlled Drugs and Substances Act*. The decision affirmed that the criminal law power encompassed 'laws that are designed to promote public peace, safety, order, health or other legitimate public purpose' (para. 74). According to the Court, 'legitimate public purposes' included the desire to protect vulnerable groups (such as young people) and to enforce morality (defined as 'societal values beyond the simply prurient or prudish'). Various justices noted that to justify the use of criminal law jurisdiction there is only a minimal burden of proof on Parliament to demonstrate that there is more than a hypothetical threat to health or vulnerable groups.

The scope of the criminal law power has also been explored in cases where provincial laws have been challenged for infringing on federal jurisdiction over criminal law. Before the introduction of the Charter of Rights, in some cases it appeared that certain judges voted to strike down provincial laws as *ultra vires* on federalism grounds in order to protect rights and liberties. For example, in both the *Alberta Press Case* (1938)—involving limits on freedom of the press by the Alberta government—and the *Saumur* (1953) case—involving limits on the distribution of religious pamphlets in Quebec—some judges on the Canadian Supreme Court struck down the laws on the grounds that only the federal government could place such restrictions on liberties under the criminal law power. Although these judges are credited with helping to defend civil liberties, their reasoning 'tended to confuse the jurisprudence of both federalism and civil liberties' (Morton 2002, 481).

The more general trend, however, has been for the Court to allow provincial regulations that have punishments attached to them. Provincial offences involving careless driving, failing to remain at the scene of an accident, offering false information in a prospectus, film censorship, and prohibitions on public assemblies have all been upheld (Hogg 2003, 489). Nevertheless, as Hogg notes, certain cases serve as reminders that the ancillary power the provinces have to create offences for violations of provincial laws is not as broad as the free-standing federal power to create criminal law. In *Westendorp* (1983), the Supreme Court, somewhat unexpectedly, struck down a municipal by-law that prohibited a person from remaining on the street for the purpose of prostitution (Hogg 2003, 489). A decade later the Court struck down Nova Scotia's prohibitions on private abortion clinics in the province, arguing that the law infringed on a matter historically considered to be part of the federal power over criminal law (*Morgentaler* 1993).

Charter of Rights

The entrenchment of the Charter of Rights in 1982 gave judges the constitutional power to strike down laws that violated Charter rights and liberties even if those laws were within the proper federal or provincial sphere of jurisdiction. The Morgentaler example above reveals that the courts now have much more power to review and shape the substance of criminal law than they did before the introduction of the Charter. Indeed, during the past two decades, Charter cases have featured the most controversial provisions of the criminal law, including abortion, pornography, child pornography, the definition of murder, hate speech, physician-assisted suicide, spanking of children, marijuana prohibitions, anti-terrorism laws, and mandatory minimum sentences. Judges must confront difficult issues in Charter cases where criminal laws are challenged as unconstitutional: how broadly rights in the Charter, such as freedom of expression or liberty, should be defined; what justifications (morality, harm, equality, community standards, and so on) can legitimately limit rights; how competing rights and interests are to be ranked (for example, the degree, if any, to which individual rights should prevail over the protection of vulnerable groups); and whether the government or the individual must demonstrate that restrictions on rights are just or reasonable or unjust and unreasonable.

The *Keegstra* (1990) case, which involved a Charter challenge to the 'hate speech' provisions in the *Criminal Code*, provides a good example of these challenges and reveals that judges can disagree with one another on these issues. The lower courts were divided as to whether the right to free expression in the Charter actually included the right to express hatred. At the Supreme Court, all seven judges who decided the case agreed that free expression should be read broadly in a free and democratic country to include all expression not communicated through violence. However, the judges were badly divided (4–3) over the question of whether the hate speech law was a 'reasonable limit' on the right to free expression.[6] The majority argued that the law served an important objective (protecting vulnerable groups and promoting equality) and did so in a well-tailored way that impaired the right to free speech only minimally. Although the dissent agreed that the law served important objectives, they argued that it would unduly constrain speech because the definition of hate speech was vague and could capture too much speech. They also argued that the law was potentially bad policy in that it could inadvertently help promote hate by making martyrs out of those who were prosecuted.[7]

The power of the courts to shape the content of criminal law was demonstrated most recently in connection with anti-terrorism policy. In October 2006, an Ontario trial court judge ruled that the anti-terrorism provisions in the *Criminal Code* were neither vague nor overbroad and were therefore not contrary to section 7 of the Charter, but he struck down a part of the law that stipulated that terrorism offences (murder, property damage, and so on) were 'in whole or in part for a political, religious or ideological purpose, objective or cause . . .'. The judge determined that the provision would lead the police and security forces to focus their efforts on people of Arab background, which would diminish their ability to express themselves, practise their religion, and associate with one another and therefore violate rights in s. 2 of the Charter. Under the s. 1 'reasonable limits' test, he found no compelling justification for having the provision in the law (*Khawaja* 2006).

In addition to giving judges more power to define what kinds of actions or motives should be criminalized, the Charter also has given judges more power to determine what kinds of punishments are suitable for criminal offences and under what conditions. In a number of s. 7 cases, the Supreme Court has ruled that the criminal law cannot impose a punishment of imprisonment without proof of fault. For example, the Court held that the 'principles of fundamental justice' were violated by a provision in *the Criminal Code* that made it an offence, punishable by life in prison, to have sexual relations with a girl under fourteen years of age even if the accused honestly believed that the girl was older and had consented (*Hess* 1990). Parliament then passed new laws that required the accused to have taken all reasonable steps to ascertain the age of the other person (and also to obtain her consent) (Sharpe and Roach 2005, 236–7).[8]

Mandatory minimum sentences also have attracted the Court's attention (see Roach 2005, 354–6). In *Smith* (1987), the Court struck down a mandatory minimum sentence of seven years for importing narcotics. The Court argued that the possibility that a person could be sent to prison for bringing a single marijuana cigarette across the border violated the right against 'cruel and unusual punishment' in s. 12 and was not saved by s. 1, because it would result in a sentence that was 'grossly disproportionate'.[9] Justice McIntyre's dissent argued that s. 12 sets only the outer limits of what is 'cruel and unusual punishment' and that a certain deference should be shown to Parliament's attempts to achieve social aims. Since then the Court has been deferential when reviewing sentences prescribed by Parliament. A minimum four-year sentence for criminal negligence causing death with a firearm was upheld in recognition of Parliament's attempt to deter gun crime (*Morrisey* 2000). In its high-profile *Latimer* (2001) decision, the Court upheld the mandatory sentence for second-degree murder of life imprisonment and eligibility for parole only after ten years. The Court also refused to grant a constitutional exemption to Latimer even though he argued that he euthanized his severely disabled daughter for compassionate reasons.[10]

Statutory Interpretation

Although the power of courts to define the criminal law is most prominent in Charter cases, courts have long played a role in shaping the meaning and application of criminal law through their interpretation of the *Criminal Code* and other criminal law legislation. A good illustration is the case of Robin Sharpe, who was charged with possessing child pornography and possessing child pornography for the purposes of distribution. Sharpe challenged the child pornography law in the *Criminal Code* (s. 163) as a violation of the Charter's right to free expression. When the Supreme Court upheld the law, it not only read in two exceptions—written stories for personal use and video recordings of lawful sexual activity—but it also instructed trial judges to read the possible defences built into the law liberally, such as not limiting the 'artistic merit' defence (s. 163 (6)). At his new trial following the Supreme Court decision, Sharpe was acquitted of some of the charges against him because the trial judge found that his personal writings had 'artistic merit'. Justice Shaw contended that a Crown expert witness's opinion that Sharpe's writing was 'boring' and 'disgusting' imported standards of morality that were not permitted according to the Supreme Court's interpretation of the *Criminal Code* (Sauvageau, Schneiderman, and Taras 2006, 192).

The *Sharpe* decision also illustrates a common law tradition of reading criminal laws in such a way that any ambiguity in them favours the accused. This principle of 'strict construction' developed hundreds of years ago in England because then even relatively minor crimes, such as theft, were often subject to capital punishment (Roach 2004, 76). The doctrine has been a guiding influence in the interpretation of laws by Canadian courts. A well-known example was the *R. v. Boucher* (1951) decision by the Supreme Court. Boucher was charged with 'seditious libel' under s. 133 of the *Criminal Code* for distributing Jehovah's Witnesses pamphlets that were very critical of the Catholic Church and the Quebec government. A jury found Boucher guilty of 'seditious libel' at trial, but a majority of the Supreme Court overturned the conviction on the ground that the *Criminal Code* provisions about seditious libel needed to be read against the 'background of free criticism as a constituent of modern democratic government.'

Of course, interpretations favouring the accused must be within reason. The Supreme Court ruled, for example, that a decision by the Ontario Court of Appeal that acquitted a man of 'break and enter' because the door to the home was left open wide enough for him to slip in was incorrect. Not only was the purpose of the law clear, but the Ontario Court of Appeal judgment would have had the unusual effect of distinguishing between fatter and thinner burglars. There have also been some cases where the Supreme Court has rejected a restrictive reading of the law that favoured the accused, preferring instead, a purposive interpretation of the law that better captured Parliament's intent in defining crime (Paciocco 1999, 13–14).[11]

The role of the courts in interpreting what constitutes a crime under the *Criminal Code* is further illustrated in Box 9.1, which examines the question of whether engaging in sexual contact when knowingly HIV-positive is sexual assault or not.

Box 9.1   Defining Sexual Assault

In 1983, Parliament amended the *Criminal Code* to modernize the law concerning sexual assault. Parliament reclassified the crimes of 'indecent assault' and 'rape' into 'sexual assaults' and in doing so, according to Justice L'Heureux-Dubé, 'sensitiz[ed] the law's approach to sexual offences, which are predominantly perpetrated by men against women' (*Cuerrier* 1998 at para. 4). The prohibited act (*actus reus*) was broadened to 'include all intentional applications of force without consent in circumstances that were objectively sexual', and the marital rape exception was also repealed (Roach 2005, 87). Before 1983, the *Criminal Code* had held that consent could not be obtained through various means, including 'by false and fraudulent representations as to the nature and quality of the act'. The 1983 amendments included a new consent provision that applied to sexual and non-sexual assaults. This revised version of the Code included a list of ways through which consent to the act would be vitiated, including 'fraud'. No mention was made of the 'nature and quality of the act'.

Controversy developed thereafter as to how to interpret the amended *Criminal Code*—for example, did fraud still only apply to the 'nature and quality of the act'? Lower courts said it did. For example, a man was acquitted of sexual assault for promising to pay $100 for sexual services without having any intention to pay. Because the man was not misleading about the fact that he wanted sex, he was not fraudulent about 'the nature and quality of the act'. In the mid-1990s, lower courts acquitted Henry Cuerrier of sexual assault for having unprotected sex with a number of partners when he knew that he was HIV-positive but did not disclose this to his partners. Despite the fact that he did not follow the instructions by the health authorities to reveal his HIV-positive status to prospective sexual partners and to wear a condom during sex, the lower courts ruled that there was no fraud about the 'nature and quality of the act'.

The Supreme Court disagreed with the lower courts (*Cuerrier* 1998). It said that, because the *Criminal Code* now used the word 'fraud' but did not include 'the nature and quality of the act', the term fraud could include not informing a prospective partner about a disease that carried 'significant risk of serious bodily harm'. But the Crown would have to prove that individuals would not have consented had they known about the disease.

The *Cuerrier* precedent has been applied in subsequent cases. Each time a decision is made in this area, it builds upon the body of precedent that judges rely on to apply the rules written by Parliament in the *Criminal Code*. For example, in 2002 a trial judge acquitted a man of sexual assault for not telling his partner that he had hepatitis C. The trial judge ruled that the *Cuerrier* precedent required a 'significant risk' of harm, and expert testimony during the trial revealed that the chances of spreading hepatitis C through sexual contact are very low (*Jones* 2002).

Conclusions

Intervener groups in *Cuerrier* argued that criminalizing the transmission of HIV could have the unfortunate consequence of undermining public health initiatives to combat HIV because people might not get themselves tested in order to guard against possible criminal consequences should they be infected. Justice Cory responded by arguing that the criminal law could be useful in deterring individuals from recklessly transmitting the disease and that most people who wanted to seek treatment would still do so (at paras. 140–7). If Parliament were to decide that the public policy repercussions of *Cuerrier* or any other interpretations of the criminal law in other cases were undesirable, it could amend the *Criminal Code* or other federal criminal law statutes. After Sharpe's acquittal on some charges of child pornography as discussed above, for example, Parliament amended the *Criminal Code* to narrow the defences available to the accused in child pornography cases.

Since 1982, however, Parliament's ability to make law within its criminal law jurisdiction has been circumscribed by the Charter of Rights and its interpretation by judges. Indeed, it is expected that Parliament's changes to the child pornography law will generate new Charter challenges that will work their way up the judicial hierarchy. The role of judges in shaping criminal law is part of the broader debate about judicial policy-making (see Chapter 11).

Investigation of Crime

The powers given to state authorities to prevent and investigate criminal activity as defined in the law are ultimately political. They play a key role in regulating the relationship between citizens and the state, and there is disagreement, based on competing values, about how much power should be given to state authorities, particularly the police, to control crime. These competing values are represented by two models of criminal justice: the crime control model and the due process model (Packer 1964). The *crime control* model of criminal justice values efficiency, convictions for those who are guilty, and public safety, and it leads to calls for greater latitude for the police to search, detain, and interrogate. By contrast, the values of the *due process* model are to protect individual rights from police power, prevent the conviction of those who are innocent, and ensure equal treatment of individuals within the system. This model calls for more restrictions on the police in the exercise of their authority.

Both the courts and legislatures have a voice in defining police power and therefore in deciding on the right balance between crime control and due process. Legislatures set out police powers in various criminal and quasi-criminal statutes. Provincial highway traffic acts, for instance, set out under what circumstances a police officer may stop a vehicle and what powers he or she has to question the driver or search the vehicle once the vehicle is stopped. Parliament defines various police powers and the limits on those powers in the *Criminal Code*, the *Controlled Drugs and Substances Act*, and other federal criminal statutes. For example, in response to concerns that there was no legal authority for the police to collect DNA samples from suspects of crime, Parliament amended the *Criminal Code* in the mid-1990s to authorize the police to do so. There were important limits placed on this power, however. The police would have to convince a s. 92 (provincial) court judge that there were 'reasonable grounds' to believe that the suspect had committed a designated offence (primarily serious violent and sexual offences are designated) and that bodily substances found at the scene of the crime would help to determine whether the targeted suspect was the source of the substances.[12] The courts define police power through judge-made common law, the interpretation of police powers in criminal law, and quasi-criminal law statutes, and since 1982, by interpreting and enforcing the legal rights enshrined in the Charter of Rights.

Before the introduction of the Charter, Canada was somewhat closer to the crime control model in the context of police powers (Harvie and Foster 1990). The Charter of Rights—particularly the right 'to retain and instruct counsel without delay and to be informed of that right' upon arrest or detention (s. 10(b)), the right against 'unreasonable search and seizure' (s. 8), and the right against 'arbitrary detention' (s. 9)—and judicial interpretation of the Charter have moved Canada more towards the due-process side of the spectrum. The Court signalled this shift in its early Charter jurisprudence. In *Therens* (1985), the Court reversed one of its early 1960 Bill of Rights decisions by ruling that a person asked by the police to go to the station for a breathalyzer test is considered to be 'detained' because of the psychological pressure exerted by the police and, therefore, is entitled to contact a lawyer. Since expanding the scope of when a person is entitled to the right to counsel, the Court has added a number of obligations on the part of the police under s. 10(b). The police must inform a person not only of his or her right to contact counsel, but also of the availability of legal aid and duty counsel and must give suspects a reasonable opportunity to contact counsel. Waiver of the right to counsel must be voluntary and done with an awareness of the possible consequences. Similarly, the Court has placed greater restrictions on searches and seizures, particularly by requiring warrants for searches that did not previously require them.

There are some caveats, however, to the conclusion that Canada's system is more oriented toward due process. First, some decisions under the Charter have been more oriented toward crime control. One man lost a right-to-counsel case when the Supreme Court ruled that he was not diligent enough in trying to exercise his right to counsel (Smith, 1989). Provincial laws authorizing the police to conduct roadside stops to look for drunk drivers were upheld as a reasonable and justified limit on rights. In search and seizure cases, the Court has concluded that the rules of search and seizure do not apply to the same extent in situations where there is a lower 'reasonable expectation of privacy', including searches at the border, searches of schools and cars (especially of non-owner passengers), and searches that detect heat radiating from homes. And in a series of common law and Charter decisions, Canadian courts, including the Supreme Court, have recognized a police power to detain individuals briefly for investigative purposes (Stribopoulos 2007).

A second caveat about Canada's increased due-process focus is that when an individual's legal right has been violated, evidence is not automatically excluded from trial. Section 24(2) of the Charter instructs judges to exclude evidence only if it would 'bring the administration of justice into disrepute.' Table 9.1 sets out the three-part guideline developed by the Supreme Court to help judges determine whether evidence should be excluded or not under s. 24(2).

The exclusionary rule is extremely controversial, and opinions often reflect either a crime-control or a due-process approach. Those who believe that only irrelevant or unreliable evidence should be excluded argue that the administration of justice is undermined when a person can escape justice because 'the constable blundered' (Parfett 2002).[13] Others argue that a robust standard for excluding evidence is necessary to protect against wrongful conviction, to deter the police from violating rights in the future, and to uphold the principles of the legal system, which apply to both the innocent and the guilty (Stuart 1999; Kamisar 2003).

Table 9.1   The s. 24(2) Exclusion-of-Evidence Test

Factor	Evidence More Likely to Be Admitted	Evidence More Likely to Be Excluded
Fairness of the trial	*Non-conscriptive evidence* that could have been found independently of the violation of an accused's Charter rights is less likely to affect the fairness of the trial.	*Conscriptive evidence* that emanates from the accused (such as confessions or blood samples), or is produced by the participation of the accused in an investigation during which time there has been a violation of his or her Charter rights is more likely to affect the fairness of the trial adversely, since the Charter violation leads to the accused producing evidence against him- or herself.
Seriousness of the Charter breach	The police acted in good faith, committed only a trivial violation of the Charter, or violated the Charter in an emergency situation.	The police violated rights in a serious and flagrant manner, particularly in a non-emergency.
The effect on the administration of justice	The evidence is central to substantiating a criminal charge and the breach of the Charter was trivial.	There is a criminal charge with the potential for serious penalties and the police flagrantly violated the Charter.

Note:
The table is based on Supreme Court of Canada s. 24(2) decisions, particularly *R. v. Collins* (1987) and *R. v. Stillman* (1997).

A third caveat is that both judges and legislators will disagree amongst themselves and with one another about the right balance between crime control and due process. The Feeney decision and its aftermath, presented in Box 9.2, reveals how deep these divisions can be and how the balance between crime control and due process is often in flux.

Box. 9.2   The Feeney Decision and Its Aftermath

On the morning of 8 June 1991 the body of 85-year-old Frank Boyle was found in his home in the small community of Likely, British Columbia. He had died from severe blows to the head from an iron pipe or similar object. At the crime scene, bystanders told the police that Boyle's truck had been seen crashed in a ditch at 6:45 that morning and that 'Michael' had been seen walking near the scene of the accident holding something in his hand, possibly a beer bottle. Another person reported that Michael Feeney had stolen a different truck earlier in the day and crashed it in almost the same place where Boyle's truck was found. The police went to where Michael was staying. His sister and her partner told the police that Michael had returned at about 7 a.m. and was asleep in the trailer he was renting located behind the house. RCMP Staff Sergeant Madrigga knocked on the door of the trailer and yelled, 'Police'. After receiving no response Madrigga drew his gun and entered the trailer with two other officers. Seeing a man lying on the bed asleep he went over and shook Feeney's leg and said, 'Wake up, police. I want to talk to you.' Once Feeney got up he was asked to move into the light coming from the doorway. After he did so the police could see that there was blood spattered on the T-shirt he was wearing. Feeney was arrested and handcuffed and an officer read Feeney his right to counsel, including informing him about the existence of legal-aid duty counsel. After being asked for a second time if he understood his rights, Feeney responded, 'Of course, what do you think I am, illiterate?' The police then asked Feeney about how he had got the blood on himself. Feeney replied that he was struck in the face with a baseball, though he did not have any noticeable injuries on his face. The police also asked about the shoes he was wearing the night before.

Feeney's shirt was taken off him, and he was then taken to the RCMP detachment. At a little after noon, Feeney left a message at a lawyer's office asking him to contact him. Feeney was then left in an observation cell for over eight hours until two detectives started to question him shortly after 9 p.m. Soon after the interview began, Feeney said, 'I should have a lawyer', but the interview continued. Under questioning, Feeney admitted to striking Boyle and stealing his cigarettes, beer, and cash. The police then obtained a search warrant from a justice of the peace authorizing them to seize Feeney's shoes, the cigarettes, and the money (which Feeney said was hidden under the mattress). Feeney was interviewed again at 3 in the morning and was fingerprinted twice later in the morning. Between those fingerprinting sessions he met for the first time with his lawyer.

At a pre-trial hearing (*voir dire*), Feeney's lawyer argued that his client's right to counsel and right against unreasonable search and seizure had been violated and that his statements and the evidence collected from Feeney and his trailer should be excluded from evidence. The trial judge excluded only the statements that had Feeney made at the station. At the trial, a jury found Feeney guilty of second-degree murder. The British Columbia Court of Appeal upheld the trial judge's Charter decision and Feeney's conviction.

The case was appealed to the Supreme Court of Canda. By a 5–4 decision the Court overturned the decisions of the trial judge and the British Columbia Court of Appeal. The majority argued that Feeney's right to counsel was violated at his trailer because he was not immediately told of his right to counsel when roused from the bed. Furthermore, once his rights were read to him, he was not given a reasonable opportunity to use a phone to call a lawyer before the police started questioning him about how he had got the blood on him and about his shoes.

The majority then argued that the T-shirt seized from Feeney resulted from an illegal arrest. Transcripts of the cross-examination of staff sergeant Madrigga by Feeney's lawyer during the pre-trial hearing revealed that Madrigga said that he was 'suspicious' that Feeney was the perpetrator but he did not have grounds for an arrest at that time. The majority argued that such an arrest was not legal under common law rules and that the Charter provided even greater rights protection than the common law. For this reason, a warrant would be required for future warrantless arrests in homes except in cases of hot pursuit. Since the arrest was illegal, the search and seizure of Feeney's T-shirt (and later his fingerprints) violated his right not to be subjected to unreasonable search and seizure. Furthermore, because the police used information gained from an illegal arrest to ask for the search warrant to search Feeney's trailer, the warrant was invalid. Therefore, the shoes, cigarettes, and money found in Feeney's trailer resulted from an unreasonable search and seizure.

The majority decided that the evidence should be excluded under s. 24(2) of the Charter. Feeney's statements and fingerprints emanated from him (and, therefore, constituted 'conscriptive' evidence), and their admission could result in an unfair trial. The T-shirt, shoes, cigarettes, and money, although non-conscriptive evidence, were the result of serious rights violations by the police and thus to admit them into the trial as evidence would bring the administration of justice into disrepute.

The dissent argued that Feeney's rights had not been violated. They argued that the police are allowed to make sure the scene is secure before reading a person the right to counsel. They also argued that it is somewhat incumbent on the accused to assert that he wanted to use his right to counsel, but that Feeney did not do so in the trailer. As for the search and seizure, the dissent maintained that the initial arrest of Feeney was legal. The dissent argued that the context needed to be taken into account, especially the fact that the community was a very small one. They also cited various parts of the transcript of Madrigga's testimony to buttress their conclusion that it appeared that Madrigga had 'reasonable and probable grounds' to enter Feeney's trailer, even though he did not use legal terminology with the precision of a lawyer or judge. It was 'unrealistic', according to the dissent, not to allow the police to make warrantless arrests in homes except when in 'hot pursuit'. Other 'exigent circumstances', such as trying to preserve evidence, would also justify warrantless arrests in dwelling places. Finally, the dissent argued that even if Feeney's rights had been violated, to exclude the evidence in a case that involved a brutal murder and in which the police acted diligently and commendably would bring the administration of justice into disrepute.

The decision was met by criticism from the media and the public. Governments and police agencies were concerned about the effects of the ruling. In response, Parliament amended the *Criminal Code* to provide for warrants to be obtained (through 'telecommunication') for entrance into a dwelling place to execute an arrest. Parliament also allowed police officers to make warrantless arrests in homes in 'exigent circumstances', which included, but were not limited to, preventing bodily harm or death and preventing the imminent destruction of evidence. In making this law, Parliament followed the view of the dissent in how to balance rights against effective law enforcement.

Finally, although legal changes have generally made Canada more due-process-oriented, what happens 'on the ground' may not necessarily agree with the law 'on the books'. Research from the US suggests that rights violations by the police are not uncommon because of breakdowns in training or leadership, a lack of incentives to follow the rules, the low visibility of most police encounters with the public, and a police culture that emphasizes the control of crime regardless of the formal rules (Rosenberg 1991, chap. 11; Gould and Mastrowski 2004). Little research has been done on the topic of police compliance with the Charter in Canada, but the evidence so far appears mixed (Moore 1992). There is also evidence to suggest, contrary to the due process model, that the police disproportionately target visible minorities, especially blacks and Aboriginals, in their efforts to control and investigate crime (Wortley and Tanner 2003; Manitoba, Aboriginal Justice Inquiry 1991). The existence of racial bias has been acknowledged by Canadian courts, especially by the Ontario Court of Appeal, which has recognized that both individual and systematic racism in policing is a social reality (*Brown* 2003). However, that court has also made it clear that a 'full appreciation of the relevant social reality also extends to an understanding that not every claim of racism, even where honestly made, is valid' (*Peart* 2006, at para. 42). Arguments continue about under what circumstances race might be an appropriate consideration in police investigations and what standards the courts should apply when dealing with questions of racial profiling (Tanovich 2006; *Globe and Mail* 2007).

The ability of courts to monitor police conduct is limited by the fact that many police encounters with the public do not result in criminal charges. The reasons why charges are not filed even if the police do find evidence that criminal or quasi-criminal laws are being broken include possible inadmissibility of evidence owing to police conduct, lack of sufficient evidence, reluctant victims or witnesses, resource implications, the availability of pre-charge diversion programs, and possibly even political considerations (see Chapter 8) (Griffiths 2007, 192). With regard to a young person alleged to have committed an offence, the *Youth Criminal Justice Act* requires the police to consider whether non-court alternatives would be sufficient (Sprott and Doob 2008). Sometimes the objectives of the police, such as removing drugs from the street, may not require a criminal charge (a seizure of illegal drugs would suffice). For example, from 1997 to 2000 in British Columbia, charges were laid in an average of only 55 per cent of the cases in which the police seized marijuana plants (Plecas et al. 2002).

Pre-trial Stage

The process at work after a criminal charge has been laid depends on whether a person has been charged with a *summary* or an *indictable* offence. Summary offences tend to be less serious offences that are tried only before provincial (s. 92) courts. Examples include causing a disturbance, defacing coins, and communicating for the purposes of prostitution. Indictable offences tend to be more serious offences, such as murder, aggravated sexual assault, and theft over $5,000. The fines and terms of imprisonment are higher for indictable offences (they can include a life sentence) than for summary offences (recall, though, that only the federal government can create indictable offences). A number of offences in the *Criminal Code* are *hybrid* (or elective) offences that allow the Crown to decide whether the charge will be summary or indictable. These offences include theft under $5,000, sexual assault, and impaired driving.

Not only does the choice made by the Crown between a summary and an indictable charge have implications for the punishment if the accused is convicted, but there are also procedural implications. Whereas all summary convictions are tried in a s. 92 provincial court before a judge (there are no juries in provincial court), the process for indictable offences is more complicated. As explained in Chapter 2, for the least serious indictable offences (and least serious hybrid offences where the Crown has elected to make the charge an indictable one), the accused has no choice but to be tried before a s. 92 provincial court judge. For the most serious indictable offences, such as murder or treason, the accused must be tried before a judge and jury in s. 96 superior trial court.[14] For most indictable offences (and hybrid offences if the Crown has elected to make the charge an indictable one), the accused has a choice of: (a) trial by a s. 92 provincial court judge, (b) trial by s. 96 superior court judge, or (c) trial by a s. 96 superior trial court judge and jury. Trials in s. 96 superior courts (before a judge or a judge and jury) are often preceded by a preliminary inquiry before a s. 92 provincial court judge, where the Crown must satisfy the judge that there is at least a plausible case to be made against the accused.[15] The criminal justice process (for accused adults) is outlined in Figure 9.1.

It should be noted that for young persons, most trials are held before s. 92 provincial youth court judges and follow the procedures for summary conviction offences. In certain circumstances, such as for serious offences like murder or manslaughter, an accused youth will have a choice of trial before a provincial youth court judge, a superior trial court judge, or a superior trial court judge and jury (*Youth Criminal Justice Act*, s. 67).[16] As with adults, if a youth chooses to be tried in superior court the trial is normally preceded by a preliminary inquiry (by a s. 92 youth court judge).

According to the most recently available adult court statistics from Statistics Canada, in 2006/7, 372,084 criminal cases were initiated against accused individuals (and businesses) involving more than one million criminal charges. The proportion of cases comprising multiple charges continues to climb (60 per cent of cases in 2006/7 involved multiple charges compared to only 44 per cent of cases in 1994/5) (Thomas 2004; Marth 2008). This trend suggests that criminal cases are becoming increasingly complex.[17] A significant number of those cases (30 per cent) were disposed of by the Crown's staying or withdrawing the charges (Marth 2008).

Figure 9.1   The Canadian Criminal Justice Process

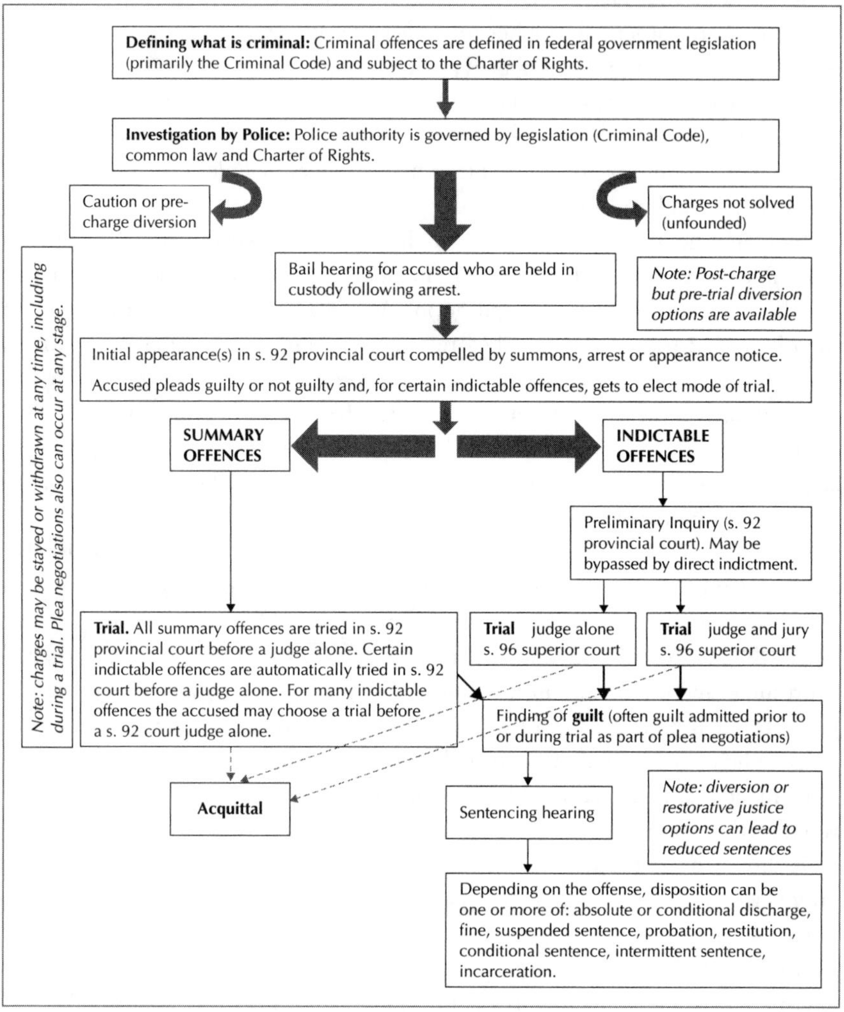

Defining what is criminal: Criminal offences are defined in federal government legislation (primarily the Criminal Code) and subject to the Charter of Rights.

Investigation by Police: Police authority is governed by legislation (Criminal Code), common law and Charter of Rights.

Caution or pre-charge diversion

Charges not solved (unfounded)

Bail hearing for accused who are held in custody following arrest.

Note: Post-charge but pre-trial diversion options are available

Initial appearance(s) in s. 92 provincial court compelled by summons, arrest or appearance notice. Accused pleads guilty or not guilty and, for certain indictable offences, gets to elect mode of trial.

Note: charges may be stayed or withdrawn at any time, including during a trial. Plea negotiations also can occur at any stage.

SUMMARY OFFENCES

INDICTABLE OFFENCES

Preliminary Inquiry (s. 92 provincial court). May be bypassed by direct indictment.

Trial. All summary offences are tried in s. 92 provincial court before a judge alone. Certain indictable offences are automatically tried in s. 92 court before a judge alone. For many indictable offences the accused may choose a trial before a s. 92 court judge alone.

Trial judge alone s. 96 superior court

Trial judge and jury s. 96 superior court

Finding of **guilt** (often guilt admitted prior to or during trial as part of plea negotiations)

Acquittal

Sentencing hearing

Note: diversion or restorative justice options can lead to reduced sentences

Depending on the offense, disposition can be one or more of: absolute or conditional discharge, fine, suspended sentence, probation, restitution, conditional sentence, intermittent sentence, incarceration.

Source: Adapted from Griffiths (2007, 207); Mihorean and Kong (2008, 19); and Brockman and Rose (2006, 27).

Stay and Withdrawal of Charges

Charges may be stayed or withdrawn for a number of reasons. The Crown may believe that there is not sufficient evidence to result in a conviction (for example, partly because of unco-operative or unreliable witnesses) or that the evidence collected by the police will be ruled inadmissible. In some cases, the Crown may opt to stay or withdraw the charges pending the completion of a diversion program before trial. Such diversion programs may take various forms, from mental health treatment, to drug treatment, to victim–offender mediation programs. For example, after 'Ruby' was arrested and charged for attacking her abusive spouse with a weapon in Campbellford, Ontario, in 2005, the Crown agreed to allow her to participate in a mental health program offered by the Canadian Mental Health Association. Ruby was diagnosed with schizophrenia and received medication to help control the effects of her illness. She also received counselling related to her mental illness and alcohol addiction. After six months, the Crown was satisfied with her progress and agreed to stay the charges against her (Eagle 2007). Pre-trial diversion programs are normally used for less serious charges than those Ruby faced, but the *Criminal Code* specifically allows for pre-trial use of 'alternative measures'.[18] The *Youth Criminal Justice Act* encourages the use of pre-trial diversion options for young offenders.

Judicial Interim Release (Bail)

For accused who are kept in custody after being arrested, the likelihood of the charges being withdrawn by the Crown increases if bail is granted (Kellough and Wortley 2002). Since reforms in the early 1970s, many accused are not held in custody before having to appear in court,[19] but for those who are held, the *Criminal Code* specifies that a bail hearing should take place within twenty-four hours or as soon as possible thereafter. Although most detained youth in one study met the twenty-four-hour standard (Moyer 2006), the Ontario Criminal Justice Review found that one-third of detained accused adults in its sample had to appear three or more times before a ruling was made (Ontario, Attorney General Ontario 1999). The presumption is that bail will be granted unless the Crown decides to 'show cause' why bail should be denied (perhaps because of previous instances where the accused failed to appear in court). In certain circumstances outlined in the *Criminal Code*, there is a 'reverse onus' on the accused to show why he or she should be released on bail. These circumstances include being charged with murder, drug trafficking, terrorism, or an offence involving organized crime or being charged with an offence while out on bail. Early in 2008, Parliament passed an omnibus anti-crime bill, proposed by the Harper government, that makes certain offences involving firearms or other regulated weapons also subject to 'reverse onus' bail provisions (Valiquet 2007; *Globe and Mail* 2008). The Supreme Court had previously decided that 'reverse onus' clauses do not necessarily violate an individual's s. 11(e) Charter right not to be denied bail without reasonable cause (*Pearson* 1992; *Morales* 1992).

The bulk of bail hearings are held before justices of the peace, though superior court judges preside over bail hearings held for serious charges, such as murder. Whether bail is granted or not and with what conditions varies between jurisdictions even within the same province (Allen 2007).[20] Research by Kellough and Wortley (2002) found that factors such as how many charges the accused was facing, whether the accused had a permanent address, and the information supplied to the Crown by the police about the accused's legal history and moral character were statistically significant in explaining whether bail was granted or not. The gender of the accused was also a significant factor (men are much more likely to be denied bail); race was not, though Kellough and Wortley argue that the statistical models suggest that the police tend to be more negative in their legal and moral assessments of blacks, so that race plays at least an indirect role in the process. Kellough and Wortley's analysis also reveals that being denied bail and remanded to custody increases the likelihood that an accused will accept a plea bargain.

Plea Agreements

Estimates suggest that approximately 80 to 90 per cent of cases not stayed or dismissed by the Crown are ended through a plea agreement, that is, 'an agreement by the accused to plead guilty in return for the prosecutor's agreeing to take or refrain from taking a particular course of action' (Law Commission of Canada, 1989, 3–4). Such agreements are usually arrived at through negotiations or discussions about one or more of the following issues: the nature of the charges to be laid or pursued (charge bargaining); the nature of the sentence (sentence bargaining); and the nature of the facts that the Crown may bring before the trial judge (fact bargaining) (Verdun-Jones 2008, 129–30). Until the late 1970s, plea bargaining was not acknowledged to exist or was viewed with disdain by legal elites, but more recently these negotiations have been deemed legitimate. And, although some research suggests otherwise, many consider plea negotiations to be necessary for the efficient operation of the criminal justice system (Verdun-Jones and Tijerino 2004; Di Luca 2005).[21]

Another argument in favour of plea bargaining is that it allows the accused to expedite the process and, in doing so, possibly receive some benefit in the form of fewer charges or a less punitive sentence. It is also possible that a plea agreement could provide investigators with information about other persons who might be involved in criminal activities. And plea bargains allow victims to avoid having to face the accused in court.

Nevertheless, controversy continues to swirl around the practice of plea bargaining. Critics argue that plea bargains could lead to some accused not getting their just punishment—the highest-profile example is probably the relatively light sentence that Karla Homolka received in 1993 for her part in the death of two Ontario teenage girls as part of her plea agreement.[22] Alternatively, plea negotiations have been argued to be detrimental to the accused, who are not afforded the same due-process protections against the power of the state that they would have during a trial. There is concern that the accused, even innocent ones (or ones that would have a valid legal defence), will be compelled to plead guilty when confronted by such possibilities as over-charging by the police or Crown, lengthy pre-trial waits (especially for those who remain in custody and are denied bail), and receiving a longer sentence if they are found guilty following a trial (Kellough and Wortley 2002; Piccinato 2004, 3–5; Di Luca 2005, 36–40). These problems are compounded for people who do not have a lawyer or are represented by over-worked (and possibly less competent) lawyers, particularly duty counsel, who may be tempted to encourage the acceptance of plea bargains out of self-interest (Ericson and Baranek 1982, chaps. 4–5). Owing to the relatively disadvantaged position of most accused in plea negotiations and the fact that plea discussions are now the norm, it is likely that 'bargains', such as the one obtained by Karla Homolka, are rather exceptional.

However, because the practice of plea bargaining is relatively unregulated and closed to public scrutiny, it is difficult to gauge its consequences. This lack of open-ness is compounded by the absence of meaningful opportunities for victims of crime to participate in plea negotiations (Verdun-Jones and Tijerino 2004). Recommendations have been made to make plea agreements more transparent and open to scrutiny (Martin Committee Report 1993, Verdun-Jones 2008). Criminologist Simon Verdun-Jones (2008) proposes a policy, based on US models (especially in state prosecutions), of giving judges more explicit responsibility for reviewing plea agreements to determine whether they serve the best interests of the various parties (including the accused, the victim(s), and the community at large). Currently the part played by judges in such proceedings is minimal. Pre-trial con-ferences allow for plea discussions to take place before a judge, but such discussions are not mandatory.[23] During the sentencing phase, since 1992, s. 606(1) of the *Criminal Code* has required that trial judges ensure that the accused is pleading guilty voluntarily, understands what a plea agreement is, and recognizes that the court is not bound by the agreement. Otherwise, trial judges have the discretion to inquire more deeply into the factual and legal circumstances surrounding a plea bargain beyond what is presented in open court (Piccinato 2004, 7). Some trial judges have expressed frustration at not being given adequate background to why the lawyers agreed on the plea (Griffiths 2007, 203), but researchers have suggested that Canadian courts also have been reluctant to use their discretion to investigate the circumstances of a plea (Griffiths and Verdun-Jones 1999, 83–4). Though judges are not bound to accept a plea recommendation made by the Crown, appel-late courts have strongly encouraged trial judges to accept joint sentence recom-mendations developed by the defence and Crown unless the submission would 'bring the administration of justice into disrepute' (Piccinato 2004, 8–9).

Disclosure of Evidence

The Supreme Court believed that plea bargaining would be facilitated by earlier and more thorough disclosure of the Crown's evidence to the defence. That was one of the justifications the Court gave for requiring full and timely disclosure of Crown evidence to the defence in its seminal *Stinchcombe* (1991) decision. The Court also argued that earlier and fuller disclosure of evidence by the Crown could help to prevent wrongful convictions.[24] Indeed, a lack of full disclosure of evidence to the defence has been called a contributing factor to a number of high-profile wrongful convictions in Canada, including those of Donald Marshall, Jr, David Milgaard, and Thomas Sophonow (Barrett 2007, Denov and Campbell 2008).

The argument that the defence should also be required to provide disclosure to the prosecution outlining the legal arguments and evidence (including experts) on which it intends to rely at trial was renewed after it was discovered that Paul Bernardo's defence lawyer had kept videotape evidence that implicated his client in the sexual assaults and murder of two Ontario teenagers. Other jurisdictions, such as some US states and England, have defence disclosure requirements. Proponents argue that such a rule would increase efficiency and assist in finding the truth, while opponents counter that such a rule would violate the due-process rights of the accused (namely, the right not to incriminate oneself) and would limit or even redefine the role of the defence as an adversary against the power of the state (Brockman and Rose 2006, 89–90).

So far, Canada continues to have only Crown disclosure,[25] but the extent to which it is practised depends to some degree on police practices and co-operation between the police and the Crown. Enforcing disclosure can be difficult for courts because they may be reluctant to use a drastic measure such as dismissal of a case for slow or inadequate disclosure by the Crown (Roach 1996). From the Crown's perspective, disclosure requirements are complicated by the need to protect the privacy and safety of victims, witnesses, and informants (Canada, Department of Justice 2004). Government officials have also expressed concern that disclosure obligations create increased costs and delays in the criminal justice system, especially for complex cases (Canada, Department of Justice 2004).

Pre-Trial Delay and Possible Solutions

Delays in getting to trial have been spotlighted recently. For example, in a 2007 speech Beverley McLachlin, Chief Justice of the Supreme Court, listed delays in the system (both criminal and civil) as one of four key challenges that the justice system faces (McLachlin 2007). Various reasons have been flagged as contributing to delay in getting to trial, including lack of adequate resources, disclosure requirements, increasingly complex cases, and inadequate pre-trial case management (Ontario Superior Court of Justice 2006). In a controversial speech in 2005, Justice Moldaver of the Ontario Court of Appeal blamed some of the delay in criminal trials on defence counsel who make too many frivolous Charter of Rights claims that needed to be dealt with by judges before the trial could start (see Moldaver 2006). Not surprisingly, though, Justice Moldaver's view has been met with criticism and concern from some quarters that it would have a chilling effect on efforts to enforce constitutional rights (Stuart 2006). Solutions offered to address pre-trial delay include more resources and more effective use of pre-trial conferences to discuss 'both resolution and case management issues [clarifying points of agreement and disagreement and so on]' (Ontario Superior Court of Justice 2006).[26]

Trial

Because of the high number of charges that are dealt with by a plea bargain or withdrawal or stay by the Crown, there are few trials compared to the number of charges laid. Estimates suggest that only about 10 per cent of criminal cases result in a trial. Nevertheless, given the sheer volume of cases initiated every year (about 400,000) there are still many trials.[27] In contrast to the American system, the majority of criminal cases in Canada do not feature a jury. A significant reason is that most criminal cases (both adult and youth) are heard in s. 92 provincial courts, which do not have juries. However, for murder cases and when an accused has chosen to be tried before a judge and jury in s. 96 superior trial court, the first step in the trial process is to empanel a jury.

Jury Selection

Juries are selected from pools of citizens summoned randomly to be potential jurors from electoral rolls in the province or local community. Jurors are expected to be impartial in their deliberations. According to the *Criminal Code*, judges are empowered to excuse individuals from jury duty who have a personal interest in the matter to be tried (s. 632(a)). The *Criminal Code* also allows both the Crown and defence to challenge potential jurors 'for cause'—a challenge suggesting that they will not be impartial in their decision making (s. 638). Each side is allowed to make an unlimited number of such challenges. Two persons who have already been selected for the jury act as 'triers' to determine whether a challenge for cause should succeed or not.[28] In the 1990s, both the Ontario Court of Appeal and the Supreme Court of Canada decided that it is permissible for the accused to challenge potential jurors for cause about racial biases if there is a widespread racial prejudice in the community. The trial judge has discretion as to whether such questions can be raised. Trial judges have also allowed challenges for cause based on the potential jurors' attitudes about sexual orientation, HIV status, and violence against women (Vidmar 1999, 162–3). If such questions are permitted, it is then up to the triers to determine whether a potential juror should be empanelled or not.

The Crown and the defence also each have a set of 'peremptory challenges' that allow jurors to be dismissed without cause. Each side is allowed twenty peremptory challenges for cases of murder or high treason, twelve for cases involving offences carrying a maximum penalty exceeding five years in prison, and four for cases involving all other offences (s. 634(2)).[29]

In the United States, jury-selection experts are sometimes employed by defendants to help them best use their challenges. The use of such experts is facilitated by the fact that in the US rather extensive questioning of the potential jurors is allowed. During the 1994 trial of ex-NFL star O.J. Simpson, for example, the defence, which employed a jury-selection expert, required potential jurors to fill out a questionnaire that ran over seventy-five pages.[30] In Canada, use of jury selection experts is much less prevalent. In part, this is because the norm in Canada is to permit generally only a few questions to be posed to a prospective juror (Vidmar 1999). Nevertheless, experts are sometimes used in Canada. In the Morgentaler case described in the introduction to this chapter, the defence made use of such an expert. When this was reported in the media, it generated considerable controversy (Morton 1992, 194–6). Whether jury-selection experts help to select a jury that is truly unbiased by rejecting people who are hostile to the accused, whether they stack the jury in favour of the accused, or whether they make any difference at all to the outcomes of trials remains an open question (Morton 1992, 198–9; Neubauer 1997, 363–4). The question is further complicated by the fact that the Crown, which is considered to be a quasi-judicial officer, is not entitled to make use of such experts.

As to whether a jury needs to be demographically representative in order to be perceived as impartial, the answer is generally that it does not. For example, in the Supreme Court's *Biddle* (1995) decision, only one justice was critical of what appeared to be an attempt by the Crown to get an all-female jury for a sexual assault case.[31] And trial courts have not been very receptive to requests by aboriginal offenders to have trials moved to their local communities in part to have access to a pool of aboriginal jurors (Martin 1996, 103–4).

Finding a jury that will be viewed as impartial can be quite difficult in small, remote communities, especially in the north, since many prospective jurors may be related to the accused or the victim. Local political struggles between families or ruling cliques may also compromise the empanelling of an impartial jury because some people may fear retaliation after a verdict is returned. Change of venues have been granted occasionally by judges in recognition of these difficulties (Gora 1993, 171–2)

Trial Processes, Evidence, and Defences

Trials in many remote and northern areas are held in 'circuit' courts, either with a judge and jury or a judge alone. A circuit court is composed of a judge, a court clerk, a defence lawyer, a Crown counsel, and perhaps a translator who travel (often by airplane) to communities on a fixed schedule and hold court in suitable buildings, such as community centres. There are concerns that circuit courts are too backlogged with cases, that personnel are too overworked to prepare effectively, and that a shortage of interpreters makes communication difficult (Griffiths 2007, 179). However, many of these problems are afflicting courts in various Canadian cities as well (Ontario Superior Court of Justice 2006).

Regardless of whether the trial is before a judge or judge and jury and whether it is held in a community centre in a remote settlement or in a large, modern building in a major urban centre, the common law tradition of criminal justice has evolved such that the accused is presumed innocent and the burden is on the Crown to prove, beyond a reasonable doubt, that the accused committed a guilty act or failed to take required action (*actus reus*) and did so with the required degree of fault (*mens rea*).[32] At the end of the Crown's presentation, the defence has three basic options: (1) file a motion arguing that the Crown has not provided enough proof to make its case; (2) try to demonstrate that the accused is factually innocent (for example, by leading evidence to show that the accused had an alibi for the time of the crime); or (3) offer a defence that is recognized in legislation or in common law that excuses the accused's actions (Griffiths 2007). Accused individuals have the choice to testify on their own behalf or not at the trial. The introduction of evidence by both sides is governed by rules in legislation, such as the *Canada Evidence Act,* and in common law decisions (Paciocco and Streusser 2003). These evidentiary rules are subject to the principles enshrined in the Charter of Rights as interpreted in court decisions, particularly by the Supreme Court. The most basic aims of rules of evidence are to ensure that evidence is relevant and reliable. For that reason, each side is allowed to cross-examine the other side's witnesses, and hearsay testimony—testimony about what a third party said in relation to the case—is generally not admissible.[33] Since the process is an adversarial one, the judge (and in some cases the jury) is expected to be neutral and relatively passive during the proceedings.

The adversarial system of common law criminal justice differs markedly from the civil law 'inquisitorial' system that developed on continental Europe, where in serious cases, investigating magistrates gather and evaluate evidence that is provided to the judge overseeing a criminal trial. Both the defence and prosecution have access to this written record and make oral presentations in public to the judge (and a jury in certain cases) during a 'trial' that is quite different than in the common law model. Lawyers for the prosecution and defence have a more limited role than in the adversarial process, whereas the presiding judge has a more prominent role and is allowed to question both sides. In fact the proceedings usually start with the presiding judge asking questions of the accused. The burden of proof is on the prosecution, but since the trial is the culmination of an investigation conducted by an independent magistrate who sends cases to trial if there is evidence of guilt, the 'presumption of innocence' is not central in the inquisitorial system of criminal justice.

There are debates about which system is superior (Langbein 2003; Walpin 2003; Weigend 2003). Whatever the merits of each side, it is important to realize that rules about presumptions of innocence or guilt, burdens of proof, the role of the judge, and whether juries can make decisions that run counter to the law (jury nullification), are social policies and not fixed truths (Shapiro 1981, 47). Since social policies, including those governing criminal trials, often try to reconcile various values and objectives, it is not surprising that they are often controversial and contested and change over time. Recently developed, specialized courts, for example, have been praised by some as a method of slowing the 'revolving door' of the criminal justice system by offering a team-based approach to treating various problems, such as drug abuse, but have been criticized by others for depriving individuals of procedural protections against the power of the state or, conversely, for not providing the same punishments as others guilty of the same offence. Many rules of evidence try to balance the search for truth with the promotion of other values, including privacy, equality, or due-process rights, so it is not surprising that discussions about the objectives and values of these rules are often politically charged. Under what circumstances, if any, should defence lawyers be able to present the alleged victim's sexual history or psychological records in sexual assault cases? To what extent should public and media access to the presentation of evidence be restricted to protect the privacy of victims or state secrets? These are but two of the many difficult policy questions related to evidence that have been debated recently.

Likewise, the kinds of defences that can be raised at trial, such as duress, self-defence, consent, not being criminally responsible on account of mental disorder, or the defence of necessity contain policy considerations and associated value implications. This is well illustrated by Box 9.3, which discusses the creation of the 'too drunk' defence by the Supreme Court and the aftermath of that decision. The case study also highlights how defences can be defined in legislation and in common law decisions, both of which must conform to principles enshrined in the Charter of Rights.

Box 9.3   'Too Drunk' Defence

On 30 May 1989 Henri Daviault, a chronic alcoholic, drank eight bottles of beer and then proceeded to visit a 65-year-old female acquaintance who was confined to a wheelchair. After sharing a glass of brandy with Daviault the woman fell asleep. When she awoke, Daviault wheeled her into the bedroom, lifted her onto the bed and, despite her protestations, tried to have sex with her. Once Daviault had left at about 4 a.m., she discovered an empty forty-ounce bottle of brandy that he had brought to the home. Daviault was charged with sexual assault. At trial, he argued that he was so intoxicated that he had no recollection of anything that happened between when he finished the bottle of brandy and when he awoke nude in the woman's bed in the early morning.

The trial judge found that the accused had committed the offence, but that his extreme state of intoxication cast doubt on whether he possessed the minimal degree of fault required for sexual assault. When Daviault's case reached the

Supreme Court, the majority upheld his acquittal. They argued that convicting someone like Daviault would violate both s. 7 and s. 11(d) of the Charter because the voluntariness or consciousness of the act was in question.[34] The majority said that in such situations it would be up to accused to prove on a balance of probabilities that he was so intoxicated that he was in a state of automatism. The majority thought that successful use of this common law (judge-made) defence of extreme intoxication would be rare. The dissenting judges in *Daviault* argued that people who drink themselves into a state of automatism and then commit a crime like sexual assault should still be held morally blameworthy, but the majority argued that it would be unfair to substitute the fault requirement of getting intoxicated with the fault requirement for an offence like sexual assault. Daviault was granted a new trial during which he could try to prove that he was in a state of automatism.

There was strong public criticism of the decision, and women's groups argued that the decision did not take into consideration that it is primarily men who become drunk and commit crimes against women (and children). The negative reaction to the decision was intensified when it came to light that at least five people had been acquitted at trial of assault or sexual assault within six months of the *Daviault* decision. There were some commentators, however, who objected to the media's characterization of the decision and subsequent events. They tried to explain why it was important to uphold the principle that people should not be found guilty of crimes which they did not intend to commit. It is the same principle, for example, that prevents a person from being convicted when he accidentally takes the wrong jacket home from a party. Some legal commentators also expressed disappointment that the Supreme Court placed the burden of proof on the accused to prove his lack of blameworthiness.

Rather than respond to *Daviault* with a law that created a crime of being 'drunk and dangerous', the Liberal government proposed a law that basically restored the old common law rule that a person would be convicted of a general intent offence no matter how intoxicated. Fault would not be negated in assaults or other crimes interfering with bodily integrity when a person departs from a reasonable standard of care by becoming extremely intoxicated. The bill received all-party support in the House of Commons, and some even suggested that it should be passed without the usual step of sending a bill to committee for review. Justice Minister Alan Rock, who rejected this suggestion, said he wanted the law to be backed up by a strong foundation of evidence in case the law was challenged in court. Scientists who testified before the

Standing Committee on Justice and Legal Affairs disputed the theory that alcohol could induce a robotic-like state of brain functioning. When the law was passed, it contained a preamble that expressed doubt about the link between intoxication and automatism and conveyed Parliament's concern with violence, especially against women and children. Some critics contended that the law was unconstitutional and resulted from politicians placating public opinion while sacrificing principles of fundamental justice.

Subsequently, the law has been upheld by some trial judges but struck down by others. One trial judge, in striking the law down, said that it essentially replaces the old common law rule that was held to be unconstitutional. The Supreme Court will very likely rule on this issue again, and the debate about how to balance the rights of the accused in the administration of justice with other societal interests will continue.

Sources: Hiebert (2002, 96–107); Paciocco (1999, 343–50); and Roach (2005, 222–36).

Other defences, or at least explanations of behaviour, such as the battered womens syndrome (BWS) and culture-based defences, have also engendered similar debates about principles of justice and criminal justice policy.[35] Does the availability of these options to the defence undermine individual responsibility and the Canadian justice system, or do they enhance justice by allowing judges (and juries) to consider the context in which individuals from historically disadvantaged groups live? Do such defences stereotype individuals and groups and divert attention away from the need for real social change, as some feminist scholars have argued with respect to BWS (Paciocco 1999, 297–324; Tang 2003)?

Despite the controversy over criminal defences, it should be noted that acquittals are relatively infrequent. According to the most recent data on trial outcomes, only about 5 per cent of adult cases and only 2 per cent of youth cases ended in an acquittal (Marth 2008; Thomas 2008).[36]

Post-trial Stage

The next step after a finding of guilt is for a sanction to be imposed on the offender by a judge following a sentencing hearing. Although technically the sentencing process is considered to be 'merely a phase of the trial process', it is included in the 'post-trial' section of the chapter in recognition of the fact that the process is quite different from the trial.

Sentencing

Most sentencing hearings are quite informal when compared to a trial, especially in provincial courts, where approximately 98 per cent of sentences are imposed. Sometimes, though, a pre-sentence report about the offender is requested by a judge or counsel, which adds some time and formality to the process (Roberts and Cole 1999). Also, unlike at trial, victims are given the right to participate in the proceedings at the sentencing stage by presenting a victim impact statement. The *Criminal Code* was amended in 1996 to require judges to take victim impact statements into consideration during sentencing (though victims are not allowed to make recommendations about the sentence itself in their statement).

The sentencing options available to the judiciary are set out in the *Criminal Code*. These options are described briefly in Box 9.4.

Box 9.4   Sentencing Options

Incarceration (Imprisonment): The offender is sentenced to a period of imprisonment in either a provincial correctional facility (for sentences of less than two years' imprisonment) or a federal correctional facility (for sentences of two years or longer). For convictions on multiple charges, judges may order that terms of imprisonment be served concurrently or consecutively. Judges often credit time served in pre-trial custody towards the sentence, and offenders usually serve less time imprisoned than the sentence imposed upon them because they are often released on parole after either one-third or two-thirds of their sentence. Offenders who are designated 'dangerous offenders' after a judicial hearing may be incarcerated indefinitely (there is no fixed time for their release).

Intermittent Sentence: For sentences of ninety days or less, offenders are allowed to serve their time of incarceration intermittently, usually on weekends. This allows offenders to continue in employment, education, or other activities.

Conditional Sentence: If a judge would otherwise sentence an offender to incarceration for two years or less, he or she may allow the offender to serve a conditional sentence of imprisonment in the community. Some conditions are compulsory (for example, keeping the peace and being of good behaviour), but other conditions (for example, participation in a treatment program or house arrest) can be imposed by the judge.

Suspended Sentence: A judge can suspend the passing of a sentence conditional upon the successful completion of a period of probation.

Probation: The offender is bound to abide by certain compulsory conditions—to keep the peace and be of good behaviour; to appear in court when required; and to notify the court or probation officer of pending changes in name, address, or employment—and additional conditions that the judge may impose. These optional conditions can include orders to abstain from drugs or alcohol, undertake community service, report to a probation officer, participate in a treatment program (if agreed to by an offender), abstain from owning or possessing a weapon, and any other reasonable order that the judge may see fit to impose.

Fine: The offender is ordered to pay a certain amount of money (subject to maximums set out in the *Criminal Code*) within a certain amount of time.

Restitution: The offender is required to compensate victims (including secondary victims), usually through cash payments (for young offenders it can be through services 'in kind'), most often for damaged or stolen property or loss of income due to personal injury.

Absolute and Conditional Discharges: The offender is considered not to have been convicted if given a discharge. Absolute discharges are immediate, whereas conditional discharges require the offender to abide by certain conditions for a certain length of time before the discharge becomes permanent.

According to available adult court data from 2006 to 2007, in 34 per cent of the approximately 250,000 cases where the accused was found guilty, incarceration was the most serious sentence imposed (followed by probation (28 per cent) and fines (26 per cent)).[37] A conditional sentence was the most serious sentence imposed in only 4 per cent of cases (Marth 2008). Probation was the most frequent sentence in youth cases (59 per cent) (Thomas 2008).

How do judges decide upon which option or combination of options should be used and to what extent when sentencing an offender? As outlined in Chapter 4, judicial decisions can be shaped by legal or non-legal factors. Studies reveal that the amount of discretion legally available to judges in sentencing contributes to different sentences being meted out for similar offences committed by similar offenders in similar circumstances (Brantingham 1985; Palys and Divorski 1986). Biases towards particular groups of individuals may be a factor in sentencing. One researcher has found that this was not relevant in the sentencing of aboriginal

offenders (La Prairie 1999), though another found that it had a small but independent effect on the sentencing of blacks as well as an indirect effect (sentences
are influenced by employment status or pre-trial custody which disproportionately
affected blacks) (Williams 1999).

The final report of the Canadian Sentencing Commission Report in 1987 recommended greater legal guidance to constrain sentencing and reduce disparities in
sentencing. Parliament did introduce sentencing reforms in 1996. A fundamental
principle of sentencing was added to the *Criminal Code* in s. 718.1: 'A sentence
must be proportionate to the gravity of the offence and the degree of responsibility of the offender.' Another section was added that instructs judges to impose
similar sentences for similar offenders for similar offences committed in similar circumstances (s. 718.2(b)). s. 718 of the *Criminal Code* also lists the general purposes
of sentencing: denunciation, deterrence, incapacitation, rehabilitation, reparations,
and promoting a sense of responsibility. Likewise, the *Youth Criminal Justice Act*
emphasizes general principles for the sentencing of young offenders.

More specific legal guidance is also provided in legislation, that is, the *Criminal
Code*, the *Youth Criminal Justice Act*, and the *Controlled Drugs and Substances Act*.
Certain sentencing options can be used only in specific circumstances. Probation
alone, for example, can be used only for offences with no minimum sentence and
can be used in conjunction with a term of imprisonment only if the length of
imprisonment is two years or less. A limited, but growing, number of offences
contain mandatory minimum punishments. Murder, committing an offence with
the use of a firearm, and a second conviction for impaired driving all carry mandatory minimum sentences. The *Criminal Code* also specifies the maximum sentences for criminal offences. Summary conviction offences carry a maximum
sentence of a $2,000 fine and/or six months' incarceration.[38] Maximum sentences
for indictable offences are two years, five years, fourteen years, or life depending
on the particular offence.

Appellate court decisions, as well as the *Criminal Code*, also state that certain
factors should be considered 'aggravating' factors in sentencing (for example,
injury to the victim) and that others should be considered 'mitigating' factors in
sentencing (for example, not having a criminal record). Controversy has sur-
rounded s. 718.2(e) of the *Criminal Code* (added by Parliament in the 1996 sentencing reform legislation), which instructs judges that 'all available sanctions
other than imprisonment that are reasonable in the circumstances should be considered for all offenders, with particular attention to the circumstances of aboriginal offenders.' The Supreme Court ruled that the section requires trial judges to
consider both the systemic factors that may have contributed to the aboriginal
offender's behaviour and the possibility that restorative justice practices might be
more suitable for the individual aboriginal offender (*Gladue* 1999). Since then,
there have been mixed signals from appellate courts about the mitigating role that
race (and gender) should play in sentencing for aboriginals and other minority

groups.[39] The Supreme Court subsequently emphasized that s. 718.2(e) does not automatically require judges to give the greatest weight to restorative justice over other sentencing options, nor does it change the duty of a trial judge to impose a sentence fit for the offence and offender (*Wells* 2000).

The issue recently came to public attention again when the British Columbia Court of Appeal unanimously lowered the sentence of an aboriginal youth from nine to seven years in prison for dragging a gas station attendant to his death with his car after robbing the gas station. The Court argued that an adult manslaughter sentence (beyond the three-year sentence called for in the *Youth Criminal Justice Act*) was appropriate in this case given the horrific details of the crime and the offender's previous record, but that the trial judge should have paid more attention to the offender's age, his aboriginal status (including his disadvantaged background and lack of schooling past age 15), and his prospect for reintegration into society (*Pratt* 2007). The decision was condemned by politicians and the victim's father, who criticized what he considered to be a racially based, two-tiered system of justice (Matas 2007; Mickleburgh 2007). Supporters of taking the social context of historically disadvantaged groups into account during sentencing argue that it enhances justice by recognizing factors that may have contributed to the commission of the offence, such as poverty resulting at least in part from systematic racism (or gender bias), whereas detractors argue that such considerations undermine justice and its equal application to all Canadians (CBC 2003).

Evidence to date suggests that sentencing disparities remain common after the 1996 reforms. Roberts (2002), for example, found considerable variation across provinces in the use of conditional sentences for certain categories of offences.[40] Continued disparity in sentencing is not surprising. Parliament did not provide clearer statutory guidance by reducing the maximum punishments for indictable offences (which are often far beyond what is normally given for the offences) or by creating sentencing guidelines for offences (Doob 1999).

The Conservative government has passed legislation that seeks to reduce some discretion in sentencing in a way that encourages greater punishment. For example, in response to public and media outrage over the imposition of conditional sentences for violent offences against people (Griffiths 2007, 249–50), Parliament amended the *Criminal Code* to create a presumption against the imposition of a conditional sentence for certain offences, particularly serious personal-injury offences (including sexual assaults) (Canada, Department of Justice 2006). In the wake of the fatal shooting of teenager Jane Creba in downtown Toronto on Boxing Day 2005, legislation was passed to introduce new or longer mandatory minimums for gun-related crime. These legislative initiatives have drawn praise from some quarters, but critics argue that harsher punishments and mandatory sentences do not deter crime.[41] They also point out that strict mandatory minimum rules like the 'three strikes' law in several US states have led to unjust sentences in certain circumstances, increased prison populations, and a disproportionate impact on disadvantaged groups, especially in the case of drug crimes (Gabor and Crutcher 2002). Finally, piecemeal adjustments to sentencing laws can lead to more incoherence in sentencing policy. Doob (1999, 355) asks, 'Does it really make sense to impose a mandatory minimum sentence on someone who uses a firearm to threaten a woman whose breasts he touches, but not on a man who brutally rapes a woman and cuts her face with a knife?'

The Canadian Sentencing Commission in its 1987 report recommended the elimination of mandatory minimum sentences and the adoption of a comprehensive system of presumptive sentencing guidelines with some room for discretion. The guidelines would be created by a sentencing commission as is done in numerous US jurisdictions as well as other countries such as England. Support for or opposition to guidelines would depend somewhat on whether they reflect people's values about the goals and nature of sentencing. In the US, a major impetus for guidelines came from conservative criticisms of what were considered to be overly lenient sentences handed out by judges who emphasized 'rehabilitation' rather than 'retribution' or 'incapacitation'. Now, though, there are arguments that offenders are treated too harshly and rigidly under such systems, especially under the US federal sentencing guidelines. After the federal guidelines were introduced, average prison times for federal offences, particularly drug offences, increased dramatically (Tarr 2006, 201–5).[42]

There are also value-laden procedural questions surrounding the use of guidelines. Since 2000, for example, the US Supreme Court has taken a 'due-process' approach to the application of sentencing guidelines by requiring that any facts (such as treating a victim with 'deliberate cruelty') that the law allows or requires to be used to increase a sentence be subject to a jury decision based upon proof beyond a 'reasonable doubt'. Because the federal guidelines did not incorporate these due-process protections, the US Supreme Court in 2005 declared them to be 'advisory' rather than 'binding' on federal judges (Frase 2007).[43]

Behind these substantive and procedural issues is the important question of the degree to which guidelines reduce (or shift) discretion within the system. Studies of sentencing guidelines in Minnesota and other jurisdictions suggest that judicial discretion has been reduced but that as time goes on judges seem less reluctant to deviate from the guidelines. There are also signs that prosecutors are increasingly using their discretion to circumvent the guidelines (see Goff 2004, 223–4; Bushway and Piehl 2007).

Appeals

Compared to courts in countries that use sentencing guidelines, appellate courts in Canada play a more significant role in shaping acceptable sentencing ranges for various offences and the circumstances surrounding those offences (such as the background of the offender) (Greene et al. 1998, 49). Either the Crown or the offender can appeal sentences.[44] The Supreme Court of Canada has provided important guiding principles about sentencing in various precedents but has admonished appeal courts to change a sentence only if it is 'demonstrably unfit' or 'clearly unreasonable' (*Shropshire* 1995).

Prosecutors in Canada have greater latitude than their American counterparts to appeal trial verdicts. Both the prosecution and defence have a general right to appeal summary-conviction offences to a s. 96 superior court. Up until 1977, an appeal involving a summary offence was a trial *de novo* (new trial), but now, except in extraordinary circumstances, the s. 96 trial judge acts as an appellate judge (Brockman and Rose 2006, 142). The prosecution is more limited than the defence in the ability to appeal cases involving indictable offences.[45] Unlike appeals of summary offence cases, which go from s. 92 provincial court to the s. 96 superior trial court level and then up to the provincial court of appeal only if that court grants permission (leave), cases involving indictable offences are appealed directly to provincial courts of appeal.

Data collected by Greene et al. (1998) revealed that fewer criminal appeals were reaching the provincial courts of appeal level in relation to the number of criminal charges being laid.[46] Possible explanations for this trend include increased financial constraints on the accused (especially with pressure on legal aid budgets), an increase in plea bargaining, and changes to the *Criminal Code* that gave prosecutors more discretion to treat offences as summary offences to be tried in s. 92 provincial court (with the first appeal being to the s. 96 trial level) (Greene et al. 1998, 46–7). Appeals from provincial courts of appeal to the Supreme Court are generally limited to leave by appeal (see Chapter 4), except when there is a dissent on a question of law in the court of appeal decision.

Restorative Justice and Diversion Programs

A number of different types of programs, from victim–offender reconciliation meetings to community service programs to anger management classes, are often referred to as diversion programs. Such programs are used at various points in the criminal justice process: (a) at the pre-charge stage, when the police or Crowns can choose to send someone to a diversion program rather than charge them; (b) after charging but before the trial, when the charge is stayed or withdrawn after completion of a diversion program; and (c) at the post-plea or post-trial stage, when offenders are diverted from a term of incarceration in exchange for participation in a diversion program. The increased use of specialized courts for drug treatment, domestic violence, and mental health (see Chapter 3) is indicative of this trend. These courts are based on the premise that successful completion of a program (for example, drug treatment in the case of drug courts) will result in a stay of the charges in the case of a charge of simple possession, or a lighter sentence in the case of a guilty plea by an offender with a prior record or somewhat more serious charges. Greater use of diversion programs at all stages of the process for young offenders is called for explicitly in the *Youth Criminal Justice Act*.

Questions remain about what kinds of diversion programs or processes are to be considered to be part of the broader concept of 'restorative justice' (Johnstone 2003, 1–2). According to Elliott (2008), restorative justice entails a fundamentally different approach to justice that may not be captured by diversion programs that operate within or as an add-on to the existing system of criminal justice. This view of restorative justice sees it as one that attempts to address the harms suffered by victims, offer support for offenders while encouraging them to accept responsibility for their actions, and promote restoration or the creation of relationships within families and communities (Elliott 2008). Three of the most common forms of restorative justice processes are victim–offender mediation, family group conferences, and sentencing circles. Victim–offender meetings were first used in Kitchener–Waterloo, Ontario, and have since been used in other provinces. The meetings, which are voluntary for both the victim and the accused, can be used at the post-charge but pre-trial stage, after a trial, and sometimes even after sentencing. Family-group conferences, which are used in child-protection cases and in youth justice cases, involve the youth in question, family members, community professionals, and sometimes victims. Sentencing circles are common in aboriginal communities but are not exclusive to them. Sitting in a circle, the offender and victim and their supporters, community leaders, and justice officials (judge, lawyers, and police) discuss the best way to dispose of a case so as to accommodate the values of restorative justice described above. This process generally is used only for offenders who plead guilty.[47]

Restorative justice or diversion programs have showed some signs of success as measured by victim and offender satisfaction with the legal process, rates of re-offending, and commitments to community (Braithwaite 2003; Clairmont 2005). However, studies have also shown that victims tend to show less satisfaction with such initiatives than other participants (though it often remains higher than with the regular process), recidivism remains a problem, and it can be difficult to achieve satisfactory outcomes for all the stakeholders (offenders, victims, and the community) (Clairmont 2005; Braithwaite 2003; Goff 2004, 228). Concerns have been raised about possible power imbalances between offenders and victims, particularly in small aboriginal communities where local leadership or kinship ties may serve to silence the women and children (Elliott 2008, 314). From the accused's perspective, being offered the possibility of a stay or a sentence reduction in exchange for participation in a restorative justice program can be coercive and possibly elicit guilty pleas from those who are innocent. There is also the question of whether it is fair that offenders might be treated differently depending on whether the victim agrees to participate in a program or whether a particular community has government or volunteer agencies that operate programs. Finally, others have questioned whether proponents of modern restorative justice exaggerate parallels to the justice practices of ancient cultures (especially aboriginal ones) and create false dichotomies between 'restorative' and 'retributive' justice systems in order to further their political agenda (Daly 2002).

Conclusions

The addition of diversion and restorative justice programs to Canada's criminal justice system make it even more complex and multi-faceted. In order to make sense of this complexity, different theoretical frameworks have been created that explain the criminal justice system and the role of the courts. Three common frameworks will be surveyed in the conclusion: critical, pluralist-majoritarian, and institutional. The critical framework contains various theoretical approaches, but a common theme is that courts, criminal law, and the overall criminal justice system facilitate the repression of disadvantage groups and the maintenance of the dominant socio-economic elite, often considered to be wealthy, white males. Michael Mandel (1996, 378–9), for example, argues that the Charter of Rights and due-process decisions by the courts legitimate the repressive system of criminal law that continues to incarcerate a growing proportion of the population, especially those from disadvantaged socio-economic groups such as aboriginal peoples. In this view, the courts must see themselves as being independent of the executive power so that justice conforms to 'neutral' rules and process; meanwhile, however, the inequality and poverty that lead to both criminal activity and victimization are not addressed.

Feminist and race-based critical analyses of criminal justice are based less on class than Mandel's analysis and more on identity, but the argument remains that the criminal justice system makes possible the repression of disadvantaged groups even if criminal law and courts can occasionally be used for positive change. Dianne Martin (1998), for example, argues that feminists have provided more equality for women by successfully lobbying Parliament for important changes to outdated rape laws, but she worries that the successes have come largely by portraying women as victims and that this perspective will only reinforce the retributive and patriarchal traditional criminal justice system.

That the criminal justice system is an apparatus for controlling and repressing disadvantaged groups is a theme that also emerges in analyses that suggest that modes of reasoning, bodies of knowledge, and discourse are used by those in position of authority to regulate individuals and groups in society. Richard Ericson's (1982, 8) study of police work, for instance, concluded that police work is not about crime prevention or law enforcement but about using rules and commands to create a sense of 'normalcy' so that the 'ranks of society are preserved'. In other studies of which Ericson was a part, courts and even defence counsel were considered to be part of the system of control exercised by the criminal justice system (Ericson and Baranek 1982). In a more recent article on the rise of therapeutic or problem-solving courts, Sirotich (2006) makes a similar claim. He argues that such courts are based on the knowledge and discourse of behavioural-science experts, such as psychiatrists, and that these courts may portend a new attempt by the state to control 'at risk' populations through psychology, psychiatry, and social work.

Although Russell (1984) appreciates that critical studies are valuable for pointing out the potentially political nature of the criminal justice system and its limits in addressing social ills, he argues that critical theorists assume that the criminal justice system makes control and repression possible and that they ignore or downplay evidence to the contrary. He is not the only one to make this claim. Doob and Sprott (2006), for example, argue that Hogeveen's (2005) assertion that the *Youth Criminal Justice Act* was meant to be a repressive system of youth justice is not borne out by the words of the law or the results it has produced.

The underlying assumptions and logic of critical theorists have also have been challenged (Russell 1984), as has the obscure language that many critical theorists use to express their ideas (Boyd 2007). Roach, for instance, agrees with Mandel that due-process decisions may not have restrained crime-control overall, but he finds the claim that due process was needed to legitimate crime control more questionable. Roach wonders why the whole criminal justice system did not suffer a 'crisis of legitimacy' before the Charter when the courts were more oriented toward crime control (1999, 23–4). Russell argues that the critical theory fails to contemplate the fact that many people desire a certain amount of social order and control so that they can enjoy their lives and property in peace. Moreover, although many critical theorists allow for the possibility of using the law and courts to achieve social reforms, their pessimism seems to preclude the possibility of meaningful reforms (Russell 1984, 282).

In contrast to the view that the criminal justice system reflects or constitutes unequal power relationships that result in repression, the pluralist-majoritarian model explains that criminal justice policy is driven largely by public opinion and lobbying by interest groups. In this model, it is possible that the public and groups might come to support less punitive measures (such as decriminalization of marijuana); however, the model assumes that it is more likely that 'law and order' politicians will exploit fear and a desire for retribution by offering 'get tough' policies (Levine 1995). Sensationalized and incomplete media reporting can contribute to this trend (Roberts and Doob 1990). Examples of law and order policies include provincial justice-related policies, such as sex offender registries and forfeiture-of-assets laws (even without a criminal conviction), and recent federal initiatives concerning mandatory minimums, new criminal offences (terrorism, street racing, and videotaping movies in the theatre), limits on the defences available to those accused of sexual assault or child pornography, and restrictions on the use of conditional sentences. Such policies are often supported by victim's groups that have been active in Canada (Roach 1999, 29–32). In some instances, Parliament has overturned a due process-oriented judicial decision in favour of a policy that is more crime control-oriented, often in reaction to public opinion and the reaction of victims' groups and other interest groups. The aftermath of both the *Feeney* (Box 9.1) and *Daviault* (Box 9.2) decisions are examples of this phenomenon.

The courts themselves are not immune from the potential influence of public opinion and groups (see Chapter 4). For example, former Chief Justice Lamer acknowledged that the Court was aware of public support for the child pornography law not long before it began deliberating about whether the law should be upheld under the Charter of Rights (Makin 1999)—the law was ultimately upheld with two exceptions. Recent public sentiment related to the threat of gun violence has led courts to be more deferential to the police in gun-related cases where a Charter argument has been raised, according to Frank Addario (2007).

However, contrary to the predictions of the pluralist-majoritarian model, there are numerous cases where courts have been vigilant in protecting the rights of unpopular accused, including in the *Feeney*, *Boucher*, *Daviault*, and *Pratt* decisions described above. Sometimes legislatures try to reverse such decisions, but often governments have simply amended a law in light of a due-process decision by a court. This was the case when the Supreme Court ruled that the police needed judicial authorization to record conversations with suspects during undercover operations. There are also examples of governments independently adopting less punitive policies that may not be popular, such as the *Youth Criminal Justice Act*, the introduction of conditional sentences, and special consideration for the social context of aboriginal offenders. Restorative justice programs are being established by both government and non-government groups, sometimes even with at least conditional support from victims' groups.

Neither the critical model nor the pluralist-majoritarian model seems to capture the variability that marks criminal justice policies and the criminal justice system. The institutional model does allow for greater variability by focusing on the institutional rules (formal and informal) and organizational features of the criminal justice system. This institutional emphasis results in a number of observations and explanations:

(1) There is a diverse array of actors in the criminal justice system—police organizations, Crown prosecutors, defence lawyers, courts, and provincial and federal justice departments and correctional agencies. Each actor is independent, yet all are interdependent. This means, for example, that a trial court judge's role and influence in the criminal justice system will be affected by the habits of the police or Crowns, the arguments advanced by defence counsel, appellate court rulings, legislation drafted by governments, and even whether community groups offer diversion programs.

(2) The current rules and organizational arrangements in Canadian criminal justice give much discretion to all actors in the system, and that can lead to significant variation in criminal justice practices and outcomes between provinces and

even within provinces. There are differences between provinces in decisions to investigate certain crimes by the police, decisions about charges by Crowns, bail decisions by justices of the peace, sentencing practices by judges, and rates of criminal appeals. There are also variations within provinces as particular areas develop particular cultures and norms of behaviour.

(3) Criminal justice reforms, including those aimed at reducing discretion within the system may not be effective or may have unintended consequences. There is the possibility, for example, that more emphasis on diversion programs may lead the police to bring people into the criminal justice system for minor offences that would have been overlooked in the past. Some US studies of sentencing guidelines have shown that the discretion formerly held by judges before the introduction of guidelines is simply shifted elsewhere in the system, particularly to prosecutors.

(4) Institutional rules and the actions of actors within the system can shape processes and outcomes at least somewhat independently from social forces (interest groups, dominant elites, or public opinion). The institutional model, for example, would highlight the fact that the rules of judicial independence give judges some latitude to make unpopular decisions and decisions that support disadvantaged groups. The parliamentary system of government allows cabinet members to introduce controversial legislation, such as the gun registry law, and, particularly in times of majority government, to have it passed even in the face of vocal opposition (Pal 2000). The federal–provincial division of powers has an important influence on the shaping of criminal justice process and policy in Canada.[48] And, as this chapter makes clear, the Charter of Rights and judicial interpretation of the Charter have affected criminal justice policies and processes. Though some of these trends and changes in criminal justice might have occurred without the introduction of the Charter, the Charter and Charter decisions have undoubtedly had an independent effect on the policies and process of the criminal justice system.

(5) Actors within the system may take steps to preserve or enhance their autonomy and influence. Superior court judges, for example, effectively lobbied against amalgamating provincial and superior criminal courts into one criminal court. The opposition of judges and Crown prosecutors to sentencing guidelines because such guidelines would reduce their discretion was the main reason why guidelines were not introduced after being recommended by the Canadian Sentencing Commission (Doob 1999).

(6) There is a delicate balance in trying to better integrate and co-ordinate actors better in the criminal justice system (and criminal justice agencies with other agencies) for efficiency and effectiveness, while maintaining checks and balances (Gordon and Kinney 2006). Ontario's creation of an anti-gang and -gun team of police and Crown prosecutors may be useful in complex criminal investigations and cases against serious threats, but it also may detract from the Crown's ability to

be an 'officer of the court' and a check on police practices. The team-based approach of specialized courts, as noted above, faces similar challenges in balancing effectiveness with due process.

The disadvantage of using the institutional approach to analyze courts and the criminal justice system is that it is not as theoretically elegant as the other two approaches. Proponents of the institutional framework argue that there is an interaction between social forces and institutions that helps to explain processes and outcomes. Sometimes this kind of analysis can shade towards description, but this may be the price that needs to be paid to explain adequately the complexity and unevenness of the criminal justice policies and processes that have been documented in this chapter.

Chapter 10

Civil Justice: Private Disputes, Public Consequences

> Until Justin was twelve years old, he lived a pretty normal life. We were so glad when concentrated blood-clotting factor came on the scene. It gave him a chance to do a lot of things that he probably wouldn't have been able to do otherwise. We thought it was great. We didn't realize that the same thing we thought was so great was going to take his life away. (In Parsons 1995, 8)

Justin Marche was one of over 1,000 Canadian hemophiliacs—roughly 40 per cent of our hemophiliac population—who contracted HIV/AIDS in the 1980s from transfusions and blood products that were contaminated with the virus.[1] Over a thousand more non-hemophiliacs were similarly infected from transfusions during surgery (Picard 1998; Orsini 2002). Blood transfusion, it turns out, is the most efficient way to transmit HIV, 'with an infection rate of over 90 per cent from a single exposure' (Parsons 1995, 244). Moreover, before they had been diagnosed, many of these people unwittingly passed on the virus to their spouses through sexual contact, as tragically illustrated by hemophiliac Randy Connors (who died in 1994) and his wife Janet Connors, who remains a powerful spokesperson for AIDS patients. In those early days of AIDS, diagnosis of HIV infection was often slow and treatment less effective than today (although the effectiveness of current treatments should not be overemphasized, and a cure remains elusive), with the result that the majority of those infected by tainted blood have already died from AIDS (Arnold, Julian, and Walker 2006). Adding to the catastrophe is the fact that many of the same people infected with HIV by contaminated blood—along with perhaps 30,000 others (Picard 1998)—were also infected with the hepatitis C virus (HCV), a liver disease that in some cases (such as in those whose health is already compromised by AIDS) can be severely debilitating and even cause death through liver failure. All told, about 8,000 of those who received bad blood are expected to die as a result (Picard 1998).

That this was a tragedy is beyond doubt. But it was also something else: a scandal, which implicated manufacturers of blood products, the federal and provincial governments, and the Red Cross Society, which administered the 'blood system'. For as Rita Marche, Justin's mother, stated: 'There were so many things that could have been done to prevent it that weren't done. I think that's what makes me so bitter. It didn't have to happen' (Parsons 1995, 8). In 1993 the federal government set up the Commission of Inquiry on the Blood System in Canada, headed by Justice Horace Krever, to determine the cause of the catastrophe. The commission identified the blood system's many failings, most of which were caused by political inaction and officials' desire to save money. These included (Picard 1998):

- Delays in purchasing safer, heat-treated blood products for hemophiliacs prompted by a desire to use up the inventory of contaminated products;
- The Red Cross's refusal to screen out high-risk donors when AIDS first appeared, for fear of blood shortages;
- Delays in implementing HIV testing;
- Importing of cheap US plasma collected from high-risk communities in prisons and San Francisco at the height of the AIDS epidemic;
- The provinces' abortive attempt to build a network of blood-manufacturing plants, which necessitated the importation of high-risk plasma from the US;
- The refusal, for four years (1986–90) to use a test that would have prevented almost 90 per cent of hepatitis C cases;
- The failure to track down those who had received tainted blood so they could receive treatment and avoid passing on the viruses to others, even after officials realized the extent of the problem with the blood supply.

Before the Krever Inquiry was even launched, and long before its damning findings were made public, several lawsuits were pursued by those infected with HIV against the Red Cross, blood-product manufacturers, and the federal and provincial governments. Many foundered or were dropped by legal counsel, however, mostly because of the prohibitive cost and time they would take—those infected were expected to live only about four years. The Canadian Hemophiliac Society, other groups, and even individuals (most notably the Connors in Nova Scotia) focused instead on lobbying the federal and provincial governments for compensation, or at least 'emergency medical assistance' with their mounting health care and pharmaceutical costs as they simultaneously became too sick to work. This yielded some results: in 1989, after virtually no prior negotiation with the affected groups, Ottawa created a $150 million 'Extraordinary Assistance Plan' for 1,250 Canadians infected with HIV from tainted blood, offering $30,000 per year to each person for a maximum of four years. In return, however, victims had to waive the right to sue the federal government, the Red Cross, and pharmaceutical companies. Given their dire financial and medical situation, most signed.

The same scenario played out four years later when the provinces, after initially stonewalling but then—probably in anticipation of Krever's report—negotiating with the victims, offered another $150 million to those infected with HIV in exchange for a comprehensive waiver. Once again, though frustrated by feeling railroaded by the government and the blood system, most agreed to the conditions. The few who did not and instead opted to sue the Red Cross and government for negligence have had mixed success. For example, some victims (or their estates after they died) have secured rulings in the Supreme Court of Canada that the Red Cross should have done more to screen out high-risk donors before HIV testing was available (*Walker Estate v. York Finch General Hospital* 2001). In contrast, the Ontario Court of Appeal rejected another case by three hemophiliacs on the rather shameful grounds that the Red Cross did not have a duty 'to do everything possible' to introduce safer blood products, nor that the federal government should have expedited its regulatory processes for approving the new, safer products (*Robb Estate v. Canadian Red Cross Society* 2001); their application for leave to appeal this to the Supreme Court of Canada was denied. Moreover, those who launched the suit (the *plaintiffs*) were ordered to pay the legal costs of the Red Cross and the pharmaceutical company (the *defendants*) they had unsuccessfully sued.

Things have played out rather differently for those infected with HCV, who mobilized later than the HIV group. This delay had two important consequences: first, they had the benefit of the Krever inquiry's public hearings and findings, which unequivocally found the blood system at fault and recommended the immediate creation of a comprehensive no-fault compensation plan to all victims of tainted blood, a recommendation that the federal and provincial governments rejected. Second, new laws in several provinces (most notably Ontario in 1992 and British Columbia in 1996) permitted *class-action suits*, which allow many individuals with the same legal dispute to combine their resources into a single claim that is handled by the same lawyer or law firm and that is heard before the same judge. Class actions are discussed in more detail later in this chapter, but suffice it to say here that class actions save litigants time and money and facilitate lawsuits. Such suits were filed in both provinces, as well as in Quebec (which has allowed class actions since 1978), against the Red Cross and the federal and respective provincial governments. This prompted the governments to negotiate a $1.1 billion compensation package, approved in 1999,[2] for those infected with HCV by tainted blood between 1986 and 1990, the years when a screening test for the disease existed but was not used. This prompted more class-action suits on behalf of those infected by tainted blood outside the 1986–90 period which produced two further negotiated settlements. The first involved the Red Cross, which had declared bankruptcy before the 1999 compensation package and had seen its half-century-old administration of the blood system removed to two new government-created agencies—Canadian Blood Services and Héma Québec. In 2000 an Ontario Superior Court Judge (*Canadian Red Cross Society* 2000) approved the Red Cross's bankruptcy plan to compensate victims infected with HIV and HCV (before 1986 and after 1990 for the latter) with $79 million earmarked for compensating transfusion claimants, who had voted overwhelmingly in favour of the plan.[3] The second package, which came from the federal government under Prime Minister Stephen Harper in 2006, provided $1 billion to be dispersed to the 5,500 HCV victims who had contracted the disease before 1986 and after 1990 or to their next-of-kin. This settlement was approved in June 2007 by courts in Alberta, British Columbia, Ontario, and Quebec.[4] Nonetheless, some cases are still in progress, including several about the fees charged by some of the law firms (including their share of the settlements in *contingency fees*[5]) and the governments' attempts to claw back some of the compensation through income tax.[6]

The tainted blood scandal illustrates several aspects of the Canadian civil justice system.

1. *Federal (or decentralized) civil justice system.* Canada does not have a civil justice 'system' so much as a collection of fourteen systems, one for each of the provincial, territorial, and federal governments; that explains why the rules for class actions vary from one province to another. As the reader will recall from the last chapter, this contrasts with the Canadian *criminal* justice system, with its national *Criminal Code*. The reason is rooted in the *Constitution Act, 1867*, which assigns the provinces jurisdiction over 'property and civil rights' in s. 92(13) (this jurisdiction has been effectively assumed by the territorial governments as well). Notably, the phrase 'property and civil rights' does not mean rights in a Charter sense or a US-style 'right to own property'. To the Fathers of Confederation, it was a familiar legal phrase that referred to the 'whole body of law governing relationships between individuals'—in other words, what we described in Chapter 1 as 'private' or 'civil' law (Hogg 2003, 510). That said, s. 91 of the constitution assigns responsibility to the federal government for a number of specific issues related to civil law, including banking, trade and commerce, currency, bankruptcy, copyright and patents, and marriage and divorce.

   Although all provinces have their own systems of civil justice, Quebec is particularly exceptional because its system is in the form of a single Civil Code (*Code civil du Québec*), like most Continental and Latin American countries and the state of Louisiana in the US (see Chapter 1). Modelled on France's Napoleonic Code, this was adopted in 1866 as a means of reforming and preserving the distinct civil justice system of predominantly French-speaking Canada East (shortly to become the province of Quebec through Confederation), a system that had become, according to the Durham Report in 1839, 'a mass of incoherent and conflicting laws, part French, part English, and with the line between each very confusedly drawn' (in Gall 1990, 171). The Code underwent major revisions in 1955 and 1992 and is updated regularly by the

Assemblé nationale du Québec (Quebec's legislature) as legal and social developments require.

The 'federal' character of civil law in Canada is reinforced by the fact that most cases in this area are heard and resolved by provincial courts, as noted in Chapter 2. That said, on occasion the Supreme Court of Canada intervenes to clarify civil law rules, as it did when it ruled that hosts of private parties are not liable for injuries caused to others by guests who drove after leaving the party drunk (*Childs v. Desormeaux* 2006).

2. *Diversity of parties.* With very few exceptions, criminal cases (like many forms of public law—see Chapter 1) involve a dispute between the state (as represented by a Crown Attorney) and a private individual or organization. In the criminal justice system, cases are initiated by the state through a prosecution. Civil cases, on the other hand, technically involve disputes between 'private' parties, any of whom could initiate a case. However—and here is where it gets confusing—those parties can be governments or quasi-governmental public institutions like the Red Cross, in addition to the more obvious parties like individuals, small businesses, unions, and large corporations.

3. *Importance of negotiation and out-of-court settlement.* Litigation from the tainted blood scandal ultimately produced five large compensation packages, totalling $3.1 billion, from governments, the Red Cross, and pharmaceutical companies; four were the product of negotiation between these parties and victims' groups and their lawyers. The Attorney General of Ontario estimates that over 90 per cent of civil cases end in a settlement (or are abandoned) before the case even reaches the trial phase.[7] The fact that either side can decide to pursue the case in court encourages both sides to negotiate, a process that is almost always faster and usually cheaper for both sides.

4. *Concerns about access to justice.* As the early HIV-infected litigants discovered, meaningful access to the civil justice system requires time, money, and (especially if the dispute is complex) legal representation. The sickest victims did not have the first two and as a consequence had trouble finding the third. Moreover, as we saw in the failed *Robb Estate* case, which is described in more detail later in this chapter, Canadian law discourages litigation with its 'loser pays' approach to legal fees. On the other hand, as demonstrated by the HCV cases, class actions (and contingency fees) enhance access to justice, although there is a vigorous debate in the United States about whether these same reforms have produced a hyper-litigious society.

5. *Power and accountability*. Viewed from a social-science perspective, the tainted blood litigation and settlements have important lessons about who has power (or authority) in society and whether they are held accountable for the exercise of that power (if sometimes only financially). Are governments and large corporations held accountable when their action—or inaction—harms the public? Or when executives mishandle the assets of investors or shareholders in their companies, or union leaders their members' dues and pension funds? The criminal law is one way of holding people to account, and for governments (or other institutions with elected leadership, like unions, and corporations with shareholders), elections and voting provide another. The civil justice system is yet another way. Under certain circumstances, litigation can publicize wrong-doing or institutional failure and can prompt policy and institutional reform, such as when the administration of the blood system was taken away from the Red Cross and given to new government agencies.

The Scope and Substance of Civil Law

It is important to emphasize that our focus in this chapter is on disputes under civil (or private) law, which governs relations between 'private' individuals, even though, as noted above, this can include governments and other collective institutions. In contrast, as explained in Chapter 1, the 'civil justice system' includes all cases that do not involve the prosecution of offences, that is, the 'criminal justice system'. Thus, the civil justice system deals with many cases involving *public law*, most notably administrative law (especially immigration and refugee claims) and civil challenges to legislation under the Constitution.[8] Since it is beyond the scope of a single chapter—or this book, for that matter—to canvass the entire spectrum of disputes under the civil justice system, we have elected to focus here on private disputes, to complement the focus on public law disputes in Chapter 9, on criminal justice. Nonetheless, cases involving administrative law and civil challenges under the Constitution are discussed throughout the book, particularly in Chapters 3, 7, 8, and 11.

Even if we focus only on civil or private disputes rather than on the civil justice system more broadly, such civil litigation comes in virtually unlimited shapes and sizes, and ranges from highly complex cases like those seen in the tainted blood scandal to simple cases of one person suing another for minor property damage (most likely in a smalls claims court). Lawyers who practise in this area tend to specialize in particular fields of civil law, such as corporate law, commercial law, estate law, property law, and so on. Alternatively, some lawyers specialize in issue areas that combine these traditional fields, such as 'sports law', which draws on contract law (for relations between players and owners), commercial and corporate law (for the rules regarding sports franchises, including anti-combine laws), torts (for injuries suffered by players), and even international law (which governs the Olympics and other international sporting events and bodies). Regardless of their complexity or subject matter, disputes under civil law can be categorized according to the types described in Box 10.1.

Box 10.1   The Diversity of Civil Litigation

As hinted at in the examples throughout this chapter, civil disputes come in a wide variety of forms, which are rooted in the types of private law introduced in Chapter 1. These are, briefly, the following:

Torts ('responsabilité civile' in Quebec law)—Torts involve harm between private individuals, including physical, psychological, emotional or economic harm, or damage to property or personal reputation (this was the type of claim launched by tainted blood victims). Though many torts (such as assault, negligence causing death, and so on) can also be prosecuted by the state as crimes, the two types of proceedings use different processes, terminologies, standards of evidence, and—most notably—remedies. These differences are summarized later in the chapter, but suffice it to say here that the person found in the wrong has to compensate his or her victim directly in a tort, whereas those found guilty in criminal law pay their penalty to the state and society as a whole though fines, incarceration, or community service.

Contractual disputes—Contracts form legitimate and binding agreements between two or more parties, usually to pay a specified amount in return for a specified service or good. Contractual disputes arise when one or both parties renege on the agreement. *Labour law*, concerning the contractual relations between employers and employees, forms a sub-field of contract law although labour relations are now so heavily regulated by government that Hogg (2003, 511) argues it has become a branch of public law.

Property disputes—Disputes often arise over how people use or manage their property (for example, between neighbours over new buildings), or over the transfer of property from one party to another, including through wills. There is an entire sub-field of law, known as *estate law*, related to property transfers and the administration of assets when someone dies either with or without a will. The many disputes between landlords and tenants—usually over the mutual obligations the property owner and the lessee owe to one other—are also governed by property (and contract) law.

Admiralty law disputes—Admiralty, or maritime, law is a long-recognized subset of law combining elements of tort, contract, and property law pertaining to shipping; it governs such things as salvage, collisions, loss of cargo, navigation, the operation and maintenance of vessels, and the use of docks and canals.

Family law disputes—Though often distinguished from other forms of civil law, family law nevertheless concerns relations between private individuals, including the rights and obligations pertaining to marriage and other spousal relationships, divorce and separation, adoption, and child custody.

Civil disputes are primarily governed by statutes or common law rules. One of the confusing aspects of 'private' law is that disputes between private actors, such as individuals and businesses, are nevertheless governed by rules passed by 'public' authorities in legislatures and bureaucracy and are frequently enforced by 'public' officials of the state. There are a massive number of laws and regulations governing everything from safety and environmental standards, to corporate organization and the stock market, to libel and negligence. For example, the *Alberta Family Law Act* sets out the rules of family law in Alberta, the *Manitoba Sale of Goods Act* regulates various contractual exchanges in that province, and the *Canada Employment Equity Act* creates employment rules for industries, such as banks, under federal jurisdiction. Outside of Quebec, common law (judge-made) rules are extremely important in some areas—particularly torts—but play only a supplementary role to legislation in others. To use the example cited earlier, it was a common law decision that determined that persons who hosted a party at their home were not responsible for damage caused by guests who drove away while intoxicated. Another common law decision ruled that bar owners, in contrast, *are* liable for such damage.

It should also be stressed that governments have chosen to divert entire categories of civil disputes out of the regular judicial system, often into alternative dispute resolution or other specialized institutions. One major example is discrimination claims. Beginning with Ontario in the 1940s, all provinces and the federal parliament passed *statutory* human rights codes (for example, the *Ontario Human Rights Code* and Alberta's *Human Rights, Citizenship and Multiculturalism Act*) that prohibit discrimination by private individuals and organizations as well as by public institutions. (In contrast, the Canadian *Charter of Rights and Freedoms* applies only directly to state actors (s. 32)—see Chapter 11). Since the 1960s, governments have also created specialized tribunals or commissions, such as the Ontario Human Rights Commission (as of 2008, the Human Rights Tribunal of Ontario), to hear complaints arising under these codes.[9] Similarly, some provinces have created specialized tribunals to resolve the large number of landlord–tenant disputes (recall the discussion of the *Residential Tenancies Act Reference* in Chapter 2), many of which involve relatively small sums of money owed by tenants, or demands by tenants for property owners to comply with building and safety standards or to deliver services promised in the lease. In Ontario, for example, this body is known as the Landlord and Tenant Board, and in Quebec the Régie du logement. Some provinces that have not created standing tribunals, such as Alberta and Nova Scotia, now offer optional alternative dispute resolution (ADR) in selected areas to resolve landlord–tenant disputes. A final type of dispute worth mentioning is those involving damage, that is, torts, from automobile accidents, which some provinces have removed from the judicial system altogether. Under a 'fault-based' system, one can sue, in court, the person responsible (or his or her insurance company) for vehicle damage and personal injury—a costly and time-consuming process. Some provinces, such as Quebec, have replaced this system with 'no-fault insurance', in which the driver's insurance company or the public insurer, such as Manitoba's Autopac, will pay for the damage to the driver's car and any injuries he or she sustained (usually up to a limit), regardless of who was at fault for the accident, and any other drivers involved will be covered by their own insurance policies or, again, the public insurer. (Notably, 'fault' is not totally ignored in this system, for the persons responsible for the accident will see it reflected in their insurance and driving record, usually in the form of higher insurance premiums or licencing fees.) In addition to Quebec, which uses a pure no-fault system, British Columbia, Ontario, Manitoba, and Saskatchewan have elements of no-fault insurance. For example, some provinces provide the option of suing the person responsible instead, or allow regular litigation if the amounts claimed are above a certain amount or if there was personal injury rather than just vehicle damage. Whatever the precise design, no-fault systems are intended to limit litigation in the regular court system.

Legislation governing civil disputes must conform to the broad legal framework established by the Constitution, including both the Charter of Rights and Freedoms and, more important, the federal division of powers. Provincial and federal laws regarding private disputes are subject to Charter review because they are statutes passed by government. In 1999, for instance, the Supreme Court of Canada ruled that Ontario's *Family Law Act* violated the equality rights provisions in the Charter by limiting spousal support payments after a relationship has ended only to opposite-sex couples (*M. v. H.* 1999). Similarly, in *Vriend* (1998) the Court ruled that statutory human rights codes and tribunals—as products of legislatures and governments—must comply with the Charter. Because the Charter applies only to Parliament, provincial legislatures, and governments (s. 32), however, the Supreme Court has generally been reluctant to apply the Charter to *common law* rules that govern private disputes. In purely private cases, the Court has said that the common law should reflect 'Charter values' but that the Charter does not apply directly. As for court orders made in private litigation, the Court initially was reluctant to apply the Charter to such orders (see *RWDSU v. Dolphin Delivery* 1986) but did subsequently apply the Charter to scrutinize a lower-court injunction against a union that prevented picketing at a courthouse (*B.C.G.E.U. v. British Columbia* 1988) (See MacIvor 2006, 20–3).

Such Charter influence aside, the primary role of constitutional law in civil disputes is through the federal division of powers, which specifies which unit of government, federal or provincial, has the authority to regulate a particular field of private law. Unfortunately, the text of the *Constitution Act, 1867* is confusing in this regard. Ss. 92(13) and 92(16) respectively gave the provinces authority over 'Property and Civil Rights in the Province' and 'Generally all Matters of a merely local or private Nature in the Province', but 91(2) gives the federal Parliament the power to make laws for the 'Regulation of Trade and Commerce'; in addition, as indicated above, Ottawa may regulate shipping (s. 91(10)), banking (s. 91(15) and (16)), interest (s. 91(19)), bankruptcy (s. 91(21)), patents (s. 91(22)), copyrights (s. 91(23)), and marriage and divorce (s. 91(26))—all of which are activities that may give rise to disputes between private actors.[10] As Hogg (2003, 494) notes, the greatest uncertainty is raised by the 'Trade and Commerce' and 'Property and Civil Rights' clauses, which appear to overlap: 'trade and commerce is [*sic*] carried on by means of contracts which give rise to "civil rights" over "property"'.

There have been numerous and fierce disputes between the federal and provincial governments on how to interpret these clauses, with the regulation of large parts of the economy or entire industries at stake (alcohol—in part because of the temperance movement—has repeatedly played a starring role in such disputes). As with many other jurisdictional disputes in Canada's history, the courts—and in particular, the Judicial Committee of the Privy Council—provided the solution, which was to narrow the scope of each power. As it currently stands, intraprovincial trade and commerce (that is, that which is entirely within the province) is under provincial jurisdiction, and the federal government may regulate only interprovincial and international trade and commerce (see Hogg 2003, 494–508; Baier 2006).[11] Thus, 'the law related to property, succession, the family, contracts and torts is mainly within provincial jurisdiction under s. 92(13)' (Hogg 2003, 511). Although there are some important federal statutes governing private law, such as those defining marriage and divorce, governing international or interprovincial commerce, or defining human rights in federally regulated industries, most legislation governing private disputes is therefore passed by provincial legislatures. Likewise, common law rules are shaped mostly by each province's Court of Appeal, unless the Supreme Court makes a common law ruling in a private disputes which is binding on all jurisdictions (see Chapter 2). All of these factors contribute to the highly 'federal' nature of civil law in Canada noted earlier;[12] similarly, because of provincial predominance over private law disputes, the legal reforms affecting civil litigation discussed throughout this chapter have been introduced by provincial governments.

How Do Civil Cases Arise?

As noted earlier, civil cases are most commonly defined as disputes between private parties. As US socio-legal scholars (for example, Felstiner, Abel, and Sarat 1980–1; Miller and Sarat 1980–1) recognized several years ago, however, disputes have a longer genealogy, and not all disputes proceed to litigation and resolution in a court of law—most, in fact, do not. As illustrated in Figure 10.1, the 'developmental theory of litigation' (Kritzer, Bogart, and Vidmar 1991) states that the process begins when someone recognizes that they have sustained an *injury*, typically a physical or psychological harm, or economic loss. There is often a delay between the actual injury and its recognition, as with the tainted blood victims who were not diagnosed with HIV or HCV for some time—in some cases, not for years. Some injuries are simply accepted as accidents or bad luck. For example, if a hockey player loses several teeth when a puck deflects off the goalie, this is likely to be accepted as bad luck. The same is not true, however, if a player is nearly crippled when his head is deliberately slammed to the ice from behind by another player after the whistle. The latter example has the necessary ingredients for the injury to become a *grievance*: the injured party perceives that another party, through his or her unjust actions, is to blame. Note that for a grievance to exist, blame need only be perceived—it is quite possible that the injured party's perception is wrong. It is also important to emphasize that the other party's actions must be unjust *as defined by the law*. Tarr (2003, 220) gives the example of a pizza parlour owner who loses revenue (an economic 'injury') because of sales lost to a new competitor. This is not a grievable injury, he states, because the law gives businesses no right to a fixed level of sales or profits.[13] The law has expanded the range of unjust actions over the years, however, in response to public opinion based on advances in science and technology. These advances have made the public more aware of risks but have also raised expectations about, for example, product safety (Friedman 1985; Lieberman 1981). It should also be noted that some cases arise because people realize that they might be able to argue that they have sustained a grievable injury—even though they know they have not—or to exaggerate the extent of their injury. These are known as 'nuisance suits', and they are essentially fraudulent, but not uncommon. As well, some nuisance suits, known as 'SLAPPs' (see Box 10.2), are meritless claims made to intimidate or discourage opposition from community groups that lack financial resources.

Box 10.2 'SLAPPing Down Citizen Participation'

A particular type of nuisance suit or 'meritless action' has become known as a 'SLAPP': Strategic Litigation against Public Participation (Canan and Pring

1988). Unlike exaggerated or fraudulent claims for compensation, such as those following car accidents or against doctors, SLAPPs are typically brought by people in power or by corporations with deep pockets to intimidate those relatively poorer or weaker individuals and groups that oppose them. In other words, SLAPPs 'use civil tort action to stifle political expression' (Canan and Pring 1988, 506). Originally a US phenomenon, an increasingly common form of SLAPP being brought in Canada is against community groups that oppose the plans of real estate developers, such as occurred in *Fraser v. Saanich* (1999) when a nursing home director sued individuals and community groups that opposed a proposed expansion of the facility. In that case—as with many SLAPPs—the judge threw out the plaintiff's claim as 'vexatious' and 'reprehensible', because it had no merit and 'has been used as an attempt to stifle the democratic activities of the defendants, the neighbourhood residents' (*Fraser v. Saanich*, para. 52). Though most SLAPPs lose in court, however, they are often successful in practical terms. As noted recently by Smith and Page (2008, AA6), 'defending a SLAPP, even when the legal defence is strong, requires a substantial investment of money, time and resources. The resulting effect is a "chill" on public participation in, and open debate on, important public issues.' They continue, 'This chilling effect is not limited to the SLAPP target(s): fearful of being the target of future litigation, others refrain from speaking on, or participating in, issues of public concern.' Indeed, unlike other plaintiffs, a SLAPP filer's main concern is, by definition, not to win monetary compensation or other legal remedy, but simply to deter opposition now and in the future (Tollefson 1994, 206).

Concerns about the harmful effects of SLAPPs on citizen participation in public affairs have led several US states and the provinces of Alberta and British Columbia to pass legislation curtailing the practice. Alberta's recent *Judicature Amendment Act, 2007* permits courts to stop proceedings of vexatious lawsuits immediately and allows defendants to make counter-applications against the party that initiated the lawsuit (Peden 2007). Quebec, Nova Scotia, and New Brunswick are considering similar legislation. Given the potential for SLAPPs to undermine democratic participation by citizens in issues directly related to their communities, SLAPPs illustrate the broader political importance of 'private' civil disputes.

Once an injury is transformed into a grievance, the injured party has three possible responses. The first is to do nothing ('inaction'), perhaps because of a desire to avoid confrontation, legal costs, or social costs (the other party might be a friend or family member, for instance). The second is to avoid future contact with that person, business, or institution. Neither of these would result in any compen-

Figure 10.1   The Developmental Theory of Civil Litigation

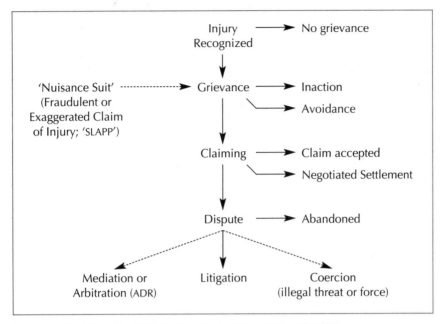

Source: Adapted from Miller and Sarat (1980–1), Kritzer, Bogart, and Vidmar (1991), and Tarr (2003).

sation for the injury, however—for that, one would need to make a *claim*. Examples of this occur every day, from a relatively minor case of sending your dinner back when the waiter brings you the wrong dish, to a more financially serious case of demanding that your building contractor repair defective workmanship on your home or return your money. A claim might be accepted outright (such as when the waiter returns with the correct order), or it might provoke a counter-offer of a compromise (such as your contractor repaying only their labour costs but not the cost of materials), which becomes a 'negotiated settlement' if you accept. If a claim or settlement is ultimately rejected, however, it becomes a full-blown *dispute*. If not abandoned at this point, disputes can be pursued via litigation, ADR (see Chapter 3), or outside of the justice system through threats or use of force. How many grievances proceed to litigation? Comparable studies do not exist in Canada, but those in the United States (Miller and Sarat 1980–1) found a steep drop in numbers at each stage of the process, as the cost (both financial and social) and pre-trial resolution increasingly filtered out potential litigants. Their findings are reproduced in Figure 10.2.[14]

It must be stressed that a court filing is only the beginning of the formal litigation process, and the overwhelming majority of filings never come to trial—in Ontario, since 1978 only between *1 and 10 per cent* of filings reach the trial stage per year (Kritzer 2004, 751).

Figure 10.2   From Grievances to Litigation, Declining Numbers

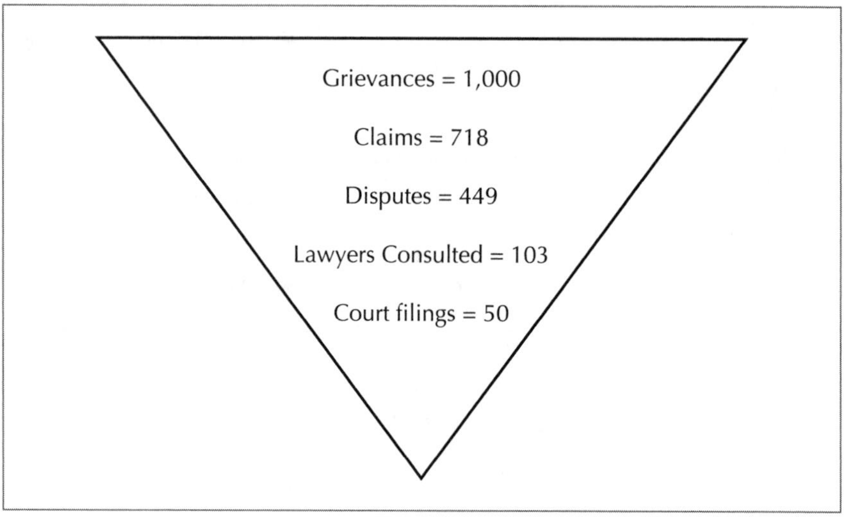

Grievances = 1,000

Claims = 718

Disputes = 449

Lawyers Consulted = 103

Court filings = 50

Source: Miller and Sarat (1980–1), in Tarr (2003, 222).

The Civil Litigation Process

Tarr (2003, 223) describes three sets of rules that govern civil litigation: substantive legal standards, jurisdictional rules, and procedural rules for lawyers. The substantive rules are those applied by judges when deciding cases, such as the laws regarding inheritance in a case concerning a will, or regulations requiring a corporation to disclose financial information about the company to its shareholders. Jurisdictional rules dictate which court is the proper venue in which to bring a case. As explained in Chapter 2, for example, the federal government must initiate suits against another party, such as a building contractor for breach of contract, in the s. 96 provincial courts, whereas someone suing the federal government may do so in either a s. 96 court or the s. 101 federal court. Procedural rules establish the process that lawyers must adhere to when filing and arguing a case in the courts, as well as during any potential appeals. There is a bewildering array of such procedural rules, which also differ for each type of court and in each province. Consequently we attempt to describe only the fundamental steps that are common to a typical example of civil litigation (see Figure 10.3). It should be noted that there are two main ways to initiate a civil case, the law in question dictating which is used. The first is by a plaintiff's 'statement of claim' (also known in some provinces as a 'writ of summons') against a defendant. The second is by 'application', which is used, for example, when one is seeking a remedy under the Charter of Rights and Freedoms or the court's advice about administering a deceased person's estate. (See, for example, Ontario *Rules of Civil Procedure*.) This is also how landlord–tenant disputes, which make up the majority of applications in Ontario, are usually initiated (Brookbank, Kingsley, and Leonard 1999, 39). In cases initiated by application, the parties are called the 'applicant' and 'respondent' instead of 'plaintiff' and 'defendant'. (In some provinces, a third way of initiating a civil case, specific to family law, is by a divorce petition.) As well, cases involving small claims use a simplified procedure, the maximum claim amount and procedure varying by province; in Ontario's small claims court, for example, there is no discovery, or cross-examination of witnesses at trial.

Several things have to happen before a civil trial actually starts.[15] The first is that the plaintiff submits to the defendant and court a statement of claim that briefly summarizes the legally significant facts upon which the plaintiff's claim relies and the remedy sought. Usually, the defendant then gives the plaintiff and the court a statement of defence, which lays out the facts on which he or she will rely. Taken

Figure 10.3   Steps in the Civil Litigation Process

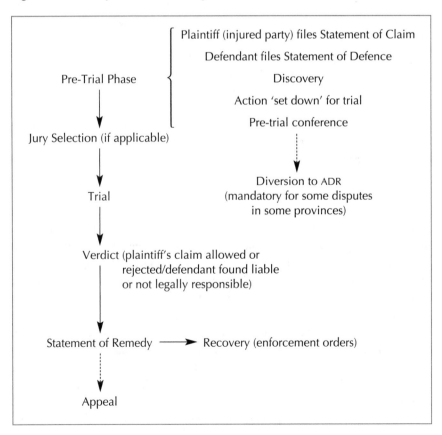

together, the statements of claim and defence are known as the *pleadings*. If the defendant offers no defence, the plaintiff can obtain 'default judgment' from the court; that is, he or she wins by default. It is also common in civil litigation, especially contract disputes, for the defendant to counterclaim against the plaintiff or to make a claim against a third party. The tainted blood cases provide an example of a third-party claim since the Red Cross, upon being sued by those infected with HIV, in turn sued the federal government for not approving new drugs and blood products more quickly. As one might imagine, all these claims and counter-claims can produce extremely complex cases for judges to disentangle at trial.

Soon after the pleadings, each party is required to deliver to the others a list of all the documents he or she possesses that are relevant to the case, and copies of the documents are made available upon request—this exchange of information is known as *discovery*. It is also at this stage that each party can compel the other to submit to an interview under oath. If, after discovery is complete, neither side has conceded, either the plaintiff or defendant can *set an action down for trial* by filing the trial record with the court. A trial record includes a copy of all pleadings and orders related to the trial. (In this case, 'orders' refers to judicial rulings on *motions*, which are requests by counsel for the judge to take a specific action or to make a decision. Examples include requests to change venue, to clarify or amend the statement of claim, or to order disclosure of particular documents.) The final step before trial is that the judge or parties can request a *pre-trial conference* between the parties and the judge or other officer of the court in an attempt to settle the case or narrow the issues (see Chapter 3). As Tarr (2003, 226–7) observes, a conference not only speeds up trials, but also actively encourages settlement because the judge may help the parties recognize the strengths and weaknesses of each side's case, and a judicially endorsed settlement is more likely to be seen as fair. The judge may also encourage the parties to make further use of ADR mechanisms. And in Ontario, for example, there are pilot projects in Toronto, Ottawa, and Windsor *requiring* mediation for some non-family law disputes.

If pre-trial conferencing fails, the case usually proceeds to *trial*, either before a judge and jury or before a judge alone (the latter is known as a 'bench' trial). In stark contrast with the US, but mirroring the trend in Great Britain, juries are rare in Canadian civil cases, being used in only 10 to 15 per cent of trials in Ontario (Bogart 1999; Kritzer 2004),[16] and not at all in Quebec and the federal courts, where they are prohibited (see Box 10.3). If the litigants can and do opt for a jury trial, *jury selection* becomes the first order of business. Civil juries are smaller than their criminal counterparts—there are only six jurors compared to twelve—and only five of the six need to agree on a verdict rather than the unanimity required in a criminal trial. Once the jury is selected ('empanelled')—or straight away in bench trials—each side presents its arguments and evidence, calls witnesses in support of its case, and cross-examines the witnesses called by the other side in the hopes of undermining their influence on the judge or jury.

Box 10.3   W(h)ither Civil Juries in Canada?

A little over 150 years ago in the British common law legal system, juries were mandatory in all civil trials. This was also the case in Canada at Confederation in 1867, but only a year later, in response to concerns about corruption and jury 'packing' by government authorities, they were made available in Ontario only on request of one of the parties (Bogart 1999, 306). The use of civil juries has gradually diminished in both Britain and Canada and has been abolished in the federal courts and Quebec (where they conflicted with the continental European-influenced civil law). Today, though still rare, they are most common in Ontario[17] and British Columbia, but in every province where they are allowed there are strict limits on their use, and judges often have the discretion to conduct a trial without one. In most provinces civil juries are available for only certain types of claims, usually those claiming over a certain minimum amount of money (in 2006, the British Columbia Justice Review Task Force recommended an increase to *$100,000*), or in specific types of disputes. In Alberta, for instance, juries are available by right only in cases involving torts and property and where more than $75,000 is claimed.

Opinion is divided over civil juries, which have both virtues and additional costs compared to trial by judge alone. On the positive side, juries inject courtrooms with a dose of democracy by involving citizens from diverse backgrounds and breaking the legal elite's monopoly over proceedings. As one judge (Bouck 2003) who supports the use of civil juries put it, 'Lawyers and judges may be experts in the law but we have no monopoly on justice.' Though the Ontario Law Reform Commission (OLRC) (1996) found that many people also see juries as a check on governmental abuses of authority, the reality is that juries are prohibited, by legislation, in suits against all levels of government. Another advantage is that to win before a jury one has to convince several people rather than just one judge, a procedure which arguably fosters fairer decisions and greater acceptance by the parties of the result. By the same token, juries are held to insulate the justice system from allegations of elitism, judicial bias, and political influence, thereby promoting broader public acceptance of decisions, especially unpopular ones (Bouck 2002). Jury duty also serves an important educational function for those who serve and helps to publicize the work of the court.

On the negative side, jury trials can take longer, because of the jury-selection process and because judges must take time to instruct juries. Mostly for this same reason, jury trials that go to verdict usually cost the parties and tax-payers more financially. In some provinces, including Alberta and British Columbia, some of this increase is artificial, since the state levies what is effectively a 'jury tax', in the form of jury hearing fees—in British Columbia, this can come to $16,000 for a three-week trial (Bouck 2003). On the other hand, the presence of a jury tends to promote settlement more frequently and faster than in bench trials (Bogart 1999, 312–13). Given that the vast majority of trials end in settlement, it is unlikely that juries actually lengthen trials overall or cost more (Ontario Law Reform Commission 1996). Two other common criticisms of juries that have little empirical support are that they are ill-suited for 'complex' trials and that they are 'unpredictable', especially with respect to remedies (Ontario Law Reform Commission 1996). In reality, verdicts by juries are usually consistent with those by judges alone (in Bogart 1999, 315), and the evidence from the US—where juries routinely deal with complex scientific and medical information—is that they are at least as com-petent decision makers as judges, if not better because of their collective input (in Bogart 1999, 315). As Judge Bouck (2003) jokes, 'many lawyers and judges studied law because we recognized we were not very good at science or math.'

Notwithstanding the actual evidence, these critiques have been used histori-cally to justify curtailing or prohibiting the use of civil juries in areas such as medical malpractice. In some provinces, judges are able to deny a litigant's request for trial by jury, or even dismiss a sitting jury, on the grounds that the case involves too much technical scientific data, and with no legal guide-lines this determination is a subjective one left entirely to the judge. This power is currently being challenged in Ontario as a violation of the Charter's rights to equality and life, liberty, and security of the person (see Makin 2007a, A4). Juries do give rise to legitimate legal concerns, however, for, unlike judges they do not give reasons for their decisions. This means that their decisions cannot develop common law precedents, and, as the Alberta Court of Appeal observed recently, 'the losing party in a civil case is largely deprived of the ability to challenge the decision' through an appeal (*Purba v. Ryan* 2006, at para. 43). Finally, though jury service may have benefits, financial gain is not one of them: indeed, service usually involves significant financial hardship (in Alberta, for example, jurors are paid only $50 per day), not to mention time away from work, family, and other responsibilities.

At present, the jury is still out on civil juries.

On the basis of all of this, the judge (or jury) issues a *verdict*, either upholding or rejecting the plaintiff's claim. Like the names of parties, different terminology is used in civil and criminal law with respect to verdicts. In civil law, we say the defendant is either *liable* or not legally responsible, rather than 'guilty' or 'acquitted'. Moreover, the two systems use different standards of proof, for in civil cases liability must only be demonstrated 'on a balance of probabilities', a somewhat slippery standard (roughly meaning it is more likely than not that the defendant committed the disputed action) that is less demanding than the criminal law's (also slippery) 'guilt beyond a reasonable doubt'. The best-known illustration of this distinction is the different verdicts in the two infamous O.J. Simpson trials in the US regarding the deaths of Simpson's ex-wife and her friend. Acquitted by a jury of criminal murder charges, Simpson was found civilly liable for their 'wrongful death' (a category of tort) by a different jury.

If the defendant is found liable, the court must decide what *remedy* to grant the plaintiff—it has wide discretion in this regard and is not bound by what the plaintiff requested in his or her statement of claim. Remedies can take many forms, but the most common are *damages* (money), *declarations of relief*, and *injunctions*. Damages come in three categories: *special*, *general*, and *punitive damages*. Special damages are designed to compensate the plaintiff for the direct costs of their injury, such as medical expenses, lost property, or lost income while recovering from a physical or psychological injury. General damages are also intended to compensate the plaintiff but for non-specified damages that are not easily quantified, such as 'future earnings' and 'pain and suffering'. Punitive damages, on the other hand, are not so much intended to compensate the plaintiff as to punish the defendant who has been found liable for behaviour that particularly offends society and to deter similar behaviour by others. Punitive damages are therefore an anomaly in the civil justice system—which is premised on compensating the plaintiff—and bear a closer resemblance to criminal sentences.

Large rewards by juries for punitive damages, most notably the $2.7 million given to Stella Liebeck in the widely known 'McDonald's coffee case' (see Box 10.4)—have contributed most to the view that the American civil justice system has experienced a 'litigation explosion' (Olson 1991) and is in need of tort reform to discourage litigation. However, as the true story of Stella Liebeck's case illustrates, this view is based more on myths generated by the media than by facts (Haltom and McCann 2004). (The debate over the 'litigation explosion', and why no 'explosion' has occurred in Canada, are discussed later in this chapter.) Moreover, popular misconceptions about cases like Stella's have actually influenced American juries to award significantly *less* in punitive damages since the early 1990s (Haltom and McCann 2004, 297–8). Punitive damages are relatively rare in Canada—they did not even exist in Quebec's system until recently—and the amounts are also comparatively low. For example, the Supreme Court of Canada's decision in *Whiten v. Pilot Insurance Co.* (2002) to uphold an Ontario jury's $1 million award for punitive damages was seen as remarkable, and the amount unprecedented. *Whiten* does not appear to have heralded a new period in expansive punitive damages, however, for only a few years later, in a somewhat similar case, the Supreme Court announced much tighter criteria for awarding such damages and emphasized their 'exceptional' nature (*Fidler v. Sun Life Assurance Co. of Canada* 2006).[18]

Box 10.4   The Truth behind the 'McDonald's Coffee' Case

The 'McDonald's coffee' case. We have all heard it: a woman spills McDonald's coffee, sues and gets $3 million. Here are the facts of this widely misreported and misunderstood case:

Stella Liebeck, 79 years old, was sitting in the passenger seat of her grandson's car having purchased a cup of McDonald's coffee. After the car stopped, she tried to hold the cup securely between her knees while removing the lid. However, the cup tipped over, pouring scalding hot coffee onto her. She received third-degree burns over 16 per cent of her body, necessitating hospitalization for eight days, whirlpool treatment for debridement of her wounds, skin grafting, scarring, and disability for more than two years. Despite these extensive injuries, she offered to settle with McDonald's for $20,000—the amount needed to pay her medical bills and the wages of a family member who had taken time off work to care for her. However, McDonald's refused to settle. The jury awarded Liebeck $200,000 in compensatory damages—reduced to $160,000 because the jury found her 20 per cent at fault—and $2.7 million in punitive damages for McDonald's callous conduct. (To put this in perspective, McDonald's revenue from coffee sales alone is in excess of $1.3 million a day.) The trial judge reduced the punitive damages to $480,000. Subsequently, the parties entered a post-verdict settlement. According to Stella Liebeck's attorney, S. Reed Morgan, the jury heard the following evidence in the case:

1. By corporate specifications, McDonald's sells its coffee at 180 to 190 degrees Fahrenheit.
2. Coffee at that temperature, if spilled, causes third-degree burns (the skin is burned away down to the muscle and fatty tissue layer) in two to seven seconds.
3. Third-degree burns do not heal without skin grafting, debridement and whirlpool treatments that cost tens of thousands of dollars and result in

permanent disfigurement, extreme pain and disability of the victim for many months, and in some cases, years.

4. The chairman of the department of mechanical engineering and bio-mechanical engineering at the University of Texas testified that this risk of harm is unacceptable, as did a widely recognized expert on burns, the editor-in-chief of the leading scholarly publication in the specialty, the *Journal of Burn Care and Rehabilitation*.

5. McDonald's admitted that it has known about the risk of serious burns from its scalding hot coffee for more than ten years—the risk was brought to its attention through numerous other claims and suits, to no avail.

6. From 1982 to 1992, McDonald's coffee burned more than 700 people, many receiving severe burns to the genital area, perineum, inner thighs, and buttocks.

7. Not only men and women, but also children and infants, have been burned by McDonald's scalding hot coffee, in some instances due to inadvertent spillage by McDonald's employees.

8. At least one woman had coffee dropped in her lap through the service window, causing third-degree burns to her inner thighs and other sensitive areas, which resulted in disability for years.

9. Witnesses for McDonald's admitted in court that consumers are unaware of the extent of the risk of serious burns from spilled coffee served at McDonald's required temperature.

10. McDonald's admitted that it did not warn customers of the nature and extent of this risk and could offer no explanation as to why it did not.

11. McDonald's witnesses testified that it did not intend to turn down the heat—as one witness put it: 'No, there is no current plan to change the procedure that we're using in that regard right now.'

12. McDonald's admitted that its coffee is 'not fit for consumption' when sold because it causes severe scalds if spilled or drunk.

13. Liebeck's treating physician testified that her injury was one of the worst scald burns he had ever seen.

Moreover, the Shriner's Burn Institute in Cincinnati had published warnings to the franchise food industry that its members were unnecessarily causing serious scald burns by serving beverages above 130 degrees Fahrenheit.

In refusing to grant a new trial in the case, Judge Robert Scott called McDonald's behavior 'callous'. Moreover, 'the day after the verdict, the news media documented that coffee at the McDonald's in Albuquerque [where Liebeck was burned] is now sold at 158 degrees. This will cause third-degree burns in about sixty seconds, rather than in two to seven seconds [so that], the margin of safety has been increased as a direct consequence of this verdict.' (Morgan 1994)

From 'Mythbuster! The "McDonald's Coffee Case" and Other Fictions', Center for Justice and Democracy at http://www.centerjd.org/ free/mythbusters-free/MB_mcdonalds.htm. Center for Justice and Democracy.

These details are confirmed in *Distorting the Law* (Haltom and McCann 2004), which won awards from the American Political Science Association and Law & Society Association for the best book published in 2005 on law and courts.

According to its website, 'The Center for Justice & Democracy is a non-profit, non-partisan public interest organization that works to educate the public about the importance of the civil justice system, and fights to protect the right to trial by jury and an independent judiciary for all Americans.' CJ&D is funded by individual contributions and foundations, and 'is not connected to any business or trial lawyer organization'.

Declarations of relief or 'declaratory remedies' simply state the rights of the parties, as when the court decides who the rightful owner is in a property dispute. We also see declarations of relief when the court interprets legal documents, such as contracts, wills, or laws in the common law and legislation. In essence, courts issue declarations of relief to acknowledge that the plaintiff's right under law has been violated but without granting any specific remedy. When a court *does* issue a specific order, this is known as an injunction.[19] For example, at the request of Winnipeg Child and Family Services (CFS), a trial court judge ordered on the basis of tort law that a pregnant woman addicted to glue sniffing (which can cause birth defects) be placed in the custody of CFS and detained in a health centre for treatment until the birth of her child (the injunction was later overturned on appeal; *Winnipeg Child and Family Services v. G. (D.F.)* 1997). Injunctions are also commonly used to *block* a particular action, such as the injunction barring Chantal Daigle from getting an abortion without the father's consent (an injunction which she successfully challenged in *Tremblay v. Daigle* 1989). Other common examples include injunctions to halt construction until a proper environmental assessment or public consultation has occurred, or to prohibit protesters from picketing a business.[20]

Usually, the final step in the litigation process is recovery, or enforcement of the judgment (only a miniscule number—fewer than 1 per cent—of civil trial decisions are appealed). In cases of declaratory relief and injunctions, if the liable party does not follow the court's orders, the plaintiff has to take him or her back to court. Where the remedy was for damages (or child support or alimony payments in family law), it may involve court-appointed debt collectors or garnishment of wages (where amounts are deducted directly from one's pay cheque). It is not uncommon for liable parties to declare bankruptcy if they are unable (or unwilling) to pay, and though there is a complex set of laws governing this possibility, it usually means that the plaintiff will not collect all, or even any, of the money owed to them. Regardless of the type of remedy, the court can find noncomplying liable parties in *contempt of court* and can fine or jail them, or both (in the case of imprisonment, they would be released immediately upon complying with the court's orders).

There is, of course, the possibility that one or both sides will appeal the trial judge's verdict to a higher court. The losing party may appeal in the hopes of overturning the verdict but also to delay resolution of the case and enforcement, especially if large sums of money or institutional reforms are involved. Thus, 'an appeal by the losing party may simply begin the next stage of bargaining and negotiation' (Greene et al. 1998, 56). The winning side may appeal because it is not completely satisfied with the remedy. In addition, either side may appeal to challenge a particular interpretation of the common-law or statutory rules governing the dispute.

Civil Litigation in Canada: A Snapshot

As noted earlier, comprehensive statistics for civil litigation do not exist, either across Canada or within individual provinces.[21] A major complicating factor in data collection is that civil jurisdiction is spread across different types of courts, even within a single province, as outlined in Chapter 2. Consider the situation in Alberta: the s. 92 Provincial Court has a Civil Division that hears small claims (under $25,000) and a Family Division for custody and child support disputes; the s. 96 Court of Queen's Bench hears civil trials for damages (regardless of the amount), divorce, adoption, foreclosure, bankruptcy, wills, and any civil jury trials; and the s. 101 Federal Court can hear civil cases filed against the federal government. Nevertheless, there is enough information from selected jurisdictions to provide some insights into the disputes that arise in the civil justice system. That said, the picture that emerges is one of remarkable diversity between provinces, within provinces, and over time. The most recent study comparing provincial courts (Brookbank, Kingsley, and Leonard 1999) is not, unfortunately, very up to date, for the data are now over a decade old and predate some major reforms to the civil justice system, such as the introduction of contingency fees in Ontario and class-action suits elsewhere. Moreover, the study focuses primarily on claims filed with the courts rather than actual trial outcomes, though this is understandable given the massive proportion of claims (usually in the 90 to 99 per cent range, depending on type) that end in default judgment, settlement, abandonment, or diversion to ADR without reaching trial.[22] Nevertheless, this section provides some sample information about the types of civil cases that historically have been filed in provincial courts, the frequency of each, how long disputes take to resolve, the amount of money claimed and awarded, and some characteristics of the parties involved.

Figure 10.4 shows a comparative breakdown of civil cases by subject across a sample of several provincial courts, using the most recent comparative study (Brookbank, Kingsley, and Leonard 1999). The figures clearly illustrate the diversity of litigation mentioned above, and the way in which cross-provincial comparisons are frustrated by inconsistencies in jurisdiction and reporting methods. Similarly, there is considerable variation among provinces in how civil cases are initiated. In Ottawa in 1994, for example, more cases were initiated by application (44 per cent) than a plaintiff's statement of claim (33 per cent) or divorce petition (23 per cent), whereas in Nova Scotia and Alberta plaintiffs either outnumbered or equalled applicants.

Without better data we cannot definitively conclude whether there are overall trends in rates of civil litigation, but *claims* do not appear to be declining[23] and those related to family law seem to be on the rise, explosively in some places (by 77 per cent in British Columbia from 1993 to 2001), more modestly elsewhere (2 per cent from 2000 to 2005 in the Ontario Superior Court, 8 per cent in the Ontario Court of Justice).[24] Small claims have witnessed a mixed record, perhaps because the threshold amount and procedure varies from province to province: they have experienced a modest and steady increase in Ontario (by 7.5 per cent since 2000), but a steep and steady drop in British Columbia (of 35 per cent from 1995 to 2000). Data from Ottawa in the mid-1990s revealed that many statements of claim result in a default judgment (30 per cent), but this rate increases dramatically for those initiated by application (69 per cent) or petitions for divorce (63 per cent). Similarly, there is some evidence that the number of cases going to trial is dropping. British Columbia's Justice Review Task Force (2006) found that between 1996 and 2002, the number of trials decreased by half while the average length doubled, mirroring trends in the US and Great Britain. Kritzer (2004) draws a similar conclusion about trials in Ontario, but his findings are not directly comparable because he excludes small claims courts from his analysis. That said, he finds an interesting pattern in the ratio of trials to (non-small) claims, which has fluctuated between 2 and 6 per cent since the late 1970s, with the ratio dropping during recessions—perhaps because people cannot afford the legal fees associated with trials—and recovering briskly when they end. Of claims that actually proceeded to trial in the Ottawa study, however, only about a fifth (but 29 per cent in divorce cases) went to judgment after trial; the rest were settled (20 per cent), dismissed by the judge (10 per cent), or abandoned by the initiating party (8 per cent).

Figure 10.4   Sample Breakdown of Civil Claims (Filings Only)

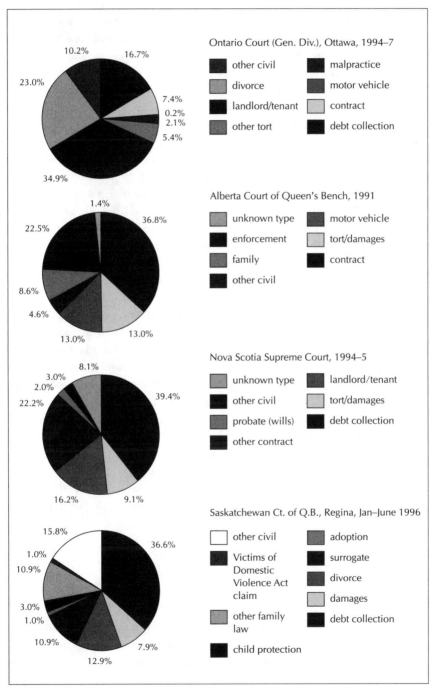

Ontario Court (Gen. Div.), Ottawa, 1994–7

- other civil
- divorce
- landlord/tenant
- other tort
- malpractice
- motor vehicle
- contract
- debt collection

Alberta Court of Queen's Bench, 1991

- unknown type
- enforcement
- family
- other civil
- motor vehicle
- tort/damages
- contract

Nova Scotia Supreme Court, 1994–5

- unknown type
- other civil
- probate (wills)
- other contract
- landlord/tenant
- tort/damages
- debt collection

Saskatchewan Ct. of Q.B., Regina, Jan–June 1996

- other civil
- Victims of Domestic Violence Act claim
- other family law
- child protection
- adoption
- surrogate
- divorce
- damages
- debt collection

Based on data in Brookbank, Kingsley, and Leonard 1999.

Civil cases have a reputation for taking a long time to resolve, but the available data provide only mixed support for this view. In the longest period for which data are available (1991–7), a study of courts in Calgary and Edmonton did find long delays between when a case was initiated and when it actually reached trial or resolution. The median waiting time for a trial to begin was roughly two years, whereas resolution by settlement took a median time of just under ten months. Once a trial actually began, about half lasted over two years, and a small fraction (5 per cent) lasted over five years. However, the time actually spent in court (or 'hearings') is much less than this suggests, usually about only four days. The rest of the 'trial time' is spent waiting for hearings and for judgment. The type of civil case clearly matters in this regard, however. In Ottawa, virtually all applications and divorce matters initiated in 1994 were resolved by 1997, compared to only about half of those initiated by a statement of claim. Cases initiated by statement of claim also took three to five times as long to resolve as other civil cases. There is also variation among the different kinds of cases initiated by statement of claim. In Calgary, family cases had the shortest median elapsed time until trial (404 days), and motor vehicle cases had the longest (1,250 days). In Nova Scotia, among cases initiated in 1994/5, tort (damages) cases took the longest to resolve (295 days), almost 2.5 times as long as the next-longest category of cases (employment disputes, at 128 days).[25] This fact has prompted many provinces to experiment with *case management*, which sorts cases by their complexity early in the litigation process and fast-tracks simpler or time-sensitive cases. A crucial aspect of case management is the heavy use—mandatory in some jurisdictions—of mediation hearings or settlement conferences, which are intended to resolve the dispute before trial, and the enforcement of strict timetables for the litigation process. Among cases initiated in 1994/5 in Nova Scotia, for example, most landlord–tenant and debt-collection disputes (86 and 84 per cent) and the majority of other contract (62 per cent) and employment (50 per cent) disputes were fast-tracked, whereas most tort cases (85 per cent) were labelled 'standard track'. Ontario has been experimenting with mandatory case management in Ottawa, Windsor, and (until May 2008) Toronto, and is currently considering expanding the system province-wide (Ministry of the Attorney General 2006a).

Outcomes of Civil Litigation

Who is suing whom in civil cases? And more to the point, who is winning? To help us answer these questions, it is useful to recall Marc Galanter's (1974) categories of litigants introduced in Chapters 7 and 8, of 'repeat player' (RP) and 'one-shot' (OS) litigants. As the name suggests, RP litigants go to court frequently and accordingly possess experience—and usually financial and personnel resources, not to mention some mutual familiarity with the judges—that give them an edge over one-shotters. Large governments are the ultimate RP litigants (although much of their litigation in the civil justice system involves public rather than private law), but large corporations or businesses are also usually RPs, whereas individuals or small grass-roots organizations are usually OSs. True to the predictions of Galanter's theory, litigants in the RP category are the most likely to resort to litigation in Canada as plaintiff or applicant, although the gap is razor-thin. In Alberta, businesses represented about half of plaintiffs (mostly in contract cases, which constitute the vast majority of business-initiated claims), roughly the same share as in Ottawa.[26] One interesting finding from Ottawa is that although statements of claim by businesses outnumber those by individuals, businesses are less likely to proceed to trial. This might be because defendants are more likely to concede when 'outgunned' by a business plaintiff, or businesses may decline to litigate because cost-benefit analysis dictates that course of action when the amount sought is relatively low. Businesses were also the most frequent category of applicants in Ottawa, the only jurisdiction for which we have applicant information. The exception to the pattern is, not surprisingly, divorce petitions, where both the petitioner and respondent are individual OS litigants.

The pattern was reversed and augmented for defendants in Alberta, where individuals outnumbered business defendants two-to-one (businesses were most often sued for contract disputes or for torts and damages). Similar findings were made in Saskatchewan. Though litigant category figures were not collected for Nova Scotia, it is likely that individuals are the most common type of defendant since two of the most common forms of civil litigation there—debt collection and landlord–tenant disputes—typically involve businesses (usually RPs) suing (OS) individuals. In Ottawa, this pattern was only true of cases begun by application, most of which involve landlord–tenant disputes, a pattern that again suggests landlords frequently take individual tenants to court (Brookbank, Kingsley, and Leonard 1999, 32). For statement of claim cases in Ottawa, however, businesses were even more prevalent among defendants than they were among plaintiffs, and cases with business defendants were more likely to proceed to trial than those with individuals.

The Ottawa study also tracked the most common combinations of plaintiffs and defendants, and here again the RP litigant theory was confirmed, for a business suing another business (RP versus RP) is the most frequent match-up (accounting for 30 per cent of all statement of claim cases). Moreover, almost three-quarters of all statement of claim cases involved businesses as plaintiff or defendant or both; other frequent litigant combinations were businesses versus men and women (9 per cent), men versus businesses (9 per cent), businesses versus men (8 per cent), and women versus businesses (5 per cent). As these last findings suggest, there is also some evidence that rates of litigation involving individuals is influenced by gender. On the plaintiff side, although women and men in the Ottawa study filed roughly the same number of statements of claim, women were only two-thirds as likely as men to take the case to trial. Applications and divorce saw a greater gender difference, for men were seven times as likely to file an application as women, but women were almost twice as likely to file for divorce (and more likely to go to trial for divorce than men). On the defendant or respondent side, men were almost twice as likely to be sued as women, regardless of whether by statement of claim, application, or divorce petition.

On the crucial question of who is *winning* in civil litigation, we unfortunately have little information. According to data from Ottawa, it is overwhelmingly the plaintiff (84 per cent) or applicant (99 per cent), who is more often than not a business (RP).[27] The majority of these victories come in the form of default judgments; that is, the defendants did not even attempt to defend themselves. When they did, and pushed the dispute to trial, the plaintiff success rate fell only slightly (to 80 per cent for statement of claim cases). In the Saskatchewan study, of the plaintiffs who claimed monetary damages, 71 per cent received an award. On a final note, it may surprise some readers to learn that the amount of money claimed in civil cases is usually quite modest, median amounts being in the $3,000–4,000 range (Brookbank, Kingsley, and Leonard 1999), although Ontario's Civil Justice Review (1996) found a higher median claim, of $32,000. There is a huge gap, however, between cases initiated by a statement of claim (which includes torts)—which run to tens of thousands of dollars—and those by application (mostly landlord–tenant disputes), where most of the claims are for less than $1,000 (Brookbank, Kingsley, and Leonard 1999). Also, there is usually a gap between what is claimed and what is awarded,[28] but the gap is significantly wider for plaintiffs than applicants. In the Ottawa study, plaintiffs received only about 40 per cent of their claim (the median award was $29,000), whereas applicants got almost all (96.5 per cent) of their (much smaller) claims. There is likely significant provincial variation on this matter, as illustrated by the only other jurisdiction for which we have information: Saskatchewan, where plaintiffs received about three-quarters of their median claim, the largest gap being for torts (67 per cent) and the smallest for debt collectors (95 per cent, perhaps reflecting the fact that the latter's damages are easier to quantify and support with evidence).

While these data are suggestive, it must be stressed that this is only a very incomplete snapshot of civil litigation in Canada. There is much more room for improvement in data collection and public reporting of this important dimension of the overall justice system, as has been repeatedly lamented by researchers in this field (for example, Canadian Bar Association 1996; Lippert, Easton, and Yirush 1997; Bogart 1999; Kritzer 2004).

The Cost of Civil Justice

Chief Justice Beverley McLachlin of the Supreme Court of Canada made headlines in 2007 for repeatedly raising the alarm about the high financial cost of

seeking justice, pointing to the justice system's low accessibility for the vast majority of Canadians and the troubling growth of self-represented litigants (McLachlin
2007; in Tyler 2007a), who make up as many as 46 per cent of those appearing in
Ontario's family courts (Langan 2005). Similarly, Roy McMurtry, the then Chief
Justice of Ontario, identified access to justice as the most important issue facing
the legal system (in Tyler 2007b, A1). Describing access to justice 'a basic right'
and the system's high cost a 'crisis', McLachlin called on the legal community to
look for solutions.

McLachlin's first salvo on this issue came shortly after a high-profile story in
the *Toronto Star* (Tyler 2007b) about an extremely expensive wrongful-dismissal
suit, which noted that a three-day trial with an average-priced lawyer is likely to
cost over $60,000, while median family income in Canada is just $58,000.
Moreover, as the story notes, civil trials frequently take more than three days.
That the justice system is expensive is hardly news, however. The figures cited by
the *Toronto Star* article actually came from a study of Ontario civil justice system
conducted in the mid-1990s (Ontario Civil Justice Review 1995, 1996), and the
system's reputation as 'being only for the wealthy' has existed for centuries.

> 'If a man stopped me in the street, and demanded of me my watch, I
> should refuse to give it to him. If he threatened to take it by force, I feel
> I should, though not a fighting man, do my best to protect it. If, on the
> other hand, he should assert his intention of trying to obtain it by means
> of an action in any court of law, I should take it out of my pocket and
> hand it to him, and think I had got off cheaply'.
>
> British humorist Jerome K. Jerome
> (1859–1927)

Why is the system so expensive? The most significant factor is the cost of hiring a lawyer. Even ten years ago, the average lawyer in Ontario charged $195 per
hour (Ontario Civil Justice Review 1995); today, experienced civil and family
lawyers charge from $250 to (in Toronto, the most expensive region) $800 an
hour, with even an articling student costing $60 per hour (Tyler 2007b). Those
hours add up quite quickly when one considers that many hours are spent preparing a statement of claim, producing and reading the documents for discovery,
interviewing witnesses during discovery, and preparing for and participating in
pre-trial hearings and motions before finally preparing for and conducting the
trial. Lawyers' fees are hardly the end of a litigant's legal expenses, however. There
are also court filing fees, photocopying costs for discovery documents, court transcript fees ($1,000 for the transcript of just one day), postage and long-distance
phone charges, and expert-witness fees. Moreover, the losing party may have to
pay some or all of his or her *opponent's* legal costs (this is known as 'loser pays' or

fee reversal). The potential for fee reversal is seen as a major disincentive to launching a civil suit, because median awards for the costs of opposing counsel were approximately $4,300 in 1996 (Ontario Civil Justice Review 1995). A case that proceeds to appeal can cost additional tens of thousands of dollars.

Broadly speaking, there are two possible ways to lower the high cost of seeking justice through litigation. The first is 'diversion', or encouraging parties to resolve their disputes outside of the traditional justice system—this is the principal goal of ADR and (in part) case-management initiatives, which have already been discussed in this and earlier chapters. Although diversion is generally believed to be cheaper than regular litigation, it is certainly not free, and it may even increase the costs if mandatory ADR mechanisms lengthen the overall resolution process. The increasing 'judicialization' of ADR and tribunal proceedings has also meant that participants increasingly need legal counsel, a development which thus off-sets the biggest cost saving of avoiding the courts (Morrison and Mosher 1996, 659–60). The second strategy is to enhance access to the 'regular' court system by making it more affordable or by subsidizing litigants in financial need. Several methods fall into this latter category, most notably the following:

Legal Aid for Low-Income Litigants

Legal aid is currently reserved for the very poor, and in most provinces it is rarely given for civil cases, or only for family law cases. In 1999, the Supreme Court of Canada ruled that low-income people (in this case, indigent and on Social Assistance) involved in serious family law disputes where the welfare of children is at stake have a constitutional right to legal aid under the Charter of Rights (*New Brunswick v. G. (J.)* 1999). A claim by crusading lawyer Dugald Christie (who died in 2006) for a more general right to civil legal aid for the poor was successful at trial and before the British Columbia Court of Appeal, but in 2007 the Supreme Court overturned these rulings (*British Columbia v. Christie* 2007).[29] In 2005, after a four-year period in which the British Columbia government cut legal aid by 40 per cent, another case was initiated claiming a right to civil legal aid, this time by the Canadian Bar Association and focusing on the Charter's rights to equality and life, liberty, and security of the person. This case was dismissed by a British Columbia lower court in 2006 for lack of standing and for having an unreasonably broad statement of claim (to be fair, if successful the claim would have entailed a revolutionary change in the way civil litigation is paid for in Canada).

Cut Taxes on Lawyers' Fees

Dugald Christie's case actually began as a challenge to a special 7 per cent tax on legal fees that British Columbia introduced in 1993 and which is used to fund legal aid and the justice system. The tax had undermined Christie's practice since his primarily low-income clients often could not afford the tax, and with an annual income of only $30,000, Christie could not afford to pay it on their behalf. This, he argued innovatively (but ultimately unsuccessfully) undermined an unwritten constitutional principle of 'access to justice'. Provincially, only Alberta and Ontario do not tax legal fees. At its annual meeting in 2007, the Canadian Bar Association endorsed a motion calling on the federal government to eliminate the GST on lawyers' fees (Tyler 2007d). In theory, this would lower such fees by 5 per cent, but whether that would be borne out in practice is another matter—in other industries, the proportion of tax cut is often replaced shortly thereafter by an increase in base price. If such a proposal were to have any meaningful effect, then, lawyers' fees would have to be frozen for some time.[30]

Class-Action Suits

Class actions were referred to earlier as a mechanism that allows many individuals with the same legal dispute to combine their resources into a single claim handled by the same lawyer or law firm and heard before the same judge. Class actions have long been associated with improved access to the court system, since they facilitate cases where an individual plaintiff would not recoup enough in damages to cover his or her legal costs, or where individual claims are so complex that it would not make economic sense to press the claim individually (for example, the tainted blood case). By sharing a lawyer or legal team, individual plaintiffs in a class action enjoy economies of scale that make litigation financially viable, and the pooling of information strengthens all of their claims. In essence, class actions allow individual 'one-shot' litigants to enjoy the advantages of a 'repeat player', especially since class-action lawyers tend to specialize in that area. Moreover, being a member of a class action is considerably easier than being an individual plaintiff because class members are rarely interviewed by the defence during discovery or asked to testify in court. Instead, most of one's participation is through sworn affidavits and mail or phone contact with the class action's legal team. Finally, a large class enjoys more leverage over the defendant at the negotiating table than a single claimant—indeed, most class actions which are approved in Canada (in most provinces, judicial approval is required) are settled before going to trial.

Class actions were first permitted in Quebec in 1978, with New Brunswick following in the 1980s, Ontario and British Columbia in the 1990s, and Newfoundland, Saskatchewan, and Alberta since 2000. Alberta's legislation in 2004 is noteworthy because it was the direct result of a Supreme Court of Canada ruling (*Western Canada Shopping Centres Inc. v. Dutton* 2001) ordering Alberta to loosen its restrictions on class actions, by removing the need to assess the damages for each individual in the class. On the other hand, in 2007 the Supreme Court struck a blow against consumer class-action suits by upholding provisions in contracts between businesses and their customers that prevent customers from suing the business via class actions and requiring them to seek arbitration instead (*Dell Computer Corp. v. Union des consommateurs* 2007; *Rogers Wireless Inc. v. Muroff* 2007).[31] These decisions have sparked criticism by consumer advocates and some legal academics (Ziegel 2007), who point out that such provisions allow businesses to 'pick off' individual plaintiffs who have the time and money to pursue their own claims and ignore the others—the very problem class actions are designed to counter. (For this reason, governments in Ontario and Quebec—and the courts in British Columbia—have outlawed 'mandatory-arbitration' provisions in consumer contracts.) Nonetheless, class actions appear to be on the rise, 200 having been initiated from 1992 to 2001 in Ontario (Watson 2001, 278) and 75 across Canada in the first seven months of 2007 alone (Canadian Bar Association National Class Action Database); it must be stressed, however, that this is a very small portion of all civil litigation. The main categories of defendants named are big businesses, including pharmaceutical and medical-product manufacturers, financial institutions, communications conglomerates, and computer and electronics manufacturers.

One criticism of class actions in Canada today is that they contain a 'fundamental contradiction' (Crosariol 2007): they are designed to facilitate and streamline litigation involving similar claims, yet provincial jurisdiction over civil law means that class actions are limited by provincial boundaries and governed by different rules. The result is the duplication of identical cases in multiple provinces, which weakens the class and undermines the efficiencies associated with class actions. Since 2007, the Canadian Bar Association has hosted an on-line National Class Action Database (http://www.cba.org/ClassActions/main/gate/index/default. aspx) to help potential plaintiffs in different provinces co-ordinate litigation, but what is ultimately sought by some legal reformers is an interprovincial agreement to create a truly national class-action system. Jurisdictional divisions and different legal systems will likely make this quite difficult, both technically and politically.

Contingency Fees

As also noted earlier in this chapter, contingency fees refer to an arrangement where the client pays his or her lawyer's fees only if the case is successful. This system is seen as a potential alternative to hourly billing by lawyers, which, while providing more transparency to clients, may encourage lawyers to prolong cases unnecessarily. A contingency fee system has obvious benefits for a client who is not independently wealthy, but its appeal to lawyers depends on the rules for contingency fees. If legal counsel receive only their regular fees should they win, contingency fees entail higher financial risk for lawyers, who will therefore be *less* likely to take cases that are complex or whose outcome is unclear. Moreover, contingency fees do not remove the disincentive to litigate inherent in the 'fee-reversal' system. On the other hand, in most contingency fee systems in the US, the lawyer is paid a pre-negotiated percentage of any settlement or judge's award.

In this 'pure percentage' arrangement, lawyers will gravitate towards cases with higher potential awards (for example, wrongful dismissal or personal injury), but such a system will do little to improve legal representation for others kinds of cases. Finally, contingency fees can be used to 'top up' the regular (or discounted) hourly fee structure, creating a financial incentive for lawyers to take on even less-lucrative cases. Ontario was the last province to permit the use of contingency fees, in 2002, most of the others having done so in the 1970s. Like most provinces, Ontario's legislation does not dictate the details of contingency fees or the maximum share of award, except in class actions, where the 'top-up' method is required. Notably, contingency fees are most likely to encourage litigation when the 'top-up' or 'pure percentage' varieties are combined with class action suits, since the large reward typically sought in a class-action creates a powerful incentive for lawyers to take the case.

Legal Expenses Insurance

In the US and many European countries, individuals can obtain insurance to cover legal expenses in case they need legal representation. This is sometimes an employee benefit or an additional provision of a home insurance policy (Marchant 2007). Although such insurance is not generally available in Canada, it has been endorsed by the Quebec bar, is being considered by the Ontario Bar Association in a series of 'town halls' across Ontario on access to justice, and was referred to by Chief Justice McLachlin (2007) in her speech on the same topic. Such a reform, however, raises questions about how premiums are assessed, whether related changes would be needed in the way that lawyers bill their clients, and about the very role of lawyers in the justice system.

Case Management

Although case management encourages diversion through pre-trial settlements or ADR, it also aims to expedite those cases that do go to trial, thus resulting in lower fees for the many litigants who pay their lawyer by the hour.

Small Claims Courts

Small claims courts have been described elsewhere in this book, but to summarize, they are specialized courts that use streamlined procedures—such as limited discovery, no expert witnesses, or no legal counsel—to resolve civil disputes involving relatively small sums of money quickly. While the specific features differ in each province, small claims courts represent a compromise between the two ways of reducing the high cost of civil justice, by diverting simpler cases out of 'full' trials, yet enhancing access to a judge rather than some form of ADR.

One reform that does not appear to be among those being considered seriously by the legal establishment is, ironically, the one that seems the most obvious: compel lawyers to cut their rates. Although all lawyers must belong to the law (or barristers') society of the province in which they practice,[32] the societies do not set the rates of their members. Consequently, lawyers and legal firms compete with one other on the open market, and fees vary widely depending on specialization, experience, reputation, and so forth. This system could, arguably, be changed by introducing hourly-fee caps through the law societies' regulations or shifting from hourly billing to 'block' billing for specific tasks (as is now sometimes done for criminal law cases in Canada and is the system in Germany). Like any form of price control, however, this can present significant challenges for implementation and compliance, but the biggest barrier to such a change is almost certainly the lawyers themselves, for obvious reasons.

So far, when discussing the 'costs' of civil justice we have been referring only to the financial dimension. However, the high financial costs of the system are problematic primarily because of their larger social and political implications: many people are unable to protect their legal rights and legitimate interests through the justice system. As Chief Justice McLachlin (2007) notes, 'The result may be injustice. A person injured by the wrongful act of another may decide not to pursue compensation. A parent seeking custody of or access to the children of a broken relationship may decide he or she cannot afford to carry on the struggle— sometimes to the detriment not only of the parent but the children. When couples split up, assets that should go to the care of the children are used up in litigation; the family's financial resources are dissipated. Such outcomes can only with great difficulty be called "just".' Moreover, self-representation—a growing trend—undermines the litigant's ability to present his or her case; as the old saying goes, 'a man who is his own lawyer has a fool for a client'. Self-represented litigants also tend to slow the justice system down, because judges must spend more time explaining the rules and guiding the litigant, thus expanding case backlogs and exacerbating the problem of inaccessibility (Tyler 2007e).

Not everyone agrees, however, that greater access to the court system is socially beneficial. The most well-known detractor, the US legal commentator Walter Olson, characterizes this view as the 'invisible fist' theory, a play on Adam Smith's famous 'invisible hand' theory of market economics. According to Smith, a system of people acting in their own financial self-interest produces, as if by 'an invisible hand', greater social welfare than other economic systems, because competition and free choice keep prices as low as is reasonable and the quality of goods and services is improved. In other words, self-interest, paradoxically, benefits everyone. According to Olson (1991, 53), proponents of more litigation put a 'bold new twist' on Smith's idea by asserting that 'private *quarrels* also lead to public benefit; the more fights you get into, the better a place you make the world for everyone else.'[33] This, it is argued, is because plaintiffs' claiming their rights and holding others accountable for harm promotes justice and deters future wrong-doing. Olson contends that this mindset—which he rejects as a simplified decep-tion—provides the moral justification for the growth of civil cases in the US over the past three decades, a trend he provocatively characterizes as a 'litigation explo-sion'. He argues that the 'invisible fist' theory ignores the fact that many lawsuits are frivolous and designed to extort settlements from businesses that are guilty of nothing more than having deep pockets but that wish to avoid the high cost and bad publicity associated with a trial. This artificially drives up the cost of doing business—by imposing what some pundits in the US refer to as a 'tort tax' (Huber 1990)—and especially for smaller businesses and individuals (such as doctors accused of malpractice), litigation is often emotionally draining. Others (Huber 1991) maintain that the risks of litigation and related cost of insurance discourage people from entering risky but socially necessary professions, such as anesthesiol-ogy or other medical fields. Other social costs attributed to the 'litigation explo-sion' are a growing culture of entitlement and greater social divisiveness, which are not matched (let alone exceeded) by the deterrence of misconduct or promo-tion of greater socio-economic justice.

These critiques have had a powerful impact on public consciousness because they have been adopted and amplified by media outlets, governments, conserva-tive politicians, and the 'tort reform' movement, all of which happen to be extremely well-financed by the very corporations most at risk of being sued (Galanter 1999; Haltom and McCann 2004). This has translated into lower awards by judges and civil juries for successful plaintiffs (Haltom and McCann 2004), an increase in the number of summary judgments and dismissal of claims by judges without trial (Miller 2003), cuts to legal aid, and political attacks on class-action suits, contingency fees, and punitive damages (which have been capped in several jurisdictions). As Galanter (1999, 1116–17) observes, 'We have seen a 20-year barrage of attacks on rules and devices that give some clout to 'have nots' and nothing that impairs in the slightest the capacity of corporate entities to use the legal system either defensively or offensively.' These responses to the 'litigation explosion' would be understandable, however, if such a crisis actually existed—only it does not. Although the number of claims filed has increased over the past few decades, the growing body of academically rigorous literature (see, most notably, Haltom and McCann 2004) proves that the worst offences cited by Olson and other critics of expanding litigation are either truly exceptional, or dis-tortions of the facts (by reporting claims or jury awards instead of what the judge or appeal court ultimately decided—see also Box 10.4), or outright myths and urban legends. Moreover, despite the widespread public acceptance of the 'litiga-tion explosion' myth, most people still paradoxically believe that the court system favours corporate interests and the wealthy (Galanter 1999, 1120–1).

Why No 'Litigation Explosion' Debate in Canada?

Although Canadians are well aware of the reputation of the American system for runaway civil litigation—not surprisingly, since we share their media—the often acrimonious debate about civil law has had no parallel in Canada. This is despite the fact that claims in Canada are rising, as is spending on legal services (Lippert, Easton, and Yirush 1997). As well, although civil justice reform is on the political agenda (see our comments in the conclusion to this chapter), proposals are almost entirely in the direction of *enhancing* access to court, and contingency fees and class actions have been adopted relatively recently here to that end. Walter Olson himself (1997) has warned that Canada is not immune to a US-style litigation explosion, and he argues that the very institutional reforms we have adopted—particularly the combination of class actions and contingency fees—are likely to produce just such a result. On the other hand, because of several institutional differences between the two countries, the incentives to litigate that exist in the US do not exist in Canada. The most important of these is that unlike the US, Canada has retained fee reversal, which is widely held to be the greatest disincentive to litigate. Among the other significant differences:

- Since a set of 1978 decisions by the Supreme Court of Canada, general damages in personal injury suits (such as for 'pain and suffering') have been capped in Canada, originally at $100,000 indexed to inflation, or $280,000 in current dollars (*Andrews v. Grand & Toy Alberta Ltd.*, *Thornton v. School Dist. No. 57 (Prince George)*, *Arnold v. Teno* 1978). The Court has refused to extend this cap, however, to cases of libel and slander (*Hill v. Church of Scientology of Toronto* 1995) or negligence harming career prospects (*Young v. Bella* 2006).
- As noted earlier, punitive damages in Canada are rare (and non-existent in Quebec) and have never reached amounts in the hundreds of millions seen in the US. This probably also explains why—and also unlike in the US—punitive damages have not been capped by legislation, constitutional law, or common law in Canada.
- The rarity of civil jury trials in Canada has been cited as a factor by some, including lawyers experienced in civil litigation (Morris 2003), because civil juries have a reputation for greater susceptibility to 'emotional appeals' by plaintiffs and hostility to big businesses and government. However, the impact of this factor is questionable, since studies (see Haltom and McCann 2004, 297–301) have repeatedly found that jurors (and judges, for that matter) are actually quite critical of 'over-litigation' and frivolous suits, suggesting that when they *do* find for plaintiffs, it was *despite* these attitudes—in other words, because the plaintiff's case had merit.

- Since Canadian trial court judges are appointed rather than elected, they are more insulated against public hostility to big business and the incentive to 'make headlines' with high-profile rulings than their peers on state trial courts south of the border. This can, of course, cut the other way, given that the public is also very hostile to what it regards as frivolous lawsuits against 'deep-pocketed' defendants.

Besides institutional differences, it has also been argued that Americans have an extremely litigious culture compared to Canada (Lipset 1989). Comparative studies of the US and Europe (including Britain) have cast doubt on this argument (Epp 2003), and while litigation rates are higher in the US than Canada (Bogart and Vidmar 1990; Dewees, Trebilcock, and Coyte 1991; Kritzer, Bogart, and Vidmar 1991; Kagan 1994), no one has empirically confirmed that this is due to cultural (rather than institutional) reasons.

Conclusions

Civil disputes may occur between 'private' entities, but they clearly have public consequences—for families, consumers, employers and employees, and those affected by particular government policies. It is also important to remember that the court system that is often used to settle such disputes is an expensive public good, paid for by taxpayers. Thus, unequal access to the civil justice system is a matter of concern for society at large, and to the extent the system is dominated by disputes between relatively wealthy 'repeat player' litigants, it invites the question of whether the public at large should be subsidizing such disputes instead of diverting them to private ADR. This said, many civil disputes raise important questions of law which are properly considered publicly by trained judges, and ADR 'privatizes' disputes, which risks allowing 'those with power . . . to circumvent public policies, accountability and notions of basic procedural fairness' (Farrow 2006, 16). Moreover, in our common law system (outside Quebec, at least), judicial rulings on civil law are made in public and they create the rules by which similar disputes will be resolved in the future. Because ADR takes place in secret, it 'privatiz[es] a significant way in which we make law and order our public and private affairs' (Farrow 2006, 16). On the other hand, there is a tension between having a system which is genuinely accessible for individuals and groups seeking redress for civil wrongs committed against them by others, and creating too many incentives for costly and socially destructive nuisance litigation.

We close this chapter by noting that the Canadian civil justice system is in a considerable state of flux. Major reforms are being evaluated, for example, by Ontario's Civil Justice Reform Project and Nova Scotia's Rules Revision Project, and in 2006 the British Columbia Justice Review Task Force proposed changes to that province's civil justice system. In 1996, the Canadian Bar Association set up the Canadian Forum on Civil Justice as a permanent body to study and recommend changes to the civil justice system in Canada. Its 2006 national conference, for example, collected research papers under the theme 'Into the Future: The Agenda for Civil Justice Reform'. Suggested reforms in all of these initiatives include either scrapping or limiting civil juries even more, implementing province-wide case management and mandatory mediation (beyond the existing pilot projects), changing the way in which lawyers bill clients, putting strict time limits on cases, limiting the number of expert witnesses, streamlining the discovery process, and increasing the use of ADR generally. These efforts should not be dismissed lightly, because previous reform movements in the mid-1990s resulted in many changes to the civil justice system, including the expansion of simplified small claims courts, the introduction of contingency fees in Ontario, and the pilot projects on mandatory mediation and case management mentioned above. And in the past ten years, laws permitting or expanding class-action suits have been passed in all provinces except Prince Edward Island (where a proposal was considered and withdrawn). Unfortunately for such an important aspect of public policy, these discussions tend to be quite insular and politically low-profile: although the input of the judiciary and legal community is obviously crucial, theirs should not be the only contribution to this debate.

Chapter 11

Courts, Policy-Making, and Judicial Impact

Public policy involves developing objectives to address issues or problems and selecting means to achieve those objectives. Political choices need to be made amongst competing objectives and the means used to achieve them—choices that involve value considerations as well as considerations of efficiency and effectiveness. The government of Ontario, for example, decided that a minimum wage law was a useful mechanism to help reach the goal of social equality in society, even though some economists argued that such laws undermine economic efficiency and could actually harm lower-income workers by forcing businesses to eliminate jobs. In creating its minimum wage law, the Ontario government also sought to protect the agricultural sector from any negative economic effects of the law. Therefore, the law exempted employers from having to pay minimum wage to any 'person employed on a farm whose employment is directly related to primary production of eggs, milk, grain . . . vegetables . . . honey, pigs' (see Waddams 1987, 120–1).

This was not the end of the policy-making story though, for the issue wound up in court when some mushroom workers argued that they should still get minimum wage. When students are asked in class about how they would decide this dispute if they were a judge in the case, some respond that they would declare the law unfair and discriminatory. However, when the dispute was before the courts in the 1970s, the judges had no legal authority to decree the law null and void or to include agricultural workers in the law because there were no constitutionally entrenched rights and no corresponding powers to remedy constitutional wrongs. Judges could only declare laws unconstitutional on federalism grounds and Ontario was clearly within its jurisdiction to pass such a law. Hence, the judges' task in this case was limited to interpreting and applying the law. The Ontario Divisional Court panel that heard the case were split in their interpretations (*Ontario Mushroom Co. v. Learie* 1977). One judge, using the 'literal' rule of statutory interpretation, declared that mushrooms were fungi and that judges could not make them vegetables; therefore, mushroom workers were not agricultural workers, and they should receive minimum wage like most other workers in the province. The other two judges looked more to the context of the law and decided that because mushrooms were similar to the other agricultural products listed in the legislation, it was to be assumed that the government would want mushroom workers to be exempt from receiving minimum wage (see Waddams 1987, 120–1).

The *Ontario Mushroom Co.* case illustrates that when judges are asked to adjudicate disputes, it is often unavoidable that they shape law and policy as a by-product of interpreting how the law applies to a particular situation (sometimes referred to as 'interstitial' rule making). In this instance, the minimum-wage rules were clarified by extending the exemptions to include mushroom workers. In other cases, judges have adapted rules incrementally to suit new situations created by social, economic, or technological change. Judges can also go beyond internal clarification or incremental changes to law and policy when making their decisions and engage more fully in creating rules or policy. This is true in non-constitutional law (tort law, contract law, criminal law, administrative law, and so on), but the potential for creating rules is greater in constitutional cases, when judges are asked to rule whether ordinary laws conform to the constitution. Imagine, for example, if the case were to take place in the Charter era. The mushroom workers (and maybe all agricultural workers) would very likely challenge the law for violating their rights to equality (s. 15 of the Charter) and perhaps also for threatening their 'security of the person' (s. 7 of the Charter). Because the case had the potential to shape labour policy, it is likely that other governments and organized groups (such as labour unions and business associations) would ask for permission to intervene in the case. Both sides of the case would probably supply social-fact evidence to the court about such matters as the socio-economic realities of farm workers and what impact minimum wage laws would have on farms, especially family farms. With various groups appearing before the court presenting social facts, the court would resemble more a legislative committee meeting (used in provincial legislatures or the federal Parliament to make recommendations about policy objectives and the best way of achieving those objectives) than a traditional adjudicative court that hears concrete legal disputes between two parties on the basis of historical facts.

However, even if the court took more of a policy-making approach by allowing interveners and using social facts (and perhaps allowing the case to be brought by a party not directly affected by the law), the judges hearing the case would still have choices about how to interpret the Charter rights and whether the rights claimant or the government would win. If the court decided in favour of the rights claimant, it would have to decide on a remedy, such as striking down the law or reading into the law a minimum wage for agricultural workers. This kind of decision would see the judges actively shaping public policy.

It turns out that a Charter of Rights case similar to the one just described was launched by agricultural workers in Ontario after the newly elected Conservative government in 1995 repealed a piece of legislation that had extended trade union and collective bargaining rights to agricultural workers in the province. Some individual workers, including Tom Dunmore, on behalf of themselves and the United Food and Commercial Workers International Union, argued in court that the policy violated their right to freedom of association (found in s. 2(d) of the Charter) and their right to equality (found in s. 15 of the Charter). When the

Dunmore case reached the Supreme Court, the Canadian Labour Congress and the provinces of Quebec and Alberta were allowed to intervene. Numerous studies containing social facts were referred to by the Court, such as a 'Profile on Ontario Farm Labour' and reports from Ontario's Task Force on Agricultural Labour Relations. The majority decided that the s. 2(d) rights of Dunmore and others were violated. In support of this conclusion, Justice Bastarache argued that in the absence of protective legislation, no agricultural workers' union could be formed in Ontario and, moreover, 'agricultural workers had suffered repeated attacks on their attempts to unionize' (at para. 42). According to Justice Bastarache, statistics from other provinces showed higher rates of unionization amongst agricultural workers in provinces that included agricultural workers in a regime of labour-relations rights (at para. 42).

After finding that s. 2(d) was violated, Justice Bastarache discussed whether the law could be justified under the s. 1 'reasonable limits' clause of the Charter. In this case, he found that the government did have important objectives behind the law, mainly to protect family farms in Ontario and more generally to protect the economic viability of the agricultural industry in Ontario—an industry that was volatile and competitive. However, Justice Bastarche found that the means used to achieve those objectives—removing agricultural workers from the protection of the *Labour Relations Act*—were not proportional to meeting those objectives. He argued that it seemed arbitrary to exclude one group of workers from labour-law protection for economic purposes given that many other industries also faced competitive markets, especially in a globalized economy. He also maintained that in denying every aspect of the right of association in every sector of agriculture, the government had not tried sufficiently to tailor the means to achieve their objectives while limiting the right to association as little as reasonably possible. Among other things, the government failed, in Justice Bastarache's view, to consider adequately that the agricultural industry was changing rapidly in Ontario with more corporate farming and more complex agri-businesses—even the 'family farm' was becoming a sophisticated and rather large business enterprise.

As for the remedy, Justice Bastarche decided to strike down the clause of the law that excluded agricultural workers from all aspects of labour-relations protection. However he noted that the government did not necessarily have to extend all collective bargaining rights to agricultural workers. At a minimum the statutory freedom to organize ought to be extended to agricultural workers, 'along with protections judged essential to its meaningful exercise, such as freedom to assemble, to participate in the lawful activities of the association and to make representations, and the right to be free from interference, coercion and discrimination in the exercise of these freedoms' (at para. 67). He gave the government eighteen months to change the law. This decision would be characterized as an *activist* one in that it required the government to alter its policy, even though the new policy did not necessarily have to give agricultural workers as many rights as they would have desired. The decision added to the debate about the degree to which courts should be deferential to government policy when making Charter decisions. In this case the government of Ontario had urged the Court to be sensitive to the fact that excluding a given occupation from the *Labour Relations Act* 'involves a weighing of complex values and policy considerations that are often difficult to balance' and that how the value and policy considerations are balanced 'will in large part depend upon the particular perspective, priorities, views, and assumptions of the policy-makers, as well as the political and economic theory to which they subscribe' (quoted by Bastarache at para. 57). Although Justice Bastarache generally agreed with this observation, he concluded nevertheless that judicial deference to government policy was not justified in this case. Critics of judicial activism have mentioned the decision has an example of policy-making by unaccountable judges (Seeman 2003).

The Conservative government responded to the *Dunmore* decision by introducing the *Agricultural Employees Protection Act* (AEPA) in 2002. The legislation allowed agricultural workers in Ontario to form associations, but not unions, and they were not given collective-bargaining rights. Agricultural workers' associations could take their complaints to their employer, but the employer was not required to reply. Not satisfied with the legislative response, the United Food and Commercial Workers (UFCW) Canada union argued that the new legislation did not fulfill the changes to the law required by the Supreme Court in *Dunmore*. It launched a Charter challenge against the new law. In January 2006, an Ontario trial judge ruled against the union, stating that the law fulfilled the minimal requirements of the Charter (*Fraser v. Ontario* 2006). The UFCW Canada has appealed the decision to the Ontario Court of Appeal and is hopeful that it will succeed in light of a 2007 Supreme Court judgment that interpreted s. 2(d) of the Charter to include a procedural right (at least for public sector employees) to bargain collectively (see *Health Services and Support — Facilities Subsector Bargaining Assn v. British Columbia* 2007). After this most recent Supreme Court decision, the president of the UFCW Canada (Local 175) called on the Liberal government of Dalton McGuinty to change the law restricting agricultural workers from unionizing and bargaining collectively.[1]

The Dunmore case and its aftermath illustrate various dimensions of the courts and policy-making that will be explored in the chapter. The case is an example of the propensity of courts, especially the Supreme Court, to adopt a policy-making model. As discussed in Chapter 3, this includes a greater willingness to relax the rules concerning standing, mootness, and political questions; to allow interveners; to use social facts; and to shape the law. The next section of the chapter focuses on the judicial law-making aspect of the policy-making model by asking two questions: how much do courts shape laws when making decisions, and should courts actively shape law and policy? The chapter examines these empirical and normative issues in both non-constitutional and constitutional contexts. Particular attention is paid, however, to the relationship between courts and legislatures in the era of the Charter of Rights. Has the Charter resulted in 'judicial supremacy' whereby 'activist' courts determine the meaning of the Charter and make policy, or has the Charter resulted in a healthy system of institutional checks and balances by facilitating a 'dialogue' between courts and elected officials over the meaning and application of rights?

The *Dunmore* decision and its aftermath also underscore how the policy and longer-term social impact of legal mobilization and judicial decisions depends on numerous factors and can be difficult to predict. The third section of the chapter discusses various factors that have been found to help explain how judicial decisions affect policy; those factors include the attitudes of government officials that are responsible for implementing the decision and the reactions of interest groups, the media, the public, and lower courts to decisions. This section of the chapter also notes that the long-term influence of the law and judicial decisions on social, economic, and political activists is very difficult to predict but may not matter as much as is popularly believed. For example, it may be that the socio-economic conditions of agricultural workers will be influenced far more by long-term changes in the agricultural sector, including the trends toward corporate farming and globalization, than by changes to labour laws.

The concluding section of the chapter begins by exploring some of the theories that have been advanced for explaining the rise of judicial policy-making in Canada and elsewhere. The chapter ends with a discussion of how the changing role of the judiciary, towards more of a policy-making model, poses challenges for the judicial and political systems and their relationship to one another. This is done with specific reference to issues and concepts covered earlier in the book, such as judicial selection and independence.

Courts and Policy-Making

Answering the question about *what judges do*—do they simply declare what the law is, do they incrementally create law in interpreting and applying the law, or do they play a relatively greater role in law-making—is extremely difficult given the sheer number of decisions that are made and the fact that the results may depend on the type of court (trial, appeal, or highest court), the historical time period, the type of law, and individual judges. Although some systematic attempts have been made to get at this question through surveys of judges or statistical analyses of case outcomes, these studies are limited by court, time frame, type of law, and so on, so we often need to resort to looking at broad trends and various individual cases to get some sense of what judges do.

Assessing the question of *what judges should do* is perhaps even more vexing. This is because the question involves various value judgments and assessments about the theory and practice of liberal-democratic governance. Whereas the adjudicative model of courts emphasizes that the judicial development of law should be limited and incremental and be based on existing legal principles in order to be legitimate, the policy-making model of courts is more comfortable with judges basing their decisions on promoting fairness, balancing interests, and keeping the law 'in tune with the times' (perhaps with aid of social facts) with less emphasis on the application of existing legal principles. Therefore, the policy-making model envisions a more prominent role for the courts in shaping policy with less deference to the legislative and executive branches. Which of these models is considered more appropriate may depend somewhat on what level or type of court is being discussed and how judges are appointed or held accountable. It may also depend on the type of case at issue. In looking at what judges do and what they should do in this section, we separate the discussion by non-constitutional and constitutional cases. We begin with the former.

Non-constitutional Cases

In order to explore questions about judicial policy-making in non-constitutional cases, it is helpful to put them in historical perspective. As explained in Chapter 1, common law courts in England had an important role in creating rules—the common law—that governed various aspects of life beginning in about the twelfth century. The notion that the common law was found in judicial decisions was not terribly controversial at first. Early in the history of the common law, judges were said to be simply applying the rules contained in local customs, so they were not 'creating' law per se. When judges started applying common law precedents across Britain, thereby centralizing law-making in the King's courts and relying less on local customs as a source of law, the rationale behind development of the common law changed. Lord Blackstone, in his famous *Commentaries* on the common law, claimed that judges only acted as 'oracles' who declared pre-existing rules grounded in reason about such things as the nature of marriage, contractual obligations, and the power of sheriffs to search citizens—they did not create common law principles. The notion that common law rules existed 'in the sky' to be 'discovered' by judges, rather than being fashioned by judges based on experience and social contexts, was rejected by some, however (Posner 1976).[2]

One of Blackstone's fiercest critics, Jeremy Bentham, favoured Parliament as the chief law-maker. He argued that laws should be 'codified' in legislation rather than found in various common law precedents (Posner 1976). Advocates for codification suggested that judges who made decisions on a case-by-case basis could easily avoid following established precedent by distinguishing the present case from past ones (see Chapter 4); in other words, they could not only usurp legislative power but could also make their decisions according to their personal biases. It was claimed that legislatures were better positioned to represent the views of the population and to create general rules (Scalia 1997). Blackstone, though, was skeptical about the ability of legislatures to develop a comprehensive set of rules. While he acknowledged that laws in statute form would trump common law if the two conflicted, he thought it would be better if Parliament were to develop statutes to fill in the gaps in the common law rather than create an exhaustive set of laws (Posner 1976). Other opponents of codification suggested that law-making by judges trained in the law was an important bulwark against legislative bodies that might respond to the whims of the masses when making decisions (Scalia 1997).

Over time, and especially since the early twentieth century, legislation has become the most important source of legal rules in Canada and other advanced democracies (Bogart 2002, 28–9; Yates et al. 2000, 35–40). Recall from Chapter 9, for instance, that crimes in Canada are no longer defined by the common law but are found in federal statutes like the *Criminal Code* and the *Controlled Drugs and Substances Act*. The accelerated growth of legislation and regulations coincided with the rise of the administrative state, in which legislatures delegated rule-making and adjudicative powers to various administrative agencies, such as the Immigration and Refugee Board, the Canadian Radio-Telecommunications Commission (CRTC), the Nova Scotia Labour Relations Board, and the Alberta Utilities Commission. Although outside of Quebec common law rules remain a significant source of law (especially in private law matters such as family law, contract law, and tort law), does the prominence of legislation and regulations in forming law and policy mean that courts have relatively less policy-making influence than in the past (setting aside for now the power of courts to strike down laws under the constitution)? Possibly, but courts still shape law and policy in four important ways in non-constitutional cases.

First, courts perform a policy-making function in overseeing decisions made by administrative tribunals. As noted in Chapter 3, courts review the procedural aspects of administrative tribunal decision making (such as whether the tribunal followed the requirements of procedural fairness and so on) and assess the substantive decisions that tribunals make. Chapter 3 also noted, however, that the scope of this review and how carefully the courts scrutinize decisions by administrative tribunal depends on a host of factors. These include whether the administrative tribunal's enabling statute (the law that created the agency and set out its authority) contains a privative clause (which prohibits judicial review of the board's procedures) or allows for appeals of the tribunal's substantive decisions to a court; the expertise of the tribunal relative to the courts; and the nature of the dispute.[3] The recent trend has been for courts to be somewhat deferential to decisions made by administrative tribunals, and this trend continued in the *Council of Canadians with Disabilities* (2007) ruling in which the Supreme Court narrowly (5–4) upheld an order by the Canadian Transportation Agency that required VIA Rail to modify more of its rail cars to accommodate passengers with disabilities, particularly those in wheelchairs.[4]

Despite this trend, though, courts still play a meaningful policy-making role in reviewing decisions by administrative agencies. Even some decisions that uphold administrative decisions contain seeds of judicial policy-making. For example, in its 2001 *Hudson* decision all nine Supreme Court judges said that the town of Hudson, Quebec, was within its authority to create a by-law banning the use of pesticides for aesthetic purposes; however, the majority based its decision in part on international agreements and statements that promoted the 'precautionary principle', which states that governments must anticipate and prevent environmental degradation. A lawyer specializing in administrative law argued that the decision would stoke the debate about judicial activism because the majority endorsed a particular view of environmental policy and seemingly set a precedent that principles of international law should be incorporated into Canadian administrative law (Bantey 2001).[5] And, of course, courts do not always accept the substantive decisions of administrative actors. Recently, for instance, the Federal Court of Appeal set aside a decision of the Immigration Appeal Division of the Immigration and Refugee Board that had denied an application by Sukhvir Singh Khosa to remain in Canada on humanitarian and compassionate grounds (*Khosa* 2007). Finally, even if judges review only the procedural aspects of administrative tribunal decision making rather than the substance, this can still have important policy implications (Tarr 2006, 286–7). An example of this was provided in Chapter 3, which described how the Supreme Court's *Singh* (1985) decision required the federal government to overhaul its refugee determination system, a decision that proved very costly and contributed to a growing backlog of refugee claimants.

The second way that courts have a policy-making role in non-constitutional cases is cumulatively. The decisions that judges make in 'routine' cases when applying legislative or common law rules, which often leave room for discretion, can forge policy in the aggregate (Tarr 2006, 289). In criminal law, for example, owing to the sentencing discretion that judges have (see Chapter 9), the sentences that judges hand out over time will establish a certain range of punishment that will usually be given for particular crimes. Changes in those patterns can signal a change in judicial policy. In British Columbia, for instance, the number of people going to jail after being convicted for growing marijuana declined from 19 to 10 per cent from 1997 to 2003 (Skelton 2005).[6] In family law, judges are often instructed in legislation to make decisions about child custody and other issues based on 'the best interests of the child'. It is mostly up to judges to fill in what the 'best interests of the child' are over successive decisions.[7] For instance, court-ordered child custody awards still tend to support the mother's claims in a majority of cases, but the number of joint-custody awards has been growing over the last couple of decades. Appellate courts help to set general guidelines for criminal sentences, child custody arrangements, and a host of other issues, but the sheer number of cases decided by trial court judges, combined with the relative infrequency of appeals, means that trial court judges also have an important part in making policy in the aggregate.

A third and related way in which judges shape policies is through clarifying the law or filling in the gaps of law when applying common law precedents or legislation to specific cases. This task is necessitated by poorly drafted legislation or because rules (in legislation or common law) cannot be written so precisely as to cover every possible situation that may give rise to a legal dispute. In such cases where the law is not clear, judges must make the rules, at least interstitially, no matter what method of statutory interpretation they use or how they use precedents (see Chapter 4). The case of the mushroom workers wanting minimum wage was an example of this kind of policy-making. Many others abound. Here are a few recent examples from the Supreme Court:

a) In *Childs v. Desormeaux* (2006), the Court had to decide whether, under common law rules of tort, persons who hosted a party are liable for damages caused by one of their guests who drove away from the party impaired. A unanimous Court declared that, unlike commercial bar owners, social hosts generally did not owe a duty of care to a person injured by one of their guests who had drunk alcohol.

b) In *Amateur Youth Soccer Association* (2007), the Court had to determine if a regional youth soccer association qualified as a 'charitable organization' for the purposes of the *Income Tax Act*. The Court decided that it did not because its purpose and activities were not centrally 'charitable' in nature.

c) In *Lumbermens Mutual Casualty Co.* (2007), the Court was asked to rule on whether automobile insurance policies that provide coverage for damage 'directly or indirectly' related to the operation of a motor vehicle would cover injuries in the following circumstance: a person was shot in the woods by a hunter who stopped his truck on the way to a hunting party and shot at what he thought was a deer that appeared in the headlights (ironically, the 'deer' turned out to be a fellow member of the hunting party). The Court ruled that the term 'indirectly' in the *Ontario Insurance Act* did not stretch so far as to cover incidents in which the use of a vehicle was only incidental to the real cause of the damages—in this case, negligently firing a gun at a target that was not clearly seen.

Each of these decisions could have important policy consequences. The *Lumbermens* decision, for instance, will likely help insurance companies avoid paying out more auto insurance claims, a decision which may save auto insurance customers money. However, it may leave victims in these kinds of cases unable to pay for all of their medical expenses. It is assumed that appellate courts, in their capacity of providing leadership on unsettled questions of law, will generally have a larger part than trial courts in this kind of policy-making.

The final way in which judges can make policy is to deviate from applying legal rules that are laid out fairly clearly in common law precedents or legislation. This is the most controversial method of judicial policy-making. The Supreme Court's decision in *Harrison v. Carswell* (1976) featured a famous debate between Chief Justice Laskin and Justice Dickson about whether it was appropriate for judges to engage in this kind of law-making (see Sharpe and Roach 2003, 148–52). Sophie Carswell had appealed a $40 fine that she received under the *Manitoba Trespass Act*, which essentially enshrined well-established common law rules about trespass into a piece of legislation. Carswell had been fined under the Act for picketing a Dominion grocery store in a mall in Winnipeg as part of a strike action. Chief Justice Bora Laskin argued that the case raised two important questions: 'whether this Court must pay mechanical deference to *stare decisis* [ruling according to precedent] and, second, whether this Court has a balancing role to play, without yielding place to the Legislature, where an ancient doctrine, in this case trespass, is invoked in a setting to suppress a lawful activity [picketing] supported by both legislation and by a well-understood legislative policy [labour legislation and policy]. . . .' Laskin answered those questions from a policy-making perspective. He suggested that the Court should recognize the new social reality of shopping malls that issued an open invitation to the public. He argued that allowing labour picketing at a mall, an otherwise lawful activity, while still allowing removal of people for misbehaviour would best reconcile the interests of the shopping mall owner and the public (including labour interests). Laskin urged his colleagues not to mechanically apply a precedent that upheld a trespass conviction for a consumer who was picketing a Safeway store in a shopping centre in an effort to boycott California grapes, because the present case involved a labour strike.

Justice Dickson, who would later become Chief Justice, disagreed with Laskin and wrote for the majority to uphold the conviction. Dickson argued from the adjudicatory perspective:

> The submission that this Court should weigh and determine the respective values to society of the right to property and the right to picket raises important and difficult political and socio-economic issues, the resolution of which must, by their very nature, be arbitrary and embody personal economic and social beliefs. It also raises fundamental questions as to the role of this Court under the Canadian constitution. The duty of the Court, as I envisage it, is to proceed in the discharge of its adjudicative function in a reasoned way from principled decision and established concepts.

Dickson acknowledged that judges 'do and must legislate' but must only do so interstitially and on the basis of existing legal principles. In this case, Dickson argued that the *Manitoba Trespass Act* clearly gave the shopping centre manager the legal right to ask Carswell to leave. Any change in the rules, to balance differently the interests of shopping centre management, the public, and labour should be made by 'the Legislature, which is representative of the people and designed to manifest the political will, and not by the Court'.[8]

The debate over the proper role of courts, even in non-constitutional cases, remains a passionate one. A recent example of this comes from a case revolving around the question of whether a child can have more than two legally recognized parents. The controversy is outlined in Box 11.1

Box 11.1   Can a child have more than two parents?

In 1999, two lesbian women, A.A. and C.C., who wanted to start a family, did so with the help of a male friend, B.B. B.B. and C.C. were recognized as the biological parents of a little boy (D.D.). In 2003, with the support of the biological mother and father, A.A. filed an application under Ontario's *Children's Law Reform Act* (*CLRA*) to be declared a legal parent of D.D. (The two women could not file a request to adopt D.D. without eliminating the father as one of the parents, something that they did not want to do.) Legal recognition under the *CLRA* would entitle A.A. to the full rights and obligations of parents under the law, including the right to apply for legal documents for the child (such as a passport) and to register the child in schools. The trial judge expressed sympathy for the application, noting that A.A. was already fully committed to the parental role and that the child, who appeared to be 'thriving in a loving family', referred to A.A. as one of his mothers (*A.A. v. B.B.* 2003 at para. 5). However, the trial judge argued that the *CLRA* was very clear that a child could have only two legal parents. He asked, 'If a child can have three parents, why not four or six or a dozen? What about all the adults in a commune or a religious organization or sect?' (at para. 41). In a nod to the adjudicatory approach to decision making, he added: 'Polarized views exist concerning the definition of the modern family. Court decisions may sometimes necessarily impact on that debate. . . . However, when it comes to creating or shaping social policy, political considerations belong to the legislature' (at para 42).

The case was appealed to the Ontario Court of Appeal. Intervener groups were allowed to argue for and against the application given its potential policy repercussions. In a unanimous (3–0) decision, the Ontario Court of Appeal overturned the trial judge's decision and decided to grant the application, thereby effectively allowing a child in Ontario to have (at least) three legal parents. The Court argued that there was a 'gap' in the legislation. The judges observed that the *CLRA* was progressive legislation, but it was 'a product of its time'. According to the Court, the law was intended to improve the equality of status of children who had suffered the stigma of being born 'illegitimately', but 'the possibility of legally and socially recognized same-sex unions and the implications of advances in reproductive technology were not on the radar screen. The Act does not deal with, nor contemplate, the disadvantages that a child born into a relationship of two mothers, two fathers or as in this case two mothers and one father might suffer' (at para. 21). Because of this gap that it identified in the law, the court argued that it was justified in using its *parens patriae* jurisdiction to make an order that would further the 'best interests of the child'.

Reactions to the decision were quite polarized. Joseph Ben-Ami, the executive director of the Institute for Canadian Values, described the decision as 'naked judicial activism'. He argued that '[a]ll areas of social policy that the court are not competent to rule on belong in the hands of legislatures and legislators who are responsible and fully accountable to the people who are electing them' (quoted in Hanes 2007). Conversely, Kaj Hasselriis, executive director of the same-sex rights group EGALE, applauded the ruling for recognizing the legal rights and obligations of various types of modern-day family structures, including those involving gays and lesbians. 'This [decision] just demonstrates that the courts are catching up with reality in Canada,' he said (quoted in Hanes 2007).

Of course, there is not always a clear line separating an appropriate incremental change to the law to keep it abreast of new social or technological developments, and more wholesale creation of rules by judges, which is often considered to be outside the boundaries of the judicial function. Court watchers and judges themselves will sometimes disagree over this question even in the context of the same case.[9] Distinguishing between what is an incremental or more significant change to the law is part of the larger difficulty in assessing how much judges mostly interpret and apply the law as opposed to making it. Although systematic empirical studies are lacking, those who have carefully observed judicial decision making in Canada over time claim that Canadian courts tended to be closer to the adjudicatory model—interpreting and applying the law with only incremental changes—before Bora Laskin's appointment of Chief Justice of the Canadian Supreme Court in the 1970s (see his opinion in *Harrison v. Carswell* above, for example) and the introduction of the Charter of Rights and Freedoms in 1982 (Russell 1987, Chap. 14). As pointed out below, most commentators agree that the Charter has moved the courts at least somewhat closer to the policy-making model. One appellate court judge claims that his colleagues are now also more prone to changing the common law since the introduction of the Charter (Greene et al. 1998, 186).

However, for a couple of reasons, non-constitutional decisions often do not generate the same sustained intense debate over legitimacy as do constitutional decisions, especially Charter ones. First, in some areas of non-constitutional law legislators appear to deliberately leave room for copious amounts of judicial discretion and policy-making, such as in criminal sentencing and family law. Second, if a legislative body does not agree with a policy created by judges in a non-constitutional decision, then it has the option of passing a law to usher in its preferred rules. Parliament or provincial legislatures do not necessarily have the same ability simply to override the courts in federalism or Charter cases given that the courts are making a decision based on the supreme law of the land.

Constitutional Cases

From 1867 onward, courts were empowered to strike down laws for violating the federal–provincial division of powers set out principally in sections 91 and 92 of the *Constitution Act, 1867* (formerly the *British North America (BNA) Act, 1867*).[10] However, it was not until the Charter of Rights was added to the constitution in 1982 that judges were given clear legal authority to declare laws to be in violation of the constitution or to provide other remedies for violations of rights. Before that, judges generally did not believe that the 1960 Bill of Rights—an ordinary piece of legislation that applied only to the federal government—gave them the power to strike down laws. The notion that the there was an 'implied Bill of Rights' in the *Constitution Act, 1867* that allowed judges to strike down laws did not obtain the support of a majority of Supreme Court justices until the 1997 *Remuneration Reference* (see Chapter 6).

Charter of Rights decisions tend to have more potential to influence policy because, under the Charter, courts have the ability to declare that laws are unconstitutional even if those laws were passed within the proper jurisdiction according to the federal–provincial division of powers. In federalism cases, if a court rules that a law passed by a provincial legislature or the federal Parliament is outside of the jurisdiction allotted by the *Constitution Act, 1867*, then in theory the government that does have jurisdiction (federal or provincial) could legally pass the identical law.

However, as noted in the next section of this chapter, federalism decisions can influence policy indirectly by constraining government options and distributing power between the federal and provincial governments. And, when the Supreme Court has decided questions involving federalism and constitutional change, it has rather directly implicated itself in constitutional policy-making. For example, in its 1998 *Quebec Secession Reference* decision the Court argued that, although Quebec does not have the legal authority under the Canadian constitution or international law to secede unilaterally, the federal government would be obligated to negotiate with Quebec if a clear majority voted in favour of secession on the basis of a clear question. The Court based its reasoning on the key 'principles' of Canadian constitutionalism: federalism, democracy, constitutionalism and the rule of law, and respect for minorities. Some commentators were surprised that the Court decided to rule on the case, because it raised such political questions and that it did so based significantly on its own estimation of key constitutional 'principles' rather than 'law'.[11] Similar reactions were given to the Court's famous 1981 *Patriation Reference* decision. The Court claimed that the federal government legally could patriate the Constitution unilaterally (without provincial consent); to do so, however, without majority support from the provinces would violate constitutional conventions. Peter Russell (1983) described the decision as 'bold statescraft, questionable jurisprudence'. He called it 'questionable jurisprudence' because the judges gave legal weight to a particular interpretation of contested constitutional conventions (about how much, if any, provincial consent was needed) and was not logically consistent as a whole, but 'bold statescraft' because it did provide an impetus for the provinces and federal government to go back to the negotiating table—the result was a series of constitutional changes made in the early 1980s that resulted in the entrenchment of the Charter of Rights.

The Charter of Rights

Commentators believed that the Charter of Rights would allow for a greater policy-making role for judges because it empowered them to review the constitutionality of provincial or federal government laws even if those laws were in accordance with the federal–provincial division of powers. How actively involved the Supreme Court and lower courts would be in shaping policy, though, depended on a number of factors: how easy would it be for individuals and organizations to make a Charter claim in court, how broadly would the courts define the rights contained in the Charter, which side (the rights claimant or the government) would have the bulk of the burden of proof in Charter cases, would the Charter apply to common law as well as legislation, and what kind of remedies would the courts provide for rights claimants whose rights have been violated? In looking at these factors more closely we concentrate on the Supreme Court, because its decisions are legally binding on lower courts across Canada and its Charter decisions have been analyzed much more thoroughly than other courts. Figure 11.1 illustrates the Charter process.

Making a Charter Claim   As shown in Figure 11.1 the first step in the Charter process is to claim that a law (such as the Criminal Code) or action by a state official (such as the actions of the police during an investigation) violates one or more of the rights in the Charter. As noted in Chapters 3 and 7, the Supreme Court has relaxed the rules of standing and mootness so that there are lower procedural barriers to getting into court. Chapter 3 also pointed out that the Supreme Court largely has rejected the doctrine that some issues are so inherently 'political' that they cannot be adjudicated under the Charter (*Operation Dismantle* 1985). The Court has also interpreted s. 32 of the Charter—the section that states that the Charter applies to the Parliament and government of Canada (and the territories) and the legislature and government of each province—somewhat flexibly (if not entirely clearly and consistently), thereby expanding somewhat the scope for judicial review under the Charter. In addition to laws and regulations, the decisions of an individual or organization operating under statutory authority, such as a school

Figure 11.1   Charter of Rights Process

1) Individual, group or corporation claims that a government law or action has violated one or more Charter rights.

2) Does the rights claimant meet procedural requirements for having a court hear and decide their particular Charter grievance?
- Does the case involve a purely political, rather than legal, dispute?
- Does the rights claimant have standing to initiate the case?
- Does the case involve a live legal dispute or is it moot?
- Does the Charter of Rights apply? The Charter can only be used against the 'state'—it cannot be used against non-state entities, such as churches, businesses, or groups.

If NO, case dismissed (rights claimant loses)

3) The judge(s) must define the particular Charter right and determine whether a law or action by a state official (such as a police officer or border guard) violates that right. For example:
- Is the right to 'freedom of expression' violated by a law that makes it a criminal offence to possess child pornography?
- Is the right to 'liberty' violated by a law that prohibits doctor-assisted suicide?
- Is the right against 'unreasonable search and seizure' violated by police using infrared radar to look for a grow-op in a house without a warrant?
- Is the right to 'equality' violated if a government does not offer sign language interpretation at a hospital facility?

If NO, rights claimant loses

3(a) If a law violates a Charter right, the judge(s) must determine if it is a 'reasonable limit' under section 1 of the Charter. See Box 11.2 for a discussion of the test judges use to determine if a law should be upheld under section 1.

If law is upheld under s. 1, then rights claimant loses

4) Rights claimant wins and a remedy may be provided by the judge(s). Some remedies include:
- declaration that the law is invlaid under the Charter
- 'reading in' to the law to fix the law's defect

4) Rights claimant wins and a remedy may be provided by the judge(s). For actions of the police (or other state agents), evidence collected in violation of constitutional rules may be excluded from use at trial if 'having regard to all the circumstances' its admission at trial would 'bring the administration of justice into disrepute' (section 24(2) of the Charter).

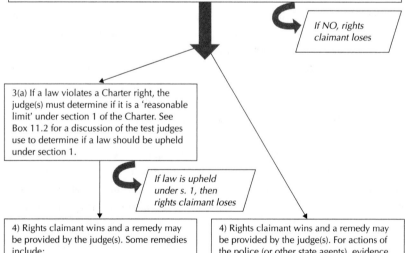

board or a labour arbitrator, will be subject to Charter scrutiny.[12] The Charter applies to the common law in the context of criminal law but not in the context of purely private litigation; however, court orders concerning criminal or private litigation (such as an order preventing a union from picketing a court house) may incur Charter scrutiny.[13] If a 'para-public' institution, such as a university or hospital, is acting to implement government policy (for example, by providing health-care services) the Charter will apply, though the Charter was held not to apply when such organizations were engaged in contractual activities (for example, creating employment contracts with doctors that contained a mandatory retirement clause).[14] This potentially murky distinction between private and public activity on the part of government or quasi-government (para-public) agencies was blurred further when Justice LaForest contended in a 1991 case (*Lavigne*) that the contemporary reality was that governments often pursued policy objectives through commercial or private transactions and that as expressions of policy such activities should be subject to the Charter (see MacIvor 2006, 20–4, for a discussion). The degree to which the Charter applies to Canadian government officials operating outside of Canada also remains a grey area (see Roach, forthcoming). Although the boundaries of the Charter's application are still somewhat in flux and some would prefer an expansion of these boundaries, the Court has been willing to hear Charter cases involving disputes beyond those that simply challenge a law or the actions of the police.

Defining Charter Rights   Even if the hurdles of getting a court to hear a Charter claim are overcome, however, the chances of a rights claimant winning a Charter case depend on how broadly courts are willing to interpret the rights in the Charter and whether the burden of proof in Charter cases rests more with the rights claimant or the government. It turns out that the Supreme Court has operationalized the Charter in ways that favour rights claimants. This, in turn, increases the possibility that courts will find in favour of the rights claimant and require changes to government policy.

Early its Charter jurisprudence, the Court said that Charter rights deserve a 'broad and purposive' or 'large and liberal' interpretation.[15] The Court has also tended to emphasize a 'living tree' approach to rights interpretation rather than relying on 'framers' intent' (see Chapter 4). For example, the Court has read in 'sexual orientation' to the list of prohibited grounds of discrimination in the s. 15 equality-rights provision. The right to 'liberty' in s. 7 of the Charter has been read relatively broadly to go beyond just freedom from physical restraint to include a certain degree of autonomy in making life choices. Furthermore, when a rights claimant invokes s. 7 to attack a law, the Court is willing to look at the substantive fairness and justice of the law rather than just whether the law has sufficient procedural safeguards (such as the ability to defend oneself in an impartial court for violating the law). In free speech cases like *Keegstra* (1990) and *Sharpe* (2001), the

Court argued that the right to free expression should include all expression (except for expression through violent actions), even hate speech and child pornography. And even though the aboriginal rights in s. 35 of the *Constitution Act, 1982* are technically not part of the Charter of Rights, the Court has read that section rather broadly and purposively such that historical government practices are not considered to have extinguished aboriginal fishing, hunting, or land rights (*Sparrow* 1990; *Delgamuukw* 1997).

There have been some exceptions, however, to the trend of the Supreme Court reading rights broadly. In the *Auton* (2004) decision, the Court took what some considered to be an overly narrow view of equality rights when it ruled that the British Columbia government did not violate s. 15 when declining to fund a therapeutic program for autistic children. The Court has also taken some of the built-in limitations on rights seriously. For instance, s. 7 allows government to limit the rights to 'life, liberty and security of the person' if those limits are 'in accordance with the principles of fundamental justice'. The Court has been hesitant to find that governments are acting outside the boundaries of 'the principles of fundamental justice' if they do not provide a certain level social welfare benefits (see *Gosselin* 2002).[16] In a s. 8 case involving the police taking infrared pictures of a home without a warrant to determine if there was a 'grow op' inside, the Court said that this was not an 'unreasonable' search and seizure under s. 8 of the Charter, because the homeowner did not have a reasonable expectation of privacy regarding heat waves emanating off of his home (*Tessling* 2004).

Overall, though, the Court has been much more willing to give expansive definitions to rights under the Charter than it did under the 1960 Bill of Rights.

Burden of Proof in Charter Cases and the s. 1 'Reasonable Limits' Clause
In addition to reading rights relatively broadly, the second way in which the Court has made it easier for rights claimants is by shifting the burden of proof to the government to justify that limits on rights are reasonable under s. 1 of the Charter, which states that the rights and freedoms set out in the Charter are subject 'to such reasonable limits prescribed by law as can be demonstrably justified in a free and democratic society'. Furthermore, in its *Oakes* (1986) decision, the Court set out a test that—on its face at least—made it relatively difficult for governments to justify limits on rights under s. 1. The Oakes test and the case that led to its creation are described in Box 11.2

Box 11.2   The s. 1 'Oakes' test

The 'Oakes' test was created in a case where David Edwin Oakes argued that the *Narcotics Control Act* violated the right to be presumed innocent in s.

11(d) of the Charter. The law stated that individuals who have been found to be possessing narcotics are presumed to have those drugs for the purposes of trafficking unless they could convince a judge otherwise. The Court found that the law violated s. 11(d) of the Charter. In doing so, the Court disagreed with the Court of Appeal's approach of using the s. 1 'reasonable limits' clause as a guide to interpreting s. 11(d). The Court maintained that the definition of rights should be analytically distinct from the reasonableness test under s. 1. Once the rights claimant has shown that a right is violated (a task made easier by not having built-in limitations), the Court maintained that the next step is for the government (or agency acting with government authority) to prove, on a balance of probabilities, that the law, including regulations and rules made under statutory authority, is reasonable under s. 1.

In *Oakes*, the Court established the test that would be used to determine whether the impugned 'law' was a reasonable limit demonstrably justified in a free and democratic society:

1) Does the law have a 'pressing and substantial' objective in a free and democratic society?

2) Does the law have means that are 'proportional' to meet that objective?
    a) are the means 'rationally connected' to the end?
    b) do the means impair the right as little as possible?
    c) are the effects of the measure (means) proportional to the objective (that is, are the costs to the individual rights claimants outweighed by the collective benefits of the legislation)?

In this case, the Court found that the law did have a pressing and substantial objective—to protect society against the 'grave ills' associated with drug trafficking. However, the Court argued that the means—assuming a person found in possession of illegal drugs is guilty of trafficking—were not proportional to the objective. In particular, the Court argued that under the law as written, even someone possessing a very small amount of drugs would be assumed to be a trafficker, and that was not a rational way to curb trafficking.

If applied strictly, the Oakes test makes it very difficult for government actors to justify limitations on rights. That the Court struck down the 'reverse onus' clause of the *Narcotics Control Act* challenged in *Oakes* is suggestive of its stringency. The test has not always been applied strictly, however. The 'minimal impairment' test was changed soon after *Oakes* such that the means would have to impair the rights 'as little as *reasonably* possible' (*Edwards Books* 1986). The test has been applied such that context has been taken into account in some cases, such as when the Court gave some latitude to the Quebec government by upholding a law under s. 1 that purported to protect children by prohibiting commercial advertising aimed at children under thirteen years of age (*Irwin Toy* 1989). The Court, though, has not been consistent in application of s. 1 (Manfredi 2001, 42). The Oakes test has been applied differently in different cases and by different judges in the same case.

Regardless of the inconsistencies in its use, the Oakes test, by requiring judges to evaluate the objectives and means of public policy, embroils judges in a 'quintessentially legislative task' (Monahan 1987, 53; see also Knopff and Morton 1992, 152–61). Even former Chief Justice Antonio Lamer acknowledged that under s. 1 judges are making 'essentially what used to be a political call' (quoted in Morton 2002, 368). This policy-making potential is fuelled by the need to examine and analyze social-fact data to some degree in the s. 1 analysis.[17]

An Example of a Charter Claim: The *Chaoulli* (2005) Decision   The policy-making potential given to courts by decisions that made it reasonably easy to get into court to argue a Charter claim, that defined rights broadly, and that called for analysis of the means and ends of policy under s. 1 was vividly displayed in the Supreme Court's *Chaoulli* (2005) decision. As discussed in Chapter 4, this decision also illustrates the discretion that judges have in deciding how to use this policy-making potential. The case arose from an appeal primarily concerning whether Quebec's policy of prohibiting private health-care insurance violated the right to 'life, liberty and security' in s. 7 of the Charter. The rights claimants were a man who had experienced delays receiving medical procedures, particularly hip operations, in the public health-care system (George Zeliotis) and a doctor who was not allowed to establish a private medical clinic (Jacques Chaoulli). Even though Zeliotis had already received the hip replacement surgery he was seeking, his action was not declared moot (Manfredi and Maioni, 2005). Moreover, all of the judges rejected suggestions that they should not hear the case because the claimants did not have standing (since they were no more personally affected by Quebec's policy than anyone else) and that the case involved such inherently political issues that it was not justiciable. In addition to allowing Zeliotis and Chaoulli to challenge the policy in the judicial arena, the Court allowed numerous interveners, including provincial governments, Senators, medical associations, anti-poverty groups, and private medical clinics.

By a 4–3 decision, the Court declared that Quebec's prohibition of private medical insurance violated rights. The three judges who voted to strike the law down under the Charter (one judge referred only to Quebec's human rights legislation to justify her decision to strike down the policy) argued that s. 7 allowed judges to look at the substantive fairness of the law (taking a 'living tree' approach to rights interpretation).[18] These judges argued that to deny at least some access to private health-care insurance in view of the waiting lists in the public health-care system was 'arbitrary', thereby restricting rights to 'security of the person' in ways that were not compatible with the 'principles of fundamental justice'. According to these judges, the violation of s. 7 could not be justified under the Oakes test. The judges argued that although preserving the public health-care system may be an important objective, a prohibition on private health-care insurance was not proportional in meeting those objectives. With reference to research reports on health care in countries with 'mixed' public and private health systems, these judges argued that some allowance for private medical care would not destroy the public system but would protect better the rights of citizens to 'security of the person'. The judges in the majority argued that courts must protect rights if governments failed to act.

Though the dissenting judges had agreed that the case should be heard, they were much more cautious about intervening in the complex field of health-care policy. According to the dissent, 'Designing, financing and operating the public health system of a modern democratic society remains a challenging task and calls for difficult choices. Shifting the design of the health system to the courts is not a wise outcome.' They argued that it was not possible to devise a legal standard for 'reasonable' access to health care that would be considered 'in accordance with the principles of fundamental justice' in s. 7 of the Charter. Moreover, the dissent pointed to the findings of the trial judge and the Romanow Report on health care that the public system could be gravely jeopardized by the addition of a private health-care sector.

The Quebec government requested an 18-month stay of the decision so that it could formulate and implement a health-care policy that responded to the Court's ruling. A 12-month stay was granted.

Remedies under the Charter

A 'declaration' that a law (or regulation or administrative order) violates the Constitution is only one of various remedies that courts can provide to successful rights claimants.[19] In certain circumstances judges may choose to 'read in' to the law or 'sever' part of a law rather than declare the entire law unconstitutional (see *Schachter*, 1992 and the discussion below on *Vriend*, 1998). More individualized remedies can be granted under s. 24(1) of the Charter, which gives courts the power to provide remedies that are 'appropriate and just in the circumstances'. Subsection 2 of s. 24 of the Charter gives judges the power to exclude evidence gathered unconstitutionally by the police and other state officials if allowing the evidence would 'bring the administration of justice into disrepute' (see Chapter 9).

The issue of remedies is important when one is analyzing how much courts do or should make policy because, even if a court rules in favour of the rights claimant, the remedy that is provided can involve courts more or less in creating policy. Take the controversy sparked by the Court's *Vriend* (1998) decision, for example. In *Vriend*, the Court found that because the Alberta government had not included sexual orientation as a prohibited grounds of discrimination in its human rights law, the law violated the Charter's guarantee of equality (in s. 15); instead of declaring the law invalid, however, the Court decided to 'read in' sexual orientation as a prohibited ground of discrimination to Alberta's *Individual's Rights Protection Act (IRPA)*. Critics accused the Court of being overly activist in *Vriend*. Not only did the Court find that the omission of government action (which had been deliberate) was unconstitutional, but it reformulated the law itself (Manfredi 2001). Justice Major dissented on the remedial aspect in *Vriend*, saying that it should be up to government to craft its response, which might even include a decision to scrap the entire law rather than include sexual orientation.

Clearly decisions about remedies raise larger questions about the role of the courts in the governance process and the relationship between the judicial, legislative, and executive branches of government. Over time the Court has tried to provide some guidance on their use in Charter cases. For example, the Court has said that judges should exercise particular caution before 'reading in' or otherwise altering legislation involving social welfare distribution. That does not preclude this kind of remedy, though, as demonstrated in *Tétreault-Gadoury* (1991), where the Court changed the *Unemployment Insurance Act* (as it was then called) to include workers over 65 who had qualified for benefits.[20] In *Doucet-Boudreau* (2003) the Court was very divided (5–4) about whether it was appropriate for the trial judge, after deciding that the claimants' Charter rights had been violated by the lack of progress on francophone schools that had been promised by the government and the school board, to order that government and school officials meet with him periodically to provide updates about the construction of francophone schools in the area. The majority supported the trial judge's decision to retain jurisdiction over the case and to require reporting. In doing so, the majority emphasized that the remedial powers in s. 24(1) require judges to be flexible and responsive in order to vindicate Charter rights. The majority argued that the rights in question—the official minority language education rights in s. 23—were remedial in nature and designed to address linguistic assimilation and a history of delay in providing francophone education. In this context the trial judge's order was appropriate and did not overstep the boundaries of judicial authority. The dissent, in contrast, argued that the trial judge's order violated the separation of powers between the judiciary, legislative, and executive branch. By undertaking to supervise the construction schedule for the French schools, the judge was performing the executive's function of public administration. Alternatives, such as relying on contempt-of-court proceedings if the schools were not built, would have been procedurally more fair to both parties and would be more in keeping with the role of courts in the system of governance.

Debates about Judicial Policy-Making under the Charter

The *Doucet-Boudreau* decision is one among many examples that highlights how Canadian courts are more prone to be activist than before the Charter. Statistical analyses confirm this trend. Under the statutory 1960 Bill of Rights, the rights claimant won, in the Supreme Court, 15 per cent of the time, which is less than half of the victory rate of approximately 33 per cent for rights claimants in Supreme Court Charter decisions. The Supreme Court struck down only one law under the 1960 Bill of Rights but had already invalidated over sixty laws under the Charter by 2003 (Kelly 2005). Half of all appellate court judges (and four of five Supreme Court judges) surveyed by Greene et al. believed that the Charter had moved them closer to the 'law-making' side of the continuum (the other side being 'law-interpreter') (Greene et al. 1998, 187–8).

While it is clear that judges have increased their policy-making in the Charter era, there is little consensus as to whether the rate of activism is proper and, more generally, whether the increased judicial policy-making under the Charter has been beneficial. Critics offered the following arguments for being skeptical about judicial policy-making under the Charter:

- The Charter and the way it has been operationalized (that is, by a broad definition of rights followed by the application of the Oakes test to legislation being challenged) encourages unelected and unaccountable judges to make decisions about policy matters more rightly reserved for elected politicians. Greater use of the s. 33 notwithstanding clause is encouraged. [21]

- Critics on the right argue that the Charter and judicial decisions have allowed post-materialist interest groups (such as feminists and 'equality'-seeking groups) to circumvent the regular political process to achieve their policy goals (Morton and Knopff 2000). Critics on the left argue that the Charter is most beneficial to those with existing socio-economic power (see Chapter 7 for a fuller treatment of these arguments) (Mandel 1994; Hutchinson 1995).

- Critics on both the left and right argue that the Charter and its expansive interpretation has 'politicized the judiciary' and 'legalized politics'. A related effect is the increased use of rights discourse, which has enervated the willingness and ability of citizens to engage in democratic discussion and compromise.

- Concerns have been raised about the 'institutional capacity' of courts, especially compared to other branches of government, to decide policy questions. Unlike the executive or legislative branches, which can rely on bureaucrats to study policy options or can invite parties to legislative hearings, judges mostly rely on legal arguments and any accompanying social-science evidence presented by the parties (and possibly interveners).

Policy analysis and the interpretation of social science generally are not a part of judicial expertise (see Box 3.1 in Chapter 3 for an example of how this lack of expertise had disastrous results in the *Askov* decision). And, even though courts have become more creative in creating remedies, they still lack the flexible powers accorded to the executive—courts cannot, for example, create a new administrative agency to help solve a social problem. Nor are courts well-equipped to monitor or follow the effects of their decisions. They must wait to hear subsequent cases that may or may not be representative of social or economic reality (Knopff and Morton 1992; Manfredi 2001).[22]

Supporters of a more active form of judicial review under the Charter have responded to these criticisms with a variety of arguments:

- The Charter was entrenched by elected politicians, and besides, litigation to protect rights and judicial policy-making existed before the Charter (Roach 2001). Some go farther to argue that the Charter was meant to upset the social status quo (Wienrib 1999) and have wished that the Supreme Court had gone further in some cases, especially those involving funding for social programs. There are misgivings about the s. 33 override clause in the Charter.
- Because judges do not have to worry about votes and make decisions on the basis of constitutional law, Charter review can inject an element of principled and reasoned decision making that may be lacking in the legislative and executive branches. A corollary of this observation is that Charter review can enhance liberal democracy by advancing the goals of protection of minority rights and social equality, especially for disadvantaged groups that may be marginalized in the traditional political process because they lack political power or popularity (Sigurdson 1993; Greene 2006).
- Critics of Charter review tend to have an overly simplistic or idealized view of democratic policy-making (Smith 2002a). The Canadian parliamentary system is dominated by the executive and is not very democratic. Governments often fail to act, thereby necessitating judicial action (Roach 2001); or politicians themselves sometimes use the courts to achieve policy goals (see Chapter 8). Furthermore, opinion polls suggest that the public prefers courts rather than politicians to make final decisions about rights (for data see Fletcher and Howe 2001).
- Similarly, when skeptics are critical of the policy-making capabilities of courts they may be comparing it to an idealized view of policy-making by other branches. There have been numerous examples of ill-conceived or poorly implemented policies that did not involve courts. And in modern states policy-making is already diffused (administrative

tribunals, public-private entities, and other organizations make policy).[23] Furthermore, changes to the judicial process, such as allowing more interveners and properly introducing social-fact evidence (including allowing it to be examined by both sides), can improve the policy-making capacity of courts.

Critics and others who were at least uneasy about the courts' exercise of power under the Charter were not persuaded, however. They argued that judges have ignored the limits on judicial power envisioned by the politicians who entrenched the Charter by downplaying the importance of the framers' intent.[24] A related argument is that while some judicial policy-making is inevitable, judicial policy-making under the Charter is quantitatively and qualitatively different from that in past eras. In response to the claim that Charter decisions are more principled, critics argue that most Charter cases are not about 'core' rights (such as whether individuals or groups should be allowed to distribute political pamphlets), but involve complex issues that require the balancing of various rights and social interests (such as whether individuals or groups should be allowed to distribute pamphlets that contain hate speech directed at certain groups) (Knopff and Morton 1992; Hiebert 2002). Reasonable people will disagree over how policy balances should be achieved owing to different policy assessments and political philosophies—this is why the Supreme Court is often so divided on controversial cases like the Keegstra case involving hate speech (where the vote was 4–3), the *Chaoulli* case involving private health care (4–3 vote) and others. Finally, Charter skeptics argue that if the political process is flawed, the solution should be to improve democratic input and strengthen the checks and balances within Parliament (such as by the reduction of party discipline or the introduction of an elected Senate) (Knopff 1998).

Relationship between Courts and Legislatures

The focus of the debate, which tended to be centred on the Court, shifted somewhat after an influential article by Peter Hogg and Allison Bushell (later Thornton) in 1997 that emphasized the relationship between the courts and other branches of government under the Charter. Hogg and Bushell argued that concerns over the undemocratic power of judicial review downplayed the capacity of elected officials 'to devise a response that is properly respectful of the Charter values that have been identified by the Court, but which accomplishes the social or economic objectives that the judicial decision has impeded' (1997, 79–80). The s. 1 'reasonable limits' clause, built-in limitations on other rights, and the s. 33 'notwithstanding' clause were identified as particularly important in facilitating dialogue. For example, Hogg and Thornton found that judges usually accepted the policy objectives of a law under the s. 1 Oakes test—most laws that failed the test did so because the judges concluded that there were other means available to achieve the objective that better respected rights. They also argued that if the legislature does not use the s. 33 notwithstanding clause after a controversial decision, such as *Vriend* (1998), then this suggests that there was strong support for the decision within the political community (Hogg, Thornton, and Wright 2007).

James Kelly (2005) also tried to assuage concerns that judges were dictating policy through Charter review by taking a more holistic view of the governance process. He argued that bureaucratic vetting of rights issues in the policy-development phase gave the executive branch an important role in defining rights and balancing rights with other social interests and objectives. More recently, Jeremy Clarke (2006) has drawn attention to a 'federalist dialogue' in which the Supreme Court is responding to provincial arguments in Charter cases that they deserve some policy latitude owing to the principle of federalism.

Though it has been accepted that the legislative and, particularly, the executive branches of government have an opportunity to influence the balancing of rights and interests by considering rights in the policy-development stage or by reversing, modifying, or avoiding the interpretation given to the Charter in a court decision (for examples, see below), serious disagreement has arisen as to how often and how much influence is really exerted by other branches and how desirable it is for them to do so (see Petter 2007a). One of the central complaints about Hogg and Thornton's model is that their definition of dialogue makes it appear as if elected branches have more influence over defining rights and shaping the balance between rights and other interests than they actually do. For instance, Hogg and Thornton's analysis has been criticized for counting virtually any response to a judicial decision as 'dialogue' even if the legislative branch simply enacted a law that incorporated judicial decisions almost verbatim. According to Manfredi and Kelly (1999), this is more like 'ventriloquism' than a genuine 'dialogue'. When counting only legislative responses that meaningfully differed from a judicial decision, such as the law that Parliament passed that eliminated the 'too drunk' defence created by the Supreme Court's reading of the Charter's legal rights in its *Daviault* decision (see Box 9.3 in Chapter 9), the number of cases considered to be dialogue under Hogg and Thornton's definition dropped considerably.[25] Commentators have also pointed out that the unpopularity of the s. 33 override clause, because of a misunderstanding amongst the public (and some elites) about its utility in Canada's constitutional scheme, diminishes greatly its potential for facilitating dialogue. It has also been asked whether Kelly's research demonstrates an independent role for government in shaping policy in the context of the Charter or whether it shows bureaucrats trying to anticipate how courts will rule on the law in a Charter case (Hennigar 2004, 16–17).

A related critique of the 'dialogue' model proposed by Hogg and Thornton was that it did not properly account for the possibility of 'policy distortion', whereby elected officials would refrain from introducing or passing legislation that might be constitutionally valid for fear of its being invalidated by the courts (Manfredi and Kelly 1999). Furthermore, from a policy-making perspective, it is not always easy to separate objectives from means in policy formation, nor is it as easy to find less restrictive means of achieving a policy goal as Hogg and Thornton and others suggest (Manfredi 2001). In the *Sharpe* (2001) case, for example, Justice L'Heureux-Dubé criticized her colleagues for reading in an exception to the child pornography law for works of the imagination created for personal use. Whereas the majority claimed that this exception would allow the government to achieve its goal of protecting children while impairing free expression rights to a lesser degree, L'Heureux-Dubé argued that Parliament's policy goals might be undermined since materials kept for personal use could fuel the fantasies of pedophiles.

Despite criticisms of the 'dialogue' metaphor, the Supreme Court and lower courts have referred to the concept in a number of decisions. Interestingly, sometimes the metaphor has been used to justify activism (on the premise that legislatures can respond to change a decision) and sometimes deference to legislative choices (Hogg, Thornton, and Wright 2007; Haigh and Sobkin 2007). An example of the latter is the Supreme Court's decision in *Mills* (1999) to uphold Parliament's legislation that strictly limited defence counsel's access to third-party medical and therapeutic records in sexual assault cases—the legislation closely followed the *dissenting* opinion in a previous Supreme Court decision on the subject (*O'Connor* 1995). The Supreme Court, however, is not always willing to be deferential to government in 'second-look' cases.[26] In *Sauvé II* (2002), a sharply divided Court struck down a federal law disenfranchising certain inmates even though the law disenfranchised only inmates convicted of an indictable offence whereas the previous law, which was struck down by the Court in 1993 (*Sauvé I*), had disqualified all prisoners from voting in federal elections. Not surprisingly, debates about the empirical and normative questions surrounding judicial policy-making, especially under the Charter, remain rather intractable (see the special 2007 edition of the *Osgoode Hall Law Journal* on the tenth anniversary of the dialogue model). Think back to the description of the *Dunmore* decision about the collective-bargaining rights of agricultural workers in Ontario in the introduction to the chapter. Is it an example of effective dialogue between the Ontario government and the courts that allowed the government to meet its objectives in a somewhat flexible manner while better respecting the right to freedom of assembly—a right that had been defined on the basis of an unbiased interpretation of the Charter by the Supreme Court? Or does it exemplify a legislature implementing what the Supreme Court asked for in a split decision in a complex policy area that depended on the political and economic perspectives of the judges—legislation that was upheld by a trial court because it conformed to what the Supreme Court wanted?

Policy Impact and Aftermath of Judicial Decisions

As indicated in the introduction, the labour union that supported Dunmore's case appealed the trial court's decision that upheld the new Ontario law giving minimal collective bargaining rights to agricultural workers; the union has also lobbied the government to improve the law. A recent decision by the Supreme Court favouring labour rights is being relied upon both in the legal and political arenas. What might happen as a result of this legal and political mobilization? Much of the literature on judicial policy-making in Canada, such as the dialogue literature, is less concerned with trying to explain or predict the effect on policy of legal mobilization and judicial decisions than with trying to determine how much power courts do have or should have vis-à-vis the other branches in making policy decisions.

Scholars in the US have been much more interested in studying the question of what actually happens after a judicial decision or series of decisions. Some of the literature in the US is concerned with legal decisions in private law, such as whether punitive awards for damages in tort litigation offer better protection for consumers or whether such awards inhibit innovation and unduly increase business costs. Other work has been done on the effects of litigation involving human rights legislation, as exemplified by McCann's study on legal mobilization by women's groups for pay equity (McCann 1994). However, constitutional rights decisions get the bulk of attention from scholars. We look at the debates in the US literature before reviewing briefly some of the few Canadian studies that have addressed these questions.

One of the most influential studies on judicial impact in the US remains Gerald Rosenberg's book *The Hollow Hope* (1991). As the title of the book suggests, Rosenberg was pessimistic about the ability of litigation and the courts to achieve policy and social change. For example, he noted that ten years after the US Supreme Court's famous *Brown v. Board of Education* (1954) decision that declared segregated schools to be unconstitutional, only 2.3 per cent of African American children were attending schools with whites (1991, 50). Rosenberg (1991, Chap. 1) proposed that because courts are 'constrained' by a variety of institutional limitations, particularly their lack of enforcement tools, they can produce social change only when the following conditions are met: (1) there is ample legal precedent for change; (2) there is support for change from Congress and the executive branch; and (3) there is support or little opposition in the public, and incentives are offered to implementers to induce them to comply (or administrators are willing to hide behind the court decisions in order to implement reforms). In his case studies, he also allows for the fact that judicial decisions, especially by the Supreme Court, may influence policy indirectly by generating media attention or mobilizing interest groups. His framework rests on several assumptions that were previously established in the literature (Wasby 1970; Levine 1970; Johnson and Canon 1984), though Rosenberg omits certain factors that previous studies have shown to be significant, including the clarity and forcefulness of a judicial decision.

While Rosenberg can be criticized for leaving out some potential explanatory factors, more fundamental critiques have been levelled against his theoretical model. Feeley and Rubin suggest that Rosenberg sets up a straw man to make his point. They note that many attempts to create significant social change have been disappointing to some degree, no matter which agency of government initiated the process; furthermore, they argue that policy implementation often involves the support of multiple organizations within a modern administrative state (1998, 316–23). In their study of prison reform litigation, Feeley and Rubin (1998, Chap. 9) conclude that federal court trial judges used many common administrative practices, such as meeting and negotiating with interested parties, to effect some changes in prison conditions in conjunction with other actors and more general social trends.

A somewhat related critique comes from a group of scholars, particularly Michael McCann (1992, 1994, 1996), who argue that Rosenberg's model assumes a 'top-down' and 'scientific' perspective that seeks to explain or predict the effects of Supreme Court decisions according to whether certain conditions are met (such as whether the decision is supported by public opinion). An alternative approach to evaluating judicial impact analyzes legal and political disputes more contextually and with the assumption that law, judicial decisions, and institutions more generally are 'constitutive' in that they can shape norms and goals that guide behaviour. This 'bottom-up' approach seeks to analyze how legal claims and judicial decisions are received, interpreted, utilized, or circumvented by bureaucrats, lower court judges, interest groups, and the media (see Wasby 1970; Scheingold 1974; McCann 1992, 1994; Mertz 1994). Although scholars in this camp tend to be skeptical about how much legal mobilization and courts can alter the existing social and political power dynamics, many argue that disadvantaged groups can use legal mobilization and courts as part of a broader strategy to further their causes, at least incrementally. Such tactics may have such interrelated benefits as bestowing legitimacy on a group's demands; raising the political and social profile of an issue; altering the perceptions of adversaries and the public; and, more instrumentally, providing bargaining leverage (Scheingold 1974; McCann 1992, 1994; Simon 1992). Though McCann (1994, 291 n. 12) concedes that Rosenberg's consideration of the 'indirect' effects of judicial decisions (such as examining the number of newspaper articles or public opinion before and after a decision) is a step forward, he argues that the model still focuses primarily on judicial capacity to initiate behavioral changes rather than on relational dynamics generated over time by legal mobilization and judicial decisions.[27]

Conversely, Rosenberg (1996) argues that bottom-up research is difficult to replicate and the results are difficult to generalize or validate. McCann's study of the pay-equity struggle, according to Rosenberg, seems to suggest that union organization and mobilization contribute more than legal mobilization to pay-equity policy change and the way that women view their role and identity in the job market. Yet, because McCann's study lacked an appropriate mixture of cases—most of McCann's examples, for instance, featured union organization—

there is no way to separate out the influence of legal mobilization on the results (Rosenberg 1996, 450–1).

As noted above, there have not been as many impact studies in Canada that try to analyze and explain impact rather than describe what happened after judicial decisions were made. One such study, however, found that elements of both the 'top-down' approach and the 'bottom-up' approach are useful in explaining policy outcomes. Riddell (2004) investigated the effect of legal mobilization under s. 23 of the Charter—the official minority language education provision—on francophone education outside of Quebec. He tried to explain why every province outside Quebec had established more homogenous French schools and created francophone school boards despite initial opposition from many provincial governments and even disagreements within francophone communities about the desirability of policy change. In keeping with the 'top-down' model he found two factors that were critical to policy success. First, the Supreme Court read s. 23 broadly and contrary to the original intent by finding that it included the right to 'management and control' of French-language instruction and francophone schools by the students' parents (*Mahé* 1990). Second, federal government funding was crucial. The federal Court Challenges Program helped pay for s. 23 litigation, and the federal government gave the provinces hundreds of millions of dollars to help provide French-language instruction and francophone schools and school governance. To look only at these factors, however, would paint a misleading and incomplete picture of the reasons for policy change. In the wake of government delays in implementing *Mahé* (for reasons identified by Rosenberg and others, such as financial considerations, fear of a public backlash and some lack of forcefulness in the decision), francophone groups outside Quebec had to lobby bureaucrats and politicians, generate favourable media coverage, initiate follow-up litigation, and try to convince more francophones that separate schools and school boards were a good idea and the best fit with their collective identity under the Charter. The use of rights discourse by advocates of separate francophone schools and school boards to win over their opponents was important. Over time, as provincial and local policies began to change, francophone groups started launching, and winning, s. 23 cases that featured more specific remedies to fill in the policy gaps. The *Doucet-Boudreau* case discussed above, where the trial judge kept jurisdiction of the case to monitor the construction of francophone schools, was the most extreme example of this phenomenon.

In an initial study of the effect on policy of the *Auton* and *Chaoulli* decisions on health-care issues (see above), Manfredi and Maioni (2005) also found that both top-down and bottom-up approaches were useful in explaining subsequent events and policy dynamics. In a study of the reaction of two Ontario police agencies to a couple of Supreme Court decisions, Moore (1992) concluded that the clarity of the decision and the organizational support system available to each police agency helped to explain the timing and degree of implementation. McCormick (1994, 180–7), using a model of impact from the US, very briefly illustrated the effect on policy of three Charter decisions.[28]

Despite the scarcity of formal impact studies in Canada, there is some useful research that can help us gain insight into the effects of judicial decisions even if they are not necessarily full-fledged 'judicial impact' studies. In his study of the Women's Legal Education and Action Fund (LEAF) in the Supreme Court, Manfredi (2004) looked at whether any policy or social change resulted from cases in which LEAF was involved. Miriam Smith's (1999, 2002b) work on gay and lesbian social movements is replete with analysis of the effects of rights discourse and institutional rules, including the Charter and judicial decisions, on social movements and public policy. Flanagan (1997) explained that there was no legislative response to the Supreme Court's 1988 *Morgentaler* decision because it removed the status-quo policy option (by striking down the law that prohibited abortion unless excused by a Therapeutic Abortion Committee to save the life or health of the mother) and then Parliament was unable to agree on a new abortion law because a compromise between pro-life and pro-choice viewpoints proved very difficult. Flanagan's more general argument is that when courts strike down existing policies, this leaves a policy void that may be difficult to fill since the policy process cycles through various options that do not attract enough support from politicians and organized interests to become the new policy. The Alberta government's attempts to limit access to abortion services after the Supreme Court's *Morgentaler* decision can be explained, according to Urquhart (1989), by two factors: first, Alberta and other provinces are responsible for health care under the constitutional division of powers; and, second, the Alberta government was trying to satisfy the ideological preferences of its supporters.[29] The analysis by Sauvageau, Schneiderman, and Taras (2006) of media coverage of Supreme Court decisions can help us to understand the effects of judicial decisions. For example, the chaos and violence that ensued on the east coast after the Supreme Court's *Marshall* decision (see the introduction to Chapter 2) can be traced in large part to some ambiguity in the Supreme Court's decision and media reporting of the decision that emphasized conflict and downplayed the fact that the Court had said in the decision that the aboriginal right to fish could still be regulated by the government (Sauvageau, Schneiderman, and Taras 2006, Chap. 4).

In reference to federalism decisions, Monahan (1987) has argued that even if one level of government (federal or provincial) loses a federalism case, there are often other options available to them to reach its policy goals, even if the means are less efficient. For example, after Saskatchewan was told by the Supreme Court that under the federal division of powers it could not tax each individual barrel of oil created in the province (*Canadian Industrial Gas and Oil Limited* 1978), the province introduced a general oil well income tax on oil companies. However, such a scheme was more difficult to administer and it made it somewhat easier for companies to avoid taxation. Meanwhile, Russell (1985) and others have pointed out that Supreme Court federalism decisions, by setting the limits of jurisdictional power, can influence federal–provincial negotiations in various policy areas.

As suggested by the Rosenberg and McCann debates and subsequent Canadian studies, it is difficult to assess the effects on policy of legal mobilization and court decisions, but it is even more difficult to evaluate the long-term socio-economic and political effects (Bogart 2002). For example, to what degree will French-language instruction and francophone schools contribute to the preservation and promotion of francophone language and culture outside Quebec in the face of an English-dominated culture and media in North America? What will the long-term effects on the environment be of the Supreme Court's decision to give the federal government some authority to legislate on environmental issues under its Peace, Order and Good Government (POGG) power (see *Crown Zellerbach* 1988) and its criminal law power (see *Hydro-Quebec* 1997)? Answering such questions is extremely challenging because there are numerous and often related factors that could affect long-term outcomes.

Nevertheless, some scholars have tried to ascertain the longer-term socio-economic and political impacts of laws and judicial decisions. In a provocatively titled article, 'Does the Charter Matter?' Harry Arthurs and Brent Arnold (2005) investigated whether the Charter and judicial decisions have led to socio-economic and political progress for women, aboriginals, and visible minorities. In the case of women, Arthurs and Arnold argue that the Charter has had little long-term effect. They argue that more liberal access to abortion after *Morgentaler* did 'matter' but it mattered 'more in some parts of the country than in others' depending on how provincial governments, hospitals, and doctors reacted. Arthurs and Arnold argue that women's socio-economic status and opportunities are explained more by labour markets, social welfare policy, and child-care policy than by the Charter and that the Charter has had little influence over these factors, because courts have been reluctant to read social and economic rights into the Charter. Turning to women's participation in the political arena, Arthurs and Arnold (2005, 77) argue that the Charter's significance has been 'marginal at best': 'The Charter has no doubt symbolically reinforced the political mobilization of Canadian women. However, judging by the greater electoral progress in other countries that have no constitutional charter—for example, the Scandinavian countries and the Netherlands—it may have done less than is assumed.'

Although the conclusions of impact studies are necessarily tentative and are often disputed, they are valuable for highlighting the need to study law and courts within a larger political context. As noted in the conclusion, the shift to a more policy-making role by Canadian courts needs to be explained with reference to the political process, and the implications for this new role need to be connected to the larger governing process.

Conclusion

The increased policy-making role of courts is not unique to Canada. Around the world there has been a growth of judicial power (Tate and Vallinder 1995; Ginsburg 2003; Goldstein 2004). Different political explanations have been offered for this phenomenon in Canada and elsewhere. Charles Epp (1998) argues that a necessary but not sufficient condition for 'rights revolutions' that feature significant judicial policy-making is a set of well-organized rights advocates with resources and the support of skilled lawyers. The presence of a constitutionally entrenched rights document, judicial independence, and popular support for rights also are factors that explain why a country has a rights revolution. According to Epp, these conditions were satisfied more in Canada than they were in the United Kingdom. In Canada, lobbying by organized interest groups (with help from the federal government) was necessary to entrench the Charter of Rights, and then groups used the Charter to press rights claims (see Chapter 7). An independent judiciary and a Supreme Court that was willing to engage in activism along with a supportive public undergirded the rights revolution in Canada.

A somewhat different explanation is offered by Ran Hirschl (2004). He traces the rise in judicial power in some countries to hegemonic elites who react to significant threats to their power and the political regime by placing authority in the courts. For example, in Israel the threat came from religious elements in society that were demanding a more or less theocratic state, whereas in Canada the threat came from Quebec separatists. In both countries the elites ceded some power to the courts under an entrenched constitutional document to preserve the political system and their place in it. Morton and Knopff (2000), however, attribute the rise of judicial power in Canada, not to socio-economic and political elites that wanted to preserve their power, but to an interconnected 'Court Party' of law professors, 'post-materialist' interest groups, and sympathetic federal bureaucrats. According to Morton and Knopff, the Court Party lobbied vigorously for the entrenchment of the Charter and then urged the courts to make decisions that would not preserve existing social and political structures, but would refashion policies (involving abortion, same-sex marriage, aboriginal self-government, and so on) along the lines they preferred.

A greater understanding of the debate over the Court Party thesis and, more generally, of the use of the Charter and the courts by organized interests to defend or advance certain policy positions comes from Chapter 7 of this book. Likewise, Chapter 8 helps us to understand better the strategies employed by governments or particular individual within governments, such as the Attorney General, to defend their policies or perhaps to achieve their policy goals by hiding behind judicial decisions or legal opinions about what the Charter requires. Those strategies include government decisions about whether to appeal Charter losses (see Hennigar 2004).[30]

Whatever the explanation for the greater policy-making role of Canada's courts, it increases pressure for more transparent appointment systems and greater accountability for judges, perhaps even direct democratic input into who sits on the bench (see Chapter 5). However, such options could jeopardize judicial independence and thereby undermine one of the reasons for having a judicial branch at arm's length from the other branches of government (see Chapter 6). One of the difficulties in finding a way out of this conundrum is that Canadian courts at all levels make decisions involving both constitutional and non-constitutional law (see Chapter 2). Hence, if one tries to make a court more accountable for taking more of a policy-making approach in Charter cases where the results seem to depend more on policy considerations (backed by social facts and interveners) than on 'law', that same court might be less able to make an impartial and legally informed decision involving a more technical aspect of law. Perhaps one solution is to create a separate constitutional court, as a number of European countries have. The appointment systems used for those constitutional courts reflects their special nature—legislators play an important role in choosing the judges and there are often term limits on appointments. Meanwhile, if a 'regular' court adopts a policy-making approach to reading ordinary legislation or the common law (or the Civil Code in Quebec) involving torts, family law, criminal law, or other non-constitutional law, governments would have the option of passing legislation to override a court decision.

Of course, one should not only look at potential changes to judicial processes when thinking about solutions to challenges raised by the policy-making role of courts, particularly under the Charter. Janet Hiebert (2002), for example, has suggested a greater role for legislative committees in debating rights issues before the passage of a law. This would have two salutary effects. First, it would make the legislative process less executive-centred and more democratic. Second, it would signal to the courts that a legislative body has thought seriously about defining rights and reconciling them with other social interests, thereby leading to greater deference by the courts to legislative choices. While Hiebert's proposal has much to recommend it, it faces a couple of serious hurdles. Prime Ministers and Premiers and their cabinets are very reluctant to give up their power to the legislative branch. There is also some concern that law-makers who focus on individual rights will do so to the detriment of the collective good (Glendon 1991). And there are those who argue strongly against the notion that the legislative and executive branches deserve equal (or co-ordinate) status with the courts in defining constitutional rights (Hogg, Thornton, and Wright 2007).

Whether one agrees or not with Hiebert's suggestion, it is clear that we cannot look at courts in isolation from the rest of the political system. A more holistic perspective not only helps us to understand both the judicial and political processes better, but also helps to restrain us from concentrating on the courts too much and exaggerating their influence. Although courts are important institutions to study (hence the time and effort we put into writing this book), we remind our readers of two things: how much judicial decisions actually make a difference in shaping policy and broader socio-economic and political trends depends on a host of factors; and, as noted in Chapter 3, much dispute resolution and associated rule-making takes place outside of the judicial system in administrative tribunals and in alternative dispute resolution (ADR).

Notes

Chapter 1

1. It is not unheard of for an expectant mother who is clinically depressed to carry a child to full term without being aware that she is pregnant. David Paciocco (1999, 96–7), however, argues that it is difficult to accept that Brenda Drummond would have fired a pellet gun into her vagina if she had not known that she was pregnant—it would have been the most bizarre suicide attempt in history.

2. Since the Supreme Court had struck down Canada's abortion law in its 1988 *Morgentaler* decision, Brenda Drummond could not be charged with trying to obtain an abortion illegally.

3. Brenda Drummond spent seven months in a psychiatric facility. She pled guilty to 'failing to provide the necessities of life' by not telling the doctors about the pellet and thus endangering the baby's life; she received a suspended sentence and thirty months of probation.

4. Some reaction was supportive. For instance, the Pro-Choice Action Network of British Columbia expressed sympathy for the injured child but had strong reservations about altering the policy balance as it existed, and it therefore, favoured the decision: 'How do we prevent women from harming their late-term fetuses, yet at the same time, ensure they have full rights to terminate their pregnancies? Where do we draw the line? Do we prosecute only if the woman uses a lethal weapon like a gun, or do we extend the law to encompass anything that might harm the fetus, including cigarettes or alcohol?' The group concluded that there are 'serious and unwanted implications' to changing policy on fetal rights. (http://www.prochoiceaction network-canada.org/prochoicepress/9697win.shtml#drummond). Other reaction was more negative. The LifeSite website (which is closely affiliated with the Campaign Life Coalition), for example, maintained that 'pro-life observers across the country are united in the belief that the current election campaign is a good opportunity to build on the increased awareness of the plight of the unborn which has come about as result of these tragedies [including the Drummond case]' (www.life site.net/election_97/issues.html).

5. See, for example, Andrew Coyne (1996).

6. The *Chaouilli v. Quebec* case was heard by seven judges. Three judges argued that laws which limit access to private health care do violate the Canadian Charter of Rights; three judges argued that such laws were not unconstitutional under the Charter. One judge preferred not to decide the case using the Charter of Rights and instead based her decision solely on Quebec's human rights law. Justice Deschamps argued that Quebec's limits on access to private health care violated the province's human rights law; therefore, a total of four judges argued that the current law in Quebec violated rights.

7. This popular definition of politics was first put forth by Harold Laswell (1936).

8. A.V. Dicey (2002) argued that the system of law, based on the legal system developed in England, reflected this notion of the 'rule of law' much more than the civil law system developed in Continental Europe, because the system applied the general

precepts of law to government authorities, whereas the civil law system had a special system of administrative law that applied only to state officials. See the discussion below on common law and civil law systems.

9. There is increasing overlap between positivist and natural law positions on this question. Contemporary natural law theorists like John Finnis (2007) argue against defining law according to whether it meets certain moral criteria, while positivists like H.L.A Hart (1961, 203) acknowledged that some law was 'too iniquitous to be applied or obeyed'.

10. It is possible to explain the outcome according to positivist perspectives—the tribunal was applying positive law (which contained moral precepts)—but given that the moral rules were crucial and seemed to be derived from a basic understanding of how people deserve to be treated across all time and places, it seems that the natural law account is more satisfactory. See Finnis (2007).

11. Dworkin has written extensively about rights, especially in relation to American constitutional law, and has even presented legal arguments to the US Supreme Court on topics such as the right to physician-assisted suicide. See, for example, Dworkin et al. (1997).

12. See Hall (2001) for a discussion of international law from natural law and positivist perspectives.

13. Some natural law theorists hope that international law can be used to promote the common good of humanity in both international and domestic situations, though specifying and applying natural law principles, including 'human rights', remains problematic. Hall (2001) is a proponent of natural law in international law, but he warns that trying specifically to list human rights in various international human rights documents imports too much of the positivist approach (that is, detailing rules in a document passed by an authoritative decision-making body) and could lead to the politicization and trivialization of 'human rights'.

14. The concepts of private and public law grew out of the civil law legal system discussed below; however, the distinction is also used to aid in understanding the law in systems as well (for example, see Tarr 2006).

15. The civil law system, which is a 'system' of law based on codes of law, should not be confused with references to 'civil law' which is the term sometimes used to mean private law disputes or all disputes other than criminal law disputes. In other words, both common law 'systems' (as found in Britain, for example) and civil law 'systems' (as found in France, for example) have rules to govern both public and private (or 'civil') disputes—in the latter system the rules are found in codes and in the former the rules are found in judge made (common) law and in legislation.

16. For example, the Civil Code of Lower Canada did not contain articles pertaining to divorce as did the Napoleonic Code (see Tetley 2000, 695–6).

17. In civil law systems, codes are also used for certain public law or quasi-public law matters such as criminal law or labour law. In other matters of public law, relationships and disputes involving the state are governed by legislation or regulations passed by legislative or executive bodies. The mixture of codes and legislation tends to vary from country to country, as does the precise classification of private versus public law (Apple and Deyling 1995). Most civil law countries also have a written constitution that serves as an overarching supreme law that establishes the system and rules of government and sets out the rights of individuals (or groups) which other laws must respect.

18. At that time, however, the 'common law' was not a substantive body of law that judges applied strictly to arrive at decisions. Glenn (2007) argues that the idea that

previous judicial decisions were binding on present cases (the concept of *stare decisis*) started only in the nineteenth century. Until then, cases 'were part of a body of common experience, to be used in further reasoning, but in no way constituting unalterable law' (Glenn 2007, 238). This partly had to do with the common law philosophy of decision making as well as practical issues, such as the haphazard reporting of cases, use of juries (along with the illiteracy of most jury members), and the lack of a judicial hierarchy.

19. Access to the king's courts required a 'writ' from the monarch (or the monarch's representative) authorizing a particular action to commence. The factual situations that each writ covered were quite specific.

20. The subcategories of writs concerning trespass included *trespass de bonis asportatis* (for damages to the plaintiff's goods that had been 'carried away'), *trespass quare clausum fregit* (where the defendant physically intruded onto the plaintiff's land) and the *trespass vi et armis* (for those other tort actions by which the plaintiff suffered injury to person or property by virtue of the defendant's direct and forceful misconduct) (see Martin 2001). The promise by Henry III to the nobility that no new writs would be created also greatly restricted the flexibility of the common law (see Yates, Yates and Bain 2000, 9).

21. It should be noted that rules which were developed and used by merchant guilds trading between continental Europe and England were eventually adopted and applied by the Admiralty courts of Britain. After common law courts took over adjudicating disputes involving merchants, judges simply incorporated merchant law into the overall body of law. This is why some mercantile laws do not follow common law legal principles (Yates, Yates and Bain 2000, 11).

22. In some civil law countries, judges make select references to past cases in their decisions, while in other countries, such as France, judges look to past decisions but do not note this formally in their decisions.

23. A good illustration of the differences in formal decision making in France (under the civil law system) and the United States (under the common law system) can be found in Wells (1994).

24. The sacred texts of the world's two largest religions, Christianity and Islam, do not contain many laws per se. The Old Testament contains some law (such as the Ten Commandments), but the Christian New Testament contains no laws. Only about 3 per cent of the Koran contains legal provisions, most of them dealing with family law and inheritance (Badr 1978, 188–9). These religious texts deal primarily with the nature of God, individual and communal relationships with God, relationships between believers, and the treatment of others. Canon law, which was developed by Church authorities to govern personal relationships, was based on their interpretation of the principles of the Christian church, while Islamic law was developed by scholars of the Koran and the life and teachings of the Prophet Mohammed.

25. During the Middle Ages, many people were considered to be clergy. Often these people preferred to be tried before ecclesiastical courts because the penalties in those courts tended to be less severe than those in the civil courts.

26. In Sunni Islam, four schools of law developed: Hanafi, Shfi'i, Maliki, and Hanabali. In each school, the reasoning used to arrive at legal rules is somewhat of a hybrid of the common and civil law systems. Legal scholars derive legal principles by reasoning from analogy (as in common law). However, at certain intervals, important cases and commentaries on their principles are collected into digests, the importance of which parallels the central role that legal treatises play in the civil law system. Although Islamic law is often referred to as Sharia law, technically Sharia law is the divine law, whereas the law created by Muslim clergy and lawyers attempting to interpret the

divine law from the Koran and the life and teachings of the Prophet Mohammed is known as Fiqh (Vogel 2003).

27. Again, it deserves mention that this does not mean that there are no debates about the role of religious principles in public life in these countries. In Israel, for example, some political parties advocate a system of government that would be largely theocratic. In the United States, the 'religious right' has had some success in advocating public policies that are based on Christian principles. In Poland, some judges have seemingly ignored constitutional provisions on abortion because they conflict with Catholic doctrine.

28. After the revolution, Sharia law replaced legislation; it contains rules of family law that disadvantaged women, such as giving men the right to divorce their wife (or wives) unilaterally; however, political lobbying by women who argued for a different interpretation of Sharia law (or in some cases for secular law) and rulings favourable to women even in the special (religious) civil courts led to changes in the laws of marriage and divorce by legislation that in some respects were more favourable than in pre-revolutionary times (Halper 2005).

29. Quebec also has a number of statutes that deal with private law matters. The creation and interpretation of such statutes are guided by the general principles of the Civil Code. An increasing reliance on precedents in private law cases in Quebec can be attributed to various factors, including a 'spill-over' effect from the use of common law in public law disputes and systemic factors, such as the use of signed decisions by judges, use of dissents, and widespread use of previous decisions (which can be accessed electronically). However, the use of precedent for private (civil) law cases in Quebec is not unproblematic since it is difficult to apply common law methods—reasoning from example and creating rules incrementally on the basis of factual circumstances—within a civil law framework. See Brierley and Macdonald (1993, Chap. 4) and Macdonald (1985).

30. In fact, some government policies recognize this limitation; for example, certain Canadian provinces and American states have introduced 'no fault' insurance for automobile accidents, which is due in some part to the acknowledgment that court trials are costly and it is often difficult to determine exactly who was responsible for an accident and to what degree (Shapiro 1981, 48).

31. S. 1(1) of the *Ontario Highway Traffic Act*, R.S.O. 1990, defined a 'vehicle' as including a 'motor vehicle, trailer, traction engine, farm tractor, road-building machine, bicycle and any vehicle drawn, propelled or driven by any kind of power, including muscular power', but specifically did not include a 'motorized snow vehicle' or 'street car'. According to Vittala (1994), charges for violations of the *Ontario Highway Traffic Act* committed by rollerbladers tended to be thrown out of court, but fines were sometimes levied against rollerbladers for violating local traffic bylaws.

32. Neo-Marxist theory in political science and critical legal studies theory are similar in that they argue that the law and courts tend to aid the privileged groups in society at the expense of the underprivileged. However, in some Marxist theory, law and judicial process are considered to be epiphenomenal (a result of the capitalist economic system), whereas in CLS theory, law and judicial process help to constitute (act as building blocks for) a system that privileges elites. Some Marxist scholars, though, argue that both theories could agree on a balanced approach that see law as constitutive to some degree but constrained by larger socio-economic forces (Sciaraffa 1999, 218).

33. Some NI scholars, such as McCann, are somewhat close to the CLS school in that they believe that laws most often help the dominant groups in politics, society, and

the economy. However, NI scholars like McCann believe that at times law can provide leverage for disadvantaged groups. The effects of the law overall are somewhat contingent on various factors.

Chapter 2

1. Though the Supreme Court has nine members, the Chief Justice assigned only seven of them to hear the case (as is fairly common—see below).
2. That said, it is not unheard of for appeal courts—even the Supreme Court of Canada—to second-guess a trial judge's factual findings.
3. Regular administrative tribunals, which are found in every province and at the federal level as well, resemble courts in that they are designed to resolve disputes that arise under specific laws and regulations. For example, the Landlord Tenant Board was created to resolve disputes between residential landlords and tenants. However, although tribunals are 'quasi-judicial', they are part of the executive, or public administration, branch of the state and not the judiciary. As well, tribunal members are appointed by the government for only a fairly short term, and are not usually judges. Instead, they have a variety of educational and work backgrounds, often related in some way to the subject area of the tribunal. The decisions of tribunals are reviewable by courts, although there is a great deal of variation by province and tribunal regarding where review authority is located. Tribunals and other quasi-judicial institutions are discussed in greater detail in Chapter 3.
4. Alberta remains the only province with no statutory requirement of legal training or experience for its s. 92 courts. Nonetheless, most judicial appointees have legal experience.
5. The Judicial Committee of the Privy Council (JCPC) was the British court—more accurately, a board of the British Privy Council with members drawn from the House of Lords ('Law Lords') and eventually some judges from Commonwealth countries—that served as Canada's highest court until 1949.
6. Notably, the Yukon and Northwest Territories also have and appoint their own Territorial Courts, which though not technically 'section 92 courts', are analogous. However, Nunavut is an exception—it has only a single s. 96 Unified Court at the trial level, appointed by the federal government.
7. The least serious indictable offences in the *Criminal Code* are listed in s. 553, the most serious in s. 469. Notably, if the Crown and the accused both consent, the jury requirement for the latter can be waived (*Criminal Code*, s. 473).
8. It should be noted that in addition to the full-time s. 96 judges, there were over 60 'supernumerary' judges in 2006, who had retired but returned to work part-time.
9. Professional associations, such as the Canadian Medical Association and Canadian Bar Association (and their provincial counterparts), are permitted a large degree of self-regulation. They are empowered by law to set rules and regulations for their members and to enforce them internally through sanction, fine, or expulsion.
10. Quebec also has an institution, the Quebec Human Rights Tribunal, which is a cross between a court and an administrative tribunal (see above). The QHRT, which rules on complaints concerning discrimination under Quebec's *Charter of Human Rights and Freedoms*, is noteworthy for being composed of both judges and laypersons.
11. For example, Saskatchewan and Manitoba. While Ontario does not bar lawyers, it does not require legal training either.
12. 'Events' include all trials, pre-trials, motions, and other hearings; thus there are many events for each case. Unfortunately, Ontario does not report the number of

individual cases, although it is currently in the process of adopting a new reporting method that will.

13. As explained in the next section on s. 96 courts, New Brunswick and Ontario have the most developed 'unified family courts' at the s. 96 level. As well, Ontario's small claims courts are s. 96 courts, but in most provinces they are s. 92 courts.

14. Disallowance empowers the Governor General, on the advice of the federal cabinet, to override (cancel) provincial legislation that is deemed to be *ultra vires*, or beyond the jurisdictional authority of the provinces. Reservation entails Ottawa 'requesting' (in practice, requiring) a province's Lieutenant Governor to withhold his or her signature from a bill—for without this Royal Assent, the bill would not become law. Although both powers are still in the Constitution Act, 1867, they fell into disuse over sixty years ago, and it is almost impossible to imagine circumstances in which they would be exercised today. The POGG clause (s. 91) grants the federal Parliament that authority 'to make Laws for the Peace, Order, and Good Government of Canada, in relation to all Matters not coming within the Classes of Subjects by this Act assigned exclusively to the Legislatures of the Provinces'.

15. Most notably, *Reference re Adoption Act and Other Acts* (1938), but regarding inferior courts rather than tribunals; *Labour Relations Board of Saskatchewan v. John East Iron Works, Ltd.* (1949); and *Tomko v. Labour Relations Board of Nova Scotia* (1977).

16. As McCormick (1994, 35) observes, 'it was, of course, logically possible for this historical inquiry to yield different results in different provinces.' This happened initially, with the Supreme Court striking down Ontario's *Residential Tenancies Act* (*Reference re Residential Tenancies Act* 1981) but upholding Quebec's virtually identical statute in *AG Quebec v. Grondin* (1983). The Supreme Court's solution, McCormick further notes, was 'to fall back on an examination of the "general historical conditions in all four original confederating provinces"—i.e., a fictional composite' (35).

17. Peter Hogg gives the example of 'labour relations', which was historically within s. 96 court jurisdiction, and the narrower issue of 'unjust dismissal', which was not (Hogg 2003, 214).

18. Notably, the Supreme Court has ruled that 'disputes between residential landlords and tenants' are 'novel jurisdiction' and therefore pass the historical inquiry test (*Reference re Amendments to the Residential Tenancies Act (Nova Scotia)* 1996). This seems an astonishing claim to make, but the Court made a somewhat tortured argument that because Nova Scotia was overwhelmingly rural in 1867 there were few urban landlords. This would seem to limit the ruling's application to provinces with levels of urbanization in 1867 comparable to that of Nova Scotia.

19. Outside of Nunavut, Quebec has gone the furthest towards criminal trial court unification, but in the s. 92 Cour du Québec. It has been given jurisdiction by the province and the federal Parliament to hear all offences—provincial and federal—except those explicitly assigned to the s. 96 superior court. As we will see shortly, while this is not significantly different in practice from the workload distribution of criminal cases in other provinces, it is yet another symbol of 'asymmetrical federalism' in Canada.

20. One of Healy's strongest arguments is that the 'inferior' s. 96 county and district courts heard jury trials before they were merged into the superior courts. Therefore, jury trials cannot possibly be constitutionally restricted to superior courts on the basis of the latter's historically 'inherent jurisdiction'.

21. For example, see Friedland (2003), Webster and Doob (2003), Russell (2007b).

22. For example, Alberta's Court of Appeal sits in Calgary and Edmonton, Quebec's in Montreal and Quebec City, Saskatchewan's in Regina and Saskatoon, and B.C.'s occasionally in Victoria, Kamloops, and Kelowna, but usually in Vancouver.

23. In Nunavut, the first appeal from a summary offence conviction is before a single judge of the Alberta Court of Appeal, since Nunavut does not have its own intermediate appeal court. Thereafter, appeals are to a full panel of the Nunavut Court of Appeal.

24. According to Baar (2007) and Tyson (2007), small claims court judges are usually part-time judges only nominally attached to s. 96 courts.

25. Furthermore, many appeals that are initiated are abandoned ('not perfected') by the appellant—as many as 40 per cent to 50 per cent, perhaps more (Greene et al. 1998, 56).

26. That is the case, for example, in France, Germany, Italy, Spain, many African countries, all of the former Soviet Bloc countries of Eastern Europe and Russia, and all Central and South American countries.

27. In another example, the *Federal Court Act* assigned general jurisdiction over civil claims by and against the federal government. *Quebec North Shore* concerned a breach of contract to build a marine terminal, which was part of a larger system for transporting newsprint from Canada to the US. The case therefore involved international trade, which is a federal responsibility. However, the federal government had not enacted any laws regarding the contract in question. *Fuller Construction* involved construction of a federal building and concerned the federal government suing a third-party contractor. The government had been sued for breach of contract by another contractor, which was working on a different part of the building, and the government blamed its failure to meet that contractual obligation on the third party. The Supreme Court ruled that because there was no federal statute about third party liability, the Federal Court could not hear that part of the case.

28. Confusingly, the Tax Court of Canada refers to its cases as 'appeals' because they are usually appeals from various administrative bodies. However, these are technically matters of original jurisdiction (that is, trials).

29. This last situation arises primarily in cases involving Quebec's *Civil Code*, because the *Supreme Court Act* requires only that three justices be trained in that area.

30. *Immigration and Refugee Protection Act (IRPA)*, as reported in *Federal Court of Canada 2002–03 Report* (2003, 14).

31. The Supreme Court does not report the specific breakdown of Charter cases; figures were calculated from the Lexum archive of Supreme Court rulings (http://scc.lexum.umontreal.ca).

Chapter 3

1. The divorcing couple and their dispute-resolution process can be read about in Perrin (2002). One of the many stories about the hockey-playing sisters can be found at CTV (2006). The arbitration between Newfoundland doctors and the provincial government was highlighted on CBC (2002). Marcel was featured in a CBC (2006) documentary on the Vancouver drug court. The lesbian couple who broke up gave rise to the *M. v. H.* case that went to the Supreme Court. The case can be found at [1999] 2 S.C.R. 3 (the second volume of the 1999 Supreme Court reports starting at p. 3).

2. In drug treatment courts, depending on the offender and the nature of the offence (i.e. simple possession versus more serious drug charges), those who complete treatment successfully either have the charges stayed or withdrawn, or receive a non-custodial sentence.

3. See Morton (1992, 98–103) for more detail.

4. The Court stated that he was genuinely interested in the validity of a law that affects all Quebec residents and it is unlikely that a systematic challenge to the law would be

brought in another way. For example, a seriously ill person would likely challenge health policy in light of their own circumstances and not target the entire health system.

5. Interestingly, the case actually involved a person who had received more than the minimum penalty for trying to smuggle cocaine into Canada (*Smith* 1987).

6. Recall from the discussion above, however, that although the Supreme Court heard the challenge to the federal government's decision to allow US cruise missiles to be tested in Canada, the rights claimants ultimately lost because the Court argued that there was no way to prove sufficiently that the decision would increase the chances of nuclear war.

7. Four of the seven Supreme Court judges ruled that Quebec's law violated the right to 'life and personal inviolability' found in Quebec's human rights legislation. Three of these judges also argued that Quebec's law violated the right to 'life, liberty and security of the person' in the Canadian Charter of Rights and Freedoms. In dissent, three judges argued that Quebec's law violated neither Quebec's human rights law nor the constitutionally entrenched Charter.

8. Some of these observations were made by Professor Julie Macfarlane during a telephone conversation about judicial dispute resolution (15 Sept. 2006). We thank her for sharing these insights with us.

9. The judges who participate in these sessions are not allowed to preside over the trial (or appeal) if the dispute continues. Assessments or recommendations made by judges during such pre-trial or pre-hearing sessions are kept confidential and are not allowed to be presented to court if the case continues to trial (or to appeal).

10. Certain non-family cases are excluded from mandatory mediation in both provinces. Also, parties can apply to a judge to be excused from having to go to mediation.

11. The methodological difficulties include establishing 'control' groups for comparison among different kinds of dispute-resolution processes (both inside and outside of the formal judicial process) for similar kinds of cases and trying to determine what is a 'fair' or 'good' process or outcome, particularly given that this can be rather subjective and different stakeholders (governments, judges, lawyers, mediators, and each party in the dispute) may have different perspectives and objectives (Mack 2003, 17–22).

12. Mandatory mediation is for non-family, civil cases in the superior trial court in Ontario. At the time of the evaluation, the program was available only in Toronto and Ottawa.

13. Ironically, however, ADR processes run the risk of becoming like the adversarial process if they are subject to too many conditions, which may undermine its effectiveness and reduce the options for litigants (Landerkin and Pirie 2003).

14. The Task Force argues that the degree of activity and informality by the judge should be based on what is at stake at trial. In other words, the style of trial should be 'proportional' to the issues raised at trial and the needs of the litigants.

15. According to a report on therapeutic justice published by the National Judicial Institute (2005, 13) 'active listening' involves such things as giving individuals the opportunity to speak; not rushing speakers; and interrupting infrequently, as well as 'asking clarifying questions and making comments that acknowledge they want to know about and understand a person's position'.

16. In civil (non-criminal) litigation, judges in the civil law system oversee the exchange of documents between the parties and can question witnesses, but what documents are produced and what witnesses are called is left to the parties to the dispute. In criminal law, civil law judges have more influence over what evidence is collected and what witnesses are called (see Damaska 1986, 124–5).

17. Appeals from decisions by magistrates or justices of the peace in common law systems are often new trials.

18. Interviews with appellate judges in the early 1990s confirmed that they were willing to examine the facts of cases, though the degree to which they were willing to do so varied (Greene et al. 1998, 192).

19. Justice Stevens dissented and argued that the Court should not have reviewed the video *de novo* to make factual conclusions. He maintained that the judge and jury were in the best position to analyze the tape in light of the local circumstances.

20. As Damaska notes, the almost intractable debate has been going on for nearly two centuries (1986, 122–3). For an attempt to use a social science study to determine which system might better uncover the facts see Block, Parker, and Dusek 2000.

21. In Canada, although provincial and federal governments produce legislation concerning evidence (such as the *Canada Evidence Act*), the courts, particularly the Supreme Court, remain mostly responsible for rules of evidence through statutory interpretation and common law rules. In the United States, the Supreme Court also plays a considerable role in shaping rules of evidence but legislation, such as the *Federal Rules of Evidence*, is more influential than in Canada.

22. Precedents about the notice requirement for job termination had emphasized that more senior and specialized workers would have more trouble finding other work. The trial judge disputed these assumptions on the basis of his reading of two Ontario Council of University studies and an article in the *Economist* magazine. See *Cronk v. Canadian General Insurance Co.* (1995).

23. It appears that a number of Supreme Court judges take a somewhat more liberal position on judicial notice, perhaps owing to their place at the top of the judicial hierarchy. Justice LaForest, for example, in a case about Sunday-closing laws and freedom of religion, stated: 'I do not accept that in dealing with broad social and economic facts the Court is bound to rely solely on those presented by counsel. The admonition in Oakes and other cases to present evidence in Charter cases does not remove from the courts the power, where it deems expedient, to take notice of broad social and economic facts and to take the necessary steps to inform themselves about them' (quoted in Jamal 2005, n. 30).

24. In the Supreme Court's *Young v. Young* (1993) decision, for example, Justices L'Heureux-Dubé and McLachlin took judicial notice of 'diametrically opposed literature on access and child development' to support their conclusions (Thompson 2003, 33).

25. Use of the Jewish Beis Din court (as it is called in Ontario) was relatively infrequent, but in about thirty cases a year the court was called upon to deal with all issues surrounding a marriage breakdown, including access and custody issues. Enforcement of the decisions was based on the *Arbitration Act*. Boyd notes that although the Catholic and Anglican churches have rules about marriage and when they can be annulled, they used panels only for a limited number of things (like marriage and annulment) but not to make decisions about property, support, or custody under the *Arbitration Act* (2004, 39–40).

26. Note that some misunderstanding seemed to develop after the release of the Boyd report with the result that incorrect assertions were made that Christian groups used arbitration panels to decide family law issues.

27. It should be noted that Mullan is not opposed entirely to greater procedural requirements being imposed on administrative tribunals. In fact, he supports the *Singh* decision for upholding procedural fairness (2005, 10).

28. The degree of deference that the courts will show to the merits of decisions depends on various factors, especially the expertise of a tribunal relative to the court (Bryant and Sossin 2002, 160–1).

Chapter 4

1. Over the decade that followed, Tremblay was repeatedly convicted of abusing other girlfriends, but the Crown's request in 2000 that he be declared a 'dangerous offender' and given an indeterminate sentence was denied by the sentencing judge.

2. See Chapters 9 and 10 for some discussion of trial court decision making in the areas of criminal and civil law.

3. As discussed in the previous chapter, the methods used to ascertain the 'facts' of a case have changed considerably. And, since rules of evidence try to balance various interests (trying to obtain the truth, privacy, equality, efficiency, and so on), these rules allow for certain 'facts', but not others, to be introduced at trial.

4. Appellate courts may also hear a case as a trial *de novo*, which is essentially a new trial. This occurs in limited situations, such as when the court of first instance is staffed by a lay judge or when the court has not kept a record of the trial proceedings (Greene et al. 1998, 43). In a trial *de novo* it is as if the first court action had not occurred.

5. 'Appeals as of right' are also allowed in cases involving indictable offences if there is a dissenting opinion on a question of law at the lower appeals court or in civil cases in very limited circumstances (for example, in disputes between governments). For a more detailed account of the rules surrounding appeals as of right see Crane and Brown 2004.

6. It should be noted that the Supreme Court also accepts all reference cases sent to it by the federal government. Reference cases are 'advisory opinions', in which the Court is asked to address questions without an actual dispute being before it. For a more detailed discussion of reference cases see Chapter 2.

7. Before Flemming, little research was done in Canada on the decision to appeal. Flemming suggests that the desire of lawyers to improve their professional standing can have an independent effect on the decision (2004, 19–42).

8. At the United States Supreme Court, the clerks of eight of the justices (the exception is the oldest justice, John Paul Stevens) participate in a 'cert pool'. The clerks in this 'pool' divide the appeals between themselves, so that one clerk writes a memo summarizing a case's facts, issues, and potential for appeal and distributes it to all eight justices.

9. This is a relatively recent development. Up until the mid-1990s, the justices' clerks were responsible for summarizing and evaluating the leave applications. Most law clerks are only a year removed from law school and will serve as a law clerk for only a year.

10. Once the justices make their decision, they place the application on one of three lists. The 'C' list is for applications about which the panel is delaying a decision because a case with similar issues is already pending before the Court. The 'B' list is for applications for which the panel has voted to grant leave. The applications on this list will be discussed at a conference of all nine justices if the decision of the panel is not unanimous or if a justice who was not on the panel asks the Court to review the decision on a case. Finally, panels place the applications they would deny on a list and circulate that to their colleagues. If a justice disagrees with this decision, he or she can place the application on the 'D' list. Applications on this list will also be discussed at a conference of all the Court's justices.

11. The conference may moderate these potential differences, but much depends on how much deference is given to the original panel that reviewed the application.

12. These submissions must conform to strict deadlines and numerous other instructions outlined by each court. The Supreme Court, for example, requires respondent factums to be filed within eight weeks of the appellant's factum, and it has detailed rules on how the documents should be submitted (Supreme Court of Canada 2006).

13. A factum is the written legal arguments of the parties in the case. Each factum generally consists of a statement of facts, points in issue, detailed legal arguments, and the order requested. The Supreme Court has strict rules regarding the content and presentation of factums. These rules cover everything from how many words may be on a page (no more than 500), to the proper presentation of headings and the table of contents (Supreme Court of Canada 2006).

14. The Federal Court of Appeal also normally sits in panels of three judges. On rare occasions the provincial and federal appeals courts may sit in panels as large as five. This might be done for cases of high 'public importance' or for cases where the possibility exists that the court may overrule one of its own precedents (Greene et al. 1998, 67). The larger courts of appeal may hear cases in panels of five, but do so only a few times a year. The British Columbia Court of Appeal, for example, sat as a panel of five on only four occasions in 2004, only twice during 2005, and not at all in 2006 (British Columbia, Court of Appeal 2006).

15. In Alberta, a judge from the provincial s. 96 trial court (the Court of Queen's Bench) is often assigned to the three-judge appeal court panel in criminal cases (usually in cases dealing with sentencing appeals). Supporters of this practice suggest it helps educate trial judges about the position and problems of appeal court judges, while alerting appeal court judges to the concerns of trial judges. It also helps reduce the workload of the appeal court and lessen the need for additional judges. Detractors worry, however, that the presence of sitting trial court judges on appeal panels could interfere with the impartiality of appeal court judges (this discussion relies on Greene et al. 1998, 61, 66).

16. These numbers are changing slightly under the current Chief Justice, Beverley McLachlin, with some years having an average panel size as high as 7.7 (Ostberg and Wetstein 2007, 212).

17. The case was heard by a panel of only seven justices because of two vacancies on the Court due to retirements.

18. Justices who sit on a panel deciding whether to grant an application for appeal are also very likely to sit on the panel hearing the case on its merits. Flemming's study found 70 per cent of case panels included all three justices from the leave-to-appeal stage (2004, 92, 109).

19. The difference in time limits between the Supreme Court and the lower courts is not as pronounced today, because lower appeal courts have started instituting tighter time limits. For example, when Roy McMurtry was Chief Justice of the Ontario Court of Appeal (1996–2007), he adopted new time limits in an effort to reduce the backlog of cases facing the court.

20. In British Columbia, for example, 42 per cent of all cases were reserved for judgment in 2006 (BC Court of Appeal, Annual Report 2006).

21. What we do know has come primarily from interviews with the justices like those by Ian Greene and Peter McCormick (see, for example, Greene et al. 1998).

22. Most scholars studying the courts attribute to the justices a desire to have as large a majority as possible. The negotiations between justices, and the changes that majority-opinion writers often appear to make to their decisions to satisfy colleagues, gives some support for this assumption. However, it should be noted that justices also see value in dissent (see the discussion below), and opinion writers are often supported by only a slim majority of the justices (5 out of 9, for example). Supreme Court decisions can also be rendered without a majority opinion. In these cases the opinion with the most judicial signatures, the plurality opinion, carries the day.

23. The rate of dissent in the Canadian Supreme Court today is much lower than that of the United States Supreme Court, where, in 2004 for example, over 60 per cent of cases had a dissent (Baum 2007, 111). However, the rate is much higher than in many European courts. The French Constitutional Court and the European Court of Justice, for example, make it a practice always to deliver unanimous opinions.

24. Concurring opinions are also written by justices for other reasons, such as to clarify a particular point or to place emphasis on something said by the Court.

25. The structure of this part of the chapter is informed, to some extent, by Baum 2007.

26. As mentioned earlier, the provincial and federal courts of appeal hear most of their cases 'as of right' and are concerned primarily with correcting errors. This suggests that many of their cases may be relatively straightforward with little room for outside influences on their decisions. Their spot in the hierarchy of courts should also ensure that lower appeals court judges are more constrained in their decision making. Of course, balancing this is the relative obscurity of these courts of appeal. Much less attention is paid to their decisions by the media and the public, and that may make them feel more able to decide cases as they wish (Baum 2008a).

27. For an interesting critique of the umpire metaphor, see McCormick 1994. Among other things, McCormick argues that while the umpire's rulings are 'secondary to the point of the game (which is to score enough goals or touchdowns . . .), the judge's rulings in some sense *are* the game' (McCormick 1994, 50).

28. The discussion in this section is influenced by Baum 2007 and Baum 2008a.

29. These 'invitations' to the legislature to change the court's decisions have been studied in the American context. An example is provided by Justice Marshall's majority opinion in *Mansell v. Mansell* (1989), 'We realize that reading the statute literally may inflict economic harm. . . . But we decline to misread the statute in order to reach a sympathetic result. . . . Congress chose the language that requires us to decide as we do, and Congress is free to change it' (594). See the discussion in Hausegger and Baum 1999.

30. Since 1949, however, the Supreme Court has not considered itself *bound* by its previous decisions (Hogg 2006b).

31. As discussed earlier in the chapter, such different decisions can serve as a trigger for Supreme Court review, and indeed these cases were heard by the Supreme Court in 1990. The Supreme Court upheld the legislation under s. 1 of the Charter.

32. However, there is some suggestion that the *obiter* statements of the Supreme Court should be followed: see the discussion in Gall 2004, 453.

33. Hogg (2006b) argues this is particularly true for constitutional cases. Since judicial decisions in the constitutional area are much more difficult for the legislature to change (since a constitutional amendment is required), the Court should be more willing to overturn precedent in this area to keep constitutional law 'abreast of new technology and new social and economic needs' (Hogg 2006b, 80). The Supreme Court of Canada, however, has not made distinctions between constitutional and non-constitutional cases in terms of observing precedent.

34. Cairns (1971), however, has argued that the JCPC decisions, which tended to be protective of provincial autonomy, did reflect the social realities of Canada in that the country had serious linguistic and regional divisions that might have ruptured if the provinces had not been given sufficient latitude.

35. The Court does speak in terms of legislative intent in the statutory area. Statutes are supposed to be interpreted in ways that best further their objective (Gall 2004). See the discussion in the next section.

36. Morton and Knopff argue that the exclusion was made deliberately to prevent the controversy it might create among the public—controversy that government advisers feared might destroy the support for the constitutional package as a whole (2000, 43).

37. In 2007, the Supreme Court ruled that the collective bargaining process was protected by section 2(d) of the Charter—the freedom-of-association clause (*Health Services and Support-Facilities Subsector Bargaining Assn. v. British Columbia* 2007). This represented a significant shift from their earlier opinions. The Court did not, however, discuss the right to strike in that opinion.

38. The rules for the interpretation of the Civil Code in Quebec are similar to those for the interpretation of ordinary legislation outside of Quebec. According to Brierley and Macdonald, the primary tendency of judges in interpreting the Code is to look at literal and logical interpretations. However, judges can also undertake a historical examination of why the language in the Code was used or try to read the text in a way that reflects contemporary social justice (1993, 136).

39. This contrast, however, may be lessening since the current US Supreme Court contains a vocal opponent to the use of legislative history, Justice Antonin Scalia, and the incidence of its use has declined in recent years (Brudney and Ditslear 2006).

40. Sullivan notes, however, that the justices have not always been consistent in their approaches (1998, 195–6).

41. Sullivan (1998) actually prefers an approach she calls pragmatism. This approach differs from textualism in that it does not just focus on legislative intent. Textualism considers the proper interpretation of a disputed text to be one that complies with the intention of the legislature. Pragmatism, by contrast, considers the proper interpretation of the text to be one that solves the dispute in an 'appropriate way'—producing a result that is 'just and reasonable' (Sullivan 1998, 184).

42. Ideology is relatively straightforward in civil liberties issues: votes for the rights of criminal defendants and for freedom of religion, freedom of expression, and the like are considered liberal votes. Things are often not as straightforward in economic and other types of cases. Generally, however, votes for government policies and for economic 'underdogs' are coded as liberal (Baum 2007, 122).

43. The Binnie and LeDain quotations are adopted from Ostberg and Wetstein 2007.

44. Ostberg and Wetstein also test the influence of the party of the appointing Prime Minister on the justice. They discover that party is not a good predictor of ideological votes in any of the issue areas. This finding is interesting since American studies of judicial decision making often include the party of the appointing President as a 'stand in' measure for ideology—with significant results. Ostberg and Wetstein suggest that this measure may not work as well outside the United States, particularly where more moderate justices are being appointed. They argue that the newspaper measure (which is based on work by Segal and Cover in the United States) is able 'to capture more nuanced ideological distinctions because it is based on journalistic interviews with legal experts in the field and so provides a more accurate, fine-tuned account of the true ideological tendencies of individual justices once they are on the high court' (2007, 217).

45. This literature suggests the justices act strategically to achieve their goals, but it does not always equate those goals with achieving good policy. While most of the literature does focus on policy goals, some leave open the possibility that legal principles may be the motivation (see the discussion in Epstein and Knight 1998). Whatever, the goal being pursued by justices, proponents of this model agree, that the justices are constrained in their decision making.

46. Interestingly, the studies not finding differences between the genders tend to be older (see, for example, Gottschall 1983; Gryski and Main 1986). This has led some to speculate that the selection of early female judges may have resulted in women with similar viewpoints to their male colleagues, or that early female judges—as lone representatives of their gender—may have felt pressure to avoid standing out, with the

result that they voted with their male colleagues more often than their preferences would suggest (Peresie 2005).

47. Songer and Crews-Meyer (2000) found that male and female judges voted significantly differently on civil rights cases at the state supreme court level as well.

48. Regardless of the male judge's ideology, having a female judge on the panel with him doubled the likelihood the male judge would vote for the plaintiff in sexual harassment cases, and almost tripled the likelihood in sex discrimination cases (Peresie 2005, 1778).

49. The Supreme Court does occasionally decide cases with only a plurality of justices, rather than a majority. However, this still requires the opinion writers to attract more justices than an opposing side. Justices would prefer to reach majority decisions, since plurality opinions do not provide clear cues to lower courts on the legal principles at stake.

50. Not all justices value consensus, however. Justice Wilson, for example, disliked it when her colleagues engaged in 'repugnant' lobbying to ensure that there would be a majority on issues they considered important' (Sauvageau, Schneiderman, and Taras 2006, 210). This was not always a popular position to take, as evidenced by Chief Justice Lamer's suggestion that Wilson was 'stubborn as a mule' [unwilling] to engage in the kind of 'horse-trading that unites judges and results in strong common opinions' (quoted in Sauvageau, Schneiderman, and Taras 2006, 210, from original sources).

51. In the United States, scholars have attempted to measure the influence of justices on one another by examining changes in the justices' votes from the initial conference to the final decision, and changes in opinion drafts that are made in response to colleagues' comments (Maltzman, Spriggs, and Wahlbeck 2000). Unfortunately, systematic records of the justices' votes in conference and their numerous written messages back and forth to each other after a draft is circulated are not available in Canada. Although interviews with Supreme Court justices have been done, there is not specific evidence on a high number of cases, over time.

52. Justice Bertha Wilson, for example, was suspicious of the media after reading several news stories on her speeches which she argued 'distorted her remarks' (Sharpe and Roach 2003, 294).

53. The references to legal scholarship by the Quebec Court of Appeal may reflect the importance placed on legal treatises in the Civil Law system of law. See Brierley and Macdonald (1993, 125–6).

Chapter 5

1. Clarence Thomas was accused of sexual harassment by Anita Hill, a law professor who had worked for Thomas at the Equal Employment Opportunity Commission. When these allegations were made public, the Senate held special hearings to investigate the matter (at this point the Senate Judiciary Committee had already sent Thomas's nomination to the floor of the Senate with 'no recommendation') (Baum 2007). The hearings were televised for three days and provided enough racy details to catch the public's attention.

2. The description of the hearing comes from the authors' notes taken while watching the event. For a more detailed account of the hearing—and a reprint of the actual speech given by the moderator—see the account by Peter W. Hogg (2006a) in the *Osgoode Hall Law Journal*.

3. Of course what is meant by competence may be a debate in itself.

4. This power was spelled out in the *Maritime Bank Case* decided by the Judicial Committee of the Privy Council in 1892.

5. A filibuster is a tactic used to delay a vote in the Senate where one or more Senators talks continuously to prevent a vote from taking place (Welch et al. 2008). Filibusters can be stopped by a vote of cloture, which requires the support of sixty senators. A vote of cloture does not actually stop a filibuster immediately. Rather it limits debate to twenty more hours (Welch et al. 2008). Filibusters of judicial nominees are a relatively new phenomenon. The first use occurred in 1968 in an effort to stall President Johnson's elevation of Abe Fortas to Chief Justice of the Supreme Court (Epstein and Segal 2005).

6. Epstein and Segal (2005) argue that ideology and partisanship have always played a role in federal appointments.

7. In New Jersey, for example, the governor appoints judges for an initial seven-year term, after which the judge must be reappointed and confirmed by the Senate. If this is successful the judge may then keep his seat until the age of seventy (Tarr 2006, 60).

8. State judicial selection methods tend to have a historical basis. Judicial elections were very rare early in American history, and it is probably no coincidence that the few states using executive appointment and legislative elections are primarily states that were part of the original thirteen colonies (Baum 2008a; Berkson 1980).

9. Depending on the state, this committee is either a screening committee (which sorts through names provided by the executive) or a nominating committee (which accepts nominations and applications itself).

10. A blatant example of the problem is provided by Texas. While Pennzoil had an $11 billion lawsuit against Texas pending before the state's Supreme Court, Pennzoil's lawyers contributed over $315,000 to the justices' campaigns (Tarr 2006, 63).

11. One former chief justice of the Idaho Supreme Court made it clear that he deliberately resigned before the end of his term in order to let the Idaho governor choose an interim replacement and give that person an advantage in the coming election (speech to Boise State University students; see also Popkey 2007). In Idaho, in the case of an interim appointment, a judicial council receives applications from prospective judges and forwards a list of names to the governor. The former justice thought this resulted in a better process and better judges than straight election. Thus, he deliberately instituted a kind of end run around the process.

12. The advantage of incumbency tends to vary by selection method and by level of court. A study by Melinda Gann Hall (2001) discovered a significant difference between partisan elections and retention elections. Whereas state supreme court judges in partisan elections had a 19 per cent rate of defeat, this same level of judge had only a 2 per cent rate of defeat in retention elections. This study also suggested that state lower court judges tend to fare better than state supreme court judges (Hall 2001).

13. Interestingly, Quebec respondents have demonstrated the highest level of support for elected judges (Makin 2007b).

14. As mentioned earlier, nominating committees are made up of lawyers and lay people. Governors are usually responsible for selecting the lay members of the committee, while state bar associations choose the lawyers for the committee.

15. Although one study did conclude that merit selection at least prevented the selection of 'very poor judges' (Reddick 2002, 743).

16. The description of judicial selection in France is based on 'ordinary' judges (primarily of the civil and criminal courts) and does not apply to judicial selection to the Constitutional Council. The Constitutional Council is the only body in France with

the power of judicial review—although it is limited to reviewing proposed laws that are referred to it by the other branches of government. There are nine members of this Council; the President of the Republic, the President of the National Assembly, and the President of the Senate nominate three each. Members tend to be former politicians or other high-profile people although to date all members have had some legal experience (Provine and Garapon 2006).

17. In 2003, Prime Minister Tony Blair announced substantial changes to the British judicial system, including the creation of a new Supreme Court. This Court begins hearing cases in 2009. Its members are chosen by a different commission from that described here.

18. The four provinces are British Columbia, Alberta, Saskatchewan, and Quebec. The other provinces are close, with Manitoba appointing the same number of judges and New Brunswick appointing only two fewer judges than the federal government in that province (see Chapter 2).

19. The lay people members of the committee have tended to be very active in the community. The current chair of the committee, for example, is an engineer who is also a member of the Ontario Panel of the Canadian Broadcast Standards Council, the President of the Council of the Muslim Community of Canada, the Past Co-Chair of the National Muslim Christian Liaison Committee, and past President of the Ontario Advisory Council on Multiculturalism and Citizenship.

20. The Yukon and the Northwest Territories also follow this system.

21. The Alberta Judicial Council is made up of the Chief Justice of Alberta (or a designate), the Chief Judge of the Provincial Court of Alberta (or a designate), the Chief Judge of the Court of Queen's Bench (or a designate), the President of the Law Society of Alberta (or a designate), and no more than two other people selected by the Attorney General (Alberta 2008).

22. The chief justices of the provincial superior courts are generally appointed by the Prime Minister rather than the Minister of Justice.

23. And it is probable that appointments made with an emphasis on patronage will not produce the best possible candidates. For example, Russell and Ziegel discovered that ten of the thirteen judges rated as only 'fair' or 'poor' by the evaluators in their study had major or minor connections to the party that appointed them (1991, 25).

24. The process of judicial appointment described here for the s. 96 provincial superior courts is the same process used for the s. 101 Federal Courts of Canada (trial and appeal courts). Therefore, these courts are included in this section rather than with the Supreme Court (the other s. 101 court). The Tax Court of Canada followed the same process as the s. 96 courts until November 2006, when a pilot project was introduced. Under the pilot project, Tax Court candidates are evaluated by a new five-person Judicial Advisory Committee, which includes a judge of the Tax Court and four nominees chosen by the Minister of Justice after consulting with the Chief Justice of the Tax Court (Commissioner for Federal Judicial Affairs 2008).

25. This category was used at least until 2006. However, it currently does not appear on the Commissioner's website.

26. Before this point, committees rated candidates as either 'qualified' or 'not qualified'.

27. One prominent example of this occurred in 1998, when Justice Minister Anne McLellan reportedly asked the Nova Scotia advisory committee to reconsider its 'not recommended' rating of her friend and fellow Dalhousie Law School graduate, Heather Robertson (Meek 1998). Robertson was appointed to the Nova Scotia Supreme Court.

28. This number excludes sitting judges who were promoted to a higher court.

29. The donors were identified by matching judicial names to Elections Canada's 'Contributions to Political Parties' data. They were actually labelled probable donors since 100 per cent certainty cannot be achieved. However, to be included as a match (and, therefore, a probable donor), the name had to be either very unusual or a complete match: first, middle, and last names.

30. Russell argues, however, that these political considerations were in the form of party and personal connections to the appointing government, rather than connections in ideology—something that sets the Canadian process apart from the American (2007a).

31. Indeed, anecdotal evidence suggests that patronage continues to be a heavy consideration under the Conservative government. For example, the elevation of J.D. Bruce McDonald from Alberta's provincial court to its Court of Queen's Bench caused controversy in 2006. McDonald had been heavily involved in the Conservative Party and its predecessors, the Alliance and Reform parties. Among other roles, he had been chief financial officer for the Reform Party of Alberta and the main organizer of fundraising dinners to benefit Stockwell Day (who at the time of McDonald's appointment was Public Security Minister) (Galloway 2006). McDonald's daughter was also a special assistant in the Prime Minister's Office at the time of his appointment.

32. Lamer and retired law professor Jacob Ziegel, who also testified before the committee, may not have got their point across. Lamer suggested that criminal cases may make up only 2 per cent of these courts' caseloads. In response to their testimony, however, Alberta MP Myron Thompson said, 'I got a pretty good idea about what I'd like to see for a judge. It wouldn't be a softie. It would be a hard man who would say the punishment's got to fit the crime' (Telus 2007).

33. Actual numbers of minorities and aboriginal judges are not available.

34. It is possible that the 'two from the West' convention has developed into one justice from British Columbia and one justice from the prairies (because of the population distribution). This will definitely be indicated if Chief Justice Beverley McLachlin is replaced by someone also from British Columbia when she retires (our thanks to the anonymous reviewers for suggesting this possibility).

35. This procedure is violated only rarely. In 1979, for example, an Ontario justice was replaced with an appointee from British Columbia in order to quiet the BC bar, which felt the province was being ignored (Sharpe and Roach 2003, 187). However, the Ontario Attorney General was assured that when the Alberta justice retired in 1982, his spot would be filled with someone from Ontario (Sharpe and Roach 2003, 1987). This was done, thus restoring the regional balance on the bench.

36. For example, the latest retiree from the Supreme Court, Justice Michel Bastarache, was only sixty-one when he left the bench on 30 June 2008. Speculation often surrounds these early retirements. In Justice Bastarache's case there is a suggestion that his health may have played a role since he had undergone coronary angioplasty before announcing his retirement (MacCharles 2008).

37. Indeed, in 1954, Justice Abbott was appointed while a member of the federal cabinet (McCormick 2005a).

38. There is some suggestion that Michel Bastarache had partisan ties to the Liberal party, which appointed him in 1997. Bastarache had been a lawyer in Prime Minister Jean Chrétien's law firm and had been an election adviser to the Liberal party during the 1993 election (Thorsell 1997).

39. Two American law professors provoked widespread debate when they suggested that objective measures could be used to rate lower-court judges on their performance (arguably this would be a merit assessment), the winner being awarded the Supreme Court appointment (Choi and Gulati 2004). These measures included factors such as

the number of citations to a judge's opinion made by the Supreme Court and legal academics, as well as a judge's rate of reversal.

40. In earlier years, religion, in terms of the balance between Protestants and Catholics, played a role in appointments. However, this consideration is no longer thought to influence appointments.

41. This tradition has been broken occasionally. In 1984, Prime Minister Trudeau appointed Brian Dickson Chief Justice instead of the most senior francophone justice on the bench, Jean Beetz. Sharpe and Roach (2003) argue, however, that this was done out of necessity since Beetz had suffered a heart attack a few years previously and was uninterested in the job of Chief Justice, with all of its administrative and ceremonial duties (particularly the public appearances and speeches). Dickson was the most senior justice at the time and had been performing the necessary day-to-day administrative tasks on the Court during the illness of the previous Chief Justice (Bora Laskin) (Sharpe and Roach 2003, 285).

Chapter 6

1. Justice Barry Strayer, *Gratton v. Canadian Judicial Council* (1994, para. 16).

2. The original wording is 'justice should not only be done but should manifestly and undoubtedly be seen to be done,' from *R. v. Justices of Sussex, Ex parte McCarthy* (1924, 259).

3. As Martin Shapiro (1981) observes, in the earliest historical versions of courts, the parties to the dispute would mutually consent to the selection of a judge and to the rules by which the dispute would be resolved. In that context, judicial independence meant that the judge had to be independent from (and impartial to) the two parties. Although parties still choose the third party in some forms of alternative dispute resolution, as discussed in Chapter 3, this is no longer done in courts of law. Canadian judges are appointed to the bench by the executive branch of government and assigned to specific cases either by the Chief Justice of their court or by lottery. And, of course, the parties no longer get to pick the 'rules of the game'. Instead, cases are adjudicated on the basis of pre-existing laws passed by Parliament or regulatory agencies or on judicially crafted precedents in the common law. Thus, we have substituted 'law and office for consent' (Shapiro 1981, 5). In the process, judges acquired the crucial function of enforcing without prejudice or favour the laws passed by the legislative branch—the cornerstone of the rule of law.

4. Choi, Gulati, and Posner (2007) provocatively conclude that elected judges in the United States are no less independent than their appointed brethren. Though their study is interesting, how they operationalize the definition of 'independence' leaves much to be desired and it calls their conclusions into doubt. Moreover, their evidence does not refute previous studies that demonstrate that the prospect of an election alters judicial behaviour (see the discussion in Chapter 5).

5. The Act covered only the judges on the top courts in London, the three traditional common law courts, the equity courts, and specialty courts (the Admiralty). In 1750, there were only twelve common law court judges, two equity, and one Admiralty. In 1867 only fifteen common law judges were protected, and even as of 1974 (after various court reforms and mergers) only seventy. The bulk of cases until the nineteenth century were handled by justices of the peace, who had no formal protections, or later by judges on the county courts or circuit courts. See Able-Smith and Stevens (1967) and Shetreet (1976). Even today, according to the Lord Chief Justice of

England and Wales, 90 per cent of criminal cases are heard before the country's 30,000 magistrates, who are unpaid, have no legal training, and are not protected by the Act (Lord Phillips of Worth Matravers 2006).

6. In a rather more contorted argument, Hogg (2003, 204) contends that they are not protected, but his position is based not on the wording of ss. 99 and 100, but on the context provided by the surrounding sections, including s. 101. Since ss. 97 and 98 refer explicitly to provincial courts, it would be constitutionally permissible for the federal government to appoint to s. 101 courts judges who were not members of the bar; s. 101 gives Ottawa the power to create federal courts 'notwithstanding anything in this Act', a power which Hogg argues exempts them from ss. 99 and 100. Although Hogg's argument raises some interesting points, it is difficult to ignore the explicit wording of ss. 99 and 100, which supports Lederman's position. Moreover, the fact that the federal government appoints the judges of both the s. 96 and s. 101 courts suggests they should be treated in the same fashion. Finally, the status of the Supreme Court of Canada as the highest court in the land (and, for that matter, of the Federal Court of Appeal as a senior appellate court) suggests that any doubt regarding their institutional independence should be resolved in their favour.

7. Indeed, it is unclear that such a challenge *could* have been made since the *Canadian Bill of Rights* applies only to the federal government and Acts of Parliament. Although s. 92 courts enforce the *Criminal Code* (a federal statute), these courts are actually established by provincial statutes, which contain the provisions regarding removal, salaries, and court administration that might violate independence.

8. New Brunswick was the last to do so, in 1985. With only three provincially appointed judges, it is not surprising that Prince Edward Island does not have a judicial council to investigate complaints against these judges. Instead, complaints against provincially appointed judges are investigated by a judge of that province's s. 96 Supreme Court. The system is susceptible to executive abuse, however, because investigations are formally initiated by the 'Lieutenant Governor in Council'—i.e., the cabinet, or even more accurately, the Attorney General and Premier—who also selects the investigating judge. A preferable system would be to allow the public to lodge complaints and have the s. 96 and 92 judges in the province work together to select the investigating judge (or judges) or to merge with one of the judicial councils in a neighbouring province.

9. In the case of the CJC, senior judges (Chief Justices and Associate Chief Justices of the superior s. 96 and s. 101 courts) may appoint as their representative to the CJC a more junior colleague from their bench.

10. The CJC recommended the removal of s. 96 court judge Jean Bienvenue in 1996 for his sexist and anti-Semitic comments, and the New Brunswick Judicial Council recommended removing s. 92 court judge Jocelyne Moreau-Bérubé in 1999 for her slurs against Acadians living in her district. Both cases are discussed later in this chapter.

11. Judge Kerry Evans of the Ontario Court of Justice resigned in 2004 just as the Ontario Judicial Council was set to recommend his suspension or removal for his sexual harassment of several courthouse staff.

12. This was the issue in the Landreville affair discussed later in this chapter.

13. The transaction in question was quite interesting: the seventy-five property owners on Île-Dorval, a small island near Montreal, offered the town council $250,000 to buy all publicly held property on the island. Their plan was to then dissolve the municipal government and thereby avoid forced amalgamation with neighbouring Dorval. Flynn's wife was a cottage owner on the island and also a member of the town council, which accepted the deal.

14. Complaints to the CJC usually pass through a four-stage screening process. Cosgrove was challenging the constitutionality of section 63(1) of the *Judges Act*, which allows provincial Attorneys General to bypass this process.

15. It is somewhat curious that the FCA did not simply strike down s. 63(1) of the *Judges Act*, since the Court itself noted that the section now 'serves no practical purpose' (para. 84).

16. Although he subsequently distanced himself from these remarks and assured Alberta's top judge in a letter that no threat to judicial independence was intended, Klein's comments largely precipitated the litigation that ultimately reached the Supreme Court as the *Remuneration Reference*, discussed later in this chapter.

17. For example, Judge Ruffo once ordered two teenagers to sleep in the office of the Quebec social service minister in Quebec City to highlight the lack of available foster-care beds; appeared in a television commercial for Via Rail; accepted a speaker's fee of $1,500 to talk at a conference about New Age medicine; and failed to disclose her friendship with an expert witness who appeared before her (CBC 2006).

18. As this only applies to the s. 92 courts and tribunals in Quebec, the official version is only in French; the regulation is the *Judicial code of ethics*, R.Q. c. T-16, r. 4.1. The French version and this English translation appear on the official website of the Conseil de la magistrature du Québec. The same versions appear on Canlii: http://www.canlii.org/qc/laws/regu/t-16r.4.1/20080515/whole.html.

19. Notably, this included one of the authors of this book, who was on a provincial government scholarship at the time!

20. Claiming a violation of judicial independence, the Chief Justice of the superior court sued the government and obtained an injunction blocking the firings. The matter was settled out of court by court staff and the government.

21. The most serious incident of the 'Judges Affair' involved Minister of Public Works Bud Drury, who telephoned the judge hearing a contempt-of-court case against another minister, André Ouellet. Ouellet had been cited for contempt after publicly calling a court ruling (involving his department) 'silly' and 'a complete disgrace'. Drury called to see if an apology from Ouellet would resolve the matter, while also suggesting that the contempt charge represented a 'ganging-up of the English-speaking establishment [the judge in question was English] against French Canadians [Ouellet]' (Russell 1987, 79). The judge dismissed Drury's offer as improper, and the entire story later appeared in the *Globe and Mail*, sparking a major political crisis for the Liberals. See Russell (1987, 79–80) for more detail on these incidents.

22. A recent study by Riddell, Hausegger, and Hennigar (2008) of federal judicial appointments since 1988 found that 76 per cent of appointments to the (s. 96) provincial courts of appeal, 71 per cent of those to the (s. 101) Federal Court of Appeal, and eleven of twelve Supreme Court of Canada appointments were elevations. The number of elevations to the s. 96 Court of Appeal has thus increased from 60 per cent during the 1984–8 period (Russell and Ziegel 1991). The proportion of s. 96 trial court appointments that were elevations from the s. 92 provincial trial courts has stayed at about 10 per cent, however, in contrast to Russell's (1987) expectations.

23. For a review of the CJC's treatment of the issue of judicial free speech, see Ratushny (2000).

24. See last chapter's discussion of the 'Missouri Plan' judicial appointment system, which in some US states includes a 'retention' vote by the legislature or voters after a set period of service.

25. See Wyman (2001) for an argument that the constitutional protections for judicial independence should not be extended to all administrative tribunals.

Chapter 7

1. In Canada, the official term for brief is 'factum'. However for the sake of convenience, this chapter uses the terms brief and factum interchangeably.
2. LEAF's brief was also signed by the Barbra Schlifer Commemorative Clinic, the Women's College Hospital Sexual Assault Care Centre, the Metropolitan Toronto Special Committee on Child Abuse, the Metro Action Committee on Public Violence Against Women and Children, and the Ontario Coalition of Rape Crisis Centres.
3. The CCLA argued that s. 277 should be upheld but that s. 276 should be struck down as an unconstitutional infringement on the accused's right to a fair trial.
4. Section 7 of the Charter of Rights and Freedoms states, 'Everyone has the right to life, liberty and security of the person and the right not to be deprived thereof except in accordance with the principles of fundamental justice.' Section 11(d) states, 'Any person charged with an offence has the right to be presumed innocent until proven guilty according to law in a fair and public hearing by an independent and impartial tribunal.'
5. The success of governments before the courts has received more attention in the United States political science literature. The US federal government, in particular, has been found to be extremely successful before its Supreme Court (see for example, McGuire 1998, Salokar 1992, and Segal and Reedy 1988), and state governments have also enjoyed a high (and, more recently, increasing) success rate before the US Supreme Court (Waltenburg and Swinford 1999a). See Chapter 8 for information on Canadian government success rates.
6. For a description of this group and its litigation see Razack 1991 and Manfredi 2004.
7. In 2001 EGALE changed its name to EGALE Canada Inc. (Smith 2005, 351–2). For a description of this group and its litigation see Smith 2005.
8. Cases often take several years to make their way through the courts. For example, in *Seaboyer*, LEAF and the CCLA first appeared before the Ontario Court of Appeal in 1987, but the case was not heard by the Supreme Court until 1991.
9. Many of the early studies of interest groups concentrated on groups representing the interests of disadvantaged groups such as African Americans or women.
10. In fact, the case described in the introduction to this chapter, *R. v. Seaboyer,* could also be used as an example here since LEAF went to court in that case to support legislation that favoured its interests in protecting complainants in sexual assault cases.
11. Indeed, in the United States, one state supreme court justice reported that his court's librarian tracks (and posts for the justices) law-review articles commenting on the court's decisions. This justice told law-review editors, 'You grade us . . . and we pay attention' (Baum 2006, 100).
12. Contrary to the Court's membership for its first 100 years, the last 30 years have seen the appointment of several justices who have been law professors at some point in their careers (this list includes Justices Beetz, Chouinard, Lamer, LeDain, LaForest, McLachlin, Stevenson, Iacobucci, Bastarache, Arbour, and Charron).
13. Critics of the NJI suggest that it now functions to 'indoctrinate' participants to specific viewpoints—particularly the feminist viewpoint of the Charter. Morton and Knopff, for example, argue that the 'unbalanced character of judicial education seminars and the heavy involvement of LEAF activists have raised concerns about judicial independence' (2000, 127).
14. Morton and Knopff (2000) suggest that EGALE was given the short list of candidates being considered by the Justice Department, access that other groups—particularly conservative groups—did not enjoy.

15. This is not to say that groups have not appeared before the courts as direct parties in a case. See for example, *Sierra Club of Canada v. Canada (Minister of Finance)* 2002.

16. Indeed LEAF faced a similar dilemma in *Tremblay v. Daigle*, a major abortion case with less than favourable facts for the group. Chantel Daigle, who was well past the first trimester of her pregnancy by the time this case made it way up through the courts, was not a victim of rape but rather had deliberately got pregnant and sought an abortion only after breaking up with her boyfriend (although charges of abuse by Tremblay were made at court) (see Morton 1992).

17. For example, in 1986 LEAF sponsored a party in a case before the Supreme Court of Ontario, Divisional Court. The case, *Melita M. Chittenden, Avelina M. Villanueva, the Toronto Organization for Domestic Workers' Rights v. AG of Ontario*, challenged the exclusion of domestic workers from minimum-wage protections. LEAF has also sponsored cases before the Ontario Human Rights Commission, the Workers' Compensation Board, and other courts.

18. For example, the American equivalent of intervener briefs—amicus curiae briefs—have been estimated to cost $20,000 per case (Caldeira and Wright 1988). While this figure may be daunting to some groups, it compares favourably to the cost of sponsoring a case.

19. According to Alan Levy, lawyers in the common law system often served the function of interveners by providing information to judges. Since precedent is so important in the common law, judges need to be cognizant of past decisions. Before recent advances in information technology, a judge had to rely on his own memory of precedent, and so there was room for error. Thus 'lawyers, awaiting hearing of their own cases, would speak out to assist the judge in his recollection' (Levy 1972, 94; Brodie 2002, 19).

20. Chief Justice Bora Laskin, who had been so instrumental in opening up the Court to interveners in the 1970s, suffered from a serious illness in 1983. Justice Brian Dickson, who at least initially was less predisposed towards interveners, took over the Chief Justice's responsibilities during this time. Laskin died in March 1984.

21. One exception to the greater receptivity in public law cases is that intervener status is granted only rarely in criminal cases—except where larger constitutional issues are at stake. For example, a trial judge in British Columbia used precedents establishing this exception to deny intervener status to the CCLA, which wanted to make presentations about the 'artistic-merit' defence in a child pornography case (*R. v. Sharpe* 2002).

22. This debate is related to the political-disadvantage theory discussed earlier in this chapter. As noted, the accuracy of this description of litigating interest groups has come under question in both the United States and Canada. Brodie (2000) takes this further to suggest not only that other groups are using the Court but also that the groups traditionally considered politically disadvantaged are not in fact disadvantaged at all. Thus he contests one justification often used for allowing interest-group participation before the courts.

    Coming from a far different ideological point of view (often classified as neo-Marxist), Michael Mandel (1994) also casts doubt on the idea that the politically disadvantaged benefit from court action. Mandel argues that leftist groups should not waste their resources on the courts because he believes courts are rooted in the status quo and will never benefit the truly disadvantaged.

23. Interestingly, however, interveners are still absent from a large number of Supreme Court cases. For example, 52 per cent of cases decided in 2006 had no interveners. This is a much higher percentage than that seen in the United States, where in most years over 90 per cent of Supreme Court cases have some amicus curiae participation.

24. Government prosecutors litigate under the title of 'the Queen'—see the chapters on governments and criminal justice for more details.

Chapter 8

1. Some sections of this chapter are adapted from Lori Hausegger, 'Participation of Governments before the Supreme Court of Canada', a paper presented at the Annual Meeting of the Midwest Political Science Association, Chicago, IL in 2002; Matthew A. Hennigar, 'Players and the Process: Charter Litigation and the Federal Government', *Windsor Yearbook of Access to Justice* 21 (2002): 91–109; Matthew A. Hennigar, 'Why Does the Federal Government Appeal to the Supreme Court of Canada in Charter of Rights Cases?: A Strategic Explanation', *Law and Society Review* 41(1) (2007): 225–50; and Matthew A. Hennigar, 'Conceptualizing Attorney General Conduct in Charter Litigation: From Independence to Central Agency', *Canadian Public Administration* 51(2) (2008): 193–215.

2. The original reference asked only if the proposed change was constitutional, and not the more salient question of whether such a change was constitutionally *necessary* under the Charter's equality rights. The latter question was added six months later, on 28 January 2004.

3. Canada's monarch is, of course, simultaneously the British monarch, and is represented in Canada by the Governor General and provincial Lieutenant Governors. This also explains the unique way we name criminal cases, 'R. v. [accused's name]', such as *R. v. Morgentaler*: the 'R.' stands for 'Regina' or 'Rex', Latin for Queen or King.

4. Such offences, which are specifically identified in the *Criminal Code*, include illegal possession of unregistered firearms (s. 103(3)), belonging to a criminal organization (anti-gang laws, ss. 467.1–467.2), and war crimes and crimes against humanity (s. 7(3.75), which links these to terrorism).

5. In Alberta, the federal and provincial governments agreed to allow special provincial constables to enforce provisions of the federal *Indian Act* on Indian reserves; in the case unsuccessfully challenging this (*R. v. Whiskeyjack and Whiskeyjack* 1984), Alberta was the prosecution, the Government of Canada appearing as an intervener.

6. S. 2 ('Attorney General', (b)) reads: '. . . proceedings commenced at the instance of the Government of Canada and conducted by or on behalf of that Government in respect of a contravention of, a conspiracy or attempt to contravene or counselling the contravention of any Act of Parliament *other than this Act* [that is, other than the *Criminal Code*] or any regulation made under any such Act, means the Attorney General of Canada and includes his lawful deputy' (emphasis added). For offences related to terrorism, and against diplomatic officials and international property (such as the UN's), the federal government's authority to prosecute is shared with provincial governments, so either level of government can initiate proceedings.

7. For example, *R. v. Aziz* (1978) [reversed 1981], *R. v. Parrot* (1979), *R. v. Sacobie* (1979) [affirmed 1983], *R. v. Hauser* (1977) [reversed 1979].

8. Paraphrasing, s. 91 states that any matters *not* clearly assigned to the provinces elsewhere in the Constitution fall within the federal Parliament's jurisdiction. Thus, the Court argued that narcotics were not a public policy issue in 1867 but a genuinely 'new' issue when the first narcotics offences were created, as telecommunications regulations were in the 1930s. Notably, despite the Court's finding in *Hauser*, the federal government has agreements with the governments of Quebec and New Brunswick which permit those provinces to prosecute drug-related offences, except

where the RCMP has laid the charges (Canada, Federal Prosecution Service 2005, I-2–7; Canada, Department of Justice 2001, 3).

9. The Supreme Court surprisingly argued that the 'service' clause in the Constitution required Canada only to build the railway but not to operate it.

10. 53. (1) The Governor in Council may refer to the Court for hearing and consideration important questions of law or fact concerning:
    (a) the interpretation of the Constitution Acts;
    (b) the constitutionality or interpretation of any federal or provincial legislation;
    (c) the appellate jurisdiction respecting educational matters, by the Constitution Act, 1867, or by any other Act or law vested in the Governor in Council; or
    (d) the powers of the Parliament of Canada, or of the legislatures of the provinces, or of the respective governments thereof, whether or not the particular power in question has been or is proposed to be exercised.

11. Hogg (2003, 241, n. 76) notes that the Supreme Court raised a 'doubt' about the constitutional validity of provinces' referring federal legislation but without discussing or resolving the issue in *McEvoy v. New Brunswick (A.G.)* (1983); Hogg (2003) and Strayer (1988) contrarily argue that there is no doubt that the scope of the provincial reference power mirrors that of the federal government.

12. S. 8(7) of the Ontario *Courts of Justice Act*, for example, classifies rulings in reference cases as equivalent to regular judicial decisions and thus appealable like any other 'judgement of the court', and since 1922 the *Supreme Court Act* has similarly classified references initiated by provinces the same way (currently, see s. 36).

13. Robert Frater, Senior General Counsel, Criminal Law Section, Department of Justice Canada, e-mail correspondence with the author, 18 July 2007.

14. Calculated by the authors from publicly accessible data on http://scc.lexum.u montreal.ca.

15. Calculated by the authors from publicly accessible data on http://scc.lexum.u montreal.ca.

16. See, for example, *Rules of the Supreme Court of Canada*, s. 61(4).

17. Deborah MacNair (2001, 130, n. 10) identifies several of the exceptions to this monopoly, including the lawyers for the Canadian International Trade Tribunal, the Judge Advocate General (National Defence), the Canadian Human Rights Commission, the Office of the Information and Privacy Commissioners, the Senate, and House of Commons (see also Brunet (2000, 67)).

18. In 2001, another 763 agents were hired, mostly to conduct prosecutions for narcotics (Canada, Department of Justice 2001, 3).

19. According to Section 2(2) of the *Department of Justice Act*, the Minister of Justice 'is *ex officio* Her Majesty's Attorney General of Canada, holds office during pleasure and has the management and direction of the Department.' Thus, the AG simultaneously sits in cabinet, acts as the official legal advisor to the Governor General, and is responsible for the administration of justice.

20. In this case, the Supreme Court of Canada ruled that Duplessis had violated the rule of law when he arbitrarily revoked the liquor licence of a tavern owner (Roncarelli) solely because Roncarelli had paid bail for Jehovah's Witnesses who had been arrested for solicitation (that is, handing out pamphlets and going door-to-door).

21. This is part of the Crown's broader duty to uphold the integrity of the justice system and the fairness of trials; that may include lowering or dropping charges, seeking lighter sentences in particular cases, or disclosing evidence to the accused that may help them get acquitted. In contrast, defence counsel's only job is to try, as much as the law permits, to acquit his or her client by raising reasonable doubt of their guilt

—they have no reciprocal duty to disclose evidence to Crown that would help the prosecution.

22. This was despite the fact that Morgentaler openly admitted breaking the law and invited prosecution, because he sought to challenge the constitutionality of the ban on abortions. The refusal by juries, on conscientious grounds, to enforce validly enacted laws is known as 'jury nullification', and the practice has been upheld by the Supreme Court of Canada (*R. v. Morgentaler* 1988; *R. v. Krieger* 2006).

23. This said, the decision to prosecute Latimer for second-degree murder rather than *first*-degree murder is also an interesting example of prosecutorial discretion. It is likely that the Crown thought that Latimer's extenuating circumstances made prosecuting to the fullest extent of the law inappropriate (or unlikely to succeed with the jury) and that the public interest would be served by the lesser murder charge (which still carries a ten-year mandatory minimum sentence).

24. Rarely is not, however, never. In 2008, a judge of the Ontario Superior Court stayed charges against six former Toronto police drug squad officers accused of corruption, blaming 'the glacial progress' of the prosecution, which had violated the officers' Charter right to be tried within a reasonable time.

25. Although the claim was for defamation (and $50 million in damages) rather than malicious prosecution, it should be noted that former Prime Minister Brian Mulroney was able to compel the Chrétien government to settle out of court in 1997 after the latter's investigation into alleged kickbacks paid by Karlheinz Schreiber to Mulroney for his government's purchase of Airbus aircraft. The recent revelations of Schreiber's clandestine transactions with the former Prime Minister suggest that the Chrétien government's decision to settle may have been in error (a view now shared by Allan Rock, the Liberal Minister of Justice at the time of the settlement).

26. Free (2002) notes that the factors influencing the decision to prosecute can include, for example, the strength of evidence collected by the police, the severity of the crime, and the race of the victim. To give just one example of how these can combine to frustrate any general conclusions, studies in the US found that blacks are sometimes prosecuted at the same or *lower* levels than whites, but that the majority of victims of black crime are themselves black. Thus, the lower prosecution rates might, ironically, indicate racism (toward victims)—or, conversely, that prosecutors are acting as an effective check on biased or weak policing.

27. Disallowance permitted the federal Parliament to pass a law nullifying provincial legislation; reservation entailed Ottawa's 'requesting' (in practice, requiring) a province's Lieutenant Governor to withhold his or her signature from a bill—for without this Royal Assent, the bill would not become law. Although both powers are still in the Constitution, it is almost impossible to imagine circumstances in which they would be exercised today.

28. Russell's (1983) criticism of the *Patriation Reference*, for example, is on precisely these grounds.

29. Our thanks to Graham Garton, Senior Counsel (Civil Litigation) at the Department of Justice Canada for showing parts of this document to one of this book's authors. Unlike its sister volume, the *Federal Prosecution Service Deskbook*, it was not publicly available on the Department's website at that time.

30. The U.S. Solicitor General seeks appeal only about 12 per cent of the time (Zorn 2002, 157). However, the figures for the two countries are not directly comparable because the studies in each country did not examine the same types of cases or the same time period. (Only Charter cases were studied in Canada and from 1982 to 2000, whereas all types of cases were studied in the U.S., but only from 1993 to 1994).

31. The best-known example of judicial amendment is probably in *Vriend v. Alberta* (1998), when the Supreme Court 'interpreted' the Alberta *Individual Rights Protection Act* to include protection against discrimination based on sexual orientation, even though this wording had been specifically resisted by the Act's framers. This remedy is more commonly known as 'reading in' or 'judicial extension'. Another form of judicial amendment occurs when judges 'read out' or 'sever' a particular word or phrase but otherwise leave the statute in place, even though the removal might completely change the meaning of the law (for example, severing the word 'not' in the sentence, 'Police offers do not need a warrant to search a dwelling-house').

32. The full text of s.1 reads: 'The *Canadian Charter of Rights and Freedoms* guarantees the rights and freedoms set out in it subject only to such reasonable limits prescribed by law as can be demonstrably justified in a free and democratic society.'

33. The US Solicitor General has, however, become more overtly tied to the President and Attorney General over the years, beginning with the Reagan administration. Reagan pushed his first Solicitor General, Rex Lee, to resign when Lee would not ask the US Supreme Court to overturn its 1973 decision in *Roe v. Wade* legalizing abortion. His replacement, Charles Fried, was appointed because he was willing to do what Lee would not, and Fried held the post until the end of Reagan's presidency.

34. This scenario occurred in Ontario in the mid-1990s. After a free vote in which the Ontario legislature rejected sweeping amendments proposed by the NDP government that would have extended rights and obligations to same-sex couples equivalent to those of opposite-sex couples, the then AG Marion Boyd declared that she might refuse to defend the unamended laws. She did just that when the government filed its trial factum in *M. v. H.* (1996). After the NDP's electoral defeat, the new Progressive Conservative government under Mike Harris withdrew Boyd's factum and refiled with an argument that defended the challenged law.

35. This incident points to another problem with Edwards's argument: the AG's assessment of what the 'Constitution requires' may be wrong in the eyes of the court. Indeed, the argument that the Constitution 'requires' a particular course of action betrays an overly simplistic view that rights are fixed and unequivocal. As former United States Supreme Court Justice William Brennan, Jr. once wrote, 'the Constitution does not take the form of a litany of specifics. There are, therefore, very few cases where the constitutional answers are clear.' The same is true in Canada, as evidenced by the frequent disagreements between judges over constitutional interpretation.

36. The success rate was on 'case disposition'—that is, whether an appellant's appeal was allowed, or whether an appeal was dismissed. Recall that in appeals, the party that initiates the appeal is called the 'appellant', and the opposing party is called the 'respondent.' Thus, if you are the respondent, you 'win' on case disposition if the other party's appeal is dismissed.

37. However, as Solberg and Ray's (2005) evidence demonstrates, there are considerable differences between states' success rates; the same is probably true in Canada, for Ontario in particular is probably more successful than average in the higher appeal courts.

38. Figures calculated by the authors.

39. The couple lost on the pension claim because they actually received more money by applying as separate individuals than as spouses. As a result, they were not actually materially disadvantaged by the law.

40. Take, for example, the interpretation of the Charter's s. 2(b) 'freedom of thought, belief, opinion and expression, including freedom of the press and other media of communication'. Does this protect hate speech, child pornography, lies, violent

expression, or commercial advertising? The text of s. 2(b) does not tell us, and the question has been decided on a case-by-case basis by judges. (The answer, incidentally, is 'yes' for everything except violent expression, but in most cases the court has found that it is 'reasonable' under s. 1 of the Charter to limit freedom of expression.)

41. Notably, in the case of the US even Sheehan, Mishler, and Songer (1992) found that governmental litigants were disproportionately successful and individuals, especially poor ones, extremely unsuccessful, consistent with party capability theory. However, big businesses fared worse than the theory would predict, whereas unions and minorities did better.

42. The part of Bill 101 that was successfully challenged was the prohibition on English language schooling in Quebec for children of anglophone parents who were born in Canada but outside Quebec.

Chapter 9

1. Morgentaler and two other doctors were charged with 'conspiring' to break s. 251 of the *Criminal Code* rather than with actually violating s. 251 of the *Criminal Code*. The prosecutors did this to prevent Morgentaler's lawyer from putting sympathetic witnesses on the stand as he had done during his trials in the 1970s in Quebec with the result that he was acquitted (Morton 1992). 'Conspiracies' are 'inchoate' crimes in that they are partial or unfulfilled crimes. The agreement to commit a crime and the subsequent actions to put that plan into effect constitute the criminal act.

2. Two judges—Justices Beetz and Estey—said that the lack of availability of Therapeutic Abortion Committees (TACs) in various places in Canada could lead to women's s.7 right to 'security of the person' being violated. Furthermore, they argued that the uneven availability of an excusing mechanism to a crime (in this instance, TAC approval to excuse an abortion) was not in accordance with the 'principles of fundamental justice' as required by s. 7. Chief Justice Dickson and Justice Lamer agreed with this assessment and added that forcing women before a panel of strangers to discuss such an intimate subject could cause psychological stress and further jeopardize their right to security of the person. Dickson and Lamer also said that the term 'health' would have to be clarified if Parliament tried to pass another abortion law.

3. At this time the line between civil and criminal law was not as distinct as today, but criminal laws were beginning to be recognized as distinct from civil (private) laws in the medieval period (Lieberman 2002).

4. As Verdun-Jones notes, the *Criminal Code* is not a 'code' of law in the way that the civil law system would use the term. Rather than being a coherent statement of general principles of criminal law, the *Criminal Code* is a complex document with specific rules that has been changed in a piecemeal fashion over time (2002, 19–23).

5. Before the *Margarine Reference* (1951), the JCPC had ruled that a law needed only to have penal consequences to be considered a criminal law (*Property and Trade Articles Association*, 1931). The decision in the *Margarine Reference* added that a law needed a criminal public purpose in addition to penal consequences to be considered criminal law. As Hogg notes, however, the list of what constitutes a 'criminal law' purpose was left open-ended and the JCPC had upheld other laws aimed at business competition and price fixing under the criminal law power.

6. Section 1 of the Charter allows for 'reasonable limits' to be put on rights that are 'demonstrably justified' in a 'free and democratic society'. As developed in the *Oakes*

(1986) case and subsequent decisions, the s. 1 analysis requires governments to demonstrate that they have a 'pressing and substantial' objective behind the law and that the means used to achieve those objectives are proportional.

7. By a 4–2 vote the judges also argued that the law violated the right to be presumed innocent in section 11(d) of the Charter because it forced accused to prove that their statements were true in order to avoid conviction.

8. Regulatory offences (involving the environment, health, business competition, and so on) do not require the same degree of subjective fault as do criminal laws. Criminal laws that are serious but do not have quite the same moral stigma attached as murder and some other offences often require only proof of fault based on an objective standard. For example, offences like dangerous driving or manslaughter would require only proof that a 'reasonable person' would have foreseen the consequences of their actions (Sharpe and Roach 2005, 238–39).

9. The accused was actually caught importing seven and a half ounces of cocaine. As noted in Chapter 2, this decision reflects more the policy-making model of courts rather than the adjudicative model, which adheres more closely to the historical facts of the case.

10. The Court's recent decision in *R. v. Ferguson* (2008) reinforced both its position against providing constitutional exemptions and its support of mandatory minimums for gun-related crimes. The Court disagreed with a trial judge's decision to give a police officer who had shot a detainee during an altercation at a RCMP detachment a lesser sentence than the mandatory minimum of fours years' imprisonment.

11. This happened in the *Paré* case (1987). Paré argued that he could not be convicted of first degree murder because he did not murder a young boy 'while committing' an indecent assault as required by the *Criminal Code*—he murdered the boy after the sexual assault, which would constitute second-degree murder. The Court argued, however, that it would be reasonable to conclude that the wording used by Parliament for first-degree murder was meant to capture actions that formed one continuous sequence of events (Paciocco 1999, 114).

12. The courts have ruled that the police can collect DNA without a warrant if a person leaves bodily substances in public areas, such as by throwing the pop can that he or she had been drinking from into a garbage bin at a park. The Supreme Court ruled that since there is less 'expectation of privacy' in such public places, there is no need for a warrant (*Stillman* 1997)

13. Critics of the exclusionary rule also argue that the rule does little to deter police officers from unconstitutional investigations. Some suggest that administrative rules that would affect an officer's personnel evaluation or pay or would introduce the possibility of being sued would be more effective at deterring police without disrupting the search for truth to the extent that the exclusionary rule does.

14. The jury requirement can be waived upon agreement from both the Crown and the accused.

15. Preliminary inquiries can be useful to the defence in that it sees a preview of the Crown's case. However, preliminary inquiries can be bypassed by the use of a preferred indictment by the Attorney General.

16. If the choice is to have the trial in a superior court that court is designated to be a 'youth court' so that the special provisions of the Youth Criminal Justice Act apply.

17. Most, but not all, criminal court jurisdictions reported to Statistics Canada. For details, see Marth (2008).

18. The Saskatchewan Diversion Program policy manual, for example, states that cases involving the use or threatened use of a weapon are ineligible for pre-trial diversion.

In British Columbia, more serious cases require the approval of more senior administrators for diversion (see Moyer and Basic 2004, 28). And Drug Treatment Courts allow for pre-plea diversion stream (before admission of guilt to a judge) only for cases of simple drug possession.

19. It should be noted that the police are given considerable discretion in most instances, except when the accused is accused of murder, as to whether or not to release a suspect before trial. The Ontario Criminal Justice Review Committee report noted that there was considerable variation across Ontario as to how frequently this was done.

20. Accused who are released following a bail hearing may be required to pay an amount of money to the Crown if they do not re-appear in court for their trial (known as a recognizance). An accused also may be required to have a surety—a person who promises to supervise the accused before trial and who may also have to pay money to the Crown if the accused does not show up as required. In some circumstances (such as if a person lives far from the place of custody), a deposit may be required from the accused or surety; however, unlike in the US, private bail bondsmen—individuals who pay an accused's bail bond in exchange for a fee (and who track down the relatively few accused who do not show up for court)—are prohibited in Canada (Liptak 2008).

21. The notion that the justice system would be overwhelmed if plea bargaining was to be discontinued has been placed in question by some studies from the US in jurisdictions that did ban the use of plea bargaining. Studies found that greater pre-charge screening and a continued willingness by many accused to plead guilty led to only relatively minor increases in the number of trials. However, certain methodological elements of the studies have led to questions about their validity, particularly concerning whether the plea bargaining was driven further down the system (Di Luca 2005, 25–8).

22. Karla Homolka's plea bargain occurred after she told the police that she and Paul Bernardo had sexually assaulted and tortured teenagers Leslie Mahaffy and Kristen French in 1991 and 1992; however, Homolka claimed that is was Bernardo's abusive behaviour that led her to help him and that Bernardo was solely responsible for the murder of the two girls. In exchange for her confession, willingness to help the police find evidence, and testimony against Bernardo, Homolka received a deal in which she pled guilty to two charges of manslaughter to be served by concurrent 12-year maximum sentences. The agreement was considered by many in the public and the media to be too lenient, particularly after videotapes of the crimes surfaced that showed Homolka to have been a willing participant in the abuses perpetrated against the girls and in view of the fact that Homolka admitted, during the plea negotiations, to having contributed to her sister's death by drugging and sexually assaulting her with Bernardo. The Galligan Report (1996), commissioned by the Ontario government, concluded that the plea bargain was justified because, at the time of the plea agreement, the police did not have the videotapes of the crime and therefore needed Homolka's testimony. For a critique of the plea bargain, along with the police investigation and the actions of many Crown lawyers associated with the case, see Williams (2003).

23. If such discussions do take place, judges are not allowed to participate actively though they may facilitate such negotiations by giving an opinion on a proposed sentence (Piccinato 2004, 9–10). As noted in Chapter 3, the judge who presides over a pre-trial conference is not allowed to participate in the substantive courtroom proceedings of a case.

24. Rules of disclosure do not apply in the same way to the defence. Communication between a lawyer and their client is considered to be privileged. There are questions

surrounding the ethics of what defence counsel should do if they are given physical, 'smoking-gun' evidence of the guilt of their client. Debates on this topic were renewed in the 1990s when it was revealed that Paul Bernardo's lawyer, Ken Murray, had kept tapes that implicated his client in the kidnapping, sexual assault, and eventual murder of Kristen French and Leslie Mahaffy. Murray was charged with 'obstruction of justice' for not divulging the existence of the tapes sooner, but was acquitted. The trial judge ruled that Murray had kept the tapes as a strategy to surprise and undermine the Crown's star witness against his client (Karla Homolka). The tapes show that Homolka appeared to have at least an equal role in the crimes.

25. There is an argument that defence disclosure does exist to a limited extent in Canada by the *Criminal Code* requirement that either side give the other thirty days' notice when it plans to call an expert witness (Brockman and Rose 2006, 90).

26. The more effective use of pre-trial conferences, especially for complex summary cases in provincial court and most, if not all, cases in superior courts is considered critical to effective case management (Provincial Court of British Columbia 2005; Ontario Superior Court of Justice 2006). The *Criminal Code* mandates pre-trial conferences for jury trials (s. 625) and allows superior courts and provincial courts (the latter with the permission of the provincial Lieutenant-Governor) to make rules of court for criminal proceedings that include pre-trial conferences (s. 482). A recent report prepared for the Ontario Superior Court of Justice by various stakeholders lamented the fact that these conferences, which are mandatory for all criminal cases according to Rule 28 of the Superior Court, are often not taken seriously enough by Crown or defence counsel and even judges. However, as discussed in Chapter 3, there are some who question whether pre-trial conferences adequately protect procedural rights and allow for open and accountable justice.

27. According to court statistics from Statistics Canada, 445,650 criminal cases were initiated against accused individuals (and businesses) in 2003/4 and 372,084 cases in 2006/7 (see Thomas 2004 and Marth 2008). However, since not all court jurisdictions report their data, these numbers even underestimate the total number of cases in any given year (see Thomas 2004 and Warth 2008 for descriptions of their methodology).

28. If a 'challenge for cause' is made before two people have been selected for the jury, the court can call on two lay people at random who are part of the jury pool to act as triers.

29. The Crown also used to be able to 'stand aside' a number of potential jurors without exercising its peremptory challenges, but because this option was not available to the defence, the Supreme Court ruled that the practice violated the right to a fair trial in the Charter (*Bain* 1992).

30. The questionnaire distributed to potential jurors for the O.J. Simpson trial can be viewed at http://www.vortex.com/privacy/simpson-jq.

31. Six of the nine judges in *Biddle* did not comment on the issue except to say that the 'stand-aside' power used by the Crown during jury selection had been subsequently ruled unconstitutional in an earlier case (see note 29 above). Two of the justices, Beverley McLachlin and Claire L'Heureux-Dubé, wrote that it could not be inferred that an all-female jury would be partial or appear to be partial to the Crown's and that jury representativeness was not an essential feature of a jury. Only Justice Gonthier criticized the Crown's actions and wrote in support of jury representativeness (see Martin 1996: 102). In December 2006, the Ontario Court of Appeal rejected an appeal that raised a similar issue from a different perspective. Defence for the accused argued that the trial judge went too far in responding to accusations of racial bias in the justice system and speculation that the Crown was going to try to get an all-white jury by dividing up the jury pool in such a way that it favoured the

selection of black jurors from the panel. Lawyer Gregory Lafontaine argued that his black client in the racially charged case involving a bungled burglary that led to the death of a white woman in the Just Desserts café in Toronto may have actually been harmed by the inclusion of two black jurors, since media reports suggested that many members of the black community had expressed anger at the crime. The Court of Appeal said that it was 'ill-advised' of the trial judge to deviate from normal selection practices but that it did not bias the outcome of the case (Makin 2006a). In a few instances, however, new jury 'arrays' (pools of prospective jurors) have been ordered when too few women appeared in the initial pool. Yet new arrays have not been ordered when there were too few ethnic minorities in the pools of jurors unless there were irregularities in the selection process (Vidmar 1999, 149).

32. A frequent distinction is made between subjective fault requirements and objective fault requirements. To get a conviction for murder, the Crown must prove that an accused had subjective foresight that his or her actions were likely to cause death. For other crimes, which require only an objective requirement of fault, the Crown must show only that the accused behaved in a way that marked a significant departure from what a 'reasonable person' would have done under the circumstances. This would be the case for manslaughter, for example. For most regulatory offences, once the Crown demonstrates that a prohibited action (or inaction) took place, it is up to the accused to demonstrate that there was no negligence. A corporation charged with a pollution offence, for instance, would have to show on a balance of probabilities that it took reasonable precautions to prevent pollution (see Roach 2005, 8–16).

33. The hearsay rule was somewhat relaxed by the Supreme Court in *R. v. Khan* (1990), but this decision was modified and the rules made somewhat less flexible in *R. v. Khelawon* (2006).

34. The majority argued that this held true even for 'general intent' offences like sexual assault. The distinction between 'general' intent and 'specific' intent offences is a legal fiction that attempts to distinguish between offences on the basis of mental awareness and sophistication required to commit a crime (for example, murder is a specific intent offence while manslaughter is a general intent offence). This distinction has been criticized by some. As Paciocco points out, it probably takes no more mental sophistication to commit a murder than it does to cause damage to property, but the former is a 'specific' intent crime and the latter is a 'general' intent crime (1999, 345–6). The distinction between the two types of crimes has been eliminated in some Commonwealth jurisdictions, such as Australia and New Zealand (Roach 2005).

35. Battered Women Syndrome (BWS) and cultural defences try to provide a context for explaining why the accused acted as he or she did. In the case of BWS, the argument is that after women endure multiple cycles of violence they fall into a condition of learned helplessness that prevents them from seeking outside help. They come to believe that there is no alternative but to kill the male abuser.

36. The data are from 2006/7. See Warth (2008) and Thomas (2008) for an explanation of the data collection. The percentages reported here are derived by taking out the cases that were 'stayed' or 'withdrawn' from the 'total number of cases processed' as reported in Warth (2008) and Thomas (2008).

37. Note that cases can have more than one sentence. Because probation is often used in conjunction with other sentences, probation was the most frequently used adult sentence (in 43 per cent of the cases in 2006/7). However, as noted in the text, it is the most serious sentence given in only 28 per cent of the cases (Marth 2008).

38. However, for sexual assaults that are treated as summary offences there is an eighteen-month maximum term of incarceration.

39. The Ontario Court of Appeal has said in cases involving black defendants that the principles in s. 718.2(e) 'are sufficiently broad and flexible to enable a sentencing court in appropriate cases to consider both the systemic and background factors that may have played a role in the commission of the offence and the values of the community from which the offender comes' (*Brown* 2003). Nevertheless, the court in *Brown* refused to lower the sentence imposed by the trial judge, and in a subsequent case it chastised a trial judge for imposing, on the basis of his own research into systemic racism and gender bias in society, only a conditional sentence, rather than incarceration, on two poor, black single mothers convicted of importing cocaine (*Hamilton and Mason* 2007).

40. For cases involving violence, judges in PEI gave the fewest conditional sentences (12 per cent), whereas judges in Manitoba gave the most (43 per cent). The situation was reversed in cases involving property. Judges in PEI gave a conditional sentence most frequently (52 per cent), whereas judges in Manitoba gave the fewest conditional sentences (28 per cent).

41. Paciocco (1999) is critical of those who downplay the need for retribution as a legitimate goal of the criminal justice system. However, he would prefer that politicians be straightforward in advancing retribution as a goal rather than arguing that stiffer penalties will help to reduce crime (which in most cases will not be the result).

42. Tarr (2006, 205) notes that some federal judges began exercising their discretion to depart downwards from the federal guidelines, but Congress enacted a new law in 2003 that restricted the ability of judges to do so.

43. In *Brooker* II (the remedial phase of the Booker decision) the US Supreme Court considered grafting these procedural protections on to the federal guidelines but opted instead to declare the guidelines advisory because advisory guidelines are, oddly perhaps, exempt from these protections (see Frase 2007). The repercussions of this decision and similar ones that apply to the states will have significant repercussions on sentencing in the US.

44. Sentences for indictable offences can be appealed with leave (permission) of the appeal court, whereas there is an automatic right of appeal for summary conviction sentences to the s. 96 superior court (trial) level.

45. For indictable cases the Crown has a right to appeal only on a question of law, such as whether evidence should have been excluded or not, whether or not a judge instructed the jury properly, or whether the judge interpreted the legislation correctly. The accused has a right to appeal on questions of law but if given leave by the court of appeal (or by the trial judge who sends the case to the court of appeal), can also appeal on questions of fact or questions mixed law and fact. The Court of Appeal is also given broad discretion to grant leave to appeal to an accused for any other ground that appears to be sufficient to warrant an appeal.

46. Notwithstanding this overall trend, Greene et al. (1998) emphasized that there were variations between provincial courts of appeal in the relative number of criminal cases that they heard. A possible cause of this variation is that some appellate courts seemed more willing than others to review sentences handed out by trial courts (Greene et al. 1998, 49–50). The Alberta government provided information about the appeal process to incarcerated offenders, and that may help explain why Alberta had a relatively high rate of criminal law appeals (Greene et al. 1998, 203).

47. Trial judges retain the power not to accept the recommendations of the sentencing circle, although in many healing circles the judge takes part in the discussions that lead to a sentence recommendation. Appeals of sentences handed out by sentencing

circles are rare, but there have been instances where appellate courts have found such sentences to be unacceptable (Goff 2004, 226–7).

48. For example, Doob and Sprott (2008) suggest that Canada does not have a more punitive youth criminal justice system because the province of Quebec would oppose such a policy and the federal government needs provincial support for its youth justice policy.

Chapter 10

1. Hemophiliacs have a genetic disorder that impairs their bodies' ability to produce the blood-clotting factors (including platelets and more than twenty different chemical compounds) that stop bleeding. Consequently, cuts and internal bruises that heal relatively easily in healthy people can cause a person with severe hemophilia to bleed to death. Hemophiliacs used to require lengthy and regular transfusions (and had to avoid even minor injuries), but the development of concentrated blood-clotting factors (derived from whole blood) was hailed as a 'miracle' because it allowed many hemophiliacs to live relatively healthy, normal lives. Justin Marche died in 1992 from AIDS-related illness, after suffering from AIDS dementia for three years.

2. *Endean v. Canadian Red Cross Society* 1999; *Parsons v. Canadian Red Cross Society* 1999; *Honhon v. Canada (Procureur général)* 1999.

3. Funds for the plan came from governments, insurance companies, and the sale to Canadian Blood Services and Héma Québec of the Red Cross's assets relating to the blood system.

4. *Adrian v. Canada (Minister of Health)* 2007; *Killough v. The Canadian Red Cross Society* 2007; *McCarthy v. Canadian Red Cross Society* 2007; *Desjardins c. Canada (Procureur général)* 2007.

5. 'Contingency fees' are lawyers' fees that are paid by the client only if the case is won. They usually come out of the settlement or judge's remedy in the form of a pre-negotiated percentage. Contingency fees are discussed later in this chapter.

6. In an attempt to undo the loss in *Robb*, those infected with HIV have launched a class action of their own against the federal government, claiming that the litigation waivers they (or their now deceased relative) signed are void because they were obtained by fraud. Specifically, the plaintiffs claim that the government destroyed certain documents from 1989 that might have been beneficial to the victims' case. At the time of writing, the class action has not yet been approved by the court, but is set to be heard in Toronto (*Leblanc v. Canada (Health)* 2007).

7. http://www.attorneygeneral.jus.gov.on.ca/english/courts/manmed/notice.asp.

8. In Chapter 8, we described how most challenges to statutes under the Charter of Rights arise in the course of criminal prosecutions, as exemplified in *Morgentaler*. Challenges based on the federal division of powers in the constitution have also usually come from those being prosecuted or regulated under the law in question. However, individuals and groups that are not being prosecuted can still challenge the constitutionality of laws—including, it should be noted, the *Criminal Code*—through the civil justice system if they can show that they have 'standing'. Since standing rules have been significantly relaxed since the mid-1970s (see Chapter 3), this is now fairly easy to do. For example, Joe Borowski challenged the *Criminal Code* provision allowing abortions in certain circumstances on the grounds that it violated the fetus's 'right to life' under s. 7 of the Charter. Individuals or groups likely to be directly affected

by a new law might also launch a civil challenge, as one tobacco company did shortly after the federal government passed new legislation prohibiting some forms of tobacco advertising and requiring graphic health warnings on packages (see *RJR-MacDonald Inc. v. Canada* 1995). Another major source of constitutional challenges in the civil justice system is aboriginal rights claims (under s. 35 of the *Constitution Act, 1982*), usually claims for land or compensation from governments as a result of treaties. Such public law cases in the civil justice system are discussed in Chapters 7, 8, and 11.

9. Human rights commissions do tend to blur the distinction between 'public' and 'private' disputes, however, when the commission itself becomes a party to the dispute, rather than simply acting as an adjudicating third party. The recent changes in Ontario formalize and reinforce this trend, for the Ontario Human Rights Commission will be separate from the new Human Rights Tribunal of Ontario. Whereas the tribunal will function primarily as a body of third-party dispute resolution, the commission will be able to initiate complaints and investigations against private actors before the tribunal and appear as a party in the actual hearing. This closely parallels the role of the state in the criminal justice system and may more properly be seen at that point as a *public* law dispute.

10. In addition, federal and provincial governments have explicitly shared jurisdiction over agriculture (s. 95), although federal laws are paramount in cases of conflict.

11. Hogg also notes a narrow federal power to regulate 'general trade and commerce', which had historically been given only a paper-thin reading by the courts. However, in *General Motors v. City National Leasing* (1989) the Supreme Court of Canada upheld on this ground federal anti-price-fixing legislation which applied to intraprovincial trade and commerce.

12. It should be noted that there has been an ongoing movement in Canada to achieve some uniformity between jurisdictions in private law disputes (and other areas of law). See the Uniform Law Conference of Canada website for more information: http://www.ulcc.ca/en/.

13. However, this scenario *could* give rise to a grievance under certain circumstances— for example, if a competitor were 'dumping' its product by selling large quantities well below production cost (as has occurred in international trade), or if a monopoly used 'predatory pricing' (below-cost pricing) to drive new rivals out of the market (as Air Canada and Bell Canada did, in the early days of market deregulation).

14. In a sample of cases from Ontario involving personal (physical) injuries, Kritzer et al. (1991) found rates of claiming (60–70 per cent) comparable to that in Figure 10.2. However, the same study found claiming rates in the US for all personal injuries to be twenty-five percentage points higher than in Ontario and almost thirty points higher (88 per cent) for injuries sustained in traffic accidents.

15. What follows in this section regarding the pre-trial phase is based on publicly available information from the Ministry of the Attorney General of Ontario, 'An Introduction to Civil Cases in the Superior Court of Justice'. http://www.attorney general.jus.gov.on.ca/english/courts/civil/intro2civilcasesinscj.asp (accessed 21 Aug. 2007).

16. Echoing our complaints in Chapter 2 about the shortage of data on provincial courts, researchers in this area (e.g., Canadian Bar Association 1996; Ontario Law Reform Commission 1996; Bogart 1999; Kritzer 2004) agree that there has been very little systematic reporting of Canadian civil justice system statistics. A study by the Centre for Justice System Statistics (Brookbank, Kingsley, and Leonard 1999)—a unit of Statistics Canada—of civil cases in five medium-sized Canadian cities (Calgary,

Edmonton, Halifax, Ottawa, Regina, and Saskatoon) only slightly improved the situation and reported no information on the prevalence of civil jury trials.

17. According to the most recent figures available, in 2005/6 just under 1,600 civil jury trials were heard in Ontario, representing 23 per cent of all civil trials in the province; of these, 74 per cent cases were related to motor vehicle accidents (Ontario Civil Justice Reform Project 2007, 54).

18. Both *Whiten* and *Fidler* concerned insurance companies that had obstinately denied policyholders benefits that had been owed to them for years. In *Whiten*, the company's actions included interfering with experts assigned to assess the claims by giving them misleading information (and this was after dismissing previous experts who had supported the policyholders) and attempting to exploit the claimants' financial difficulties to extract a settlement favourable to the company (an attempt that failed).

19. A fourth kind of remedy, closely related to injunctions, is known as '*specific performance*'. This also requires a person to do something and is most commonly used when the defendant has breached a contract with the plaintiff. For example, if the court finds that the defendant has broken a contract to sell his car to the plaintiff (say, by later insisting on a higher price than agreed upon or refusing to turn the car over), the judge could order the defendant to sell the car to the plaintiff at the price agreed upon.

20. The remedies of declarative relief and injunction also exist for disputes under public law, including the constitution. For example, someone who wants to challenge legislation under the Charter of Rights might sue the government in the hopes of obtaining a 'declaration of unconstitutionality' from the courts—in essence, an order that the law is unconstitutional and therefore unenforceable, as the tobacco companies did in *RJR-Macdonald* (1995). Or they might ask the court to order the government to provide a particular good or service, such as French-language education at public expense under s. 23 of the Charter, as seen in *Doucet-Boudreau v. Nova Scotia* (2003).

21. A cross-provincial study of civil courts, using consistent measures, is currently underway by the Canadian Centre for Judicial Statistics, and it promises to improve the situation. As of this writing, however, we cannot assess the degree to which this promise will be met.

22. At the high end of this range, for example, 99.7 per cent of divorce petitions filed in Ottawa in 1994 were resolved without a trial hearing (Brookbank, Kingsley, and Leonard 1999, 10).

23. In Newfoundland and Labrador's Provincial Court, however, civil claims fell by 85 per cent and family claims by 40 per cent from 1997 to 2006, with steep drops beginning in 2001. Whether this is because civil cases were genuinely in decline or because of changes in reporting method—or whether cases were pursued in the (s. 96) Supreme Court instead—is unclear (Provincial Court of Newfoundland and Labrador 2006, Appendix B).

24. Unless otherwise indicated, all statistics in this section are drawn from the following sources: Brookbank, Kingsley, and Leonard (1999); Ontario, Ministry of the Attorney General (2006b); Provincial Court of Newfoundland and Labrador (2006); Supreme Court of British Columbia (2006).

25. Surprisingly, cases in Nova Scotia appear to have taken longer to settle than to resolve through the court: the comparable median time taken for cases to reach settlement was 287 days (versus only 56 days for completion of litigated cases), and 338 for torts and damages.

26. In contrast, individuals made up a majority (51 per cent) of plaintiffs in Saskatchewan, with businesses (35 per cent) next and then governments (12 per cent). However, it is likely these data are skewed by the fact that Saskatchewan did

not distinguish divorce and family law cases—which are necessarily initiated by individuals—from other forms of civil litigation.

27. Ninety-one per cent of divorce petitioners were successful, and 75 per cent of the case went to trial.

28. The Ontario Civil Justice Review (1996) found a median award of $15,000, or less than half of the median claim.

29. While finding that a right to counsel may exist in certain circumstances, the Court ruled that there is no 'absolute' right to access the courts, and s. 92(14) of the constitution empowers a legislature 'to impose at least some conditions on how and when people have a right to access the courts.' Moreover, '[g]eneral access to legal services is also not a currently recognized aspect of, or a precondition to, the rule of law.'

30. Given the exorbitant hourly rates of even average-priced lawyers, the argument that they would have to raise their rates to keep pace with regular inflation is not persuasive.

31. In *Dell Computers*, a class of plaintiffs had tried to sue Dell for failing to honour bargain prices it had mistakenly posted on its website for hand-held computers. In *Rogers Wireless*, subscribers tried to challenge the validity of $4 per minute roaming charges in parts of the US.

32. For example, the Law Society of Upper Canada, the Nova Scotia Barristers' Society, the Barreau du Québec, etc.

33. Emphasis in original.

Chapter 11

1. This information was taken from an undated letter posted on the UFCW Canada website by the President of the Union (Local 175), Wayne Hanley. (See http://www.ufcw175.com/News/President/index.shtml.)

2. US Supreme Court Justice Oliver Wendell Holmes, for example, said that 'the life of the law has not been logic; it has been experience.' Posner argues that a careful reading of Blackstone shows that he had a more nuanced understanding of legal development that recognized the need to develop rules in response to social conditions. To some degree at least, the notion that judges 'discovered' pre-existing rules was used to provide a cover for judicial law-making. For example, Blackstone argued that the creation of common laws rules involving transfer of real property were necessary to overcome rules that had started in feudal times and that inhibited the growth of a free market for property transactions (such as rules requiring that conveyance of real property transferred with it military and other service obligations that related to the land).

3. The Supreme Court continues to struggle somewhat in developing and consistently applying an analytical framework for reviewing the decisions of administrative tribunals. In *Dunsmuir* (2008), a majority of the court argued that there should be only two possible 'standards of review' for administrative tribunal decisions: 'reasonableness' and 'correctness'. The majority also argued that there should be more flexibility in determining which standard should be used—the one that gives relatively more latitude to the administrative tribunal ('reasonableness') or the one that gives relatively less latitude ('correctness').

4. The majority of the Supreme Court concluded that in the circumstances, courts should overturn the Agency's decision only if it was 'patently unreasonable' (*Council of Canadians with Disabilities* 2007). The majority argued that the decision was not 'patently unreasonable' and that the CTA's decision against VIA Rail (in favour of the Council of Canadians with Disabilities) should stand. The dissent, however, argued

that in this case courts should not be as deferential to the CTA (arguing that the standard should be one of 'correctness') and they would have overturned the CTA's decision.

5. Bantey (2007) argued that the concurring decision was much more restrained because it simply analyzed whether the town of Hudson had the legal authority to ban pesticides under Quebec's *Cities and Towns Act*.

6. The Chief Justice of the British Columbia Provincial Court has argued that judges are responding to the 1996 *Criminal Code* reforms and subsequent Supreme Court decisions that have encouraged judges to use imprisonment more as a last resort.

7. Certain jurisdictions try to offer further general guidelines in their legislation. In New Brunswick, for example, judges may look at the 'stability of the home' and the 'love, affection and ties between a child and a parent'.

8. In their biography of Justice (and then Chief Justice) Dickson, Sharpe and Roach note a 'subtle shift' in Dickson's philosophy: before the introduction of the Charter of Rights, Dickson was more open to making decisions that better reflected changing social and economic conditions so long as the decisions were supported by legal principles and aimed to achieve adjudicative rather than distributive justice (2003, 152). In the Charter era, Sharpe and Roach argue, Dickson occupied a middle ground on the Supreme Court between judges who read Charter rights narrowly and tried to avoid policy-making and judges who read Charter rights broadly and were not hesitant to engage in policy-making (2003, 376).

9. For example, the Supreme Court judges split over this question in a 1997 case involving the question of whether a woman who was five-months pregnant and addicted to glue sniffing could be ordered by a trial judge, partly on the basis of common law tort principles, to be detained in a health facility to undergo treatment (*Winnipeg Child and Family Services* 1997). The majority argued that the trial judge did not have such authority because tort rules stipulate that the child must be 'born alive' before seeking an injunction or compensation for injuries. The majority argued that 'as a general rule, judicial change to common law principles is confined to incremental change based largely on the mechanism of extending an existing principle to new circumstances. Courts will not extend the common law where the revision is major and its ramifications complex.' The dissent, though, called the 'born alive' rule a legal anachronism that existed only because before advances in neonatal technology, science could not determine the status of the fetus inside the womb. According to the dissent, the rule no longer makes sense and its abolition would not alter the substantial rules of tort allowing for claims to be based on harm or potential harm caused by others.

10. From 1867 until the 1930s the basis of judicial review on federalism grounds rested on imperial grounds. The *British North America (BNA) Act* was a British statute and the *Colonial Laws Validity Act* required that all British colonies had to abide by British laws; hence, the federal government and provinces had to obey the division of powers set out in the *BNA Act*. When Canada and other British colonies were granted their legal independence in the 1930s, the basis of judicial review shifted to federalism—Canadian leaders requested that the *BNA Act* still be enforced because they feared that otherwise the provinces or federal government would be able to change the division of powers unilaterally. The basis of judicial review on federalism grounds shifted to constitutionalism in 1982 with the introduction of an amending formula, which prevented either the provinces or federal government from changing the division of powers unilaterally, and the addition of s. 52 of the *Constitution Act*, which gave judges the authority to strike down laws that violate the Constitution (see Morton 2002, 424–6).

11. For a full range of reactions to the decision, see Schneiderman 1999.

12. However, administrative guidelines and policy manuals that help officials apply laws are not themselves subject to Charter review (see Sossin 2003).

13. As noted in Chapter 10, the Court said that in purely private cases the common law should reflect 'Charter values' but that the Charter does not apply directly. As for court orders made in private litigation, the Court initially was reluctant to apply the Charter to such orders (see *Dolphin Delivery* 1986), but did subsequently apply the Charter to scrutinize a lower-court injunction against the picketing of a courthouse by a union (*BCGEU* 1988). (See MacIvor 2006, 20–3.)

14. In *McKinney v. University of Guelph* (1990) and *Stoffman v. Vancouver Hospital* (1990), the Court said that the Charter does not apply to employment contracts entered into by these organizations. However, in *Eldridge* (1997) the Court applied the Charter against a hospital when some individuals complained that their equality rights in the Charter had been violated by the failure of a hospital to provide sign language interpretation.

15. For some examples of broad interpretations of legal rights, see Chapter 9.

16. In another s. 7 case (*Rodriguez* 1993), a majority of the Court found that the law prohibiting assisted suicide comported with 'the principles of fundamental justice' because the law has a long history and can help protect vulnerable groups such as the elderly.

17. The Court has not been consistent about how strong the social-science data have to be to justify a government objective or the means to achieve that objective. As part of its s. 1 analysis in *Irwin Toy*, the majority said that in cases such as this where governments were trying to balance interests (by protecting children), the Court should not hold government to exacting standards of social-science proof to justify their objectives or the means chosen to meet those objectives. Yet in the *RJR-Macdonald* (1995) case, the Court struck down limits on tobacco advertising, which were designed to curtail the harmful effects of smoking, in large part because of dissatisfaction with the expert testimony and studies that the government used to justify its law.

18. In the *B.C. Motor Vehicle Reference* (1985) case, the Court decided that the phrase 'principles of fundamental justice' in s. 7 empowers judges to look at the substantive fairness and justice of a law that limits the rights to 'life, liberty and security of the person' rather than at just the procedural fairness of the law. One of the Court's responses to the argument that the framers of the Charter only wanted to give judges the power to examine 'procedural due process', not 'substantive due process,' was to argue that only 'minimal weight' should be given to the framers' intent and that a 'living tree' approach to rights interpretation was preferable.

19. As discussed below, there is some debate about whether a law that a court has declared to be in violation of constitutional rights should be considered to be invalid under the constitution. S. 52 of the *Constitution Act, 1982* states that laws that violate the constitution are of 'no force or effect'. However, if a court declares a law to be in violation of the constitution but Parliament or a provincial legislature disagrees with this interpretation of the constitution, should the court's view automatically triumph, thereby leaving the law null and void? Or should the ruling apply only to the individual litigant in the court case, rather than constituting a binding declaration about the status of the law more generally? For a discussion of this question see Baker (2007, Chap. 8). In the US, Abraham Lincoln made this argument in relation to *Dred Scott* (the decision that upheld the practice of slavery) in his first inaugural address: 'The candid citizen must confess that if the policy of the government, upon vital questions affecting the whole people, is to be irrevocably fixed by decisions of the Supreme Court, the instant that they are made, *in ordinary litigation between parties in personal actions*, the people will have ceased to be their own rulers, having to that extent practically resigned

the government into the hands of that eminent tribunal.' See Manfredi (2001, 21–4) for a discussion of Lincoln's argument in the Canadian context.

20. The Court was influenced by the fact that by the time the case was heard Parliament had repealed the age restriction (see Hogg 2003, 846).

21. The s. 33 notwithstanding clause allows Parliament or a provincial legislature to pass a law that overrides Charter rights in s. 2 (fundamental freedoms), ss. 7–14 (legal rights), and s. 15 (equality rights) for a period of up to five years.

22. In the US this argument was made most forcefully by Donald Horowitz (1977).

23. This point has been made in the US by Feeley and Rubin (1998). Although the US features more independent-style administrative agencies than in Canada, their general point about diffused policy-making would also apply generally in Canada.

24. See Chapter 4 for a discussion of the arguments for and against relying on framers' intent in the context of the Charter.

25. However, as Hennigar (2004) has pointed out, Manfredi and Kelly's definition of dialogue seems to preclude the possibility of genuine agreement resulting from institutional dialogue between courts and legislatures.

26. In its 2007 decision to uphold a law that forbids 'lifestyle' tobacco advertising (*JTI-Macdonald Corp*), which had been passed after the Supreme Court struck down a wider-ranging tobacco advertising ban in 1995 (*RJR-MacDonald Inc.* 1995), the Court quoted approvingly from Hogg, Thornton, and Wright (2007) to the effect that the dialogue metaphor does not suggest that the Court should be more or less deferential when viewing a revised law. It could be argued that the Court decided to uphold the new law because it reflected what the Court suggested in its 1995 decision. This would not be counted as an example of genuine dialogue under Manfredi and Kelly's definition.

27. Likewise, McCann (1994, 291 n. 11) argued that a model introduced by Johnson and Canon was a positive development, but he maintained that it still 'retained a relatively mechanical stimulus-response view of causality and impact.' The Johnson and Canon model rests on analyzing the interrelated actions of five 'populations': decision-maker population (appellate court or Supreme Court), interpreting population (primarily lower-court judges), implementing population (usually public bureaucracies such as school boards), consumer population (affected individuals, such as black and white parents affected by desegregation orders), and the secondary population (executive and legislative branches of government, media, local elites, and the public). (See Johnson and Canon 1999.)

28. McCormick used the Johnson and Canon model—see note 25 above.

29. Urquhart (1989) briefly examined Alberta's receptiveness to other Charter issues as well in a later piece.

30. As Hennigar (2004) points out, a government decision to appeal a Charter loss should be considered to be part of an expanded conception of 'dialogue' (including 'intra-institutional' dialogue within the judiciary as a higher court reviews a lower court decision).

References

Able-Smith, Brian, and Robert Stevens. 1967. *Lawyers and the Courts: A Sociological Study of the English Legal System 1750–1965*. London: Heinemann Educational Books.

Abraham, Henry J. 1993. *The Judicial Process*. 6th edn. New York: Oxford.

Addario, Frank. 2007. 'Judges are Constitutional Guardians, Not Cheerleaders for the Police', *Globe and Mail*, 17 Sept. http://www.theglobeandmail.com/servlet/story/RT GAM.20070917.wcofrisk17/BNStory/specialComment/home.

Agrios, Justice John A. 2004. *A Handbook on Judicial Dispute Resolution for Canadian Lawyers*. www.cba.org/alberta/PDF/JDR%20Handbook.pdf.

Aikins Report 2002. *Judicially Assisted Dispute Resolution in the Manitoba Court of Queen's Bench* (Fall). http://www.aikins.com/publications/fall02/2.htm.

Alberta Court of Queen's Bench. 2006. *Q.B. Family Law Practice Note No. 5 Family Law Pretrial Conferences*. http://www.albertacourts.ab.ca/qb/practicenotes/familylaw/note 5.pdf.

Alberta. 2008. 'Justice—Courts'. http://www.justice.gov.ab.ca/courts.

Allen, Judge Elliott. Personal communication with authors.10 Sept. 2007.

Anderson, Ellen. 2001. *Judging Bertha Wilson: Law as Large as Life*. Toronto: Osgoode Society and University of Toronto Press.

Apple, James G., and Robert P. Deyling. 1995. 'A Primer on the Civil Law System'. Federal Judicial Center. http://www.fjc.gov/public/home.nsf (accessed 12 Aug. 2005).

Arnold, Donald M., Jim A. Julian, and Irwin R. Walker. 2006. 'Mortality Rates and Causes of Death among All HIV-Positive Individuals with Hemophilia in Canada over 21 Years of Follow-Up', *Blood* 108 (2): 460–4.

Arshi, Mona, and Colm O'Cinneide. 2004. 'Third-Party Interventions: The Public Interest Reaffirmed', *Public Law* Spring.: 69–77.

Arthurs, Harry, and Brent Arnold. 2005. 'Does the Charter Matter?' *Review of Constitutional Studies* 11: 37–117.

Atcheson, M. Elizabeth, Mary Eberts, and Beth Symes. 1984. *Women and Legal Action: Precedents, Resources and Strategies for the Future*. Ottawa: Canadian Advisory Council on the Status of Women.

Atkins, Burton. 1991. 'Party Capability Theory as an Explanation for Intervention Behavior in the English Court of Appeal', *American Journal of Political Science* 35(4): 881–903.

Audain, Linz. 1992. 'Critical Legal Studies, Feminism, Law and Economics and the Veil of Intellectual Tolerance: A Tentative Case for Cross-Jurisprudential Dialogue', *Hofstra Law Review* 20: 1017–1105.

Avery, Simon. 2005. 'RIM Faces Loss of US Market for Blackberry', *Globe and Mail*, 7 Oct. Accessed online.

Baar, Carl. 1996. 'Court Systems in the Provinces'. In Christopher Dunn, ed., *Provinces: Canadian Provincial Politics*. Peterborough, Ont.: Broadview Press.

———. 1998. 'Judicial Independence and Judicial Administration: The Case of Provincial Court Judges', *Constitutional Forum* 9(4): 114–9.

———. 2002. 'Social Facts, Court Delay and the *Charter*'. In F.L. Morton, ed., *Law, Politics and the Judicial Process in Canada*. Calgary: University of Calgary Press.

————. 2006. 'Court Systems in the Provinces'. In Christopher Dunn, ed., *Provinces*. 2nd edn. Peterborough, Ont.: Broadview Press.

————. 2007. 'Trial Court Organization in Canada: Alternative Futures'. In Peter H. Russell, ed., *Canada's Trial Courts: Two Tiers or One?* Toronto: University of Toronto Press.

Badr, Gamal Moursi. 1977–8. 'Islamic Law: Its Relation to Other Legal Systems', *American Journal of Comparative Law* 26: 187–98.

Baier, Gerald. 2006. *Courts and Federalism: Judicial Doctrine in the United States, Australia, and Canada*. Vancouver: UBC Press.

Baker, Dennis. 2007. 'Not Quite Supreme: The Courts and Coordinate Constitutional Interpretation'. PhD dissertation, University of Calgary.

Bakht, Natasha. 2005. 'Problem Solving Courts as Agents of Change', *Criminal Law Quarterly* 50: 224–54.

Bantey, Mark. 2001. 'Green Judicial Activism', *National Post*, 26 July, C16.

Barker, Paul. 2008. *Public Administration in Canada*. Brief edn. Toronto: Thomson Nelson.

Barrett, Tom. 2007. 'Landmark Alberta Charter Case Requires All Vital Evidence Be Shared with Defence', *Edmonton Journal*, 27 Aug. http://www.canada.com/edmonton journal/story.html?id=5067d05a-e8e5-4d36-a2d8-4af42b5b8f6d.

Bastarache, Michel. 2007. 'Decision-making in the Supreme Court of Canada', *University of New Brunswick Law Journal* 56: 328–33.

Bateman, Thomas M.J. 2002. 'Liberal versus Post-liberal Constitutionalism: Applying the *Charter* to Civil Society'. In F.L. Morton, ed., *Law, Politics and the Judicial Process in Canada*. 3rd edn. Calgary: University of Calgary Press.

Baum, Lawrence. 1995. 'Electing Judges'. In Lee Epstein, ed., *Contemplating Courts*. Washington DC: CQ Press.

————. 2001. *American Courts: Process and Policy*. 5th edn. Boston: Houghton Mifflin.

————. 2006. *Judges and Their Audiences: A Perspective on Judicial Behavior*. Princeton: Princeton University Press.

————. 2007. *The Supreme Court*. 9th edn. Washington, DC: CQ Press.

————. 2008a. *American Courts: Process and Policy*. Boston: Houghton Mifflin.

————. 2008b. 'Ways of Thinking About Precedent', *Law and Courts* 18: 11–12.

Berkson, Larry C. 1980. 'Judicial Selection in the United States: A Special Report', *Judicature* 64: 176–93.

Berman, Greg, and John Feinblatt. 2001. 'Problem-Solving Courts: A Brief Primer', *Law and Policy* 23: 125–140.

Berry, Jeffrey. 1989. *The Interest Group Society*. 2nd edn. Boston: Little, Brown.

Block, Michael K., Jeffrey S. Parker, and Labor Dusek. 2000. 'An Experimental Comparison of Adversarial versus Inquisitorial Procedural Regimes', *American Law and Economics Review* 2: 170–94.

Bogart, W.A. 1999. '"Guardian of Civil Rights . . . Medieval Relic": The Civil Jury in Canada', *Law and Contemporary Problems* 62 (2): 305–19.

————. 2002. *Consequences: The Impact of Law and Its Complexity*. Toronto: University of Toronto Press.

————, and Neil Vidmar. 1990. 'Problems and Experience with the Ontario Civil Justice System: An Empirical Assessment'. In A. Hutchinson, ed., *Access to Justice*. Toronto: Carswell.

Bork, Robert. 1971. 'Neutral Principles and Some First Amendment Problems', *Indiana Law Journal* 47: 1–35.

Bouck, John C. 2002. 'Civil Jury Trials—Assessing Non-Pecuniary Damages—Civil Jury Reform', *Canadian Bar Review* 81 (3): 493–528.

———. 2003. 'The Future of Civil Jury Trials'. Vancouver: Continuing Legal Education Society of British Columbia. http://www.cle.bc.ca/CLE/Analysis/Collection/ 03-civiljurytrials?\practiceAreaMessage=true&practiceArea=Personal%20Injury.

Boyd, Marion. 2004. *Dispute Resolution in Family Law: Protecting Choice, Promoting Inclusion.* http://www.attorneygeneral.jus.gov.on.ca/english/about/pubs/boyd/fullreport.pdf.

Boyd, Neil. 2007. Letter to the Editor. *Canadian Journal of Criminology and Criminal Justice* 49: 125–6.

Brace, Paul, and Brent D. Boyea. 2007. 'Judicial Selection Methods and Capital Punishment in the American States'. In Matthew J. Streb, ed., *Running for Judge: The Rising Political, Financial and Legal Stakes of Judicial Elections.* New York: NYU Press.

Bradbeer, Ronald, and Stewart Shackleton. 2005. 'The Only Alternative'. Lawyer.com (15 Aug.). http://www.thelawyer.com/cgi-bin/item.cgi?id=116416&d=122&h=24&f=46.

Braithwaite, John. 2003. 'Does Restorative Justice Work?' In Gerry Johnstone, ed., *A Restorative Justice Reader: Texts, Sources, Context.* Portland, Oreg.: Willan.

Brantingham, Patricia. 1985. 'Sentencing Disparity: An Analysis of Judicial Consistency', *Journal of Quantitative Criminology* 1: 281–305.

Brettel-Dawson, T. 2002. 'Women's Studies and Feminist Legal Studies: A Primer'. In T. Brettel Dawson, ed., *Women, Law and Social Change: Core Readings and Current Issues.* 4th edn. Concord, Ont.: Captus Press.

Brierley, John E.C., and Roderick A. Macdonald, eds. 1993. *Quebec Civil Law.* Toronto: Emond Montgomery.

British Columbia Court of Appeal. 2006. *2006 Annual Report.* http://www.courts.gov. bc.ca/ca/annual%20reports/2006%20Annual%20Report%20Final.pdf.

British Columbia Judicial Council. Judicial Council Annual Report 2004, 2005, 2006. www.provincialcourt.bc.ca/judicialcouncil/index.html.

British Columbia Justice Review Task Force. 2006. *Effective and Affordable Civil Justice.* Report of the Civil Justice Reform Working Group to the Justice Review Task Force. Vancouver: Law Society of British Columbia.

Brockman, Joan and V. Gordon Rose. 2006. *An Introduction to Canadian Criminal Procedure and Evidence.* 3rd edn. Toronto: Nelson.

———. 2005. *A New Justice System for Families and Children.* http://www.bcjustice review.org/.

———. 2006. *Effective and Affordable Civil Justice.* http://www.bcjusticereview.org/.

Brodie, Ian. 2001. 'Interest Group Litigation and the Embedded State: Canada's Court Challenges Program', *Canadian Journal of Political Science* 34: 357–76.

———. 2002. *Friends of the Court: The Privileging of Interest Group Litigants in Canada.* Albany: SUNY Press.

Brookbank, C.B. Kingsley, and T. Leonard. 1999. *Civil Courts Study Report, Canadian Centre for Justice Statistics.* Statistics Canada cat. no. 85–549–XIE. Ottawa: Minister of Industry.

Brown, Desmond. 1989. *The Genesis of the Canadian Criminal Code of 1892.* Toronto: University of Toronto Press.

Brudney, James J., and Corey Ditslear. 2006. 'The Decline and Fall of Legislative History? Patterns of Supreme Court Reliance in the Burger and Rehnquist Eras', *Judicature* 89: 220–9.

———, Sara Schiavoni, and Deborah J. Merritt. 1999. 'Judicial Hostility toward Labor Unions? Applying the Social Background Model to a Celebrated Concern', *Ohio State Law Journal* 60: 1675–771.

Brunet, Mélanie. 2000. *Out of the Shadows: The Civil Law Tradition in the Department of Justice Canada, 1868–2000.* Ottawa: Department of Justice.

Bryant, Michael, and Lorne Sossin. 2002. *Public Law.* Toronto: Carswell.

Bryden, Philip L. 1987. 'Public Interest Intervention in the Courts', *Canadian Bar Review* 66: 490–528.

Burbank, Stephen B. 2007. 'Judicial Independence, Judicial Accountability and Interbranch Relations', *Georgetown Law Journal* 95 (4): 909–28.

————, and Barry Friedman. 2002. 'Reconsidering Judicial Independence'. In S. Burbank and B. Friedman, eds, *Judicial Independence at the Cross-Roads: An Interdisciplinary Approach*. Thousand Oaks, Calif.: Sage.

Bushnell, Ian. 1992. *The Captive Court: A Study of the Supreme Court of Canada*. Montreal: McGill-Queen's University Press.

————. 1997. *The Federal Court of Canada: A History, 1875–1992*. Toronto: University of Toronto Press (for the Osgoode Society for Canadian Legal History).

Bushway, Shawn D., and Anne Morrison Piehl. 2007. 'Social Science Research and the Legal Threat to Presumptive Sentencing Guidelines'. *Criminology and Public Policy* 6: 461–82.

Cairns, Alan. 1971. 'The Judicial Committee and Its Critics', *Canadian Journal of Political Science* 4: 301–45.

————. 1992. *Charter versus Federalism: The Dilemmas of Constitutional Reform*. Montreal: McGill-Queen's University Press.

Caldeira, Gregory, and John Wright. 1988. 'Organized Interests and Agenda Setting in the U.S. Supreme Court', *American Political Science Review* 82: 1109–27.

————, and ————. 1998. 'Lobbying for Justice: Organized Interests, Supreme Court Nominations and the United States Senate', *American Journal of Political Science* 42: 499–523.

————, Marie Hojnacki, and John Wright. 2000. 'The Lobbying Activities of Organized Interests in Federal Judicial Nominations', *Journal of Politics* 62: 51–69.

Cameron, Alex. 2006. 'Recognition of Invasion of Privacy As a Tort in Its Own Right: Has Gordias' Ox Cart Been Freed in Ontario?' Ontario Bar Association. http:// www.oba. org/en/pri/may06/PrintHtml.aspx?DocId=9428 (accessed 19 Dec. 2006).

Cameron, Jamie. 2003. *Victim Privacy and the Open Court Principle*. Ottawa: Department of Justice.

Canada, Department of Justice. 2001. *Serving Canadians: Report of the Federal Prosecution Service Review*. Ottawa: Department of Justice.

————. 2003. 'Civil Litigation Deskbook'. Unpublished internal document.

————. 2004. *Disclosure Reform: Consultation Paper*. http://www.justice.gc.ca/en/cons/ disc-ref/disc_ref.pdf.

————. 2005. 'Expanding Drug Treatment Courts in Canada'. http://www.justice.gc.ca/ en/news/nr/2005/doc_31552.htm.

————. 2006. *Departmental Performance Report, 2005–2006*. Ottawa: Department of Justice. http://www.justice.gc.ca/en/dept/pub/dpr/2005-2006/section1c.html (last accessed 20 July 2007).

Canada, Federal Prosecution Service. 2005. *Federal Prosecution Service Deskbook*. Ottawa: Minister of Justice. http://www.justice.gc.ca/en/dept/pub/fps/fpd/toc.html (last accessed 18 July 2007).

Canadian Bar Association (CBA). 1985. *The Appointment of Judges in Canada*. Toronto: CBA.

————. National Class Action Database. http://www.cba.org/ClassActions/main/gate/ index/default.aspx (last accessed 30 Aug. 2007).

————. 1996. *Report of the Task Force on Systems of Civil Justice*. Ottawa, ON: Canadian Bar Association.

Canadian Judicial Council (CJC). 1997. *CJC Annual Report 1996–97*. Ottawa: Canadian Judicial Council.

———. 1998. *Ethical Principles for Judges*. Ottawa: Canadian Judicial Council.

———. 2002. *CJC Annual Report 2001–02: Thirty Years*. Ottawa: Canadian Judicial Council.

———. 2006a. *Alternative Models of Court Administration*. Ottawa: Canadian Judicial Council.

———. 2006b. 'Canadian Judicial Council Calls on Government to Consult on Proposed Changes'. Ottawa: CJC. 9 Nov. http://www.cjc-ccm.gc.ca/article.asp?id=3029.

———. 2007. 'Judicial Appointments: Perspective from the Canadian Judicial Council'. Ottawa: Canadian Judicial Council Media. 20 Feb. http://www.cjc-ccm.gc.ca/article.asp?id=3072 (accessed 20 Feb. 2008).

———. 2008. *Report of the Inquiry Committee concerning the Hon. P. Theodore Matlow*. Ottawa: Canadian Judicial Council.

Canadian Sentencing Commission. 1987. *Sentencing Reform: A Canadian Approach*. Ottawa: Minister of Supply and Services.

Canan, Penelope, and George W. Pring. (1988) 'Strategic Lawsuits against Public Participation', *Social Problems* 35 (5): 506–19.

Carney, Gerard. 1997. 'Comment—The Role of the Attorney-General', *Bond Law Review* 9: 1–9.

CBA. *See* Canadian Bar Association.

CBC. 2000. *News*. 'Outspoken Judge Praises Court Decision', 6 Sept. http://www.cbc.ca/news/story/2000/09/06/rllywins000906.html (accessed 9 July 2007).

———. 2002. *News*. 'Striking Newfoundland Doctors Agree to Arbitration'. 16 Oct. http://www.cbc.ca/canada/story/2002/10/15/doctors_021015.html.

———. 2003. *News*. 'Judges Advised to Take Race, Background into Account in Sentencing'. 13 Feb. http://www.cbc.ca/canada/story/2003/02/13/court030213.html.

———. 2004. *News*. 'Ontario Report Criticized by Shariah Opponents'. 20 Dec. http://www.cbc.ca/canada/story/2004/12/20/sharia-boyd041220.html.

———. 2006. *News*. 'Quebec Judge Quits After Top Court Declines Case' 18 May. http://www.cbc.ca/canada/story/2006/05/18/judge-ruffo.html.

CBC Radio. 2006. 'Breaking the Cycle'. Documentary. Reporter: Frédéric Zalac Producer: Marie Belzil.

CCLA. 1991. Factum Submitted to the Supreme Court of Canada in *R. v. Seaboyer*.

Cheek, Kyle, and Anthony Champagne. 2000. 'Money in Texas Supreme Court Elections: 1980–1998', *Judicature* 84: 20–5.

Choi, Stephen J., G. Mitu Gulati, and Eric A. Posner. 2007. 'Professionals or Politicians: The Uncertain Empirical Case for an Elected Rather Than Appointed Judiciary'. John M. Olin Law and Economics Working Paper No. 357, 2nd ser. Chicago: University of Chicago, Law School. http://www.law.uchicago.edu/Lawecon/index.html.

———, and ———. 2004. 'Choosing the Next Supreme Court Justice: An Empirical Ranking of Judge Performance', *Southern California Law Review* 78: 23–118.

Chwialkowska, Luiza. 2000. 'Rein in Lobby Groups, Senior Judges Suggest', *National Post*, 6 Apr., A1.

CJC. *See* Canadian Judicial Council.

Clairmont, Don. 2005. 'Penetrating the Walls: Implementing a System-Wide Restorative Justice Approach in the Justice System'. In Elizabeth Elliott and Robert M. Gordon, eds, *New Directions in Restorative Justice: Issues, Practice, Evaluation*. Portland, Oreg.: Willan.

Clark, Campbell. 2007a. 'Partisans Filling Judge Nomination Committees', *Globe and Mail*, 12 Feb., A1.

————. 2007b. 'Legal Community Takes Stand against Partisan Appointments', *Globe and Mail*, 13 Feb., A8.

Clark, Edward. 2005. 'The Needs of the Many and the Needs of the Few: A New System of Public Interest Intervention for New Zealand', *Victoria University of Wellington Law Review* 36: 71–103.

Clarke, Jeremy. 2006. 'Beyond the Democratic Dialogue, and towards a Federalist One: Provincial Arguments and Supreme Court Responses in Charter Litigation', *Canadian Journal of Political Science* 39 (2): 293–314.

Cole, Judge David P. 2008. 'A Day in the Life of a Judge'. In Julian V. Roberts and Michelle Grossman, eds, *Criminal Justice in Canada: A Reader*. 3rd edn. Toronto: Thomson Nelson.

Commissioner for Federal Judicial Affairs. 2008. http//www.fja.gc.ca.

Cooley, John W. 1986. 'Arbitration vs. Mediation: Explaining the Differences', *Judicature* 69: 263–9.

Cortner, Richard. 1968. 'Strategies and Tactics of Litigants in Constitutional Cases', *Journal of Public Law* 17: 287–307.

Cotler, Irwin. 2004. 'Presentation to Justice Committee Supreme Court of Canada Appointments Process'. 30 Mar.

Court Administration Service. 2006. *Annual Report, 2005–06*. Ottawa: Court Administration Service.

Cowan, Ruth B. 1976. 'Women's Rights through Litigation: An Examination of the American Civil Liberties Union Women's Rights Project, 1971–1976', *Columbia Human Rights Law Review* 8: 373–412.

Coyne, Andrew. 1996. 'Lack of Protection for Unborn a Stain on Society; Cases Add Up to Urgent Plea for Parliament to Act', *Edmonton Journal*, 28 Dec. 1996. Accessed online.

Craig, John D.R. 1997. 'Invasion of Privacy and Charter Values: The Common Law Tort Awakens', *McGill Law Journal* 42: 355–400.

Crane, Brian A., and Henry S. Brown. 2004. *Supreme Court of Canada Practice, 2005*. Toronto: Thomson Carswell.

Crosariol, Beppi. 2007. 'Growing Chorus Advocates Streamlining of Class Actions', *Globe and Mail*, 31 Jan., B9.

CTV. 2005. 'Protestors March against Sharia Law in Canada'. 9 Sept. http://www.ctv.ca/servlet/ArticleNews/story/CTVNews/1126181967010_31/?hub=TopStories.

————. 2006. 'Sisters Win Right to Play Hockey with the Boys'. 22 Sept. http://www.ctv.ca/servlet/ArticleNews/story/CTVNews/20060922/girls_hockey_060922?s_name=&no_ads=.

Currie, A.W. 2004. 'A Burden on the Court? Self-Representing Accused in Canadian Criminal Courts', *JustResearch* 11: 5. Ottawa: Department of Justice.

Cushman, Barry. 1998. *Rethinking the New Deal Court: The Structure of a Constitutional Revolution*. Oxford: Oxford University Press.

Daly, Kathleen. 2002. 'Restorative Justice: The Real Story', *Punishment and Society* 4: 55–79.

Damaska, Mirjan R. 1986. The Faces of Justice and State Authority: A Comparative Approach to the Legal Process. New Haven: Yale University Press.

Daubney, David, and Gordon Parry. 1999. 'An Overview of Bill C-41 (The Sentencing Reform Act)'. In Julian V. Roberts and David P. Cole, eds, *Making Sense of Sentencing*. Toronto: University of Toronto Press.

Davis, Sue. 1990. 'Power on the Court: Chief Justice Rehnquist's Opinion Assignments', *Judicature* 74: 66–72.

————, Susan Haire, and Donald R. Songer. 1993. 'Voting Behavior and Gender on the US Courts of Appeals', *Judicature* 77: 129–33.

Dawson, R. MacGregor. 1954. *The Government of Canada*. Toronto: University of Toronto Press.

DeMarco, Jerry V. 2005. 'Assessing the Impact of Public Interest Interventions on the Environmental Law Jurisprudence of the Supreme Court of Canada: A Quantitative and Qualitative Analysis', *Supreme Court Law Review*, 2nd ser., 30: 299–332.

Denov, Myriam, and Kathryn Campbell. 2008. 'When Justice Fails: Understanding Miscarriages of Justice'. In Julian V. Roberts and Michelle Grossman, eds, *Criminal Justice in Canada: A Reader*. 3rd edn. Thomson Nelson.

Deschênes, Jules (with Carl Baar). 1981. *Masters in Their Own House: A Study on the Independent Judicial Administration of the Courts*. Ottawa: Canadian Judicial Council.

Devlin, Richard F. 1994. 'Mapping Legal Theory', *Alberta Law Review* 32: 602–21.

———, A. Wayne MacKay, and Natasha Kim. 2000. 'Reducing the Democratic Deficit: Representation, Diversity and the Canadian Judiciary, or Towards a 'Triple P' Judiciary', *Alberta Law Review* 38: 734–866.

Devonshire, Reginald A. 1995. 'The Effects of Supreme Court *Charter* Decisions on Policing: More Beneficial Than Detrimental?' *Criminal Reports*, 4th ser., 31: 82–104.

Dewees, Donald N., Michael J. Trebilcock, and Peter C. Coyte. 1991. 'The Medical Malpractice Crisis: A Comparative Empirical Perspective', *Law and Contemporary Problems* 53 (1): 217–51.

Dicey, A.V.C. 2002. 'The Rule of Law'. In F.L. Morton, ed., *Law, Politics and the Judicial Process in Canada*. 3rd edn. Calgary: University of Calgary Press.

Dickson, Brian. 2000. 'A Life in the Law: The Process of Judging', *Saskatchewan Law Review* 63: 373–88.

Di Luca, Joseph. 2005. 'Expedient McJustice or Principled Alternative Dispute Resolution? A Review of Plea Bargaining in Canada', *Criminal Law Quarterly* 50: 14–66.

Dobrota, Alex. 2007. 'Tories Consider Softening Gun Bill', *Globe and Mail*, 17 Apr. http://www.theglobeandmail.com/servlet/story/LAC.20070417.COPS17.

Doob, Anthony N. 1999. 'Sentencing Reform: Where Are We Now?' In Julian V. Roberts and David P. Cole, eds, *Making Sense of Sentencing*. Toronto: University of Toronto Press.

———, and Jane B. Sprott. 2006. 'Punishing Youth Crime in Canada: The Blind Men and the Elephant', *Punishment and Society* 8: 223–33.

Doolittle, Robyn. 2007. 'Record-editing Judge Scolded', *Toronto Star*, 24 May. www.thestar.com.

Dotan, Yoav. 1999. 'Do the "Haves" Still Come Out Ahead? Resource Inequalities in Ideological Courts: The Case of the Israeli High Court of Justice', *Law and Society Review* 33: 1059–80.

Dowling, Timothy J. 2008. 'Suspect Seminars', *Daily Journal: Focus & Forum* (14 Jan.), http://www.communityrights.org/Newsroom/OpEdsLetters/DJ_1_2008.pdf.

Dworkin, Ronald. 1978. *Taking Rights Seriously*. Cambridge, Mass.: Harvard University Press.

———, and Thomas Nagel, Robert Nozick, John Rawls, T.M. Scanlon, Judith Jarvis Thomson. 1997. 'Assisted Suicide: The Philosophers' Brief. *New York Review of Books* 44 (27 Mar.). http://www.nybooks.com/articles/1237.

Eagle, Galen. 2007. 'Court Diversion Program Helps Mentally Ill Navigate Court System', *Peterborough Examiner*, 10 Aug. http://www.thepeterboroughexaminer.com/.

Easton, David. 1971. *The Political System: An Inquiry into the State of Political Science*. 2nd edn. New York: Knopf.

Eaton, Leslie, and Leslie Kaufman. 2005. 'In Problem-solving Court, Judges Turn Therapist', *New York Times*, 26 April. http:www.nytimes.com/2005/04/26/nyregion/26courts.html.

Eberts, Mary. 1986. 'A Strategy for Equality Rights Litigation under the Charter of Rights and Freedoms'. In Joseph M. Weiler and Robin M. Elliot, eds, *Litigating the Values of a Nation: The Canadian Charter of Rights and Freedoms*. Toronto: Carswell.

Edgar, Allen. 1999. 'Sentencing Options in Canada'. In Julian V. Roberts and David P. Cole, eds, *Making Sense of Sentencing*. Toronto: University of Toronto Press.

Edwards, John Ll. J. 1987. 'The Attorney General and the Charter of Rights'. In Robert J. Sharpe, ed., *Charter Litigation*. Toronto: Butterworths.

———. 1995. 'The Office of the Attorney General—New Levels of Public Expectations and Accountability'. In Philip C. Stenning, ed., *Accountability for Criminal Justice: Selected Essays*. Toronto: University of Toronto Press.

Elliott, Liz. 2008. 'Restorative Justice in Canada'. In Julian V. Roberts and Michelle Grossman, eds, *Criminal Justice in Canada: A Reader*. 3rd edn. Toronto: Thomson Nelson.

Epp, Charles. 1998. *The Rights Revolution: Lawyers, Activists, and Supreme Courts in Comparative Perspective*. Chicago: University of Chicago Press.

———. 2003. 'The Judge over Your Shoulder: Is Adversarial Legalism Exceptionally American?' *Law and Social Inquiry* 28(3): 743–70.

Epstein, Lee. 1985. *Conservatives in Court*. Knoxville: University of Tennessee Press.

———, and Jack Knight. 1998. *The Choices Justices Make*. Washington, DC: CQ Press.

———, and Joseph F. Kobylka. 1992. *The Supreme Court and Legal Change: Abortion and the Death Penalty*. Chapel Hill: University of North Carolina Press.

———, and C.K. Rowland. 1991. 'Debunking the Myth of Interest Group Invincibility in the Courts', *American Political Science Review* 85: 205–17.

———, and Jeffrey A. Segal. 2005. *Advice and Consent: The Politics of Judicial Appointments*. New York: Oxford University Press.

———, and Thomas G. Walker. 2004. *Constitutional Law for a Changing America: Rights, Liberties and Justice*. 5th edn. Washington, DC: CQ Press.

———, and ———. 2007. *Constitutional Law for a Changing American: Rights, Liberties and Justice*. 6th edn. Washington, DC: CQ Press.

———, ———, Jeffrey A. Segal, and Harold J. Spaeth. 2006. *Supreme Court Compendium*. 4th edn. Washington DC: CQ Press.

Ericson, Richard. 1982. *Reproducing Order: A Study of Police Patrol Work*. Toronto: University of Toronto Press.

———, and Patricia Baranek. 1982. *The Ordering of Justice*. Toronto: University of Toronto Press.

Eskridge, William N. Jr, and Philip P. Frickey. 1994. 'Forward: Law as Equilibrium', *Harvard Law Review* 108: 26–108.

Farhang, Sean, and Gregory Wawro. 2004. 'Institutional Dynamics on the US Courts of Appeals: Minority Representation under Panel Decision Making', *Journal of Law, Economics and Organization* 20: 299–330.

Farole, Donald J., Jr. 1999. 'Reexamining Litigant Success in State Supreme Courts', *Law & Society Review* 33: 1043–58.

———, Nora Puffett, Michael Rempel, and Francine Byrne. 2005. 'Applying Problem Solving Principles in Mainstream Courts: Lessons for State Courts', *Justice System Journal* 26: 57–75.

Farrow, Trevor C.W. 2005. 'Dispute Resolution, Access to Civil Justice and Legal Education', *Alberta Law Review* 42: 741–801.

———. 2006. 'Privatizing our Public Civil Justice System', *News and Views on Civil Justice Reform: Canadian Forum on Civil Justice* 9: 16–7. http://cfcj-fcjc.org/publications/.

Federal Court of Canada. 2003. *Federal Court of Canada 2002–03 Report*. Ottawa: Federal Court of Canada.

Feeley, Malcolm M., and Edward L. Rubin. 1998. *Judicial Policy Making and the Modern State*. Cambridge: Cambridge University Press.

Felstiner, William L. F., Richard L. Abel, and Austin Sarat. 1980–81. 'The Emergence and Transformation of Disputes: Naming, Blaming, Claiming', *Law and Society Review* 15: 631–53.

Finkel, Jodi S. 2008. *Judicial Reform as Political Insurance: Argentina, Peru, and Mexico in the 1990s*. Notre Dame, Indiana: University of Notre Dame Press.

Finnis, John. 1980. *Natural Law and Natural Rights*. Oxford: Clarendon Press.

———. 2007. 'Natural Law Theories'. In Edward N. Zalta, ed., *The Stanford Encyclopedia of Philosophy*, Spring 2007 edn. http://plato.stanford.edu/archives/spr2007/entries/natural-law-theories/.

Fiss, Owen. 1984. 'Against Settlement', *Yale Law Journal* 93: 1073–90.

Flanagan, Thomas. 1985. 'Policy-Making by Exegesis: The Abolition of 'Mandatory Retirement' in Manitoba', *Canadian Public Policy* 11: 40–53.

———. 1997. 'The Staying Power of the Legislative Status Quo: Collective Choice in Canada's Parliament after Morgentaler', *Canadian Journal of Political Science* 30: 31–54.

Flemming, Roy B. 2000. 'Processing Appeals for Judicial Review: The Institutions of Agenda Setting in the Supreme Courts of Canada and the United States'. In Hugh Mellon and Martin Westmacott, eds, *Political Dispute and Judicial Review: Assessing the Work of the Supreme Court of Canada*. Scarborough, Ont.: Nelson Thomson Learning.

———. 2004. *Tournament of Appeals: Granting Judicial Review in Canada*. Vancouver: UBC Press.

———, and Glen S. Krutz. 2002a. 'Repeat Litigators and Agenda Setting on the Supreme Court of Canada', *Canadian Journal of Political Science* 35: 811–33.

———, and Glen S. Krutz. 2002b. 'Selecting Appeals for Judicial Review in Canada: A Replication and Multivariate Test of American Hypotheses', *Journal of Politics* 64: 232–48.

———, and D. Dan Wood. 1997. 'The Public and the Supreme Court: Individual Justice Responsiveness to American Public Moods', *American Journal of Political Science* 41: 468–98.

Fletcher, Joseph F., and Paul Howe. 2001. 'Public Opinion and Canada's Courts'. In Paul Howe and Peter H. Russell, eds, *Judicial Power and Canadian Democracy*. Montreal: McGill-Queen's University Press.

Frase, Richard S. 2007. 'The *Apprendi-Blakely* Cases: Sentencing Reform Counter-Revolution?' *Criminology and Public Policy* 6: 403–32.

Frater, Robert. 2007. Senior General Counsel, Criminal Law Section, Department of Justice Canada, e-mail correspondence, 18 July.

Free, Marvin D., Jr. 2002. 'Race and Presentencing Decisions in the United States: A Summary and Critique of the Literature', *Criminal Justice Review* 27 (2): 203–32.

Freeze, Colin, and Karen Howlett. 2005. 'McGuinty Government Rules Out Use of Sharia Law', *Globe and Mail*, 12 Sept. www.globeandmail.com.

Freiman, Mark. 2002. 'Convergence of Law and Policy and the Role of the Attorney General', *Supreme Court Law Review*, 2nd ser., 16: 335–41.

Friedland, Martin L. 1995. *A Place Apart: Judicial Independence and Accountability in Canada*. Ottawa: Canadian Judicial Council.

———. 2003. 'The Provincial Court and the Criminal Law', *Criminal Law Quarterly* 48: 15–30.

Friedman, Lawrence M. 1985. *Total Justice*. New York: Russell Sage Foundation.

Fudge, Judy. 1987. 'The Public/Private Distinction and the Possibilities of the and the Limits to the Use of Charter Litigation to Further Feminist Struggles', *Osgoode Hall Law Journal* 25: 485–554.

Fuller, Lon. 1969. *The Morality of Law*. Rev. edn. New Haven: Yale University Press.

Gabor, Thomas, and Nicole Crutcher. 2002. Mandatory Minimum Penalties: Their Effects on Crime, Sentencing Disparities, and Justice System Expenditures. Ottawa: Department of Justice Canada.

Galanter, Marc. 1974. 'Why the 'Haves' Come Out Ahead: Speculations on the Limits of Legal Change', *Law and Society Review* 9: 95–160.

———. 1999. 'Do the 'Haves' Still Come Out Ahead?', *Law and Society Review* 33 (4): 1113–23.

Gall, Gerald L. 1990. *The Canadian Legal System*. 3rd edn. Toronto: Carswell.

———. 2004. *The Canadian Legal System*. 5th edn. Toronto: Thomson Carswell.

Gallagher, Sheila A. 1993. 'The Public Policy Process and Charter Litigation'. In Patrick Monahan and Marie Finkelstein, eds, *The Impact of the Charter on the Public Policy Process*. North York, Ont.: York University Centre for Public Law and Public Policy.

Galligan, Patrick T. 1996. *Report to the Attorney-General of Ontario on Certain Matters Related to Karla Homolka*. Toronto: Ministry of the Attorney General.

Galloway, Gloria. 2006. 'Alberta Judge's Promotion a Patronage Job, Liberals Say', *Globe and Mail*, 2 Oct.

Geyh, Charles Gardner. 2002. 'Customary Independence'. In S. Burbank and B. Friedman, eds, *Judicial Independence at the Cross-Roads: An Interdisciplinary Approach*. Thousand Oaks, Calif.: Sage.

Gibson, James L. 1983. 'From Simplicity to Complexity: The Development of Theory in the Study of Judicial Behavior', *Political Behavior* 5: 7–49.

Ginsburg, Tom. 2003. *Judicial Review in New Democracies: Constitutional Courts in Asian Cases*. Cambridge: Cambridge University Press.

Glendon, Mary Ann. 1991. *Rights Talk: The Impoverishment of Political Discourse*. New York: Free Press.

Glenn, H. Patrick. 2007. *Legal Traditions of the World*. 3rd edn. Oxford: Oxford University Press.

Globe and Mail. 2004. 'Islamic Arbitration, by the Rules All Follow', 22 Dec.

———. 2007. 'Policing and Profiling'. 9 May. http://www.theglobeandmail.com/servlet/story/RTGAM.20070509.weracial09/BNStory/National/.

———. 2008. 'Senate passes anti-crime bill'. 27 Feb. http://www.theglobeandmail.com/servlet/story/RTGAM.20080227.wcrimebill0227/BNStory/National.

Goff, Colin. 2004. *Criminal Justice in Canada*. 3rd edn. Scarborough, Ont.: Thomson Nelson.

Gold, Marc. 1985. 'The Mask of Objectivity: Politics and Rhetoric in the Supreme Court of Canada', *Supreme Court Law Review* 7: 455–504.

Goldstein, Leslie Friedman. 2004. 'From Democracy to Juristocracy', *Law and Society Review* 38 (2004): 611–29.

Gora, Christopher. 1993. 'Jury Trials in the Small Communities of the Northwest Territories'. *Windsor Yearbook of Access to Justice* 13: 156–81.

Gordon, Robert M., and J. Bryan Kinney. 2006. *Reducing Crime and Improving Criminal Justice in British Columbia: Recommendations for Change*. Vancouver: British Columbia Progress Board.

Gottschall, Jon. 1983. 'Carter's Judicial Appointments: The Influence of Affirmative Action and Merit Selection on Voting on the US Courts of Appeals', *Judicature* 67: 164–73.

Gottsfield, Robert L., and Mitch Michkowski. 2007. 'Settlement Conferences Help Resolve Criminal Cases', *Judicature* 90: 196–9, 235.

Gould, Jon B., and Stephen Mastrowski. 2004. 'Suspect Searches: Assessing Police Behaviour under the US Constitution', *Criminology and Public Policy* 3: 316–62.

Goundry, Sandra, Yvonne Peters, and Rosalind Currie. 1998. Family Mediation in Canada: Implications for Women's Equality. Ottawa: Status of Women Canada.

Graber, Mark. 1993. 'The Nonmajoritarian Difficulty: Legislative Deference to the Judiciary', *Studies in American Political Development* 7: 35–73.

Greene, Ian. 1995. 'Judicial Accountability in Canada'. In Philip Stenning, ed., *Accountability for Criminal Justice: Selected Essays*. Toronto: University of Toronto Press.

———. 2006. *The Courts*. The Canadian Democratic Audit series, No. 9. Vancouver: UBC Press.

———, Carl Baar, Peter McCormick, George Szablowski, and Martin Thomas. 1998. *Final Appeal: Decision-Making in Canadian Courts of Appeal*. Toronto: Lorimer.

Griffiths, Curt T. 2007. *Canadian Criminal Justice: A Primer*. 3rd edn. Toronto: Thomson Nelson.

Gryski, Gerard S., and Eleanor C. Main. 1986. 'Social Backgrounds as Predictors of Votes on State Courts of Last Resort: The Case of Sex Discrimination', *Western Political Quarterly* 39: 528–37.

Guarnieri, Carlo. 2001 'Judicial Independence in Latin Countries of Western Europe'. In Peter H. Russell and David M. O'Brien, eds, *Judicial Independence in the Age of Democracy: Critical Perspectives from around the World*. Charlottesville: University of Virginia Press.

———, and Patrizia Pederzoli. 2002. *The Power of Judges: A Comparative Study of Courts and Democracy*. Oxford Socio-Legal Studies series. Oxford: Oxford University Press.

Haigh, Richard, and Michael Sobkin. 2007. 'Does the Observer Have an Effect? An Analysis of the Use of the Dialogue Metaphor in Canada's Courts', *Osgoode Hall Law Journal* 45: 67–90.

Hall, Melinda Gann. 1992. 'Electoral Politics and Strategic Voting in State Supreme Courts', *Journal of Politics* 54: 427–46.

———. 1995. 'Justices as Representatives: Elections and Judicial Politics in the American States', *American Politics Quarterly* 23: 485–503.

———. 2001. 'State Supreme Courts in American Democracy: Probing the Myths of Judicial Reform', *American Political Science Review* 95: 315–30.

Hall, Stephen. 2001. 'The Persistent Spectre: Natural Law, International Order and the Limits of Legal Positivism', *European Journal of International Law* 12: 269–307.

Halper, Louise. 2005. 'Law and Women's Agency in Post-Revolutionary Iran', *Harvard Journal of Law and Gender* 28: 85–142.

Haltom, William, and Michael McCann. 2004. *Distorting the Law: Politics, Media, and the Litigation Crisis*. Chicago: University of Chicago Press.

Hamilton, Alexander, James Madison, and John Jay. 1787–8. *The Federalist Papers*. Washington, DC: Library of Congress. http://thomas.loc.gov/home/histdox/fed papers.html.

Hanes, Allison. 2007. 'Critics Decry Three Parents and a Baby', *National Post*, 4 Jan. http://www.canada.com.

Hann, Robert G. and Baar, Carl. 2001. *Evaluation of the Ontario Mandatory Mediation Program (Rule 24.1): Executive Summary and Recommendations*. Toronto: Queen's Printer.

Hart, H.L.A. 1961. *The Concept of Law*. Oxford: Oxford University Press.

Harvie, Robert, and Hamar Foster. 1990. 'Ties That Bind? The Supreme Court of Canada, American Jurisprudence, and the Revision of Canadian Criminal Law under the Charter', *Osgoode Hall Law Journal* 28 (4): 729–88.

Hausegger, Lori. 1999. 'The Impact of Interest Groups on Judicial Decision Making: A Comparison of Women's Groups in the U.S. and Canada'. PhD. dissertation, Ohio State University.

————. 2000. 'Panel Selection and the Canadian Supreme Court: Neutral Assignment or the Exercise of Power'. Paper presented at the Annual Meeting of the Southern Political Science Association, Atlanta.

————. 2002. 'Participation of Governments before the Supreme Court of Canada'. Paper presented at the Annual Meeting of the Midwest Political Science Association, Chicago.

————, and Lawrence Baum. 1999. 'Inviting Congressional Action: A Study of Supreme Court Motivations in Statutory Interpretation', *American Journal of Political Science* 43: 162–85.

————, and Stacia Haynie. 2003. 'Judicial Decisionmaking and the Use of Panels in the Canadian Supreme Court and the South African Appellate Division', *Law and Society Review* 37: 635–57.

Haynie, Stacia, and Kaitlyn L. Sill. 2007. 'Repeat Players in the South African Supreme Court of Appeal', *Political Research Quarterly* 60 (3): 443–53.

————, C. Neal Tate, Reginald Sheehan, and Donald Songer. 2001. 'Winners and Losers: A Comparative Analysis of Appellate Courts and Litigation Outcomes'. Paper presented at the Annual Meeting of the American Political Science Association, San Francisco.

Healy, Patrick. 2003. 'Constitutional Limitations upon the Allocation of Trial Jurisdiction to the Superior or Provincial Court in Criminal Matters', *Criminal Law Quarterly* 48: 31–76.

Hein, Gregory. 2000. 'Interest Group Litigation and Canadian Democracy', *Choices* 6: 3–32.

————. 2001. 'Interest Group Litigation and Canadian Democracy'. In P. Howe and P. Russell, eds, *Judicial Power and Canadian Democracy*. Montreal: McGill-Queen's University Press.

Hennigar, Matthew A. 1996. 'Litigating Pan-Canadianism: The Constitutional Litigation Strategy of the Canadian Federal Government in Charter Cases, 1982–1993'. MA thesis, University of Calgary.

————. 2002. 'Players and the Process: Charter Litigation and the Federal Government', *Windsor Yearbook of Access to Justice* 21: 91–109.

————. 2004. 'Expanding the 'Dialogue' Debate: Canadian Federal Government Responses to Lower Court Charter Decisions', *Canadian Journal of Political Science* 37: 3–21.

————. 2007. 'Why Does the Federal Government Appeal to the Supreme Court of Canada in Charter of Rights Cases? A Strategic Explanation', *Law and Society Review* 41: 225–50.

————. 2008. 'Conceptualizing Attorney General Conduct in Charter Litigation: From Independence to Central Agenda, *Canadian Public Administration* 51(2): 193–215.

Hiebert, Janet L. 1996. *Limiting Rights: The Dilemma of Judicial Review*. Montreal: McGill-Queen's University Press.

————. 2002. *Charter Conflicts: What Is Parliament's Role?* Montreal: McGill-Queen's University Press.

Hill, Casey. 1996. 'The Role of Fault in s. 24(2) of the Charter'. In Jamie Cameron, ed., *The Charter's Impact on the Criminal Justice System*. Toronto: Carswell.

Himma, Kenneth Einar. 2002. 'Positivism, Naturalism, and the Obligation to Obey Law', *Southern Journal of Philosophy* 36: 145–61.

Hirschl, Ran. 2004. *Towards Juristocracy: The Origins and Consequences of the New Constitutionalism*. Cambridge: Harvard University Press.

Ho, Shawn. 1994. 'The Macro- and Micro-Constitutional Strategies of Provincial Governments in Charter Politics: A Study of Alberta, Saskatchewan and Ontario, 1982–1992'. MA thesis, University of Calgary.

Hogeveen, Brian. 2005. 'If We Are Tough on Crime, If We Punish Crime, Then People Will Get the Message: Constructing and Governing the Punishable Young Offender in Canada during the Late 1990s'. *Punishment and Society* 7: 73–89.

Hogg, Peter W. 1987. 'Legislative History in Constitutional Cases'. In Robert J. Sharpe, ed., *Charter Litigation*. Toronto: Butterworths.

———. 2003. *Constitutional Law of Canada*. Student edn. Toronto: Thomson Carswell.

———. 2006a. 'Appointment of Justice Marshall Rothstein to the Supreme Court of Canada', *Osgoode Hall Law Journal* 44: 527–38.

———. 2006b. 'Canada: Privy Council to Supreme Court'. In Jeffrey Goldsworthy, ed., *Interpreting Constitutions: A Comparative Study*. New York: Oxford University Press.

———, and Allison A. Bushell. 1997. 'The Charter Dialogue between Courts and Legislatures (or Perhaps the Charter Isn't Such a Bad Thing after All)', *Osgoode Hall Law Journal* 35: 75–124.

———, ———, and Wade K. Wright. 2007. '*Charter* Dialogue Revisited—or "Much Ado About Metaphors"', *Osgoode Hall Law Journal* 45: 1–65.

Horowitz, Donald. 1977. *The Courts and Social Policy*. Washington, DC: Brookings Institution.

Huber, Gregory A., and Charles C. Gordon. 2004. 'Accountability and Coercion: Is Justice Blind When It Runs for Office?' *American Journal of Political Science* 48: 247–63.

Huber, Peter. 1990. 'Cockroaches in Court', *Forbes*, 1 Oct., 248.

———. 1991. *Galileo's Revenge: Junk Science in the Courtroom*. New York: Basic Books.

Hughes, Patricia. 2001. 'Judicial Independence: Contemporary Pressures and Appropriate Responses', *Canadian Bar Review* 80: 181–208.

Huscroft, Grant. 1996. 'The Attorney General and Charter Challenges to Legislation: Advocate or Adjudicator?', *National Journal of Constitutional Law* 5: 125–62.

———. 2004. '"Thank God We're Here": Judicial Exclusivity in Charter Interpretation and Its Consequences', *Supreme Court Law Review*, 2nd ser., 25: 241–67.

Hutchinson, Allan. 1995. *Waiting for Coraf: A Critique of Law and Rights*. Toronto: University of Toronto Press.

Iacobucci, Frank. 2002. 'The Charter: Twenty Years Later', *Windsor Yearbook of Access to Justice* 21: 3–32.

Jacobs, Laverne. 2003. 'The Place of Administrative Tribunals: Linking Our Past to Future Prospects'. Presented at the Annual Conference of the Canadian Council of Administrative Tribunals (June). http://www.ccat-ctac.org/en/conferences/docs/2003_jacobs.pdf.

Jai, Julie. 1998. 'Policy, Politics and Law: Changing Relationships in Light of the Charter', *National Journal of Constitutional Law* 9: 1–25.

Jamal, Muhamed. 2005. 'Legislative Facts in Charter Litigation: Where are We Now?' *National Journal of Constitutional Law* 17: 1–12.

Johnson, Charles A., and Bradley C. Canon. 1999. *Judicial Policies: Implementation and Impact*. 2nd edn. Washington, DC: *Congressional Quarterly*.

Johnstone, Gerry. 2003. 'Introduction: Restorative Approaches to Criminal Justice'. In Gerry Johnstone, ed., *A Restorative Justice Reader: Texts, Sources, Context*. Portland, Oreg.: Willan.

Kagan, Robert. 1994. 'Do Lawyers Cause Adversarial Legalism? A Preliminary Inquiry', *Law and Social Inquiry* 19 (1): 1–62.

Kamisar, Yale. 2003. 'In Defense of the Search and Seizure Exclusionary Rule', *Harvard Journal of Law and Public Policy* 26: 119–40.

Kellough, Gail, and Scot Wortley. 2002. 'Remand for Plea: Bail Decisions and Plea Bargaining as Commensurate Decisions', *British Journal of Criminology* 42: 186–210.

Kelly, James B. 2005. *Governing with the Charter: Legislative and Judicial Activism and Framers' Intent.* Vancouver: UBC Press.

Kirkpatrick, David D. 2005. 'A Year of Work to Sell Roberts to Conservatives', *New York Times.* 22 July, A14.

Knopff, Rainer. 1998. 'Populism and the Politics of Rights: The Dual Attack on Representative Democracy'. *Canadian Journal of Political Science* 31: 683–706.

———, and F.L. Morton. 1992. *Charter Politics.* Toronto: Nelson Canada.

Kritzer, Herbert M. 2003a. 'Martin Shapiro: Anticipating the New Institutionalism'. In Nancy Maveety, ed., *The Pioneers of Judicial Behavior.* Ann Arbor: University of Michigan Press.

———. 2003b. 'The Government Gorilla'. In H. Kritzer and S. Silbey, eds, *In Litigation: Do the 'Haves' Still Come Out Ahead?* Stanford, Calif.: Stanford University Press.

———. 2004. 'Disappearing Trials? A Comparative Perspective', *Journal of Empirical Legal Studies* 1(3): 735–54.

———, and Susan Silbey, eds. 2003. *In Litigation: Do the 'Haves' Still Come Out Ahead?* Stanford, Calif.: Stanford University Press.

———, W.A. Bogart, and Neil Vidmar. 1991. 'The Aftermath of Injury: Cultural Factors in Compensation Seeking in Canada and the U.S.', *Law and Society Review* 25: 499–543.

Landerkin, Hugh F., and Andrew J. Pirie. 2003. 'Judges as Mediators: What's the Problem with Judicial Dispute Resolution in Canada?' *Canadian Bar Review* 82: 249–98.

Langan, Anne-Marie. 2005. 'Threatening the Balance of the Scales of Justice: Unrepresented Litigants in the Family Courts of Ontario', *Queen's Law Journal* 30: 825–59.

Langbein, John H. 2003. *The Origins of Adversary Criminal Trial.* Oxford: Oxford University Press.

Langer, Laura. 2002. *Judicial Review in State Supreme Courts: A Comparative Study.* Albany: State University of New York Press.

LaPrairie, Carol. 1999. 'Sentencing Aboriginal Offenders: Some Critical Issues'. In Julian V. Roberts and David P. Cole, eds, *Making Sense of Sentencing.* Toronto: University of Toronto Press.

Laswell, Harold. 1936. *Politics: Who Gets What, When, How.* New York: McGraw-Hill.

Law Reform Commission of Canada. 1989. *Plea Discussions and Agreements.* Working Paper 61. Ottawa: Law Reform Commission of Canada.

———. 1990. *Controlling Criminal Prosecutions: The Attorney General and the Crown Prosecutor.* Working Paper 62. Ottawa: Law Reform Commission of Canada.

LEAF. 1993. Factum Submitted to the Supreme Court of Canada in *Conway v. Canada.*

———. 1991. Factum Submitted to the Supreme Court of Canada in *R. v. Seaboyer.*

Lederman, William R. 1956. 'The Independence of the Judiciary', *Canadian Bar Review* 34: 769–809; 1139–79.

Levine, James P. 1970. 'Methodological Concerns in Studying Supreme Court Efficacy', *Law and Society Review* 4: 583–611.

———. 2005. 'Federal Crime Legislation through the Eyes of Alexis de Tocqueville', *Crime, Law and Social Change* 23: 175–89.

Levy, Alan. 1972. 'The Amicus Curiae (An Offer of Assistance to the Court),' *Chitty's Law Journal* 20: 94–103, 135–40.

Lieberman, David. 2002. 'Mapping Criminal Law: Blackstone and the Categories of English Jurisprudence'. In Norma Landau, ed., *Law, Crime and English Society, 1660–1840*. Cambridge: Cambridge University Press.

Lieberman, Jethro K. 1981. *The Litigious Society*. New York: Basic Books.

Lindgren, April, and Tim Naumetz. 2003. 'Ontario Defies Gun Registry Law: 5 Provinces Now Refuse to "Persecute" Gun Owners', *Ottawa Citizen*, 4 June, A1.

Lippert, Owen, Stephen Easton, and Craig Yirush. 1997. 'The State of Canadian Judicial Statistics: Trends in Canadian Civil Justice'. In John Robson and Owen Lippert, eds, *Law and Markets: Is Canada Inheriting America's Litigious Legacy?* Vancouver: Fraser Institute.

Lipset, Seymour Martin. 1989. *Continental Divide: The Values and Institutions of the United States and Canada*. New York: Routledge.

Liptak, Adam. 2008. 'Illegal Globally, Bail for Profit Remains in the US', *New York Times*, 29 Jan. http://www.nytimes. com/2008/01/29/us/29bail.html.

Lowery, David, and Holly Brasher. 2004. *Organized Interests and American Government*. Boston: McGraw-Hill.

MacCharles, Tonda. 2004. 'It Was an Issue of Rights', *Toronto Star*, 2 Oct., H1, H4.

———. 2008. 'Supreme Court Loses Its Expert on Languages', *Toronto Star*, 10 Apr.

Macdonald, Roderick. 1985. 'Understanding Civil Law Scholarship in Quebec', *Osgoode Hall Law Journal* 23: 573–608.

———, ed. 1995. *Study Paper on Prospects for Civil Justice*. Toronto: Ontario Law Reform Commission.

Macfarlane, Julie. 2008. *The New Lawyer*. Vancouver: University of British Columbia Press.

MacIvor, Heather. 2006. *Canadian Politics and Government in the Charter Era*. Toronto: Thomson Nelson.

Mack, Kathy. 2003. Court Referral to ADR: Criteria and Research Australian Institute of Judicial Administration and the National Dispute Resolution Advisory Council. www.nadrac.gov.au.

MacLean, Pamela A. 2006. 'Judges Warned about Seminars', *The National Law Journal*, 29 May. Accessed on-line 2 July 2007 via Academic OneFile @ Knowledge Ontario, Brock University library.

MacNair, Deborah. 2001. 'The Role of the Federal Public Sector Lawyer: From Polyester to Silk', *University of New Brunswick Law Journal* 50: 125–65.

———. 2002. 'Crown Prosecutors and Conflict of Interest: A Canadian Perspective', *Canadian Criminal Law Review* 7: 257–97.

MacPherson, Jim. 1986. 'The Case for the Defendant Government in Charter Litigation'. In Joseph Weiler and Robin Elliot, eds, *Litigating the Values of a Nation: The Canadian Charter of Rights and Freedoms*. Toronto: Carswell.

Makin, Kirk. 1999. 'Lamer Worries about Public Backlash', *Globe and Mail*, 6 Feb., A1.

———. 2003. 'In the Back Halls of Justice', *Globe and Mail*, 26 Apr., F6.

———. 2005. 'Trial Judges Usually Get Last Word, Air India Shows', *Globe and Mail*, 6 May. www.theglobeandmail.com/servlet/story/LAC.2005/05/06/.

———. 2006a. 'Appeal Rejected in Just Desserts Case', *Globe and Mail*, 23 Dec. http://www.theglobeandmail.com/servlet/story/LAC.20061223.DESSERTS23.

———. 2006b. 'Dramatic Drop In Supreme Court Rulings Fuels Questions', *Globe and Mail*, 30 Dec., A4.

———. 2006c. 'Top Judges Rebuke Tories', *Globe and Mail*, 10 Nov., A1.

———. 2007a. 'Civil Court Rule Allowing Judges to Jettison Juries Faces Challenge', *Globe and Mail*, 13 Sept., A4.

———. 2007b. 'Two-thirds Back Electing Judges', *Globe and Mail*, 9 Apr., A1.

Mallan, Caroline. 2004. 'Report Called 'Betrayal' of Women', *Toronto Star*. 21 Dec., A1.

Malleson, Kate. 2006. 'The New Judicial Appointments Commission in England and Wales'. In Kate Malleson and Peter H. Russell. eds, *Appointing Judges in an Age of Judicial Power: Critical Perspective from around the World*. Toronto: University of Toronto Press.

Maltzman, Forrest, James F. Spriggs, and Paul J. Wahlbeck. 2000. *Crafting the Law on the Supreme Court: The Collegial Game*. New York: Cambridge University Press.

Mandel, Michael. 1994. *The Charter of Rights and the Legalization of Politics in Canada*. Rev. edn. Toronto: Thompson Educational.

————. 1996. '"Fundamental Justice", Repression and Social Power'. In Jamie Cameron, ed., *The Charter's Impact on the Criminal Justice System*. Toronto: Carswell.

Manfredi, Christopher P. 1994. 'Constitutional Rights and Interest Advocacy: Litigating Educational Reform in Canada and the United States'. In F. Leslie Seidle, ed., *Equity and Community: The Charter, Interest Advocacy and Representation* Montreal: Institute for Research on Public Policy.

————. 1997. 'Institutional Design and the Politics of Constitutional Modification: Understanding Amendment Failure in the United States and Canada', *Law and Society Review* 31: 111–36.

————. 2001. *Judicial Power and the Charter: Canada and the Paradox of Liberal Constitutionalism*. 2nd edn. Don Mills, Ont.: Oxford.

————. 2004. *Feminist Activism in the Supreme Court: Legal Mobilization and the Women's Legal Education and Action Fund*. Vancouver: UBC Press.

————. 2007. 'The Day the Dialogue Died: A Comment on *Sauvé v. Canada*', *Osgoode Hall Law Journal* 45: 105–22.

————, and James B. Kelly. 1999. 'Six Degrees of Dialogue: A Response to Hogg and Bushell', *Osgoode Hall Law Journal* 37: 513–27.

————, and Antonia Maioni. 2005. 'Litigating Innovation: Health Care Policy and the Canadian Charter of Rights and Freedoms'. Paper presented to the Annual Meeting of the Canadian Political Science Association.

————, and ————. 2006. 'The Last Line of Defence for Citizens: Litigating Private Health Insurance in *Chaoulli v. Quebec*', *Osgoode Hall Law Journal* 44: 249–71.

Manitoba, Aboriginal Justice Inquiry. 1991. *Report*. Winnipeg: Queen's Printer.

Marchant, Kenning. 2007. 'Insurance Could Help Ensure Justice for All', *Toronto Star*, 24 Mar., A21.

Marth, Michael. 2008. 'Adult Court Statistics, 2006/07', *Juristat* 28. Statistics Canada cat. no. 85-002-XIE. Ottawa: Minister of Industry.

Martin, Dianne L. 1996. 'Rising Expectations: Slippery Slope or New Horizon? The Constitutionalization of Criminal Trials in Canada'. In Jamie Cameron, ed., *The Charter's Impact on the Criminal Justice System*. Toronto: Carswell.

————. 1998. 'Retribution Revisited: A Reconsideration of Feminist Criminal Law Strategies'. *Osgoode Hall Law Journal* 36: 151–88.

Martin, Edward C. 2001. 'Historical Background: The Common Law Writ System'. http://www.samford.edu/schools/netlaw/Martin/torts1/writhistory.htm.

Matas, Robert. 2007. '"We Need This Native Card Taken Out" of Courts, Slain Man's Father Says', *Globe and Mail*, 10 Apr. http://www.theglobeandmail.com/servlet/story/LAC.20070410.BCDRAG10/TPStory/?query=Patie.

Matisz, Derek. 2005. 'Appointment of Section 92 Judges in Canada'. Major research paper, University of Guelph.

Maute, Judith L. 2007. 'English Reforms to Judicial Selection: Comparative Lessons for American States', *Fordham Urban Law Journal* 34: 387–423.

McAllister, Debra M. 2002. 'The Attorney General's Role as Guardian of the Public Interest in *Charter* Litigation', *Windsor Yearbook of Access to Justice* 21: 47–90.

McCann, Michael W. 1992. 'Reform Litigation on Trial', *Law and Social Inquiry* 17: 715–43.

———. 1994. *Rights at Work*. Chicago: University of Chicago Press.

———. 1996. 'Causal versus Constitutive Explanations', *Law and Social Inquiry* 21: 457–82.

———. 1999. 'How the Supreme Court Matters in American Politics: New Institutionalist Perspectives'. In Howard Gillman and Cornell Clayton, eds, *The Supreme Court in American Politics: New Institutionalist Interpretations*. Lawrence, Kan.: University of Kansas Press.

McCormick, Peter. 1993. 'Party Capability Theory and Appellate Success in the Supreme Court of Canada, 1949–1992', *Canadian Journal of Political Science* 26 (3): 523–40.

———. 1994. *Canada's Courts*. Toronto: Lorimer.

———. 1998a. 'Do Judges Read Books, Too? Academic Citations by the Supreme Court of Canada 1991–97', *Supreme Court Law Review*, 2nd ser., 9: 463–96.

———. 1998b. 'Twelve Paradoxes of Judicial Discipline', *Constitutional Forum* 9: 105–13.

———. 2000. *Supreme at Last: The Evolution of the Supreme Court of Canada*. Toronto: Lorimer.

———. 2004a. 'Blocs, Swarms and Outliers: Conceptualizing Disagreement on the Modern Supreme Court of Canada', *Osgoode Hall Law Journal* 42: 99–138.

———. 2004b. 'New Questions about an Old Concept: The Supreme Court of Canada's Judicial Independence Decisions', *Canadian Journal of Political Science*, 37: 839–62.

———. 2005a. 'Selecting the Supremes: The Appointment of Judges to the Supreme Court of Canada', *Journal of Appellate Practice and Process* 7: 1–42.

———. 2005b. 'The Choral Court: Separate Concurrence and the McLachlin Court, 2000–2004', *Ottawa Law Review* 37: 1–33.

———, and Ian Greene. 1990. *Judges and Judging: Inside the Canadian Judicial System*. Toronto: Lorimer.

———, and Twyla Job. 1993. 'Do Women Judges Make a Difference? An Analysis by Appeal Court Data', *Canadian Journal of Law and Society* 8: 135–48.

McGuire, Kevin T. 1993. *The Supreme Court Bar: Legal Elites in the Washington Community*. Charlottesville: University Press of Virginia.

———. 1995. 'Repeat Players in the Supreme Court: The Role of Experienced Lawyers in Litigation Success', *Journal of Politics* 57: 187–96.

———. 1998. 'Explaining Executive Success in the US Supreme Court', *Political Research Quarterly* 51: 505–26.

McLachlin, Chief Justice Beverley. 2006. 'Judicial Accountability'. Remarks presented at the Law and Parliament Conference, Ottawa, 2 Nov. 2006. http://www.scc-csc.gc.ca/About Court/judges/speeches/Ju_Resp_e.asp.

———. 2007. 'The Challenges We Face'. Speech to the Empire Club of Canada, Toronto, 8 Mar. http://www.scc-csc.gc.ca/aboutcourt/judges/speeches/ Challenges_e.asp.

Meek, Jim. 1998. 'Justice Heather Robertson: 'Not Recommended'', *Halifax Chronicle Herald*, 14 July.

Menkel-Meadow, Carrie J. 2005. 'Is the Adversary System Really Dead? Dilemmas of Legal Ethics As Legal Institutions and Roles Evolve'. In Jane Holder, Colm O'Cinneide, and Michael Freeman, eds, *Current Legal Problems 2004*, Vol. 57. New York: Oxford.

Mertz, Elizabeth. 1994. 'A New Social Constructionism for Sociolegal Studies', *Law and Society Review* 28: 1243–65.

Mewett, Alan W. 1988. 'The Criminal Law, 1867–1967', In R.C. Macleod, ed, *Lawful Authority: Readings on the History of Criminal Justice in Canada*. Toronto: Copp Clark Pitman.

Michell, Paul. 2007. 'Class Actions Aren't Dead Yet', *National Post*, 9 Aug., FP13.

Mickleburgh, Robert. 2007. 'Sentence Reduction Sparks Outrage', *Globe and Mail*, 4 Apr. http://www.theglobeandmail.com/servlet/story/LAC.20070404.BCSENTENCE04/T PStory/?query=Patie.

Mihorean, Karen, and Rebecca Kong. 2008. 'Criminal Justice Trends in Canada'. In Julian V. Roberts and Michelle Grossman, eds, *Criminal Justice in Canada: A Reader*. 3rd edn. Toronto: Thomson Nelson.

Millar, Andre S. 2000. 'The 'New' Federal Judicial Appointments Process: The First Ten Years', *Alberta Law Review* 38: 616–53.

Miller, Arthur R. 2003. 'The Pretrial Rush to Judgment: Are the 'Litigation Explosion', 'Liability Crisis', and Efficiency Clichés Eroding Our Day in Court and Jury Trial Commitments?' *New York University Law Review* 78: 982–1134.

Miller, Richard E., and Austin Sarat. 1980–1. 'Grievances, Claims, and Disputes: Assessing the Adversary Culture', *Law and Society Review* 15: 524–65. Blackwell Publishing.

Ministry of the Attorney General, Court Services Division. 2006. *Annual Report 2004/05*. Toronto: Queen's Printer for Ontario.

Mishler, William, and Reginald S. Sheehan. 1993. 'The Supreme Court as a Counter-majoritarian Institution? The Impact of Public Opinion on Supreme Court Decisions', *American Political Science Review* 87: 87–101.

Mitchell, Graeme G. 1993. 'The Impact of the Charter on the Public Policy Process: The Attorney General'. In Patrick Monahan and Marie Finkelstein, eds, *The Impact of the Charter on the Public Policy Process*. North York, Ont.: York University Centre for Public Law and Public Policy.

Moldaver, Hon. Justice Michael. 2006. 'Long Criminal Trials: Masters of a System They Are Meant to Serve', *Criminal Reports*, 6th ser., 32: 316–23.

Monahan, Patrick. 1987. *Politics and the Constitution: The Charter, Federalism and the Supreme Court of Canada*. Toronto: Carswell/Methuen.

Moore, Kathryn. 1992. 'Police Implementation of Supreme Court of Canada Charter Decisions: An Empirical Study', *Osgoode Hall Law Journal* 30: 547–77.

Morgan, S. Reed. 1994. 'Verdict against McDonald's Is Fully Justified'. Letter to the *National Law Journal* 17 (8), 24 Oct., A20.

Morris, S. Wayne. 2003. 'A Comparison of Legal Systems: Canada and the United States'. www.projecteagle.com/articles/pe001.pdf.

Morrison, Ian, and Janet Mosher. 1996. 'Barriers to Access to Civil Justice for Disadvantaged Groups'. In *Rethinking Civil Justice: Research Studies for the Civil Justice Review*, Vol. 2. Toronto: Ontario Law Reform Commission.

Morton, F.L. 1992. *Morgentaler v. Borowski: Abortion, the Charter and the Courts*. Toronto: McLelland and Stewart.

———. 2002. *Law, Politics and the Judicial Process in Canada*. 3rd edn. Calgary: University of Calgary Press.

———. 2006. 'Judicial Appointments in Post Charter Canada: A System in Transition'. In Kate Malleson and Peter H. Russell, eds, *Appointing Judges in an Age of Judicial Power: Critical Perspective from around the World*. Toronto: University of Toronto Press.

———, and Avril Allen. 2001. 'Feminists and the Courts: Measuring Success in Interest Group Litigation in Canada', *Canadian Journal of Political Science* 34: 55–84.

———, and Rainer Knopff. 2000. *The Charter Revolution and the Court Party*. Peterborough: Broadview Press.

———, Matthew Hennigar, and Shawn Ho. 1996. 'The Role of Governments in Charter Litigation: Charter Politics as Centre-Periphery Politics'. Presented at the annual meeting of the Canadian Political Science Association, St Catharines, Ont.

————, Peter Russell, and Troy Riddell. 1994. 'The Canadian Charter of Rights and Freedoms: A Descriptive Analysis of the First Decade, 1982–1992', *National Journal of Constitutional Law* 5: 1–58.

Moyer, Sharon. 2006. *YCJA Monitoring Study*. Ottawa: Department of Justice Canada.

————, and Maryanna Basic. 2004. *Crown Decision-Making under the Youth Criminal Justice Act*. Ottawa: Department of Justice Canada. http://www.justice.gc.ca/en/ps/rs/rep/2004/rr04yj-2/rr04yj-2.pdf.

Mullan, David. 2005. 'Tribunals Imitating Courts—Foolish Flattery or Sound Policy?' *Dalhousie Law Journal* 28: 1–25.

Murphy, Jeffrie G., and Jules L. Coleman. 1990. *Philosophy of Law: An Introduction to Jurisprudence*. Boulder, CO: Westview Press.

National Judicial Institute (Canada). 2005. 'Judging for the 21st Century: A Problem-solving Approach'. www.nji.ca.

Nejatian, Kasra. 2007. 'Report Back from "The Future of Freedom"', *The Court*, 23 Oct. http://www.thecourt.ca.

Neubauer, David W. 1997. *Judicial Process: Law, Courts and Politics in the United States*. 2nd edn. New York: Harcourt Brace.

Nevitte, Neil. 1996. *The Decline of Deference: Canadian Value Change in Cross National Perspective*. Peterborough: Broadview Press.

Nova Scotia, Royal Commission on the Donald Marshall, Jr. Prosecution. 1989. *Findings and Recommendations*. Halifax: The Royal Commission.

Nova Scotia. Department of Justice [Kaufman, Fred]. 1998. *Review of the Public Prosecution Service: Interim Report*. Halifax, N.S.: Department of Justice.

O'Brien, David, and Yasuo Ohkoski. 2001. 'Stifling Judicial Independence from Within: The Japanese Judiciary'. In P. Russell and D. O'Brien, eds, *Judicial Independence in the Age of Democracy: Critical Perspectives from around the World*. Charlottesville: University Press of Virginia.

O'Connor, Karen. 1980. *Women's Organizations' Use of the Courts*. Lexington: D.C. Heath and Co.

Office of the Commissioner for Federal Judicial Affairs. 2008. www.fja.gc.ca/fja-cmf/ja-am/com/index-eng.html.

Olson, Susan. 1990. 'Interest Group Litigation in Federal District Court: Beyond the Political Disadvantage Theory', *Journal of Politics* 52: 854–82.

Olson, Walter K. 1991. *The Litigation Explosion: What Happened When America Unleashed the Lawsuit*. New York: Truman Talley.

————. 1997. 'How America Got Its Litigation Explosion: Why Canada Should Not Consider Itself Immune'. In John Robson and Owen Lippert, eds, *Law and Markets: Is Canada Inheriting America's Litigious Legacy?* Vancouver: Fraser Institute.

Ontario. 1968. *Royal Commission Inquiry into Civil Rights* (McRuer Report), vols 1–5. Toronto: Queen's Printer.

Ontario, Attorney General. 1993. *Report of the Advisory Committee on Screening of Criminal Charges, Resolution Discussions and Disclosure* (Martin Report). Toronto: Queen's Printer for Ontario.

————. 1999. *Report of the Criminal Justice Review Committee*. Toronto: Queen's Printer for Ontario.

————. 2006. *Crown Policy Manual—2005*. Toronto: Queen's Printer for Ontario. http://www.attorneygeneral.jus.gov.on.ca/english/crim/cpm/default.asp (last accessed 2 Aug. 2007).

Ontario Civil Justice Review. 1995. *Civil Justice Review: First Report*. Toronto: Ontario Civil Justice Review.

———. 1996. *Civil Justice Review: Supplemental and Final Report*. Toronto: Ontario Civil Justice Review.

Ontario, Commission on Systemic Racism in the Ontario Criminal Justice System. 1995. *Report*. Toronto: Queen's Printer for Ontario.

Ontario Courts Inquiry. 1987. *Report* (Zuber Report). Toronto: Queen's Printer.

Ontario Judicial Council. 1996. 'Principles of Judicial Office'. Toronto: Ontario Judicial Council. http://www.ontariocourts.on.ca/ontario_court_justice/principlesjudicial.pdf.

Ontario Law Reform Commission. 1996. *Report on the Use of Jury Trials in Civil Cases*. Toronto: Ontario Law Reform Commission.

Ontario, Ministry of the Attorney General. 2006a. *Civil Justice Reform Project: Consultation Paper*. http://www.civiljusticereform.jus.gov.on.ca/english/consultation.asp.

———. 2006b. *Court Services Division: Annual Report 2004/05*. Toronto: Queen's Printer for Ontario.

———. 2006c. *Published Results-Based Plan 2007–8*. Toronto: Queen's Printer for Ontario. http://www.attorneygeneral.jus.gov.on.ca/english/about/pubs/mag_annual/rbp-partI-mag-2007-8.asp (last accessed 20 July 2007).

———. 2007. *Civil Justice Reform Project: Summary of Findings and Recommendations*. Toronto: Ministry of the Attorney General.

Ontario Superior Court of Justice. 2006. *New Approaches to Criminal Trials*. http://www.ontariocourts on.ca/superior_court_justice/reports/CTR/CTReport.htm#_Toc141087521.

Orsini, Michael. 2002. 'The Politics of Naming, Blaming and Claiming: HIV, Hepatitis C and the Emergence of Blood Activism in Canada', 35 *Canadian Journal of Political Science* 35: 475–98.

Ostberg, Cynthia L., and Matthew E. Wetstein. 2007. *Attitudinal Decision Making in the Supreme Court of Canada*. Vancouver: UBC Press.

———, M.E. Wetstein, and C.R. Ducat. 2002. 'Attitudinal Dimensions of Supreme Court Decision-Making in Canada: The Lamer Court, 1991–1995', *Political Research Quarterly* 55 (1): 235–56.

Ottawa Citizen. 1984. 'PM Names LeDain to High Court', 30 May, A1, A12.

———. 1998. 'Judge: Critics Argue Time for Another Woman', 9 Jan., D2.

Pacelle, Richard. 2003. *Between Law and Politics: The Solicitor General and the Structuring of Race, Gender, and Reproductive Rights Litigation*. College Station, Tex.: Texas A&M University Press.

Paciocco, David M. 1999. *Getting Away with Murder: The Canadian Criminal Justice System*. Toronto: Irwin Law.

———, and Lee Streusser. 2003. *The Law of Evidence*. 3rd edn. Toronto: Irwin Law.

Packer, Herbert. 1964. 'Two Models of the Criminal Process'. *University of Pennsylvania Law Review* 113: 1–68.

Pal, Leslie A. 2000. 'Between the Sights: Gun Control in Canada and the United States'. In David M. Thomas, ed., *Canada and the United States: Differences that Count*, Toronto: Broadview Press.

Palys, Ted S., and Stan Divorski. 1986. 'Explaining Sentencing Disparity', *Canadian Journal of Criminology* 28: 347–62.

Parfett, Juianne. 2002. 'A Triumph of Liberalism: The Supreme Court of Canada and the Exclusion of Evidence', *Alberta Law Review* 40: 299–332.

Parsons, Vic. 1995. *Bad Blood: The Tragedy of the Canadian Tainted Blood Scandal*. Toronto: Lester.

Peden, Martha. 2007. 'Reducing the Number of Frivolous Lawsuits'. Edmonton: Centre for Constitutional Studies, University of Alberta (30 July). http://www.law.ualberta.ca/centres/ccs/Current-Constitutional-Issues/Reducing-the-Number-of-Frivolous-Lawsuits.php.

Peresie, Jennifer L. 2005. 'Female Judges Matter: Gender and Collegial Decisionmaking in the Federal Appellate Courts', *Yale Law Journal* 114: 1759–90.

Perrin, Terri. 2002. 'The Best Place to Get Divorced in Canada', *Canadian Living*, June, 155–60.

Petter, Andrew. 2007a. 'Taking Dialogue Theory Much Too Seriously (or Perhaps Charter Dialogue Isn't Such a Good Thing After All)', *Osgoode Hall Law Journal* 45: 147–68.

———. 2007b. 'The State of Canadian Democracy', speech to the Annual Conference of the McGill Institute for the Study of Canada, 'The Charter @ 25', Montreal, 15 Feb.

Phillips of Worth Matravers, Lord. (Lord Chief Justice of England and Wales). 2006. Webcast interview by Marcel Berlins, 6 Apr. http://clients.westminster-digital.co.uk/judiciary/.

Picard, André. 1998. *The Gift of Death: Confronting Canada's Tainted-Blood Tragedy*. Rev. edn. Toronto: HarperCollins Canada.

Piccinato, Milica Potrebic. 2004. 'Plea Bargaining'. Ottawa: International Cooperation Group, Department of Justice.

Plecas, Darryl, Yvon Dandurand, Vivienne Chen, and Tim Segger. 2002. 'Marijuana Growing Operations in British Columbia: An Empirical Survey (1997–2000).' Vancouver: International Centre for Criminal Law Reform and Criminal Justice Policy. http://www.icclr.law.ubc.ca/Publications/Reports/Grow.PDF.

Popkey, Dan. 2007. 'A Better Way to Select Our Supreme Court Justices', *Idaho Statesman*, 13 June. www.idahostatesman.com.

Posner, Richard A. 1976. 'Blackstone and Bentham', *Journal of Law and Economics* 19: 569–606.

Provincial Court of Newfoundland and Labrador. 2006. *Annual Report 2005–2006*. http://www.court.nl.ca/provincial/ar05_06.pdf.

Provine, Doris Marie, and Antoine Garapon. 2006. 'The Selection of Judges in France: Searching for a New Legitimacy'. In Kate Malleson and Peter H. Russell, eds, *Appointing Judges in an Age of Judicial Power: Critical Perspective from around the World*. Toronto: University of Toronto Press.

Raaflaub, Wade. 2004. 'Bill S-10: Federal Law–Civil Law Harmonization Act No. 2'. Parliamentary Research Branch, Law and Government Section. http://www.parl.gc.ca/common/Bills_ls.asp?Parl=38&Ses=1&ls=S10#6txt (accessed 12 Aug. 2005).

Ramseyer, J. Mark, and Eric B. Rasmusen. 2003. *Measuring Judicial Independence: The Political Economy of Judging in Japan*. Chicago: University of Chicago Press.

Ratushny, Ed. 2000. 'Speaking As Judges: How Far Can They Go?', *National Journal of Constitutional Law* 11: 293–410.

Razack, Sherene. 1991. *Canadian Feminism and the Law: The Women's Legal Education and Action Fund and the Pursuit of Equality*. Toronto: Second Story Press.

Reddick, Malia. 2002. 'Merit Selection: A Review of the Social Scientific Literature', *Dickinson Law Review* 106: 729–45.

René, David, and John E.C. Brierley. 1985. *Major Legal Systems in the World Today: An Introduction to the Comparative Study of Law*. 3rd edn. London: Stevens and Sons.

Renke, Wayne. 1998. 'The Independence and Impartiality of Provincial Court Judges: Rapporteur's Report', *Constitutional Forum* 9: 121–6.

Renteln, Alison Dundes. 2005. 'Use and Abuse of the Cultural Defence', *Canadian Journal of Law and Society* 20: 47–67.

Revesz, Richard L. 2000. 'Litigation and Settlement in the Federal Appellate Courts: Impact of Panel Selection Procedures on Ideologically Divided Courts', *Journal of Legal Studies* 29: 685–710.

Riddell, Troy Q. 2004. 'The Impact of Legal Mobilization and Judicial Decisions: The Case of Official Minority-Language Education Policy in Canada for Francophones outside Quebec', *Law and Society Review* 38: 583–610.

———, and F.L. Morton. 1998. 'Reasonable Limitations, Distinct Society and the Canada Clause: Interpretive Clauses and the Competition for Constitutional Advantage', *Canadian Journal of Political Science* 31: 467–93.

———, and ———. 2004. 'Government Use of Strategic Litigation: the Alberta Exported Gas Tax Reference', *American Review of Canadian Studies* 34 (3): 485–509.

———, Lori Hausegger, and Matthew Hennigar. 2008. 'Federal Judicial Appointments: A Look at Patronage in Federal Appointments since 1988', *University of Toronto Law Journal* 58: 39–74.

Roach, Kent. 1993. 'The Role of Litigation and the Charter in Interest Advocacy'. In F. Leslie Seidle, ed., *Equity and Community: The Charter, Interest Advocacy and Representation*. Ottawa: Institute for Research on Public Policy.

———. 1996. 'Institutional Choice, Co-operation, and Struggle in the Age of the Charter'. In Jamie Cameron, ed., *The Charter's Impact on the Criminal Justice System*. Toronto: Carswell.

———. 1999. *Due Process and Victims' Rights*. Toronto: University Toronto Press.

———. 2000. 'The Attorney General and the Charter Revisited', *University of Toronto Law Review* 50: 1–40.

———. 2001. *The Supreme Court on Trial: Judicial Activism or Democratic Dialogue*.

———. 2005. *Criminal Law*. 3rd edn. Toronto: Irwin Law.

———. 2006. 'Not Just the Government's Lawyer: the Attorney General as Defender of the Rule of Law', *Queen's Law Journal* 31: 598–643.

———. Forthcoming. 'National Security and the Charter'. In James Kelly and Christopher Manfredi, eds, *Contested Constitutionalism: Reflections on the Charter of Rights and Freedoms*. Vancouver: UBC Press.

Roberts, Julian V. 2002. 'The Evolution of Conditional Sentencing: An Empirical Analysis', *Criminal Reports*, 6th ser., 3: 267–83.

———, and Anthony N. Doob. 1990. *Law and Human Behaviour* 14: 451–68.

———, Nicole Crutcher, and Paul Verbrugge. 2007. 'Public Attitudes to Sentencing in Canada: Exploring Recent Findings', *Canadian Journal of Criminology and Criminal Justice* 49: 75–107.

Roberts, Julian V., and David P. Cole, eds. 1999. *Making Sense of Sentencing*. Toronto: University of Toronto Press.

Rosenberg, Gerald N. 1991. *The Hollow Hope: Can Courts Bring About Social Change?* Chicago: University of Chicago Press.

———. 1996. 'Positivism, Interpretivism, and the Study of Law', *Law and Social Inquiry* 21: 435–55.

Rosenberg, Morris. 2003. 'An Inside Look: A Message from the Deputy Minister', *Serving Canadians: Justice Canada* 1 (1): 1.

Russell, Peter H. 1983. 'Bold Statecraft, Questionable Jurisprudence'. In Keith Banting and Richard Simeon, eds, *And No One Cheered: Federalism, Democracy and the Constitution Act*. Toronto: Methuen.

————. 1984a. 'Constitutional Reform of the Judicial Branch: Symbolic vs. Operational Considerations', *Canadian Journal of Political Science* 17: 227–52.

————. 1984b. 'The Political Theory of Contrology'. In Anthony N. Doob and Edward L. Greenspan, eds, *Perspectives in Criminal Law: Essays in Honour of John LL.J. Edwards*. Aurora, Ont.: Canada Law Book.

————. 1985. 'The Supreme Court and Federal Provincial Relations: The Political Use of Legal Resources', *Canadian Public Policy* 11: 161–70.

————. 1987. *The Judiciary in Canada: The Third Branch of Government*. Toronto: McGraw-Hill Ryerson.

————. 2001. 'Toward a General Theory of Judicial Independence'. In P. Russell and D. O'Brien, eds, *Judicial Independence in the Age of Democracy: Critical Perspectives from around the World*. Charlottesville: University Press of Virginia.

————. 2004a. 'A Parliamentary Approach to Reforming the Process of Filling Vacancies on the Supreme Court of Canada'. Submission to Standing Committee on Justice, Human Rights, Public Safety and Emergency Preparedness, 23 Mar.

————. 2004b. *Constitutional Odyssey: Can Canadians Become a Sovereign People?* 3rd edn. Toronto: University of Toronto Press.

————. 2007a. 'An Error of Judgment', *Globe and Mail*, 27 Feb., A21.

————, ed., 2007b. *Canada's Trial Courts: Two Tiers or One?* Toronto: University of Toronto Press.

————, and Jacob Ziegel. 1991. 'Federal Judicial Appointments: An Appraisal of the First Mulroney Governments Appointments and the New Judicial Advisory Committees', *University of Toronto Law Journal* 41(1): 4–37.

Salokar, Rebecca Mae. 1992. *The Solicitor General: The Politics of Law*. Philadelphia: Temple University Press.

Sauvageau, Florian, David Schneiderman, and David Taras. 2006. *The Last Word: Media Coverage of the Supreme Court of Canada*. Vancouver: UBC Press.

Scalia, Antonin. 1997. *A Matter of Interpretation: Federal Courts and the Law*. Princeton: Princeton University Press.

Scheingold, Stuart. 1974. *The Politics of Rights: Lawyers, Public Policy and Political Change*. New Haven, Conn.: Yale University Press.

Scheppele, Kim Lane, and Jack L. Walker. 1991. 'The Litigation Strategies of Interest Groups'. In Jack L. Walker, ed., *Mobilizing Interest Groups in America*. Ann Arbor: University of Michigan Press.

Scherer, Nancy. 2003. 'The Judicial Confirmation Process: Mobilizing Elites, Mobilizing Masses', *Judicature* 86: 240–50.

Schlozman, Kay Lehman, and John T. Tierney. 1986. *Organized Interests and American Democracy*. New York: Harper and Row.

Schmitz, Cristin. 2007. 'Judge Defends Right to Speak Out in Public', *Lawyers Weekly*, 7 July. http://www.lawyersweekly.ca/index.php?section=article&articleid=464.

Schneiderman, David, ed. 1999. *The Quebec Decision: Perspectives on the Supreme Court Ruling on Secession*. Toronto: James Lorimer.

Sciaraffa, Stefan. 1999. 'Critical Legal Studies: A Marxist Rejoinder', *Legal Theory* 5: 201–19.

Scott, Ian. 1989. 'Law, Policy and the Role of the Attorney General: Constancy and Change in the 1980s', *University of Toronto Law Journal* 39: 109–26.

Seeman, Neil. 2003. 'Taking Judicial Activism Seriously', *Fraser Forum* (August): 3–19.

Segal, Jeffrey A. 1984. 'Predicting Supreme Court Cases Probabilistically: The Search and Seizure Cases, 1962–1981', *American Political Science Review* 78: 891–900.

————, and Albert D. Cover. 1989. 'Ideological Values and Votes of US Supreme Court Justices', *American Political Science Review* 83: 557–65.

————, and Cheryl Reedy. 1988. 'The Supreme Court and Sex Discrimination: The Role of the Solicitor General', *Western Political Quarterly* 41: 553–68.

————, and Harold J. Spaeth. 2002. *The Supreme Court and the Attitudinal Model Revisited.* New York: Cambridge University Press.

Shapiro, Martin. 1981. *Courts: A Comparative and Political Analysis.* Chicago: University of Chicago Press.

Sharpe, Robert J., and Patricia I. McMahon. 2007. *The Persons Case: The Origins and Legacy of the Fight for Legal Personhood.* Toronto: University of Toronto Press.

————, and Kent Roach. 2003. *Brian Dickson: A Judge's Journey.* Toronto: University of Toronto Press (for The Osgoode Society of Canadian Legal History).

————, and Kent Roach. 2005. *The Charter of Rights and Freedoms.* 3rd edn. Toronto: Irwin Law.

Sheehan, Reginald S., William Mishler, and Donald R. Songer. 1992. 'Ideology, Status, and the Differential Success of Direct Parties before the Supreme Court', *American Political Science Review* 86(2): 464–71.

Sheldon, Charles H., and Nicholas P. Lovrich, Jr. 1999. 'Voter Knowledge, Behavior and Attitudes in Primary and General Judicial Elections', *Judicature* 82: 216–23.

Shetreet, Shimon. 1976. *Judges on Trial: A Study of the Appointment and Accountability of the English Judiciary.* Oxford: North-Holland.

Sieder, Rachel, Line Schjolden, and Alan Angell, eds. 2005. *The Judicialization of Politics in Latin America.* London: Palgrave Macmillan.

Sigurdson, Richard. 1993. 'Left- and Right-Wing Charterphobia in Canada: A Critique of the Critics', *International Journal of Canadian Studies* 7–8: 95–115.

Simon, Jonathon. 1992. '"The Long Walk Home" to Politics', *Law and Society Review* 26: 923–41.

Simpson, Jeffrey. 1988. *The Spoils of Power: The Politics of Patronage.* Toronto: Collins.

————. 2004. 'Our Refugee System Costs More Than We Think', *Globe and Mail*, 7 Jan., A17.

Sirotich, Frank. 2006. 'Reconfiguring Crime Control and Criminal Justice: Governmentality and Problem-Solving Courts', *University of New Brunswick Law Journal* 55: 11–26.

Skelton, Chad. 2005. 'Out of Control: Criminal Justice System "on the Brink of Imploding"', *Vancouver Sun*, 11 Mar.

Smith, Charles W. 2006. 'The Provincial State and Keynesian Labour Policy in Ontario, 1949–1961'. Paper presented at the Annual Meeting of the Canadian Political Science Association, York University. http://www.cpsa-acsp.ca/papers-2006/Smith,%20Charles.pdf.

Smith, Heather J. (Chief Justice). 2007. 'Remarks, Opening of the Courts of Ontario', 10 Jan. http://www.ontariocourts.on.ca/superior_court_justice/opening_speeches/2007 scjrep.htm.

Smith, Jennifer. 1983. 'The Origins of Judicial Review in Canada', *Canadian Journal of Political Science* 16 (1): 115–34.

Smith, Miriam. 1999. *Lesbian and Gay Rights in Canada: Social Movements and Equality-Seeking, 1971–1995.* Toronto: University of Toronto Press.

————. 2002a. 'Ghosts of the JCPC: Group Politics and Charter Litigation in Canadian Political Science', *Canadian Journal of Political Science* 35: 3–30.

————. 2002b. 'Recognizing Same-Sex Relationships: The Evolution of Recent Federal and Provincial Policies', *Canadian Public Administration* 45: 1–23.

————. 2005. 'Social Movements and Judicial Empowerment: Courts, Public Policy and Lesbian and Gay Organizing in Canada', *Politics and Society* 33: 327–53.

Smith, Rick, and Devon Page. 2008. 'Developers and Citizens: Democracy Suffers under Barrage of Strategic Lawsuits', *Toronto Star*, 26 Feb., AA6.

Smyth, Russell. 2000. 'The 'Haves' and the 'Have Nots': An Empirical Study of the Rational Actor and Party Capability Hypotheses in the High Court 1948–99', *Australian Journal of Political Science* 35: 255–74.

Snell, James G., and Frederick Vaughan. 1985. *The Supreme Court of Canada: History of the Institution*. Toronto: University of Toronto Press.

Sniderman, Paul M., Joseph F. Fletcher, Peter H. Russell, and Phillip E. Tetlock. 1996. *The Clash of Rights: Liberty, Equality, and Legitimacy in a Pluralist Democracy*. New Haven: Yale University Press.

Solberg, Rorie Spill, and Leonard Ray. 2005. 'Capacity, Attitudes, and Case Attributes: The Differential Success of the States before the United States Courts of Appeals', *State Politics and Policy Quarterly* 5: 147–67.

Solum, Lawrence. 2003. 'The Recall, Standards of Review and Transsubstantive Procedure', lsolum.blogspot.com, 24 Sept.

Songer, Donald, and Ashlyn Kuersten. 1995. 'The Success of Amici in State Supreme Courts', *Political Research Quarterly* 48: 31–42.

Songer, Donald, and Reginald S. Sheehan. 1993. 'Interest Group Success in the Courts: Amicus Participation in the Supreme Court', *Political Research Quarterly* 46: 339–54.

Songer, Donald R., and Kelly Crews-Meyer. 2000. 'Does Judge Gender Matter? Decision Making in the State Supreme Courts', *Social Science Quarterly* 81: 750–62.

Songer, Donald R., and Susan W. Johnson. 2007. 'Judicial Decision Making in the Supreme Court of Canada: Updating the Personal Attribute Model', *Canadian Journal of Political Science* 40: 911–34.

Songer, Donald R., Sue Davis, and Susan Haire. 1994. 'A Reappraisal of Diversification in the Federal Courts: Gender Effects in the Courts of Appeals', *Journal of Politics* 56: 425–39.

Songer, Donald, and Ashlyn Kuersten. 1995. 'The Success of Amici in State Supreme Courts', *Political Research Quarterly* 48: 31–42.

Songer, Donald, and Reginald S. Sheehan. 1992. 'Who Wins on Appeal? Upperdogs and Underdogs in the United States Courts of Appeals', *American Journal of Political Science* 36: 235–58.

Songer, Donald, and Reginald S. Sheehan. 1993. 'Interest Group Success in the Courts: Amicus Participation in the Supreme Court', *Political Research Quarterly* 46: 339–54.

Songer, Donald, Reginald Sheehan, and Susan Brodie Haire. 1999. 'Do the Haves Come Out Ahead Over Time?' *Law and Society Review* 33: 811–32.

Sopinka, John. 1996. 'Must a Judge Be a Monk—Revisited', *University of New Brunswick Law* Journal 45: 167–74.

Sossin, Lorne. 1999. *Boundaries of Judicial Review: The Law of Justiciability in Canada*. Toronto: Carswell.

Sossin, Lorne. 2003. 'Discretion Unbound: Reconciling the *Charter* and Soft Law', *Canadian Public Administration* 45: 465–89.

Sprott, Jane B., and Anthony Doob. 2008. 'The Use of Court and Custody under the *Youth Criminal Justice Act*'. In Julian V. Roberts and Michelle Grossman, eds, *Criminal Justice in Canada: A Reader*. 3rd edn. Toronto: Thomson Nelson.

Sterling, Lori, and Heather Mackay. 2003. 'Constitutional Recognition of the Role of the Attorney General in Criminal Prosecutions: *Krieger v. Law Society of Alberta*', *Supreme Court Law Review*, 2nd ser., 20: 169–96.

Stier, Marc, and Saul Brenner. 2008. 'Does Precedent Influence the Justices' Voting on the US Supreme Court? A Theoretical Argument', *Law and Courts* 18 (Winter): 4–10.

Stimson, James A., Michael B. MacKuen, and Robert S. Erikson. 1995. 'Dynamic Representation', *American Political Science Review* 89: 543–65.

Strayer, Barry L. 1988. *The Canadian Constitution and the Courts: The Function and Scope of Judicial Review.* 3rd edn. Toronto: Butterworths.

Stribopolous, James. 2007. 'The Limits of Judicially Created Police Powers: Investigative Detention after *Mann*', *Criminal Law Quarterly* 52: 299–326.

Stribopoulos, James, and Moin A. Yahya. 2007. 'Does a Judge's Party of Appointment or Gender Matter to Case Outcomes? An Empirical Study of the Court of Appeal for Ontario', *Osgoode Hall Law Journal* 45: 315–63.

Stuart, Don. 1995. 'Prosecutorial Accountability in Canada'. In Philip C. Stenning, ed., *Accountability for Criminal Justice: Selected Essays.* Toronto: University of Toronto Press.

———. 1999. 'The Unfortunate Dilution of Section 8 Protection: Some Teeth Remain', *Queen's Law Journal* 25: 65–94.

———. 2006. 'The Charter Is a Vital Living Tree Not a Weed to Be Stunted—Justice Moldaver Has Overstated', *Criminal Reports*, 6th ser., 40: 280–9.

Sullivan, Ruth. 1998–9. 'Statutory Interpretation in the Supreme Court of Canada', *Ottawa Law Review* 30: 175–227.

Summers, Robert S. 1999. 'Formal Legal Truth and Substantive Truth in Judicial Decision-making: Their Justified Divergence in Some Particular Cases', *Law and Philosophy* 18: 497–511.

Supreme Court of British Columbia. 2006. *Annual Report 2005.* http://www.courts.gov. bc.ca/sc/whats% 20new/Supreme%20Court%202005%20Annual%20Report.pdf.

Supreme Court of Canada. 2006. 'Statistics 1995–2005'. *Bulletin of Proceedings: Special Edition.* Ottawa: Supreme Court of Canada.

———. 2008a. 'Statistics 1997–2007'. *Bulletin of Proceedings: Special Edition.* Ottawa: Supreme Court of Canada.

———. 2008b. http//www.scc-csc.gc.ca/aboutcourt.

Swinton, Katherine. 1996. *Report to the National Judicial Institute on Social Context Education for Judges.* Ottawa: National Judicial Institute.

Szmer, John, Susan W. Johnson, and Tammy A. Sarver. 2007. 'Does the Lawyer Matter? Influencing Outcomes on the Supreme Court of Canada', *Law and Society Review* 41 (2): 279–304.

Tang, Kwong-leung. 2003. 'Battered Woman Syndrome Testimony in Canada: Its Development and Lingering Issues', *International Journal of Offender Therapy and Comparative Criminology* 47: 618–29.

Tanovich, David M. 2006. 'The Further Erasure of Race in Charter Cases', *Criminal Reports*, 6th ser., 38: 84–103.

Tarr, G. Alan. 2003. *Judicial Process and Judicial Policymaking.* 3rd edn. Belmont, Calif.: Wadsworth/Thomson Learning.

———. 2006. *Judicial Process and Judicial Policymaking.* 4th edn. Belmont, Calif.: Wadsworth/Thomson Learning.

Tate, C. Neal, and Roger Handberg. 1991. 'Time Binding and Theory Building in Personal Attribute Models of Supreme Court Voting Behavior', *American Journal of Political Science* 35: 460–80.

———, and P. Sittiwong. 1989. 'Decision-Making in the Canadian Supreme Court: Extending the Personal Attributes Model across Nation', *Journal of Politics* 51 (4): 900–16.

————, and Torbjorn Vallinder, eds. 1995. *The Global Expansion of Judicial Power*. New York: New York University Press.

Tauber, Steven C. 1998. 'On Behalf of the Condemned? The Impact of the NAACP Legal Defense Fund on Capital Punishment Decision Making in the US Court of Appeals', *Political Research Quarterly* 51: 191–219.

Telus. 2007. 'Former Top Judge Slams Tory Changes to Judicial Appointments as "Useless"'. www.mytelus.com, 19 Apr.

Tetley, William. 2000. 'Mixed Jurisdictions: Common Law vs. Civil Law (Codified and Uncodified)', *Louisiana Law Journal* 60: 677–738.

Thomas, Jennifer. 2008. 'Youth Court Statistics, 2006/07', *Juristat* 28. Statistics Canada cat. no. 85-002-XIE. Ottawa: Minister of Industry.

Thomas, Mikhail. 2004. 'Adult Criminal Court Statistics, 2003/4', *Juristat* 24. Statistics Canada cat. no. 85-002-XPE. Ottawa: Minister of Industry.

Thompson, Rollie D.A. 2003. 'Are There Any Rules of Evidence in Family Law?' *Canadian Family Law Quarterly* 21: 245. Accessed through WestLaw. (Page numbers cited refer to the WestLaw document.)

————. 2005. 'Judge as Counsel', *News and Views on Civil Justice Reform*, Spring: 3–6. Canadian Forum on Civil Justice. http://cfcj-fcjc.org/publications/.

Thorsell, William. 1997. 'What to Look For, and Guard Against, in a Supreme Court Judge', *Globe and Mail*, 20 Dec., D6.

Tollefson, Chris. 1994. 'Strategic Lawsuits against Public Participation: Developing a Canadian Response', *Canadian Bar Review* 73 (2): 200–33.

Tyler, Tracey. 2007a. 'Access to Justice a 'Basic Right': Country's Top Judge Says the System's High Cost Is an 'Urgent' Problem That Must Be Addressed', *Toronto Star*, 12 Aug., A1–A2.

————. 2007b. 'The Dark Side of Justice', *Toronto Star*, 3 Mar., A1, A25.

————. 2007c. 'Judge Says His Free Speech Is on Trial', Toronto Star, 24 Feb., B1.

————. 2007d. 'Lawyers Seek Break from GST', *Toronto Star*, 11 Aug., A4.

————. 2007e. 'Taking Your Own Counsel', *Toronto Star*, 7 Mar., A3.

Tyson, Marion. 2007. 'Trial Court Restructuring: A Court Administrator's Perspective', in Peter H. Russell, ed., *Canada's Trial Courts: Two Tiers or One?* Toronto: University of Toronto Press.

United States Government Accountability Office. 2005. *Adult Drug Courts* (GAO-05-219) http://www.gao.gov/new.items/d05219.pdf.

Urquhart, Ian. 1989. 'Federalism, Ideology, and Charter Review: Alberta's Response to Morgentaler', *Canadian Journal of Law and Society* 4: 157–73.

————. 1997. 'Infertile Soil? Sowing the Charter in Alberta'. In Schneiderman and Sutherland, eds, *Charting the Consequences: The Impact of Charter Rights on Canadian Law and Politics*. Toronto: University of Toronto Press.

Vago, Steven, and Adie Nelson. 2004. *Law and Society: Canadian Edition*. Toronto: Pearson Education.

Verdun-Jones, Simon. 2002. *Criminal Law in Canada: Cases, Questions, and the Code*. 3rd edn. Toronto: Harcourt Canada.

————. 2008. 'Plea Bargaining'. In Julian V. Roberts and Michelle Grossman, eds, *Criminal Justice in Canada: A Reader*. 3rd edn. Toronto: Thomson Nelson.

————, and Adamira A. Tijerino. 2004. 'Four Models of Victim Involvement during Plea Negotiations: Bridging the Gap between Legal Reforms and Current Legal Practice', *Canadian Journal of Criminology and Criminal Justice* 46: 471–500.

Vidmar, Neil. 1999. 'The Canadian Criminal Jury: Searching for a Middle Ground', *Law and Contemporary Problems* 62: 141–72.

Vittala, Kalyani. 1994. 'In-line Skates Make Traffic By-laws Stumble', *Globe and Mail*, 5 July, A1.

Vogel, Frank. 2003. 'An Introduction to Law of the Islamic World', *International Journal of Legal Information* 31: 353–69.

Volcansek, Mary L. 2006. 'Judicial Selection in Italy: A Civil Service Model with Partisan Results'. In Kate Malleson and Peter H. Russell, eds, *Appointing Judges in an Age of Judicial Power: Critical Perspective from around the World*. Toronto: University of Toronto Press.

Valiquet, Dominique. 2007. Bill C-35: An Act to Amend the Criminal Code (reverse onus in bail hearings for firearm related offences). Library of Parliament, Legislative Summaries LS-549E. http://www.parl.gc.ca/common/Bills_ls.asp?lang=E&ls=c35&source=library_prb&Parl=39&Ses=1.

Vose, Clement E. 1972. *Constitutional Change*. Lexington: Lexington Books, D.C. Heath.

Waddams, S.M. 1987. *Introduction to the Study of Law*. 3rd edn. Toronto: Carswell.

Walker, Judge David C. 2006. 'Mental Health Court in New Brunswick', *Provincial Judges' Journal* 29: 41.

Walpin, Gerald. 2003. 'America's Adversarial and Jury System: More Likely to So Justice', *Harvard Journal of Law and Public Policy* 26: 175–86.

Waltenburg, Eric N., and Bill Swinford. 1999a. *Litigating Federalism: The States before the US Supreme Court*. Westport, Conn.: Greenwood Press.

———, and ———. 1999b. 'The Supreme Court as a Policy Arena: The Strategies and Tactics of State Attorneys General', *Policy Studies Journal* 27: 242–59.

Walton, Luanne A. 2001. 'Making Sense of Canadian Constitutional Interpretation', *National Journal of Constitutional Law* 12: 315–51.

Wasby, Stephen L. 1970. *The Impact of the United States Supreme Court*. Homewood, Ill.: Dorsey Press.

———. 1988. *The Supreme Court in the Federal Judicial System*. 3rd edn. Chicago: Nelson-Hall.

Watson, Garry D. 2001. 'Class Actions: The Canadian Experience', *Duke Journal of Comparative and International Law* 11: 269–87.

Weber, Max. 1965. *Politics as a Vocation*. Trans. H.H. Gerth and C. Wright Mills. Philadelphia: Fortress.

Webster, Cheryl M., and Anthony N. Doob. 2003. 'The Superior/Provincial Criminal Court Distinction: Historical Anachronism or Empirical Reality?' *Criminal Law Quarterly* 48: 77–109.

Weigend, Thomas. 2003. 'Is the Criminal Process about Truth? A German Perspective', *Harvard Journal of Law and Public Policy* 26: 157–73.

Weiler, Paul. 1968. 'Two Models of Judicial Decision-making', *Canadian Bar Review* 46: 406–71.

———. 2002. 'Architect of the Common Law'. In F.L. Morton, ed, *Law, Politics and the Judicial Process in Canada*. Calgary: University of Calgary Press.

Weinrib, Lorraine. 'The Activist Constitution', *Policy Options*, April 1999: 27–30.

Welch, Jillian. 1985. 'No Room at the Top: Interest Group Intervenors and Charter Litigation in the Supreme Court of Canada', *University of Toronto Faculty of Law Review* 43: 204–31.

Welch, Susan, John Gruhl, John Comer, and Susan M. Rigdon. 2008. *Understanding American Government*. 11th edn. Belmont, Calif.: Thomson Wadsworth.

Wells, Michael. 1994. 'French and American Legal Opinions', *Yale Journal of International Law* 19: 85–103.

Wente, Margaret. 2004. 'The State Should Not Give Its Blessing to Muslim Courts', *Globe and Mail*, 23 Dec. www.globeandmail.com.

Wheeler, Stanton, Bliss Cartwright, Robert Kagan, and Lawrence Friedman. 1987. 'Do the 'Haves' Come Out Ahead? Winning and Losing in State Supreme Courts 1870–1970', *Law and Society Review* 21: 413–45.

Williams, James R. 1996. 'Grasping a Thorny Baton: A Trial Judge Looks at Judicial Notice and Courts' Acquisition of Social Science', *Canadian Family Law Quarterly* 14: 179–232.

Williams, Stephen. 2003. *Karla: Pact with the Devil*. Toronto: Seal Books.

Williams, Toni. 1999. 'Sentencing Black Offenders in the Ontario Criminal Justice System'. In Julian V. Roberts and David P. Cole, eds, *Making Sense of Sentencing*. Toronto: University of Toronto Press.

Wilson, Bertha. 1990. 'Will Women Judges Really Make a Difference?' *Osgoode Hall Law Journal* 28: 507–22.

Wolpert, Robin M. 1991. 'Explaining and Predicting Supreme Court Decision Making: The Gender Discrimination Cases, 1971–1987'. Presented at the Annual Meeting of the Midwest Political Science Association, Chicago.

Women's Legal Education and Action Fund. *See* LEAF.

Wortley, Scot, and Julian Tanner. 2003. 'Data, Denials, and Confusion: The Racial Profiling Debate in Toronto', *Canadian Journal of Criminology and Criminal Justice* 45: 367–90.

Wyman, Katrina Miriam. 2001. 'The Independence of Administrative Tribunals in an Era of Ever Expansive Judicial Independence', *Canadian Journal of Administrative Law and Practice* 14: 61–125.

Yates, Richard A., Ruth Whidden Yates, and Penny Bain. 2000. *An Introduction to Law in Canada*. 2nd edn. Scarborough, Ont.: Prentice Hall; Allyn and Bacon.

Ziegel, Jacob S. 1999. 'Merit Selection and Democratization of Appointments to the Supreme Court of Canada', *IRPP Choices: Courts and Legislatures* 5: 3–23.

———. 2006. 'A New Era in the Selection of Supreme Court Judges?' *Osgoode Hall Law Journal* 44: 547–55.

———. 2007. 'Supreme Sellout: Canada's Top Court Has Sold Out Consumers by Handing Businesses an Easy Way to Avoid Class Action Suits', *National Post*, 9 Aug., FP13.

Zorn, Christopher. 2002. 'US Government Litigation Strategies in the Federal Appellate Courts', *Political Research Quarterly* 55: 145–66.

Cases Cited

114957 Canada Ltée (Spraytech, Société d'arrosage) v. Hudson (Town), [2001] 2 S.C.R. 241
A.A. v. B.B., 2003 CarswellOnt 1353 (ON S.C.J.)
A.A. v. B.B., (2007) 278 D.L.R. (4th) 519 (ON C.A.)
A.G. (Can.) v. Can. Nat. Transportation, Ltd., [1983] 2 S.C.R. 206
A.G. Canada v. Canard, [1976] 1 S.C.R. 170
A.G. Ontario v. A.G. Canada, [1912] AC 571 (P.C.)
A.G. Quebec v. Farrah, [1978] 2 S.C.R. 638
A.G. Quebec v. Grondin, [1983] 2 S.C.R. 364
A.Y.S.A. Amateur Youth Soccer Association v. Canada (Revenue Agency), 2007 SCC 42
Addy v. Canada, [1985] 2 F.C. 452 (Fed. Ct. Trial Div.)
Adrian v. Canada (Minister of Health), 2007 ABQB 376 (CanLII)
Andrews v. Grand & Toy Alberta Ltd., [1978] 2 S.C.R. 229
Anti-Inflation Reference, [1976] 2 S.C.R. 373
Arnold v. Teno, [1978] 2 S.C.R. 287
Attorney General of Manitoba v. Manitoba Egg and Poultry Association et al. [Chicken and Egg Reference], [1971] 1 S.C.R. 689
Attorney General of Quebec v. Association of Quebec Protestant School Boards, [1984] 2 S.C.R. 66
Auton (Guardian ad litem of) v. British Columbia (Attorney General), [2004] 3 S.C.R. 657
B.C.G.E.U. v. British Columbia (Attorney General), [1988] 2 S.C.R. 214
Baker v. Carr, 369 U.S. 186 (1962)
Beauregard v. Canada, [1986] 2 S.C.R. 56
Bodner v. Alberta; Provincial Court Judges' Assn. of New Brunswick v. New Brunswick (Minister of Justice; Ontario Judges' Assn. v. Ontario (Management Board); Conférence des juges du Québec v. Quebec (Attorney General); Minc v. Quebec (Attorney General), [2005] 2 S.C.R. 286
Borowski v. Canada (Attorney General), [1989] 1 S.C.R. 342
Boucher v. The King, [1951] S.C.R. 265
British Columbia (Attorney General) v. Canada (Attorney General); An Act respecting the Vancouver Island Railway (Re), [1994] 2 S.C.R. 41
British Columbia (Attorney General) v. Christie, [2007] 1 S.C.R. 873
British Columbia v. Imperial Tobacco Canada Ltd., [2005] 2 S.C.R. 473
Brown v. Board of Education, 347 U.S. 483 (1954)
Bush v. Gore, 531 U.S. 98 (2000)
Canada (Attorney General) v. JTI-Macdonald Corp., [2007] 2 S.C.R. 610
Canada (Minister of Citizenship and Immigration) v. Tobiass, [1997] 3 S.C.R. 391
The Canadian Bar Association v. The Queen et al., (2006) 144 C.R.R. (2d) 291 (BC S.C.)
Canadian Council of Churches v. Canada (Minister of Employment and Immigration), [1992] 1 S.C.R. 236
Canadian Federation of Agriculture v. Quebec (Attorney General) [Margarine Reference], [1951] A.C. 179 (P.C.)
Canadian Industrial Gas and Oil Limited v. Saskatchewan, [1978] 2 S.C.R. 545
Chaoulli v. Quebec (Attorney General), [2005] 1 S.C.R. 791
Charkaoui v. Canada (Citizenship and Immigration), [2007] 1 S.C.R. 350
Childs v. Desormeaux, [2006] 1 S.C.R. 643

CLRB v. Paul L'Anglais, [1983] 1 S.C.R. 147

The Corporation of the City of Mississauga v. The Regional Municipality of Peel et al., [1979] 2 S.C.R. 244

Cosgrove v. Canadian Judicial Council, (2007) 279 D.L.R. (4th) 352 (F.C.A.)

Council of Canadian with Disabilities v. Via Rail Canada Inc., [2007] 1 S.C.R. 650

Crevier v. A.G. Quebec, [1981] 2 S.C.R. 220

Cronk v. Canadian General Insurance Co., (1995) 128 D.L.R. (4th) 147 (ON C.A.)

Delgamuukw v. British Columbia, [1997] 3 S.C.R. 1010

Dell Computer Corp. v. Union des consommateurs, 2007 SCC 34

Desjardins c. Canada (Procureur général), 2007 CarswellQue 5142 (QC C.S.)

Doucet-Boudreau v. Nova Scotia (Minister of Education), [2003] 3 S.C.R. 3

Dunmore v. Ontario (Attorney General), [2001] 3 S.C.R. 1016

Dunsmuir v. New Brunswick, 2008 SCC 9

EGALE Canada v. Canada (Attorney General) [sub nom Barbeau v. Canada], (2003) 228 D.L.R. (4th) 416 (BC C.A.)

Egan v. Canada, [1995] 2 S.C.R. 513

Eldridge v. British Columbia (Attorney General), [1997] 3 S.C.R. 624

Ell v. Alberta, [2003] 1 S.C.R. 857

Endean v. Canadian Red Cross Society, (1999) 68 B.C.L.R. (3d) 350 (BC S.C.)

Fidler v. Sun Life Assurance Co. of Canada, [2006] 2 S.C.R. 3

Fleming v. Atkinson (Cattle Trespass Case), [1959] S.C.R. 513

Fraser v. Ontario (Attorney General), (2006) 263 D.L.R. (4th) 425 (ON S.C.J.)

Fraser v. Saanich (District), (1999) M.P.L.R. (3d) 80 (BC S.C.)

General Motors v. City National Leasing, [1989] 1 S.C.R. 641

Godbout v. Longueuil (City), [1997] 3 S.C.R. 844

Gosselin v. Québec (Attorney General), [2002] 4 S.C.R. 429

Gratton v. Canadian Judicial Council, [1994] 2 F.C. 769 (Fed. Ct. Trial Div.)

H.L. v. Canada (Attorney General), [2005] 1 S.C.R. 401

Haig v. Canada, (1992) 94 D.L.R. (4th) 1 (ON C.A.)

Halpern v. Canada (Attorney General), (2003) 65 O.R. (3d) 161 (ON C.A.)

Harrison v. Carswell, [1976] 2 S.C.R. 200

Health Services and Support—Facilities Subsector Bargaining Assn v. British Columbia, [2007] 2 S.C.R. 391

Henrietta Muir Edwards et al. v. Attorney General for Canada, [1930] A.C. 124 (P.C.)

Hill v. Church of Scientology of Toronto, [1995] 2 S.C.R. 1130

Honhon c. Canada (Procureur général), [1999] J.Q. No. 4370 (QC C.S.)

Housen v. Nikolaisen, [2002] 2 S.C.R. 235

Hunter v. Southam, [1984] 2 S.C.R. 145

Irwin Toy Ltd. v. Quebec (Attorney General), [1989] 1 S.C.R. 927

Killough v. The Canadian Red Cross Society, 2007 BCSC 836 (CanLII)

Krieger v. Law Society of Alberta, [2002] 3 S.C.R. 372

Labour Relations Board of Saskatchewan v. John East Iron Works, Ltd., [1949] A.C. 134 (P.C.)

Landreville v. Canada, [1977] 1 F.C. 419 (Fed. Ct. Trial Div.)

Landreville v. The Queen (No. 2), (1977) 75 D.L.R. (3d) 380 (Fed. Ct. Trial Div.)

Lavell v. Canada (Attorney General), [1974] S.C.R. 1349

Lavigne v. Ontario Public Service Employees Union, [1991] 2 S.C.R. 211

Leblanc v. Canada (Health), 2007 CanLII 12689 (ON S.C.J.)

Liquidators of the Maritime Bank v. Receiver General of New Brunswick, [1892] A.C. 437 (P.C.)

Lovelace v. Ontario, [2000] 1 S.C.R. 950

Lumbermens Mutual Casualty Co. v. Herbison, 2007 SCC 47

M. v. H., (1996) 27 O.R. (3d) 593 (ON Ct. (Gen. Div.))

M. v. H., [1999] 2 S.C.R. 3

MacKay v. Manitoba, [1989] 2 S.C.R. 357

Mackeigan v. Hickman, [1989] 2 S.C.R. 796

Mackin v. New Brunswick, [2002] 1 S.C.R. 405

MacMillan Bloedel v. Simpson, [1995] 4 S.C.R. 725

Mahe v. Alberta, [1990] 1 S.C.R. 342

Mansell v. Mansell, 490 U.S. 581 (1989)

Manulife Bank of Canada v. Conlin, [1996] 3 S.C.R. 415

Mapp v. Ohio, 367 U.S. 643 (1961)

Marshall v. The Queen, [1999a] 3 S.C.R. 456

Marshall v. The Queen, [1999b] 3 S.C.R. 533

McCarthy v. Canadian Red Cross Society, 2007 CanLII 21606 (ON S.C.J.)

McEvoy v. Attorney General for New Brunswick et al. [*Reference re Court of Unified Criminal Jurisdiction*], [1983] 1 S.C.R. 704

McKinney v. University of Guelph, [1990] 3 S.C.R. 229

McNamara Construction v. The Queen, [1977] 2 S.C.R. 654

McNeil v. Nova Scotia Board of Censors, [1976] 2 S.C.R. 265

Melita M. Chittenden, Avelina M. Villanueva, The Toronto Organization for Domestic Workers' Rights (Intercede) v. Attorney General of Ontario, 1996 (ON S.C. (Div. Ct.))

Minister of Justice of Canada v. Borowski, [1981] 2 S.C.R. 575

Moreau-Bérubé v. New Brunswick (Judicial Council), [2002] 1 S.C.R. 249

Morgentaler v. The Queen, [1976] 1 S.C.R. 616

Motherwell v. Motherwell, (1976) 73 D.L.R. (3d) 62 (AB S.C. (App. Div.))

Nelles v. Ontario, [1989] 2 S.C.R. 170

New Brunswick (Minister of Health and Community Services) v. G. (J.), [1999] 3 S.C.R. 46

Ocean Port Hotel v. British Columbia (General Manager, Liquor Control and Licensing Branch), [2001] 2 S.C.R. 781

Ontario v. Canadian Pacific Ltd., [1995] 2 S.C.R. 1031

Ontario Conference of Judges v. Ontario (Chair of Management Board), (2004) 71 O.R. (3d) 528 (ON S.C.J. (Div.Ct.))

Ontario Mushroom Co. v. Learie, (1977) 15 O.R. (2d) 639 (ON H.C.J. (Div. Ct.))

Operation Dismantle v. The Queen, [1985] 1 S.C.R. 441

Parsons v. Canadian Red Cross Society, [1999] O.J. No. 3572 (ON S.C.J.)

Patriation Reference, [1981] 1 S.C.R. 753

Peart v. Peel Regional Police Services, 2006 CanLII 37566 (ON C.A.)

Peel (Regional Municipality) v. Canada; Peel (Regional Municipality) v. Ontario, [1992] 3 S.C.R. 762

Propriety and Trade Articles Assn. v. A.G. Canada [Reference re: The Combines Investigation Act (Can.) s.36], [1931] A.C. 310 (P.C.)

Provincial Court Judges' Assn. of New Brunswick v. New Brunswick (Minister of Justice); Ontario Judges' Assn. v. Ontario (Management Board); Bodner v. Alberta; Conférence des juges du Québec v. Quebec (Attorney General); Minc v. Quebec (Attorney General), [2005] 2 S.C.R. 286

Purba v. Ryan, (2006) 61 Alta. L.R. (4th) 112 (AB C.A.)

Quebec North Shore Paper Co. v. Canadian Pacific, [1977] 2 S.C.R. 1054

R. v. Andrews, (1988) 65 O.R. (2d) 161 (ON C.A.)

R. v. Askov, [1990] 2 S.C.R. 1199

R. v. Aziz, (1978) 88 D.L.R. (3d) 712 (QC C.A.)

R. v. Aziz, [1981] 1 S.C.R. 188

R. v. Bain, [1992] 1 S.C.R. 91

R. v. Biddle, [1995] 1 S.C.R. 761

R. v. Brown, 2003 CanLII 52142 (ON C.A.)

R. v. Crown Zellerbach Canada Ltd., [1988] 1 S.C.R. 401

R. v. Cuerrier, [1998] 2 S.C.R. 371

R. v. Daviault, [1994] 3 S.C.R. 63

R. v. Drummond, (1996) 143 D.L.R. (4th) 368 (ON C.J. (Prov. Div.))

R. v. Edwards Books and Art Ltd., [1986] 2 S.C.R, 713

R. v. Elliot, [1999] O.J. No. 3265 (ON S.C.J.)

R. v. Feeney, [1997] 2 S.C.R. 13

R. v. Ferguson, 2008 SCC 6

R. v. Généreux, [1992] 1 S.C.R. 259

R. v. Gladue, [1999] 1 S.C.R. 688

R. v. Hamilton, (2004) 241 D.L.R. (4th) 490 (ON C.A.)

R. v. Hauser, (1977) 37 C.C.C. (2d) 129 (AB S.C. (App. Div.))

R. v. Hauser, [1979] 1 S.C.R. 984

R. v. Hydro-Québec, [1997] 3 S.C.R. 213

R. v. Jones, [2002] N.B.J. No. 375 (NB Q.B. (Trial Div.))

R. v. Justices of Sussex, Ex parte McCarthy, [1924] 1 K.B. 265 (U.K.)

R. v. Keegstra, (1988) 60 Alta. L.R. (2d) 1 (AB C.A.)

R. v. Keegstra, [1990] 3 S.C.R. 697

R. v. Khan, [1990] 2 S.C.R. 531

R. v. Khawaja, [2006] O.J. No. 4245 (ON S.C.J.)

R. v. Khelawon, [2006] 2 S.C.R. 787

R. v. Krieger, [2006] 2 S.C.R. 501

R. v. Latimer, [2001] 1 S.C.R. 3

R. v. Lippé, [1991] 2 S.C.R. 114

R. v. Mills, [1999] 3 S.C.R. 668

R. v. Morales, [1992] 3 S.C.R. 711

R. v. Morgentaler, [1984] O.J. No. 1314 (ON H.C.J.)

R. v. Morgentaler, [1976] 1 S.C.R. 616

R. v. Morgentaler, [1988] 1 S.C.R. 30

R. v. Morgentaler, [1993] 3 S.C.R. 463

R. v. Morrisey, [2000] 2 S.C.R. 90

R. v. O'Connor, [1995] 4 S.C.R. 411

R. v. Oakes, [1986] 1 S.C.R. 103

R. v. Osolin, [1993] 2 S.C.R. 313

R. v. Parrot, (1979) 106 D.L.R. (3d) 296 (ON C.A.)

R. v. Pearson, [1992] 3 S.C.R. 665

R. v. Pratt, (2007) 218 C.C.C. (3d) 298 (BC C.A.)

R. v. Richard, [1996] 3 S.C.R. 525

R. v. Sacobie, (1979) 51 C.C.C. (2d) 430 (NB C.A.)

R. v. Sacobie, [1983] 1 S.C.R. 241

R. v. Seaboyer; R. v. Gayme, [1991] 2 S.C.R. 577

R. v. Sharpe, [2001] 1 S.C.R. 45

R. v. Sheppard, [2002] 1 S.C.R. 869

R. v. Shropshire, [1995] 4 S.C.R. 227

R. v. Smith, [1987] 1 S.C.R. 1045

R. v. Smith [1989], 2 S.C.R. 368

R. v. Sparrow, [1990] 1 S.C.R. 1075

R. v. Tessling, [2004] 3 S.C.R. 432

R. v. Therens, [1985] 1 S.C.R. 613

R. v. Thomas Fuller Construction, [1980] 1 S.C.R. 695

R. v. Trochym, [2007] 1 S.C.R. 239

R. v. Vaillancourt, [1987] 2 S.C.R. 636

R. v. Valente, [1985] 2 S.C.R. 673

R. v. Wells, [2000] 1 S.C.R. 207

R. v. Wetmore, [1983] 2 S.C.R. 284

R. v. Whiskeyjack, (1984) 16 D.L.R. (4th) 231 (AB C.A.)

Re B.C. Motor Vehicle Act, [1985] 2 S.C.R. 486

Re Blainey and Ontario Hockey Association et al., (1985) 52 O.R. (2d) 225 (ON H.C.J.)

Re Canadian Red Cross Society, [2000] OJ No. 3421 (ON S.C.J.)

Re Seaboyer and the Queen, (1987) 61 O.R. (2d) 290 (ON C.A.)

Re Therrien, [2001] 2 S.C.R. 3

Reference re Adoption Act and Other Acts, [1938] S.C.R. 393

Reference re Alberta Statutes [Alberta Press Case], [1938] S.C.R. 100

Reference re Amendments to the Residential Tenancies Act (Nova Scotia), [1996] 1 S.C.R. 186

Reference re B.C. Family Relations Act, [1982] 1 S.C.R. 62

Reference re Firearms Act (Canada), [2000] 1 S.C.R. 783

Reference re Newfoundland Continental Shelf, [1984] 1 S.C.R. 86

Reference re Proposed Federal Tax on Exported Natural Gas, [1982] 1 S.C.R. 1004

Reference re Public Service Employee Relations Act (Alta.), [1987] 1 S.C.R. 313

Reference re Residential Tenancies Act, [1981] 1 S.C.R. 714

Reference re Resolution to amend the Constitution, [1981] 1 S.C.R. 753

Reference re Same-Sex Marriage, [2004] 3 S.C.R. 698

Reference re Secession of Quebec, [1998] 2 S.C.R. 217

Remuneration Reference, [1997] 3 S.C.R. 3

Riggs v. Palmer, 115 N.Y. 506 (1889)

RJR-MacDonald Inc. v. Canada (Attorney General), [1995] 3 S.C.R. 199

Robb Estate v. Canadian Red Cross Society, [2001] 152 O.A.C. 60 (ON C.A.)

Rogers Wireless Inc. v. Muroff, 2007 SCC 35

Roncarelli v. Duplessis, [1959] 1 S.C.R. 121

Ruffo v. Conseil de la magistrature, [1995] 4 S.C.R. 267

RWDSU v. Dolphin Delivery Ltd., [1986] 2 S.C.R. 573

Saumur v. A.G. Quebec, [1964] 2 S.C.R. 252

Saumur v. The City of Quebec, [1953] 2 S.C.R. 299

Sauvé v. Canada (Attorney General), [1993] 2 S.C.R. 438

Sauvé v. Canada (Chief Electoral Officer), [2002] 3 S.C.R. 519

Schachter v. Canada, [1992] 2 S.C.R. 679

Scott v. Harris, 550 U.S. ___ (2007)

Sierra Club of Canada v. Canada (Minister of Finance), [2002] 2 S.C.R. 522

Singh v. Minister of Employment and Immigration, [1985] 1 S.C.R. 177

Smith v. Ontario Attorney General, [1924] S.C.R. 331

Société des Acadiens v. Association of Parents, [1986] 1 S.C.R. 549

Solski v. Quebec, [2005] 1 S.C.R. 201

Somwar v. McDonald's Restaurants of Canada Ltd., (2006) 263 D.L.R. (4th) 752 (ON S.C.J.)

Stoffman v. Vancouver General Hospital, [1990] 3 S.C.R. 483

Sukhvir Singh Khosa v. Minister of Immigration and Citizenship, (2007) 376 D.L.R. (4th) 369 (F.C.A.)

Tétreault-Gadoury v. Canada (Employment and Immigration Commission), [1991] 2 S.C.R. 22

Thornton v. School Dist. No. 57 (Prince George), [1978] 2 S.C.R. 267

Thorson v. A.G. Canada, [1975] 1 S.C.R. 138
Tomko v. Labour Relations Board of Nova Scotia, [1977] 1 S.C.R. 112
Toronto (City) v. York (City), [1938] A.C. 415 (P.C.)
Tremblay v. Daigle, [1989] 2 S.C.R. 530
United States v. Booker, 543 U.S. 220 (2005)
Vieth v. Jubelirer, 541 U.S. 267 (2004)
Vriend v. Alberta, [1998] 1 S.C.R. 493
Walker Estate v. York Finch General Hospital, [2001] 1 S.C.R. 647
Weatherall v. Canada (Attorney General), [1993] 2 S.C.R. 872
Westendorp v. The Queen, [1983] 1 S.C.R. 43
Western Canadian Shopping Centres Inc. v. Dutton, [2001] 2 S.C.R. 534
Whiten v. Pilot Insurance Co., [2002] 1 S.C.R. 595
Winnipeg Child and Family Services (Northwest Area) v. G. (D.F.), [1997] 3 S.C.R. 925
Young v. Bella, [2006] 1 S.C.R. 108
Young v. Young, [1993] 4 S.C.R. 3

Index